This is a state-of-the-art review on children's eyewitness memory and child forensic interviews that is dedicated to Dr. Karen J. Saywitz, who devoted her entire career to scientific research in this area and to advocacy for children. I have no doubt that both researchers and practitioners in the fields of developmental, clinical, and forensic psychology will benefit from reading this holistic overview.

—**Yoojin Chae, PhD,** Department of Human Development & Family Sciences, Texas Tech University, Lubbock

Judges, lawyers, social workers—indeed, all legal professionals—risk contributing to injustice when they rely on intuition or untested assumptions in their work. In the field of child abuse, this handbook offers a vital corrective. Authored by leading experts on children and the law, it presents the most up-to-date, comprehensive synthesis of foundational and applied research, making it essential reading for any legal professional who is committed to advancing justice.

—**Donna Shestowsky, JD, PhD,** Senior Associate Dean for Academic Affairs and Martin Luther King Jr. Professor of Law, School of Law, University of California, Davis

Handbook on Child Witnesses

Handbook on Child Witnesses

Improving Psychological Science and Legal Practice

Edited by Gail S. Goodman, Thomas D. Lyon,
Sue D. Hobbs, and Rayna Enriquez

AMERICAN PSYCHOLOGICAL ASSOCIATION

Published by
American Psychological Association
750 First Street, NE
Washington, DC 20002
https://www.apa.org

Order Department
https://www.apa.org/pubs/books
order@apa.org

Typeset in Meridien and Ortodoxa by Circle Graphics, Inc., Reisterstown, MD

Printer: Gasch Printing, Odenton, MD
Cover Designer: Beth Schlenoff Design, Bethesda, MD

Library of Congress Cataloging-in-Publication Data

Names: Goodman, Gail S. editor | Lyon, Thomas D. editor | Hobbs, Sue D. editor | Enriquez, Rayna editor
Title: Handbook on child witnesses : improving psychological science and legal practice / Gail S. Goodman, Thomas D. Lyon, Sue D. Hobbs, Rayna Enriquez.
Description: Washington : American Psychological Association, 2026. | Series: American psychology-law series | Includes bibliographical references and index.
Identifiers: LCCN 2026001457 (print) | LCCN 2026001458 (ebook) | ISBN 9781433842658 paperback | ISBN 9781433843389 epub | ISBN 9781433850202 pdf
Subjects: LCSH: Child witnesses | Forensic psychology | Child abuse--Psychological aspects | Child sexual abuse--Psychological aspects | Witnesses--Psychological aspects | Evidence, Expert | Jurors--Psychology
Classification: LCC K2271.5 .H36 2026 (print) | LCC K2271.5 (ebook)
LC record available at https://lccn.loc.gov/2026001457
LC ebook record available at https://lccn.loc.gov/2026001458

https://doi.org/10.1037/0000492-000

Printed in the United States of America

10 9 8 7 6 5 4 3 2 1

This handbook is dedicated to the memory of Dr. Karen J. Saywitz, our long-time collaborator and dear friend, who passed away in 2018. She was a giant in this field of study, and her work is still influential today. Dr. Saywitz trained as both a developmental scientist and a child clinician. She was a guiding force in the child witness research field from its inception. Many of her studies were groundbreaking, inspiring a generation of researchers. She invented narrative practice as a nonleading way to obtain children's reports, as summarized in her 2014 book Evidence-Based Child Forensic Interviewing: The Developmental Narrative Elaboration Interview. *Her research, sensitivity, and thinking are in every child forensic interview at children's advocacy centers today, where children are interviewed about trauma.*

After her tragic death at the age of 61, we thought about what we could do to honor her, and we decided on this handbook. It provides state-of-the-art thinking on child forensic interviews, focusing on allegations of child sexual abuse (CSA). Many contributors to this book worked with Dr. Saywitz or knew her and her research. We (the editors) represent colleagues, collaborators, and students who worked directly with Dr. Saywitz or her disciples. We still miss her!

Why focus on CSA? The primary reason is that this is the crime about which most child witnesses testify. The topic of children's reports of CSA is controversial. Dr. Saywitz's scientific research and clinical knowledge were aimed at bringing balance to this controversial topic. We also hope to emulate Dr. Saywitz's goal in this handbook.

CONTENTS

CONTRIBUTORS

Uri Blasbalg, PhD, Department of Psychology, University of Cambridge, Cambridge, United Kingdom

Stephanie D. Block, PhD, Department of Psychology, University of Massachusetts Lowell, Lowell, MA, United States

Sherille Bosfield, MA, Department of Psychology, The Pennsylvania State University, University Park, PA, United States

Deirdre A. Brown, PhD, Department of Psychology, University of Otago, Dunedin, New Zealand

Sonja P. Brubacher, PhD, Centre for Investigative Interviewing, Griffith Criminology Institute, Griffith University, Brisbane, QLD, Australia

Charlotte Bücken, PhD, Leuven Institute of Criminology, KU Leuven, Leuven, Belgium

Kelly C. Burke, PhD, Department of Psychology, University of Texas at El Paso, El Paso, TX, United States

Lorinda B. Camparo, PhD, Emerita, Department of Psychological Sciences, Whittier College, Whittier, CA, United States

Angela M. Crossman, PhD, Department of Psychology, John Jay College, City University of New York, New York, NY, United States

Sarah L. Deck, PhD, Centre for Investigative Interviewing, Griffith Criminology Institute, Griffith University, Brisbane, QLD, Australia

Rachel E. Dianiska, PhD, Department of Psychology, University of California, Irvine, Irvine, CA, United States

Victoria W. Dykstra, PhD, Department of Psychology, Memorial University of Newfoundland, St. John's, NL, Canada

Rayna Enriquez, PhD, Department of Psychology, University of California, Davis, Davis, CA, United States

Martine Fredrickson, MS, College of Arts, Sciences and Education, Department of Psychology, Florida International University, Miami, FL, United States

Deborah Goldfarb, JD, PhD, College of Arts, Sciences and Education, Department of Psychology, Florida International University, Miami, FL, United States

Jonathan M. Golding, PhD, Department of Psychology, University of Kentucky, Lexington, KY, United States

Gail S. Goodman, PhD, Department of Psychology and Center for Public Policy Research, University of California, Davis, Davis, CA, United States

Lucy A. Henry, DPhil, Centre for Language and Communication Science Research, City St George's, University of London, London, United Kingdom

Juan Pablo Hernandez Aldaco, MA, Department of Psychology, University of California, Davis, Davis, CA, United States

Irit Hershkowitz, PhD, School of Social Work, Faculty of Social Welfare & Health Sciences, University of Haifa, Haifa, Israel

Sue D. Hobbs, PhD, Child and Adolescent Development, College of Education, California State University, Sacramento, Sacramento, CA, United States

Mark L. Howe, PhD, Faculty of Psychology and Neuroscience, Maastricht University, the Netherlands; Department of Psychology and Neuroscience, City St George's, University of London, London, United Kingdom

Yo Jackson, PhD, ABPP, Department of Psychology, Tulane University, New Orleans, LA, United States

Hannah M. Johnson, PhD, Department of Psychology, University of Massachusetts Lowell, Lowell, MA, United States

Yael Karni-Visel, PhD, School of Social Work, Bar-Ilan University, Ramat Gan, Israel

Michael E. Lamb, PhD, Department of Psychology, University of Cambridge, Cambridge, United Kingdom

Rakel P. Larson, PhD, Gould School of Law, University of Southern California, Los Angeles, CA; Social and Behavioral Sciences Department, Riverside City College, Riverside, CA, United States

Mary M. Levi, MS, Department of Psychology, University of Kentucky, Lexington, KY, United States

Thomas D. Lyon, JD, PhD, Gould School of Law and Department of Psychology, University of Southern California, Los Angeles, CA, United States

Katie Maras, PhD, Department of Psychology, Center for Applied Autism Research, and Institute for Digital Security and Behaviour, University of Bath, Bath, United Kingdom

Nathalie Moriarty, MA, Department of Psychology Memory and Development Lab, University of California, Davis, Davis, CA, United States

Rebecca Nathanson, PhD, College of Education and Boyd School of Law, University of Nevada, Las Vegas, Las Vegas, NV, United States

Henry Otgaar, PhD, Faculty of Psychology and Neuroscience, Maastricht University, the Netherlands; Leuven Institute of Criminology, KU Leuven, Leuven, Belgium

Martine B. Powell, PhD, Centre for Investigative Interviewing, Griffith Criminology Institute, Griffith University, Brisbane, QLD, Australia

Jodi A. Quas, PhD, Department of Psychology, University of California, Irvine, Irvine, CA, United States

Michaela G. Ramsey, MA, Department of Psychology, University of Massachusetts Lowell, Lowell, MA, United States

Ben T. Reeb, PhD, Department of Psychology, University of California, Davis, Davis, CA, United States

Lea Sobrilsky, MS, New College of Interdisciplinary Arts and Sciences, Arizona State University, Phoenix, AZ, United States

Avery Stackle, MS, College of Arts, Sciences and Education, Department of Psychology, Florida International University, Miami, FL, United States

Margaret C. Stevenson, PhD, Department of Psychology, Kenyon College, Gambier, OH, United States

Stacia N. Stolzenberg, PhD, School of Criminology & Criminal Justice, Arizona State University, Phoenix, AZ, United States

Sara Such, MS, Department of Psychology, The Pennsylvania State University, University Park, PA, United States

Colleen E. Sullivan, PhD, Gould School of Law, University of Southern California, Los Angeles, CA, United States

Zsofia A. Szojka, PhD, School of Law and Criminology, University of Greenwich, London, United Kingdom

Victoria Talwar, PhD, Department of Educational and Counselling Psychology, McGill University, Montréal, QC, Canada

Christine R. Wells, PhD, Office of Advanced Research Computing, University of California, Los Angeles, Los Angeles, CA, United States

Alexandria P. Winstead, BS, Department of Psychology, University of Massachusetts Lowell, Lowell, MA, United States

Yuerui Wu, PhD, Department of Psychology, New York University Shanghai, Shanghai, China

Breanne E. Wylie, PhD, Department of Psychology, North Carolina State University, Raleigh, NC, United States

SERIES FOREWORD

Jemour A. Maddux

As series associate editor of the American Psychology–Law Society's (AP-LS's; American Psychological Association's Division 41) book series, it is my pleasure to introduce the *Handbook on Child Witnesses: Improving Psychological Science and Legal Practice,* edited by Gail S. Goodman, Thomas D. Lyon, Sue D. Hobbs, and Rayna Enriquez.

Through its book series, the AP-LS seeks to advance and disseminate the science of psychology and law; advance the practice of psychology in legal contexts and establish contemporary best practices; promote human rights, dignity, and justice in our multicultural, pluralistic society; and actively encourage mentoring in the profession through knowledge dissemination and the publication process.

The AP-LS Book Series seeks proposals from authors and editors across the spectrum of psychology and law, both science and practice. The editorial team is particularly focused on authored and edited volumes involving authors and editors from traditionally underrepresented groups; collaborations between psychologists and lawyers/legal scholars; and collaborations between veteran and early-career scientists and/or practitioners. The editorial team hopes its published volumes will inform scholars and practitioners as to the current state of the science at the nexus of psychology and law. In doing so, the series is intended to encourage unbiased science and best practices that promote well-being and prevent discrimination and injustice.

Perhaps nowhere is this intersection between psychology and law more critical than in the realm of child witnesses, where children's safety and access to justice depend directly on professionals from diverse disciplines having access to the most cutting-edge and recent research to inform their practice.

This handbook is particularly impactful in this regard because it addresses not only the most current research but does so inclusively; for example, by dedicating attention to children with autism spectrum disorder as well as survivors of child sexual abuse who are now adults seeking justice through lookback windows that remove the statute of limitations. The comprehensive scope of this volume reflects the multifaceted nature of child witness work. It spans foundational research on child memory, suggestibility, and trauma in addition to applied research concerning interview techniques and courtroom dynamics. Each chapter contributes essential knowledge, ultimately giving children a voice while providing key research to inform practices that uphold their rights. Experts evaluating children in various forensic contexts will find useful guidance both for engaging child examinees and creating opportunities for them to tell their stories as completely, accurately, and defensibly as possible.

In closing, I would like to end by thanking the members of the editorial board who do the work of recruiting and reviewing proposals for the series: Series Editor Monica K. Miller, and Associate Editor Monique Bowen. They are esteemed leaders in the field, generously contributing their time and expertise to drive meaningful progress in the specialty. I would also like to thank Chris Kelaher, senior acquisitions editor for APA Books, who provided thoughtful direction and support from start to finish. This team made this important work possible.

Handbook on Child Witnesses

1

Child Witness Research

Introduction

Gail S. Goodman, Thomas D. Lyon, Sue D. Hobbs, and Rayna Enriquez

Our futures reside in our childhood memories. Moreover, childhood memories of trauma are of legal and societal significance. When children experience the trauma of a sexual assault or the trauma of a false report, society at large suffers. Traumas such as these in childhood have lasting mental and physical effects on children, their families, and communities. Although we cannot yet avoid child victimization, we need to hear victims' voices to take appropriate action so we can protect children, prevent future occurrences, and avoid false reports. That's where forensic interviewing comes into play, as does basic research on memory, suggestibility, linguistic, and social/emotional development.

This handbook provides the most up-to-date science- and practice-based information on child forensic interviewing, especially in child abuse cases. Eliciting descriptions of childhood assaults—from children, adolescents, and adults—is a daunting task. Each age period poses its own challenges: For example, young children may be susceptible to influence, may fail to disclose abusive experiences, or their descriptions of events might be ignored. Adolescence is a time of sexual experimentation in which exploitation by adults can be confused with love and affection. Adults who describe childhood trauma may suffer from depression and fading memory of the events at issue, which can undermine their claims about their childhood.

In this area of study and practice, we have seen excessive concerns about both false denials and false allegations. Fortunately, evidence-informed protocols

https://doi.org/10.1037/0000492-001
Handbook on Child Witnesses: Improving Psychological Science and Legal Practice,
G. S. Goodman, T. D. Lyon, S. D. Hobbs, and R. Enriquez (Editors)

have been developed that seek a balance, including the Developmental Narrative Elaboration (DNE) interview (Saywitz & Camparo, 2014), the Ten Step Investigative Interview (Lyon, 2021), the cognitive interview (Fisher & Geiselman, 1992), and the National Institute of Child Health and Human Development (NICHD) revised investigative interview protocol (Lamb et al., 2018). Yet, there is still much to learn about child forensic interviewing. For example, how much social support and rapport building is required for disclosure, and do these protocols sufficiently foster the optimal amounts of disclosure? Is too much rapport harmful for some subgroups? What predicts accurate disclosure versus too much parental influence? Even basic questions—such as how reconstructive memory is for unforgettable, traumatic events—need to be addressed. There are many questions yet to explore. Yet experimental work is inherently limited, because for ethical reasons, research on children's reports focuses on nontraumatic events. Observational work examining issues such as disclosure of abuse is often hampered by uncertainties over the accuracy of the reports.

Nevertheless, we expect the chapters included in this handbook will help the field learn about children's abilities and needs, as well as what works and what does not work. We also hope the research findings will stimulate new research and growth in this field of study.

BASIC RESEARCH AND APPLICATIONS

We start with a chapter by Yo Jackson and colleagues from Tulane and Penn State Universities, respectively. Like Dr. Saywitz, Dr. Jackson is a child clinician who specializes in research on child maltreatment and trauma. In this chapter, Jackson and her colleagues, Sherille Bosfield and Sara Such, lay important groundwork as to correlates of childhood trauma often found by psychologists using standardized tests, which can influence court and clinical evaluations: This includes cognitive and educational problems, emotional issues, and psychopathology symptoms.

We dive into another view in the chapter by Yuerui Wu and colleagues. Working at New York University Shanghai and educated at the University of California campuses in the United States, Wu and her colleagues, Nathalie Moriarty, Juan Pablo Hernandez Aldaco, Ben T. Reeb, and Gail S. Goodman, present an "adaptation" view informed by evolutionary psychology and anthropology (e.g., Ellis et al., 2017). Adaptation theories explain how childhood trauma heightens memory for trauma cues, while also explaining the findings of memory deficits that Jackson et al. reviewed. Wu et al. discuss several studies of children's memory and suggestibility for abuse-related information through the lens of adaptation theories.

In contrast to the focus on children in Wu et al.'s chapter, developmental psychologist and attorney Deborah Goldfarb and her colleagues Avery Stackle and Martine Fredrickson focus on adults' long-term memories of childhood abuse-related events. Because children often fail to disclose sexual abuse in childhood but realize in adulthood they should take legal action (as demonstrated by the Jeffrey Epstein and Ghislaine Maxwell cases), research on adults' long-term memory of childhood trauma is particularly important. Goldfarb and colleagues find that adults can remember the central features of stressful, child abuse-related events, such as forensic genital examinations, especially if the adult has trauma-related symptoms.

Dr. Goldfarb met Dr. Saywitz at a conference in Los Angeles, and some of the research Dr. Goldfarb reviews was inspired by Saywitz and colleagues' research on memory for genital touch (Saywitz et al., 1991). That research was novel in examining the effects of different types of questions on both true and false allegations, reminding researchers that efforts at reducing false reports often entail reducing true reports as well. Moreover, although the study's focus was on memory, it found that older children were less inclined to recall genital touch than younger children, highlighting the need to consider reluctance and denial as well as memory in understanding nondisclosure.

Unfortunately, abuse, including child sexual abuse (CSA), is often repeated. The chapter by Sarah L. Deck, Sonja P. Brubacher, and Martine B. Powell addresses research on children's memory and suggestibility for repeated events. Deck et al. utilize the source monitoring framework (Johnson et al., 1993) and "script theory" (Schank & Abelson, 1977) to help explain some of what we know about children's memory and suggestibility for repeated events. They provide suggestions on how to interview children who have experienced repeated abuse.

Thomas D. Lyon, one of the editors of this handbook, was a postdoctoral fellow with Dr. Saywitz in the mid-1990s, which led to a longstanding collaboration. Lyon and his coauthors, Breanne E. Wylie and Zsofia A. Szojka, review research on children's denial of abuse and show how denial is underestimated because suspicion and substantiation of abuse are largely dependent on disclosure. Uncovering high rates of nondisclosure and denial, they discuss the implications for expert testimony explaining disclosure dynamics to jurors. They also note how reluctance to disclose embarrassing and abusive genital touch undermines the generalizability of suggestibility research examining nonabusive events.

Closing out this section of the book is a chapter by Henry Otgaar, Mark L. Howe, and Charlotte Bücken on highly suggestive techniques that led society to question child forensic interviewing. The authors review several CSA cases (e.g., the McMartin case in the United States during the 1980s and the 1993 Peter Ellis case in New Zealand) that are controversial yet widely considered by scientific researchers to represent false reports. They mention the benefits of having scientific memory-development researchers as expert witnesses in court (see also Goodman et al., 2025; Quas et al., 2025, for the advantages of clinical and scientific experts in CSA cases).

IMPROVING CHILDREN'S REPORTS

How best to interview children is still debated, and interview protocols are being refined to better fit children's needs. We start this section of the book with Lorinda B. Camparo's review of the Developmental Narrative Elaboration (DNE) interview and research that supports it. Dr. Saywitz first developed the technique in the mid 1990s (Saywitz & Snyder, 1996; Saywitz et al., 1996), and it has been studied with over 1,000 children from 3 to 12 years of age in the United States, Australia, New Zealand, and Canada (Saywitz & Camparo, 2014). In addition to outlining a training procedure for assisting children to recall events with reminder cards, the technique includes a verbal-labels approach that has spawned a great deal of research identifying cued recall questions that increase productivity without increasing error (Brown & Pipe, 2003; Canning & Peterson, 2020). The chapter refers readers to the Saywitz and Camparo book (2014) that provides full details of the technique.

Another important innovation in forensic interviewing is narrative practice, in which the interviewer asks the child to narrate a nonabusive event so the child can practice providing narrative information in response to open-ended questions before the interviewer asks about the allegation. Dr. Saywitz first demonstrated the benefits of this technique in her work adapting the Cognitive Interview for children (Saywitz et al., 1992) and included it in the DNE interview (Saywitz & Camparo, 2014).

Narrative practice has been incorporated into numerous protocols, including the revised NICHD interviewing protocol developed by Michael E. Lamb and colleagues (Lamb et al., 2018). In their chapter, Lamb and his coauthors Irit Hershkowitz, Yael Karni-Visel, and Uri Blasbalg discuss the increases in productivity related to the use of narrative practice, and they argue (and we agree) that "[b]efore seeking to elicit information from children about personal experiences that might have been frightening, embarrassing, confusing, or shameful, interviewers need to ensure" that children feel "comfortable with the interviewer to discuss such personal information" (p. 164). The revised NICHD Interviewing Protocol is having a tremendous impact on child forensic interviewing worldwide.

A common component of interviewing protocols and practice guidelines (DNE, NICHD, Ten Step) are ground rules that the interviewer presents toward the beginning of the interview, including "don't know," "don't understand," and "interviewer ignorance" (Saywitz & Camparo, 2014). These provide a type of coordination between the interviewer and the child, one of the foundations of rapport building (Dianiska et al., 2024). Sonya P. Brubacher and Deirdre A. Brown discuss the latest research on ground rules in their chapter. They note that "Saywitz's work laid an important foundation for the evidence base underpinning the use of ground rules" (p. 182; Saywitz & Moan-Hardie, 1994; Saywitz & Nathanson, 1993; Saywitz et al., 1999). Their review stresses the importance of practicing ground rules, but also notes their limitations, particularly with younger children. They emphasize the overarching importance of asking the right questions during the substantive phase of the interview and call for much-needed research on how to make instructions more effective.

Victoria W. Dykstra, Rachel E. Dianiska, and Jodi A. Quas describe some of the dilemmas of interviewing adolescents. They rightly argue that much of the research is oriented to young children rather than adolescents, who may be particularly difficult to interview if they have been sexually trafficked. The chapter authors point out the difficulties of interviewing teenagers and offer ideas for successful interviewing.

The authors of our next chapter are Sue D. Hobbs, Rakel P. Larson, and Christine R. Wells, all of whom worked closely with Dr. Saywitz on systematic literature reviews and a meta-analysis on social support and rapport building (Saywitz et al., 2015, 2016). There is relatively little basic research on supportive interviewing, including on rapport building, even though some people, like Dr. Saywitz, mastered it. Yet, Hobbs et al. present convincing theoretical and research-based evidence demonstrating the importance of support and rapport building for successful child interviewing.

Angela M. Crossman and Victoria Talwar review the research on children's ability and proclivity to lie and to conceal information. Crossman and Talwar discuss how younger children are less capable of lying and maintaining secrets, and outline the factors that influence children to deceive. The chapter authors suggest ways in which understanding children's cognitive and social development can assist interviewers in encouraging honesty.

Rayna Enriquez from the University of California, Davis and her coauthors Katie Maras and Lucy A. Henry, both from the United Kingdom, have a special interest in autism and how to interview children with this developmental disorder. The chapter authors argued that with proper supports, children and teenagers on the autism spectrum, if verbal and high functioning, can be accurate witnesses when interviewed.

PERCEPTIONS OF CHILDREN IN COURT

In some of her earliest published work, Dr. Saywitz questioned children about courtroom processes, demonstrating their limited understanding (Saywitz, 1989; Saywitz et al., 1990). Years later, these studies helped convince the U.S. Supreme Court that young children's complaints of abuse should not require that they later appear in court and testify (*Ohio v. Clark*, 2015). Dr. Saywitz also developed a task for sensitively assessing children's ability to answer questions about truth-telling and lying (Lyon & Saywitz, 1999, 2000), a mainstay of American court procedure. However, surviving the competency questions is only the first challenge for child witnesses. Stacia N. Stolzenberg and Colleen E. Sullivan, and their student Lea Sobrilsky, review the legal requirements for child witness competency and the psychological research that identifies the best procedures for establishing competency. They also review research on courtroom questioning and demonstrate the many ways in which both prosecutors and defense attorneys ask developmentally inappropriate questions.

This handbook would not be complete without a review of jurors' reactions to child witnesses. Jonathan M. Golding, Margaret C. Stevenson, Kelly C. Burke, and Mary M. Levi provide a thoughtful review of research on jurors' views of children in CSA trials and other alleged child victims. Golding et al. call for further research on non-CSA cases on the effects of jury deliberation and research that investigates racial disparities for child victims and witnesses of color.

EMOTIONAL REACTIONS AND COURT PREPARATION PROGRAMS

Dr. Saywitz experimentally demonstrated how the stress of being questioned in the courtroom impairs children's performance (Saywitz & Nathanson, 1993). Stephanie D. Block, along with her colleagues Hannah M. Johnson, Michaela G. Ramsey, and Alexandria P. Winstead review the literature on children's emotional reactions to the prospect of appearing and actually appearing in court. Dr. Block has conducted well-known research on the prosecution of CSA cases and uses her findings as a backdrop to review the possible negative and positive effects when children take the stand.

Working with Rebecca Nathanson, Dr. Saywitz developed procedures for reducing child witnesses' stress in court (Nathanson & Saywitz, 2003). In her chapter, Dr. Nathanson describes the court preparation school that she directs at the University of Nevada, Las Vegas. Creating a program to evaluate and support children's preparation to take the stand, then doing so without treading on the legal process, is tricky. However, the school achieves this goal with positive effects. The preparation program might well be copied in other jurisdictions.

We have many professionals to thank in our quest to illuminate child forensic interviewing. First, we thank Monica Miller, PhD, JD, for her support of this book, sponsored by Division 41 (American Psychology–Law Society [AP-LS]) of the American Psychological Association (APA). Dr. Miller chaired the AP-LS Publication Board at the time our proposal was accepted, and she provided guidance throughout. We also thank Christopher Kelaher from the APA Publication Office for his advocacy and help, and for providing us with additional motivation to publish the enclosed chapters. We thank Krissy Jones and Meghan Quinn for their fine editing. We thank our colleagues, friends, and families. Most of all, we thank Dr. Karen J. Saywitz for all that she did for traumatized youth, for researchers and clinicians, for society, and for being such an amazing person and dear friend.

REFERENCES

Brown, D., & Pipe, M. E. (2003). Individual differences in children's event memory reports and the narrative elaboration technique. *Journal of Applied Psychology, 88*(2), 195–206. https://doi.org/10.1037/0021-9010.88.2.195

Canning, H. S., & Peterson, C. (2020). Encouraging more open-ended recall in child interviews. *Psychiatry, Psychology and Law, 27*(1), 81–94, 1687045. https://doi.org/10.1080/13218719.2019.1687045

Dianiska, R. E., Quas, J. A., & Lyon, T. D. (2024). Using rapport building to improve information yield when interviewing adolescents: A systematic review and call for research. *Child Abuse & Neglect, 154*, 106898. https://doi.org/10.1016/j.chiabu.2024.106898

Ellis, B. J., Bianchi, J., Griskevicius, V., & Frankenhuis, W. E. (2017). Beyond risk and protective factors: An adaptation-based approach to resilience. *Perspectives on Psychological Science, 12*(4), 561–587. https://doi.org/10.1177/1745691617693054

Fisher, R. P., & Geiselman, R. E. (1992). *Memory enhancing techniques for investigative interviewing: The cognitive interview*. Charles C. Thomas.

Goodman, G. S., Quas, J. A., Bulkley, J., & Shapiro, C. (1999). Innovations for child witnesses: A national survey. *Psychology, Public Policy, and Law, 5*(2), 255–281. https://doi.org/10.1037/1076-8971.5.2.255

Goodman, G. S., Quas, J. A., & Maltby, L. (2025, August 18–21). *The advantages of both clinical and scientific expert witnesses on child sexual abuse in US courts* [Paper presentation]. Institute on Violence, Abuse, and Trauma Annual Conference, San Diego, CA, United States.

Johnson, M. K., Hashtroudi, S., & Lindsay, D. S. (1993). Source monitoring. *Psychological Bulletin, 114*(1), 3–28. https://doi.org/10.1037/0033-2909.114.1.3

Lamb, M. E., Brown, D. A., Hershkowitz, I., Orbach, Y., & Esplin, P. W. (2018). *Tell me what happened: Structured investigative interviews of child victims and witnesses* (2nd ed.). John Wiley & Sons.

Lyon, T. D. (2021). *Ten step investigative interview* (Version 3). Retrieved October 3, 2025 from https://drive.google.com/file/d/1JTrEH6eK4pHwCqr7HU5-Bg1CYFUyWrER/view?usp=sharing

Lyon, T. D., & Saywitz, K. J. (1999). Young maltreated children's competence to take the oath. *Applied Developmental Science, 3*(1), 16–27. https://doi.org/10.1207/s1532480xads0301_3

Lyon, T. D., & Saywitz, K. J. (2000). Qualifying children to take the oath: Materials for interviewing professionals. Retrieved September 21, 2025, from https://www.zeroabuseproject.org/wp-content/uploads/2019/02/NCPTC-Qualifying-Children-to-Take-the-Oath.pdf

Nathanson, R., & Saywitz, K. J. (2003). The effects of the courtroom context on children's memory and anxiety. *Journal of Psychiatry & Law, 31*(1), 67–98. https://doi.org/10.1177/009318530303100105

Ohio v. Clark, 576 U.S. 237 (2015).

Quas, J. A., Maltby, L., & Goodman, G. S. (2025). *Psychological science and clinical knowledge: Additive value when making decisions in child sexual abuse legal cases* [Manuscript submitted for publication].

Saywitz, K. J. (1989). Children's conceptions of the legal system: Court is a place to play basketball. In S. J. Ceci, D. F. Ross, & M. P. Toglia (Eds.), *Perspectives on children's testimony* (pp. 131–157). Springer. https://doi.org/10.1007/978-1-4613-8832-6_7

Saywitz, K. J., & Camparo, L. B. (2014). *Evidence-based child forensic interviewing: The developmental narrative elaboration interview*. Oxford University Press.

Saywitz, K. J., Geiselman, R. E., & Bornstein, G. K. (1992). Effects of cognitive interviewing and practice on children's recall performance. *Journal of Applied Psychology, 77*(5), 744–756. https://doi.org/10.1037/0021-9010.77.5.744

Saywitz, K. J., Goodman, G. S., Nicholas, E., & Moan, S. F. (1991). Children's memories of a physical examination involving genital touch: Implications for reports of child sexual abuse. *Journal of Consulting and Clinical Psychology, 59*(4), 682–694. https://doi.org/10.1037/0022-006X.59.5.682

Saywitz, K. J., Jaenicke, C., & Camparo, L. (1990). Children's knowledge of legal terminology. *Law and Human Behavior, 14*(6), 523–535. https://doi.org/10.1007/BF01044879

Saywitz, K. J., Larson, R. P., Hobbs, S. D., & Wells, C. R. (2015). Developing rapport with children in forensic interviews: A systematic review of experimental research. *Behavioral Sciences and the Law, 33*(4), 372–389. https://doi.org/10.1002/bsl.2186

Saywitz, K. J., & Moan-Hardie, S. (1994). Reducing the potential for distortion of childhood memories. *Consciousness & Cognition, 3*(3–4), 408–425. https://doi.org/10.1006/ccog.1994.1023

Saywitz, K., & Nathanson, R. (1993). Children's testimony and their perceptions of stress in and out of the courtroom. *Child Abuse & Neglect, 17*(5), 613–622. https://doi.org/10.1016/0145-2134(93)90083-H

Saywitz, K. J., & Snyder, L. (1996). Narrative elaboration: Test of a new procedure for interviewing children. *Journal of Consulting & Clinical Psychology, 64*(6), 1347–1357. https://doi.org/10.1037/0022-006X.64.6.1347

Saywitz, K. J., Snyder, L., & Lamphear, V. (1996). Helping children tell what happened: A follow-up study of the Narrative Elaboration procedure. *Child Maltreatment, 1*(3), 200–212. https://doi.org/10.1177/1077559596001003003

Saywitz, K. J., Snyder, L., & Nathanson, R. (1999). Facilitating the communicative competence of the child witness. *Applied Developmental Science, 3*(1), 58–68. https://doi.org/10.1207/s1532480xads0301_7

Saywitz, K. J., Wells, C. R., Larson, R. P., & Hobbs, S. D. (2016). Effects of interviewer support on children's memory and suggestibility: Systematic review and meta-analysis of experimental research. *Trauma, Violence, & Abuse, 20*(1), 22–39. https://doi.org/10.1177/1524838016683457

Schank, R., & Abelson, R. (1977). *Scripts, plans, goals, and understanding: An inquiry into human knowledge structures*. Erlbaum.

I

BASIC RESEARCH AND APPLICATION

2

Children's Mental Health and Childhood Adversity

Yo Jackson, Sherille Bosfield, and Sara Such

Adversity is, unfortunately, a common experience for youth. Recent estimates indicate that by the age of 16, the majority of youth in the United States report experiencing at least one traumatic event (Substance Abuse and Mental Health Services Administration, 2024). The kinds of exposures commonly experienced include child abuse or neglect, community or school violence, witnessing or experiencing domestic violence, sudden or violent loss of a loved one, military family-related stressors (e.g., deployment or parental loss or injury), serious accidents, or life-threatening illness (Copeland et al., 2007; Saunders & Adams, 2014). In addition, children who experience or witness violence may face further trauma when required to provide legal testimony about their experiences (e.g., Back et al., 2011; Hobbs et al., 2014; *Maryland v. Craig*, 1990).

While false reports of abuse or neglect are possible, as estimates for child maltreatment also tend to include unsubstantiated reports (Children's Bureau, 2024). For the most part, exposure to childhood adversity means that one has experienced a nonnormative event, something that is not an expected part of childhood, which has potential to influence development and well-being significantly and negatively.

Although most research on childhood adversity includes examinations of exposures like experiencing child maltreatment or the death of a parent, adversity can also include other unfortunate events like moving homes or changing schools, living with a chronic physical illness, or experiencing parental separation or parental substance abuse. For the purposes of this chapter, *adversity*

https://doi.org/10.1037/0000492-002
Handbook on Child Witnesses: Improving Psychological Science and Legal Practice,
G. S. Goodman, T. D. Lyon, S. D. Hobbs, and R. Enriquez (Editors)

will be defined as the events on which there are the greatest amount of research, especially including all forms of child maltreatment.

It is important to note that not all responses in children to adversity exposure result in negative or harmful effects. In fact, some newer research seeks to document the adaptive side of exposure, or the "hidden talents" that are enhanced in individuals after adversity (e.g., faster cognitive recognition of deception by others) for those reared in home environments marked by unpredictability (Frankenhuis et al., 2020). Research shows that, for children who grow up in environments where family or community violence is common, hypervigilance (commonly thought to be a clinical problem) develops as a skill that can serve a protective function (Phan et al., 2020). Even testifying in court can be beneficial to children if they are adequately prepared and protected (see Rush et al., 2013, for a review). These children may perceive more fairness in the legal system compared to children who do not get a chance to provide their testimony (Field & Katz, 2023; Weisz et al., 2011). Although it is possible that children exposed to adversity can adapt and develop skills that make the influence of adversity perhaps less severe, the evidence base for this work with samples of children is mixed at best. That said, the relation between exposure and maladjustment is not automatic, and the purpose of the present chapter is to detail the primary findings in relation to how adversity can and does pose a risk to healthy development for children.

The following discussion of adversity and its effects on children will describe the research base on the adversity exposure–(mal)adjustment relation and explain the evidence base for what is known about the impact of adversity on children. Specifically, we will focus in this chapter on the negative impact of adversity on children's cognitive, social, emotional, and behavioral health, given that these are the primary domains of study in the field of child adversity exposure. The discussion will include not only the immediate effects of exposure but also the long-term effects, when known, attributed to exposure to adversity in childhood. The chapter ends with legal implications and conclusions.

METHODOLOGICAL APPROACHES

The basis for the information presented in this chapter is empirical research, and as such, it is important to first discuss how most research on adversity in childhood is conducted. The approach to research on adversity, whether the sample is made up of youth or adults, can be organized into two groups: (a) research on community samples, or (b) research on targeted or known exposed groups.

Several well-known studies of community samples follow participants over time, resulting in large samples of respondents and their reports of adversity across a large time frame (longitudinal studies). An example of a community sample study is the well-known Adverse Childhood Experiences (ACE) Study (Felitti et al., 1998), which assessed childhood adversity experiences from over

19,000 adults and examined how the total scores of adversities were related to later physical and mental health problems. This landmark study is responsible for what most in the field and the lay public understand to be the negative effects of experiencing multiple adverse events early in one's development. Results from the ACE study showed that exposure to more than three adverse events (e.g., death of a parent, child maltreatment, parental substance abuse, parental mental illness) in childhood was related to a higher rate of miscarriage, diabetes, and obesity in adulthood.

As mentioned, the second type of research is on targeted or known exposed groups. Research on targeted samples includes studies that recruit youth or adults known to have experienced a specific adversity (e.g., child maltreatment) or who are at risk for exposure (e.g., families living below the poverty line). The majority of this research focuses on youth exposed to multiple events or events that are chronic in nature. For example, Wadsworth et al. (2008) evaluated the effect of multiple poverty-related stressors on adolescents' and preadolescents' mental health and well-being. They found that poverty itself was not related to youth outcomes. Instead, poverty-related stressors such as discrimination, family conflict, and exposure to violence predicted mental health, physical health, and legal problems in those who live in low socioeconomic status environments.

Understanding the mechanisms that increase or dampen the impact of exposure is an important consideration when trying to identify the trajectory from exposure to trauma and outcome effects on youth well-being. Exposure to trauma is complex, and the influence it can have on youth functioning is not always straightforward.

IMPACT OF TRAUMA ON COGNITIVE FUNCTIONING

One of the most consistently researched processes in early childhood is the development of cognitive skills. This includes children's ability to learn, think, problem-solve, memorize, develop language skills, reason, and process information, and is essential to how they understand their world. Most of the child eyewitness memory research focuses on these cognitive factors. However, the tests and stimuli used in such studies and in much of the research reviewed here are positive or neutral, rather than trauma-related.

Although the brain continues to grow and change throughout a person's life, the first years of childhood are critical for building the foundation for children's future success (Centers for Disease Control and Prevention, 2023). Children's environments are key to their healthy brain growth. Thus, exposure to trauma or nonnormative and unexpected events can have short-term and long-term negative consequences on children's cognitive development, as tested on standardized tests that are often used in assessment of children in clinical settings.

For example, a 2016 meta-analysis (Op den Kelder et al.) of over 55 studies found that youth exposed to trauma have lower executive functions, specifically in working memory and cognitive flexibility. Studies show that the negative associations with cognitive skills on standardized tests increase with the number of trauma exposures. Moreover, chronic childhood maltreatment is associated with alterations in children's processing and psychomotor speed, executive functioning, standardized memory tests, learning abilities, and overall daily functioning, but important individual differences exist (McCrory et al., 2017; Su et al., 2019). McCrory et al. (2017) stated, "studies on threat processing indicate heightened as well as depressed neural responsiveness in maltreated samples, particularly in the amygdala, thought to reflect threat hypervigilance and avoidance, respectively" (p. 338).

Individuals who have reported experiencing maltreatment are at an increased risk of having learning disabilities and difficulty concentrating (Eiberg, 2023). Some studies have also examined the effects of different types of maltreatment on children's cognitive development. Pears et al. (2008) created a cognitive functioning assessment that evaluated preschool children who have experienced multiple types of abuse. Children who experienced neglect and physical abuse had lower cognitive functioning compared to children who were sexually abused and neglected.

Furthermore, children who experienced neglect showed worse cognitive development outcomes than other types of maltreatment. In a sample of children living in foster care, Viezel et al. (2015) examined the impact of maltreatment on children's cognitive skills. Children who experienced abuse and neglect had lower overall processing speed and verbal comprehension scores compared with youth not living in foster care with no history of child maltreatment. Although it is not clear what specifically accounted for the difference (e.g., time in foster care, direct effects from the maltreatment), both child maltreatment and being placed in foster care are adverse experiences for most youth, and either or both have been related to cognitive maladjustment in childhood (e.g., on school-related tasks). These adverse relations of trauma and performance on standardized tests should be considered in clinical or forensic situations.

Complex trauma (e.g., exposure to multiple adversities at the same—or over a short period of—time) may significantly influence children's cognitive development. Over time, because multiple adversities at the same time likely activate a chronic rather than episodic fight or flight response, it is believed that complex trauma can affect the neurophysiological stress system, which can impair structural and functional areas of the brain responsible for cognitive functions (Bick & Nelson, 2016). The timing of the adversity also plays a role in children's cognitive functioning. Hambrick et al. (2019) found that children who experienced traumatic stress in infancy and early childhood had worse cognitive outcomes than those who experienced adversity in later childhood (see McGuire et al., 2021, for a longitudinal study that found a similar result). Hong et al. (2018) conducted a population-based observational study that examined how cognitive functioning varied by maltreatment experience timing, the effects of various maltreatment types on cognitive functioning, and the associations of maltreatment with cognitive functioning. Children who had a history of maltreatment in early childhood performed lower on standardized tests of cognitive skills than children who experienced maltreatment at older ages.

We should remind the reader again, however, that most of this research focuses on cognitive functioning for positive or neutral information in standardized tests. These studies' results do not mean that child maltreatment adversely affects memory for traumatic real-life events or false suggestions about such events. Moreover, the extent of maltreatment is not always considered in the studies. Children vary in their outcomes, and these studies examine average performance in a nomothetic fashion. Yet, the findings should be considered when working clinically with children who have experienced trauma. Patterns may differ in the forensic context.

Academic Outcomes

One thing is clear: Adversity exposure in childhood is linked to lower-than-expected academic achievement (Oeri & Roebers, 2022). For example, studies have found that children exposed to child maltreatment tend to be enrolled in special education at a higher rate and have poorer educational outcomes than their nonmaltreated peers (Ferrara et al., 2023). Understanding the effects of adversity on children's educational outcomes is essential, as academic achievement can shape the trajectory and success of their future lives. Adversity can potentially influence the skills children need to learn, including the development of language and communication skills, reading comprehension, paying attention in class, motivation, and the ability to retain new academic information (Mental Health America, 2022). When children do not excel in these rudimentary academic skills, their chances for short and long-term academic failure, incarceration, involvement with criminal activity, victimization, and continued experiencing of traumatic events tend to increase over time (Romano et al., 2014; Snow et al., 2020).

We describe a few studies on which these conclusions are based. In a study of over 11,835 second-grade youth with substantiated cases of neglect and unsubstantiated cases of other forms of maltreatment before entry into kindergarten, Fantuzzo et al. (2011) found that such experiences were associated with poorer school outcomes (e.g., behavior problems, low engagement, poor attendance) than in those with post-kindergarten reports. The Fantuzzo et al. study suggests that the timing of maltreatment is important, in that earlier exposure to maltreatment may create a particular risk for poor school performance.

Renner et al. (2022) examined how family violence may affect children's educational outcomes. The sample consisted of children aged 8 to 10 years who experienced or witnessed alleged physical abuse in their household. Children with a child protective services (CPS) report of physical violence maintained lower school attendance rates and lower math and reading proficiency than their nonmaltreated peers. Children who witnessed their sibling being physically abused had the same adverse educational outcomes as children who experienced the abuse directly. Findings from this study suggest that exposure to unpredictable, unstable, and violent parenting may be related to poor performance in school.

When investigating the long-term effects of adversity exposure, studies show that adolescents can succeed despite their stressors and adversities. Positive school experiences, such as feeling connected to teachers and mentors, can influence the trajectory of children's academic health. Smith et al. (2012) explored, for 14- to 18-year-olds who have experienced adverse events, whether positive school experiences protected them from criminal activity in early adulthood. These adolescents were asked about their crime history, educational aspirations, college expectations, school commitment, and grades. Overall, the results showed that the adverse relation between maltreatment exposure and later criminal activity was reduced with positive educational experiences. Specifically, maltreatment was significantly associated with participants reporting lower grade point averages and a negative outlook on their educational aspirations, but only for those who had fewer positive educational experiences. Findings from this study amplify the importance of creating positive academic experiences for youth exposed to maltreatment for long-term positive adjustment.

In summary, for youth exposed to adversity and especially child maltreatment, cognitive functioning is one of the many areas of developmental health that can be hampered by exposure. Although hypervigilance may result from maltreatment, and it may be associated with particularly accurate memory performance for traumatic information (see Chapter 3, this volume), adversity is generally associated with decreased cognitive and educational performance. It is important to consider the age at the time of exposure (Nweze et al., 2023) to best predict the degree of problems in cognitive functioning, such as for school tasks.

IMPACT OF TRAUMA ON SOCIAL FUNCTIONING

Children's social functioning often includes their abilities to embody social roles, adapt to norms, establish and maintain meaningful relationships, and avoid individual difficulties, including isolation and rejection (Michelson et al., 2013). As children often navigate several environmental contexts and continue to do so throughout development, associated social skills and interpersonal relationships within each context are salient factors that influence their immediate and future outcomes.

Effects of Childhood Trauma on Social Functioning

Following experiences of early trauma, scholars have identified loneliness, limited social competence, withdrawal, reduced interpersonal trust, and feeling different from peers as reactions and behaviors that can impede children's social functioning (de Heer et al., 2022). Studies investigating the effects of types of traumas or child maltreatment on children's early social functioning have produced interesting findings. In a study evaluating posttraumatic stress disorder (PTSD) symptoms and social functioning in adolescents who had experienced sexual abuse, higher symptom severity was associated with decreased social functioning (McLean et al., 2013). In a sample of children between the ages of 8 and 12, teachers reported higher total scores of social problems (e.g., not getting along with others, jealousy, teasing), withdrawal, and lower levels of assertion and self-control among children who experienced sexual abuse compared to children without sexual abuse histories (Blanchard-Dallaire & Hébert, 2014). Moreover, children who were sexually abused reported lower levels of interpersonal trust, a finding that could affect children in forensic interviews.

Social skills are often conceptualized as protective skills (e.g., cooperation, assertion, responsibility, self-control; Gresham & Elliot, 1990) that encourage positive interactions with others and are key to promoting social functioning (Lum et al., 2018). One social skill that promotes positive social functioning is perspective-taking, which allows children to communicate, problem solve, and empathize with others as a means of experiencing connectedness (Cigala & Mori, 2022). During an interview assessing their own and their friends' perceptions of their friendship, fewer perspective-taking skills were found among adolescents living in out-of-home care (97% of whom experienced maltreatment) compared to adolescents who did not experience child maltreatment (Kay & Green, 2016). In a sample of mother–child dyads (e.g., recruited from referrals following mothers' experiences of intimate partner violence), children who experienced frequent physical and emotional abuse also experienced poorer social support from peers and family compared to children who experienced infrequent to no abuse (Lamis et al., 2014). Early traumatic experiences may contribute to children's inability to recognize others' support or its functionality (Barrera, 1986); another explanation may be that children exposed to trauma may have difficulty developing social skills such as assertion or cooperation that contribute to social support (Lamis et al., 2014). In any case, social skill difficulties following trauma may influence children's recognition of support from peers or family and hinder children's efforts to seek such support.

Whereas trauma may negatively relate to children's immediate social functioning, early trauma can also have lasting effects. Various individual factors, such as peer rejection sensitivity (e.g., the inaccurate perception of rejection from others, the tendency to expect rejection; Liang et al., 2023), can influence children's abilities to perceive and accept social support. Liang and colleagues (2023) found a direct effect of emotional abuse on later peer victimization in adolescents. Specifically, adolescents who experienced frequent emotional abuse at younger ages were also likely to report sensitivity to peers' rejection and heightened aggressive behaviors in response to interpersonal difficulties compared to adolescents who reported less frequent emotional abuse. The authors' findings suggest that early abuse can inhibit accurate perceptions of social interactions and place children exposed to trauma at greater risk of experiencing adversity or difficulties building lasting friendships (see also Oshri et al., 2017).

Recent literature examining the effects of childhood trauma on social functioning provides important information about interventions to prevent poor social outcomes and improve clinical practice. For example, Tyler et al. (2021) found that adolescent-aged youth exposed to high levels of adversity in early childhood had low scores on interpersonal emotional processing and problem-solving skills. Fortunately, social skills intervention targeted at these deficits was effective in improving the social functioning for youth at the highest levels of trauma exposure.

Overall, these findings highlight the need for future research to continue addressing factors that influence multifinality (having similar histories yet developmental outcomes that vary widely) and the multidirectional nature of peer and family relationships following potentially traumatic events.

RELATIONS OF TRAUMA TO SELF-REGULATION, EMOTIONAL, AND OTHER FUNCTIONING

The development of self-regulatory and adaptive functioning is critical in early childhood. Early childhood maltreatment can lead to disruptions in positive attachment relationships. These disruptions can prevent children from learning how to modulate their emotions and develop self-regulatory skills (Dvir et al., 2014). Additionally, adverse events can affect children's behavioral regulation. The ability to regulate one's behaviors is affected by stress reactivity, which is correlated with exposure to adverse events. Early childhood maltreatment has a distinctive potential negative effect on inhibitory control and poor behavioral regulation (Lipscomb et al., 2021; Marshall et al., 2016). Several of these associations, and other likely effects of child maltreatment, are discussed next.

Exposure to adversity is positively correlated with internalizing and/or externalizing disorders, including in the short term (Schroeder et al., 2018; Snyder et al., 2012). Goldenthal et al. (2023) examined the relation between potentially traumatic events and children's socioemotional and adaptive functioning, self-regulatory skills, and attentional regulation. Their study examined this association in a community-based sample of 3- to 5-year-olds who were primarily Black and Latinx. Children exposed to more maltreatment had elevated internalizing and externalizing behaviors, lower caregiver-reported adaptive behaviors, and less developed emotional, attentional, and behavioral regulation skills. Overall, the study shows the linkage between adverse events and how they may negatively affect children's socioemotional and adaptive developmental outcomes.

Childhood adversity exposure, and childhood maltreatment specifically, appears to increase children's risk of being diagnosed with anxiety, depression, and behavioral problems (Holshausen et al., 2014). Children who experience childhood maltreatment are three times more likely to be diagnosed with adverse mental health outcomes compared to children who have not experienced adverse events (Li et al., 2016). A mechanism that may underlie the association between abuse, mood disorders, and aggression in adolescents is emotional regulation (Heleniak et al., 2016).

Insecure attachment between the child and caregiver can lead to maladaptive emotional regulation strategies. When a child does not know how to cope with adversity, the child may respond by suppressing their emotions, which can lead to mood disorders and aggression (O'Mahen et al., 2015). The inability to reappraise and interpret adversity in a neutral or benign light may be related to feelings of hopelessness. It is also the case that feeling hopeless, especially when adversity exposure is chronic, is often related to the subsequent development of depression symptoms.

In terms of aggression, children who have experienced maltreatment specifically may make errors in overattributing hostile intentions to others, and this may produce an overly defensive approach to interactions with others (Hong et al., 2012; Zhu et al., 2020). Children who often display anger may also isolate themselves from others due to their low frustration tolerance, which may also lead to feelings of loneliness and depression (Galambos et al., 2018).

Childhood adversity exposure is related to changes in brain functioning associated with a tendency to be more susceptible to viewing harmless situations as threats (McLaughlin et al., 2016). As a result, some children exposed to adversity may engage in a constant "fight or flight" response, releasing stress hormones that can change brain chemistry (Koss & Gunnar, 2017). Moreover, alterations in children's stress hormones and brain chemistry are associated with the development of internalizing and externalizing disorders, at least in the short term (Agorastos et al., 2018).

There are also long-term emotional and behavioral correlates of early maltreatment on children's overall trajectory. The overall takeaway from most research is that children exposed to adversity may have a hard time adjusting to life problems and unexpected events later in life. For example, Lansford and colleagues (2002) examined whether early physical maltreatment has long-term effects on children's psychological, behavioral, and academic outcomes. Children who experienced physical maltreatment in early childhood reported more aggressive behaviors in later school years than their nonmaltreated peers. Furthermore, mothers of physically maltreated children reported that their children had high levels of depression and anxiety disorders, dissociation, delinquency, and social problems into adolescence.

Lansford and colleagues (2002) also found that gender and ethnicity played a role in the relation between physical maltreatment and both internal and external disorders. For example, girls who had experienced maltreatment had high scores for problems like anxiety, depression, aggression, and school absences. Moreover, maltreated ethnic minority participants reported more behavioral problems and were suspended from school more often than their

White peers. Perhaps because of racial biases, children of color are often perceived to have more behavioral problems when they are exhibiting the same behavior as their White peers. This can result in children of color being suspended and expelled more frequently than White children (Wood et al., 2017).

Longitudinal studies have also examined the stability of the relation between child maltreatment and anxiety and depression symptoms (Levin & Liu, 2021). For example, individuals who have experienced multiple occurrences of adversity exhibit more symptoms of anxiety and depression (Springer et al., 2007). Also, individuals with a history of childhood trauma's symptoms of anxiety and depression demonstrate a deficit in emotion regulation when assessed again around 20 years later (Young & Widom, 2014). These findings are consistent in showing that adversity exposure is related to negative worldview thinking and emotion processing and that the effects can be long-lasting.

CLINICAL ASSESSMENT AND TRAUMA EXPOSURE

Clinicians play an important role in trauma assessment. Clinical techniques might predate legal involvement in instances where the clinician discovered unreported child maltreatment; as mandated reporters, clinicians' suspicions of child maltreatment must be reported to the Child Protection Agency Hotline or to the police.

Clinical Assessment

That said, in the course of clinical assessment, clinicians often need to determine if trauma exposure has occurred. Self-report is the most common form of assessment for trauma exposure in adults and adolescents. Usually, the form of this assessment is a self-report survey or a checklist where respondents are asked to recall if an event occurred and sometimes how often or under what conditions it occurred.

Assessment of trauma in youth is typically conducted by a trained professional and includes questions about the nature of the event as well as the youth's response to the exposure. Free recall questioning, such as in the Developmental Narrative Elaboration (DNE) interview (Saywitz & Camparo, 2014) or the Ten Step Interview (Lyon, 2021), helps avoid the argument that leading questions were used in the assessment.

Of importance clinically, the assessment should include open questions that can determine if a youth is experiencing a diagnosable condition. It is also important to note that for many youth, especially those who experience more than one event or chronic types of trauma, some behavior problems may predate the trauma exposure and may not represent a change in behavior. For example, a youth might display signs of anxiety or depression before experiencing an episode of abuse, a loss in the family, or exposure to community violence, so it is important that the assessment also determine the degree to which the symptoms are a function of the new exposure or represent a longer-standing mental health condition.

From a clinical perspective, screening measures for trauma exposure should include the most commonly identified kinds of exposures (e.g., child abuse, neglect), the nature of the event (e.g., how severe, how frequent), and the age of the youth when the event occurred. Clinicians should be exceedingly careful when attempting to assess if child abuse or neglect has occurred, making sure their queries are not suggestive or insistent if children deny experiencing abuse. Such questioning can create problems when abuse is reported to law enforcement (Goodman, 2006). Assessment should also query for the most common types of traumatic stress reactions, such as avoidance of trauma-related thoughts or feelings, intrusive thoughts about the event, and hyperarousal or exaggerated startle response.

When assessing trauma exposure, who reports is important. Generally, youth over the age of 8 years can reliably respond to questions about their history of trauma exposure. Assessment of trauma directly from youth usually requires a professional who is clinically trained so that questions can be phrased in the most sensitive way possible. For some youth, recalling the events of their lives may not be as emotionally taxing as one might guess, either because those events were not perceived as threatening or because they have spoken about those events before. For example, youth in foster care are often asked by social services to recount the details of their child maltreatment experiences, and on occasion, law enforcement officials ask too. Thus, telling their "stories" to clinicians may not be as distressing as the first time the maltreatment was reported. It is important, however, to always have children's mental health in mind when assessing for trauma history, as the distress in discussing past events may not always appear immediately. Youth may seem fine only for difficult feelings associated with discussing past events to show up later. In the clinical context, when a child is young, it may be deemed more appropriate for parents or caregivers to respond on behalf of the youth, especially for younger youth. That said, for older youth, parents are not always aware of all the exposures a youth may have experienced, given the tendency to spend more time with peers and in activities outside of their parents' supervision as youth age into adolescence (Stover et al., 2010).

A range of measures are available to assess past adversity exposure, and most of these measures include a fairly long list of possible events one might experience as a child. Although self-report near or close to the time of exposure is likely the most accurate way to get a full inventory of all one has experienced, the majority of research findings are based on adult samples, where adults are asked to think back on their childhoods and recall if a given set of events occurred. The effort to include adults in adversity research is due primarily to concerns that youth might be too vulnerable to experiencing distress if asked about adverse events. However, asking adults is not without its own problems: Thinking back on events that may have occurred decades ago requires fairly strong memory skills. In either case, the standard approach is to ask youth or adults to recall their past experiences, and at least in research, the result is then computed as a total score of adversity exposures.

Legal Implications

Clinicians and forensic interviewers play different roles when dealing with traumatized children. Clinicians try to treat emotional problems; forensic interviewers try to uncover information needed for legal action. Clinicians can profit from lessons learned from forensic interviewers. The different goals may require different procedures, but clinicians should keep in mind that a legal case might be forthcoming. Saywitz et al. (2017) argued for a toolbox approach, in which experienced child clinicians can match a science-based technique to the child's needs and abilities, and still be in a good position to justify their practice to the court, should the occasion arise.

CONCLUSION

Research studies, both cross-sectional and longitudinal, make it clear that for many children, exposure to trauma, no matter the type, is associated with a host of internalizing (e.g., anxiety, depression) and externalizing (e.g., aggression) problems (Price et al., 2013) as well as developmental challenges. Moreover, without treatment, repeated childhood exposure to traumatic events can increase health-risk behaviors (e.g., smoking, eating disorders, substance use, high-risk activities). Fortunately, even when youth experience traumatic events, psychological and developmental problems do not always occur. Whether a youth develops problems is likely due to several factors, including the youth's preexposure functioning, the severity of the event, if the youth experienced the event directly or indirectly (e.g., victim of violence vs. hearing about the violence), and whether the youth has a history of exposure to adverse events.

Although early adversity exposure may have a negative impact on children's immediate and long-term social skills and functioning, the protective nature of social support and competence is well-established. Miller-Graff and colleagues (2017) found that in children between 8 and 12 years old, with documented substantiated, indicated, and unsubstantiated histories of maltreatment, social support (e.g., emotional, affiliative) from family and friends predicted greater perceived social competence. Social support from family and friends is especially important when children must participate in the legal system as a result of their traumas (e.g., Goodman et al., 1992). Together, the authors suggest that existing social support may have lasting effects on children's development of social skills even when faced with early adversity.

Perhaps most importantly, the reaction of those caretakers around youth can play a significant role if the youth develop psychological and developmental problems subsequent to exposure. Having caretakers who respond empathically and provide safety from additional exposures is key to youth recovery. Youth stand the best chance to avoid long-term maladjustment and experience short-lived symptoms after trauma exposures when the identification of exposure is swift, youth are insulated from additional trauma experiences, and they receive mental health, academic, and social support.

It is important to remember that the effects of a given exposure to adversity can and do manifest in a myriad of ways, and that there are no "sure" signs of adversity exposure. Even if the research evidence is consistent that adversity exposure places children at risk for maladjustment, for some children, this is not the case. Therefore, it is important that research continues to examine the mechanisms by which adversity exposure exerts its influence on the psychological health of children. It is also important to note that for the most part, adversity exposure is not just a child's experience, but a family experience. Children do not experience maltreatment, poverty, or any of a wide range of adversities without these events also impacting their parents and families. Thus, research and clinical efforts should also attend to the response and needs of the whole family when adversity occurs and not solely focus on children's reactions. For most children, even those involved in the legal system, recovery from exposure is dependent on the health of other members in the environment, and so the skills of parents and other adults in the child's life are important contributors to lifelong adjustment for children.

REFERENCES

Agorastos, A., Pervanidou, P., Chrousos, G. P., & Kolaitis, G. (2018). Early life stress and trauma: Developmental neuroendocrine aspects of prolonged stress system dysregulation. *Hormones, 17*(4), 507–520. https://doi.org/10.1007/s42000-018-0065-x

Back, C., Gustafsson, P. A., Larsson, I., & Bertero, C. (2011). Managing the legal proceedings: An interpretative phenomenological analysis of sexually abused children's experience with the legal process. *Child Abuse & Neglect, 35*(1), 50–57. https://doi.org/10.1016/j.chiabu.2010.08.004

Barrera, M. (1986). Distinctions between social support concepts, measures, and models. *American Journal of Community Psychology, 14*(4), 413–445. https://doi.org/10.1007/BF00922627

Bick, J., & Nelson, C. A. (2016). Early adverse experiences and the developing brain. *Neuropsychopharmacology, 41*(1), 177–196. https://doi.org/10.1038/npp.2015.252

Blanchard-Dallaire, C., & Hébert, M. (2014). Social relationships in sexually abused children: Self-reports and teachers' evaluation. *Journal of Child Sexual Abuse, 23*(3), 326–344. https://doi.org/10.1080/10538712.2014.888123

Centers for Disease Control and Prevention. (2023, February 24). *Early brain development and health.* https://archive.cdc.gov/www_cdc_gov/ncbddd/childdevelopment/early-brain-development.html

Children's Bureau. (2024). *Child maltreatment 2022.* U.S. Department of Health & Human Services, Administration for Children and Families, Administration on Children, Youth and Families. https://acf.gov/cb/report/child-maltreatment-2022

Cigala, A., & Mori, A. (2022). Perspective taking ability in psychologically maltreated children: A protective factor in peer social adjustment. *Frontiers in Psychology, 13,* Article 816514. https://doi.org/10.3389/fpsyg.2022.816514

Copeland, W. E., Keeler, G., Angold, A., & Costello, E. J. (2007). Traumatic events and posttraumatic stress in childhood. *Archives of General Psychiatry, 64*(5), 577–584. https://doi.org/10.1001/archpsyc.64.5.577

de Heer, C., Bi, S., Finkenauer, C., Alink, L., & Maes, M. (2022). The association between child maltreatment and loneliness across the lifespan: A systematic review and multi-level meta-analysis. *Child Maltreatment, 29*(2), 388–404. https://doi.org/10.1177/10775595221103420

Dvir, Y., Ford, J. D., Hill, M., & Frazier, J. A. (2014). Childhood maltreatment, emotional dysregulation, and psychiatric comorbidities. *Harvard Review of Psychiatry, 22*(3), 149–161. https://doi.org/10.1097/hrp.0000000000000014

Eiberg, M. (2023). Cognitive functioning of children in out-of-home care. *Journal of Child and Adolescent Trauma, 17*(2), 217–230. https://doi.org/10.1007/s40653-023-00580-8

Fantuzzo, J. W., Perlman, S. M., & Dobbins, E. K. (2011). Types and timing of child maltreatment and early school success: A population-based investigation. *Children and Youth Services Review, 33*(8), 1404–1411. https://doi.org/10.1016/j.childyouth.2011.04.010

Felitti, V. J., Anda, R. F., Nordenberg, D., Williamson, D. F., Spitz, A. M., Edwards, V., Koss, M. P., & Marks, J. S. (1998). Relationship of childhood abuse and household dysfunction to many of the leading causes of death in adults: The Adverse Childhood Experiences (ACE) study. *American Journal of Preventive Medicine, 14*(4), 245–258. https://doi.org/10.1016/s0749-3797(98)00017-8

Ferrara, A. M., Mullins, C. A., Ellner, S., & Van Meter, P. (2023). Early child maltreatment and reading processes, abilities, and achievement: A systematic review. *Child Abuse & Neglect, 142*(Part 1), 1–11. https://doi.org/10.1016/j.chiabu.2022.105857

Field, N., & Katz, C. (2023). The experiences and perceptions of sexually abused children as participants in the legal process: Key conclusions from a scoping literature review. *Trauma, Violence, & Abuse, 24*(4), 2758–2771. https://doi.org/10.1177/15248380221111463

Frankenhuis, W. E., Young, E. S., & Ellis, B. J. (2020). The hidden talents approach: Theoretical and methodological challenges. *Trends in Cognitive Science, 24*(7), 569–581. https://doi.org/10.1016/j.tics.2020.03.007

Galambos, N. L., Johnson, M. D., & Krahn, H. J. (2018). The anger–depression connection: Between-persons and within-person associations from late adolescence to midlife. *Developmental Psychology, 54*(10), 1940–1953. https://doi.org/10.1037/dev0000568

Goldenthal, H. J., Gouze, K., Russo, J., Raviv, T., Holley, C., & Cicchetti, C. (2023). Potentially traumatic events, socioemotional and adaptive functioning: Associations with self-regulatory skills in a community sample of primarily Black and Latinx 3–5-year-olds. *Child Psychiatry & Human Development, 56*(3), 669–682. https://doi.org/10.1007/s10578-023-01595-w

Goodman, G. S. (2006). Children's eyewitness memory: A modern history and contemporary commentary. *Journal of Social Issues, 62*(4), 811–832. https://doi.org/10.1111/j.1540-4560.2006.00488.x

Goodman, G. S., Taub, E. P., Jones, D. P. H., England, P., Port, L. K., Rudy, L., & Prado, L. (1992). Testifying in criminal court: Emotional effects on child sexual assault victims. *Monographs of the Society for Research in Child Development, 57*(5), i–159. https://doi.org/10.2307/1166127

Gresham, F. M., & Elliot, S. N. (1990). *Social skills rating system*. American Guidance Service.

Hambrick, E. P., Brawner, T. W., Perry, B. D., Brandt, K., Hofmeister, C., & Collins, J. O. (2019). Beyond the ACE score: Examining relationships between timing of developmental adversity, relational health and developmental outcomes in children. *Archives of Psychiatric Nursing, 33*(3), 238–247. https://doi.org/10.1016/j.apnu.2018.11.001

Heleniak, C., Jenness, J. L., Vander Stoep, A., McCauley, E., & McLaughlin, K. A. (2016). Childhood maltreatment exposure and disruptions in emotion regulation: A transdiagnostic pathway to adolescent internalizing and externalizing psychopathology. *Cognitive Therapy and Research, 40*(3), 394–415. https://doi.org/10.1007/s10608-015-9735-z

Hobbs, S. D., Goodman, G. S., Block, S. D., Oran, D., Quas, J. A., Park, A., Widamin, K. F., & Baumrind, N. (2014). Child maltreatment victims' attitudes about appearing in dependency and criminal courts. *Children and Youth Services Review, 44*, 407–416. https://doi.org/10.1016/j.childyouth.2014.07.001

Holshausen, K., Bowie, C. R., & Harkness, K. L. (2014). The relation of childhood maltreatment to psychotic symptoms in adolescents and young adults with depression. *Journal of Clinical Child & Adolescent Psychology, 45*(3), 241–247. https://doi.org/10.1080/15374416.2014.952010

Hong, J. S., Kral, M. J., Espelage, D. L., & Allen-Meares, P. (2012). The social ecology of adolescent interpersonal violence. *Children and Youth Services Review, 34*(5), 831–838. https://doi.org/10.1016/j.childyouth.2012.01.021

Hong, S., Rhee, T. G., & Piescher, K. N. (2018). Longitudinal association of child maltreatment and cognitive functioning: Implications for child development. *Child Abuse & Neglect, 84*, 64–73. https://doi.org/10.1016/j.chiabu.2018.07.026

Kay, C. L., & Green, J. M. (2016). Social cognitive deficits and biases in maltreated adolescents in U.K. out-of-home care: Relation to disinhibited attachment disorder and psychopathology. *Development and Psychopathology, 28*(1), 73–83. https://doi.org/10.1017/S0954579415000292

Koss, K. J., & Gunnar, M. R. (2017). Annual research review: Early adversity, the hypothalamic–pituitary–adrenocortical axis, and child psychopathology. *Journal of Child Psychology and Psychiatry, 59*(4), 327–346. https://doi.org/10.1111/jcpp.12784

Lamis, D. A., Wilson, C. K., King, N. M., & Kaslow, N. J. (2014). Child abuse, social support, and social functioning in African American children. *Journal of Family Violence, 29*(8), 881–891. https://doi.org/10.1007/s10896-014-9639-9

Lansford, J. E., Dodge, K. A., Pettit, G. S., Bates, J. E., Crozier, J., & Kaplow, J. (2002). A 12-year prospective study of the long-term effects of early child physical maltreatment on psychological, behavioral, and academic problems in adolescence. *Archives of Pediatrics & Adolescent Medicine, 156*(8), 824–830. https://doi.org/10.1001/archpedi.156.8.824

Levin, R. Y., & Liu, R. T. (2021). Life stress, early maltreatment, and prospective associations with depression and anxiety in preadolescent children: A six-year, multiwave study. *Journal of Affective Disorders, 278*, 276–279. https://doi.org/10.1016/j.jad.2020.09.072

Li, M., D'Arcy, C., & Meng, X. (2016). Maltreatment in childhood substantially increases the risk of adult depression and anxiety in prospective cohort studies: Systematic review, meta-analysis, and proportional attributable fractions. *Psychological Medicine, 46*(4), 717–730. https://doi.org/10.1017/s0033291715002743

Liang, C., Liu, J., Gao, Y., & Liu, X. (2023). Developmental pathway from childhood abuse to adolescent peer victimization: The role of rejection sensitivity and aggression. *Journal of Youth and Adolescence, 52*(11), 2370–2383. https://doi.org/10.1007/s10964-023-01833-3

Lipscomb, S. T., Hatfield, B., Lewis, H., Goka-Dubose, E., & Abshire, C. (2021). Adverse childhood experiences and children's development in early care and education programs. *Journal of Applied Developmental Psychology, 72*, 101218. https://doi.org/10.1016/j.appdev.2020.101218

Lum, J. A., Powell, M., & Snow, P. C. (2018). The influence of maltreatment history and out-of-home care on children's language and social skills. *Child Abuse & Neglect, 76*, 65–74. https://doi.org/10.1016/j.chiabu.2017.10.008

Lyon, T. D. (2021). *Ten Step Investigative Interview* (Version 3). http://www.caichildlaw.org/Misc/Ten_Step_Investigative_Interview.pdf

Marshall, D. F., Passarotti, A. M., Ryan, K. A., Kamali, M., Saunders, E. F. H., Pester, B., McInnis, M. G., & Langenecker, S. A. (2016). Deficient inhibitory control as an outcome of childhood trauma. *Psychiatry Research, 235,* 7–12. https://doi.org/10.1016/j.psychres.2015.12.013

Maryland v. Craig, 497 U.S. 836 (1990).

McCrory, E. J., Gerin, M. I., & Viding, E. (2017). Annual research review: Childhood maltreatment, latent vulnerability and the shift to preventative psychiatry—The contribution of functional brain imaging. *Journal of Child Psychology and Psychiatry, 58*(4), 338–357. https://doi.org/10.1111/jcpp.12713

McGuire, A., Gabrielli, J., Hambrick, E., Abel, M. R., Guler, J., & Jackson, Y. (2021). Academic functioning of youth in foster care: The influence of unique sources of social support. *Child and Youth Services Review, 121,* 105867. https://doi.org/10.1016/j.childyouth.2020.105867

McLaughlin, K. A., Sheridan, M. A., Gold, A. L., Duys, A., Lambert, H. K., Peverill, M., Heleniak, C., Shechner, T., Wojcieszak, Z., & Pine, D. S. (2016). Maltreatment exposure, brain structure, and fear conditioning in children and adolescents. *Neuropsychopharmacology, 41*(8), 1956–1964. https://doi.org/10.1038/npp.2015.365

McLean, C. P., Rosenbach, S. B., Capaldi, S., & Foa, E. B. (2013). Social and academic functioning in adolescents with child sexual abuse-related PTSD. *Child Abuse & Neglect, 37*(9), 675–678. https://doi.org/10.1016/j.chiabu.2013.03.010

Mental Health America. (2022). 2022 *State of Mental Health in America report.* https://www.mhanational.org/research/2022-state-of-mental-health-in-america-report/

Michelson, L., Sugai, D. P., Wood, R. P., & Kazdin, A. E. (2013). *Social skills assessment and training with children: An empirically based handbook.* Springer.

Miller-Graff, L. E., Howell, K. H., Martinez-Torteya, C., & Grein, K. (2017). Direct and indirect effects of maltreatment and social support on children's social competence across reporters. *Child Psychiatry & Human Development, 48*(5), 1–753. https://doi.org/10.1007/s10578-016-0698-4

Nweze, T., Ezenwa, M., Ajaelu, C., Hanson, J. L., & Okoye, C. (2023). Cognitive variations following exposure to childhood adversity: Evidence from a pre-registered, longitudinal study. *eClinicalMedicine, 56,* 101784. https://doi.org/10.1016/j.eclinm.2022.101784

Oeri, N., & Roebers, C. M. (2022). Adversity in early childhood: Long-term effects on early academic skills. *Child Abuse & Neglect, 125,* 105507. https://doi.org/10.1016/j.chiabu.2022.105507

O'Mahen, H. A., Karl, A., Moberly, N., & Fedock, G. (2015). The association between childhood maltreatment and emotion regulation: Two different mechanisms contributing to depression? *Journal of Affective Disorders, 174,* 287–295. https://doi.org/10.1016/j.jad.2014.11.028

Op den Kelder, R., Van den Akker, A. L., Geurts, H. M., Lindauer, R. J. L., & Overbeek, G. (2018). Executive functions in trauma-exposed youth: A meta-analysis. *European Journal of Psychotraumatology, 9*(1), 1450595. https://doi.org/10.1080/20008198.2018.1450595

Oshri, A., Topple, T. A., & Carlson, M. W. (2017). Positive youth development and resilience: Growth patterns of social skills among youth investigated for maltreatment. *Child Development, 88*(4), 1087–1099. https://doi.org/10.1111/cdev.12865

Pears, K. C., Kim, H. K., & Fisher, P. A. (2008). Psychosocial and cognitive functioning of children with specific profiles of maltreatment. *Child Abuse & Neglect, 32*(10), 958–971. https://doi.org/10.1016/j.chiabu.2007.12.009

Phan, J., So, S., Thomas, A., & Gaylord-Harden, N. (2020). Hyperarousal and hypervigilance in African American male adolescents exposed to community violence.

Journal of Applied Developmental Psychology, 70, 101168. https://doi.org/10.1016/j.appdev.2020.101168

Price, M., Higa-McMillan, C., Kim, S., & Frueh, B. C. (2013). Trauma experience in children and adolescents: An assessment of the effects of trauma type and role of interpersonal proximity. *Journal of Anxiety Disorders, 27*(7), 652–660. https://doi.org/10.1016/j.janxdis.2013.07.009

Renner, L. M., Piescher, K. N., & Mickelson, N. L. (2022). Academic outcomes among children who experienced or were exposed to physical abuse. *Journal of Interpersonal Violence, 38*(3–4), 2510–2533. https://doi.org/10.1177/08862605221101185

Romano, E., Babchishin, L., Marquis, R., & Fréchette, S. (2014). Childhood maltreatment and educational outcomes. *Trauma, Violence, & Abuse, 16*(4), 418–437. https://doi.org/10.1177/1524838014537908

Rush, E., Quas, J. A., & McAuliff, B. D. (2013). Child witnesses' experiences of distress in criminal court: Sources, consequences, and solutions. In M. K. Miller & B. H. Bornstein (Eds.), *Stress, trauma, and wellbeing in the legal system* (pp. 89–121). Oxford University Press. https://doi.org/10.1093/acprof:oso/9780199829996.003.0005

Saunders, B. E., & Adams, Z. W. (2014). Epidemiology of traumatic experiences in childhood. *Child and Adolescent Psychiatry Clinics of North America, 23*(2), 167–184. https://doi.org/10.1016/j.chc.2013.12.003

Saywitz, K. J., & Camparo, L. B. (2014). *Evidence-based child forensic interviewing: The developmental narrative elaboration interview.* Oxford University Press.

Saywitz, K. J., Lyon, T. D., & Goodman, G. S. (2017). When interviewing children: A review and update. In J. B. Klika & J. R. Conte (Eds.), *The APSAC handbook on child maltreatment* (4th ed., pp. 310–329). SAGE.

Schroeder, A., Slopen, N., & Mittal, M. (2018). Accumulation, timing, and duration of early childhood adversity and behavior problems at age 9. *Journal of Clinical Child & Adolescent Psychology, 49*(1), 36–49. https://doi.org/10.1080/15374416.2018.1496440

Smith, C. A., Park, A., Ireland, T. O., Elwyn, L., & Thornberry, T. P. (2012). Long-term outcomes of young adults exposed to maltreatment. *Journal of Interpersonal Violence, 28*(1), 121–156. https://doi.org/10.1177/0886260512448845

Snow, P., McLean, E., & Frederico, M. (2020). The language, literacy and mental health profiles of adolescents in out-of-home care: An Australian sample. *Child Language Teaching and Therapy, 36*(3), 151–163. https://doi.org/10.1177/0265659020940360

Snyder, F. J., Roberts, Y. H., Crusto, C. A., Connell, C. M., Griffin, A., Finley, M. K., Radway, S., Marshall, T., & Kaufman, J. S. (2012). Exposure to traumatic events and the behavioral health of children enrolled in an early childhood system of care. *Journal of Traumatic Stress, 25*(6), 700–704. https://doi.org/10.1002/jts.21756

Springer, K. W., Sheridan, J., Kuo, D., & Carnes, M. (2007). Long-term physical and mental health consequences of childhood physical abuse: Results from a large population-based sample of men and women. *Child Abuse & Neglect, 31*(5), 517–530. https://doi.org/10.1016/j.chiabu.2007.01.003

Stover, C. S., Hahn, H., Im, J. J., & Berkowitz, S. (2010). Agreement of parent and child reports of trauma exposure and symptoms in the peritraumatic period. *Psychological Trauma, 2*(3), 159–168. https://doi.org/10.1037/a0019156

Su, Y., D'Arcy, C., Yuan, S., & Meng, X. (2019). How does childhood maltreatment influence ensuing cognitive functioning among people with the exposure of childhood maltreatment? A systematic review of prospective cohort studies. *Journal of Affective Disorders, 252,* 278–293. https://doi.org/10.1016/j.jad.2019.04.026

Substance Abuse and Mental Health Services Administration. (2024, May 24). *Understanding child trauma.* U.S. Department of Health and Human Services. https://www.samhsa.gov/child-trauma/understanding-child-trauma

Tyler, P. M., Aitken, A. A., Ringle, J. L., Stephenson, J. M., & Mason, W. A. (2021). Evaluating social skills training for youth with trauma symptoms in residential programs. *Psychological Trauma, 13*(1), 104–113. https://doi.org/10.1037/tra0000589

Viezel, K. D., Freer, B. D., Lowell, A., & Castillo, J. A. (2015). Cognitive abilities of maltreated children. *Psychology in the Schools, 52*(1), 92–106. https://doi.org/10.1002/pits.21809

Wadsworth, M. E., Raviv, T., Reinhard, C., Wolff, B., Santiago, C. D., & Einhorn, L. (2008). An indirect effects model of the association between poverty and child functioning: The role of children's poverty-related stress. *Journal of Loss and Trauma, 13*(2–3), 156–185. https://doi.org/10.1080/15325020701742185

Weisz, V., Wingrove, T., Beal, S. J., & Faith-Slaker, A. (2011). Children's participation in foster care hearings. *Child Abuse and Neglect, 35*(4), 267–272. https://doi.org/10.1016/j.chiabu.2010.12.007

Wood, J. L., Essien, I., & Blevins, D. (2017). Black males in kindergarten: The effect of social skills on close and conflictual relationships with teachers. *Journal of African American Males in Education, 8*(2), 30–50. https://jaamejournal.scholasticahq.com/article/18490.pdf

Young, J. C., & Widom, C. S. (2014). Long-term effects of child abuse and neglect on emotion processing in adulthood. *Child Abuse & Neglect, 38*(8), 1369–1381. https://doi.org/10.1016/j.chiabu.2014.03.008

Zhu, W., Chen, Y., & Xia, L. X. (2020). Childhood maltreatment and aggression: The mediating roles of hostile attribution bias and anger rumination. *Personality and Individual Differences, 162,* 110007. https://doi.org/10.1016/j.paid.2020.110007

3

Children's Memory and Suggestibility for Abuse-Related Events

Yuerui Wu, Nathalie Moriarty, Juan Pablo Hernandez Aldaco, Ben T. Reeb, and Gail S. Goodman

Considerable debate within psychology and law concerns the reliability of children's eyewitness memory. The issue has traditionally centered on whether children have the ability to provide accurate memory statements about past trauma, such as child maltreatment. In light of recent theories (e.g., Ellis et al., 2017, 2020; Young et al., 2022) and empirical evidence (for review, see Cleveland et al., 2022), we argue that the veracity of children's memory reports depends, in large part, on the content of the to-be-remembered information. Thus, instead of debating about whether children are reliable or unreliable witnesses, it is more informative to ask the questions of "when" and "which": *When* are children more or less accurate? And *which* type of information are they better able to remember? Addressing these questions can help scientists and practitioners to better identify, understand, and target factors that facilitate or hinder children's memory performance within legal settings.

Regarding these questions, we tend to agree with adaptation-based theories, such as that proposed by Ellis and colleagues (2017) and others: Children who experience hostile, violent, and/or inconsistent caregiving may cope in ways that facilitate survival at home but hinder functioning in other environments (e.g., school). Such adaptation can lead to content-dependent task performance (e.g., advantages in processing negative or other stress-inducing

---

We thank Wenxin Shen for her assistance.

https://doi.org/10.1037/0000492-003
Handbook on Child Witnesses: Improving Psychological Science and Legal Practice, G. S. Goodman, T. D. Lyon, S. D. Hobbs, and R. Enriquez (Editors)

event details; disadvantages in processing positive or neutral event details), rather than domain-general deficits. According to adaptation-based theories, early trauma and adversity contribute to distinct developmental pathways in children, resulting in specialized cognitive skills in survival-related domains and/or contexts (e.g., Ayoub & Fischer, 2006; Ellis et al., 2017, 2020). Children in institutionalized settings (i.e., an orphanage), compared to those who are not, are more accurate in choosing whether to trust their peers and more sensitive to the presence or absence of social reciprocation (Pitula et al., 2017). Children who have been abused, compared to children who have not been abused, show heightened attention towards potentially threatening stimuli (e.g., angry faces; Shackman et al., 2007). Children who grow up in abusive households are also better able to recount negative versus positive stories (K. W. Fischer et al., 1997). Thus, there is mounting evidence that an adverse early environment facilitates certain attentional and coping skills relevant to survival.

Adaptation-based processing may also have implications for memory. For instance, in studies involving both maltreated and nonmaltreated samples, children with maltreatment histories (compared to those without) evinced similar or even higher accuracy when asked to report on negative and/or abuse-relevant events; however, some of the nonabused children were growing up in high-crime neighborhoods and may have experienced traumatic events other than child abuse (e.g., Eisen et al., 2002, 2007; see also McWilliams et al., 2014). Research on long-term memory for a childhood maltreatment investigation also shows that adults with maltreatment histories are better able to recount childhood discussions that center on the abuse than those that center on relatively positive or neutral conversational content (Wu et al., 2023). In children, some individual differences yield variations in memory performance: For instance, trauma symptoms (e.g., depression, posttraumatic stress disorder) may benefit memory for abuse-specific event details but contribute to errors for positive and/or less personally significant information (Goldfarb et al., 2018; Young & Widom, 2014).

In the current chapter, we focus on children's eyewitness memory for events related to child sexual abuse (CSA), a type of child maltreatment that often invokes concern about possible false reports because of a lack of hard evidence and substantial barriers to disclosure (Hartman et al., 2023; Russell, 1986). We acknowledge that children, like adults, sometimes lie or make false reports, but our focus here is less on memory malleability than on the accuracy of children's memory for traumatic events. We first review research on maltreated children's memory. We then discuss how typically developing children who do not have known maltreatment histories might respond to CSA-related memory interview questions (e.g., questions about touch). Next, we consider children's suggestibility when they are questioned about different types of information. In the end, we highlight key takeaways from the chapter and provide future research directions.

MEMORY IN MALTREATED CHILDREN

Scientific inquiry into maltreated children's memory for personally experienced trauma is constrained by a major methodological challenge: Because it is neither ethical nor legal to randomly assign children to trauma versus nontrauma groups, causal effects of trauma on memory cannot be determined. To give insight into maltreated children's memory for traumatic events, researchers have mainly resorted to two alternative approaches: (a) investigation of memory for real-life trauma (where randomization to trauma vs. nontrauma groups is not possible) or (b) examination of trauma victims' memory for stressful but nontraumatic stimuli (where randomization is possible, but the experimental results are likely less generalizable to memory for trauma). Whereas studies have revealed remarkable memory durability for personally experienced trauma, including for documented CSA (Alexander et al., 2005; Goodman et al., 2014), experimental research has yielded mixed results; maltreatment histories and trauma symptoms are sometimes associated with increased errors (e.g., McWilliams et al., 2014; Windmann & Krüger, 1998). The seemingly inconsistent findings stemmed, at least in part, from the varying content of to-be-remembered information. Next, we discuss children's memory in light of variations in event content that are particularly pertinent to CSA, which is often negative, traumatic, personally significant, central, and/or taboo/secretive.

The emotional nature of content matters for how well children can remember past events. In general, negative emotions and events elicit more coherent autobiographical narratives, more elaborative conversations (in the case of CSA, these conversations might be with a trusted disclosure recipient), and greater appraisals (e.g., reflections on the causes of the emotions) in children than positive information, potentially leading to better memory encoding and retention (Baker-Ward et al., 2022; Fivush et al., 2004; Lagattuta & Wellman, 2002). Repeated, chronic experiences of negative, stressful events (e.g., child abuse) contribute to the development of "fear networks" (Foa & Kozak, 1986), a state of fear characterized by difficulties disengaging from fear-eliciting stimuli and hypervigilance towards trauma cues. Due to the activation of fear networks, maltreated children—perhaps especially when traumatized—may be skilled at remembering negative information (Eisen et al., 2007; Goodman et al., 2014; McWilliams et al., 2014; but see Brewin & Field, 2024).

However, better memory for negative information is not always the case in empirical laboratory research. For example, maltreated children can report more overly general memories (i.e., the tendency to recall events in general terms instead of reporting details about specific event incidents) than nonmaltreated children (e.g., Valentino et al., 2009). However, this task examines the speed and specificness of autobiographical memory reports in response to cue words. Maltreated children may not wish to quickly recount some of their experiences or provide details. As another example, several studies using the Deese–Roediger–McDermott paradigm (DRM; Deese, 1959; Roediger &

McDermott, 1995) revealed that maltreated children made more errors (i.e., false recognition/recall of nonpresent words) than nonmaltreated peers on negative and CSA-related word lists (Baugerud et al., 2016; Goodman et al., 2011; Otgaar et al., 2017; but see Howe et al., 2011). Word lists are unlikely to be traumatic to experience. In any case, one possibility is that event valence only completes part of the puzzle; compared to word lists (like on the DRM task), not only is abuse emotionally negative, it also tends to be intensely negative and relevant to survival. Greater stress at encoding predicts more accurate memory in children, above and beyond the effects of emotional valence (e.g., Goodman et al., 1991; Quas et al., 2016; Shields et al., 2017). Thus, with memory tasks that are minimally distressing, even when the queried information itself is negatively valenced, survival-related processing may not take place.

Another related factor to consider is the to-be-remembered event's personal significance. Whereas DRM studies typically test individuals' recall or recognition memory for word lists, eyewitness memory of abuse concerns personally involved autobiographical recollections. When childhood events are highly salient and/or personally consequential, memory tends to be well retained over long periods of time, sometimes even into adulthood (Fivush et al., 2004; Goldfarb et al., 2020; Ross et al., 2020; Wu et al., 2023). Events that are more stressful, traumatic, distinctive, and/or unexpected have greater personal significance. Adults who nominate documented CSA as the most traumatic event in their lives remember their abuse with relatively high levels of accuracy, regardless of the number of self-reported posttraumatic stress symptoms (Alexander et al., 2005). Maltreated children who have experienced an emergency child protective services removal, compared to those whose removal was planned, are also better able to provide details about high-stress phases of the removal (Baugerud & Melinder, 2012). These events are arguably negative and have substantial personal significance, particularly in acute removal cases where parents and children were not prepared.

Event content can also be differentiated into central details (e.g., information related to the stressor) versus peripheral details (e.g., information that is spatially or temporally distant from the stressor; Christianson, 1992; for other definitions of centrality, see Paz-Alonso et al., 2013). From an adaptation standpoint, information that centers on the sources of threat pertains closely to children's personal safety. As a result, central details of trauma may undergo preferential processing and rehearsal, which can in turn strengthen memories (Christianson, 1992; Neisser et al., 1996). Children who have suffered injuries serious enough to warrant emergency room treatment evince more complete recall of central versus peripheral components of the injury experiences (Peterson, 2012). Similar results have emerged for children with maltreatment histories: In one study, Eisen et al. (2007) tested a child maltreatment sample's memory for an anogenital examination that assessed—as part of a maltreatment investigation—signs of sexual trauma. Findings revealed that children were more accurate and less suggestible in remembering central details of the examination (e.g., who took off their clothes) than peripheral information (e.g., what objects were inside the room); moreover, children with substantiated CSA made fewer omission errors to CSA-related questions (e.g., about anogenital contact) than children from other maltreatment backgrounds. In fact, the experience of a traumatic event may result in children's greater focus on central and personally significant details (McWilliams et al., 2013; Pynoos & Eth, 1984).

Emotional nature, personal significance, and centrality of event content are not the only characteristics that play a role in children's memory. Experiences like CSA carry with them a wealth of socioemotional "baggage" that must also be taken into account when evaluating children's eyewitness reports; although here, incorrect omissions and/or false denials are arguably more often the issues than false reports. With prevalent feelings of fear, shame, confusion, and embarrassment following CSA, children tend to minimize or otherwise under-report their CSA experiences (Edelstein et al., 2005; Goodman et al., 2001; Hartman et al., 2023). Thus, although older children typically evince better event memory than younger children, increasing age may contribute to heightened awareness of the secretive and taboo nature of CSA. This can result in frequent omissions of abuse-related details in older children, even when interviewers ask increasingly suggestive questions (Leach et al., 2017; Saywitz et al., 1991). Children who have falsely denied an event have also been shown to evince poorer subsequent memory for event-related conversations, although memory for the target event itself tends to remain intact (Bücken et al., 2023). Increasing reluctance to provide CSA information may be particularly likely when the suspected abuse involves a familiar individual as the alleged perpetrator (e.g., parent; Kogan, 2004), as is often the case in real-life CSA experiences (Block & Williams, 2019; Children's Bureau, 2022).

Maltreated children's memory for different event content also needs to be considered in conjunction with individual difference factors. For example, some children cope with abuse through dissociation. Children and adults who attempt to limit their processing of emotionally distressing content, whether through avoidant attachment (Mikulincer & Shaver, 2016) or defensive coping strategies (e.g., functional avoidance; J. M. G. Williams et al., 2007), can have poorer encoding or less mental access to trauma-related information, and subsequently less complete and/or less accurate memory (Goodman et al., 2003, 2010; Shaver & Mikulincer, 2007). Evidence even suggests that for children with maltreatment histories, stress at encoding only benefits memory when the children demonstrate low levels of dissociation (Eisen et al., 2007). In addition, maltreatment increases children's risks for posttraumatic stress symptoms (e.g., intrusive thoughts, flashbacks). Whereas maltreatment status per se does not always predict memory, individuals with more posttraumatic stress symptoms can evince trauma-specific memory advantages, remembering personally experienced events that center on the abuse with greater accuracy (Eisen et al., 2007; Goldfarb et al., 2023; Goodman et al., 2001; McWilliams et al., 2014; Wu et al., 2023).

In summary, the emotional nature, personal significance, and centrality of event content affect maltreated children's memory, as does the taboo nature of the event. The extent and type of traumatization may also matter: Whereas avoidance-oriented coping tends to be associated with poorer memory, posttraumatic stress symptoms can potentially lead to better memory for abuse-related incidents.

MEMORY IN NONMALTREATED CHILDREN

To supplement the relatively sparse research on maltreated children's memory, we next consider how typically developing children who come from nonmaltreatment backgrounds remember and report on CSA-related experiences. Despite historically heated debates about laboratory versus ecological approaches to memory research (for review, see Kvavilashvili & Ellis, 2004), most contemporary researchers acknowledge the value and importance of both. To better understand children's memory statements related to alleged abuse, laboratory studies have tested nonmaltreated children's memory for events sharing features with traumatic events, such as CSA. Field research further examined nonmaltreated children's memory for more negative, personal, and abuse-relevant events outside of the laboratory, in the "real world." Together, this creates a body of empirical evidence—holding abuse status relatively constant—that can elucidate how children might respond to questions about experience (e.g., genital touch) that is often of interest during CSA investigations.

There is concern about whether nonmaltreated children would admit to CSA allegations. Sexual victimization can take many forms (e.g., fondling, oral sex, penetration), with inappropriate touch being one of the most recurrent violations in CSA cases (D. G. Fischer & McDonald, 1998; Negriff et al., 2014). In some laboratory studies, children are interviewed about standardized interactions that either involve or do not involve an adult touching the children in socially acceptable manners (e.g., on the arm). Few children spontaneously recall touches (e.g., Bruck, 2009; Quas et al., 2007). When cued with more specific memory prompts, as is often necessary with young children, higher rates of incorrect touches are reported, but children (including those as young as 3–4 years old) rarely disclose, at least in research studies, genital touches that have not occurred in response to nonmisleading questions (e.g., Krackow & Lynn, 2003; Morgan et al., 2013).

Note, however, that false reports can still surface when nonmaltreated children are questioned within suggestive and/or biased contexts. The use of anatomical dolls and body maps, for example, has been found to sometimes increase children's false reports of genital contact (for a review, see Poole & Bruck, 2012). Suggestive questioning, in combination with social pressure, may also result in false allegations, especially when children are young or when suggestions are posed repeatedly (e.g., Bruck et al., 1995; Bruck & Ceci, 1999; Garven et al., 1998; Schreiber et al., 2006; see also Chapter 7, this volume). Even when interviewers reportedly adhere to best-practice guidelines, confirmation bias—such as when adults are driven by prior beliefs to selectively seek evidence from children—can occur before, during, or after the interviews to increase the likelihood of children's false reports (O'Donohue & Cirlugea, 2021). To address these issues, some evidence-based recommendations have proposed the use of both structured interview protocols (e.g., the National Institute of Child Health and Human Development [NICHD] Protocol) and a hypothesis-testing approach aimed at reducing potential interviewer bias (e.g., Korkman et al., 2024; but see MacDonald et al., 2025).

Laboratory experiments on memory for touch-related actions, although informative, have their limitations. Children may remember benign physical contact that is commonly observed in everyday interactions very differently from sexual violations, which are often intrusive, embarrassing, exploitative, and traumatic (Finkelhor, 1984). Because inducing emotions is extremely difficult, and laboratories are often limited in endeavors such as implementing touches that are highly negative and/or inappropriate (Głomb, 2022), some researchers have turned to naturalistic methods that examine children's memory for more ecologically valid events outside of the laboratories. For example, several studies have queried children's abilities to remember and report on stressful medical events (e.g., inoculations, anogenital checkups), some of which involved genital contact (e.g., Chae et al., 2014; Goodman et al., 1994; Peterson, 2012; Saywitz et al., 1991). Whereas older age is associated with more accurate memory for medical procedure body contact, even very young children (e.g., preschoolers) can report details about CSA-specific actions (e.g., genital touch) with accuracy, particularly in free-recall (e.g., Chae et al., 2014; Saywitz et al., 1991).

The type of interpersonal involvement also plays a role in children's memory. Over 90% of maltreatment cases are committed by relatives, neighbors, or authority figures—individuals who are well-known to the children (Children's Bureau, 2022). However, most memory studies with nonmaltreated children test memory for briefly seen strangers, with whom there is no prior relationship or knowledge base. A handful of laboratory studies have examined the role of interpersonal familiarity on memory in children up to age 10. In two of these studies, children were randomly assigned to interact with either a familiar adult (e.g., a researcher with prior exposure) or an unfamiliar adult (e.g., a stranger without prior exposure); 1 to 3 weeks later, their memories were tested for the interactions (Cordón et al., 2016; Lepore & Sesco, 1994). On several memory measures, familiarity was associated with greater accuracy. Moreover, findings of the Wu and colleagues (in press) study revealed that familiarity with the parent was associated with more accurate and consistent memory responses when children were responding to questions about documented actions that are often of interest during CSA investigation (e.g., touching, hitting, picture taking; see also Greenhoot et al., 2005), consistent with an adaptation-based theory prediction.

When abuse does occur, the private and often secretive nature of CSA raises concerns about underreporting or false denials (Bücken et al., 2023; Eisen et al., 2021). By manipulating the content of the to-be-remembered event, research with nonmaltreated children provides insight into content-related factors that potentially contribute to incorrect omissions of CSA. Studies have used experimental paradigms to examine children's memory reports about staged transgressions (e.g., toy breaking) committed by the children themselves (e.g., S. Williams et al., 2020) or others (e.g., Mugno & Malloy, 2023). Findings suggest that children are less willing to disclose secretive compared to nonsecretive adult transgressions (Bottoms et al., 2002; Gordon et al., 2014). Identity of the "transgressor" also matters, with children being less forthcoming when the perceived transgressions are committed by more familiar or trusted adults, such as parents (Lyon et al., 2010; Mugno & Malloy, 2023). Memory responses for events related to the staged transgressions, when provided and assessed, tend to be highly accurate (Klemfuss et al., 2016; Pipe & Wilson, 1994; Stolzenberg et al., 2018).

Similar to research with maltreated children, studies of nonmaltreated children have identified important individual differences related to child–parent attachment. For example, securely attached, nonmaltreated children, who tend to use more elaborative narrative strategies to process distressing information, demonstrate more accurate (and more complete) memories for stressful events (Chae et al., 2018; Dykas & Cassidy, 2011). Of note, the positive relation between children's attachment security and memory may be specific to attachment-activating content. Memory studies using stimuli that do not necessarily activate the attachment system, such as stories and puppet shows, yielded mixed results (e.g., Alexander et al., 2010; Belsky et al., 1996). Gonzalves and colleagues (2022) interviewed 9- to 12-year-old children about a moderately stressful experience (i.e., the Strange Situation procedure; Ainsworth et al., 1978) that took place 6 to 7 years prior. Only children who reported relatively low levels of attachment anxiety manifested stress-related memory advantages. Taken together, findings suggest that children's attachment orientations might interplay with the content and/or emotional impact of the to-be-remembered event to influence memory.

In summary, nonmaltreated children are generally reluctant to generate false reports of taboo physical contact, including genital touch, unless highly and/or repeated suggestive implications and questioning techniques are used. Moreover, important relational factors must be considered. Children tend to better recount interactions with familiar versus unfamiliar adults, although a close relationship with an adult transgressor can also contribute to disclosure barriers, particularly when the to-be-remembered event is perceived as secretive. Secure attachment is associated with children's accurate reports of stressful interpersonal events.

FALSE MEMORY IN CHILDREN

Although traumatic events can be recounted, they are not immune to memory errors. Understanding how children process misinformation about CSA-related events is important because children, especially young children, are often (but not always) more suggestible than adults (Otgaar et al., 2018; see also Chapter 7, this volume). Several factors contribute to age-related vulnerability. Children have a more limited knowledge base and less developed cognitive functioning than adults. Children may be more susceptible to adults' social pressure. Compared to adults, children also tend to be less adept at using metacognitive strategies, which can facilitate the rejection of suggested false information (Brainerd et al., 2003; Moore et al., 2018). To evaluate children's suggestibility, responses need to be considered in relation to the varying sources of misinformation and memory content.

False reports can arise due to semantic associations between presented and nonpresented stimuli (e.g., categorized word lists or pictures), or exposure to postevent misinformation. Association-based memory errors—such as those elicited using the DRM paradigm—differ from suggestion-based errors, which result from externally generated misinformation and have limited reliance on the processing of meaning connections (e.g., Ost et al., 2013; Otgaar & Candel, 2011). Suggestion-based false memory (i.e., suggestibility) is particularly relevant to legal cases, because children can be exposed to misinformation (e.g., from parents) following alleged abuse, and forensic interviews may be carried out in leading or even misleading manners. Therefore, we focus on suggestion-based errors in the current chapter.

The classic misinformation paradigm that is used to assess people's susceptibility to false suggestions involves a presented or experienced event, followed by exposure to false information (e.g., inconsistent details), and then one or more memory tests (e.g., Loftus, 2005). Alternatively, through the use of misleading prompts—such as tag questions (e.g., "He forced you to do that, didn't he?") and presuppositions (e.g., "Did he touch your pee-pee over or under your clothes?" when child did not mention genital contact)—misinformation can be suggested to children during interviews or other forensic/legal contexts in both laboratory experiments and abuse investigations (e.g., Andrews & Lamb, 2021).

We first consider children's tendency to produce false memory reports in response to suggestive questioning. In laboratory studies, older compared to younger children can better resist false suggestions (e.g., Bruck & Ceci, 1999; Paz-Alonso & Goodman, 2016). However, when children's memory was tested for an analogue to CSA (i.e., an anogenital examination by a doctor), few children (with or without maltreatment histories) assented to suggestions about nonexperienced inappropriate contact, even when young children (e.g., 3-year-olds) were interviewed in suggestive manners; additionally, in those studies, CSA victims were less suggestible than controls (Eisen et al., 2002, 2007).

There is also often concern that parents or other adults would "coach" and/or inadvertently bias the children before formal interviews take place. For example, interviewers or other investigators might hold strong beliefs about the presence or absence of abuse allegations, leading to biased questioning and the subsequent production of false event details (e.g., O'Donohue & Cirlugea, 2021; Quas et al., 2007). Conversations within the family might also introduce narratives that were not initially present in the children's memory (Lawson et al., 2018; Principe & London, 2022). Potentially, this can lead to the creation of false reports (due to distorted memory and/or belief) when allegations come to light, although a majority of studies to date examined fun or noninteractive events (Chae et al., 2022). Moreover, empirical evidence of such a memory distortion effect is mixed (Galindo & Harris, 2017; McWilliams & Goodman, 2019; Schaaf et al., 2015). Here, source monitoring manipulations can help (e.g., Did your parent say something about that?).

To investigate how postevent misinformation suggested by family members might be incorporated into memory statements, some researchers have used the false memory implantation paradigm, in which individuals are asked to elaborate on false life events allegedly provided by their parents (e.g., Loftus, 2003; Scoboria et al., 2017). The rate of implanted false memory depends in part on event content. For example, several studies revealed that children have a greater tendency to incorporate misinformation into their memory reports when the suggested details are more plausible (e.g., lost in a mall [plausible] vs. receiving a rectal enema [implausible]; Pezdek & Hodge, 1999).

Studies later found that event plausibility and schematic knowledge (i.e., organized mental representations of objects, people, events) are separate but easily confounded constructs (e.g., adults are more likely to think that they experienced an implausible childhood event if they read about schematic [faked] news stories stating that the event happened to many children; Mazzoni et al., 2001). This is much like how beliefs about event occurrence and memory do not always coincide (e.g., Most adults believe they were fed as young infants, but they have no memory of it; Scoboria et al., 2004). Making an implausible event more schema-conforming (e.g., providing background information, inducing stereotypes) can increase adults' and children's susceptibility to false suggestions (Cordón et al., 2016; Leichtman & Ceci, 1995; Mazzoni et al., 2001; Moore et al., 2018; Strange et al., 2006). Note, however, that invoking negative stereotypes (e.g., "clumsy") about the target person can simultaneously boost children's correct responses (Cordón et al., 2016; Moore et al., 2018), suggesting that true and false memories are not always the flip side of each other.

Some information (e.g., self-related attributes and experiences) may also leave more enduring footprints in memory than others (e.g., Ross et al., 2020). Not only does greater memory strength protect against children's suggestibility, when initial memory is strong, repeated questioning—which is often considered highly suggestive—can still result in or reinstate accurate recollections (Marche & Howe, 1995; Peterson et al., 2004; Pezdek & Roe, 1995; Quas et al., 2007; Roediger & Abel, 2022).

Thus, although children are often more suggestible than adults, the extent of their suggestibility depends not only on the use of misleading questions but also on the content and context of the situation. Although young children (e.g., 3-year-olds) are often more suggestible than older children and adults, when memory is strong, children can resist many types of false suggestions, including those from their own parents.

FUTURE DIRECTIONS

The issue of memory content and the veracity of children's eyewitness accounts has important implications for clinical intervention strategies and legal decisions, where obtaining accurate statements is critical. This is particularly true for CSA cases, because children's memory reports often serve as the main evidence in legal actions (Goldfarb et al., 2020; Goodman et al., 2014). In the present chapter, we have integrated findings from traditionally separate scientific endeavors (e.g., laboratory studies, field experiments) to demonstrate that children can provide accurate memory responses about abuse and abuse-related events, but at times also manifest errors. The extent to which accuracy and/or inaccuracy arise depends heavily on what children are asked to remember. The same information may have different meanings to children with varying life experiences (e.g., maltreatment vs. no maltreatment); children from similar backgrounds can also process emotional materials in distinct ways. Here we highlight some of the main takeaways and offer future directions.

Empirical evidence suggests that more personally significant event details may be better remembered than peripheral or less meaningful details. This is in line with adaptation-based theories, which argue that children who have experienced trauma preferentially process and remember threat-related information, such as events related to their victimization (e.g., Ellis et al., 2017, 2020). When asked about events that center on potential trauma or abuse, maltreated children are highly accurate and sometimes less suggestible than their nonmaltreated peers (e.g., Eisen et al., 2007). Accuracy tends to decrease, and suggestibility increase, for events that are less consequential or less threatening to children's personal safety (e.g., positive or neutral interactions, peripheral event details; but see Otgaar et al., 2017). The issue of how good memory for maltreatment can be should make us think more about the veracity of alleged abuse reports, not just about false reports. Unless highly suggestive techniques and implications are used, especially with young children (e.g., misleading prompts), both maltreated and nonmaltreated children generally provide few false CSA-related memory statements (e.g., about nonexperienced genital touch) in forensic-like interview contexts, despite what "memory experts" might contend (e.g., Diamond et al., 2020). Of course, a child or adult can always lie or be mistaken, but that is often not the same as a memory malleability error about central, personally significant events, such as whether CSA happened. Then again, errors can happen.

Content of to-be-remembered information and the associated memory advantages are not only about task demands, but also about children's perception of the events. Positive activities can have negative components, and not all children find supposedly negative events stressful. Even CSA victims do not uniformly perceive their abuse as traumatic. They may be too young to understand the nature of sexual behaviors at the time, and perpetrators often normalize sexual contact through grooming (Clancy, 2009; Winters et al., 2020). Assessing stress at encoding is one way to disentangle the issues involved with how perceptions of an event might relate to children's memory (e.g., Shields et al., 2017), but there is much more to emotional encounters besides stress. Other event characteristics, such as those reviewed in the present chapter (e.g., emotional qualities, personal significance, centrality, sexual connotation, plausibility), can also play a role. However, existing research primarily focuses on single event characteristics (but see Quas et al., 2016), measured or classified mostly via adult ratings, intuitive judgments, or inconsistent criteria (e.g., Paz-Alonso et al., 2013). Future memory studies that take a multivariate approach and those that evaluate event qualities from children's perspectives are needed to help clarify some of the mixed findings within the literature.

In the current chapter, we have also discussed individual variability in how children perceive and remember different events. For example, older age is typically associated with more accurate responses and lower suggestibility in both maltreated and nonmaltreated children (Bjorklund & Causey, 2017). One future challenge is in how best to ask young children detailed questions without leading to errors. Some young children may not view genital touch as particularly unusual or embarrassing, which might reduce disclosure reluctance but also increase their CSA suggestibility. However, with CSA-related content, younger children can evince robust memory while older children (e.g., adolescents) become prone to omissions; the result may be a diminished or even vanished age effect. Moreover, other individual differences in children's trauma-related coping and dispositions—avoidance, posttraumatic stress symptoms, and attachment—also at times interact with event content to result in different memory findings. How event content and individual difference factors jointly contribute to children's eyewitness memory reports is an important avenue of future research.

Whereas our review of prior studies suggests that with increasingly abuse-specific events, children can be more resistant to suggestions, we also find evidence that children may be unwilling to report sensitive information, such as details related to CSA. Thus, a lack of details alone should not become the basis for questioning children's claims about alleged CSA. To date, much of the false memory research has focused on suggestibility. However, inaccuracy in eyewitness reports can originate from errors of omission (i.e., false exclusion of experienced events from memory reports), on top of commission (i.e., false inclusion of nonexperienced events in memory reports). Both types of errors are of great legal concern, but in different ways: On the one hand, commission errors can potentially lead to false accusations and/or wrongful convictions; on the other hand, omission errors increase the risks of not being able to intervene and protect abused children in a timely manner.

Omission errors for CSA-related events sometimes result from cognitive limitations (as in the case for young children), but other times have more to do with socioemotional dynamics than memory failures. It is thus important for scientific endeavors not only to research content-related factors that contribute to suggestibility, but also those that create or reduce disclosure barriers when children are questioned about alleged abuse (e.g., interviewer rapport and support; Saywitz et al., 2015, 2019). Moreover, only a few studies have examined children's disclosure and memory for "forbidden" versus socially accepted adult behaviors (e.g., Stolzenberg et al., 2018). Given that event secrecy seems to be associated with children's greater reluctance to discuss adult transgressions (e.g., Bottoms et al., 2002), it is important to more systematically investigate how supposedly norm-violating interactions with adults and the associated emotional impact might relate to children's eyewitness reports within accuracy-focused interview settings.

CONCLUSION

Historically, maltreated children have been treated as incompetent or inaccurate reporters in forensic contexts—regardless of their ages or histories. However, recent research arguably demonstrated that children's memory for personally significant, trauma-specific events tends to be particularly accurate and resistant to false suggestions. Varying qualities of the target events and individual differences often lead to differences in what children remember. The content of the to-be-remembered information is thus an essential component to consider when evaluating the accuracy and completeness of children's eyewitness memory.

REFERENCES

Ainsworth, M. D. S., Blehar, M. C., Waters, E., & Wall, S. (1978). *Patterns of attachment: A psychology study of the Strange Situation*. Erlbaum.

Alexander, K. W., O'Hara, K. D., Bortfeld, H. V., Anderson, S. J., Newton, E. K., & Kraft, R. H. (2010). Memory for emotional experiences in the context of attachment and social interaction style. *Cognitive Development, 25*(4), 325–338. https://doi.org/10.1016/j.cogdev.2010.08.002

Alexander, K. W., Quas, J. A., Goodman, G. S., Ghetti, S., Edelstein, R. S., Redlich, A. D., Cordon, I. M., & Jones, D. P. H. (2005). Traumatic impact predicts long-term memory for documented child sexual abuse. *Psychological Science, 16*(1), 33–40. https://doi.org/10.1111/j.0956-7976.2005.00777.x

Andrews, S. J., & Lamb, M. E. (2021). Lawyers' question repetition and children's responses in Scottish criminal courts. *Journal of Interpersonal Violence, 36*(1–2), 276–296. https://doi.org/10.1177/0886260517725739

Ayoub, C. C., & Fischer, K. W. (2006). Developmental pathways and intersections among domains of development. In K. McCartney & D. Phillips (Eds.), *Blackwell handbook of early childhood development* (pp. 62–81). Blackwell. https://doi.org/10.1002/9780470757703.ch4

Baker-Ward, L., Ornstein, P., & Thomas, T. E. (2022). Children's memory for forensically relevant experiences. In G. C. Calloway & S. M. Lee (Eds.), *Handbook of children in the legal system* (pp. 55–83). Routledge. https://doi.org/10.4324/9780429397806-3

Baugerud, G. A., Howe, M. L., Magnussen, S., & Melinder, A. (2016). Maltreated and non-maltreated children's true and false memories of neutral and emotional word lists in the Deese/Roediger–McDermott task. *Journal of Experimental Child Psychology, 143*, 102–110. https://doi.org/10.1016/j.jecp.2015.10.007

Baugerud, G. A., & Melinder, A. (2012). Maltreated children's memory of stressful removals from their biological parents. *Applied Cognitive Psychology, 26*(2), 261–270. https://doi.org/10.1002/acp.1817

Belsky, J., Spritz, B., & Crnic, K. (1996). Infant attachment security and affective–cognitive information processing at age 3. *Psychological Science, 7*(2), 111–114. https://doi.org/10.1111/j.1467-9280.1996.tb00339.x

Bjorklund, D. F., & Causey, K. B. (2017). *Children's thinking: Cognitive development and individual differences.* SAGE Publications.

Block, S. D., & Williams, L. M. (2019). *The prosecution of child sexual abuse: A partnership to improve outcomes.* U.S. Department of Justice, Office of Justice Programs, National Institute of Justice. https://www.ncjrs.gov/pdffiles1/nij/grants/252768.pdf

Bottoms, B. L., Goodman, G. S., Schwartz-Kenney, B. M., & Thomas, S. N. (2002). Understanding children's use of secrecy in the context of eyewitness reports. *Law and Human Behavior, 26*(3), 285–313. https://doi.org/10.1023/A:1015324304975

Brainerd, C. J., Reyna, V. F., Wright, R., & Mojardin, A. H. (2003). Recollection rejection: False-memory editing in children and adults. *Psychological Review, 110*(4), 762–784. https://doi.org/10.1037/0033-295X.110.4.762

Brewin, C., & Field, A. (2024). Meta-analysis shows traumatic memories in posttraumatic stress disorder lack coherence. *Clinical Psychological Science, 12*(5), 1027–1033. https://doi.org/10.1177/21677026241240456

Bruck, M. (2009). Human figure drawings and children's recall of touching. *Journal of Experimental Psychology: Applied, 15*(4), 361–374. https://doi.org/10.1037/a0017120

Bruck, M., & Ceci, S. J. (1999). The suggestibility of children's memory. *Annual Review of Psychology, 50*(1), 419–439. https://doi.org/10.1146/annurev.psych.50.1.419

Bruck, M., Ceci, S. J., Francouer, E., & Renick, A. (1995). Anatomically detailed dolls do not facilitate preschoolers' reports of a pediatric examination involving genital touching. *Journal of Experimental Psychology: Applied, 1*(2), 95–109. https://doi.org/10.1037/1076-898X.1.2.95

Bücken, C. A., Otgaar, H., London, K., Riesthuis, P., Battista, F., & Mangiulli, I. (2023). 'Nothing happened': Legal implications of false denials among abused children. *Child Abuse Review, 32*(2), Article e2791. https://doi.org/10.1002/car.2791

Chae, Y., Goodman, G. S., Larson, R. P., Augusti, E. M., Alley, D., VanMeenen, K. M., Culver, M., & Coulter, K. P. (2014). Children's memory and suggestibility about a distressing event: The role of children's and parents' attachment. *Journal of Experimental Child Psychology, 123*, 90–111. https://doi.org/10.1016/j.jecp.2014.01.005

Chae, Y., Goodman, M., Goodman, G. S., Troxel, N., McWilliams, K., Thompson, R. A., Shaver, P. R., & Widaman, K. F. (2018). How children remember the Strange Situation: The role of attachment. *Journal of Experimental Child Psychology, 166*, 360–379. https://doi.org/10.1016/j.jecp.2017.09.001

Chae, Y., Hartman, D. T., & Goodman, G. S. (2022). What children remember after talking with parents: Implications for children's memory and testimony. *Journal of Applied Research in Memory and Cognition, 11*(3), 328–333. https://doi.org/10.1037/mac0000067

Children's Bureau. (2022). *Child maltreatment 2021.* U.S. Department of Health & Human Services, Administration for Children and Families, Administration on Children, Youth and Families. https://www.acf.hhs.gov/cb/report/child-maltreatment-2021

Christianson, S. A. (1992). Emotional stress and eyewitness memory: A critical review. *Psychological Bulletin, 112*(2), 284–309. https://doi.org/10.1037/0033-2909.112.2.284

Clancy, S. A. (2009). *The trauma myth.* Basic Books.

Cleveland, K. C., Wu, Y., Hartman, D. T., Brown, L. F., & Goodman, G. S. (2022). Children's memory development: Emotion, distress, and trauma. In M. L. Courage & N. Cowan (Eds.), *The development of memory in infancy and childhood* (pp. 297–336). Psychology Press. https://doi.org/10.4324/9781003016533-13

Cordón, I. M., Silberkleit, G., & Goodman, G. S. (2016). Getting to know you: Familiarity, stereotypes, and children's eyewitness memory. *Behavioral Sciences & the Law, 34*(1), 74–94. https://doi.org/10.1002/bsl.2233

Deese, J. (1959). On the prediction of occurrence of particular verbal intrusions in immediate recall. *Journal of Experimental Psychology, 58*(1), 17–22. https://doi.org/10.1037/h0046671

Diamond, N. B., Armson, M. J., & Levine, B. (2020). The truth is out there: Accuracy in recall of verifiable real-world events. *Psychological Science, 31*(12), 1544–1556. https://doi.org/10.1177/0956797620954812

Dykas, M. J., & Cassidy, J. (2011). Attachment and the processing of social information across the life span: Theory and evidence. *Psychological Bulletin, 137*(1), 19–46. https://doi.org/10.1037/a0021367

Edelstein, R. S., Ghetti, S., Quas, J. A., Goodman, G. S., Alexander, K. W., Redlich, A. D., & Cordón, I. M. (2005). Individual differences in emotional memory: Adult attachment and long-term memory for child sexual abuse. *Personality and Social Psychology Bulletin, 31*(11), 1537–1548. https://doi.org/10.1177/0146167205277095

Eisen, M. L., Goodman, G. S., Diep, J., Lacsamana, M., Ristrom, L. J., & Qin, J. J. (2021). Disclosures of sexual and physical abuse across repeated interviews. *Journal of Child Sexual Abuse, 30*(8), 932–952. https://doi.org/10.1080/10538712.2021.1960457

Eisen, M. L., Goodman, G. S., Qin, J., Davis, S., & Crayton, J. (2007). Maltreated children's memory: Accuracy, suggestibility, and psychopathology. *Developmental Psychology, 43*(6), 1275–1294. https://doi.org/10.1037/0012-1649.43.6.1275

Eisen, M. L., Qin, J., Goodman, G. S., & Davis, S. L. (2002). Memory and suggestibility in maltreated children: Age, stress arousal, dissociation, and psychopathology. *Journal of Experimental Child Psychology, 83*(3), 167–212. https://doi.org/10.1016/S0022-0965(02)00126-1

Ellis, B. J., Abrams, L. S., Masten, A. S., Sternberg, R. J., Tottenham, N., & Frankenhuis, W. E. (2020). Hidden talents in harsh environments. *Development and Psychopathology, 34*(1), 95–113. https://doi.org/10.1017/S0954579420000887

Ellis, B. J., Bianchi, J., Griskevicius, V., & Frankenhuis, W. E. (2017). Beyond risk and protective factors: An adaptation-based approach to resilience. *Perspectives on Psychological Science, 12*(4), 561–587. https://doi.org/10.1177/1745691617693054

Finkelhor, D. (1984). *Child sexual abuse: New theory and research*. Free Press.

Fischer, D. G., & McDonald, W. L. (1998). Characteristics of intrafamilial and extrafamilial child sexual abuse. *Child Abuse & Neglect, 22*(9), 915–929. https://doi.org/10.1016/S0145-2134(98)00063-5

Fischer, K. W., Ayoub, C., Singh, I., Noam, G., Maraganore, A., & Raya, P. (1997). Psychopathology as adaptive development along distinctive pathways. *Development and Psychopathology, 9*(4), 749–779. https://doi.org/10.1017/S0954579497001429

Fivush, R., Sales, J. M., Goldberg, A., Bahrick, L., & Parker, J. (2004). Weathering the storm: Children's long-term recall of Hurricane Andrew. *Memory, 12*(1), 104–118. https://doi.org/10.1080/09658210244000397

Foa, E. B., & Kozak, M. J. (1986). Emotional processing of fear: Exposure to corrective information. *Psychological Bulletin, 99*(1), 20–35. https://doi.org/10.1037/0033-2909.99.1.20

Galindo, J. H., & Harris, P. L. (2017). Mother knows best? How children weigh their firsthand memories against their mothers' reports. *Cognitive Development, 44*, 69–84. https://doi.org/10.1016/j.cogdev.2017.08.008

Garven, S., Wood, J. M., Malpass, R. S., & Shaw, J. S., III. (1998). More than suggestion: The effect of interviewing techniques from the McMartin Preschool case. *Journal of Applied Psychology, 83*(3), 347–359. https://doi.org/10.1037/0021-9010.83.3.347

Głomb, K. (2022). How to improve eyewitness testimony research: Theoretical and methodological concerns about experiments on the impact of emotions on memory performance. *Psychological Research, 86*(1), 1–11. https://doi.org/10.1007/s00426-021-01488-4

Goldfarb, D., Goodman, G. S., Gonzalves, L., Gonzalez, A., Wang, Y., Wu, Y., & Vidales, D. (2020). The accuracy of adults' long-term memory for child sexual abuse. In M. Miller & B. Bornstein (Eds.), *Advances in psychology and law* (pp. 51–82). Springer. https://doi.org/10.1007/978-3-030-54678-6_3

Goldfarb, D., Goodman, G. S., Larson, R. P., Gonzalez, A., & Eisen, M. L. (2018). Putting children's memory and suggestibility in their place: An analysis considering person, topic, and context. In H. Otgaar & M. L. Howe (Eds.), *Finding the truth in the courtroom: Dealing with deception, lies, and memories* (pp. 137–159). Oxford University Press.

Goldfarb, D., Goodman, G. S., Wang, Y., Fisher, R. P., Vidales, D., Gonzalves, L. C., Wu, Y., Hartman, D., Qin, J., & Eisen, M. L. (2023). Adults' memory for a maltreatment-related childhood experience: Interview protocols. *Clinical Psychological Science, 11*(1), 164–184. https://doi.org/10.1177/21677026221081877

Gonzalves, L., Chae, Y., Wang, Y., Widaman, K. F., Bederian-Gardner, D., Goodman-Wilson, M., Thompson, R. A., Shaver, P. R., & Goodman, G. S. (2022). Children's memory and suggestibility years later: Age, distress, and attachment. *Applied Cognitive Psychology, 36*(5), 1034–1048. https://doi.org/10.1002/acp.3988

Goodman, G. S., Bottoms, B. L., Rudy, L., Davis, S. L., & Schwartz-Kenney, B. M. (2001). Effects of past abuse experiences on children's eyewitness memory. *Law and Human Behavior, 25*(3), 269–298. https://doi.org/10.1023/A:1010797911805

Goodman, G. S., Ghetti, S., Quas, J. A., Edelstein, R. S., Alexander, K. W., Redlich, A. D., Cordon, I. M., & Jones, D. P. H. (2003). A prospective study of memory for child sexual abuse: New findings relevant to the repressed-memory controversy. *Psychological Science, 14*(2), 113–118. https://doi.org/10.1111/1467-9280.01428

Goodman, G. S., Hirschman, J. E., Hepps, D., & Rudy, L. (1991). Children's memory for stressful events. *Merrill-Palmer Quarterly, 37*(1), 109–157.

Goodman, G. S., Ogle, C. M., Block, S. D., Harris, L. S., Larson, R. P., Augusti, E. M., Cho, Y. I., Beber, J., Timmer, S., & Urquiza, A. (2011). False memory for trauma-related Deese–Roediger–McDermott lists in adolescents and adults with histories of child sexual abuse. *Development and Psychopathology, 23*(2), 423–428. https://doi.org/10.1017/S0954579411000150

Goodman, G. S., Ogle, C. M., McWilliams, K., Narr, R., & Paz-Alonso, K. (2014). Memory development in the forensic context. In P. Bauer & R. Fivush (Eds.), *Handbook on the development of children's memory* (pp. 920–942). Wiley-Blackwell.

Goodman, G. S., Quas, J. A., Batterman-Faunce, J. M., Riddlesberger, M. M., & Kuhn, J. (1994). Predictors of accurate and inaccurate memories of traumatic events experienced in childhood. *Consciousness and Cognition, 3*(3), 269–294. https://doi.org/10.1006/ccog.1994.1016

Goodman, G. S., Quas, J. A., & Ogle, C. M. (2010). Child maltreatment and memory. *Annual Review of Psychology, 61*(1), 325–351. https://doi.org/10.1146/annurev.psych.093008.100403

Gordon, H. M., Lyon, T. D., & Lee, K. (2014). Social and cognitive factors associated with children's secret-keeping for a parent. *Child Development, 85*(6), 2374–2388. https://doi.org/10.1111/cdev.12301

Greenhoot, A. F., McCloskey, L., & Glisky, E. (2005). A longitudinal study of adolescents' recollections of family violence. *Applied Cognitive Psychology, 19*(6), 719–743. https://doi.org/10.1002/acp.1103

Hartman, D. T., Wang, Y., Wu, Y., Goldfarb, D., Vidales, D., Qin, J., Eisen, M. L., & Goodman, G. S. (2023). Childhood sexual abuse: A longitudinal study of disclosures and denials. *Child Maltreatment, 28*(3), 462–475. https://doi.org/10.1177/10775595231165335

Howe, M. L., Toth, S. L., & Cicchetti, D. (2011). Can maltreated children inhibit true and false memories for emotional information? *Child Development, 82*(3), 967–981. https://doi.org/10.1111/j.1467-8624.2011.01585.x

Klemfuss, J. Z., Rush, E. B., & Quas, J. A. (2016). Parental reminiscing style and children's suggestibility about an alleged transgression. *Cognitive Development, 40*, 33–45. https://doi.org/10.1016/j.cogdev.2016.08.003

Kogan, S. M. (2004). Disclosing unwanted sexual experiences: Results from a national sample of adolescent women. *Child Abuse & Neglect, 28*(2), 147–165. https://doi.org/10.1016/j.chiabu.2003.09.014

Korkman, J., Otgaar, H., Geven, L. M., Bull, R., Cyr, M., Hershkowitz, I., Mäkelä, J.-M., Mattison, M., Milne, R., Santtila, P., van Koppen, P., Memon, A., Danby, M., Filipovic, L., Garcia, F. J., Gewehr, E., Gomes Bell, O., Järvilehto, L., Kask, K., . . . Volbert, R. (2024). White paper on forensic child interviewing: Research-based recommendations by the European Association of Psychology and Law. *Psychology, Crime & Law, 38*(8), 987–1030. https://doi.org/10.1080/1068316X.2024.2324098

Krackow, E., & Lynn, S. J. (2003). Is there touch in the game of Twister®? The effects of innocuous touch and suggestive questions on children's eyewitness memory. *Law and Human Behavior, 27*(6), 589–604. https://doi.org/10.1023/B:LAHU.0000004888.52210.35

Kvavilashvili, L., & Ellis, J. (2004). Ecological validity and twenty years of real-life/laboratory controversy in memory research: A critical (and historical) review. *History and Philosophy of Psychology, 6*, 59–80. https://researchprofiles.herts.ac.uk/en/publications/ecological-validity-and-twenty-years-of-real-lifelaboratory-contr

Lagattuta, K. H., & Wellman, H. M. (2002). Differences in early parent–child conversations about negative versus positive emotions: Implications for the development of psychological understanding. *Developmental Psychology, 38*(4), 564–580. https://doi.org/10.1037/0012-1649.38.4.564

Lawson, M., Rodriguez-Steen, L., & London, K. (2018). A systematic review of the reliability of children's event reports after discussing experiences with a naïve, knowledgeable, or misled parent. *Developmental Review, 49*, 62–79. https://doi.org/10.1016/j.dr.2018.06.003

Leach, C., Powell, M. B., Sharman, S. J., & Anglim, J. (2017). The relationship between children's age and disclosures of sexual abuse during forensic interviews. *Child Maltreatment, 22*(1), 79–88. https://doi.org/10.1177/1077559516675723

Leichtman, M. D., & Ceci, S. J. (1995). The effects of stereotypes and suggestions on preschoolers' reports. *Developmental Psychology, 31*(4), 568–578. https://doi.org/10.1037/0012-1649.31.4.568

Lepore, S. J., & Sesco, B. (1994). Distorting children's reports and interpretations of events through suggestion. *Journal of Applied Psychology, 79*(1), 108–120. https://doi.org/10.1037/0021-9010.79.1.108

Loftus, E. F. (2003). Make-believe memories. *American Psychologist, 58*(11), 867–873. https://doi.org/10.1037/0003-066X.58.11.867

Loftus, E. F. (2005). Planting misinformation in the human mind: A 30-year investigation of the malleability of memory. *Learning & Memory, 12*(4), 361–366. https://doi.org/10.1101/lm.94705

Lyon, T. D., Ahern, E. C., Malloy, L. C., & Quas, J. A. (2010). Children's reasoning about disclosing adult transgressions: Effects of maltreatment, child age, and adult identity. *Child Development, 81*(6), 1714–1728. https://doi.org/10.1111/j.1467-8624.2010.01505.x

MacDonald, S., Price, H. L., Lamb, M., Parker, N. J., Binford, W., & Dimitropoulos, G. (2025). Questioning the expertise of "experts" who recommend active hypothesis testing in child forensic interviews. *Juvenile and Family Court Journal, 76*(4), 26–34. https://doi.org/10.1111/jfcj.70016

Marche, T. A., & Howe, M. L. (1995). Preschoolers report misinformation despite accurate memory. *Developmental Psychology, 31*(4), 554–567. https://doi.org/10.1037/0012-1649.31.4.554

Mazzoni, G. A. L., Loftus, E. F., & Kirsch, I. (2001). Changing beliefs about implausible autobiographical events: A little plausibility goes a long way. *Journal of Experimental Psychology: Applied, 7*(1), 51–59. https://doi.org/10.1037/1076-898X.7.1.51

McWilliams, K., & Goodman, G. S. (2019). Parental bias, parent-child discussion, and children's eyewitness reports. *International Journal on Child Maltreatment: Research, Policy and Practice, 2*(4), 219–237. https://doi.org/10.1007/s42448-019-00030-9

McWilliams, K., Harris, L. S., & Goodman, G. S. (2014). Child maltreatment, trauma-related psychopathology, and eyewitness memory in children and adolescents. *Behavioral Sciences & the Law, 32*(6), 702–717. https://doi.org/10.1002/bsl.2143

McWilliams, K., Narr, R., Goodman, G. S., Ruiz, S., & Mendoza, M. (2013). Children's memory for their mother's murder: Accuracy, suggestibility, and resistance to suggestion. *Memory, 21*(5), 591–598. https://doi.org/10.1080/09658211.2013.763983

Mikulincer, M., & Shaver, P. R. (2016). Adult attachment and emotion regulation. In J. Cassidy & P. R. Shaver (Eds.), *Handbook of attachment: Theory, research, and clinical applications* (Vol. 3, pp. 507–533). Guilford Press.

Moore, K. N., Lampinen, J. M., Gallo, D. A., Adams, E. J., & Bridges, A. J. (2018). Children's use of memory editing strategies to reject source misinformation. *Child Development, 89*(1), 219–234. https://doi.org/10.1111/cdev.12716

Morgan, K., Dorgan, K., & Hayne, H. (2013). Body maps do not facilitate older children's report of touch. *Scandinavian Journal of Psychology, 54*(1), 51–55. https://doi.org/10.1111/sjop.12000

Mugno, A. P., & Malloy, L. C. (2023). Interview and child factors that influence children's true disclosures of a parent's versus a stranger's wrongdoing. *Applied Developmental Science, 28*(4), 457–472. https://doi.org/10.1080/10888691.2023.2231846.

Negriff, S., Schneiderman, J. U., Smith, C., Schreyer, J. K., & Trickett, P. K. (2014). Characterizing the sexual abuse experiences of young adolescents. *Child Abuse & Neglect, 38*(2), 261–270. https://doi.org/10.1016/j.chiabu.2013.08.021

Neisser, U., Winograd, E., Bergman, E. T., Schreiber, C. A., Palmer, S. E., & Weldon, M. S. (1996). Remembering the earthquake: Direct experience vs. hearing the news. *Memory, 4*(4), 337–357. https://pubmed.ncbi.nlm.nih.gov/8817459/

O'Donohue, W., & Cirlugea, O. (2021). Controlling for confirmation bias in child sexual abuse interviews. *Journal of the American Academy of Psychiatry and the Law, 49*(3), 371–380.

Ost, J., Blank, H., Davies, J., Jones, G., Lambert, K., & Salmon, K. (2013). False memory ≠ false memory: DRM errors are unrelated to the misinformation effect. *PLOS One, 8*(4), Article e57939. https://doi.org/10.1371/journal.pone.0057939

Otgaar, H., & Candel, I. (2011). Children's false memories: Different false memory paradigms reveal different results. *Psychology, Crime & Law, 17*(6), 513–528. https://doi.org/10.1080/10683160903373392

Otgaar, H., Howe, M. L., Merckelbach, H., & Muris, P. (2018). Who is the better eyewitness? Sometimes adults but at other times children. *Current Directions in Psychological Science, 27*(5), 378–385. https://doi.org/10.1177/0963721418770998

Otgaar, H., Howe, M. L., & Muris, P. (2017). Maltreatment increases spontaneous false memories but decreases suggestion-induced false memories in children. *British Journal of Developmental Psychology, 35*(3), 376–391. https://doi.org/10.1111/bjdp.12177

Paz-Alonso, P. M., & Goodman, G. S. (2016). Developmental differences across middle childhood in memory and suggestibility for negative and positive events. *Behavioral Sciences & the Law, 34*(1), 30–54. https://doi.org/10.1002/bsl.2239

Paz-Alonso, P. M., Goodman, G. S., & Ibabe, I. (2013). Adult eyewitness memory and compliance: Effects of post-event misinformation on memory for a negative event. *Behavioral Sciences & the Law, 31*(5), 541–558. https://doi.org/10.1002/bsl.2081

Peterson, C. (2012). Children's autobiographical memories across the years: Forensic implications of childhood amnesia and eyewitness memory for stressful events. *Developmental Review, 32*(3), 287–306. https://doi.org/10.1016/j.dr.2012.06.002

Peterson, C., Parsons, T., & Dean, M. (2004). Providing misleading and reinstatement information a year after it happened: Effects on long-term memory. *Memory, 12*(1), 1–13. https://doi.org/10.1080/09658210344000468

Pezdek, K., & Hodge, D. (1999). Planting false childhood memories in children: The role of event plausibility. *Child Development, 70*(4), 887–895. https://doi.org/10.1111/1467-8624.00064

Pezdek, K., & Roe, C. (1995). The effect of memory trace strength on suggestibility. *Journal of Experimental Child Psychology, 60*(1), 116–128. https://doi.org/10.1006/jecp.1995.1034

Pipe, M. E., & Wilson, J. C. (1994). Cues and secrets: Influences on children's event reports. *Developmental Psychology, 30*(4), 515–525. https://doi.org/10.1037/0012-1649.30.4.515

Pitula, C. E., Wenner, J. A., Gunnar, M. R., & Thomas, K. M. (2017). To trust or not to trust: Social decision-making in post-institutionalized, internationally adopted youth. *Developmental Science, 20*(3), Article e12375. https://doi.org/10.1111/desc.12375

Poole, D. A., & Bruck, M. (2012). Divining testimony? The impact of interviewing props on children's reports of touching. *Developmental Review, 32*(3), 165–180. https://doi.org/10.1016/j.dr.2012.06.007

Principe, G. F., & London, K. (2022). How parents can shape what children remember: Implications for the testimony of young witnesses. *Journal of Applied Research in Memory and Cognition, 11*(3), 289–302. https://doi.org/10.1037/mac0000059

Pynoos, R. S., & Eth, S. (1984). The child as witness to homicide. *Journal of Social Issues, 40*(2), 87–108. https://doi.org/10.1111/j.1540-4560.1984.tb01095.x

Quas, J. A., Davis, E. L., Goodman, G. S., & Myers, J. E. B. (2007). Repeated questions, deception, and children's true and false reports of body touch. *Child Maltreatment, 12*(1), 60–67. https://doi.org/10.1177/1077559506296141

Quas, J. A., Malloy, L. C., Melinder, A., Goodman, G. S., D'Mello, M., & Schaaf, J. (2007). Developmental differences in the effects of repeated interviews and interviewer bias on young children's event memory and false reports. *Developmental Psychology, 43*(4), 823–837. https://doi.org/10.1037/0012-1649.43.4.823

Quas, J. A., Rush, E. B., Yim, I. S., Edelstein, R. S., Otgaar, H., & Smeets, T. (2016). Stress and emotional valence effects on children's versus adolescents' true and false memory. *Memory, 24*(5), 696–707. https://doi.org/10.1080/09658211.2015.1045909

Roediger, H. L., III, & Abel, M. (2022). The double-edged sword of memory retrieval. *Nature Reviews Psychology, 1*(12), 708–720. https://doi.org/10.1038/s44159-022-00115-2

Roediger, H. L., III, & McDermott, K. B. (1995). Creating false memories: Remembering words not presented in lists. *Journal of Experimental Psychology: Learning, Memory, and Cognition, 21*(4), 803–814. https://doi.org/10.1037/0278-7393.21.4.803

Ross, J., Hutchison, J., & Cunningham, S. J. (2020). The me in memory: The role of the self in autobiographical memory development. *Child Development, 91*(2), e299–e314. https://doi.org/10.1111/cdev.13211

Russell, D. E. H. (1986). *The secret trauma: Incest in the lives of girls and women.* Basic Books.

Saywitz, K. J., Goodman, G. S., Nicholas, E., & Moan, S. F. (1991). Children's memories of a physical examination involving genital touch: Implications for reports of child sexual abuse. *Journal of Consulting and Clinical Psychology, 59*(5), 682–691. https://doi.org/10.1037/0022-006X.59.5.682

Saywitz, K. J., Larson, R. P., Hobbs, S. D., & Wells, C. R. (2015). Developing rapport with children in forensic interviews: Systematic review of experimental research. *Behavioral Sciences & the Law, 33*(4), 372–389. https://doi.org/10.1002/bsl.2186

Saywitz, K. J., Wells, C. R., Larson, R. P., & Hobbs, S. D. (2019). Effects of interviewer support on children's memory and suggestibility: Systematic review and meta-analyses of experimental research. *Trauma, Violence, & Abuse, 20*(1), 22–39. https://doi.org/10.1177/1524838016683457

Schaaf, J. M., Bederian-Gardner, D., & Goodman, G. S. (2015). Gating out misinformation: Can young children follow instructions to ignore false information? *Behavioral Sciences & the Law, 33*(4), 390–406. https://doi.org/10.1002/bsl.2195

Schreiber, N., Bellah, L. D., Martinez, Y., McLaurin, K. A., Strok, R., Garven, S., & Wood, J. M. (2006). Suggestive interviewing in the McMartin Preschool and Kelly Michaels Daycare abuse cases: A case study. *Social Influence, 1*(1), 16–47. https://doi.org/10.1080/15534510500361739

Scoboria, A., Mazzoni, G., Kirsch, I., & Relyea, M. (2004). Plausibility and belief in autobiographical memory. *Applied Cognitive Psychology, 18*(7), 791–807. https://doi.org/10.1002/acp.1062

Scoboria, A., Wade, K. A., Lindsay, D. S., Azad, T., Strange, D., Ost, J., & Hyman, I. E. (2017). A mega-analysis of memory reports from eight peer-reviewed false memory implantation studies. *Memory, 25*(2), 146–163. https://doi.org/10.1080/09658211.2016.1260747

Shackman, J. E., Shackman, A. J., & Pollak, S. D. (2007). Physical abuse amplifies attention to threat and increases anxiety in children. *Emotion, 7*(4), 838–852. https://doi.org/10.1037/1528-3542.7.4.838

Shaver, P. R., & Mikulincer, M. (2007). Adult attachment strategies and the regulation of emotion. In J. J. Gross (Ed.), *Handbook of emotion regulation* (pp. 446–465). Guilford Press.

Shields, G. S., Sazma, M. A., McCullough, A. M., & Yonelinas, A. P. (2017). The effects of acute stress on episodic memory: A meta-analysis and integrative review. *Psychological Bulletin, 143*(6), 636–675. https://doi.org/10.1037/bul0000100

Stolzenberg, S. N., McWilliams, K., & Lyon, T. D. (2018). Children's conversational memory regarding a minor transgression and a subsequent interview. *Psychology, Public Policy, and Law, 24*(3), 379–392. https://doi.org/10.1037/law0000176

Strange, D., Sutherland, R., & Garry, M. (2006). Event plausibility does not determine children's false memories. *Memory, 14*(8), 937–951. https://doi.org/10.1080/09658210600896105

Valentino, K., Toth, S. L., & Cicchetti, D. (2009). Autobiographical memory functioning among abused, neglected, and nonmaltreated children: The overgeneral memory effect. *Journal of Child Psychology and Psychiatry, 50*(8), 1029–1038. https://doi.org/10.1111/j.1469-7610.2009.02072.x

Williams, J. M. G., Barnhofer, T., Crane, C., Herman, D., Raes, F., Watkins, E., & Dalgleish, T. (2007). Autobiographical memory specificity and emotional disorder. *Psychological Bulletin, 133*(1), 122–148. https://doi.org/10.1037/0033-2909.133.1.122

Williams, S., McWilliams, K., & Lyon, T. (2020). Children's concealment of a minor transgression: The role of age, maltreatment, and executive functioning. *Journal of Experimental Child Psychology, 191*, Article 104664. https://doi.org/10.1016/j.jecp.2019.104664

Windmann, S., & Krüger, T. (1998). Subconscious detection of threat as reflected by an enhanced response bias. *Consciousness and Cognition, 7*(4), 603–633. https://doi.org/10.1006/ccog.1998.0337

Winters, G. M., Jeglic, E. L., & Kaylor, L. E. (2020). Validation of the sexual grooming model of child sexual abusers. *Journal of Child Sexual Abuse, 29*(7), 855–875. https://doi.org/10.1080/10538712.2020.1801935

Wu, Y., Enriquez, R., Hartman, D. T., Brown, L. F., Kramer, M., Grandchamp, J., Moriarty, N., & Goodman, G. S. (in press). Caregiver familiarity and children's eyewitness memory: A pilot study. *Journal of Interpersonal Violence*.

Wu, Y., Goodman, G. S., Goldfarb, D., Wang, Y., Vidales, D., Brown, L. F., Eisen, M. L., & Qin, J. (2023). Memory accuracy after 20 years for interviews about child maltreatment. *Child Maltreatment, 28*(1), 85–96. https://doi.org/10.1177/10775595211055184

Young, E. S., Frankenhuis, W. E., DelPriore, D. J., & Ellis, B. J. (2022). Hidden talents in context: Cognitive performance with abstract versus ecological stimuli among adversity-exposed youth. *Child Development, 93*(5), 1493–1510. https://doi.org/10.1111/cdev.13766

Young, J., & Widom, C. S. (2014). Long-term effects of child abuse and neglect on emotional processing in adulthood. *Child Abuse & Neglect, 38*(8), 1369–1381. https://doi.org/10.1016/j.chiabu.2014.03.008

4

Adults' Memory for Childhood Maltreatment and Childhood Trauma

The Continued Relevance of Research on Historic Child Sexual Abuse

Avery Stackle, Martine Fredrickson, and Deborah Goldfarb

Beginning around 2002, a substantial change occurred in the United States legal system's response to delayed claims of child sexual abuse (CSA), frequently referred to as historic child sexual abuse (HCSA; see CHILD USA, 2025). HCSA can refer to incidents of CSA that were not disclosed until adulthood. However, it can also refer to abuse with a prolonged delay in disclosure, even if disclosure occurs during childhood. States lifted or modified time limits for HCSA cases; almost every state eventually modified its civil statute of limitations (the time limit within which a plaintiff must bring the case to civil court), and some states also modified criminal statutes. Thus, courts were hearing HCSA cases in almost every state.

One might assume that this shift by the legislatures and courts means that the issue of whether the courts should hear HCSA cases is settled, and, as such, the applied value of research into adults' memories for childhood events has subsequently decreased. This chapter, however, argues for the continued validity of such research from a legal and theoretical perspective. Indeed, we argue here that not only are debates about the procedural and substantive fairness of hearing HCSA cases alive and well in the courts, but numerous important unanswered empirical questions regarding memory for such events remain.

In so doing, we first lay out the current state of the law in the United States on HCSA cases to help frame the value of this research. We then review reasons

https://doi.org/10.1037/0000492-004
Handbook on Child Witnesses: Improving Psychological Science and Legal Practice,
G. S. Goodman, T. D. Lyon, S. D. Hobbs, and R. Enriquez (Editors)

that disclosure of traumatizing memories may be delayed and the research on adults' and children's abilities to remember events that occurred decades prior. Finally, we review the science on how prosecutors, lawyers, jurors, and judges react to the cases. Our goal in using this order is to mimic the legal process, starting with how the law governs such cases, moving to disclosure, and ending with investigators and the triers of fact. Ultimately, we aim to highlight the multiple points where research is needed for both civil and criminal cases.

CURRENT STATE OF LEGAL TREATMENT IN THE UNITED STATES OF HISTORIC CHILD SEXUAL ABUSE CASES

Courts in the United States have historically preferred to try cases within a reasonable time after the alleged event (Goldfarb et al., 2020). This preference, among other factors, led to the implementation of statutes of limitations in the United States and other countries. A statute of limitations sets a time limit for the courts to hear cases. The United States Supreme Court has noted that one reason for bringing cases promptly is that time can lead to "fading memories" or other loss of evidence (*U.S. v. Kubrick*, 1979).

Such time limitations are not, however, absolute bars. Courts recognize some exceptions to time limits. For example, the deadline to bring a claim can be tolled or delayed when the defendant has actively sought to conceal the existence of the harm, or the plaintiff could not be reasonably expected to have discovered the harm. Courts have accepted arguments that equity or estoppel (a legal concept that prevents an individual from contradicting their earlier actions or statements) should allow plaintiffs to bring claims outside of what might ordinarily be considered a reasonable period of time.

Arguments of equity and estoppel have been applied to survivors seeking civil suits for HCSA cases. For example, the delayed discovery rule holds in abeyance the statute of limitations deadline to bring a suit for previously undiscoverable claims until the plaintiff reasonably could have discovered their right to sue (Reilly, 2021). This rule arises from equity and common sense: One cannot do something they do not know they can do. Although some courts have been amenable to such arguments in the HCSA context, others have rejected them (see Reilly, 2021, citing *Basile v. Covenant House*).

Legislators have also accepted arguments for extending the statute of limitations for HCSA claims. In the 18 years between 2002 and 2020, the vast majority of states (48 states and the District of Columbia) changed their statute of limitations for civil CSA claims and, in some cases (as mentioned above), criminal claims (CHILD USA, 2025). Legislatures have modified or extended their statutes in various ways. Some have generally extended the time (e.g., allowing survivors to bring claims until they are 40). In contrast, others, like New York, have created lookback windows, giving survivors a set period of time (e.g., 3 years) during which they can bring expired civil claims.

This diversity in response has created a panoply of deadlines depending on the state where the harm occurred.

As of 2023, 44 states and 5 U.S. Territories had no criminal statute of limitations for HCSA. In North Dakota and Oregon, individuals must bring criminal claims before turning 40; in Nevada, New Hampshire, Ohio, and Oklahoma, the age is between 40 and 50. For civil cases, 17 states and 2 U.S. territories did not have a time limit for HCSA cases, whereas 23 states required that survivors bring the claims before turning 34. Twenty-six states and three territories had opened a window for expired claims to be brought. Such windows, however, were not always wide and fully open. In Michigan, the window only permitted expired claims against doctors.

Not all states have been receptive to extending the statute of limitations, and suits arguing the impermissibility of such extensions, particularly for previously time-barred claims, have sometimes been successful. The United States Supreme Court ruled in 2003 that criminal claims that had already expired could not be revived, as doing so violates the ex post facto clause in the United States Constitution (*Stogner v. California*, 2003). Some states have similarly established that civil claims are barred from revival. For example, in 2020, the Utah Supreme Court found that the statute extending the window for HCSA claims was unconstitutional and that "the Utah Legislature [was] constitutionally prohibited from retroactively reviving a time-barred claim in a manner depriving a defendant of a vested statute of limitations defense" (*Mitchell v. Roberts*, 2020, p. 903). Although such arguments have not gained a foothold in other federal and state courts (e.g., *A.B. vs. S.U.*, 2023), this is an area of current legal debate, and it is unclear whether statutes extending deadlines will continue to decline or, as others have argued, expand into abuse beyond CSA (La Puma, 2016).

DISCLOSURE PROCESS FOR HISTORIC CHILD SEXUAL ABUSE SURVIVORS

Delayed disclosure necessarily conflicts with legal processes that favor a statute of limitations because such delays often result in disclosures that can no longer be addressed through the legal system. Although there are logical reasons for limitations, such as the disappearance of evidence that can be used in defense of the accused, there are arguments for extending or eliminating limitations that concern the disclosure processes of survivors. The balance between the rights of the accused and the rights of survivors may be clarified by understanding how and when disclosure is delayed (for a systematic review of barriers to disclosure, see McPherson et al., 2025).

When discussing HCSA cases, we refer to victims who intentionally withheld the disclosure of abuse and not those with repressed memories (see Deferme et al., 2024, for a discussion on HCSA cases and repressed memories). Many individuals assume that HCSA cases involve repressed memories and that repressed memories have a solid empirical basis (Otgaar et al., 2021). However, in reviewing decades of HCSA cases, Connolly and Read (2006) observed that almost all complainants (94%) reported continuous memory of their abuse. People may believe that a child enduring such traumatic abuse would reach out to the adults in their lives to put an end to their suffering, but such beliefs arise from false assumptions about the experience of CSA (St. George et al., 2020). For instance, people believe that victims have the opportunity or means to safely disclose. Sadly, many children lack such resources, as abusers often target children and circumstances in which they will not get caught (Budin & Johnson, 1989; Winters et al., 2020, 2024).

Fear of Impact of Disclosure

Fear is one of the most common reasons individuals do not disclose CSA (McGill & McElvaney, 2023; Münzer et al., 2016). Fears surrounding disclosure are multifaceted, including fears about the repercussions of disclosure, fears of not being believed, fears about the response from the people to whom they are disclosing, and fears of losing control over the situation once other parties are involved. Many CSA survivors, adolescents, and adults who have experienced CSA fear that disclosure could worsen their situations (McGill & McElvaney, 2023).

Concern for parents, especially mothers, is a determining factor for disclosure in CSA cases (Goodman-Brown et al., 2003). Münzer et al. (2016) reported that 19% of their sample did not want to burden their parents. Survivors are often concerned that disclosure will aggravate parental problems, such as alcohol abuse or other mental health difficulties (McGill & McElvaney, 2023; Münzer et al., 2016; Schönbucher et al., 2012). Children also fear imposing financial strains on their families, especially since survivors are often aware that perpetrators frequently contribute to the financial stability of the family (Jensen et al., 2005; McGill & McElvaney, 2023). Abusers often remind the children about such family circumstances. Münzer et al. (2016) found that 26% of their sample had been directly threatened by their abuser to dissuade their disclosure (both threats of bodily harm and threats about what would happen to their family). For example, the abuser may be a stepfather who is providing part of the family's income and reminds the child that if the child were to share their secret, the family would have to give up their house.

Another fear many individuals do not consider in cases of CSA is the fear children have about what will happen to the perpetrator if they disclose the abuse. Children may have attachments to their abusers, making the children want to protect the perpetrator (Donalek, 2001; Goodman-Brown et al., 2003; Münzer et al., 2016). Abusers may target children who need their attention or care, which can come in many forms (e.g., understanding, presence). They will then take advantage of the child's compassion to keep the child quiet (Gemara & Katz, 2023). Intrafamilial abuse may often rely on the child's desire to protect the perpetrator, especially if the perpetrator is a significant caregiver for the child.

Many victims of CSA also fear that, even if they disclose, they will not be believed (London et al., 2008; McElvaney, 2015; Münzer et al., 2016) and, even if they are believed, they will be blamed. The fear of being blamed is far from unfounded. Münzer et al. (2016) reported that, out of the participants they interviewed who did disclose as children, 19% of them were blamed for the abuse following disclosure.

Betrayal trauma theory (Freyd, 1996; McNally, 2007) suggests that fear of these negative consequences prevents survivors from disclosing the abuse. In Australia, Hunter (2011) discovered that every interviewee in their sample who disclosed as a child suffered some negative consequence due to the disclosure, so much so that they either decided not to disclose later abuse or advised others who were being abused not to disclose. It is thought that perpetrators often exploit survivors' fears by either convincing or reminding survivors of the consequences of disclosure (Elliott et al., 1995). In this way, the fear of consequences is supported by the perpetrator's suggestions and other survivors' previous experiences.

Cultural Responses to Disclosure

Culture also influences how a child views the abuse, which can impact their decision whether to disclose. Several studies have examined cases of sexual abuse in various cultural communities (Gemara & Katz, 2023; Gerdes et al., 1996; Haboush & Alyan, 2013; McGuigan & Stephenson, 2015; Parkinson, 2014). Although most of these studies examined sexual abuse broadly, as opposed to CSA, the findings revealed that community standards can sometimes encourage codes of silence. Many communities have a code of silence that results in cases being handled through institutional structures instead of local law enforcement; cases of CSA in the Catholic Church are a notable example (McGuigan & Stephenson, 2015; Parkinson, 2014).

Cultural expectations may also play a role in how survivors view their abuse. For example, shame is often reported by many survivors, including those in collectivist cultures (Haboush & Alyan, 2013). Haboush and Alyan (2013) explain the importance of family over self in Arab cultures. The researchers showed how such values can increase feelings of shame for survivors and potentially encourage delays in disclosure. Furthermore, in some cultures, disclosing CSA would impact a family's honor, and the child does not want to harm or shame their parents in this way (Shalhoub-Kevorkian, 2005). The maintenance of family honor is a good example of how fears about how abuse disclosure will impact the family differ. In some families, children's fears for their families center around immediate familial repercussions such as financial strain or parental mental health relapses. In other families, children's fears center around familial repercussions involving the larger community, such as losing social standing.

Regardless of culture, disclosing CSA can be a nuanced and ongoing process for survivors. Many factors contribute to delays in disclosure (McPherson et al., 2025), including fears about what will happen following disclosure and shame about what has happened. These delays, however, create due process difficulties for the accused. For example, by the time a disclosure occurs, exonerating evidence may no longer exist. Survivors typically wait to disclose until they feel safer doing so, whether through time, distance from the perpetrator, or an opportunity that facilitates disclosure (Hunter, 2011; Jensen et al., 2005; McElvaney, 2015). One key question in analyzing due process issues is how time impacts both the accuracy and productivity of the survivors' memory.

ACCURACY OF HISTORIC CHILD SEXUAL ABUSE MEMORIES

Memory researchers have drawn our attention to how fallible human memory is. One reason that memory is fallible is the influence of time. Time generally degrades the quality, if not the existence, of the memory trace. Ebbinghaus (1913) illustrated this effect in his classic research, which showed the exponential memory loss of a nonsense syllables list that he had taught himself. This exponential retention curve, with considerable degradation in memory in the beginning and a general subsistence of a smaller amount of the initial trace over time, has been replicated in other studies (Murre & Dros, 2015; Roediger & DeSoto, 2014; Rubin & Wenzel, 1996; Wixted, 2004), including in studies with children: Young children who experienced a medical event forgot details in the intervening three months after the event, though they showed some memory stability after 6 months (Ornstein et al., 2006).

Research has also shown, however, that the exponential decline in memory is not absolute. Older children, and even sometimes very young children, can recall stressful medical events months, years, and even decades later (Goldfarb et al., 2023; Peterson, 2015; Quas et al., 1999). Pockets of memories thus appear to be present that are more inoculated against degradation, though, of course, they are not entirely immune. Factors predicting which memories are potentially more resistant are discussed in the following paragraphs. As this chapter concentrates on issues surrounding memories for HCSA, we focus primarily on factors that predict increased or decreased recall of memories encoded during childhood that are recalled a significant period later. Specifically, we discuss the impact of age, trauma of the event, psychopathology, and gender on recall for the event.

Age at Encoding

As children age, they further develop several skills that help them encode and store memory. For example, older children have richer language skills, knowledge bases within which to code events, and more enriched sociocognitive skills relevant to interview performance. Children who are older at the time an event occurred generally show increased memory performance, including the ability to remember additional details (Eisen et al., 2007; Goodman et al., 2001; McWilliams et al., 2014).

Perhaps not surprisingly, age also seems to relate to individuals' recall of an event decades later. Many memory researchers have noted that when individuals are asked to recall autobiographical memories, the distribution has an almost inverse U-shaped curve, with a peak in recall of memories encoded between the ages of 10 and 30 (Rathbone et al., 2008). Indeed, Bahrick and colleagues conducted classic studies on adolescents' and young adults' ability to remember information encoded in the school setting, such as classmates' faces, Spanish words, and mathematical concepts (Bahrick, 1984; Bahrick & Hall, 1991). Although some information was initially forgotten, other information, particularly well-practiced information (Bahrick & Hall, 1991), was retained and recalled decades later. Bahrick theorized that this information had reached a reasonably permanent state in memory, the permastore.

Similar age effects are found in adults' memory for sensitive childhood events. Goldfarb and colleagues (2019) interviewed adults who, as children, stayed in a forensic unit for 5 days so authorities could assess potential child abuse. As part of that assessment, all the children had a genital examination. Approximately two decades later, the children, now adults, were interviewed about the examination. The older a child was at Time 1, the less likely they were to have forgotten or to deny the genital examination. In other words, older participants were less likely than younger participants to say they had not had a genital examination when they did. Interestingly, none of the children who were older than 11 when the exam occurred forgot or denied the exam as adults.

Goldfarb and colleagues (2023) followed up on these findings with a similar sample of adults. All participants had also undergone a 5-day stay in the forensic unit. Paralleling the earlier study, younger age was associated with less complete memories for the sensitive examination, with those who were older at Time 1 remembering more than those who were younger. Older children within this sample were also more likely to consistently disclose the abuse that brought them to the forensic unit (Hartman et al., 2023).

Despite having less complete memories, age at the time of encoding did not necessarily predict inaccuracy (Goldfarb et al., 2023). Adults who were younger at the time of encoding recalled fewer details decades later, but the details they did remember were as accurate as their older counterparts'. It may be that this is a further example of Bahrick's permastore. The pieces of information that were sufficiently encoded at Time 1 were maintained within the memory over the intervening decades, and younger children adequately encoded fewer pieces of information at Time 1. The fact that children who were older at the time of encoding remembered more details than younger children does not mean that younger children can never remember the target event. Numerous studies have shown that even preschoolers can sometimes remember details of an event decades later (Goldfarb et al., 2019, 2023; Peterson, 2015; Peterson & Whalen, 2001; Wu et al., 2023). Peterson and colleagues interviewed preschoolers who had experienced an emergency room visit years prior. Although the children did show degradation in memory for the details of the medical event, they could generally accurately recall the injury or accident that brought them to the hospital. It may be that the injury itself was more traumatic than the hospital visit and thus led to increased memory performance, a theory discussed below.

Trauma of the Memory and Psychopathology

Researchers have long debated the impact of stress or emotionality on an individual's ability to remember an event (Deffenbacher et al., 2004). Longitudinal studies of traumatizing or potentially stressful events have found that individuals can recall these events many years later (Bauer et al., 2016; Goodman et al., 2003; Van Abbema & Bauer, 2005). Children who survived Hurricane Andrew, a category 4 hurricane that hit Florida in 1992 with little notice and devastating impact, were interviewed shortly after the event and then again approximately 6 years later (Fivush et al., 2004). Many of the children in the sample, even though they were all preschoolers at Time 1, recalled the event with high levels of detail years later. Of note, children often reported more information at the second interview, perhaps due to development in verbal or other abilities in the intervening years.

Recall of traumatizing events may also vary depending on the quality of the interview protocol used to elicit these memories. Goldfarb and colleagues (2023) interviewed children who were part of a forensic unit stay using three different interview protocols: (a) the Federal Law Enforcement Training Center's (FLETC's) Five-Step Interview (which focuses predominately on the who, what, when, and where of the event), (b) the cognitive interview (CI; which utilizes empirically supported mnemonic techniques to bolster recall), and (c) the CI in conjunction with physical memory reinstatement via the presentation of a contemporaneously filmed video of the forensic unit. Participants interviewed via either CI protocol recalled fewer schematically based false events than participants interviewed via the FLETC. No other effects of the interview protocol were uncovered.

The lack of an effect of interview protocol in Goldfarb and colleagues' study is somewhat surprising. Scholars (Dodier & Otgaar, 2019) have argued that interview techniques may be particularly valuable for recall of historic sexual abuse beyond the ability to suppress incorrect details and have maintained that the techniques used in the CI can bolster memories for sensitive events. One potential explanation is that Goldfarb and colleagues (2023) did not manipulate the level of rapport development between the interview techniques. When interviewers use richer rapport-building techniques, adult survivors of HCSA have revealed richer recall, including disclosing more abuse-related details (Chenier et al., 2022). Both the CI and the FLETC incorporate rapport, and, as such, any effect of interviewer rapport building washes out. Further work on the impact of interview protocol on recall for HCSA is thus needed.

In addition to the interview protocol, memories of traumatic events may be influenced by the level of psychopathology that the individual was or is currently experiencing. The relation between mental health and memory accuracy is not always clear. Some studies find that increased PTSD symptomology in adolescents and young adults predicts increased accuracy for traumatic memories (Alexander et al., 2005). Other work across age groups, however, argues that mental health symptomology, such as PTSD or depression, leads to more errors, perhaps due to overgeneral memory or a less conservative reporting criterion (Otgaar et al., 2017; Valentino, 2011; Williams & Broadbent, 1986).

Within research on recall for historic memories of sensitive events in childhood, depression has sometimes been found to be a predictor of increased memory accuracy. For example, depression predicted increased recall in adults of a childhood genital touch, which occurred during a childhood forensic medical examination (Goldfarb et al., 2019). An argument was made that perhaps those with increased depressive symptoms spent more time ruminating on the target event and, as such, increased the strength of the memory trace for the event. However, support for this argument did not hold in Goldfarb et al. (2023), as no relation between depression and memory for a CSA-related investigation was detected. PTSD, however, did predict memory accuracy in the 2023 study; participants with higher PTSD symptomology had both more correct and incorrect answers to specific questions and incorrect answers to misleading questions.

Some individuals have argued, however, that increased psychopathology may result from individuals failing to initially disclose CSA and receive much-needed services and support (Paine & Hansen, 2002). In line with this argument, Hartman and colleagues (2023) reported that participants with increased psychopathology in adulthood were more likely to reveal CSA that they had not previously discussed during a childhood forensic investigation. It is also posited that increased psychopathology in childhood could prevent disclosure, resulting in delayed disclosure. Hartman and colleagues, however, found that participants' Time 1 psychopathology symptoms did not predict their Time 2 recall as adults. Additional research is needed to understand the link between mental health and disclosure.

Other scientists maintain that it may not just be whether but how we recall an event that influences our later psychopathology. Booker and colleagues (2020) interviewed adults in the emergency department shortly after a traumatic event and one year later. They analyzed the participants' reports of the traumatic event for their narrative structure, including reports' interpretative elaboration (including details about one's interpretation of the event), and their narrative coherence (providing an overall "framework" for the event). Individuals with more elaborate and coherent descriptions of the event revealed higher later coping engagement and utilization of strategies in response to stressors, which, in turn, predicted higher mental health performance. Further work on this front within the context of HCSA-relevant memories is warranted.

Recent research elaborates and adds context to models of stressful events, psychopathology, and memory. It highlights the need to understand further individual differences in ways that individuals initially encode, create narrative structures from, and seek support in response to stressful events. This variance between event and memory may provide further support for removing statutes of limitations that presume a universality in the experience of memory degradation in favor of a more individualized approach.

Gender

Gender differences have been uncovered in emotional autobiographical memory generally (Davis, 1999) and in the recall and reporting of historic childhood events specifically. Goldfarb and colleagues' (2019) study of adults' memory of a childhood forensic unit visit found that males were less likely than females to report genital touch that had occurred as part of the exam. When interviewed about the full forensic unit stay, males in a similar sample also revealed more commission errors to free recall questions and commission errors to specific questions, whereas females were more likely to say "don't know" to suggestive questioning (Goldfarb et al., 2023).

These results may be explained not by memory failures but, at least in part, by hesitancy by males, both children and adults, to report abuse, even if the event is adequately encoded. Female participants who had been part of the forensic unit stay were more likely to consistently report the abuse that brought them to the forensic unit than were males (Hartman et al., 2023). This aligns with prior research showing that males are less likely to disclose CSA than females (Cashmore et al., 2017; Wallis & Woodworth, 2020; Widom & Morris, 1997). That being said, almost all memory research relies on reporting as the metric for memory, so recall failures in all individuals, regardless of their gender, could arise from either a failure to remember the encoded event or a hesitancy to disclose or discuss the event.

Moreover, not all studies find gender effects in long-term recall and reporting of stressful events. Fivush and colleagues' (2004) study on children's recall of Hurricane Andrew did not find any differences between male and female children. One explanation for this difference in findings is that Hurricane Andrew did not involve an abusive or sexual event. Males may be socialized to be more reluctant than females to disclose sexual abuse, which may lead to differences in error rates between the two (Ullman & Filipas, 2005; Widom & Morris, 1997). This is not to say, however, that disclosure is easy, well-accepted, or frequent for females. Individuals of any gender identity consistently report difficulty disclosing traumatizing events (Manay & Collin-Vézina, 2021). Thus, reluctance to disclose has implications for how memory failures are interpreted across genders.

Additional work is also needed within our conceptualization of gender. Research on HCSA memories has predominantly focused on a dichotomous definition of gender and sex, male or female. This partially arises from using historic medical or educational records for much of the research conducted thus far. Research, however, consistently shows that children who are transgender and gender nonconforming have a heightened risk for child abuse, including child sexual abuse (Price et al., 2019; Tobin & Delaney, 2019).

Further, as with all research, care should be shown in applying the group-based differences to the individual testifying in a particular case (Faigman et al., 2014). In other words, although males generally may show decrements in disclosing and recalling historic trauma, there is variance within gender reporting as well. As such, research revealing overall gender differences does not give us scientific certainty about the testimony of a particular male. Simply put, science tells us recall is possible, but it does not allow us to state whether this individual's recall is accurate or, alternatively, inaccurate, and if inaccurate, if the testimony should be disregarded. Understanding differences between the group and individual findings may be significant for the legal actors who decide the fate of HCSA cases, such as investigators and prosecutors.

INVESTIGATORS' AND ATTORNEYS' RESPONSE TO DISCLOSURE

Law enforcement investigators often share survivors' concerns about how individuals will react to the case or whether an individual's memory alone is sufficient evidence to prove the case. Westera and colleagues (2023) interviewed 21 investigators in Australia and New Zealand. The investigators' concerns in handling allegations of sexual assault were the difficulty in eliciting and providing evidence to meet the evidentiary requirements of sexual assault cases and the level of detail necessary to proceed. These challenges are often further compounded by the fact that CSA often occurs across multiple instances over a long period of time, but prosecuting a case requires information about specific instances of abuse (Shead, 2014).

Additional work is necessary to understand the type of support investigators need to prosecute HCSA cases, as well as how disclosure is handled at the parallel stage in civil proceedings. Given the ever-changing climate of HCSA legislation and precedent, such work is vital to understand better how these changes have impacted the interactions between survivors and legal actors.

Another challenge that legal responders encounter during the disclosure process is the need to perform a preliminary screening for the credibility of abuse claims: Officers often assess the potential credibility of disclosures (Westera et al., 2023). As sexual assaults, including cases of HCSA, tend to leave minimal amounts of physical evidence, the word of the victim is the primary evidence (Westera et al., 2023). As research continues about how legal actors respond to disclosure, it is imperative to examine the accuracy of HCSA memories so that research can help inform investigators and prosecutors about the potential credibility of such reports.

Serving as an initial judge of disclosure credibility also creates a conflict for legal actors. Investigators report that finding the balance between objectivity and compassion in their assessments of the evidence is difficult. Such a balance is essential for meeting the needs of both the legal system and the survivors. As most victims fear not being believed, these interactions can affirm their worst fears about the situation. One way to address the balance between objectivity and empathy is by using trauma-informed practices.

In the context of law enforcement, trauma-informed care means understanding that victims are bringing emotional vulnerabilities with them into investigative conversations that the words and behavior of investigators can worsen. When officers understand these vulnerabilities, they can better support survivors by providing safe environments for disclosure (Wilson et al., 2013). Along with being more empathetic towards victims, additional trauma-informed practices may include allowing victims to provide written recall and allowing less structure in their recalls. Providing an opportunity for victims to write about their victimization may allow for the disclosure of details about the assault that are uncomfortable to verbalize, and previous work has found the act of writing to diminish negative emotions or mental health problems (Antal & Range, 2005; Pennebaker et al., 1990). Thus, writing may benefit the investigation and the victim's well-being. Additionally, victims may shut down if they feel their recall is being perceived as "not good enough" by investigators (Zajac et al., 2019). Ensuring that victims feel supported in their recall (e.g., recalling any detail, in any order) could help alleviate victims' concerns about the coherence of their recall and the specificity or importance of any detail they recall.

Trauma-informed practices are not often considered for the disclosure process of HCSA because adults reporting these past events are seen more as sources of information than survivors in need of support (Mooney, 2023). A British study reported that investigations into large-scale cases of HCSA were driven more by the needs of the justice system (e.g., evidentiary requirements and the due process rights owed to the accused) than by the needs of the survivors (Colton et al., 2002). Trauma-informed care allows us to balance the defendant's rights without actively harming survivors by giving officers tools to remain objective about the facts of the case while being compassionate towards the individual disclosing. To help the investigators who handle delicate cases like those regarding HCSA, future research must focus on integrating trauma-informed care into the disclosure process.

Prosecuting Attorneys

Similar to the investigators discussed, prosecutors are frequently concerned about whether there is sufficient evidence to take an HCSA to court, particularly as the memories in these cases are often decades old. In Ireland, Bunting (2014) assessed the effect of delayed reporting on case detection, defined in this study as whether police and prosecuting attorneys deemed a CSA case strong enough to be prosecuted. Abuse that occurred during victims' teenage years had a decrease in the likelihood of detection if the abuse was reported a year or more after the incident. For children who were abused when younger than 6 years, there was a higher likelihood of detection if the reporter was an adult female than for a child who reported immediately. This is potentially due to the difficulty of going to trial with such young witnesses. For male reporters, delaying disclosure did not relate to an increase in perceptions that the case was strong enough to prosecute; for males, age at the time of disclosure was not a significant factor.

The effect of delay of disclosure on the likelihood of proceeding to trial, however, is not necessarily consistent across jurisdictions. Two Australian states (i.e., New South Wales, South Australia), for example, have been shown to differ on what characteristics led to prosecution in HCSA cases (Cashmore et al., 2017). In New South Wales, the likelihood of prosecution increased with longer reporting delays, especially as the child's age at the time of the offense increased. In South Australia, however, immediate reporting was more likely to result in prosecution. These differences may reflect variations in prosecutorial discretion across jurisdictions. Furthermore, the only common characteristic between both states was that the perpetrator's authority over the victim increased the likelihood of prosecution.

Chenier and colleagues (2024) additionally examined the progress of cases with indigenous adults in a northern Canadian territory. They reported that cases progressed when victims were female, when victims were 11 to 14 at the time of the abuse, and there were multiple complainants in the case. Another key component in a prosecutor's decision to prosecute a case is consistency. In examining HCSA and CSA cases, Martschuk and colleagues (2024) found that any inconsistency by the victim diminished their perceived credibility and subsequently the progression of the case.

Defense Attorneys

For insight into how defense attorneys treat adults' memories of childhood abuse, we must look to CSA research, as less research has considered this issue in HCSA cases. CSA often relies heavily on the testimony and memory of the victim. Thus, cross-examination provides the defense with an avenue to cast doubt on this crucial evidence. Research has indicated that defense attorneys use CSA myths when questioning victims. Questions regarding CSA myths were found to home in on disclosure (e.g., delays or partial disclosure; Davies et al., 1997; Denne et al., 2023). Defense attorney cross-examination questions also often ask about the plausibility of the abuse either generally (e.g., reactions to the abuse) or specifically (e.g., body position or clothing worn when the abuse occurred) or to develop an alternative explanation (e.g., accidental or mistaken identity; St. George et al., 2022b). Prince and colleagues (2018) further indicated that children who were older at the time of the trial also faced more victim-blaming questions or questions that were sympathetic toward the defendant (e.g., having a good character). Additionally, if the defendant was anyone other than the child's father or stepfather, there were numerous questions about why disclosure was delayed.

Rape myths have also been found in the defense's cross-examination of survivors in CSA or assault cases, including questions regarding whether the victim had a motive to lie (e.g., revenge; St. George et al., 2022a). Stolzenberg and Lyon (2014) examined CSA cases. They reported that an acquittal was more likely in cases with evidence related to rape stereotypes, specifically lack of force or the victim's continued contact with the defendant. Acquittals were also more likely if hearsay testimony was offered by the defense about statements made by the victim or if there was a character witness who testified about either the victim or another prosecution witness.

Less is known about how cross-examination affects the accuracy of victims' testimony. Previous research with children showed that cross-examination decreased their accuracy (Fogliati & Bussey, 2014; Zajac et al., 2012). For HCSA victims, it has been suggested that there should be limits on the length of cross-examination (Shead, 2014). Although this suggests cross-examination may be similarly detrimental for HCSA victims, research in this area is needed and, as noted by others, should also consider how one balances the need for advocacy for the defendant (see Martschuk et al., 2024).

JURORS' AND JUDGES' REACTIONS TO CASES INVOLVING HISTORIC CHILD SEXUAL ABUSE MEMORIES

When a case proceeds to trial, the next vital question is what factors influence the judgments of triers of fact, both jurors and judges, in cases of HCSA and how their judgments compare to one another.

Jurors' Reactions

Jury-eligible participants indicate that they believe victims of CSA significantly delay disclosure of their abuse (McGuire & London, 2017; Morison & Greene, 1992; Quas et al., 2005). Despite this knowledge, delayed disclosure has mixed results on juror decision making. Pozzulo and colleagues (2010) presented participants with mock trial transcripts in which the years of delay in disclosure of HCSA were varied (i.e., 2, 15, 30). Shorter delays (i.e., two years) resulted in higher guilty ratings and longer sentence recommendations than longer delays in reporting (i.e., 30 years). Although dichotomous verdicts (guilt vs. innocence) and the participants' ratings of the complainant's or defendant's credibility were not affected by the delay length in the Pozzulo study (see also Myers et al., 1999), a recent study (Miller et al., 2022) found that a longer delay of 10 months (vs. one day or one month) did diminish guilty verdicts, as well as ratings of the victim's credibility.

Another variable that could impact juror decision making is the relationship between the accused and the victim. Jury-eligible participants have indicated that they believe the perpetrator of the abuse is often known to the victim (McGuire & London, 2017). Pozzulo and colleagues (2010) further tested how this belief manifests in verdict decisions by varying the mock trial transcripts of an HCSA case to include two levels of familiarity in the relationship between the perpetrator and the victim. Specifically, the perpetrator was indicated to be the victim's uncle or coach. Guilty ratings were higher, and jurors were more confident in their verdict when the uncle was the perpetrator rather than the coach.

The content of the testimony by the victim can also impact juror decision making. Individuals who discuss repeated events are sometimes perceived as less honest, less cognitively competent, and less credible despite accuracy being held constant (Weinsheimer et al., 2017). The speaker's perceived confidence, consistency, and cooperation when discussing the events at least partially moderated these results. These findings forecast a negative perception of the victim's credibility, especially for an individual recalling repeated abuse. Yet abuse is often repeated (see Connolly & Read, 2006; Walker et al., 2019; Woiwod & Connolly, 2017).

Judges' Reactions

Bench trials, in which a judge alone decides the outcome of a case, sometimes occur in place of jury trials. Both bench and jury decisions have undergone an overall decline in the United States, at both the federal and state levels, in favor of other means of resolution (e.g., plea deals; Wang, 2022). Bench trials are declining at a slower rate than jury trials, though they are still less common in the United States than in other countries. In an analysis of HCSA cases in Canada, a slight majority of cases were bench trials (i.e., 57%; Connolly & Read, 2006). Thus, understanding judicial case decision making and treatment of historic memories is of great importance.

Several studies have analyzed comments within judicial decisions in HCSA cases that give insight into elements that affect judges' decision making. One category of judicial comments involves credibility, including comments about the complaint's conduct at significant case junctures, such as time of abuse or disclosure (Connolly et al., 2009, 2010). An analysis of bench trials of HCSA in Canada from 1986 to 2002 revealed that credibility comments comprised 30% of all comments in the cases (Connolly et al., 2009). Of the credibility comments, comments about the complainant's conduct at the time of the alleged abuse and their demeanor at trial (e.g., appropriate emotion) were the most frequent.

For HCSA cases, judges seem particularly concerned about the reasons for delay and how such delays impact memory. Over half of the cases analyzed by Connolly and colleagues included comments about the reason for the complainant's delayed disclosure or resistance to the alleged abuse. Such comments are more common in HCSA cases than in CSA cases (Connolly et al., 2010). Judges also commented on the survivors' memory of the offense, including the specificity of the complainant's description of the allegation (i.e., general details, e.g., the basic actions that occurred during the incident; specific details, e.g., incident setting, actions leading up to/directly after the event) and memory failures (i.e., complainant mentioned memory failures, judge mentions an inadequate level of detail was provided; Anderson et al., 2021; Connolly et al., 2009, 2010). Connolly and colleagues (2009) observed that memory for the alleged offense was discussed in almost every case, with comments regarding both specific and general details occurring frequently. Memory failures (i.e., discussing the complainant's difficulty in remembering or forgetting details of the alleged abuse) were discussed less frequently within a case, but were at least commented on in 60% of cases. Additionally, comments about memory failures were more common for HCSA cases than CSA cases. For HCSA cases, it was also more likely that memory failure comments were present in acquittal cases than in conviction cases.

Comparison of Juries' and Judges' Decisions and Beliefs About Disclosure

Given that HCSA cases could be determined by one of two different triers of fact (judges or juries), it is vital to understand how their decision making compares to one another. Read and colleagues (2006) compared HCSA cases from Canadian jury and bench trial outcomes. Overall, jury trials resulted in significantly more guilty verdicts (93.1%) than bench trials (68.6%). Complainants in this study were between 1 and 19 years old at the time of abuse, and the time to disclosure ranged from 2 to 48 years later (M = 14.03). For jury trials only, the complainant's age at the time of the alleged abuse and threats made to the child by the perpetrator affected their verdict decisions. Specifically, as the complainant's age at the time of the alleged abuse increased, so did the likelihood of an acquittal. This increase in acquittals was most pronounced for the oldest age range of 13 to 19 years of age. Physical and emotional threats accompanying the abuse, compared to the absence of threat, increased the likelihood that a jury would find the accused guilty.

Judges' decisions, conversely, were affected by the length of delay for disclosure, the intrusiveness of the abuse, and whether the memory of the abuse was allegedly repressed. Specifically, as the length of delay increased, so did the likelihood of an acquittal decision, especially if the delay was over 20 years from the time of the alleged abuse. Additionally, continuous rather than repressed memory of the alleged abuse more than doubled the likelihood of conviction for bench trials. Though it is not straightforward why there are differences between jury and bench trial outcomes, it may be related to the effects of deliberation or judges focusing on more legally relevant factors while jurors homed in on factors that had more emotional ties (e.g., threats toward the victim; Read et al., 2006).

Given the wide variety of factors that can influence triers of fact, it would be useful to determine ways to assist their decision making. However, limited research has been conducted on ways to aid triers of fact in assessing HCSA cases. Experts are one avenue to aid triers of fact. Connolly and colleagues (2006) assessed Canadian cases of HCSA to understand what factors predicted the use of social science experts. The cases in this study had complainants between 1 and 19 years old when the abuse began and were between age 5 and 64 years old when the trial of the alleged perpetrators occurred (M = 26.09).

They found that the following factors increased the likelihood of an expert testifying in a case: a higher level of offense intrusiveness (e.g., from fondling to penetration), higher frequencies of abuse (i.e., four or more incidents), when the relationship between the victim and perpetrator was parental, higher victim age, the victim being female, and if the memory was repressed. Once present in a case, however, the effect of an expert may not be as intended. Goodman-Delahunty and Martschuk (2017) tested the use of psychological expert testimony to dispel common CSA misconceptions (e.g., delays in reporting are common, inconsistencies are common). Juror CSA knowledge increased when jurors received the expert testimony compared to when they did not receive the intervention. Unfortunately, the knowledge gained from the expert testimony did not correspond to differences in victim credibility assessments or verdict decisions. Further work is thus necessary.

Jury instructions are another mode via which jurors can be given guidance. In New Zealand, a memory-focused juror instruction is used when the crime occurred over a decade before the allegations were brought forward (Cheung, 2020). The memory-focused instruction describes that memory does not act like a tape recorder, and it can be affected by elements such as the time that has passed and the emotionality of the event. Potential jurors in an HCSA case who received the memory-focused instruction were less likely to find the alleged offender guilty.

CONCLUSION

Our goal in this chapter was to highlight that much work is still to be done regarding the issues surrounding HCSA allegations and adults' memory for childhood events. The law continues to be in flux, and it is unclear what challenges extended statutes may face. Further, as some of the more limited lookback statutes expire, state legislatures will continue to debate whether, when, and how these cases should be heard. They will also grapple with the important issue regarding false accusations of HCSA and how due process procedures can help protect the accused.

Research can help support these debates by helping policymakers understand what adult survivors can and should remember. Scientists can also help establish best practices for interviewing survivors and preserving evidence in these cases. In so doing, scientists can help answer what is perhaps the most vital question of all: How can we help create an environment such that children or young adults who want to come forward and disclose feel safe to do so, while also decreasing the number of false allegations? What contextual changes can science help advocate for that can make the disclosure and the litigation process easier but also ensure we avoid wrongful convictions? Cases of HCSA are cases where children did not have their day in court. Science and the legal system can help ensure that a failure to prosecute does not result from a misunderstanding of how survivors can and do remember.

REFERENCES

A.B. v. S.U., 298 A.2d 573 (Vt., 2023).

Alexander, K. W., Quas, J. A., Goodman, G. S., Ghetti, S., Edelstein, R. S., Redlich, A. D., Cordon, I. M., & Jones, D. P. H. (2005). Traumatic impact predicts long-term memory for documented child sexual abuse. *Psychological Science, 16*(1), 33–40. https://doi.org/10.1111/j.0956-7976.2005.00777.x

Anderson, S. F., Patel, U., Harvey, M. B., Price, H. L., & Connolly, D. A. (2021). How do judges discuss memory failures in childhood sexual abuse cases? A brief report. *Journal of Child Sexual Abuse, 30*(4), 498–508. https://doi.org/10.1080/10538712.2021.1914259

Antal, H. M. A., & Range, L. M. (2005). Psychological impact of writing about abuse or positive experiences. *Violence and Victims, 20*(6), 717–728. https://doi.org/10.1891/0886-6708.20.6.717

Bahrick, H. P. (1984). Semantic memory content in permastore: Fifty years of memory for Spanish learned in school. *Journal of Experimental Psychology: General, 113*(1), 1–29. https://doi.org/10.1037/0096-3445.113.1.1

Bahrick, H. P., & Hall, L. K. (1991). Lifetime maintenance of high school mathematics content. *Journal of Experimental Psychology, 120*(1), 20–33. https://doi.org/10.1037/0096-3445.120.1.20

Bauer, P. J., Stark, E. N., Ackil, J. K., Larkina, M., Merrill, N. A., & Fivush, R. (2016). The recollective qualities of adolescents' and adults' narratives about a long-ago tornado. *Memory, 25*(3), 412–424. https://doi.org/10.1080/09658211.2016.1180396

Booker, J. A., Fivush, R., Graci, M. E., Heitz, H., Hudak, L. A., Jovanovic, T., Rothbaum, B. O., & Stevens, J. S. (2020). Longitudinal changes in trauma narratives over the first year and associations with coping and mental health. *Journal of Affective Disorders, 272*, 116–124. https://doi.org/10.1016/j.jad.2020.04.009

Budin, L. E., & Johnson, C. F. (1989). Sex abuse prevention programs: Offenders' attitudes about their efficacy. *Child Abuse & Neglect, 13*(1), 77–87. https://doi.org/10.1016/0145-2134(89)90031-8

Bunting, L. A. (2014). Exploring the influence of reporting delay on criminal justice outcomes: Comparing child and adult reporters of childhood sexual abuse. *Journal of Child Sexual Abuse, 23*(5), 577–594. https://doi.org/10.1080/10538712.2014.920457

Cashmore, J., Taylor, A., & Parkinson, P. (2017). The characteristics of reports to the police of child sexual abuse and the likelihood of cases proceeding to prosecution after delays in reporting. *Child Abuse and Neglect, 74*, 49–61. https://doi.org/10.1016/j.chiabu.2017.07.006

Chenier, K., Shawyer, A., Milne, R., & Williams, A. (2022). Police interviews with adult reporters of historical child sexual abuse: Exploring the link between verbal rapport and information obtained. *Child Abuse & Neglect, 134*, 105943. https://doi.org/10.1016/j.chiabu.2022.105943

Chenier, K., Shawyer, A., Williams, A., & Milne, R. (2024). Historical child sexual abuse cases reported to the police by Indigenous adults in a northern Canadian territory: An exploration of factors affecting the likelihood of charges and convictions. *Journal of Sexual Aggression, 31*(2), 1–23. https://doi.org/10.1080/13552600.2024.2331146

Cheung, G. (2020). *The effect of memory-focused judicial instructions on juror decision-making* [Doctoral dissertation]. Department of Psychology, University of Otago, Dunedin, New Zealand.

CHILD USA. (2025). *Child sex abuse statute of limitations reform.* The Sean P. McIlmail Statute of Limitations Research Institute at CHILD USA. https://childusa.org/sol/

Colton, M., Vanstone, M., & Walby, C. (2002). Victimization, care and justice: Reflections on the experiences of victims/survivors involved in large-scale historical investigations of child sexual abuse in residential institutions. *British Journal of Social Work, 32*(5), 541–551. https://doi.org/10.1093/bjsw/32.5.541

Connolly, D. A., Coburn, P. I., & Chong, K. (2017). Twenty-six years prosecuting historic child sexual abuse cases: Has anything changed? *Psychology, Public Policy, and Law, 23*(2), 166–177. https://doi.org/10.1037/law0000121

Connolly, D. A., Price, H. L., & Gordon, H. M. (2009). Judging the credibility of historic child sexual abuse complainants: How judges describe their decisions. *Psychology, Public Policy, and Law, 15*(2), 102–123. https://doi.org/10.1037/a0015339

Connolly, D. A., Price, H. L., & Gordon, H. M. (2010). Judicial decision making in timely and delayed prosecutions of child sexual abuse in Canada: A study of honesty and cognitive ability in assessments of credibility. *Psychology, Public Policy, and Law, 16*(2), 177–199. https://doi.org/10.1037/a0019050

Connolly, D. A., Price, H. L., & Read, J. D. (2006). Predicting expert social science testimony in criminal prosecutions of historic child sexual abuse. *Legal and Criminological Psychology, 11*(1), 55–74. https://doi.org/10.1348/135532505X50312

Connolly, D. A., & Read, J. D. (2006). Delayed prosecutions of historic child sexual abuse: Analyses of 2064 Canadian criminal complaints. *Law and Human Behavior, 30*(4), 409–434. https://doi.org/10.1007/s10979-006-9011-6

Davies, E., Henderson, E., & Seymour, F. W. (1997). In the interests of justice? The cross-examination of child complainants of sexual abuse in criminal proceedings. *Psychiatry, Psychology and Law, 4*(2), 217–229. https://doi.org/10.1080/13218719709524912

Davis, P. J. (1999). Gender differences in autobiographical memory for childhood emotional experiences. *Journal of Personality and Social Psychology, 76*(3), 498–510. https://doi.org/10.1037/0022-3514.76.3.498

Deferme, D., Otgaar, H., Dodier, O., Körner, A., Mangiulli, I., Merckelbach, H., Sauerland, M., Panzavolta, M., & Loftus, E. F. (2024). Repressed memories (of sexual abuse against minors) and statutes of limitations in Europe: Status quo and possible alternatives. *Topics in Cognitive Science, 16*(4), 630–643. https://doi.org/10.1111/tops.12715

Deffenbacher, K. A., Bornstein, B. H., Penrod, S. D., & McGorty, E. K. (2004). A meta-analytic review of the effects of high stress on eyewitness memory. *Law and Human Behavior, 28*(6), 687–706. https://doi.org/10.1007/s10979-004-0565-x

Denne, E., St George, S., & Stolzenberg, S. N. (2023). Myths and misunderstandings about child sexual abuse in criminal investigations. *Journal of Interpersonal Violence, 38*(1–2), 1893–1919. https://doi.org/10.1177/08862605221093679

Dodier, O., & Otgaar, H. (2019). The forensic and clinical relevance of evidence-based investigative interview methods in historical sexual abuse cases. *Clinical Psychological Science, 7*(6), 1244–1248. https://doi.org/10.1177/2167702619858287

Donalek, J. G. (2001). First incest disclosure. *Issues in Mental Health Nursing, 22*(6), 573–591. https://doi.org/10.1080/01612840118152

Ebbinghaus, H. (1913). *Memory: A contribution to experimental psychology* (Vol. 3). University Microfilms.

Eisen, M. L., Goodman, G. S., Qin, J., Davis, S., & Crayton, J. (2007). Maltreated children's memory: Accuracy, suggestibility, and psychopathology. *Developmental Psychology, 43*(6), 1275–1294. https://doi.org/10.1037/0012-1649.43.6.1275

Elliott, M., Browne, K., & Kilcoyne, J. (1995). Child sexual abuse prevention: What offenders tell us. *Child Abuse & Neglect, 19*(5), 579–594. https://doi.org/10.1016/0145-2134(95)00017-3

Faigman, D. L., Monahan, J., & Slobogin, C. (2014). Group to individual (G2i) inference in scientific expert testimony. *The University of Chicago Law Review, 81*(2), 417–480.

Fogliati, R., & Bussey, K. (2014). The effects of cross-examination on children's reports of neutral and transgressive events. *Legal and Criminological Psychology, 19*(2), 296–315. https://doi.org/10.1111/lcrp.12010

Fivush, R., McDermott Sales, J., Goldberg, A., Bahrick, L., & Parker, J. (2004). Weathering the storm: Children's long-term recall of Hurricane Andrew. *Memory, 12*(1), 104–118. https://doi.org/10.1080/09658210244000397

Freyd, J. J. (1996). *Betrayal trauma: The logic of forgetting childhood abuse.* Harvard University Press.

Gemara, N., & Katz, C. (2023). "It was really hard for me to tell": The gap between the child's difficulty in disclosing sexual abuse, and their perception of the disclosure recipient's response. *Journal of Interpersonal Violence, 38*(1-2), 2068–2091. https://doi.org/10.1177/08862605221099949

Gerdes, K. E., Beck, M. N., Cowan-Hancock, S., & Wilkinson-Sparks, T. (1996). Adult survivors of childhood sexual abuse: The case of Mormon women. *Affilia, 11*(1), 39–60. https://doi.org/10.1177/088610999601100104

Goldfarb, D., Goodman, G. S., Gonzalves, L., Gonzalez, A., Wang, Y., Wu, Y., & Vidales, D. (2020). The accuracy of adults' long-term memory for child sexual abuse. *Advances in Psychology and Law, 5,* 51–82. https://doi.org/10.1007/978-3-030-54678-6_3

Goldfarb, D., Goodman, G. S., Larson, R. P., Eisen, M. L., & Qin, J. (2019). Long-term memory in adults exposed to childhood violence: Remembering genital contact nearly 20 years later. *Clinical Psychological Science,* 7(2), 381–396. https://doi.org/10.1177/2167702618805742

Goldfarb, D., Goodman, G. S., Wang, Y., Fisher, R. P., Vidales, D., Gonzalves, L. C., Wu, Y., Hartman, D., Qin, J., & Eisen, M. L. (2023). Adults' memory for a maltreatment-related childhood experience: Interview protocols. *Clinical Psychological Science, 11*(1), 164–182. https://doi.org/10.1177/21677026221081877

Goodman, G. S., Bottoms, B. L., Rudy, L., Davis, S. L., & Schwartz-Kenny, B. M. (2001). Effects of past abuse experiences on children's eyewitness memory. *Law and Human Behavior, 25*(3), 269–298. https://doi.org/10.1023/A:1010797911805

Goodman, G. S., Ghetti, S., Quas, J. A., Edelstein, R. S., Alexander, K. W., Redlich, A. D., Cordon, I. M., & Jones, D. P. (2003). A prospective study of memory for child sexual abuse: New findings relevant to the repressed-memory controversy. *Psychological Science, 14*(2), 113–118. https://doi.org/10.1111/1467-9280.01428

Goodman-Brown, T. B., Edelstein, R. S., Goodman, G. S., Jones, D. P. H., & Gordon, D. S. (2003). Why children tell: A model of children's disclosure of sexual abuse. *Child Abuse and Neglect, 27*(5), 525–540. https://doi.org/10.1016/S0145-2134(03)00037-1

Goodman-Delahunty, J., & Martschuk, N. (2017). Using pretest–posttest research designs to enhance jury decisions. *Newcastle Law Review, 12,* 86–103. https://www.austlii.edu.au/au/journals/NewcLawRw/2017/6.pdf

Haboush, K. L., & Alyan, H. (2013). Who can you tell? features of Arab culture that influence conceptualization and treatment of childhood sexual abuse. *Journal of Child Sexual Abuse, 22*(5), 499–518. https://doi.org/10.1080/10538712.2013.800935

Hartman, D. T., Wang, Y., Vidales, D., Wu, Y., Goldfarb, D., Qin, J., Eisen, M. L., & Goodman, G. S. (2023). Childhood sexual abuse: A longitudinal study of disclosures and denials. *Child Maltreatment, 28*(3), 462–475. https://doi.org/10.1177/10775595231165335

Hunter, S. V. (2011). Disclosure of child sexual abuse as a life-long process: Implications for health professionals. *Australian and New Zealand Journal of Family Therapy, 32*(2), 159–172. https://doi.org/10.1375/anft.32.2.159

Jensen, T. K., Gulbrandsen, W., Mossige, S., Reichelt, S., & Tjersland, O. A. (2005). Reporting possible sexual abuse: A qualitative study on children's perspectives and the context for disclosure. *Child Abuse and Neglect, 29*(12), 1395–1413. https://doi.org/10.1016/j.chiabu.2005.07.004

La Puma, R. (2016). De-categorizing child abuse-equally devastating acts require equally solicitous statutes of limitations. *UC Davis Journal of Juvenile Law & Policy, 20,* 139–190. https://digitalcommons.law.ggu.edu/pubs/781/

London, K., Bruck, M., Wright, D. B., & Ceci, S. J. (2008). Review of the contemporary literature on how children report sexual abuse to others: Findings, methodological issues, and implications for forensic interviewers. *Memory, 16*(1), 29–47. https://doi.org/10.1080/09658210701725732

Manay, N., & Collin-Vézina, D. (2021). Recipients of children's and adolescents' disclosures of childhood sexual abuse: A systematic review. *Child Abuse & Neglect, 116*(Pt. 1), 104192. https://doi.org/10.1016/j.chiabu.2019.104192

Martschuk, N., Brubacher, S., & Powell, M. (2024). *Defense perspectives on cross-examination of child complainants* [Unpublished manuscript]. Griffith Criminology Institute, Griffith University. https://doi.org/10.2139/ssrn.5034993

Martschuk, N., Cashmore, J., Hoff, S., Parkinson, P., Goodman-Delahunty, J., Shackel, R., Cowdery, N., & Powell, M. B. (2024). The importance of consistency in complainants' evidence in the decision to prosecute child sexual abuse cases. *Child Abuse & Neglect, 158,* 107095. https://doi.org/10.1016/j.chiabu.2024.107095

McElvaney, R. (2015). Disclosure of child sexual abuse: Delays, non-disclosure and partial disclosure. What the research tells us and implications for practice. *Child Abuse Review, 24*(3), 159–169. https://doi.org/10.1002/car.2280

McGill, L., & McElvaney, R. (2023). Adult and adolescent disclosures of child sexual abuse: A comparative analysis. *Journal of Interpersonal Violence, 38*(1–2), 1163–1186. https://doi.org/10.1177/08862605221088278

McGuigan, W. M., & Stephenson, S. J. (2015). A single-case study of resiliency after extreme incest in an Old Order Amish family. *Journal of Child Sexual Abuse, 24*(5), 526–537. https://doi.org/10.1080/10538712.2015.1042182

McGuire, K., & London, K. (2017). Common beliefs about child sexual abuse and disclosure: A college sample. *Journal of Child Sexual Abuse, 26*(2), 175–194. https://doi.org/10.1080/10538712.2017.1281368

McNally, R. J. (2007). Betrayal trauma theory: A critical appraisal. *Memory, 15*(3), 280–294. https://doi.org/10.1080/09658210701256506

McPherson, L., Gatwiri, K., Graham, A., Rotumah, D., Hand, K., Modderman, C., Chubb, J., & James, S. (2025). What helps children and young people to disclose their experience of sexual abuse and what gets in the way? A systematic scoping review. *Child Youth Care Forum, 54*(2), 515–544. https://doi.org/10.1007/s10566-024-09825-5

McWilliams, K., Harris, L. S., & Goodman, G. S. (2014). Child maltreatment, trauma-related psychopathy, and eyewitness memory in children and adolescents. *Behavioral Sciences & the Law, 32*(6), 702–717. https://doi.org/10.1002/bsl.2143

Miller, Q. C., Call, A. A., & London, K. (2022). Mock jurors' perceptions of child sexual abuse cases: Investigating the role of delayed disclosure and relationship to the perpetrator. *Journal of Interpersonal Violence, 37*(23–24), 23374–23396. https://doi.org/10.1177/08862605221078812

Mitchell v. Roberts, 469 P.3d 901, 2020 U.T. 34 (Utah 2020).

Mooney, J. (2023). Personal narratives, public risk: Using Foucault's 'confessional' to examine adult retrospective disclosures of childhood abuse. *Health, Risk and Society, 25*(1–2), 61–74. https://doi.org/10.1080/13698575.2023.2166019

Morison, S., & Greene, E. (1992). Juror and expert knowledge of child sexual abuse. *Child Abuse & Neglect, 16*(4), 595–613. https://doi.org/10.1016/0145-2134(92)90075-3

Münzer, A., Fegert, J. M., Ganser, H. G., Loos, S., Witt, A., & Goldbeck, L. (2016). Please tell! Barriers to disclosing sexual victimization and subsequent social support perceived by children and adolescents. *Journal of Interpersonal Violence, 31*(2), 355–377. https://doi.org/10.1177/0886260514555371

Murre, J. M., & Dros, J. (2015). Replication and analysis of Ebbinghaus' forgetting curve. *PLOS One, 10*(7), e0120644. https://doi.org/10.1371/journal.pone.0120644

Myers, J. E. B., Prizmich, L. P., Redlich, A. D., Goodman, G. S., & Imwinkelried, E. (1999). Jurors' perceptions of hearsay in child sexual abuse cases. *Psychology, Public Policy, and Law, 5*(2), 388–419. https://doi.org/10.1037/1076-8971.5.2.388

Ornstein, P. A., Baker-Ward, L., Gordon, B. N., Pelphrey, K. A., Tyler, C. S., & Gramzow, E. (2006). The influence of prior knowledge and repeated questioning on children's long-term retention of the details of a pediatric examination. *Developmental Psychology, 42*(2), 332–344. https://doi.org/10.1037/0012-1649.42.2.332

Otgaar, H., Howe, M. L., Dodier, O., Lilienfeld, S. O., Loftus, E. F., Lynn, S. J., Merckelbach, H., & Patihis, L. (2021). Belief in unconscious repressed memory persists. *Perspectives on Psychological Science, 16*(2), 454–460. https://doi.org/10.1177/1745691621990628

Otgaar, H., Muris, P., Howe, M. L., & Merckelbach, H. (2017). What drives false memories in psychopathology? A case for associative activation. *Clinical Psychological Science, 5*(6), 1048–1069. https://doi.org/10.1177/2167702617724424

Paine, M. L., & Hansen, D. J. (2002). Factors influencing children to self-disclose sexual abuse. *Clinical Psychology Review, 22*(2), 271–295. https://doi.org/10.1016/S0272-7358(01)00091-5

Parkinson, P. (2014). Child sexual abuse and the churches: A story of moral failure? *Current Issues in Criminal Justice, 26*(1), 119–138. https://doi.org/10.1080/10345329.2014.12036010

Pennebaker, J. W., Colder, M., & Sharp, L. K. (1990). Accelerating the coping process. *Journal of Personality and Social Psychology, 58*(3), 528–537. https://doi.org/10.1037/0022-3514.58.3.528

Peterson, C. (2015). A decade later: Adolescents' memory for medical emergencies. *Applied Cognitive Psychology, 29*(6), 826–834. https://doi.org/10.1002/acp.3192

Peterson, C., & Whalen, N. (2001). Five years later: Children's memory for medical emergencies. *Applied Cognitive Psychology, 15*(7), 7–24. https://doi.org/10.1002/acp.832

Pozzulo, J. D., Dempsey, J. L., & Crescini, C. (2010). Factors affecting juror decisions in historic child sexual abuse cases involving continuous memories. *Criminal Justice and Behavior, 37*(9), 951–964. https://doi.org/10.1177/0093854810373587

Price, M., Olezeski, C., McMahon, T. J., & Hill, N. E. (2019). A developmental perspective on victimization faced by gender nonconforming youth. In H. E. Fitzgerald, D. J. Johnson, D. B. Qin, F. A. Villarruel, & J. Norder (Eds.), *Handbook of children and prejudice: Integrating research, practice, and policy* (pp. 447–461). Springer. https://doi.org/10.1007/978-3-030-12228-7_25

Prince, E. R., Andrews, S. J., Lamb, M. E., & Foster, J. L. H. (2018). The construction of allegedly abused children's narratives in Scottish criminal courts. *Psychology, Crime and Law, 24*(6), 621–651. https://doi.org/10.1080/1068316X.2017.1399395

Quas, J. A., Goodman, G. S., Bidrose, S., Pipe, M. E., Craw, S., & Ablin, D. S. (1999). Emotion and memory: Children's long-term remembering, forgetting, and suggestibility. *Journal of Experimental Child Psychology, 72*(4), 235–270. https://doi.org/10.1006/jecp.1999.2491

Quas, J. A., Thompson, W. C., Alison, K., & Stewart, C. (2005). Do jurors "know" what isn't so about child witnesses? *Law and Human Behavior, 29*(4), 425–456. https://doi.org/10.1007/s10979-005-5523-8

Rathbone, C. J., Moulin, C. J., & Conway, M. A. (2008). Self-centered memories: The reminiscence bump and the self. *Memory & Cognition, 36*(8), 1403–1414. https://doi.org/10.3758/MC.36.8.1403

Read, J. D., Connolly, D. A., & Welsh, A. (2006). An archival analysis of actual cases of historic child sexual abuse: A comparison of jury and bench trials. *Law and Human Behavior, 30*(3), 259–285. https://doi.org/10.1007/s10979-006-9010-7

Reilly, M. T. (2021). Retribution against Catholic dioceses by revival: The evolution and legacy of the New York Child Victims Act. *Albany Law Review, 84*, 735. https://www.albanylawreview.org/article/39717-retribution-against-catholic-dioceses-by-revival-the-evolution-and-legacy-of-the-new-york-child-victims-act

Roediger, H. L., & DeSoto, K. A. (2014). Forgetting the presidents. *Science, 346*(6213), 1106–1109. https://doi.org/10.1126/science.1259627

Rubin, D. C., & Wenzel, A. E. (1996). One hundred years of forgetting: A quantitative description of retention. *Psychological Review, 103*(4), 734–760. https://doi.org/10.1037/0033-295X.103.4.734

Schönbucher, V., Maier, T., Mohler-Kuo, M., Schnyder, U., & Landolt, M. A. (2012). Disclosure of child sexual abuse by adolescents: A qualitative in-depth study. *Journal of Interpersonal Violence, 27*(17), 3486–3513. https://doi.org/10.1177/0886260512445380

Shalhoub-Kevorkian, N. (2005). Disclosure of child abuse in conflict areas. *Violence Against Women, 11*(10), 1263–1291. https://doi.org/10.1177/1077801205280180

Shead, K. (2014). Responding to historical child sexual abuse: A prosecution perspective on current challenges and future directions. *Current Issues in Criminal Justice, 26*(1), 55–73. https://doi.org/10.1080/10345329.2014.12036007

St. George, S., Denne, E., & Stolzenberg, S. N. (2022a). Blaming children: How rape myths manifest in defense attorneys' questions to children testifying about child sexual abuse. *Journal of Interpersonal Violence, 37*(17-18), NP16623–NP16646.

St. George, S., Denne, E., & Stolzenberg, S. N. (2022b). "This incident happened when there were 10 people in the house?" Exploring a framework to categorize defense attorneys' plausibility questioning in CSA trials. *Psychology, Crime and Law, 30*(6), 556–582. https://doi.org/10.1080/1068316X.2022.2104277

St. George, S., Garcia-Johnson, A., Denne, E., & Stolzenberg, S. N. (2020). "Did you ever fight back?" Jurors' questions to children testifying in criminal trials about alleged sexual abuse. *Criminal Justice and Behavior, 47*(8), 1032–1054. https://doi.org/10.1177/0093854820935960

Stogner v. California, 539 U.S. 607, 123 S. Ct. 2446, 156 L. Ed. 2d 544 (2003).

Stolzenberg, S. N., & Lyon, T. D. (2014). Evidence summarized in attorneys' closing arguments predicts acquittals in criminal trials of child sexual abuse. *Child Maltreatment, 19*(2), 119–129. https://doi.org/10.1177/1077559514539388

Tobin, V., & Delaney, K. R. (2019). Child abuse victimization among transgender and gender nonconforming people: A systematic review. *Perspectives in Psychiatric Care, 55*(4), 576–583. https://doi.org/10.1111/ppc.12398

United States v. Kubrick, 444 U.S. 111, 100 S. Ct. 352, 62 L. Ed. 2d 259 (1979).

Ullman, S. E., & Filipas, H. H. (2005). Gender differences in social reactions to abuse disclosures, post-abuse coping, and PTSD of child sexual abuse survivors. *Child Abuse & Neglect, 29*(7), 767–782. https://doi.org/10.1016/j.chiabu.2005.01.005

Valentino, K. (2011). A developmental psychopathology model of overgeneral autobiographical memory. *Developmental Review, 31*(1), 32–54. https://doi.org/10.1016/j.dr.2011.05.001

Van Abbema, D., & Bauer, P. (2005). Autobiographical memory in middle childhood: Recollections of the recent and distant past. *Memory, 13*(8), 829–845. https://doi.org/10.1080/09658210444000430

Wallis, C. R., & Woodworth, M. D. (2020). Child sexual abuse: An examination of individual and abuse characteristics that may impact delays of disclosure. *Child Abuse & Neglect, 107*, 104604. https://doi.org/10.1016/j.chiabu.2020.104604

Walker, H. E., Freud, J. S., Ellis, R. A., Fraine, S. M., & Wilson, L. C. (2019). The prevalence of sexual revictimization: A meta-analytic review. *Trauma, Violence, & Abuse, 20*(1), 67–80. https://doi.org/10.1177/1524838017692364

Wang, H. Z. (2022). Rethinking evidentiary rules in an age of bench trials. *UC Irvine Law Review, 13*, 263–316. https://doi.org/10.2139/ssrn.4051991

Weinsheimer, C. C., Coburn, P. I., Chong, K., MacLean, C. L., & Connolly, D. A. (2017). Perceptions of credibility for a memory report of a single versus repeated event. *Applied Cognitive Psychology, 31*(4), 414–423. https://doi.org/10.1002/acp.3340

Westera, N., Gentle, M., Powell, M., & Zajac, R. (2023). Police investigators' perceptions of the challenges associated with interviewing adult sexual assault complainants. *Violence Against Women, 29*(2), 276–299. https://doi.org/10.1177/10778012221120447

Widom, C. S., & Morris, S. (1997). Accuracy of adult recollections of childhood victimization, Part 2: Childhood sexual abuse. *Psychological Assessment, 9*(1), 34–36. https://doi.org/10.1037/1040-3590.9.1.34

Williams, J. M., & Broadbent, K. (1986). Autobiographical memory in suicide attempters. *Journal of Abnormal Psychology, 95*(2), 144–149. https://doi.org/10.1037/0021-843X.95.2.144

Wilson, C., Pence, D. M., & Conradi, L. (2013). Trauma-informed care. In *Encyclopedia of social work.* Oxford University Press. https://doi.org/10.1093/acrefore/9780199975839.013.1063

Winters, G. M., Jeglic, E. L., & Kaylor, L. E. (2020). Validation of the sexual grooming model of child sexual abusers. *Journal of Child Sexual Abuse, 29*(7), 855–875. https://doi.org/10.1080/10538712.2020.1801935

Winters, G. M., Jeglic, E. L., & Kaylor, L. E. (2024). Sexual grooming behaviors of females who perpetrate child sexual abuse. *Victims & Offenders,* 1–25. https://doi.org/10.1080/15564886.2024.2329098

Wixted, J. T. (2004). The psychology and neuroscience of forgetting. *Annual Review of Psychology, 55*(1), 235–269. https://doi.org/10.1146/annurev.psych.55.090902.141555

Woiwod, D. M., & Connolly, D. A. (2017). Continuous child sexual abuse: Balancing defendants' rights and victims' capabilities to particularize individual acts of repeated abuse. *Criminal Justice Review, 42*(2), 206–225. https://doi.org/10.1177/0734016817704700

Wu, Y., Goodman, G. S., Goldfarb, D., Wang, Y., Vidales, D., Brown, L., Eisen, M. L., & Qin, J. (2023). Memory accuracy after 20 years for interviews about child maltreatment. *Child Maltreatment, 28*(1), 85–96. https://doi.org/10.1177/10775595211055184

Zajac, R., O'Neill, S., & Hayne, H. (2012). Disorder in the courtroom? Child witnesses under cross-examination. *Developmental Review, 32*(3), 181–204. https://doi.org/10.1016/j.dr.2012.06.006

Zajac, R., Westera, N. J., Ali, M. M., & Powell, M. (2019). Investigative interviews with adult sexual assault complainants: Challenges and future directions. In J. J. Dickinson, N. Schreiber Compo, R. Carol, B. L. Schwartz, & M. McCauley (Eds.), *Evidence-based investigative interviewing* (pp. 177–192). Routledge. https://doi.org/10.4324/9781315160276-10

5

Children's Memory for Repeated Events in Child Maltreatment Investigations

Sarah L. Deck, Sonja P. Brubacher, and Martine B. Powell

Ongoing maltreatment involves patterns of behaviors enacted over multiple episodes of abuse. These episodes often transpire in a similar way (Brubacher et al., 2013) and may become increasingly severe over time (Winters & Jeglic, 2017). In some cases, maltreatment occurs within or after a protracted period of positive contact. Take these two case examples:

> Six-year-old Anita lives with her mom and stepfather, Gus. She has a good relationship with both caregivers. She enjoys playing with Gus, who often puts her to bed when her mother works evenings. However, at bath time, Gus often tries to touch her genitals and sometimes gets into the bath naked with her. He makes her promise not to tell her mother and says he'll get in trouble if she does. Anita does not like bath time with Gus but otherwise loves him very much.

> Twelve-year-old Darnell has been playing hockey for two years. He always looked up to his coach, Rick, with whom he developed a strong friendship. Sometime in the last year, Rick started buying Darnell food and other small gifts, and then created more opportunities for them to spend time together. Darnell increasingly felt like Rick was the only person who understood him. When Rick started giving Darnell sports massages and sharing beers with him, Darnell felt mildly uncomfortable but did not protest. The massages evolved into genital touching, and Rick convinced Darnell that the youth himself wanted the relationship. Darnell has nightmares and anxiety but does not know how to end it.

The writing of this chapter was supported in part by funding from grant DP230101634 awarded to MBP and SPB.

https://doi.org/10.1037/0000492-005
Handbook on Child Witnesses: Improving Psychological Science and Legal Practice,
G. S. Goodman, T. D. Lyon, S. D. Hobbs, and R. Enriquez (Editors)

When children are interviewed in maltreatment investigations, their recollections tend to be based on multiple event episodes (potentially a mixture of positive, negative, and neutral recurring experiences), presenting an additional challenge due to the structure of memory for repeated events. This chapter provides an overview of theory and empirical findings on children's memory for repeated events and addresses interviewing considerations that could be made in this context. We conclude with an overview of children's understanding of time and number, as these concepts are particularly pertinent to investigations that involve recurring abuse.

CHILDREN'S MEMORY FOR REPEATED EVENTS

When children and adults experience events, generic representations, or scripts, may be formed. *Scripts* are temporally organized, hierarchical frameworks that include information about the people, objects, and actions involved in an event (Schank & Abelson, 1977). These cognitive representations provide an efficient scaffold for storing previous experiences with a recurring event and guide expectations for how future similar experiences will unfold.

Children show evidence of script development after a single experience, and scripts are consolidated following additional experiences with similar events (Farrar & Boyer-Pennington, 1999). Children also acquire the ability to form scripts at very young ages (Hudson & Nelson, 1986), including for repeated traumatic events (Bearison & Pacifici, 1989). With repeated experience, individual episodes of the event are incorporated into the overarching memory representation. This makes the representation more detailed and sophisticated, and strengthens memory for details that were encountered in a similar way multiple times (Hudson et al., 1992). Scripts are considered a form of semantic memory, which involves memory for concepts, meaning, and facts (Tulving, 2002).

Scripts do not typically maintain the integrity of memories for individual episodes (Hudson & Mayhew, 2009; cf. Graesser et al., 1979). This generic quality of script memory is reflected in the language children use to talk about events. Children tend to use timeless present tense to report script information, whereas episodic information is usually reported in past tense with occurrence-specific details (Hudson & Nelson, 1986), as in the following example:

SCRIPT: You mix everything in a bowl and then you bake them and eat them.

EPISODIC: We made cookies, but they burned in the oven and tasted a bit yucky.

Retrieval of individual occurrences of a repeated event relies on episodic memory. Episodic memories are embedded within a temporospatial context and can contain many sensory details. Many of these memories, especially for neutral or common events, decay relatively rapidly. People may increasingly engage in event reconstruction, based on their scripts, as accessibility to episodic information declines (e.g., after a long delay: Reyna & Brainerd, 1995). Although these processes are also true for adults, they may be particularly true for young children (Tulving, 2002), who are the focus here. To recall what happened in a particular instance, children may use their scripts to fill in details not retrieved by accessible episodic memory traces. This process supports recall: When children recall a repeated event, they often retrieve a variety of details that were experienced at some point during the event, and they rarely report information that was never experienced (Hudson & Nelson, 1986; Woiwod et al., 2019). Moreover, because they tend to reconstruct an episode by reporting details that were typically present, children may correctly recount details specific to that episode, even when relevant episodic memory traces denoting that information are not retrieved (Baker-Ward et al., 2020). In other words, many episodic details are retained, but the connection to the specific episode fades. Although the process of reconstruction can lead to recalling accurate details, it can also lead to errors.

Script theory is useful for making predictions about how much children will report about repeated events, across levels of development and under what circumstances, but it does not contain a mechanism for predicting what children will report about an individual or strongly remembered occurrence. By some notable accounts, children connect experienced details to a particular episode through *source monitoring*—a decision-making process at retrieval. According to the source-monitoring framework, people monitor the characteristics of their memories, such as perceptual, semantic, and contextual information to determine their origins, and this process can occur outside of conscious awareness or involve more effortful reasoning (Johnson et al., 1993).

The process of source monitoring is particularly difficult when competing sources are highly similar (e.g., Lindsay et al., 1991). The more implausible the detail (e.g., an elephant arrived at Uncle Jay's apartment), the more likely it will lead to a von Restorff-like effect (i.e., when something is distinctive in a given context it is more likely to be attended to and recalled; MacLeod, 2020). This effect is not unique to repeated events, but if the routine experiences are considered a homogenous background, then occurrences with highly atypical details may stand out. Better identification of occurrences with atypical details fits with the *script pointer plus tag* (SP + T) hypothesis (Schank & Abelson, 1977). This hypothesis assumes that a script consists of pointers to the event script and a set of tags that link typical actions to the generic script and atypical actions directly to a memory representation. The fate of atypical details over time depends on their characteristics. Those that are relevant to the goal, associated with goal disruption (i.e., continuous deviation), or vividly irrelevant to the story, are likely to be retained and preserved as a unique episodic memory.

Although we just presented general findings concerning script memory, there have also been many studies on how developmental factors affect memory for repeated events. We review developmental changes in memory for repeated events in the next section.

DEVELOPMENTAL CHANGES IN MEMORY FOR REPEATED EVENTS

Scripts are powerful mental structures, and their development appears to emerge early in life. At one year of age, infants can recall the order of novel action sequences, indicating that their event representations are temporally organized (Bauer & Mandler, 1992). By 2.5 years of age, children can generalize event knowledge. Bauer and Fivush (1992) found that 30-month-olds could generalize familiar action sequences to perceptually novel items which fulfilled the same function in the event (e.g., choosing a different animal to go down a toy slide). When children's language abilities are sufficiently developed, event generalization is reflected in their verbal reports. Children in early preschool (aged 3 to 4 years) provide organized verbal reports about "what usually happens" during a familiar event like eating breakfast (Sims & Morton, 2021), and at 5 years of age, children report novel activities they experienced on their first day of kindergarten in a general way (e.g., "You play and then clean up"; Fivush, 1984).

As children develop, they form scripts more rapidly, and their representations become more detailed and complex (e.g., DeMarie et al., 2000). Older children are more accurate than younger ones in attributing details to the episode they experienced, due to enhanced accessibility of relevant episodic memory traces and superior source-monitoring abilities (e.g., Odegard et al., 2009). Compared to younger children, older children are also more likely to refer to activities that changed predictably across episodes of the event (i.e., optionals: e.g., "we can bake cake or cookies"), to specify the conditions necessary for an act to occur (i.e., conditionals: e.g., "once we have put the mixture into the pan, then we can put the cake in the oven"), and to recall details that deviate from previous experiences (Farrar & Goodman, 1992; Slackman & Nelson, 1984). According to the schema confirmation deployment model, these developmental differences arise because older children are more efficient than younger ones in recognizing which details of a novel event are script components (Farrar & Goodman, 1992). Consequently, older children can progress to using their event script as a guide for processing that experience more rapidly. This reduces the need to allocate cognitive resources to script-consistent details and allows for greater processing of novel information.

Laboratory-based research designs have illuminated developmental differences in children's baseline accuracy when recalling occurrences of a repeated event. For example, Powell and colleagues (2003) conducted a series of experiments involving 4- to 5- and 6- to 8-year-olds, examining their ability to remember separate occurrences of a repeated event. At a short retention interval (1 to 7 days), older children tended to recall the first and last occurrence of a series of six events better than the middle occurrences, a pattern not observed in younger children (a similar pattern was observed in Roberts et al., 2015). In other repeated-events research demonstrating developmental differences, preschool and elementary school aged children reported their memories for one occurrence of a repeated event that had a consistent structure with slight variations across occurrences. The 4- to 5-year-olds were less accurate than 7- to 8-year-olds at attributing the varying details to the correct occurrence when specifically asked. Regarding new details, which were present on one occurrence only, younger children rarely recalled these details spontaneously, whereas 50% of the older children did so, and they were also above chance at attributing them to their correct occurrence (Brubacher, Glisic, et al., 2011).

The research on developmental differences in memory for repeated events shows, in many ways, improvements over the course of development. Yet, older children are also more susceptible to some types of false memories, such as those that are script consistent, because they use their scripts (which are comparatively stronger than those of younger children) to fill in what happened on a given episode (Otgaar et al., 2018). Indeed, Baker-Ward and colleagues (2020) found that older children were more likely than younger children to erroneously attribute typically occurring details to their most recent physical examination (e.g., that their height was measured, when this did not happen). In addition to spontaneous intrusions, older children are more vulnerable to suggestions that are consistent with the concepts embodied in their scripts (e.g., to a suggestion that they were given a train sticker, when they received a bus and boat sticker during previous experiences; Connolly & Price, 2006).

There may also be developmental differences in how disruptions to goals are recalled. Younger children (6- to 8-year-olds) correctly recalled more details that varied across occurrences when they had experienced a continuous deviation in the fourth occurrence compared to no deviation, but older (9- to 11-year-olds) children were not affected by the manipulation (Connolly et al., 2016).

The studies reviewed so far tend to be about neutral or positive events. In the next section, we consider the impact of stress on memories for repeated events.

STRESS AND REPEATED EVENT MEMORY

The relation between stress and memory is complex. That an event is traumatic or induces negative emotional arousal is not a direct predictor of better or worse memory compared to a neutral or pleasant event (Price & Connolly, 2008). Further, some parts of a stressful memory, like details integral to the stressor, may be very well remembered, although other parts, like details that are peripheral to the stressor, may be forgotten or confused (Christianson, 1992). Whereas there appears to be some impact of trauma on memory, this effect may be influenced by a variety of factors, including age of the child (at exposure to trauma or retrieval) and type of event recalled. In general, memories for stressful events follow the same developmental course as memories for nonstressful ones (e.g., Goodman et al., 1991).

Little analogue research has explored memory for stressful repeated events, and only a few studies have compared recall of a stressful event to a matched nonstressful one. In one study, children (aged 4–5 years) participated in a swimming lesson one or multiple times and were interviewed about the only/first lesson they experienced (Price & Connolly, 2007). Some children found the lessons stressful. The effect of stress did not significantly differ based on experience frequency. However, children who found the lessons stressful (anxious children) were less suggestible than nonanxious children in free recall. In another study, the effect of stress on adults' memory for a repeated event was evaluated by asking participants to imagine hypothetical relationship encounters where domestic violence was either absent or present. Stress supported recall, and this was the case regardless of event frequency (Dilevski et al., 2020). Although more research is needed, these studies suggest that the effect of stress on memory does not depend on event frequency. A problem with experimental research, however, is that even when stressful paradigms are used, they do not reach the level of emotional arousal that would be experienced in a real-life situation that threatens personal safety.

Memories for real-life repeated negative experiences should be relatively strong, especially for details that are central (Christianson, 1992; Cleveland et al., 2022) and those that are experienced the same way each time; that is, fixed details, like perpetrator identity (Price & Connolly, 2008). Some evidence to the contrary comes from clinical case studies (Terr, 1988, 1991). Terr interviewed and studied case reports of children who experienced documented trauma between age 6 months and 4.5 years. Consistent with literature on infantile amnesia (Peterson, 2021), if the trauma occurred before 28–36 months of age, children were unable to provide more than fragments, if any, of episodic memories. Terr suggested that memories for single, startling traumas tend to be vivid, while memories for repeated experience tend to fade or be spotty, due to dissociation or repression (Terr, 1991). Yet, there were many confounding factors in Terr's case studies, which limit conclusions.

The best evidence for evaluating the relation between stress and memory for repeated experiences comes from real-life events for which there are some external measures of ground truth. In one such study, forty-six 3- to 10-year-olds were interviewed about a stressful medical procedure, voiding cystourethrogram fluoroscopy (VCUG), that involves catheterization and infusion of fluid into the bladder and then voiding onto the exam table (Goodman et al., 1994). Relevant to the current chapter, 17 of the children had undergone at least one, and up to six, prior VCUGs. There were no clear effects of repeated experience on memory performance, but it was associated with more adverse emotional consequences. Instead, children's increasing age and having mothers who talked with them about the procedure were associated with better understanding of the event and greater resistance to misleading questions. This real-world example of a stressful repeated event provides additional evidence that repetition strengthens memory (for the event script, central details, and those experienced similarly across occurrences) regardless of event emotionality.

CHILD ABUSE AND MEMORY FOR REPEATED EVENTS

The dominant findings in the literature on repeated event memory in children (studies are rare in adolescents) are that children preferably report generic information, and they often confuse the source (episode) of the episodic details they report. Our understanding of repeated-event memory largely stems from studies that examine children's recall of pleasant familiar events from their lives (e.g., birthday parties; Hudson & Nelson, 1986) or from multiple staged activity sessions in which they participated (see Woiwod et al., 2019, for a review). Nevertheless, the patterns of script development and memory confusions are similar when repeated experiences are traumatic or negative (notwithstanding social factors that increase reluctance and might apply to the reporting of sensitive or traumatic events regardless of their frequency). For example, consistent with experimental research, field studies have shown that children alleging repeated sexual abuse provide overall more information than children alleging a single instance of abuse (Orbach et al., 2000; Sternberg et al., 1996) and develop routine abuse scripts (Brubacher & La Rooy, 2014; Brubacher, Malloy et al., 2013).

In the context of repeated events, each episode of abuse can be considered a separate source. Children must work out in which episode details (encountered at some point during the event) were experienced. Because the source (i.e., the episode-specific context in which particular details were experienced) is not represented in the script, the most common error children who recall a repeated event make is connecting experienced details to the wrong episode (i.e., internal intrusions). For example, a child may recall, "Uncle Chris showed me naked people on the computer" and attribute the experience to, "the second time he looked after me," when this detail happened on a different occasion.

Some cases of abuse may involve the same offender, at the same location, with a relatively routine time context (e.g., Uncle Jay looks after MacKenna at his home on Friday nights when her mom is at work). In such cases, retrieval of atypical details (e.g., one Friday night the power went out in Uncle Jay's apartment) could be facilitated due to their distinctiveness against the routine backdrop of the script (Davidson & Hoe, 1993). Atypical details that are script-consistent or plausible within the script (e.g., Uncle Jay usually washes MacKenna's hair in the bath but one time he did not), or do not seriously disrupt the goal (discrete deviation) are more likely to be forgotten or omitted in script reconstruction, at least based on memory of typical and atypical elements in stories (Davidson & Hoe, 1993; Davidson & Jergovic, 1996).

In a real-life example of a traumatic repeated child sexual abuse with corroborating evidence, four girls (ages 8, 13, 14, and 15 at the time they testified—which was within approximately a year of when the abuse began), started to work as cleaners for a man who increasingly talked to them in a sexual manner and engaged them in sexual activities with himself and other men

(Bidrose & Goodman, 2000). Researchers analyzed the girls' 11 testimonies, as well as evidence in the form of 77 audiotapes and 623 photographs. Together, they made 246 allegations, for which 194 (79%) were supported by evidence. (The remaining 21% were not disconfirmed; there simply was no supporting evidence, and these acts were usually nonsexual; they were about allegations of payment for sex and coercive activities). In contrast, there was evidence for 318 different acts; thus, the rate of supported allegations was 61% (194/318); meaning omission errors were more prevalent than possible commission errors. The girls who were involved for a longer duration made more omission errors than the girls who were involved for a shorter duration. The authors note that it is impressive how little was forgotten out of 318 acts. Like the VCUG example cited earlier, this real-world example of a traumatic repeated event provides additional evidence that repetition strengthens memory (likely for the event script).

GROOMING AND REPEATED EVENT MEMORY

Grooming is a type of repeated event that is particularly likely to include positive, negative, and neutral aspects. It occurs when someone builds a relationship, trust, and emotional connection with a child, to manipulate, exploit, and/or abuse them (Craven et al., 2006). This process involves repeated contact (of some kind). It may involve similar locations and actions and is often embedded within the child's own routine activities (Williams, 2015). Yet, grooming differs substantially from the events typically used in laboratory studies of repeated-event memory, wherein each episode is similar in structure. Consequently, it is not well understood how children represent episodes when grooming has occurred.

The grooming process likely affects script formation. If episodes are dissimilar (e.g., when grooming progresses rapidly), children are unlikely to form strong scripts and may recall episode-specific details well (Danby et al., 2019). Conversely, if grooming occurs gradually and episodes are similar, children's scripts are likely to be strong, allowing them to report generic information with ease, at the expense of difficulty reporting episodic information. How experiences later in the grooming process affect memory for earlier episodes is unclear. Children may assimilate the novel information into their existing script, meaning that their representations of earlier episodes are somewhat preserved (Piaget, 1957). Alternatively, children may engage in script accommodation, affecting how they remember earlier experiences.

In the following section, we address interviewing considerations for a repeated event; yet the extent to which interviewing guidance for repeated events applies to grooming (or child abuse generally) remains largely untested. This question is relevant to developing a comprehensive understanding of how memories for similar but evolving experiences are retained and should be a priority area for researchers studying repeated-event memory. In the context of forensic interviews, evidence about how a child was groomed can help to explain their behavior both before and after the abuse began (Winters & Jeglic, 2017). In the absence of research on interviewing practices when grooming is implicated, we provide a few preliminary suggestions that may be useful for eliciting this information where relevant.

QUESTIONING CHILDREN ABOUT A REPEATED EVENT IN INVESTIGATIONS

Worldwide, many jurisdictions require that child complainants particularize abuse by describing individual episodes with a reasonable level of detail (e.g., with respect to time, place, or another unique contextual detail). In awareness of the challenge of this requirement when children have experienced recurring abuse, several jurisdictions have relaxed these requirements, adopting continuous child sexual abuse statutes instead (Woiwod & Connolly, 2017). Yet, children often need to provide episodic details even where continuous statutes exist. This occurs for several reasons, such as the need to establish that abuse was continuous and underutilization of the new legislation (which is typically complex; Shead, 2014). Moreover, the provision of episodic information can aid investigations and enhance children's credibility (Powell et al., 2007). In forensic interviews, how children are interviewed heavily influences the potential for obtaining accurate episodic information. Interviewing children about a repeated event requires considerations that extend beyond best practice recommendations for a single event. In the following section, we provide an overview of key recommendations.

The Building Blocks: Open-Ended Questions

Open-ended questions (e.g., "Tell me what happened") promote accurate and detailed responses and support children to accurately recall episode-specific details (Brubacher et al., 2014). Although open-ended prompts allow children to search their memories and self-generate the most accessible information, specific questions request children to report details specified by the interviewer (e.g., "What underwear did you wear that day?"). Even when children retrieve relevant information (e.g., wearing green, pink, and white underwear on different days), the source of that information, which decays much more rapidly than content, may be unavailable (Powell & Thomson, 1997).

Interviewers should phrase their open-ended questions in a manner consistent with the specificity of the information they seek to elicit (Brubacher et al., 2013, 2018; Schneider et al., 2011). Prompts that are phrased generically tend to elicit script information, whereas episodic prompts elicit information about specific episodes. See Table 5.1 to compare the following examples, noting how minor changes in interview tense can transform the information elicited.

TABLE 5.1. Example of a Generic Prompt Versus an Episodic Prompt

Generic	Episodic
Interviewer: "Tell me what *usually happens* when Dan *visits*."	**Interviewer:** "Tell me what *happened* the *last time* Dan *visited*."
Child: "We *play* games."	**Child:** "We *played* the tickling game."

Even when probed episodically, children may nonetheless resort to reporting generic information, especially if their scripts are strong (e.g., Brubacher & La Rooy, 2014). Interviewers do not always follow children's shifts in language (Brubacher et al., 2013). If children revert to reporting the event generically (e.g., "He touched me on my privates, it was always the same"), interviewers can redirect them to the episode of interest if needed (e.g., "I know that you said it's always the same, but I want to know what happened the last time Dan visited").

Using Narrative Practice to Orient Children to the Relevance of Episodic Information

To elicit information about individual episodes of an event, it is important that children understand the relevance of episodic information to the interview. Among other benefits (e.g., promoting rapport; see Chapter 12, this volume), narrative practice is an effective tool for establishing children's expectations about the conversation style of the interview, including the level of detail that is valued in their responses. Recent research indicates that narrative practice may also sensitize children to the specificity of the responses; asking children about one or more episodes of a pleasant routine event during narrative practice may support the provision of episodic information in the substantive phase (Brubacher et al., 2011; Danby et al., 2017; see also Chapter 10, this volume).

Identifying and Labelling Episodes

To encourage children to provide detailed information about specific episodes of a repeated event, interviewers should ask about one episode at a time. Yet interviewers must ensure that children understand their requests to talk about an episode. Attention to how prompts are phrased can increase the likelihood that children will provide a narrative, rather than conventional time information. McWilliams et al. (2023) tested one hundred ninety-one 6- to 9-year-old maltreated children's responses to questions phrased as "Tell me *about* [one/the first/the last] time you . . ." versus "Tell me *what happened* [one/the first/the last] time . . ." (half of the children in each condition first received "when" questions like, "When do you put on your pjs?"). Children's responses to the about prompt indicated that they perceived the prompt as asking for conventional time information (e.g., day, month) 31% of the time, versus only 5% of the time to the happened prompt. When children were first asked when questions, they were even more likely to interpret the about prompt as asking for temporal information. Age was not related to likelihood of interpreting the prompt as a request for temporal information. This work suggests that interviewers should ask, "*What happened* the time . . ." to elicit episodic and narrative details.

To facilitate children's reports of specific episodes, interviewers should assign labels that distinctly refer to one episode of abuse. Labels are useful when inviting children's narratives about an event episode to focus children on the episode under discussion and to confirm whether they are still discussing the episode of interest. Episodes can be labelled in a variety of ways, and labels might be based on the following categories of information: *temporal* (e.g., "the first/last time"; "the day before Thanksgiving"), *locational* (e.g., "The time at Uncle Murray's house"), *abuse-related* ("the day there was a camera"), and *situational* (e.g., "the time there was a storm"; Brubacher et al., 2013). Ideally, these labels should be child-generated, because how children refer to episodes provides insight into how these episodes are cognitively organized, which episodes are most accessible in memory, and which are the effective retrieval cues. Children can provide labels for an episode of a repeated event themselves during a forensic interview, and they are especially likely to do so with increasing age (Brubacher et al., 2013, 2018).

In many cases, and especially with younger children, interviewers will need to identify details in children's accounts that could be used as an effective label. To reduce confusion, labels should uniquely identify an episode of abuse. When interviewers spontaneously identify details in this way, uniqueness could be confirmed by asking, "Did that happen any other times?" (Brubacher et al., 2018). Interviewing techniques that enhance reporting of differences across episodes are helpful because they provide cues for interviewers to utilize as labels to elicit a narrative about an additional event episode. When unique details have not been identified, interviewers can use a variety of strategies to generate labels. They can inquire about the last/first time the event occurred, because memory for the first and last episode of a repeated-event is often relatively strong (Roberts et al., 2015; Rubínová & Kontogianni, 2023). It may be difficult, however, for children to recall the first episode under some circumstances (e.g., when maltreatment began long ago, in cases of grooming, for younger children who have limited understanding of temporal concepts).

Eliciting a Generic Account

Thus far, we have focused on techniques that promote narratives about specific episodes; yet sometimes, "what usually happens" is of value to the interview. Attending to script information can sharpen children's awareness of differences across episodes. Several experiments show that when children are asked what usually happens early in the interview, they provide more complete information about the event and are more likely to mention differences across episodes compared to children who do not provide an initial generic account (Brubacher et al., 2012, 2018; Connolly & Gordon, 2014). Thus, when children provide generic information at the outset of an interview (which indicates strong script memory), there is value in allowing them to continue reporting in this way (Brubacher & La Rooy, 2014). Permitting an initial generic account also supports children's credibility, because the strength of their script memory is convincing to evaluators and contextualizes inconsistencies that may emerge across reports of episodes (Powell et al., 2017).

Eliciting a generic report may also provide valuable information about grooming. Indeed, prosecutors have identified that generic reports from children about their abuse often provide clues about the nature of the relationship and how it evolved (Powell et al., 2017). Yet it may be difficult for children who have been subject to a lengthy grooming process to report "what usually happens" compared to children whose experiences were less changeable over time, because of their relatively undeveloped scripts (Danby et al., 2019). This is an important consideration to address in future research.

In some situations, eliciting a generic account of events is equally or more important than finding out what happened during a specific episode. It also may be less traumatizing because recalling a specific memory of abuse involves episodic reliving, including the associated emotional state or feelings (Tulving, 2002). In the context of family law, interviewers elicit generic information that provides a broad understanding of children's daily lives, such as parenting styles, relationship dynamics between the child and parent, and issues affecting the quality of care (e.g., violence, substance use; Turoy-Smith et al., 2018). Information about the child's routines can be critical to assess the suitability of each parent to provide care. For example, a child who does not bring lunch to school one day should not be cause for concern, yet a child who routinely lacks a packed lunch could be indicative of underlying issues. Other contexts where generic information would be useful include gathering information about patterns of bullying and ongoing medical conditions.

CHILDREN'S UNDERSTANDING OF TIME, SEQUENCE, AND FREQUENCY CONCEPTS

Concepts of time, sequence, and frequency have a protracted developmental course and are relevant to most forensic interviews. Given their particular importance in cases of recurring maltreatment, we provide an overview of children's understanding of these concepts.

Children's Understanding of Time

The ability to provide temporal information appears to primarily rely on reconstructive processes, much like the reconstruction of episodes. Children and adults utilize information associated with their memory of an event to make an inference about when it occurred, rather than retrieving such information directly from memory (Friedman, 1993). Specifically, people use information contained in episodic memories (e.g., playing soccer), as well as semantic information (e.g., I took soccer practice in the spring), to make decisions about when the event occurred (e.g., Dad hit me after soccer practice, so it must have been spring). People also use impressions of the age of a memory to make temporal judgments (Jack et al., 2016).

There are developmental improvements in the ability to provide accurate temporal information, enabled by improvements in (a) the amount of detail embedded in episodic memories, which enhances the likelihood of recalling details that cue temporal context; (b) knowledge of semantic information relevant to discerning time (e.g., days of the week and associated routines); and (c) the ability to select and integrate relevant information from episodic and semantic sources to make temporal inferences (Friedman & Lyon, 2005).

Children's ability to make judgments about when an event occurred differs according to timescale (e.g., time of day, month, year). By age 4, children can use contextual information about daily routines to make inferences about when an event occurred (e.g., in the morning, because I was eating cereal; Friedman, 1991). Rapid developments in children's temporal ability occur in the following years. By 6 to 7 years of age, many children can judge the month, season, and year of a relatively recent event (e.g., Pathman, Larkina, et al., 2013). This ability appears to be more stable in middle childhood and early adolescence; those 8 to 12 years old can recall the month or season of an event that occurred a few years prior (Friedman et al., 2011). Although developments in temporal memory that arise in late childhood and early adolescence are minor compared to earlier advancements, adults outperform older children on numerous temporal tasks (e.g., sequencing events; Pathman, Doydum, et al., 2013). There are clear age-related improvements in temporal memory, yet there is considerable variability in these trends. For example, children with a history of maltreatment lag developmentally in their ability to provide temporal information (Wandrey et al., 2012) and conventional time knowledge (awareness of temporal concepts, the ability to use this information flexibly) is a better predictor of temporal memory than age (Pathman et al., 2022).

Attributing temporal information is a relatively imprecise process, even for adults (e.g., Jack et al., 2016). Particularization statutes do not require children to provide the date and time of specific episodes; a timeframe is sufficient. An effective way to determine timeframe is to elicit contextual details through children's narrative account of the event (i.e., in response to open-ended questions). Orbach and Lamb (2007) found that, in response to open-ended prompts, children (aged 4–10 years) often reported temporal information, and they were increasingly likely to do so as they aged, up until 8 years of age. Children may also reference details, such as a teacher or place of residence, which were only true of a certain temporal period, so timing can be triangulated with the information provided by a relevant adult (e.g., a caregiver). Thus, children's narrative accounts can provide information that help determine event timing. This approach avoids posing temporal questions beyond children's developmental capacities, which can result in errors that undermine their credibility, even if the content of their recall is reliable.

Children's Understanding of Sequencing Events

Sequencing and spontaneous temporal clustering of components that were experienced close together in time are observed even among young children. When 144 children (aged 4–10 years) who had participated in a five-day camp at the zoo were asked which animals they visited, even the youngest children displayed temporal clustering in their recall at above-chance levels, and there were clear developmental improvements with age (Pathman et al., 2023). The tendency to engage in temporal clustering predicted individual differences in the number of animals children correctly recalled visiting, indicating that temporal clustering is integral to effective recall of event content in children. Thus, this ability may also be predictive of the amount and accuracy of children's recall for repeated events, but whether this is the case remains an empirical question.

There are age-related, linear improvements in children's ability to accurately sequence components within an event (Canada et al., 2020). Children's ability to sequence an event is better when the event consists of a smaller number of component activities and varies according to how they are questioned. For example, Price and Evans (2021) found that 6- to 8-year-old children were more adept at sequencing activities when afforded the visual support of photographs from the event, compared to when they were asked a free recall prompt about what happened. More research is needed into whether different types of visual prompts and extensive open-ended follow-up prompts (e.g., "What was the very next thing that happened?") support children in sequencing components of an event. Previous research indicates that children are likely to be more accurate in responding to follow-up prompts that inquire about what "happened after" compared to what "happened before" (Klemfuss et al., 2020).

Other studies have explored children's ability to sequence different events. The temporal distancing effect refers to the phenomena whereby adults are better at ordering events that are separated by long, relative to short, intervals of time. This effect appears to emerge around 8 years of age; it is possible that younger children do not demonstrate this pattern because their prefrontal cortex, which is recruited for many aspects of temporal memory, is too immature (Deker & Pathman, 2021). The ability to sequence events also depends on event recency. Although young children can sequence two unique events when one occurred very recently, it is not until late childhood that children can sequence two events that both occurred in the distant past (Friedman, 1991). When the event involves multiple similar episodes, the difficulty of this task increases. Children find it difficult to sequence episodes of a repeated event, even after a short retention interval (Roberts et al., 2015). Older children (aged 6–8 years) appear to be generally more competent in this task than younger ones (aged 4–5 years; Roberts et al., 2015).

One strategy that legal practitioners employ to determine temporal information about an event is to ask about the proximity of a maltreatment experience to a landmark event (e.g., Christmas). Yet, children have trouble responding to these questions accurately. For example, when 167 maltreated children (aged 6–10 years) answered questions about the proximity of the current day to their birthday, they responded with respect to a future birthday, rather than one they had recently experienced (McWilliams et al., 2019). For example, when asked, "Right now, is it near your birthday?," children tended to respond "yes" if it was close to an upcoming birthday, but not one experienced previously.

Children's Understanding of Frequency

Children are poor at estimating the exact number of times they have experienced a recurring event. Yet, because their estimates of frequency tend to increase with the number of times they have experienced an event (e.g., Wandrey et al., 2012), a good proxy for identifying event frequency is asking whether the event occurred one time or more than one time. Indeed, when children (aged 4–8 years) who participated in staged activities one or four times were asked this question, 85% of the single-event children and all repeated-event children responded correctly (Roberts et al., 2015). However, when repeated-event children were asked the precise number of times they had participated in the activities, only 23% could do so accurately.

CONCLUSION

In some ways, children's memory for repeated events is impressive. Their memories of what usually happens are often strong, and they rarely report details that never happened. Yet in maltreatment investigations, in which episodic information is often (but not always) valuable, children (especially preadolescents) may have difficulty reporting the information required. The likelihood that children will provide accurate and detailed information about specific episodes of an event is greatly enhanced when they are questioned using evidence-based techniques, such as asking about episodes of a routine event during narrative practice, using prompts of the appropriate specificity, and labeling episodes with unique identifiers. These techniques facilitate recall by supporting children's understanding of the types of information required and providing a scaffold to help them structure their memories. It is the responsibility of adult interviewers to steward the information that children are willing to share, to minimize the risk of future harm, and to promote just outcomes in the face of maltreatment.

REFERENCES

Baker-Ward, L., Tyler, C. S., Coffman, J. L., Merritt, K. A., & Ornstein, P. A. (2020). Children's expectations and episodic reports over 12 weeks: Influences on memory for a specially designed pediatric examination. *Applied Cognitive Psychology, 34*(2), 330–342. https://doi.org/10.1002/acp.3619

Bauer, P. J., & Fivush, R. (1992). Constructing event representations: Building on a foundation of variation and enabling relations. *Cognitive Development, 7*(3), 381–401. https://doi.org/10.1016/0885-2014(92)90023-K

Bauer, P. J., & Mandler, J. M. (1992). Putting the horse before the cart: The use of temporal order in recall of events by one-year-old children. *Developmental Psychology, 28*(3), 441–452. https://doi.org/10.1037/0012-1649.28.3.441

Bearison, D. J., & Pacifici, C. (1989). Children's event knowledge of cancer treatment. *Journal of Applied Developmental Psychology, 10*(4), 469–486. https://doi.org/10.1016/0193-3973(89)90022-1

Bidrose, S., & Goodman, G. S. (2000). Testimony and evidence: A scientific case study of memory for child sexual abuse. *Applied Cognitive Psychology, 14*(3), 197–213. https://doi.org/10.1002/(SICI)1099-0720(200005/06)14:3<197::AID-ACP647>3.0.CO;2-6

Brubacher, S. P., Earhart, B., Roberts, K. P., & Powell, M. B. (2018). Effects of label training and recall order on children's reports of a repeated event. *Applied Cognitive Psychology, 32*(5), 600–609. https://doi.org/10.1002/acp.3440

Brubacher, S. P., Glisic, U., Roberts, K. P., & Powell, M. (2011). Children's ability to recall unique aspects of one occurrence of a repeated event. *Applied Cognitive Psychology, 25*(3), 351–358. https://doi.org/10.1002/acp.1696

Brubacher, S. P., & La Rooy, D. (2014). Witness recall across repeated interviews in a case of repeated abuse. *Child Abuse & Neglect, 38*(2), 202–211. https://doi.org/10.1016/j.chiabu.2013.06.010

Brubacher, S. P., Malloy, L. C., Lamb, M. E., & Roberts, K. P. (2013). How do interviewers and children discuss individual occurrences of alleged repeated abuse in forensic interviews? *Applied Cognitive Psychology, 27*(4), 443–450. https://doi.org/10.1002/acp.2920

Brubacher, S. P., Powell, M. B., & Roberts, K. P. (2014). Recommendations for interviewing children about repeated experiences. *Psychology, Public Policy, and Law, 20*(3), 325–335. https://doi.org/10.1037/law0000011

Brubacher, S. P., Roberts, K. P., & Powell, M. (2011). Effects of practicing episodic versus scripted recall on children's subsequent narratives of a repeated event. *Psychology, Public Policy, and Law, 17*(2), 286–314. https://doi.org/10.1037/a0022793

Brubacher, S. P., Roberts, K. P., & Powell, M. (2012). Retrieval of episodic versus generic information: Does the order of recall affect the amount and accuracy of details reported by children about repeated events? *Developmental Psychology, 48*(1), 111–122. https://doi.org/10.1037/a0025864

Canada, K. L., Pathman, T., & Riggins, T. (2020). Longitudinal development of memory for temporal order in early to middle childhood. *The Journal of Genetic Psychology, 181*(4), 237–254. https://doi.org/10.1080/00221325.2020.1741504

Christianson, S. Å. (1992). Emotional stress and eyewitness memory: A critical review. *Psychological Bulletin, 112*(2), 284–309. https://doi.org/10.1037/0033-2909.112.2.284

Cleveland, K. C., Wu, Y., Hartman, D., Brown, L. F., & Goodman, G. S. (2022). Children's memory development: Emotion, distress, and trauma. In M. L. Courage & N. Cowan (Eds.), *The development of memory in infancy and childhood* (3rd ed., pp. 297–336). Routledge. https://doi.org/10.4324/9781003016533-13

Connolly, D. A., & Gordon, H. M. (2014). Can order of general and specific memory prompts help children to recall an instance of a repeated event that was different from the others? *Psychology, Crime & Law, 20*(9), 852–864. https://doi.org/10.1080/1068316X.2014.885969

Connolly, D. A., Gordon, H. M., Woiwod, D. M., & Price, H. L. (2016). What children recall about a repeated event when one instance is different from the others. *Developmental Psychology, 52*(7), 1038–1051. https://doi.org/10.1037/dev0000137

Connolly, D. A., & Price, H. L. (2006). Children's suggestibility for an instance of a repeated event versus a unique event: The effect of degree of association between variable details. *Journal of Experimental Child Psychology, 93*(3), 207–223. https://doi.org/10.1016/j.jecp.2005.06.004

Craven, S., Brown, S., & Gilchrist, E. (2006). Sexual grooming of children: Review of literature and theoretical considerations. *Journal of Sexual Aggression, 12*(3), 287–299. https://doi.org/10.1080/13552600601069414

Danby, M. C., Brubacher, S. P., Sharman, S. J., & Powell, M. B. (2017). The effects of one versus two episodically oriented practice narratives on children's reports of a repeated event. *Legal and Criminological Psychology, 22*(2), 442–454. https://doi.org/10.1111/lcrp.12110

Danby, M. C., Sharman, S. J., Brubacher, S. P., & Powell, M. B. (2019). The effects of episode similarity on children's reports of a repeated event. *Memory, 27*(4), 561–567. https://doi.org/10.1080/09658211.2018.1529798

Davidson, D., & Hoe, S. (1993). Children's recall and recognition memory for typical and atypical actions in script-based stories. *Journal of Experimental Child Psychology, 55*(1), 104–126. https://doi.org/10.1006/jecp.1993.1005

Davidson, D., & Jergovic, D. (1996). Children's memory for atypical actions in script-based stories: An examination of the disruption effect. *Journal of Experimental Child Psychology, 61*(2), 134–152. https://doi.org/10.1006/jecp.1996.0009

Deker, L., & Pathman, T. (2021). Did I visit the polar bear before the giraffe? Examining memory for temporal order and the temporal distance effect in early to middle childhood. *Applied Cognitive Psychology, 35*(3), 785–794. https://doi.org/10.1002/acp.3804

DeMarie, D., Norman, A., & Abshier, D. W. (2000). Age and experience influence different verbal and nonverbal measures of children's scripts for the zoo. *Cognitive Development, 15*(2), 241–262. https://doi.org/10.1016/S0885-2014(00)00027-7

Dilevski, N., Paterson, H. M., & van Golde, C. (2020). Investigating the effect of emotional stress on adult memory for single and repeated events. *Psychology, Public Policy, and Law, 26*(4), 425–441. https://doi.org/10.1037/law0000248

Farrar, M. J., & Boyer-Pennington, M. E. (1999). Remembering specific episodes of a scripted event. *Journal of Experimental Child Psychology, 73*(4), 266–288. https://doi.org/10.1006/jecp.1999.2507

Farrar, M. J., & Goodman, G. S. (1992). Developmental changes in event memory. *Child Development, 63*(1), 173–187. https://doi.org/10.2307/1130911

Fivush, R. (1984). Learning about school: The development of kindergartners' school scripts. *Child Development, 55*(5), 1697–1709. https://doi.org/10.2307/1129917

Friedman, W. J. (1991). The development of children's memory for the time of past events. *Child Development, 62*(1), 139–155. https://doi.org/10.2307/1130710

Friedman, W. J. (1993). Memory for the time of past events. *Psychological Bulletin, 113*(1), 44–66. https://doi.org/10.1037/0033-2909.113.1.44

Friedman, W. J., & Lyon, T. D. (2005). Development of temporal–reconstructive abilities. *Child Development, 76*(6), 1202–1216. https://doi.org/10.1111/j.1467-8624.2005.00844.x-i1

Friedman, W. J., Reese, E., & Dai, X. (2011). Children's memory for the times of events from the past years. *Applied Cognitive Psychology, 25*(1), 156–165. https://doi.org/10.1002/acp.1656

Goodman, G. S., Hirschman, J. E., Hepps, D., & Rudy, L. (1991). Children's memory for stressful events. *Merrill-Palmer Quarterly, 37*(1), 109–157. http://www.jstor.org/stable/23087341

Goodman, G. S., Quas, J. A., Batterman-Faunce, J. M., Riddlesberger, M. M., & Kuhn, J. (1994). Predictors of accurate and inaccurate memories of traumatic events experienced in childhood. *Consciousness and Cognition, 3*(3–4), 269–294. https://doi.org/10.1006/ccog.1994.1016

Graesser, A. C., Gordon, S. E., & Sawyer, J. D. (1979). Recognition memory for typical and atypical actions in scripted activities: Tests of a script pointer + tag hypothesis. *Journal of Verbal Learning and Verbal Behavior, 18*(3), 319–332. https://doi.org/10.1016/S0022-5371(79)90182-8

Hudson, J., & Nelson, K. (1986). Repeated encounters of a similar kind: Effects of familiarity on children's autobiographic memory. *Cognitive Development, 1*(3), 253–271. https://doi.org/10.1016/S0885-2014(86)80004-1

Hudson, J. A., Fivush, R., & Kuebli, J. (1992). Scripts and episodes: The development of event memory. *Applied Cognitive Psychology, 6*(6), 483–505. https://doi.org/10.1002/acp.2350060604

Hudson, J. A., & Mayhew, E. M. (2009). The development of memory for recurring events. In M. Courage & N. Cowan (Eds.), *The development of memory in infancy and childhood* (pp. 69–92). Psychology Press.

Jack, F., Friedman, W., Reese, E., & Zajac, R. (2016). Age-related differences in memory for time, temporal reconstruction, and the availability and use of temporal landmarks. *Cognitive Development, 37*, 53–66. https://doi.org/10.1016/j.cogdev.2015.12.003

Johnson, M. K., Hashtroudi, S., & Lindsay, D. S. (1993). Source monitoring. *Psychological Bulletin, 114*(1), 3–28. https://doi.org/10.1037/0033-2909.114.1.3

Klemfuss, J. Z., McWilliams, K., Henderson, H. M., Olaguez, A. P., & Lyon, T. D. (2020). Order of encoding predicts young children's responses to sequencing questions. *Cognitive Development, 55*, 100927. https://doi.org/10.1016/j.cogdev.2020.100927

Lindsay, D. S., Johnson, M. K., & Kwon, P. (1991). Developmental changes in memory source monitoring. *Journal of Experimental Child Psychology, 52*(3), 297–318. https://doi.org/10.1016/0022-0965(91)90065-Z

MacLeod, C. M. (2020). Zeigarnik and von Restorff: The memory effects and the stories behind them. *Memory & Cognition, 48*(6), 1073–1088. https://doi.org/10.3758/s13421-020-01033-5

McWilliams, K., Lyon, T. D., & Quas, J. A. (2019). Maltreated children's ability to make temporal judgments using a recurring landmark event. *Journal of Interpersonal Violence, 34*(4), 873–883. https://doi.org/10.1177/0886260516645812

McWilliams, K., Williams, S., Henderson, H. M., Evans, A. D., & Lyon, T. D. (2023). Pseudotemporal invitations: 6-to 9-year-old maltreated children's tendency to misinterpret invitations referencing "time" as solely requesting conventional temporal information. *Child Maltreatment, 28*(2), 265–274. https://doi.org/10.1177/10775595221104829

Odegard, T. N., Cooper, C. M., Lampinen, J. M., Reyna, V. F., & Brainerd, C. J. (2009). Children's eyewitness memory for multiple real-life events. *Child Development, 80*(6), 1877–1890. https://doi.org/10.1111/j.1467-8624.2009.01373.x

Orbach, Y., Hershkowitz, I., Lamb, M. E., Sternberg, K. J., & Horowitz, D. (2000). Interviewing at the scene of the crime: Effects on children's recall of alleged abuse. *Legal and Criminological Psychology, 5*(1), 135–147. https://doi.org/10.1348/135532500167930

Orbach, Y., & Lamb, M. E. (2007). Young children's references to temporal attributes of allegedly experienced events in the course of forensic interviews. *Child Development, 78*(4), 1100–1120. https://doi.org/10.1111/j.1467-8624.2007.01055.x

Otgaar, H., Howe, M. L., Merckelbach, H., & Muris, P. (2018). Who is the better eyewitness? Sometimes adults but at other times children. *Current Directions in Psychological Science, 27*(5), 378–385. https://doi.org/10.1177/0963721418770998

Pathman, T., Deker, L., Coughlin, C., & Ghetti, S. (2022). Examining temporal memory and flexible retrieval of conventional time knowledge across middle to late childhood. *Journal of Cognition and Development, 23*(4), 571–589. https://doi.org/10.1080/15248372.2022.2072846

Pathman, T., Deker, L., Parmar, P. K., Adkins, M. C., & Polyn, S. M. (2023). Children's memory "in the wild": Examining the temporal organization of free recall from a week-long camp at a local zoo. *Cognitive Research: Principles and Implications, 8*(1), Article 6. https://doi.org/10.1186/s41235-022-00452-z

Pathman, T., Doydum, A., & Bauer, P. J. (2013). Bringing order to life events: Memory for the temporal order of autobiographical events over an extended period in school-aged children and adults. *Journal of Experimental Child Psychology, 115*(2), 309–325. https://doi.org/10.1016/j.jecp.2013.01.011

Pathman, T., Larkina, M., Burch, M. M., & Bauer, P. J. (2013). Young children's memory for the times of personal past events. *Journal of Cognition and Development, 14*(1), 120–140. https://doi.org/10.1080/15248372.2011.641185

Peterson, C. (2021). What is your earliest memory? It depends. *Memory, 29*(6), 811–822. https://doi.org/10.1080/09658211.2021.1918174

Piaget, J. (1957). *Construction of reality in the child.* Routledge & Kegan Paul.

Powell, M. B., Burrows, K. S., Brubacher, S. P., & Roberts, K. P. (2017). Prosecutors' perceptions on questioning children about repeated abuse. *Psychiatry, Psychology and Law, 24*(1), 74–89. https://doi.org/10.1080/13218719.2017.1273749

Powell, M., Roberts, K., & Guadagno, B. (2007). Particularisation of child abuse offences: Common problems when questioning child witnesses. *Current Issues in Criminal Justice, 19*(1), 64–74. https://doi.org/10.1080/10345329.2007.12036415

Powell, M. B., & Thomson, D. M. (1997). Contrasting memory for temporal-source and memory for content in children's discrimination of repeated events. *Applied Cognitive Psychology, 11*(4), 339–360. https://doi.org/10.1002/(SICI)1099-0720(199708)11:4%3C339::AID-ACP460%3E3.0.CO;2-O

Powell, M. B., Thomson, D. M., & Ceci, S. J. (2003). Children's memory of recurring events: Is the first event always the best remembered? *Applied Cognitive Psychology, 17*(2), 127–146. https://doi.org/10.1002/acp.864

Price, H. L., & Connolly, D. A. (2007). Anxious and nonanxious children's recall of a repeated or unique event. *Journal of Experimental Child Psychology, 98*(2), 94–112. https://doi.org/10.1016/j.jecp.2007.05.002

Price, H. L., & Connolly, D. A. (2008). Children's recall of emotionally arousing, repeated events: A review and call for further investigation. *International Journal of Law and Psychiatry, 31*(4), 337–346. https://doi.org/10.1016/j.ijlp.2008.06.002

Price, H. L., & Evans, A. D. (2021). With support, children can accurately sequence within-event components. *Applied Cognitive Psychology, 35*(4), 890–899. https://doi.org/10.1002/acp.3816

Reyna, V. F., & Brainerd, C. J. (1995). Fuzzy-trace theory: An interim synthesis. *Learning and Individual Differences, 7*(1), 1–75. https://doi.org/10.1016/1041-6080(95)90031-4

Roberts, K. P., Brubacher, S. P., Drohan-Jennings, D., Glisic, U., Powell, M. B., & Friedman, W. J. (2015). Developmental differences in the ability to provide temporal information about repeated events. *Applied Cognitive Psychology, 29*(3), 407–417. https://doi.org/10.1002/acp.3118

Rubínová, E., & Kontogianni, F. (2023). Sources and destinations of misattributions in recall of instances of repeated events. *Memory & Cognition, 51*(1), 188–202. https://doi.org/10.3758/s13421-022-01300-7

Schank, R., & Abelson, R. (1977). *Scripts, plans, goals, and understanding: An inquiry into human knowledge structures*. Erlbaum.

Schneider, L., Price, H. L., Roberts, K. P., & Hedrick, A. M. (2011). Children's episodic and generic reports of alleged abuse. *Applied Cognitive Psychology, 25*(6), 862–870. https://doi.org/10.1002/acp.1759

Shead, K. (2014). Responding to historical child sexual abuse: A prosecution perspective on current challenges and future directions. *Current Issues in Criminal Justice, 26*(1), 55–73. https://doi.org/10.1080/10345329.2014.12036007

Sims, C., & Morton, J. (2021). Remembering breakfast: How do pre-schoolers represent an everyday event? *Cognition, 213*, 104654. https://doi.org/10.1016/j.cognition.2021.104654

Slackman, E., & Nelson, K. (1984). Acquisition of an unfamiliar script in story form by young children. *Child Development, 55*(2), 329–340. https://doi.org/10.2307/1129946

Sternberg, K. J., Lamb, M. E., Hershkowitz, I., Esplin, P. W., Redlich, A., & Sunshine, N. (1996). The relation between investigative utterance types and the informativeness of child witnesses. *Journal of Applied Developmental Psychology, 17*(3), 439–451. https://doi.org/10.1016/s0193-3973(96)90036-2

Terr, L. (1988). What happens to early memories of trauma? A study of twenty children under age five at the time of documented traumatic events. *Journal of the American Academy of Child & Adolescent Psychiatry, 27*(1), 96–104. https://doi.org/10.1097/00004583-198801000-00015

Terr, L. C. (1991). Acute responses to external events and posttraumatic stress disorders. In M. Lewis (Ed.), *Child and adolescent psychiatry: A comprehensive textbook* (pp. 755–763). Williams & Wilkins Co.

Tulving, E. (2002). Episodic memory: From mind to brain. *Annual Review of Psychology, 53*(1), 1–25. https://doi.org/10.1146/annurev.psych.53.100901.135114

Turoy-Smith, K. M., Brubacher, S. P., Earhart, B., & Powell, M. B. (2018). Eliciting children's recall regarding home life and relationships. *Journal of Child Custody, 15*(4), 349–368. https://doi.org/10.1080/15379418.2018.1530629

Wandrey, L., Lyon, T. D., Quas, J. A., & Friedman, W. J. (2012). Maltreated children's ability to estimate temporal location and numerosity of placement changes and court visits. *Psychology, Public Policy, and Law, 18*(1), 79–104. https://doi.org/10.1037/a0024812

Williams, A. (2015). Child sexual victimisation: Ethnographic stories of stranger and acquaintance grooming. *Journal of Sexual Aggression, 21*(1), 28–42. https://doi.org/10.1080/13552600.2014.948085

Winters, G. M., & Jeglic, E. L. (2017). Stages of sexual grooming: Recognizing potentially predatory behaviors of child molesters. *Deviant Behavior, 38*(6), 724–733. https://doi.org/10.1080/01639625.2016.1197656

Woiwod, D. M., & Connolly, D. A. (2017). Continuous child sexual abuse: Balancing defendants' rights and victims' capabilities to particularize individual acts of repeated abuse. *Criminal Justice Review, 42*(2), 206–225. https://doi.org/10.1177/0734016817704700

Woiwod, D. M., Fitzgerald, R. J., Sheahan, C. L., Price, H. L., & Connolly, D. A. (2019). A meta-analysis of differences in children's reports of single and repeated events. *Law and Human Behavior, 43*(1), 99–116. https://doi.org/10.1037/lhb0000312

6

Initial Denial of Child Sexual Abuse

Reluctance or Suggestibility

Thomas D. Lyon, Breanne E. Wylie, and Zsofia A. Szojka

Whether and how often children who have been sexually abused deny abuse is important for understanding assessments of credibility in child sexual abuse cases. There is general agreement among researchers and practitioners that children typically delay disclosing abuse, if they disclose at all (McElvaney, 2015; Miller & London, 2020; Newlin et al., 2015). Similarly, it has long been believed that children often deny abuse when directly questioned (Azzopardi et al., 2019; Pollack, 1909), although critical reviews of the literature (London et al., 2005, 2008) and defense expert testimony (Bruck, 2017; *Ohio v. Swoboda*, 2021) have challenged the frequency with which this occurs.

We argue that the best available research demonstrates that a substantial percentage—typically about 50%—of sexually abused children deny abuse when initially questioned. However, because children who deny abuse are less likely to be seen for suspicions of abuse and less likely to be substantiated as abuse victims, clinical samples will consist of children unusually forthcoming about abuse. This has implications for factfinders who assess the credibility of children's reports, and for both researchers who study and experts who testify about the dynamics of sexual abuse disclosure and the susceptibility of children to suggestive questioning about sexual abuse.

The research supports expert testimony explaining to jurors how abused children are frequently reluctant to disclose abuse, and often deny abuse when

Preparation of this chapter was supported by Eunice Kennedy Shriver National Institute of Child Health and Human Development Grant HD101617.

https://doi.org/10.1037/0000492-006
Handbook on Child Witnesses: Improving Psychological Science and Legal Practice,
G. S. Goodman, T. D. Lyon, S. D. Hobbs, and R. Enriquez (Editors)

directly questioned, rebutting defense arguments that delays and denial undermine the credibility of children's disclosures (*California v. Flores*, 2024; *New York v. Ashton*, 2024). In addition, an understanding of the factors that lead children to be reluctant to disclose abuse challenges expert claims that false allegations in lab research easily translate into false disclosures of sexual abuse and highlights the need for suggestibility research to take account of those factors. Importantly, however, the research does not support the use of suggestive interviewing techniques with children interviewed for suspicions of abuse, in large part because those children are disproportionately likely to be children who have disclosed before and are likely to disclose again without suggestion.

There are different ways of understanding abuse denial. Initial denials by children who ultimately disclose abuse could be evidence of suggestive influences creating a false report, but they could also be evidence of reluctance to disclose actual abuse. Researchers have explored ways in which nonabused children might be led to make false claims of abuse and ways in which abused children may falsely claim they have not been abused. Of course, there are reasons besides reluctance why abused children may deny abuse (e.g., memory issues), and reasons besides suggestibility that nonabused children may allege abuse (e.g., vindictiveness), and any comprehensive assessment of children's credibility in sexual abuse cases should consider those factors. In this chapter we focus on the competing themes of reluctance and suggestibility.

We provide a framework for comparing alternative explanations for disclosures and denials. In assessing disclosure and whether it constitutes evidence for or against abuse, it is important to compare the percentage of abused children who disclose to the percentage of nonabused children who disclose. Conversely, in assessing the probative value (or evidentiary weight) of nondisclosure, one compares the percentage of nonabused children who do not disclose to abused children who fail to disclose. These percentages are connected in important ways that we will discuss.

Denial has been studied in a number of ways, and our focus is on clinical samples of children questioned about sexual abuse. If substantial percentages of children who have been abused deny abuse at some point in time, then this reduces the probative value of nondisclosure in disproving abuse. Furthermore, it highlights how suggestibility research often fails to capture reasons why nonabused children would be reluctant to make false claims of abuse. To adequately interpret these studies, however, we must confront and attempt to solve several methodological problems. First, there is the ground truth problem: How do we know whether abuse actually occurred? Second, there are selection bias problems that include substantiation selection bias and substantiation suspicion bias. To the extent that abuse is suspected and substantiated because of disclosure, samples of children questioned about suspected abuse will have inflated rates of disclosure. We can reduce these problems somewhat by examining cases with corroborative evidence of abuse. But this raises the third problem: The apparent rate of disclosure among abused children will be inflated in corroborated cases if corroboration is dependent on disclosure. We will define these problems in greater detail and demonstrate how solving these problems leads to the conclusion that denial is extremely common among sexually abused children.

DIFFERENT INTERPRETATIONS OF NONDISCLOSURE

Abused children may fail to disclose abuse and may at some point deny that abuse occurred for numerous reasons. In a systematic review of motivational barriers to sexual abuse disclosure, Lemaigre and colleagues (2017) identified an anticipated lack of support from adults (parents or professionals); perceived negative consequences for the self, including parental punishment and losing familial support; negative consequences for the suspect and the child's family; and emotional barriers such as guilt, shame, and self-blame (see also reviews by Alaggia et al., 2019; McElvaney, 2015). We refer generally to these motivational issues as *reluctance*.

From a suggestibility perspective, initial denial may be reasons to suspect that a nonabused child was subjected to suggestive pressures leading to a false allegation. There is extensive literature identifying the ways in which adults can shape children's reports (see Chapters 3 and 7, this volume; see also Principe & London, 2022—with responses by Brown & Lamb, 2022; Chae et al., 2022; and others). If a child was never abused, but adults suspected that they were, and suggestively questioned the child about abuse, then one might observe initial denial (when the child was first questioned), followed by a disclosure (when the child acquiesced to suggestiveness). Similarly, recantations, which are denials that occur after an initial disclosure, may be evidence of false allegations. The disclosure may have occurred due to suggestive questioning, and the recantation may occur when the child is questioned in a less suggestive fashion. Hence, competing views of abuse denial characterize it as evidence of reluctance or evidence of suggestibility.

Questions about whether an abuse allegation is true or false will come up in several contexts. During investigation, awareness of the likelihood of denial will help investigators weigh the significance of a child's prior silence. When interviewing the child, investigators should avoid techniques that have been proven to reduce accuracy, both false allegations and false denials. During decision making, which can include the decision whether to substantiate an allegation or the verdict in civil and criminal cases, awareness of the likelihood of denial will help factfinders decide whether the allegations are more likely true or false. In policymaking, the courts and legislators may make special provisions for expert testimony and jury instructions regarding how factfinders should evaluate denial. Researchers in developmental psychology can assist by seeking to identify how true disclosures can be increased without increasing false disclosures, keeping in mind the dynamics that are likely to influence abused children's disclosures.

HOW TO THINK ABOUT PERCENTAGES IN UNDERSTANDING DENIAL OF ABUSE

To assess research in which percentages of children make true and false allegations, or utter true and false denials, one must always keep in mind both abused and nonabused children. If a behavior is more common among abused children than nonabused children, then it is evidence that the child was abused. Conversely, if a behavior is more common among nonabused children, then it is evidence of nonabuse. If the behavior is equally common among abused and nonabused children, then it is nondiagnostic of abuse or nonabuse (Ceci & Friedman, 2000; Lyon, 2023; Wood, 1996). Disclosures of sexual abuse increase the likelihood that abuse occurred to the extent that abused children are more likely to disclose than nonabused children. Conversely, denials of sexual abuse decrease the likelihood that abuse occurred to the extent that nonabused children are more likely to deny than abused children.

The strength of the evidence depends on the ratio of percentages, also known as the *likelihood ratio*. For example, if one wishes to assess the evidentiary strength (often referred to as the probative value) of a disclosure in proving that abuse occurred, the likelihood ratio is the ratio of the percentage of abused children who disclose to the percentage of nonabused children who disclose; the true positive rate divided by the false positive rate (Lyon & Koehler, 1996; Wood, 1996). Of course, the ultimate judgment requires the factfinder to consider all the evidence in the case (Lyon et al., 2012; Wood, 1996).

Recognizing that the ratio is important enables one to avoid fallacies in reasoning. For example, the fact that a behavior is common among abused children does not automatically mean that the behavior increases the likelihood that abuse occurred. Some types of sexualized behavior are common among abused children but are almost as common among nonabused children, and therefore are only very weak evidence of abuse (Lyon & Koehler, 1996). Conversely, the fact that a behavior is uncommon among abused children does not mean that it decreases the likelihood that abuse occurred. To decrease the likelihood of abuse, the behavior must be more common among nonabused children than abused children. Indeed, behaviors that are uncommon among abused children are often strong evidence of abuse. For example, it would be absurd to point to the rarity of pregnancy in sexual abuse cases and argue that it has little probative value in proving abuse (Lyon & Koehler, 1996).

A particularly dangerous fallacy is the inverse error. In the context of sexual abuse, this includes confusing the likelihood that a child denies abuse, given they were abused, with the likelihood that a child was abused, given that they deny abuse. The inverse error has led some courts astray. For example, the Pennsylvania Supreme Court held that behaviors are irrelevant in proving abuse unless they occur in more than half of abused children, reasoning that behaviors that occur less than 50% of the time cannot make abuse more likely than not (*Pennsylvania v. Dunkle*, 1992). The court was confusing the likelihood of a behavior, given abuse, with the likelihood of abuse given a behavior. In *New Jersey v. J.L.G.* (2018), a New Jersey Supreme Court case in which the court concluded that experts should not be allowed to explain to jurors why abused children often deny abuse, the prosecutor had referenced a study in which 23% of children in a dependency court sample had recanted abuse (Malloy et al., 2007). At oral argument, one of the justices asked the prosecutor if this didn't mean that abuse allegations were true in only 23% of recantations (oral argument in *New Jersey v. J.L.G.*, 2018). The justice was confusing the likelihood of recantation given abuse with the likelihood of abuse given recantation.

False Positives and Suggestibility

Suggestibility experts acknowledge that children's disclosures can be highly probative, but only when they were elicited in a nonsuggestive way (Bruck & Ceci, 2013). Suggestibility research demonstrates that many children make false claims if suggestively questioned, and suggestibility experts argue that by extension, there is a substantial likelihood that a nonabused child would allege abuse if suggestively questioned about abuse. Suggestion thus potentially reduces the probative value of abuse disclosures. Suggestibility researchers do not claim that, in the face of suggestion, nonabused children are more likely than abused children to disclose. Rather, they argue that under suggestive conditions, a high enough percentage of nonabused children are likely to disclose abuse to render children's reports unreliable (London et al., 2020). How high is high enough has not been defined. However, it is easy to define the extreme case: If nonabused children are as likely to make a false claim as abused children are to make a true claim, then a disclosure has no probative value.

False Negatives and Reluctance

There is a parallel between suggestibility research and research into abused children's reluctance to disclose abuse. Suggestibility experts argue that the probative value of disclosure in proving abuse decreases in the face of suggestibility. Reluctance experts argue that the probative value of denial in disproving abuse decreases in the face of reluctance. In both cases, the argument is that the evidence at issue has less probative value than one would expect. Suggestibility experts argue that a surprising percentage of nonabused children allege abuse if suggestively questioned, so much so that disclosures have little probative value. Reluctance experts testify that a surprising percentage of abused children deny abuse at some point in time, so much that denial has little probative value.

In both situations, the experts do not estimate the numerator of the likelihood ratio, only the denominator. The suggestibility experts argue that because suggestiveness leads a large number of nonabused children to allege abuse (the denominator), it doesn't matter what percentage of abused children allege abuse (the numerator). Even if the percentage of abused children who allege abuse is very high, the likelihood ratio is small because of the size of the denominator. Disclosures in the face of suggestibility have limited probative value in proving abuse. The reluctance experts argue that because reluctance leads a large number of abused children to deny abuse (the denominator), it doesn't matter what percentage of nonabused children deny abuse (the numerator). Even if the percentage is very high, the likelihood ratio is small because of the size of the denominator. Denials in the face of reluctance have limited probative value in disproving abuse.

Of course, if a child persistently denies abuse, and there is no other evidence of abuse, investigators must conclude that the evidence does not support an abuse finding. But what is true of persistent denial may not be true of occasional denial. For example, consider a case in which the child initially denies abuse, but ultimately discloses. That ultimate disclosure may convince investigators and other factfinders that abuse occurred. Suggestibility experts see this pattern and suspect it is a nonabused child succumbing to suggestion. However, to the extent that this pattern is common among abused children, this challenges the suggestibility researcher's argument that the child's report has so little probative value that it should be rejected as evidence of abuse.

THE IMPLICATIONS OF RELUCTANCE FOR ASSESSING THE RELATIVE LIKELIHOOD OF FALSE ALLEGATIONS AND FALSE DENIALS

Disclosure and nondisclosure are complementary, and nondisclosures are denials if the child was directly asked about abuse and answered "no." There is thus a direct relation between the probative value of disclosure in proving abuse and the probative value of denial in disproving abuse. As the denial rate among abused children goes up, reducing the probative value of denial in disproving abuse, the disclosure rate among abused children goes down. Hence, all else being equal, reluctance to disclose among sexually abused children reduces the probative value of disclosure in proving abuse that occurred (Ceci & Friedman, 2000).

Does this mean that abused children's reluctance suggests less confidence in disclosures of abuse? Not necessarily, because this argument assumes that reluctance only reduces the likelihood that abused children disclose touch. In other words, all else is not equal. The reasons that abused children are reluctant to disclose are also often reasons why nonabused children are reluctant to make false claims. For example, embarrassment is a common reason that abuse victims give for a failure to disclose (Anderson et al., 1993; Fleming, 1997). One reason abuse is potentially embarrassing is because it involves intimate touch. A rough analog to abusive genital touch is touching during a pediatric exam. Of course, the differences between abuse and pediatric exams are obvious: During the pediatric exam a parent or chaperone accompanies the child, and the touch is socially sanctioned. Nevertheless, in their classic study, Karen Saywitz and colleagues (1991) found a significant reverse developmental effect: 7-year-old girls were less likely than 5-year-old girls to disclose genital touch during a pediatric exam in their free recall. This could not be attributable to memory ability, since 7-year-olds' recall is superior to that of 5-year-olds'. Instead, the results suggested that "emotions such as embarrassment, anxiety, or self-consciousness" interfered with children's recall (p. 689).

Recognizing that suggestibility research studying unemotional events may not translate into false abuse reports, suggestibility experts have pointed to subsequent studies eliciting false reports of touching, including genital touch (Bruck & Ceci, 2015). However, children are less likely to make false reports of genital touch than other types of touch (Brown et al., 2007; Otgaar et al., 2012; Poole et al., 2014). This supports the argument that factors that decrease true disclosures also decrease false disclosures.

Another factor that reduces true reports and is likely to reduce false reports is closeness between the child and the suspect. It is well established that closeness to the suspect reduces the likelihood that abused children acknowledge abuse (Lyon et al., 2026), in part because of their positive feelings for the suspect. Closeness should be considered in assessing the likelihood of a false allegation: Children are less likely to falsely acknowledge abuse by someone they love. This intuitive proposition was first suggested in a study examining the effects of prior knowledge and stereotypes on memory. Ceci and colleagues (1981) showed that 7- to 10-year-old children who read stories containing negative facts tended to forget those facts if the protagonists were familiar television characters with strong positive stereotypes (e.g., the Bionic Woman, the Six Million Dollar Man, James Bond, Tarzan).

Given the importance of familiarity in assessing allegations, there is surprisingly little research varying the familiarity of the "suspect" in suggestibility research. In the classic Sam Stone study, Leichtman and Ceci (1995) demonstrated that 3- to 6-year-old children's reports were seriously distorted by stereotype induction and suggestive questioning about the suspect Sam Stone. The stereotype induction involved students visiting and playing with children once per week for 4 weeks before Sam's visit to the classroom, telling them 12 stories about Sam's clumsiness, whereas the suggestive questioning involved visits with children once per week for 4 weeks after Sam's visit, including presenting children with evidence of Sam's misdeeds (a ripped book and a soiled teddy bear) and repeatedly asking questions that presupposed the misdeeds had occurred. Children's actual encounter with Sam, when he visited their classroom, lasted for 2 minutes. Lepore and Sesco (1994) tested whether 4- to 6-year-old children's responses to questions about a 5-minute interaction with a teaching assistant (TA) were influenced if they had 90 minutes of prior exposure. An initial interviewer used stereotype induction (labeling everything the TA did as bad) and suggestive questions (e.g., "Didn't he take off some of your clothes, too?"). Familiarity failed to counteract stereotype induction and suggestion but had some positive effects: Children viewed the familiar TA as more likable, and recalled more about their interaction. Cordón et al. (2016) tested whether 4- to 8-year-old children's responses to questions about a suspect camp leader were influenced if they had 6 hours of prior exposure. Parents had read their child stories relating 13 messy and clumsy actions by the camp leader. Stereotyping influenced children's susceptibility to closed-ended questions suggesting stereotypical actions, but familiarity increased children's accuracy in response to closed-ended questions and reduced their commission errors when asked stereotype-related questions. Taken together, the three studies suggest that as familiarity increases, children's susceptibility to negative stereotyping and suggestion decreases.

Hence, a lot rides on whether abused children freely disclose abuse when questioned. Their reluctance not only speaks to understanding denial when it occurs in abuse cases, but also challenges the external validity of suggestibility research, because what makes abused children reluctant to make true disclosures is likely to make nonabused children reluctant to make false disclosures.

DO ABUSED CHILDREN FREELY DISCLOSE ABUSE WHEN QUESTIONED?

One way to assess reluctance is to examine rates of denial in clinical studies of children assessed for suspected sexual abuse. However, one immediately runs into the ground truth problem: One doesn't know for sure whether children in the samples have been abused or not. For example, assume the disclosure rate in a study is 70%, and the denial rate is 30%. Should one conclude that 70% of abused children disclose abuse? No, because children who disclose abuse may not have been abused, and children who deny abuse may have been abused. Because of the ground truth problem, researchers have proposed different solutions.

Addressing the Ground Truth Problem by Identifying the Subset of Substantiated Cases

One might try to solve the ground truth problem by limiting one's analysis to substantiated cases. This is the solution offered by London and colleagues (2005, 2008). The researchers identified six child interview studies that they viewed as methodologically superior because the researchers classified cases based on certainty that abuse had occurred. Those studies, in chronological order, were Dubowitz and colleagues (1992), Elliott and Briere (1994), Keary and Fitzpatrick (1994), Gordon and Jaudes (1996), DiPietro and colleagues (1997), and Devoe and Faller (1999).

London and colleagues identified the subsamples for which researchers were confident that abuse had occurred, and they calculated an average denial rate of 14% (corresponding to an 86% disclosure rate; London et al., 2008).

These rates of denial were much lower than the denial rates of the original samples, which suggested that the original samples contained numerous cases in which abuse was falsely suspected. These numbers, along with the claim that the "methodologically superior" studies generate lower estimates of denial, have been reiterated in subsequent reviews of the sexual abuse literature (e.g., Ceci & Bruck, 2013), in critiques of expert testimony about the dynamics of abuse disclosure (Zajac et al., 2013), and in expert testimony for the defense in child sexual abuse cases (*Ohio v. Swoboda*, 2021). The New Jersey Supreme Court accepted the argument in rejecting the scientific validity of expert testimony that explains why abused children deny abuse (*New Jersey v. J.L.G.*, 2018).

The problem with this approach is that disclosure is most often the means by which abuse is substantiated (Lyon et al., 2020), a point emphasized by the authors of the original studies (e.g., Elliott & Briere, 1994, "evaluation relies heavily on the minor's statements," p. 261). Focusing on substantiated cases in estimating disclosure rates leads to a selection problem, which can be called *substantiation selection bias*. If disclosure is the primary means by which cases are substantiated, then substantiated cases will have an inflated rate of disclosure. Abused children who fail to disclose are excluded from the substantiated sample, unless there is other evidence sufficient to support a finding of abuse without disclosure. To the extent that corroborative evidence is uncommon, the disclosure rate among substantiated cases approaches 100%, no matter how frequently truly abused children deny abuse. If there is no corroborative evidence, and the abused child fails to disclose, then they are presumed to be nonabused.

A word about terminology: In earlier work, substantiation selection bias was simply called *substantiation bias* (Azzopardi et al., 2019; Lyon, 2007). We've added *selection* to emphasize that the bias describes a bias in the sample selection process and does not reflect an interpretive bias on the part of the evaluators. Unfortunately, substantiation bias has been conflated with confirmation bias (Brainerd, 2017). Confirmation bias would reflect evaluators' biased interpretation of children's statements as disclosures to confirm their assumptions that the child had been abused. This is an important but separate concern: It has been addressed in research accessing the interviews on which the evaluation was based, enabling the researchers to objectively determine whether a disclosure occurred (Eisen et al., 2021; Hershkowitz et al., 2014).

Addressing the Ground Truth and Substantiation Selection Bias Problem by Identifying the Subset of Corroborated Cases

Ironically, to the extent that suggestive questioning leads to substantial numbers of false disclosures of abuse, examining substantiated cases has an additional flaw: It fails to solve the ground truth problem. Substantiating cases based on disclosures is wrongheaded if many disclosures are false. In their 2005 review,

London et al. acknowledged the ground truth problem. They noted that there was often uncertainty about the "validity of [the] sexual abuse diagnosis": "[I]n many of the cited studies, classification of abuse was often based in part on children's disclosures; consequently, the conclusion that abused children do disclose abuse during formal interviews may be circular" (London et al., 2005, p. 217). The authors also proposed a solution: one could examine the cases in which "children are classified as abused on the basis of medical evidence or nonchild factors (confession, material evidence)" (p. 217). This is a promising approach which we endorse. One reduces the ground truth problem while that one reduces the substantiation selection bias problem. One caveat: The corroborative evidence should be independent of disclosure, an issue we discuss later.

If one takes this approach with the "methodologically superior" studies one consistently finds lower rates of disclosure. London et al. (2005) calculated an 83% disclosure rate in Dubowitz et al. (1992) and argued that "the finding that 83% of children disclosed abuse was based on the calculation of the number of children with medical findings" (p. 217). Unfortunately, London et al. (2005) confused substantiated cases with corroborated cases. In fact, the actual rate of disclosure among children with medical evidence "indicative" of abuse was 46%.

Neither the 83% number nor the 46% number is reported in the original study. To calculate these numbers, one must take a closer look at the categories of disclosure and medical evidence. First, one should be careful to calculate disclosure rather than nonverbal behaviors once believed to be evidence of abuse. Dubowitz et al. (1992) drew a distinction between full disclosure and partial disclosure, defining *partial disclosure* as "suggestive doll play or an inconclusive account of alleged abuse" (p. 690). Although there is some debate over whether children can clarify verbal disclosures with dolls or drawings to identify where touching occurred, there is general agreement that doll play (as opposed to disclosure with dolls) does not corroborate abuse (Poole & Bruck, 2012). Hence, one should exclude partial disclosures. Indeed, London et al. (2008, p. 42) themselves argued that disclosure rates will be exaggerated if children are included in the "substantiated" group "because they demonstrate ambiguous behaviors that are [wrongly] considered diagnostic of abuse (e.g., suggestive doll play, i.e., not diagnostic)." Nevertheless, London et al. (2008) included partial disclosures in their calculation of the disclosure rate in Dubowitz and colleagues (1992).

Second, one should look for the strongest corroborative evidence. This addresses both the ground truth problem and the substantiation selection bias problem. Of course, if the corroborative evidence is stronger, this increases the likelihood that the child was abused. Furthermore, if the corroborative evidence is stronger, this decreases the likelihood that substantiation was dependent on the disclosure; one could conclude that the child had been abused regardless of disclosure. Dubowitz et al. (1992) classified "hymenal scarring" as "indicative" of abuse, and hymenal abnormalities as "compatible" with sexual abuse (p. 690).

Because of variability in the appearance of a normal hymen at birth (Berenson et al., 1991), it is best to focus on the "indicative" subsample. London et al. (2008) warned that one should not classify children as "substantiated" if they "display 'soft' medical findings that are also present in non-abused children" (p. 42). If one examines the "indicative" subset of children, the disclosure rate is 46% (Lyon et al., 2020).

London et al. (2005) calculated a "substantiated" disclosure rate of 77% in the Gordon and Jaudes study (1996). They indirectly acknowledged that the study failed to find a high rate of disclosure in medically corroborated cases, citing Gordon and Jaudes (1996) with a "but see" (London et al., 2005, p. 217), but then repeated the 77% "substantiated" rate in their subsequent review (London et al., 2008). Examination of the original paper (Gordon & Jaudes, 1996, Table 2, p. 319; Lyon et al., 2020, Table 4, p. 639) reveals that the disclosure rate among children with a sexually transmitted illness was 43%. In sum, if one identifies the subsamples of the "methodologically superior" studies with strong corroborative evidence of abuse, one finds that only 43% to 46% of children disclosed sexual contact.

The Importance of Independent Corroboration for Solving the Substantiation Selection Bias Problem

Although examining cases with corroborative evidence may help overcome the substantiation selection bias problem, it is important to identify corroborative evidence that is independent of disclosure. If the corroborative evidence is dependent on disclosure, then the bias will continue to inflate disclosure rates. So, for example, if we used criminal convictions as corroboration, disclosure rates would approach 100%, because prosecutors rarely prosecute cases without a disclosure (London et al., 2020).

We can see these problems in London and colleagues' (2008) discussion of one of the "methodologically superior" subsamples. They calculated an 87% disclosure rate among 47 "corroborated cases" in Devoe and Faller (1999), which they stated were corroborated by "medical findings, material evidence, offender confession, and offender conviction" (p. 42). However, examination of the original study reveals that corroboration for these 47 cases constituted "corroborative evidence from previous reports" (DeVoe & Faller, 1999, p. 224), specifically "reports of child statements in other contexts" (p. 221). Prior disclosures are not independent of current disclosures to the extent that children who previously disclosed are more likely to disclose again. The corroboration reported by London and colleagues (2008) only applied to a smaller subsample of 25 cases for which disclosure rates were not reported (Devoe & Faller, 1999, Table 2, p. 222). The other "methodologically superior" studies either failed to report corroboration (DiPietro et al., 1997; Keary & Fitzpatrick, 1994) or included external evidence that was dependent on a disclosure (e.g., children's description of the defendant's room when the suspect had denied contact; Elliott & Briere, 1994).

There are two other ways in which disclosure rates can be inflated by a dependence between corroborative evidence and disclosure. First, disclosures can increase the likelihood of corroboration. This occurs when disclosures spur the search for corroborative evidence. To take an extreme example, if children are medically examined for physical evidence of sexual abuse only if they have disclosed, then the disclosure rate among medically corroborated cases will be 100%. In Heger and colleagues' (2002) examination of medical findings of abuse, 82% of children with diagnostic findings were referred for medical evaluation only after disclosing abuse. Hence, it is important to assess when the corroborative evidence was discovered. Ideally, it should have been discovered before the child was questioned about abuse.

Second, corroborative evidence can increase the likelihood of disclosure. When there is corroboration, interviewers may use the corroborative evidence as a tool for overcoming the child's reluctance. If the initial allegation questions fail to elicit a disclosure, the National Institute of Child Health and Human Development (NICHD) structured protocol recommends referring to external evidence (Lamb et al., 2018, e.g., "I [saw, heard] that you have/had [documented injuries, bruises] on your [body part]. Tell me everything about [those, that]."). Experimental work has shown that presenting maltreated children with evidence of their joint transgressions with adults increases disclosure (Evans & Lyon, 2019). Therefore, when the corroborative evidence was discovered before questioning, it is important to know whether the interviewers used the corroborative evidence in their questioning of children.

Internet-based abuse (also known as technology-facilitated abuse) is often discovered by concerned adults coming across digital evidence, which both corroborates the abuse and exists independently of disclosure. However, the interviewers routinely present the evidence to children as a means of overcoming reluctance (Gemara & Katz, 2023; Katz, 2013; Vale et al., 2024). Katz (2013) examined 20 cases of 11- to 14-year-olds who had been abused by strangers they met online and were questioned with the NICHD Protocol. The interviews included the presentation of digital evidence when necessary; nevertheless "[o]f the twenty children who underwent investigative interviews, eight children did not disclose any allegation even though there was strong evidence that they had been abused" (p. 1540). Even in the face of digital evidence and use of research-based interviewing methods, the disclosure rate was only 60%.

Because most cases of sexual abuse are not accompanied by physical evidence, examining cases in which evidence was presented to children inflates the likelihood of disclosure. When interviewers question children without presenting evidence, disclosure rates are lower (Evans & Lyon, 2019). To solve the two problems discussed here with respect to corroborative evidence (that disclosure leads to corroborative evidence and corroborative evidence encourages disclosure), we would ideally examine cases in which corroborative evidence was discovered prior to any disclosure and in which corroborative evidence was not presented to the child as such. These concerns mirror a related problem—suspicion selection bias—which we discuss next.

Suspicion Selection Bias: Disclosure Rates Are Inflated When Disclosure Is the Reason That Abuse Is Suspected

As previously discussed, substantiation selection bias means that disclosure rates are inflated when one focuses on the disclosure rates among substantiated cases, because substantiation is dependent on disclosure. To reduce substantiation selection bias, one needs to identify cases that can be corroborated by evidence that is independent of disclosure. In cases for which there is medical evidence of abuse, the disclosure rates drop from over 80% to under 50% (Dubowitz et al., 1992; Gordon & Jaudes, 1996). Even these rates could be inflated, however, if children's disclosure led them to be tested for a sexually transmitted illness. To understand the problem, imagine that children were only tested for sexually transmitted illness if they disclosed; in that case, the disclosure rates would be 100% among children with sexually transmitted illness.

This is an example of a broader problem that we can call suspicion selection bias. To show how suspicion selection bias is independent of substantiation selection bias, consider a medical analogy. Imagine that medical professionals want to estimate the likelihood that patients with a particular disease are symptomatic. Assume there is a test for the disease that is 100% accurate regardless of symptoms, which means that there is no ground truth problem or substantiation selection bias problem. The professionals survey medical clinics and find that virtually 100% of patients diagnosed with the disease are symptomatic. Should they conclude that 100% of individuals in the population with the disease are symptomatic? No, to the extent that symptoms lead patients and their caretakers to seek out medical care, and symptoms lead doctors to test for the disease. Asymptomatic carriers of the disease will be systematically overlooked because they won't visit the doctor, and even if they do, they won't be tested for the disease.

Now apply this logic to sexual abuse, in which one imagines that sexual abuse is the disease and disclosure is the symptom. If disclosure leads adults to suspect abuse and investigators to question children about abuse, then samples of children questioned about sexual abuse will have inflated rates of disclosure. This will occur even if the initial suspicions are aroused by facts other than disclosure (such as sexualized behavior), as long as disclosures affect adults' decisions to pursue further investigation.

Suspicion selection bias is evinced by high rates of prior disclosure in clinical samples of children questioned about suspected sexual abuse, which shows that the reason the interviewers suspected the child had been abused was because the child had disclosed abuse. In Azzopardi and colleagues' (2019) meta-analysis of clinical samples, prior disclosure was noted in 24 of the 45 studies, and the average rate of prior disclosure was 69%.

SOLVING THE METHODOLOGICAL PROBLEMS: EXAMINE CASES FOR WHICH ABUSE IS SUSPECTED ONLY AFTER CORROBORATIVE EVIDENCE IS IDENTIFIED

Since 1983, pediatric experts have consistently advised practicing pediatricians that childhood gonorrhea past infancy is sexually transmitted, because non-sexual transmission of gonorrhea has never been convincingly documented and is at most extremely rare (Committee on Child Abuse & Neglect, 1988; Committee on Early Childhood, Adoption and Dependent Care, 1983; Jenny et al., 2013; Kellogg & Committee on Child Abuse & Neglect, 2005; Kellogg et al., 2023). A diagnosis of childhood gonorrhea thus minimizes the ground truth problem, because one can be confident that the illness was due to sexual contact and substantiation selection bias, because abuse can be substantiated without relying on a disclosure. Moreover, gonorrhea in children is often detected prior to any suspicion of sexual abuse, thus reducing suspicion selection bias (Kelly, 2002).

Lyon (2007) reviewed several decades of research examining disclosure rates of children with gonorrhea. He identified 21 studies (from 1965 to 1993). In addition to reviewing those studies, we have identified two more recent studies from New Zealand, which witnessed an increase in gonorrhea starting in the late 1990s and began to report on its appearance in children (Kelly, 2002; Whaitiri & Kelly, 2011). In most studies, cases were selected on the basis that the child appeared at the hospital with symptoms of gonorrhea, with few of the cases seen for the evaluation of sexual abuse (see, e.g., Farrell et al., 1981 [2/46 seen for suspicion of abuse]; Shapiro et al., 1993 [1/22 seen for suspicion]; Kelly, 2002 [1/14 seen for suspicion]). In 21 of the 23 studies the authors clearly mentioned that the diagnosis was confirmed by culture, minimizing concerns that the diagnoses were false positives (London et al., 2020). In all the studies the authors refer to whether there was a "history" of abuse, a medical term that includes disclosure, or explicitly note that the child was questioned, minimizing concerns that children were never questioned about the source of their illness (London et al., 2020).

Based on these 23 studies, we calculated an average rate of disclosure of 43% (258/601). Whenever possible we removed children younger than 3 years of age, because they may have been too young to disclose sexual contact. If one excludes the five studies in which it was impossible to separately analyze children 3 years and older, the rate of disclosure across the remaining 16 studies was 42% (193/459). If in addition to removing the studies that included disclosure rates for children under 3 years, one excludes the studies that included teenagers (who may have become infected through consensual contact), the rate of disclosure among the remaining studies was 51% (134/261). Lyon (2007) also discussed two other studies that minimized suspicion substantiation bias by examining the disclosure rates of children for whom corroborative evidence was discovered prior to any suspicions of abuse, and disclosure rates were only about 50% in both studies (Lawson & Chaffin, 1992 [sexually transmitted illness; 43%]; Muram et al., 1991 [hymenal tears; 51%]).

These numbers are generous estimates of disclosure. First, researchers often interviewed children more than once, so that the reported disclosure rates reflected whether the child ultimately disclosed. For example, Sgroi (1979) reported that "[s]everal interviews may be necessary to enlist the confidence of the child to a degree that will permit the child to share the 'secret' of his/her sexual behavior with someone else" (p. 82). When initial disclosure rates were reported, they were always substantially lower than the ultimate disclosure rates. Farrell and colleagues (1981) ultimately obtained a 52% disclosure rate, but they noted that a history of sexual contact was only obtained in 15% of the children in the emergency room. Ingram (1994), describing his 1982 study, emphasized that "If no history of sexual contact is obtained, multiple interviews over time are necessary. In our series of cases of gonococcal disease in children, only 18% of the children who gave a history of sexual contact did so on the first interview. Two girls told us about their sexual contact eight years later when they were no longer afraid of the sexual abuser" (p. 344). Shapiro et al. (1993) reported that only one child out of the 22 (5%) evaluated disclosed to the doctor during the emergency room visit.

Second, in some cases, high rates of disclosure could be attributable to interviewers presenting children with the diagnosis as proof of abuse. The reader will recall that this inflates disclosure rates, because corroboration is no longer independent of disclosure. For example, one of the highest disclosure rates was reported by Branch and Paxton (1965; 100%), in which the interviewer "explain[ed] the mechanism" by which the child became infected during the interview (p. 349). However, because of the erroneous belief among many researchers prior to the late 1970s and early 1980s that nonsexual transmission was a common cause of infection, such as through toilet seats, bed sheets, towels, and other "fomites" (Sacco, 2002; Shore & Winkelstein, 1971), it is likely that interviewers usually treated sexual contact as a possibility rather than a foregone conclusion. As such, the studies provide an estimate of the likelihood that children will disclose or deny abuse when it is first suspected (but not presumed).

IMPLICATIONS OF THE RESEARCH FOR ASSESSING DENIAL AND FOR INTERVIEWING PROTOCOLS

In any case in which a child denied abuse early in the investigation but eventually disclosed abuse, investigators and legal decision makers must assess the likelihood that the child's behavior is likely due to reluctance or to suggestibility. The fact that denials are rare in cases of suspected and substantiated abuse in child clinical studies doesn't enable us to assess the likelihood that abused children are reluctant to disclose. Nor do the overall denial rates in those studies, in part because we don't know if the deniers were abused. To sensibly estimate the likelihood that abused children will deny abuse, we need to identify children for whom there is clear independent corroborative evidence of abuse and assess their early disclosure histories. Doing so reveals that only a small percentage of abused children are likely to disclose abuse when it is first suspected.

The apparent ease with which interviewers obtain disclosures from children suspected of being sexually abused in clinical studies of children questioned about abuse simply reflects the fact that disclosure is the primary basis for suspicion and substantiation of abuse. In other words, professionals are encountering children who are disproportionately likely to be forthcoming. Because of this fact, and because heavy-handed techniques may elicit false reports from nonabused children, interviewers' use of nonleading methods encouraging free recall of abuse is obviously warranted. But it bears repeating that when children deny abuse at some point during investigation, identification of abuse in cases free of suspicion and substantiation selection bias reveals that these are common behaviors of the abused child. As such, they constitute only weak evidence against abuse.

London and colleagues (2005, 2008) take a very different approach in reviewing research on children's disclosure. In addition to focusing on the problems previously discussed on substantiated subsamples of children questioned about abuse, they argued that the most relevant data come from studies questioning children using modern interviewing protocols. They limited their reviews to studies published since 1990, largely because of "major reforms in best practice guidelines for forensic interviewers" (London et al., 2005, p. 204; London et al., 2008, p. 30). Accordingly, they criticized the gonorrhea studies on the grounds that because most "were published before any evidence-based child forensic protocols existed, children in these studies were not interviewed according to contemporary interview guidelines" (London et al., 2020, p. 651).

The argument that one should only study denial of sexual abuse in response to research-based protocols misconceives the purpose of reviewing the literature on denial. The cases that lead to suggestibility concerns aren't those in which children deny abuse in response to state-of-the-art protocol interviews conducted by highly trained interviewers. Rather, they are cases in which nonprofessionals (such as worried parents) or poorly trained professionals question children, and children's initial denials eventually lead to a disclosure. Confronted with a case in which a child initially denied abuse, but ultimately disclosed, one needs to estimate the likelihood that an abused child questioned for the first time about abuse would deny abuse. If the likelihood is great, then this counters the assumption that such a child is a nonabused child coerced by false suspicions and suggestions of abuse.

Second, the argument assumes that modern-day protocols have solved the problem of reluctance and denial. This is a misinterpretation of what research has and has not accomplished in identifying the most productive means of questioning children about abuse. Discussing the "unwarranted assumption" that "children's disclosures of traumatic events are delayed, denied, and often recanted," Ceci and colleagues (2007, p. 322) cited the fact that among 4- to 8-year-old children interviewed with the NICHD Protocol, 83% of disclosures were elicited through free recall questions (Lamb et al., 2003), concluding that "children can provide detailed information through open-ended prompts, and if a child denies abuse when asked directly, there is no scientifically compelling evidence that the child is in denial" (p. 323). Similarly, citing Lamb and colleagues (2003), London and colleagues (2008) asserted that the NICHD Protocol "uses techniques that produce high rates of true disclosures even from young children" (p. 43).

The assertion confuses the likelihood that recall questions are productive, given abuse disclosure, with the likelihood of abuse disclosure, given recall questions. Lamb and colleagues (2003) never asserted that most abused children are forthcoming about their abuse. Rather, the authors simply excluded the 60 children who failed to disclose sexual abuse when questioned with the NICHD Protocol (out of 190, or 32%), and focused on disclosers, demonstrating that they were responsive to free recall questions. Recall questions are effective because modern interviewing protocols take advantage of the fact that most children questioned about abuse have previously disclosed. For example, in Lamb and colleagues (2003), the first allegation question was, "Tell me the reason you came to talk with me today." Subsequent allegation questions refer to prior disclosures, such as "I heard that you talked to a [. . . professional] at [time, location.] Please tell me what you talked about" (Lamb et al., 2018; see also American Professional Society on the Abuse of Children, 2023).

Of course, how many of the 60 children were abused is unknown, reminding us of the importance of assessing disclosure rates in corroborated cases. Hershkowitz and colleagues (2014) examined over 400 children referred to investigative social workers for suspicions of intrafamilial physical or sexual abuse. The study reduced ground truth and substantiation selection bias problems by limiting the sample to cases with corroborative evidence such as "suspects' admissions, disinterested eyewitness testimony, medical evidence (including observable physical injuries), and material evidence" (p. 339). Material evidence was not defined but probably included photographs. (The authors do not discuss the extent to which corroborative evidence was independent of disclosure.) The study utilized the NICHD structured protocol (Lamb et al., 2018); with most of the children receiving a revised version of the protocol with added supportive statements designed to reduce reluctance. Most of the sample was physical abuse cases, possibly because corroborative evidence is more likely in those cases, and the overall disclosure rate for those cases was 57%, which means that 43% either denied or failed to disclose. Among the smaller sample of 18 sexually abused children, the overall disclosure rate was 44%, which means that over half either denied or failed to disclose.

Clearly, the research on interview protocols has great value in informing practitioners how to conduct their interviews. The fact that open-ended questions elicit disclosures from a large percentage of children interviewed for suspected sexual abuse means that practitioners need not start their interviews with suggestive questions, which are ill-advised because of the risks that they will distort children's reports. However, the efficacy of open-ended questions with children who disclose says nothing about the abuse status of children who do not disclose.

Because denial allays suspicions and prevents the substantiation of abuse, its frequency goes unnoticed. It is only by solving the methodological problems in identifying abuse among children who are reluctant to disclose that one uncovers the sad truth that most abused children will deny abuse when initially questioned. Using abused children's initial denials in court as a means of attacking their credibility compounds the injuries inflicted by the abuse and makes it more difficult to protect them from continuing harm. We still have a long way to go in reassuring reluctant children that it is safe to disclose.

REFERENCES

Alaggia, R., Collin-Vézina, D., & Lateef, R. (2019). Facilitators and barriers to child sexual abuse (CSA) disclosures: A research update (2000–2016). *Trauma, Violence, & Abuse, 20*(2), 260–283. https://doi.org/10.1177/1524838017697312

American Professional Society on the Abuse of Children. (2023). *Forensic interviewing of children*. Association of Professionals Solving the Abuse of Children. https://apsac.org/wp-content/uploads/2024/04/30014.pdf

Anderson, J., Martin, J., Mullen, P., Romans, S., & Herbison, P. (1993). Prevalence of childhood sexual abuse experiences in a community sample of women. *Journal of the American Academy of Child & Adolescent Psychiatry, 32*(5), 911–919. https://doi.org/10.1097/00004583-199309000-00004

Azzopardi, C., Eirich, R., Rash, C. L., MacDonald, S., & Madigan, S. (2019). A meta-analysis of the prevalence of child sexual abuse disclosure in forensic settings. *Child Abuse & Neglect, 93*, 291–304. https://doi.org/10.1016/j.chiabu.2018.11.020

Berenson, A., Heger, A., & Andrews, S. (1991). Appearance of the hymen in newborns. *Pediatrics, 87*(4), 458–465. https://doi.org/10.1542/peds.87.4.458

Brainerd, C. (2017). *Interim report and expert opinion re: New Jersey v. J.L.G.*

Branch, G., & Paxton, R. (1965). A study of gonococcal infections among infants and children. *Public Health Reports, 80*(4), 347–352. https://pmc.ncbi.nlm.nih.gov/articles/PMC1919640/

Brown, D. A., & Lamb, M. E. (2022). Walking the line: What can analog studies teach us about children's memories of abusive incidents? *Journal of Applied Research in Memory and Cognition, 11*(3), 312–316. https://doi.org/10.1037/mac0000063

Brown, D. A., Pipe, M. E., Lewis, C., Lamb, M. E., & Orbach, Y. (2007). Supportive or suggestive: Do human figure drawings help 5-to 7-year-old children to report touch? *Journal of Consulting and Clinical Psychology, 75*(1), 33–42. https://doi.org/10.1037/0022-006X.75.1.33

Bruck, M. (2017). *Psychological Report, State of New Jersey v. J.L.G.*

Bruck, M., & Ceci, S. J. (2013). Expert testimony in a child sex abuse case: Translating memory development research. *Memory, 21*(5), 556–565. https://doi.org/10.1080/09658211.2013.769606

Bruck, M., & Ceci, S. J. (2015). Children's testimony: A scientific framework for evaluating the reliability of children's statements. In A. Thapar, D. S. Pine, J. F. Leckman, S. Scott, M. J. Snowling, & E. Taylor (Eds.), *Rutter's child and adolescent psychiatry* (pp. 250–260). John Wiley & Sons. https://doi.org/10.1002/9781118381953.ch20

California v. Flores, 101 Cal.App.5th 538 (Ct. App. 2024).

Ceci, S. J., & Bruck, M. (2013). Loftus's lineage in developmental forensic research: Six scientific misconceptions about children's suggestibility. In M. Garry & H. Hayne (Eds.), *Do justice and let the sky fall: Elizabeth F. Loftus and her contributions to science, law, and academic freedom* (pp. 65–77). Psychology Press.

Ceci, S. J., & Friedman, R. D. (2000). The suggestibility of children: Scientific research and legal implications. *Cornell Law Review, 86*(1), 33–108. https://scholarship.law.cornell.edu/clr/vol86/iss1/2

Ceci, S. J., Kulkofsky, S., Klemfuss, J. Z., Sweeney, C. D., & Bruck, M. (2007). Unwarranted assumptions about children's testimonial accuracy. *Annual Review of Clinical Psychology, 3*(1), 311–328. https://doi.org/10.1146/annurev.clinpsy.3.022806.091354

Chae, Y., Hartman, D. T., & Goodman, G. S. (2022). What children remember after talking with parents: Implications for children's memory and testimony. *Journal of Applied Research in Memory and Cognition, 11*(3), 328–333. https://doi.org/10.1037/mac0000067

Committee on Child Abuse & Neglect. (1988). Gonorrhea in prepubertal children. *Pediatrics, 101*(1), 134–135. https://doi.org/10.1542/peds.101.1.134

Committee on Early Childhood, Adoption, and Dependent Care. (1983). Gonorrhea in prepubertal children. *Pediatrics, 71*(4), 553. https://doi.org/10.1542/peds.71.4.553

Cordón, I. M., Silberkleit, G., & Goodman, G. S. (2016). Getting to know you: Familiarity, stereotypes, and children's eyewitness memory. *Behavioral Sciences & the Law, 34*(1), 74–94. https://doi.org/10.1002/bsl.2233

DeVoe, E. R., & Faller, K. C. (1999). The characteristics of disclosure among children who may have been sexually abused. *Child Maltreatment, 4*(3), 217–227. https://doi.org/10.1177/1077559599004003003

DiPietro, E. K., Runyan, D. K., & Fredrickson, D. D. (1997). Predictors of disclosure during medical evaluation for suspected sexual abuse. *Journal of Child Sexual Abuse, 6*(1), 133–142. https://doi.org/10.1300/J070v06n01_09

Dubowitz, H., Black, M., & Harrington, D. (1992). The diagnosis of child sexual abuse. *American Journal of Diseases of Children, 146*(6), 688–693. https://doi.org/10.1001/archpedi.1992.02160180046015

Eisen, M. L., Goodman, G. S., Diep, J., Lacsamana, M., Ristrom, L. J., & Qin, J. J. (2021). Disclosures of sexual and physical abuse across repeated interviews. *Journal of Child Sexual Abuse, 30*(8), 932–952. https://doi.org/10.1080/10538712.2021.1960457

Elliott, D. M., & Briere, J. (1994). Forensic sexual abuse evaluations of older children: Disclosures and symptomatology. *Behavioral Sciences & the Law, 12*(3), 261–277. https://doi.org/10.1002/bsl.2370120306

Evans, A. D., & Lyon, T. D. (2019). The effects of the putative confession and evidence presentation on maltreated and non-maltreated 9- to 12-year-olds' disclosures of a minor transgression. *Journal of Experimental Child Psychology, 188*. Article 104674. https://doi.org/10.1016/j.jecp.2019.104674

Farrell, M. K., Billmire, M. E., Shamroy, J. A., & Hammond, J. G. (1981). Prepubertal gonorrhea: A multidisciplinary approach. *Pediatrics, 67*(1), 151–153. https://doi.org/10.1542/peds.67.1.151

Fleming, J. M. (1997). Prevalence of childhood sexual abuse in a community sample of Australian women. *Medical Journal of Australia, 166*(2), 65–68. https://doi.org/10.5694/j.1326-5377.1997.tb138722.x

Gemara, N., & Katz, C. (2023). "It was really hard for me to tell": The gap between the child's difficulty in disclosing sexual abuse, and their perception of the disclosure recipient's response. *Journal of Interpersonal Violence, 38*(1-2), 2068–2091. https://doi.org/10.1177/08862605221099949

Gordon, S., & Jaudes, P. K. (1996). Sexual abuse evaluations in the emergency department: Is the history reliable? *Child Abuse & Neglect, 20*(4), 315–322. https://doi.org/10.1016/0145-2134(96)88716-3

Heger, A., Ticson, L., Velasquez, O., & Bernier, R. (2002). Children referred for possible sexual abuse: Medical findings in 2,384 children. *Child Abuse & Neglect, 26*(6–7), 645–659. https://doi.org/10.1016/S0145-2134(02)00339-3

Hershkowitz, I., Lamb, M. E., & Katz, C. (2014). Allegation rates in forensic child abuse investigations: Comparing the revised and standard NICHD protocols. *Psychology, Public Policy, & Law, 20*(3), 336–344. https://doi.org/10.1037/a0037391

Ingram, D. L. (1994). Neisseria gonorrhoeae in children. *Pediatric Annals, 23*(7), 341–345. https://doi.org/10.3928/0090-4481-19940701-07

Jenny, C., Crawford-Jakubiak, J. E., & Committee on Child Abuse and Neglect. (2013). The evaluation of children in the primary care setting when sexual abuse is suspected. *Pediatrics, 132*(2), 558–567. https://doi.org/10.1542/peds.2013-1741

Katz, C. (2013). Internet-related child sexual abuse: What children tell us in their testimonies. *Children and Youth Services Review, 35*(9), 1536–1542. https://doi.org/10.1016/j.childyouth.2013.06.006

Keary, K., & Fitzpatrick, C. (1994). Children's disclosure of sexual abuse during formal investigation. *Child Abuse & Neglect, 18*(7), 543–548. https://doi.org/10.1016/0145-2134(94)90080-9

Kellogg, N., & Committee on Child Abuse and Neglect. (2005). The evaluation of sexual abuse in children. *Pediatrics, 116*(2), 506–512. https://doi.org/10.1542/peds.2005-1336

Kellogg, N. D., Farst, K. J., & Adams, J. A. (2023). Interpretation of medical findings in suspected child sexual abuse: An update for 2023. *Child Abuse & Neglect, 145*, Article 106283. https://doi.org/10.1016/j.chiabu.2023.106283

Kelly, P. (2002). Childhood gonorrhoea in Auckland. *The New Zealand Medical Journal, 115*(1163), U201.

Lamb, M. E., Brown, D. A., Hershkowitz, I., Orbach, Y., & Esplin, P. W. (2018). *Tell me what happened: Structured investigative interviews of child victims and witnesses* (2nd ed.). John Wiley & Sons.

Lamb, M. E., Sternberg, K. J., Orbach, Y., Esplin, P. W., Stewart, H., & Mitchell, S. (2003). Age differences in young children's responses to open-ended invitations in the course of forensic interviews. *Journal of Consulting and Clinical Psychology, 71*(5), 926–934. https://doi.org/10.1037/0022-006X.71.5.926

Lawson, L., & Chaffin, M. (1992). False negatives in sexual abuse disclosure interviews: Incidence and influence of caretaker's belief in abuse in cases of accidental abuse discovery by diagnosis of STD. *Journal of Interpersonal Violence, 7*(4), 532–542. https://doi.org/10.1177/088626092007004008

Leichtman, M. D., & Ceci, S. J. (1995). The effects of stereotypes and suggestions on preschoolers' reports. *Developmental Psychology, 31*(4), 568–578. https://doi.org/10.1037/0012-1649.31.4.568

Lemaigre, C., Taylor, E. P., & Gittoes, C. (2017). Barriers and facilitators to disclosing sexual abuse in childhood and adolescence: A systematic review. *Child Abuse & Neglect, 70*, 39–52. https://doi.org/10.1016/j.chiabu.2017.05.009

Lepore, S. J., & Sesco, B. (1994). Distorting children's reports and interpretations of events through suggestion. *Journal of Applied Psychology, 79*(1), 108–120. https://doi.org/10.1037/0021-9010.79.1.108

London, K., Bruck, M., Ceci, S. J., & Shuman, D. W. (2005). Disclosure of child sexual abuse: What does the research tell us about the ways that children tell? *Psychology, Public Policy, and the Law, 11*(1), 194–226. https://doi.org/10.1037/1076-8971.11.1.194

London, K., Bruck, M., Miller, Q. C., & Ceci, S. J. (2020). Analyzing the scientific foundation of Child Sexual Abuse Accommodation Syndrome: A reply to Lyon et al. *Behavioral Sciences & the Law, 38*(6), 648–653. https://doi.org/10.1002/bsl.2489

London, K., Bruck, M., Wright, D. B., & Ceci, S. J. (2008). Review of the contemporary literature on how children report sexual abuse to others: Findings, methodological issues, and implications for forensic interviewers. *Memory, 16*(1), 29–47. https://doi.org/10.1080/09658210701725732

Lyon, T. D. (2007). False denials: Overcoming methodological biases in abuse disclosure research. In M. Pipe, M. Lamb, Y. Orbach, & A. Cederborg (Eds.), *Disclosing abuse: Delays, denials, retractions and incomplete accounts* (pp. 41–62). Erlbaum.

Lyon, T. D. (2023). Child maltreatment, the law, and two types of error. *Child Maltreatment, 28*(3), 403–406. https://doi.org/10.1177/10775595231176454

Lyon, T. D., Ahern, E. C., & Scurich, N. (2012). Interviewing children vs. tossing coins: Accurately assessing the diagnosticity of children's disclosures of abuse. *Journal of Child Sexual Abuse, 21*(1), 19–44. https://doi.org/10.1080/10538712.2012.642468

Lyon, T. D., & Koehler, J. J. (1996). The relevance ratio: Evaluating the probative value of expert testimony in child sexual abuse cases. *Cornell Law Review, 82*, 43–78. https://scholarship.law.cornell.edu/clr/vol82/iss1/4

Lyon, T. D., Williams, S., & Stolzenberg, S. N. (2020). Understanding expert testimony on child sexual abuse denial after New Jersey v. J.L.G.: Ground truth, disclosure suspicion bias, and disclosure substantiation bias. *Behavioral Sciences & the Law, 38*(6), 630–647. https://doi.org/10.1002/bsl.2490

Lyon, T. D., Wylie, B. E., & Szojka, Z. A. (2026). Understanding child sexual abuse: Disclosures, delays, and denials. In M. E. Lamb, I. Hershkowitz, & M.-E. Pipe (Eds.), *Child sexual abuse: Why children disclose or deny being abused* (2nd ed., pp. 15–46). Routledge.

Malloy, L. C., Lyon, T. D., & Quas, J. A. (2007). Filial dependency and recantation of child sexual abuse allegations. *Journal of the American Academy of Child and Adolescent Psychiatry, 46*(2), 162–170. https://doi.org/10.1097/01.chi.0000246067.77953.f7

McElvaney, R. (2015). Disclosure of child sexual abuse: Delays, non-disclosure and partial disclosure. What the research tells us and implications for practice. *Child Abuse Review, 24*(3), 159–169. https://doi.org/10.1002/car.2280

Miller, Q. C., & London, K. (2020). Forensic implications of delayed reports from child witnesses. In J. Pozzulo, E. Pica, & C. Sheahan (Eds.), *Memory and sexual misconduct* (pp. 100–131). Routledge.

Muram, D., Speck, P. M., & Gold, S. S. (1991). Genital abnormalities in female siblings and friends of child victims of sexual abuse. *Child Abuse & Neglect, 15*(1-2), 105–110. https://doi.org/10.1016/0145-2134(91)90095-U

New Jersey v. J.L.G., 190 A.3d 442 (2018).

Newlin, C., Steele, L. C., Chamberlin, A., Anderson, J., Kenniston, J., Russell, A., Stewart, H., & Vaughan-Eden, V. (2015). *Child forensic interviewing: Best practices*. U.S. Department of Justice, Office of Justice Programs, Office of Juvenile Justice and Delinquency Prevention. https://ojjdp.ojp.gov/sites/g/files/xyckuh176/files/pubs/248749.pdf

New York v. Ashton, 215 N.Y.S.3d 812 (4th Dept. 2024).

Ohio v. Swoboda, 180 N.E.3d 1277 (Ct. App. 2021).

Otgaar, H., Horselenberg, R., van Kampen, R., & Lalleman, K. (2012). Clothed and unclothed human figure drawings lead to more correct and incorrect reports of touch in children. *Psychology, Crime & Law, 18*(7), 641–653. https://doi.org/10.1080/1068316X.2010.532129

Oral Argument in *New Jersey v. J.L.G.* (2018). https://www.njcourts.gov/courts/supreme/appeals?filter_by=All&search=j.l.g

Pennsylvania v. Dunkle, 602 A.2d 830 (1992).

Pollack, F. (1909). The acquired venereal diseases in children: A report of 187 children treated in the women's venereal department of the Johns Hopkins Hospital Dispensary. *Johns Hopkins Hospital Bulletin, 218*, 142–149.

Poole, D. A., & Bruck, M. (2012). Divining testimony? The impact of interviewing props on children's reports of touching. *Developmental Review, 32*(3), 165–180. https://doi.org/10.1016/j.dr.2012.06.007

Poole, D. A., Dickinson, J. J., Brubacher, S. P., Liberty, A. E., & Kaake, A. M. (2014). Deficient cognitive control fuels children's exuberant false allegations. *Journal of Experimental Child Psychology, 118*, 101–109. https://doi.org/10.1016/j.jecp.2013.08.013

Principe, G. F., & London, K. (2022). How parents can shape what children remember: Implications for the testimony of young witnesses. *Journal of Applied Research in Memory and Cognition, 11*(3), 289–302. https://doi.org/10.1037/mac0000059

Sacco, L. (2002). Sanitized for your protection: Medical discourse and the denial of incest in the United States, 1890–1940. *Journal of Women's History, 14*(3), 80–104. https://doi.org/10.1353/jowh.2002.0074

Saywitz, K. J., Goodman, G. S., Nicholas, E., & Moan, S. F. (1991). Children's memories of a physical examination involving genital touch: Implications for reports of child sexual abuse. *Journal of Consulting and Clinical Psychology, 59*(5), 682–691. https://doi.org/10.1037/0022-006X.59.5.682

Sgroi, S. M. (1979). Pediatric gonorrhea beyond infancy. *Pediatric Annals, 8*(5), 326–336. https://doi.org/10.3928/0090-4481-19790501-09

Shapiro, R. A., Schubert, C. J., & Myers, P. A. (1993). Vaginal discharge as an indicator of gonorrhea and chlamydia infection in girls under 12 years old. *Pediatric Emergency Care, 9*(6), 341–345. https://doi.org/10.1097/00006565-199312000-00004

Shore, W. B., & Winkelstein, J. A. (1971). Nonvenereal transmission of gonococcal infections to children. *Journal of Pediatrics, 79*(4), 661–663. https://doi.org/10.1016/s0022-3476(71)80316-5

Vale, M., Gomes, J. P., & Matos, M. (2024). Forensic psychological procedures in cases of technology-facilitated sexual abuse among adolescents: A scoping review. *Behavioral Sciences & the Law, 42*(4), 313–337. https://doi.org/10.1002/bsl.2658

Whaitiri, S., & Kelly, P. (2011). Genital gonorrhoea in children: Determining the source and mode of infection. *Archives of Disease in Childhood, 96*(3), 247–251. https://doi.org/10.1136/adc.2009.162909

Wood, J. M. (1996). Weighing evidence in sexual abuse evaluations: An introduction to Bayes's Theorem. *Child Maltreatment, 1*(1), 25–36. https://doi.org/10.1177/1077559596001001004

Zajac, R., Garry, M., London, K., Goodyear-Smith, F., & Hayne, H. (2013). Misconceptions about childhood sexual abuse and child witnesses: Implications for psychological experts in the courtroom. *Memory, 21*(5), 608–617. https://doi.org/10.1080/09658211.2013.778287

7

The Development and Correction of Children's False Memories

Henry Otgaar, Mark L. Howe, and Charlotte Bücken

Children who are witnesses or victims of a traumatic event oftentimes talk about their experiences to a variety of parties. For example, some will talk to friends or their parents and/or will be formally interviewed by child protection services or the police. During such conversations, there is always a chance that children receive questions about details or entire events that were not part of the original experience. When this happens, memory for the original experience can become contaminated, resulting in children remembering events that they did not experience. Memories for events that were never truly experienced are called *false memories* (e.g., Loftus, 2005).

Such false memories can exert devastating consequences. To provide some examples, when false memories appear in child protection contexts, families can be torn apart because a child might incorrectly recall having been mistreated by the father (e.g., Erens et al., 2022; Wood & Garven, 2000). In legal contexts, false memories of sexual abuse might lead to false accusations and even wrongful convictions (e.g., Schreiber et al., 2006). Furthermore, such false memories can be damaging for those who have come to remember false events, as such memories feel as authentic as true memories (Bernstein & Loftus, 2009). In this chapter, we will first present a brief history of several key legal cases that catalyzed scientific research on children's false memories.[1] We will then present several lines of evidence showing how children's false memories can be formed and which factors underpin the development of such false memories.

[1]We will focus primarily on the formation of false memories induced by suggestion and will not discuss research on spontaneous false memories.

https://doi.org/10.1037/0000492-007
Handbook on Child Witnesses: Improving Psychological Science and Legal Practice,
G. S. Goodman, T. D. Lyon, S. D. Hobbs, and R. Enriquez (Editors)

Finally, we will discuss ways in which children's false memories can be prevented or corrected.

A BRIEF HISTORY ON LEGAL CASES CONCERNING CHILDREN'S FALSE MEMORIES

In the 1980s and 1990s, several countries witnessed an outbreak of legal cases in which groups of children testified that they had been (sexually) abused. These cases were also called day care abuse cases (e.g., Ceci & Bruck, 1995). These cases were characterized by highly suggestive child interviews conducted, for example, by social workers. These suggestive interviews likely led to the production of false memories in children. We will now discuss several important day care abuse cases.

McMartin Preschool Case

The McMartin Preschool case was initiated in 1983 in Manhattan Beach, California, when a parent reported that their child had been abused. A letter was then sent from the police to the families of more than 100 children attending McMartin Preschool. This letter warned parents of the possibility that their children could have been abused by teachers at the preschool. In the letter, parents were urged to interview their children about whether they were also victims of abuse. After being interviewed by their own parents, these children were questioned by social workers who used highly suggestive questions. A brief example of such a suggestive interview from the McMartin preschool case is as follows:

INTERVIEWER: Can you remember the naked pictures?

CHILD: (Shakes head "no")

INTERVIEWER: Can't remember that part?

CHILD: (Shakes head "no")

INTERVIEWER: Why don't you think about that for a while, okay? Your memory might come back to you. (Garven et al., 1998, p. 28)

These suggestive interviews led to children not only acquiescing to this pressure but also resulted in children subsequently reporting accounts of bizarre events. For example, some children reported experiencing satanic rituals, seeing witches fly on brooms, and seeing children flushed down toilets. Memory researchers argued that the suggestive questions used during the interviews might have caused false memories in these children (Garven et al., 1998).

Wee Care Nursery Case

The Wee Care Nursery case started in 1985 at a day care center in New Jersey. Kelly Michaels, a day care worker at the nursery, was accused of abusing several children at the center. Like the former case, the school sent a letter to parents to interview their children about possible abuse. In the letter, parents were told that child sexual abuse is very common. As in the McMartin Preschool Case, children sometimes made bizarre claims such as that Kelly Michaels was licking peanut butter off children's genitals, making children drink urine, and raping children with Lego blocks (Schreiber et al., 2006). Because of these allegations, Michaels was sentenced to 47 years in prison in 1988. In 1993, the conviction was overturned. The court declared that children were interviewed in a highly suggestive fashion, rendering their accounts unreliable.

Christchurch Civic Creche Case

Around the same time, a similar day care case was emerging in New Zealand. This case began on November 20, 1991, when the parent of a child attending the creche came forward with allegations of abuse by Peter Ellis, one of the teachers (for a recent overview, see Howe, 2022; for a more exhaustive account, see Hood, 2019). As the investigation progressed, over 100 children from the creche were interviewed. During a preliminary court hearing, Peter Ellis faced an initial 45 charges of indecency involving 20 children with a further 15 charges laid involving five children. These charges included accusations of having inserted his finger, penis, needles, sticks, and food into the children's vaginas, mouths, and anuses. He was also accused of making them eat his urine and feces. All the children were between 6 and 9 years of age at trial (3–6 years at the time of the alleged offences). In the end, Peter Ellis faced 23 charges involving 13 children. On June 6, 1993, Peter Ellis was found guilty on three counts of sexual violation, eight counts of indecent assault, and five counts of performing indecent acts, and was sentenced to 10 years in prison.

As in similar cases, these children may have developed false memories of abuse through a sort of contagion; that is, collaborative false memories may have emerged through repeated conversations between children and parents, among the parents, and among the children themselves. Moreover, children were exposed to various forms of therapy, including scene reconstruction techniques using dolls, drawings, and toys.

Galileo Case

Although many day care abuse cases happened in the 1980s and 1990s, such cases still happen from time to time. An illustrative example is the Dutch Galileo Case in 2009. In this case, parents of a young boy told the school that a teacher had hit their son. Like the previous cases, the school decided to send a letter to all parents of the school stating that more children could have been victimized. Parents were informed that they would receive detailed information on (behavioral) signs in children that would be indicative of abuse. After this letter was sent out, 20 children claimed to have been abused by several teachers at the school. Children were questioned about the alleged experiences by parents, therapists, and the police. These interviews led to claims of a bizarre nature. For example, a child reported that one of the teachers had cut his genitals or that one of the teachers had live crocodiles at home. Because of the possibly suggestive nature of the letter and the different conversations with the children, it was concluded that the children in this case might have reported experiences that did not actually happen (Otgaar et al., 2017).

Jakarta International School Case

Another important observation in examples of day care abuse cases is that they do not only occur in Western countries but have been occurred in Asian countries as well. A noteworthy example is the Jakarta International School Case in Indonesia starting in 2014 (Calado, 2022). In March 2014, two 6-year-olds and one 7-year-old child reported abuse by six janitors and two teachers of the Jakarta International School. However, these claims originated from a series of suggestions. That is, these children initially denied being abused but were heavily (suggestively) influenced by their parents, therapists, and the police who questioned the children about the alleged abuse. For example, children were told by parents that they were sexually abused while initially no mention was made by children about any sexually abusive acts (Calado, 2022). These statements made by the children eventually led to the conviction of the suspects. One of them, a Canadian citizen, eventually received clemency from the Indonesian president's office.

Cases such as the ones described have fueled the attention of memory scientists to study the conditions by which children can come to falsely remember autobiographical experiences. To that end, several false memory paradigms have been devised to investigate how suggestion can instill the formation of false memories.

FALSE MEMORY AND SUGGESTIBILITY PARADIGMS

One of the most well researched methods used to study (children's) false memories elicited by suggestion is the misinformation paradigm (Loftus, 2005; Loftus & Klemfuss, 2023). This paradigm generally uses the following procedure: Participants are presented with some stimuli (e.g., video of crime) or are involved in an interactive event (e.g., mock crime). After this, they receive misinformation (i.e., false suggestive information) concerning the stimuli or the event itself. Examples of such misinformation include participants being presented with a supposed eyewitness account of the stimuli/event that contains false information (e.g., stating that the culprit had a gun when in fact it was a knife), or participants receiving suggestive questions about the experiences (e.g., "The culprit was carrying a gun, right?"). Last, participants' memory for the original stimuli/event is tested. The central finding is that a significant proportion (about 30%; see Wylie et al., 2014) of participants accept the misinformation and report to have experienced it during the original stimuli/event presentation.

Such misinformation procedures have been studied with children as participants. A canonical example is the Mr. Science experiment (e.g., Poole & Lindsay, 1995). In these experiments, children (ranging oftentimes from 3 to 7 years old) interacted with Mr. Science, who previously showed the children several science demonstrations (e.g., folding different types of paper airplanes). After several months, their parents read the children stories about this interaction. These stories contained events that were experienced, but also events that were not experienced (e.g., that Mr. Science wiped children's faces with a foul-smelling wipe). Moreover, the children were asked suggestive questions about these events (e.g., "Did you make paper airplanes with Mr. Science?"). What was detected is that children made many errors, ones consistent with the suggestions, when they were interviewed about their interaction with Mr. Science.

Another procedure that has been used to induce (children's) false memories is the false memory implantation paradigm (Loftus & Pickrell, 1995). In this procedure, participants are told that they experienced several events in their childhood. Although several of these really happened and are provided by participants' parents, the experimenter fabricates one of these events. The participants' parents also confirm that these latter events have not occurred. For example, in one of the first studies, participants were falsely told that they got lost in a shopping mall when they were children. After several suggestive interviews, a quarter of participants became convinced that they experienced the false event and came up with elaborate accounts of the (false) experience.

A critique of false memory implantation studies is that they sometimes used different scoring systems which might have affected false memory propensity (e.g., Shaw, 2018; for a recent discussion on false memory implantation research, see Andrews & Brewin, 2024; Murphy & Greene, 2025; Wade et al., 2025). Therefore, Scoboria and colleagues (2017) reanalyzed previous false memory accounts using a new scoring system that was based on the latest insight into false memory production. They found that between 30% and almost 50% of participants fall prey to these suggestions in these studies and create false autobiographical memories for entire events (Scoboria et al., 2017; see also Arce et al., 2023, for a meta-analysis). Furthermore, a large variety of false events have been successfully implanted in children's and adults' memory, such as committing a crime (Shaw & Porter, 2015), receiving a rectal enema (Otgaar et al., 2010), and going on a hot air balloon ride (Wade et al., 2002).

In one such study, Pezdek and Hodge (1999) suggested to nineteen 5- to 7-year-old children and twenty 9- to 12-year-old children that they experienced two false events when they were 4 years old. Specifically, they were told that they were lost in a shopping mall and that they received a rectal enema. In general, children were more likely to falsely assent to the shopping mall narrative than to the rectal enema narrative. Specifically, while 14 children falsely remembered the plausible (but not implausible) event, only one child falsely recalled the implausible event but not plausible event. Although both the misinformation and false memory implantation paradigms have yielded false memory reports successfully with both children and adults, there are also false memory paradigms specifically designed for children. One illustrative example is the rumor mongering paradigm.

The *rumor mongering paradigm* has been developed to deal with natural conversations that occur between children or between children and their parents (Principe et al., 2006). Such conversations can sometimes be highly suggestive when they concern sensitive topics such as abuse (e.g., Principe & Schindewolf, 2012). In one of the first demonstrations, four groups of 3- to 5-year-olds watched a staged magic show at their school (Principe et al., 2006). During the magic show, a magician tried to pull a rabbit out of his hat. Despite several attempts, the magician failed, apologized, and left the school. Children were divided into four groups: overheard, classmate, witness, and control group. In the overheard group, children heard two adults talking to each other and alleging that the trick failed because the rabbit had gotten loose in the school. Children in the classmate group did not hear this conversation and were classmates of the children in the overheard group. The critical question was whether children in the classmate group would later hear about this rumor from the overheard group children and falsely recall that the rabbit had gotten loose in the school. Children in the control group were not exposed to any rumor, and children in the witness group witnessed a loose rabbit at the school.

After two weeks, all children were interviewed about the magic show. The most interesting finding was that children in the overheard and classmate groups were as susceptible to wrongly claiming to have seen the loose rabbit as children in the witness group who had seen a loose rabbit. This finding demonstrates that rumors can leak into children's recollections, thereby showing the possible suggestive nature of natural conversations (Principe et al., 2006).

Taken together, several false memory methods have been constructed to investigate the production of false memories in adults as well as in children. Apart from these false memory paradigms, several theories have been developed to explain how false memories can occur. We will not explain all of them but will discuss some selected key theories.

FALSE MEMORY THEORIES

In this section, we will describe three influential theories to explain the occurrence of false memories.

Source Monitoring Framework

One influential theory underlying the formation of false memories is the *source monitoring framework* (SMF; Johnson et al., 1993), which postulates that people make judgments about the origin or source of their memories. The source can refer to the context or circumstances by which a memory is obtained.

For example, someone who witnesses the robbery of a bank acquires a memory in the context (spatial, temporal, visual context) of this experience. Indeed, we can have memories of events that we truly experienced, such as the bank robbery (i.e., these have an external source). However, we can also have memories of events that we did not actually experience but simply imagined or dreamed (i.e., these have an internal source). People are often unable to directly retrieve the source of a memory, but they can make attributions concerning the source of their memories. These attributions stem from the phenomenology of mental representations—memories with different origins seem to differ from each other in certain phenomenological characteristics. So, for example, when a mental representation contains many visual, spatial, and auditory details, people attribute this mental representation as originating from an external source. Thereby, they decide that mental representation refers to a true memory of an event that they experienced. However, when a mental representation contains many cognitive operations (e.g., thinking or reasoning about an experience), people might attribute this representation to an internal source such as an imagined event.

The process of source monitoring is not error proof. Source monitoring errors might arise if, for example, mental representations based on internal sources contain as many memory characteristics as mental representations based on external sources. Such a situation can arise if, for example, someone is confronted with external suggestions about an event and then imagines what could have occurred. This process can then lead to a mental representation that has a phenomenology akin to that of a memory for an experienced event. In such a case, source monitoring errors can evolve in which the mental representations are then attributed to an external rather than internal source. Such a misattribution can then lead to a false memory that the suggested event was truly experienced.

Fuzzy-Trace Theory

According to the *fuzzy-trace theory* (FTT; Brainerd et al., 2008), people store two independent memory traces when experiencing an event. Specifically, FTT postulates that people store verbatim and gist traces during an experience. *Verbatim traces* refer to memories of specific details of an event. In the example of the bank robbery, a verbatim trace might be the color of the jacket of the bank robber. *Gist traces*, on the other hand, involve the storage of the underlying meaning of an event. Going back to the bank robbery example, a gist trace might be that the experience concerned a bank robbery. Verbatim traces fade rapidly over time as the details of an experience are forgotten. According to FTT, this means that people will increasingly rely on the retrieval of gist traces. Because retrieving gist traces involves the recollection of nonspecific information and the general meaning of an event, gist trace extraction fosters false memory production, leaving room for the person remembering the incident to add in (suggested) details later.

Associative Activation Theory

Associative-activation theory (AAT; Howe et al., 2009) uses the notion of spreading activation to explain the formation of false memories. AAT postulates that encoding an event leads to spreading activation across a network of related concepts (also called nodes), which can result in the activation of concepts that are related but not experienced during an event. Looking back at the bank robbery example, when the witness is thinking about or remembering the robber, the spreading activation might trigger concepts such as a weapon. Activation of the concept of weapon can lead to the remembrance that the culprit carried a gun although, in fact, the culprit had a knife (a different weapon). Hence, spreading activation can lead to the activation of related nonpresented details leading to the creation of false memories.

In sum, several theories exist to elucidate the formation of false memories. These theories have been important in the study of the different factors that might affect the propensity (of children) to form false memories.

FACTORS INVOLVED IN FALSE MEMORY CREATION

We will now discuss several factors that have been shown to affect the risk of producing false memories. Some of them have been studied because of predictions that were borne out of several false memory theories. Many of the studies conducted in suggestibility and false memory creation are lab-based. This limits the generalizability of these studies to complex cases of child sexual abuse in which a multitude of factors (e.g., social factors) might have led to false memories. Nonetheless, lab-based studies are informative as they can examine potential false memory factors in a controlled setting.

Age

An important factor when considering false memory creation is whether children or adults are more or less likely to produce false memories. Research in the area of false memories induced by suggestion seems to show a rather consistent pattern. Specifically, suggestion-based false memory development follows an age-related decrease. This means that younger children are more at risk of producing false memories than older children who are in turn more susceptible to false memories than adults (e.g., Sutherland & Hayne, 2001). The SMF, which stipulates that children experience more difficulties in monitoring the sources of their memories than adults (Lindsay et al., 1991), nicely explains this age pattern. For example, Sutherland and Hayne (2001; experiment 2) presented 11- and 12-year-olds and adults with a video (i.e., child getting lost, then found by a policeman) and presented them—among others—with misleading information. The authors found that the children were more likely to go along with the misleading information than the adult participants.

However, theories such as FTT and AAT predict a so-called developmental reversal effect, suggesting that children are less likely to form false memories than adults (Brainerd et al., 2008; Otgaar et al., 2018). In many studies on suggestion-induced false memories, the necessary ingredients are missing to find and examine such developmental reversals. That is, according to the tenets of FTT and AAT, developmental reversals in suggestion-induced false memories can appear under certain circumstances. Specifically, developmental reversals appear if the encoded stimuli contain semantically-related or associatively-related details, and when the misinformation contains false details that are associatively related to the encoded experience. Studies containing such critical ingredients have indeed found that in some contexts false memories are more likely to occur in adults rather than children, and more in older rather than younger children (Brainerd et al., 2008; Ceci et al., 2007; Goswick et al., 2013; Otgaar et al., 2016).

Plausibility

Memory scholars have argued that before false memories can be implanted, two conditions should be met (e.g., Mazzoni & Kirsch, 2002; Scoboria et al., 2004). First, people should appraise a false event as an event that could plausibly occur. Then, people need to start to believe that the false event happened. Only when such a false belief has been formed can implanted false memories be induced. If true, this theoretical position predicts that plausible false events ought to be more easily implanted than implausible false events.

False memory research has indeed revealed that false memories for plausible events are easier to be evoked than false memories for implausible events. For example, Pezdek and colleagues (1997; experiment 2) suggested to 20 adult participants that they experienced a plausible (lost in a shopping mall) and an implausible event (receiving a rectal enema) in their childhood. Fifteen percent ($n = 3$) falsely recalled the plausible event, but no one endorsed the implausible event. This finding was also replicated in children (discussed previously) in which the plausible false event was more likely to give rise to implanted false memories than the implausible event (Pezdek & Hodge, 1999).

However, Strange and colleagues (2006) argued that event plausibility can be affected by many different factors that might also influence false memory production. In their study, 6-year-olds and 10-year-olds were interviewed thrice about true events and two false events. The first false event was a hot air balloon ride, which was deemed plausible, while the implausible event concerned drinking tea with Prince Charles. Interestingly, in this study, participants received doctored photographs depicting them in the false events, rendering the events more personally plausible. The authors found that false memories were equally likely to be implanted for the plausible and implausible event (for similar results, see Otgaar et al., 2009). The argument that event plausibility can be affected by certain factors is supported by Scoboria and colleagues (2006), who showed that if participants receive information that an event happens commonly (also called prevalence information), the personal plausibility of an event increases.

Valence

Another important variable of interest in the formation of children's false memories is the valence or emotional aspect of an event. FTT and AAT would predict that negative false memories are easier to induce than neutral false memories (e.g., Bookbinder & Brainerd, 2016; Howe et al., 2010). According to FTT, emotionally negative experiences enhance gist memory thereby facilitating false memory formation. AAT stipulates that emotionally negative experiences lead to more interrelated and dense memory networks which increases the chance that spreading activation will activate nonpresented but related concepts in the memory system (Howe et al., 2010).

A recent systematic review did not reveal a consistent pattern in the link between valence and adults' false memories induced by misinformation (Sharma et al., 2023). The only finding (based on a limited set of studies) was that false memories were most likely to be produced for peripheral, negatively-valenced misinformation. Research into children's implanted false memories is also scarce. One study found that negative false memories were more easily implanted than neutral ones (Otgaar et al., 2008), but clearly more research is needed in the area of valence and suggestion-induced false memories. In this latter study, it was suggested to children that they were accused of copying off their neighbor's homework in class (i.e., negative event) or that they had to move to another classroom (i.e., neutral event). In two interviews, it was shown that children produced more false memories for the negative than neutral event.

Prior Knowledge

Another important variable that can affect (children's) false memories is having prior knowledge of an event. Castel and colleagues (2007) published an interesting demonstration of the role of prior knowledge in false memory formation. In their study, participants with low or high levels of knowledge about American football had to learn a list of animal names which were also names of American football teams (e.g., lions, broncos, bears). The participants who had more knowledge of American football not only remembered more animal names correctly but were also more likely to remember names that were related but not presented during encoding (e.g., eagles) than participants with low knowledge of American football. Clearly, this finding shows that having knowledge can come at a cost because it might amplify false memory generation. In essence, this finding is related to spreading activation accounts of false memories (e.g., Howe et al., 2009). Having elaborate knowledge goes hand in hand with an extensive knowledge base and memory network in which spreading activation can easily activate related but not presented concepts.

The role of prior knowledge has also been examined in the context of children's false memories. Pezdek and Hodge's study (1999), which showed that children were more likely to form false memories for a plausible than implausible event, was also argued to be a study in which children had more script-related knowledge (knowledge about the sequence of an event) about the plausible event than the implausible event. However, this means that it is not clear whether the false memory findings were mainly driven by plausibility or also script knowledge.

Hence, Otgaar and colleagues (2010) used two false events that were equated on levels of plausibility and valence but differed in script knowledge (receiving a rectal enema: low script; having your fingers stuck in a mousetrap: high script). The events were chosen based on a pilot study in which children were asked to report what typically happens during certain events (i.e., script knowledge). Based on this pilot study, two events were selected that statistically differed in terms of the children's amount of script knowledge. Children aged 7 and 11 were suggestively interviewed on two occasions and told that they had experienced the high or low script event when they were 4 years old. Children receiving the high script event were more susceptible to false memory generation than children in the low script group. Furthermore, 23% of the younger children ($n = 7$) falsely recalled the enema event at interview 1 and 19% ($n = 6$) at interview 2. None of the older children falsely assented to the enema event. Like Castel and colleagues' (2007) work, this study suggests that having knowledge about an event might increase children's willingness to go along with suggestion.

CORRECTING AND PREVENTING CHILDREN'S FALSE MEMORIES

An important goal in child forensic interviews is to prevent false memories from happening as they might lead to false accusations and miscarriages of justice. Several ways exist to prevent children from developing false memories. A straightforward manner is to ensure that child forensic interviewers are trained to use open-ended questions that maximize the amount of accurate reporting, and not to use suggestive questions (Korkman et al., 2024; Saywitz & Camparo, 2014). The use of open-ended questions is imperative because children can accurately recount events, even when the events are traumatic in nature (e.g., Paz-Alonso et al., 2012).

One such training method is the National Institute of Child Health and Human Development (NICHD) interview protocol. The NICHD Protocol is a proven and effective way to stimulate detailed accounts in children (e.g., Lamb et al., 2007; La Rooy et al., 2015). The NICHD Protocol has several phases. In the first phase, children receive several ground rules concerning the interview such as telling them that it is okay if they do not know the answer to a question they are asked. Following this, the interview commences with a rapport building phase. Rapport building is embedded to increase children's level of trust with the interview and interviewer (e.g., asking about hobbies or favorite foods). The idea behind rapport building is to create an environment in which children feel more comfortable talking about traumatic events. After the rapport building phase, children engage in an episodic memory training in which they are asked to provide a detailed account of an autobiographical experience (e.g., what they did the day before the interview). The rationale is that children get accustomed to retrieving autobiographical memories because they will need to retrieve them concerning an alleged traumatic event later in the interview. The most important phase is the substantive phase where children receive open-ended questions about the alleged event. Specifically, child forensic interviewers are trained in asking so-called invitation questions, which are questions in the form of "tell me what happened." The crux of these questions is that they facilitate the reporting of detailed and accurate accounts. Only after children's recall is exhausted with invitation questions can interviewers shift to the use of more closed questions such as directive (e.g., "Where did it happen?") or option-posing (e.g., "Did it happen at home or somewhere else?"). However, even when interviewers resort to the use of such closed questions, the goal of the NICHD Protocol is always to combine these questions again with invitations (also called pairing).

Research has demonstrated that when child forensic interviewers are trained in using the NICHD Protocol, they ask more invitation questions than non-trained interviewers. Furthermore, the NICHD Protocol has been shown to lead to a reduction in the use of suggestive questions, thereby protecting children against the formation of false memories (Benia et al., 2015). Equally interesting, the use of the NICHD Protocol has been associated with an increase in the number of reported details by children (e.g., Erens et al., 2022).

Although following the NICHD Protocol prevents the use of suggestive questioning in interviews, sometimes the suggestive damage has been done before any forensic interview is conducted. For example, it is not uncommon for children to talk about an alleged traumatic event with parents, caretakers, or friends (e.g., Principe & London, 2022). During such (parental) conversations, it can happen that parents ask their children in a suggestive fashion about experienced and nonexperienced incidents. A concern, then, is that children's testimony is already unduly contaminated before a formal interview at, for example, the child protection agency. Moreover, after a well-conducted child forensic interview, children might also be confronted with suggestive information. This can happen, for example, when they return home and talk with parents, caretakers, or friends (see Figure 7.1). A pivotal issue arises whether a well- conducted interview (such as one delivered via the NICHD Protocol) can counteract previously presented misinformation or protect against subsequent misinformation. Thus, apart from the fact that the use of open-ended questions (such as recommended in the NICHD Protocol) can lead to detailed accounts, it is important to know whether such recommended procedures to interview children might also have an additional benefit in editing out misinformation.

FIGURE 7.1. Schematic Representation Showing That Misinformation Can Occur Before or After an Investigative Interview

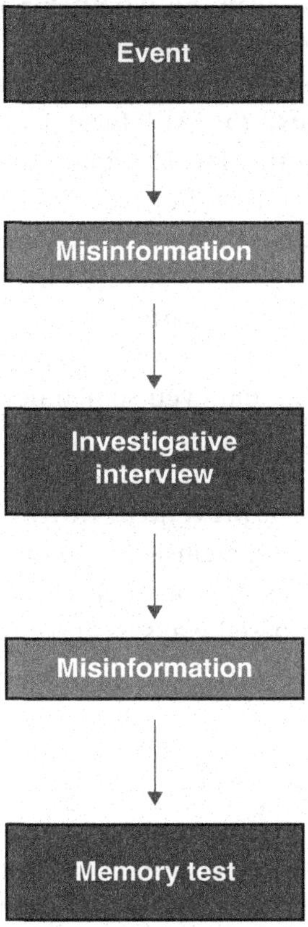

Note. Arrows show the points where misinformation can occur (before or after).

Empirical research on whether a well-conducted child interview can neutralize the debilitating effects of previously encountered misinformation has shown that such interviews can sometimes decrease children's reporting of this misinformation at a later memory test. For example, in one experiment, 4- and 8-year-old children were presented with a video of a birthday party (Holliday, 2003). After 1 day, children received misinformation regarding the video. Then, one group of children received an empirically based interview (i.e., the cognitive interview) while another group was interviewed using a control interview. Following this, children received a final memory test about the video. When children were questioned using the cognitive interview, they were less likely to report misinformation in their own accounts than those who were not interviewed by an empirically validated interview protocol (but see also Hayes & Delamothe, 1997).

This finding is reminiscent of postwarning studies on the misinformation effect (Blank & Launay, 2014). These studies have revealed that when participants are told that they, for example, have been confronted with misinformation, they are less likely to endorse this misinformation on later memory tests than participants who were not warned. Although interesting, research with children in this area is still highly limited (Blank & Launay, 2014).[2]

Another possibility is to examine whether a well-conducted interview might protect from the reporting of misinformation presented after the interview. When children are interviewed using empirically based principles (e.g., asking open-ended questions), they will form detailed and accurate accounts of an event. Remembering this level of detail might protect children from incorporating misinformation that they receive at a later stage (e.g., Brainerd et al., 2008). However, findings in this research area are mixed. Some studies found that child forensic interviews had no effect at all on the reporting of misinformation children are faced with later (e.g., Roos af Hjelmsäter et al., 2012; Holliday, 2003), whereas other studies have found that such interviews decreased (Erens et al., 2022) and even sometimes increased the reporting of misinformation (Otgaar et al., 2019).

Collectively, there are different strands of research on how children's false memories can be corrected or prevented. However, research in this area is limited and sometimes evinces inconsistent findings. Because of the obvious practical ramifications of this line of research, it is imperative that future research focuses on science-based ways to prevent or correct the production of children's false memories.

CONCLUDING REMARKS

A major reason why scientific research in the area of children's false memories commenced is that legal cases showed the corrupting effects of suggestion on children's memory reports (e.g., Garven et al., 1998). In general, research has shown that although children's memory can be highly accurate, even for traumatic events, they can also be highly vulnerable to suggestion, thereby producing false memories. This knowledge is vital for legal professionals because it shows that children can accurately talk about experienced traumatic events such as sexual abuse. Simultaneously, however, legal professionals should be wary when there are signs that children's reports were influenced by suggestion as the reliability of their reports might have been jeopardized.

Therefore, in cases where children's testimony is of high relevance for legal decision making, it is advisable to consult expert witnesses with expertise on children's memory to evaluate the reliability of children's testimony (e.g., Otgaar et al., 2017; Zajac et al., 2013). Such experts can advise the court about whether children's statements are grounded in reality or whether there are reasons to doubt these statements. Two key recommendations are important

[2]There is also research on prewarning and false memory creation. However, such work is less relevant for discussions on misinformation effects in real life cases: In such cases it is not generally known whether people will be exposed to misinformation at a later stage.

for experts working with child sexual abuse cases. First, when reading a case file concerning alleged child (sexual) abuse, it is imperative to examine the first disclosure of the alleged trauma and examine the context of this first statement. If the first statement of the child happened spontaneously, this supports the reliability of the account; however, if there are signals that children were asked suggestive questions, then there are doubts concerning the reliability of the statement. Second, in expert witness work, it is recommended to use scenarios when evaluating accounts of children (Otgaar et al., 2017). That is, when expert witnesses are asked to evaluate the reliability of children's statements, they need to find elements in a case that supports a scenario that the statements refer to an experienced event (e.g., spontaneous statement). However, they also need to consider an alternative scenario where the children's statements refer to a nonexperienced event and might be based on a false memory. Using multiple scenarios can reduce expert witnesses' likelihood of falling prey to confirmation bias—only looking at elements in a case that support one scenario, thereby neglecting the possibility of other scenarios (Korkman et al., 2024; Lidén, 2023, Chapter 3; Vredeveldt et al., 2022).

Taken together, children's false memories can have damaging consequences in different areas such as child protective contexts or the legal arena. When children are interviewed about alleged incidents of trauma, it is vital that such interviews are conducted using science-based principles thereby reducing the formation of children's false memories. Furthermore, when children's statements appear in court, memory experts can educate the court about the reliability of these statements. Such expert witness testimony can help triers of fact to base their judgments on true statements of children who were abused yet also acquit innocent suspects who have been accused based on children's false memories.

REFERENCES

Andrews, B., & Brewin, C. R. (2024). Lost in the mall? Interrogating judgements of false memory. *Applied Cognitive Psychology, 38*(6), e70012. https://doi.org/10.1002/acp.70012

Arce, R., Selaya, A., Sanmarco, J., & Fariña, F. (2023). Implanting rich autobiographical false memories: Meta-analysis for forensic practice and judicial judgment making. *International Journal of Clinical and Health Psychology, 23*(4), 100386. https://doi.org/10.1016/j.ijchp.2023.100386

Benia, L. R., Hauck-Filho, N., Dillenburg, M., & Stein, L. M. (2015). The NICHD investigative interview protocol: A meta-analytic review. *Journal of Child Sexual Abuse, 24*(3), 259–279. https://doi.org/10.1080/10538712.2015.1006749

Bernstein, D. M., & Loftus, E. F. (2009). How to tell if a particular memory is true or false. *Perspectives on Psychological Science, 4*(4), 370–374. https://doi.org/10.1111/j.1745-6924.2009.01140.x

Blank, H., & Launay, C. (2014). How to protect eyewitness memory against the misinformation effect: A meta-analysis of post-warning studies. *Journal of Applied Research in Memory and Cognition, 3*(2), 77–88. https://doi.org/10.1016/j.jarmac.2014.03.005

Bookbinder, S. H., & Brainerd, C. J. (2016). Emotion and false memory: The context–content paradox. *Psychological Bulletin, 142*(12), 1315–1351. https://doi.org/10.1037/bul0000077

Brainerd, C. J., Reyna, V. F., & Ceci, S. J. (2008). Developmental reversals in false memory: A review of data and theory. *Psychological Bulletin, 134*(3), 343–382. https://doi.org/10.1037/0033-2909.134.3.343

Calado, B. (2022). *Revictimisation and false memory formation.* [Doctoral Thesis, Maastricht University, University of Gothenburg]. ProefschriftMaken. https://doi.org/10.26481/dis.20220520bc

Castel, A. D., McCabe, D. P., Roediger, H. L., & Heitman, J. L. (2007). The dark side of expertise: Domain-specific memory errors. *Psychological Science, 18*(1), 3–5. https://doi.org/10.1111/j.1467-9280.2007.01838.x

Ceci, S. J., & Bruck, M. (1995). *Jeopardy in the courtroom: A scientific analysis of children's testimony.* American Psychological Association.

Ceci, S. J., Papierno, P. B., & Kulkofsky, S. (2007). Representational constraints on children's suggestibility. *Psychological Science, 18*(6), 503–509. https://doi.org/10.1111/j.1467-9280.2007.01930.x

Erens, B., Otgaar, H., De Ruiter, C., van Bragt, D., & Hershkowitz, I. (2022). The NICHD interview protocol used by Dutch child protection workers: Effects on interview style, children's reported information and susceptibility to suggestion. *Applied Cognitive Psychology, 36*(1), 7–18. https://doi.org/10.1002/acp.3893

Garven, S., Wood, J. M., Malpass, R. S., & Shaw, J. S., III. (1998). More than suggestion: The effect of interviewing techniques from the McMartin Preschool case. *Journal of Applied Psychology, 83*(3), 347–359. https://doi.org/10.1037/0021-9010.83.3.347

Goswick, A. E., Mullet, H. G., & Marsh, E. J. (2013). Suggestibility from stories: Can production difficulties and source monitoring explain a developmental reversal? *Journal of Cognition and Development, 14*(4), 607–616. https://doi.org/10.1080/15248372.2012.710864

Hayes, B. K., & Delamothe, K. (1997). Cognitive interviewing procedures and suggestibility in children's recall. *Journal of Applied Psychology, 82*(4), 562–577. https://doi.org/10.1037/0021-9010.82.4.562

Holliday, R. E. (2003). The effect of a prior cognitive interview on children's acceptance of misinformation. *Applied Cognitive Psychology, 17*(4), 443–457. https://doi.org/10.1002/acp.879

Hood, L. (2019). *A city possessed: The Christchurch civic creche case.* Otago University Press.

Howe, M. L. (2022). Forensic consequences of creating and shaping children's memories. *Journal of Applied Research in Memory and Cognition, 11*(3), 303–306. https://doi.org/10.1037/mac0000051

Howe, M. L., Candel, I., Otgaar, H., Malone, C., & Wimmer, M. C. (2010). Valence and the development of immediate and long-term false memory illusions. *Memory, 18*(1), 58–75. https://doi.org/10.1080/09658210903476514

Howe, M. L., Wimmer, M. C., Gagnon, N., & Plumpton, S. (2009). An associative-activation theory of children's and adults' memory illusions. *Journal of Memory and Language, 60*(2), 229–251. https://doi.org/10.1016/j.jml.2008.10.002

Johnson, M. K., Hashtroudi, S., & Lindsay, D. S. (1993). Source monitoring. *Psychological Bulletin, 114*(1), 3–28. https://doi.org/10.1037/0033-2909.114.1.3

Korkman, J., Otgaar, H., Geven, L. M., Bull, R., Cyr, M., Hershkowitz, I., Mäkelä, J.-M., Mattison, M., Milne, R., Santtila, P., van Koppen, P., Memon, A., Danby, M., Filipovic, L., Garcia, F. J., Gewehr, E., Gomes Bell, O., Järvilehto, L., Kask, K., . . . Volbert, R. (2024). White paper on forensic child interviewing: Research-based recommendations by the European Association of Psychology and Law. *Psychology, Crime & Law,* 1–44. https://doi.org/10.1080/1068316x.2024.2324098

Lamb, M. E., Orbach, Y., Hershkowitz, I., Esplin, P. W., & Horowitz, D. (2007). A structured forensic interview protocol improves the quality and informativeness of investigative interviews with children: A review of research using the NICHD investigative interview protocol. *Child Abuse & Neglect, 31*(11–12), 1201–1231. https://doi.org/10.1016/j.chiabu.2007.03.021

La Rooy, D., Brubacher, S. P., Aromäki-Stratos, A., Cyr, M., Hershkowitz, I., Korkman, J., Myklebust, T., Naka, M., Peixoto, C. E., Roberts, K. P., Stewart, H., & Lamb, M. E. (2015). The NICHD protocol: A review of an internationally-used evidence-based tool for training child forensic interviewers. *Journal of Criminological Research, Policy and Practice, 1*(2), 76–89. https://doi.org/10.1108/JCRPP-01-2015-0001

Lidén, M. (2023). *Confirmation bias in criminal cases*. Oxford University Press. https://doi.org/10.1093/oso/9780192867643.003.0003

Lindsay, D. S., Johnson, M. K., & Kwon, P. (1991). Developmental changes in memory source monitoring. *Journal of Experimental Child Psychology, 52*(3), 297–318. https://doi.org/10.1016/0022-0965(91)90065-Z

Loftus, E. F. (2005). Planting misinformation in the human mind: A 30-year investigation of the malleability of memory. *Learning & Memory, 12*(4), 361–366. https://doi.org/10.1101/lm.94705

Loftus, E. F., & Klemfuss, J. Z. (2023). Misinformation—Past, present, and future. *Psychology, Crime & Law, 30*(4), 312–318. https://doi.org/10.1080/1068316X.2023.2219813

Loftus, E. F., & Pickrell, J. E. (1995). The formation of false memories. *Psychiatric Annals, 25*(12), 720–725. https://doi.org/10.3928/0048-5713-19951201-07

Mazzoni, G., & Kirsch, I. (2002). Autobiographical memories and beliefs: A preliminary metacognitive model. *Applied Metacognition*, 121–145. https://doi.org/10.1017/cbo9780511489976.007

Murphy, G., & Greene, C. M. (2025). Who got lost in the mall? Challenges in counting and classifying false memories. *Applied Cognitive Psychology, 39*(2), e70044. https://doi.org/10.1002/acp.70044

Otgaar, H., Candel, I., & Merckelbach, H. (2008). Children's false memories: Easier to elicit for a negative than for a neutral event. *Acta Psychologica, 128*(2), 350–354. https://doi.org/10.1016/j.actpsy.2008.03.009

Otgaar, H., Candel, I., Merckelbach, H., & Wade, K. A. (2009). Abducted by a UFO: Prevalence information affects young children's false memories for an implausible event. *Applied Cognitive Psychology, 23*(1), 115–125. https://doi.org/10.1002/acp.1445

Otgaar, H., Candel, I., Scoboria, A., & Merckelbach, H. (2010). Script knowledge enhances the development of children's false memories. *Acta Psychologica, 133*(1), 57–63. https://doi.org/10.1016/j.actpsy.2009.09.002

Otgaar, H., Chan, J. C., Calado, B., & La Rooy, D. (2019). Immediate interviewing increases children's suggestibility in the short term, but not in the long term. *Legal and Criminological Psychology, 24*(1), 24–40. https://doi.org/10.1111/lcrp.12137

Otgaar, H., De Ruiter, C., Howe, M. L., Hoetmer, L., & van Reekum, P. (2017). A case concerning children's false memories of abuse: Recommendations regarding expert witness work. *Psychiatry, Psychology and Law, 24*(3), 365–378. https://doi.org/10.1080/13218719.2016.1230924

Otgaar, H., Howe, M. L., Brackmann, N., & Smeets, T. (2016). The malleability of developmental trends in neutral and negative memory illusions. *Journal of Experimental Psychology: General, 145*(1), 31–55. https://doi.org/10.1037/xge0000127

Otgaar, H., Howe, M. L., Merckelbach, H., & Muris, P. (2018). Who is the better eyewitness? Sometimes adults but at other times children. *Current Directions in Psychological Science, 27*(5), 378–385. https://doi.org/10.1177/0963721418770998

Paz-Alonso, P. M., Ogle, C. M., & Goodman, G. S. (2012). Children's memory in "scientific case studies" of child sexual abuse: A review. In B. Cooper, D. Griesel, & M. Ternes (Eds.), *Applied issues in investigative interviewing, eyewitness memory, and credibility assessment* (pp. 143–171). Springer. https://doi.org/10.1007/978-1-4614-5547-9_6

Pezdek, K., Finger, K., & Hodge, D. (1997). Planting false childhood memories: The role of event plausibility. *Psychological Science, 8*(6), 437–441. https://doi.org/10.1111/j.1467-9280.1997.tb00457.x

Pezdek, K., & Hodge, D. (1999). Planting false childhood memories in children: The role of event plausibility. *Child Development, 70*(4), 887–895. https://doi.org/10.1111/1467-8624.00064

Poole, D. A., & Lindsay, D. S. (1995). Interviewing preschoolers: Effects of nonsuggestive techniques, parental coaching, and leading questions on reports of nonexperienced events. *Journal of Experimental Child Psychology, 60*(1), 129–154. https://doi.org/10.1006/jecp.1995.1035

Principe, G. F., Kanaya, T., Ceci, S. J., & Singh, M. (2006). Believing is seeing: How rumors can engender false memories in preschoolers. *Psychological Science, 17*(3), 243–248. https://doi.org/10.1111/j.1467-9280.2006.01692.x

Principe, G. F., & London, K. (2022). How parents can shape what children remember: Implications for the testimony of young witnesses. *Journal of Applied Research in Memory and Cognition, 11*(3), 289–302. https://doi.org/10.1037/mac0000059

Principe, G. F., & Schindewolf, E. (2012). Natural conversations as a source of false memories in children: Implications for the testimony of young witnesses. *Developmental Review, 32*(3), 205–223. https://doi.org/10.1016/j.dr.2012.06.003

Roos af Hjelmsäter, E., Strömwall, L. A., & Granhag, P. A. (2012). The self-administered interview: A means of improving children's eyewitness performance? *Psychology, Crime & Law, 18*(10), 897–911. https://doi.org/10.1080/1068316X.2011.582844

Saywitz, K. J., & Camparo, L. B. (2014). Interviewing children: A primer. In G. B. Melton, A. Ben-Arieh, J. Cashmore, G. S. Goodman, & N. K. Worley (Eds.), *The SAGE handbook of child research* (pp. 371–390). Sage. https://doi.org/10.4135/9781446294758.n21

Schreiber, N., Bellah, L. D., Martinez, Y., McLaurin, K. A., Strok, R., Garven, S., & Wood, J. M. (2006). Suggestive interviewing in the McMartin Preschool and Kelly Michaels daycare abuse cases: A case study. *Social Influence, 1*(1), 16–47. https://doi.org/10.1080/15534510500361739

Scoboria, A., Mazzoni, G., Kirsch, I., & Jimenez, S. (2006). The effects of prevalence and script information on plausibility, belief, and memory of autobiographical events. *Applied Cognitive Psychology, 20*(8), 1049–1064. https://doi.org/10.1002/acp.1240

Scoboria, A., Mazzoni, G., Kirsch, I., & Relyea, M. (2004). Plausibility and belief in autobiographical memory. *Applied Cognitive Psychology, 18*(7), 791–807. https://doi.org/10.1002/acp.1062

Scoboria, A., Wade, K. A., Lindsay, D. S., Azad, T., Strange, D., Ost, J., & Hyman, I. E. (2017). A mega-analysis of memory reports from eight peer-reviewed false memory implantation studies. *Memory, 25*(2), 146–163. https://doi.org/10.1080/09658211.2016.1260747

Sharma, P. R., Wade, K. A., & Jobson, L. (2023). A systematic review of the relationship between emotion and susceptibility to misinformation. *Memory, 31*(1), 1–21. https://doi.org/10.1080/09658211.2022.2120623

Shaw, J. (2018). How can researchers tell whether someone has a false memory? Coding strategies in autobiographical false-memory research: A reply to Wade, Garry, and Pezdek (2018). *Psychological Science, 29*(3), 477–480. https://doi.org/10.1177/0956797618759552

Shaw, J., & Porter, S. (2015). Constructing rich false memories of committing crime. *Psychological Science, 26*(3), 291–301. https://doi.org/10.1177/0956797614562862

Strange, D., Sutherland, R., & Garry, M. (2006). Event plausibility does not determine children's false memories. *Memory, 14*(8), 937–951. https://doi.org/10.1080/09658210600896105

Sutherland, R., & Hayne, H. (2001). Age-related changes in the misinformation effect. *Journal of Experimental Child Psychology, 79*(4), 388–404. https://doi.org/10.1006/jecp.2000.2610

Vredeveldt, A., van Rosmalen, E. A., Van Koppen, P. J., Dror, I. E., & Otgaar, H. (2022). Legal psychologists as experts: Guidelines for minimizing bias. *Psychology, Crime & Law, 30*(7), 1–25. https://doi.org/10.1080/1068316X.2022.2114476

Wade, K. A., Garry, M., Don Read, J., & Lindsay, D. S. (2002). A picture is worth a thousand lies: Using false photographs to create false childhood memories. *Psychonomic Bulletin & Review, 9*(3), 597–603. https://doi.org/10.3758/bf03196318

Wade, K. A., Riesthuis, P., Bücken, C., Otgaar, H., & Loftus, E. F. (2025). Still lost in the mall—False memories happen and that's what matters. *Applied Cognitive Psychology, 39*(1), e70028. https://doi.org/10.1002/acp.70028

Wood, J. M., & Garven, S. (2000). How sexual abuse interviews go astray: Implications for prosecutors, police, and child protection services. *Child Maltreatment, 5*(2), 109–118. https://doi.org/10.1177/1077559500005002003

Wylie, L. E., Patihis, L., McCuller, L. L., Davis, D., Brank, E. M., Loftus, E. F., & Bornstein, B. H. (2014). Misinformation effect in older versus younger adults: A meta-analysis and review. In M. P. Toglia, D. F. Ross, J. Pozzulo, & E. Pica (Eds.), *The elderly eyewitness in court* (pp. 38–66). Psychology Press.

Zajac, R., Garry, M., London, K., Goodyear-Smith, F., & Hayne, H. (2013). Misconceptions about childhood sexual abuse and child witnesses: Implications for psychological experts in the courtroom. *Memory, 21*(5), 608–617. https://doi.org/10.1080/09658211.2013.778287

II

IMPROVING CHILDREN'S REPORTS

8

The Developmental Narrative Elaboration Interview

A Toolbox Approach for Interviewing Young Children

Lorinda B. Camparo

On July 15, 2002, Samantha Runnion was kidnapped while playing in front of her home at the Smoketree Condominium complex in Stanton, California. The next day her body was found 75 miles away on a deserted trail. The only witness to the kidnapping was her 5-year-old playmate, Sarah Ahn, who provided police with a detailed portrait of the kidnapper and his truck. Within 24 hours of discovering Samantha's body, police began checking alibis for registered sex-offenders in the area and fielding tips; however, nothing substantive was produced. Then, after circulating a composite sketch based on Sarah's description of the kidnapper and his truck, police received a phone tip identifying Alejandro Avila by name and recommending that police question him. Following up, police discovered that Avila had been acquitted in 2001 of molesting two young girls over a year-long period between 1998 and 1999; one was the daughter of Avila's then-girlfriend, and the other was the girl's cousin. Police also discovered that the daughter of Avila's girlfriend lived part-time with her father and brothers in the same Smoketree Condominium complex that Samantha lived in, and that she was friends with Samantha's older sister. The police arrested Avila within 4 days of Samantha's abduction and murder. Three years later, based on extensive DNA evidence, Alejandro Avila was convicted and sentenced to death (Note: since Avila's sentencing, the death penalty was suspended in 2019 in California).

For the child forensic interviewer, this case makes two very important points. First, police stated that Sarah Ahn's detailed and accurate descriptions of the

https://doi.org/10.1037/0000492-008
Handbook on Child Witnesses: Improving Psychological Science and Legal Practice,
G. S. Goodman, T. D. Lyon, S. D. Hobbs, and R. Enriquez (Editors)

suspect and his truck were crucial to Avila's arrest, thus demonstrating that even young children can accurately report critical details about traumatic experiences they've witnessed. Nevertheless, police stated that had the tipster not provided the police with Avila's name, their initial efforts to find Samantha's murderer would ultimately have proven fruitless because having been acquitted in the 2001 case, Avila was not a registered sex offender (Leonard & Hanley, 2002). In Avila's first trial, there was no corroborating physical or DNA evidence; a conviction would have to have been based almost exclusively on two 9-year-old girls' testimonies, which jurors were unlikely to have found very convincing after cross-examination. So, the second important point made by this case is, as one law professor told reporters, "A child's credibility can be impeached so easily" (A. Brown et al., 2002, n.p.).

Together, these two points underscore both the successes and challenges of interviewing children. Often, corroborating physical evidence does not exist, as in Avila's first trial. Consequently, adult decision makers must rely heavily on information elicited from the child to take appropriate actions, which then makes the accuracy, veracity, and reliability of children's reports particularly critical. Generally, the success or failure of the interview will be determined in large part by the way the child is interviewed and the interviewer's skill (Akca et al., 2021; Cronch et al., 2006; Lamb, 2016; see also Chapter 9, this volume). When interviewers promote children's cooperation through nonsuggestive supportive interviewing and pose nonsuggestive, open-ended questions in developmentally appropriate language (Saywitz & Camparo, 1998), even very young children, like Sarah Ahn, can and do provide relatively spontaneous and quite accurate descriptions of their experiences (Brubacher et al., 2019; Hershkowitz & Lamb, 2020; Lamb et al., 2018), and jurors/fact finders find the child and interview more credible (Bala et al., 2001; Bell & Loftus, 2006; Peterson et al., 2013). But when interviewers pose suggestive or leading forced-choice questions, use developmentally inappropriate language, or include information in their questions that the child has not previously introduced, the errors in children's responses begin to mount (Lamb, 2016).

Currently, numerous semi-structured interview protocols, all based on memory, suggestibility, social influence, and developmental research, and all focused on best practice techniques, are in use around the world. These include, but are not limited to, the Step-Wise Guidelines (Yuille et al., 2009), Cognitive Interview (Fisher & Geiselman, 1992; Fisher et al., 2011), National Institute of Child Health and Human Development (NICHD) Standard Protocol (Lamb et al., 2008) and Revised Protocol (Lamb et al., 2018), and the Developmental Narrative Elaboration interview (Saywitz & Camparo, 2014a; see Saywitz and Camparo [2014b] for a description of these and other interview protocols). The remainder of this chapter will focus on the Developmental Narrative Elaboration (DNE) interview, a semistructured, developmentally sensitive, and highly flexible protocol that accommodates varying individual and development needs of different children and respects both legal requirements and social science research (Saywitz et al., 2017). The goal of this chapter is to provide readers in the fields of psychology, mental health, child welfare, law enforcement, and law with an overview of the form, function, and evidence base of the DNE—one of many currently available protocols that offer interviewers a "toolbox of techniques at the ready from which they can select the most appropriate tools for a particular child, context, or jurisdiction—techniques that they can justify based on the best available science" (Saywitz et al., 2017, p. 310). Although a full description and explanation of all the DNE tools and guidelines in using the DNE are beyond the scope of this chapter, the interested reader can find such information in Saywitz and Camparo (2014a).

THE DEVELOPMENTAL NARRATIVE ELABORATION: A TOOLBOX APPROACH

A toolbox of science-based techniques is "an assortment of techniques shown via accepted scientific methods to promote accurate and complete memory reports. In growing numbers, these tools have been packaged into science-based protocols" (Saywitz et al., 2017, p. 310). Because children are interviewed for a multitude of reasons, the DNE was specifically designed for information-gathering in a wide range of situations, including abuse, divorce, foster care, neglect, immigration, car accidents, or as a witness to violent or nonviolent crimes. In allegations where children are suspected to be victims and/or witnesses to a crime, accuracy and completeness of children's memories for a potentially traumatic event may be paramount. In cases of pending divorce and custody planning or placement in foster care, children's perceptions of caretaking, household chaos or structure, or how well their educational, social-emotional, and medical needs are being met may be critical. Thus, the goals of the interview will vary. To accommodate these various goals, the DNE provides the interviewer with a variety of tools that can be deployed as needed within the guidance of a semi-structured interview protocol.

Closing the Gap

The DNE was designed to address a problem all interviewers face—an inherent gap between the demands of the forensic interview and the capabilities of young children. Regarding children's cognitive and communicative capabilities, the DNE provides the scaffolding, structure, and guidance young children typically need to perform at a more advanced level than their developmental limitations normally allow (Vygotsky & Cole, 1978). Closing this gap is accomplished through a core template that lowers task demands to a child's developmental level and provides the child with a set of unbiased retrieval and communication strategies to help them organize their memory search and narrative. It also provides the interviewer with a variety of optional instructions and activities to enhance retrieval and reduce the potential for miscommunication and suggestibility.

The DNE was further designed to help the interviewer close the gap between the demands of the interview and the child's psychosocial needs. Saywitz and Camparo (2014a) noted that "Forensic interviews require a level of honesty, openness, and effort from children that is rare in their interactions with strangers" (p. 61). Closing this gap is accomplished by creating the physical, psychological, and social atmosphere that is so important to meeting the child's socioemotional needs. Research indicates that children's cooperation and motivation during the interview, the accuracy and completeness of their testimony, and their resistance to suggestive questions are all positively related to interviewers' ability to establish and maintain rapport through noncontingent, nonsuggestive social support (Hershkowitz et al., 2017; Lamb, 2016; Lamb et al., 2018; see Saywitz et al., 2019 for a review). Consequently, the DNE provides interviewers with recommendations (and a checklist) for how to create a physical setting that is private and safe with minimal distractions. It also provides interviewers with sample language for instructions to support persons if the child needs them to be present during the interview, as well as sample language that can be used to reassure the child of their safety. The interviewer is provided with guidelines for creating a nonsuggestive psychosocial atmosphere through

- smiling and maintaining eye contact and a relaxed body posture
- using a warm and friendly tone of voice
- demonstrating patience by tolerating the child's silence, not interrupting the child, and not helping the child by supplying words
- adopting an objective and nonjudgmental stance by avoiding derogatory or evaluative comments and not overreacting to any statements by the child
- acknowledging the child's effort without selectively reinforcing the content of any of the child's responses that might fit the interviewer's *a priori* beliefs
- being clear, unambiguous, and sincere in all utterances and facial expressions
- creating a working alliance by letting the child know that the interviewer needs the child's help because the interviewer was not present at the alleged event and has no special knowledge about the event.

As should be clear from these guidelines, the DNE approach to creating a nonsuggestive psychosocial atmosphere spans the full length of the interview, from before the child enters the room to the moments after the child leaves the room. Additionally, the DNE expands on these guidelines by providing sample language and activities the interviewer can use to break the ice, reduce reluctance in the child, and build rapport with children of all ages (see Chapters 3 and 4 in Saywitz & Camparo, 2014a).

Overview and Format

Consistent with most interview protocols that conform to best practices, the DNE is a three-phase interview process: a preparatory phase involving introductions, ground rules and instructions, rapport development, and narrative practice (phase 1); a substantive-questioning/information-gathering phase involving open-ended free-recall and follow-up questions (phase 2); and a closure phase during which the interviewer addresses the child's questions and assists with recomposure if the child is upset (phase 3). This chapter will focus on phases 1 and 2, but that is not meant to diminish the importance of closure during phase 3.

The DNE interview is best described as a toolbox approach because it offers an array of individual evidence-based options or tools that can be embedded into phases 1 or 2 of the interview at the interviewer's discretion (see Saywitz & Camparo, 2014a for a complete list of all tools and a guide to the use of the DNE). This approach does not suggest that every child should receive every instruction listed, however. Instead, the DNE toolbox approach demands that only those tools that the interviewer deems necessary or beneficial for a given child during a given interview will be deployed for that child during that interview. Just as a carpenter would not use every tool in their toolbox to build a child's drawing table or use the same tools to build a small table as they would to build a complex schoolyard play set, the interviewer should not expect to use every tool in their DNE toolbox for every interview or the same tools for every child. Indeed, the only tool that has been used in every study of the DNE is the instruction encouraging complete, accurate, and detailed answers (Saywitz & Camparo, 2014a).

During phase 2, the substantive-questioning and information-gathering phase, the DNE provides a three-step core template for questioning the child. The core template follows the commonly recommended practice of beginning, in step 1, with an open-ended invitation for an initial spontaneous statement about the target event by the child in the child's own words. After the child has exhausted their free recall response, it is step 2 that distinguishes the core template of the DNE from every other interview protocol—all of which move directly from the child's free recall of the event to the interviewer's more detailed follow-up questions. In contrast, during step 2 of the DNE core template, the interviewer provides the child with an additional opportunity to further elaborate on the target event in the child's own words; however, this time the interviewer scaffolds the process by helping the child organize and structure their responses around four forensically relevant story-grammar categories of information that were derived from script theories of children's event knowledge (Mandler & Johnson, 1977; Singer & Donlan, 1982; Stein & Glenn, 1978): the people present at the target event, the location or setting of the event, actions during the event, and conversations and affective states relevant to the event (Saywitz & Camparo, 2014a). The interviewer may choose to use verbal cues (e.g., "Tell me more about the people that were there and how they looked") or visual cues for the four story-grammar categories to scaffold the child's elaboration during this step (see Appendices A and B in Saywitz & Camparo, 2014a). Finally, based on the information gathered during the child's free recall in step 1 and the additional information gathered during the open-ended cued elaboration of step 2, the interviewer can then formulate better informed, and potentially less biased, follow-up questions for step 3.

Empirical Basis

During the nearly 40 years since the McMartin Preschool trial and the 35 years since the adoption of the United Nations Convention on the Rights of the Child (U.N. General Assembly, 1989), research on child interviewing has expanded massively; in the area of child forensic interviewing, much has been learned, and consequently, much has changed (Lamb, 2016; Saywitz & Camparo, 2009; Saywitz et al., 2017). There is now broad and strong international consensus among practitioners and researchers for numerous best-practice recommendations for interviewing children using a developmental perspective (e.g., American Professional Society on the Abuse of Children, 2012; Cronch et al., 2006; Jones et al., 2005; Larsson & Lamb, 2009; McWilliams, 2016; Newlin et al., 2015; Saywitz & Camparo, 2009; Saywitz et al., 2010; World Health Organization, 2006; Wyman et al., 2019).

The DNE's unique core template and optional tools were derived from three sources: The longstanding literature on normative language, cognitive, and socioemotional development in preschool and school-age children; contemporary research on child forensic interviewing; and studies of Saywitz's innovative strategies for improving children's recall and communication of forensically relevant information and reducing their acquiescence to suggestion (Saywitz & Moan-Hardie, 1994; Saywitz et al., 1999). The DNE has been studied in the United States, Australia, New Zealand, Canada, and South Korea with more than 1200 children ranging from 3- to 15-years of age regarding memory for staged events (Bowen & Howie, 2002; D. Brown & Pipe, 2003b; Camparo et al., 2001; Canning & Peterson, 2020; Chae et al., 2014; Kulkofsky, 2010; Lee & Shin, 2025; Saywitz & Snyder, 1996; Saywitz et al., 1996), highly stressful naturally occurring events, like injuries requiring emergency department treatment (Peterson et al., 2013) or physically painful events (Briere & Marche, 2023), and false events to test suggestibility effects (Camparo et al., 2001). The DNE has also been tested within different populations, including typically developing children and children with learning disabilities (Nathanson et al., 2007), varied levels of intelligence and vocabulary skills (D. Brown & Pipe, 2003a; Chae et al., 2014; Kulkofsky, 2010), and varied levels of socioeconomic status (Chae et al., 2014; Dorado & Saywitz, 2001). Overall, these studies have found that children perform better with the DNE than with a standard interview protocol.

Saywitz's original studies of the efficacy of the DNE focused on the amount and accuracy/inaccuracy of information children recalled about staged events after receiving training and practice in the use of the memory and narrative strategies (Saywitz & Snyder, 1996; Saywitz et al., 1996). These studies incorporated six evidence-based experimental procedures administered to school-age children over two separate meetings:

1. Memory strategy instruction
2. Organized guidance according to category cues
3. External memory aids (i.e., visual cue cards, presented to the children as reminder cards, consisting of generic line drawings on four separate cards)
4. Rationale for strategy usefulness
5. Practice in the use of the reminder cards with feedback and modeling
6. Reminders to use the reminder cards on subsequent trials

Compared to children who were not given training and practice with feedback and modeling in the use of the reminder cards, children in the DNE condition demonstrated a 53% increase in recall without compromising accuracy, and the 7- to 8-year-old children in the DNE condition performed at the level of the 10- to 11-year-old children in the control condition (Saywitz & Snyder, 1996). Saywitz and colleagues' (1996) follow-up study, which randomized the order of the reminder cards for the story-grammar categories in the step 2 cued elaboration and used different assistants for the training in the memory strategy versus the interview, found similar results: Children in the DNE condition recalled significantly more information during the step 2 cued elaboration than did children in the control condition who were not trained in the use of cue cards but were presented with each card and simply asked, "Does this card help remind you to tell anything else?" Most importantly, use of the reminder cards did not increase the amount of inaccurate information the children provided.

Following these original studies, several labs developed and examined the efficacy of different streamlined versions of the DNE. Saywitz's original studies (Saywitz & Snyder, 1996; Saywitz et al., 1996) required a 45-minute training and practice with feedback and modeling session using a story book and videotaped stimuli two days before a review session was administered just before starting the information-gathering interview about the staged event. This original version of the DNE, therefore, has been criticized as too long and cumbersome for actual forensic interviews in the field (Chae et al., 2014; Kulkofsky, 2010). The first attempt to streamline the DNE included a shortened training and practice session in the use of the reminder cards that was administered at the end of phase 1 on the same day that the information-gathering interview in phase 2 was conducted (Camparo et al., 2001). This streamlined training and practice with feedback and modeling lasted only 20 minutes and did not require a story book or any videotaped stimuli. However, it still provided the children with a rationale for the use of memory strategies, training in the use of the reminder cards, a shorter practice session in the use of the reminder cards with feedback and modeling, and a reminder to use the memory strategy in future tasks. Consistent with Saywitz's original findings, results indicated that first to sixth-grade children in the streamlined DNE condition recalled 54% more accurate information across the entire interview (free recall + cued elaboration + specific questions) than did the children in the Standard Protocol control group who received no training and were not shown the cue cards. This finding is particularly compelling given that accurate and inaccurate information was coded only once during the entire interview; such that, for example, if a child in the DNE condition provided accurate (or inaccurate) information during the free recall (step 1) and then repeated it during the cued elaboration (step 2), that information was not counted again. Thus, all accurate and inaccurate information was unique information. Finally, as in Saywitz's original studies, there were no significant differences in the amount of inaccurate information provided by children in the DNE versus the control condition.

Other labs beyond Saywitz's and Camparo's have tested even more streamlined versions of the DNE, either eliminating the rationale for the new memory strategy but retaining the training for the four reminder cards with feedback and modeling (Bowen & Howie, 2002) or completely eliminating the training and practice with the reminder cards during phase 1 as well as the use of the reminder cards in phase 2. Instead, the child is prompted verbally (referred to as verbal labels or VL) about the four story-grammar categories following free recall in phase 2 (D. Brown & Pipe, 2003a). In the VL condition, following the free recall, the interviewers simply asked four open-ended standardized questions relevant to the four categories of information, giving the children time to respond fully to each question before moving to the next question (e.g., "Tell me more about the people who were there and how they looked."). Both Bowen and Howie's (2002) and D. Brown and Pipe's (2003a) streamlined versions were found to be as effective as Saywitz's original DNE, with children recalling a significantly greater amount of accurate, but not inaccurate, information in comparison to children in their control conditions. As a result of these studies, the DNE now offers both a VL version and a streamlined reminder cards version for step 2 of the core template as empirically supported tools in the DNE toolbox (Saywitz & Camparo, 2014a).

In addition to research assessing the efficacy of streamlined versions of the original DNE, recent research has tested an expanded version. The Comprehensive Narrative Elaboration Technique (CNET) was designed specifically to elicit children's autobiographical memories for emotional and physically painful events (Briere & Marche, 2023). The CNET expands the number of categories of information prompted by the DNE from four to six:

1. sensory/somatosensory (e.g., information related to the five senses, bodily sensations, autonomic reactions)
2. emotional/affective (e.g., feelings and affective reactions, physiological changes)
3. cognitive (e.g., awareness, judgment, mental processes)
4. contextual (e.g., details related to environment, time, people)
5. procedural/temporal (e.g., steps involved in the unfolding of an event)
6. behavioral (e.g., actions, reactions, responses to stimuli)

To cue children's autobiographical memories of physically painful events for these categories of information, the CNET involves the use of eight reminder cards—feelings, time, senses, places, actions, people, thoughts, and sayings—with each card depicting drawings representing the card's category (Briere &

Marche, 2023). Thus, the CNET includes several categories of information and reminder cards from the DNE (feelings, sayings, places, actions, people) and three that are new (time, thoughts, senses). Briere and Marche did not compare the effects of the CNET to the DNE, and they were not able to assess the accuracy of the children's reports of the two painful memories; however, their results indicated that the 7- to 15-year-old participants reported a significantly greater amount of new information during the CNET step of the substantive interview about two physically painful memories than they did during the free recall step. This finding is consistent with previous findings for the original DNE and streamlined versions of the DNE. Analyses further indicated that the CNET reminder card that elicited the greatest amount of new information was the senses card; this is not surprising given that the two memories the children were prompted to recall were about "a time that they felt the most physical pain that they could remember" (Briere & Marche, 2023, p. 764). Nevertheless, the people and places cards, which are included in the DNE, also elicited a significant amount of contextual and procedural/temporal information.

Because step 2 of the DNE core template was specifically designed to encourage children to provide more elaborate narratives about events, there was concern that the DNE could inadvertently prompt children to report information about events that they did not experience (i.e., false reports). To address this serious concern, Camparo and colleagues (2001) used their streamlined version of the DNE and a standard interview protocol (free recall + scripted follow-up questions) to interview 1st- to 6th-grade children about both a staged event they experienced as well as a fictitious, but plausible event they were known to have not experienced (within-subject design; see Camparo et al., 2001, for scripted questions in each step of phase 2). The order of the events they were interviewed about was counterbalanced, and the interviewers were blind to all elements of the staged event including the fact that one of the events was fictitious. For both the staged and the fictitious event, the interviewers invited free recall using up to three scripted prompts. For the fictitious event, the script read, "Tell me about that time your class took the bus with your teacher to the desert to gather desert plants." If the child indicated they did not recall the event, the script prompted the interviewer to say, "You know, that time you and other students all went together on the school bus to the desert and collected plants?" And if the child still indicated they did not recall the event, the script read, "Is there anything you can tell me about that time?" (Camparo et al., 2001). Overall, results indicated that children in the DNE condition did not report significantly more false information about the fictitious event than did children in the control condition. In fact, 98% of all children denied experiencing the fictitious event after the first prompt. However, two younger children (first or second grade) in the DNE condition who were interviewed about the fictitious event first stated that they remembered the fictitious event after the first prompt. One of these children immediately recanted but then provided details of the fictitious event during all three steps of phase 2 (free recall, cued elaboration, and follow-up questions). The other child did not recant after stating they recalled the event in response to the first free recall prompt; however, although this child provided no information during free recall or cued elaboration (steps 1 and 2), they provided 161 inaccurate units of information during the specific questioning (step 3).

Given that some children in the DNE and control conditions provided false reports, my colleagues and I (Camparo et al., 2001) stated,

> [T]he children's reports to the fictitious event heightened our awareness of the need to respect children's denials of experiencing an event. Children may deny experiencing an event for a variety of reasons unrelated to memory (e.g., they actually did not experience the event, poor rapport development, or lack of empathy in interviewer). In these cases, repeated probing or presentation of "reminder cards" may not be an appropriate course of action. (p. 78)

These findings highlight the need for more research using fictitious events given that concern about false reports may be applicable to any interview protocol designed to enhance children's narratives and increase the likelihood that they will make an allegation of abuse.

Research on the efficacy of the DNE has primarily focused on the quantity of information and the accuracy and inaccuracy of children's reports during substantive questioning. Based on the memory literature, however, Kulkofsky (2010) and Chae and colleagues (2014) proposed that the use of D. Brown and Pipe's (2003a) VL version of the DNE during step 2 cued elaboration may serve to improve children's memory for events during step 3 direct questioning (i.e., in addition to simply providing more information during step 2), because step 2 forces children to rehearse the original event beyond what they could do without it. These researchers predicted that, relative to a control condition with no step 2 cued elaboration, children interviewed with the VL version of the DNE would provide a greater number of accurate responses to direct open-ended questions (Chae et al., 2014; Kulkofsky, 2010) and misleading questions (Kulkofsky, 2010) during subsequent step 3 follow-up questioning. Furthermore, based on previous findings that children with lower language skills are less accurate when answering direct questions (see Kulkofsky, 2010, for a brief review), Kulkofsky (2010) and Chae and colleagues (2014) also examined the effectiveness of the VL version of the DNE for improving reports by children with low language skills.

Consistent with these predictions, Kulkofsky (2010) found that, across all vocabulary-skill levels, 3- to 5-year-old children in the VL condition gave a proportionally greater number of correct answers to open-ended direct questions during step 3 than did children in the control condition; there was no condition by vocabulary skill interaction for direct questions. Importantly, Kulkofsky also found that in addition to the predicted main effects for interview condition and vocabulary skill level for the proportion of correct answers to step 3 misleading questions, there was a significant interaction: low vocabulary skill children interviewed with the VL version correctly answered nearly three times more misleading questions than did low vocabulary-skill children in the control condition, and they correctly answered the same number of misleading questions as the average and high vocabulary skill children in the VL condition.

Whereas Chae and colleagues (2014) included the same interview conditions as Kulkofsky (2010) to examine potential memory-enhancing effects of VL on children's responses to direct questions (no misleading questions), Chae and colleagues sampled only low socioeconomic status (SES) 3- to 5-year-old children and grouped them only by low vs. average/high vocabulary skills. In contrast to Kulkofsky, Chae and colleagues did not find the same interview condition main effects for proportion of correct responses to direct questions, and similar to Kulkofsky, they did not find any interactions. However, when analyzing proportion of correct responses in VL versus control conditions for each vocabulary skill group separately, they found that children with low vocabulary skills in the VL condition provided a greater proportion of correct responses to direct questions than did children with low vocabulary skills in the control condition.

One important caveat to these positive VL effects is that, inconsistent with D. Brown and Pipe (2003a) who sampled school-age children, both Kulkofsky (2010) and Chae and colleagues (2014) found that preschoolers in the VL condition made more errors. Although these increased error rates in the VL condition did not result in an increase in the proportion of incorrect responses to direct and misleading questions in the VL condition in either study, Chae and colleagues found that the low vocabulary children in the VL condition provided a decreased proportion of correct information during spontaneous recall (i.e., free recall + cued elaboration). Given these findings, Chae and colleagues (2014) suggested that "simply asking children to talk about different categories of information during the interview [as in D. Brown & Pipe's, 2003a VL version] seems to be less beneficial for young children" (p. 742) than including the DNE training in the use of the reminder cards as in Dorado and Saywitz's (2001) study with preschool children. Research needs to examine the efficacy of the VL version versus a streamlined training version of the DNE (e.g., Bowen & Howie, 2002; Camparo et al., 2001) with low SES preschoolers of different vocabulary levels to answer this question.

Another area of DNE research that has produced positive results has focused on the quality of the information provided by children who were interviewed with the DNE. Although the quantity and accuracy of the information children report with the DNE has obvious investigative benefits, research indicates that more fully elaborated witness reports are perceived as more credible by mock jurors (Bell & Loftus, 2006), and children who provide such reports may be more likely to be believed as witnesses (Bala et al., 2001; Peterson et al., 2013). Moreover, Kulkofsky and Klemfuss (2008) found that children who provided reports about a staged event that were higher in descriptive quality were more resistant to suggestive questioning about that event, and, importantly, the descriptive quality of the children's narrative superseded age as a predictor of resistance to suggestive questions. To explore the effect of the DNE on the quality, and not only the quantity and accuracy of children's reports, Camparo and Camparo (2011) examined the descriptive quality of 4- to 12-year-old children's narrative reports about a staged event, and Peterson and colleagues (2013) examined the causal connectives (e.g., because, if, so); temporal connectives (first, next, later, before, after); and contextual embedding (specification of location) of 3- to 7-year-old children's narrative reports about a serious injury.

Consistent with their predictions, Camparo and Camparo (2011) found that children interviewed with the DNE produced seven times more accurate descriptors in response to free recall prompts (free recall + cued elaboration) than did children interviewed with a Standard Protocol, and across the entire interview (including specific questions in step 3), children in the DNE condition produced twice as many accurate descriptors with no significant differences in inaccurate descriptors. Similarly, Peterson and colleagues (2013) found that children interviewed with the DNE about a serious injury produced longer, more emotionally evaluated, more descriptive, and more coherent reports during open-ended free recall (free recall + cued elaboration) than did children in the control group, although there were no significant group differences for causal or temporal connectives. These findings are especially important given that, as noted earlier, narrative quality is associated with perceptions of greater credibility and may be more strongly associated than age with resistance to suggestive questioning about the same event.

Whereas most of this research has examined the efficacy of the DNE after relatively short delays (e.g., 2 weeks) between when the children experienced the event and were interviewed about it, D. Brown and Pipe (2003b) investigated whether positive results for the DNE found after only a 2-week delay in study 1 could be replicated in a sample of children interviewed for the first time after a 9-month delay in study 2. Results of study 2 indicated that children in the DNE condition reported a greater number of correct items, summed across the entire interview, than did children in the control condition (DNE *mean [M]* = 39.73, *standard error [SE]* = 12.72; control $M = 13.73$, $SE = 4.44$). However, this effect was only marginally significant ($p = 0.07$), perhaps due to the small sample size ($n = 11$ in each condition) and the large standard deviation for the DNE group. Analyses of each individual interview stage indicated that there were no significant differences in the number of correct items provided during free recall for children in the DNE ($M = 10.27$, $SE = 2.75$) and control ($M = 6.82$, $SE = 1.88$) conditions and no significant differences in the mean number of correct answers children gave to the 10 specific follow-up questions concerning details of the event (DNE = 6.5 questions answered correctly and control = 6.9 questions answered correctly). Finally, although children trained in the DNE provided significantly more correct information in response to the people card and setting card than did the children in the control condition, they also reported more incorrect information in response to the people card and the conversation/affect card. An examination of the type of errors children made in response to the people card in the DNE condition indicated they were mostly related to descriptions of the clothing people had worn during the event. Consequently, the authors suggested exercising caution about eliciting information about clothing from children after long delays. Nevertheless, D. Brown and Pipe (2003b) concluded that

> it is encouraging to see that these errors were largely confined to descriptions of attire rather than incorrectly reporting that certain people were present or absent for activities. None of the errors made would lead to the incorrect assumption that any of the people from the event did things that did not actually happen. (p. 393)

In summary, approximately 30 years of research in multiple labs with randomized trials using different step 2 core template options on a range of populations about staged events, serious injuries, physically painful memories, and fictitious events has found that the DNE results in an increased quantity and quality of proportionally accurate information without increases in proportionally inaccurate information or reports of false events. However, as noted above, more research is needed to further examine the effectiveness of the VL version with low vocabulary skill preschoolers from low SES samples.

CONNECTING THE PRESENT TO THE FUTURE

The remainder of this chapter will begin by unpacking some thorny challenges still plaguing child forensic interviewing and will conclude by proposing potential child- and interviewer-friendly strategies going forward.

The Present

The experiences of child witnesses today are very different from those of child witnesses 30 years ago. In the United States alone, we now have over 900 children's advocacy centers using multidisciplinary teams to coordinate the investigation, treatment, and prosecution of child abuse cases (Ryan, 2021). Child forensic research conducted in the laboratory and the field has informed best practice guidelines by many professional groups and jurisdictions around the world. As noted above, we also have a wide range of evidence-based, structured interview protocols (Poole & Dickinson, 2005) that can be used very effectively with even preschool-aged children. Despite these exciting advances, however, recent research has uncovered two thorny challenges (Lamb, 2016): (a) Even when using these evidence-based interview protocols, many children are still reluctant to disclose abuse, especially younger victims of intrafamilial abuse (London et al., 2008); and (b) children's reluctance to disclose and apparent lack of cooperation often lead interviewers to abandon training in best practice interview techniques and use fewer open-ended questions and more directive or suggestive questions in an effort to elicit a disclosure (Lamb, 2016). To address these interrelated challenges, much research is now focused on increasing interviewers' adherence to best practice interview guidelines and reducing children's reluctance to disclose.

Adhering to Best Practice Guidelines

Poole and Dickinson (2013) argued that "investigative interviewing is a specialized skill because the way trained interviewers talk is not how adults usually talk" (p. 161). They reasoned that because children learn conversational turn-taking as early as infancy, they develop expectations when talking with adults that include saying a little, but not too much, and then passing the ball to the adult, who is expected to then say a little, but not too much, and pass the ball back to the child. Poole and Dickinson called these conversational turn-taking expectations "the bane of investigative interviewing because witnesses rarely tell everything they know about a topic and interviewers have trouble suppressing the habit of talking" (2013, p. 161). Consequently, interviewers inadvertently dominate the interview by asking a lot of specific questions to elicit the amount of information and detail necessary for legal decision making and/or disclosure. Unfortunately, it is just these types of questions, in combination with adults' universal cognitive tendency toward confirmation bias (Melinder et al., 2020), that can become "a recipe for disaster" (Poole & Dickinson, p. 164). Indeed, my colleagues and I (Camparo et al., 2001) found that, when questioned about a fictitious event that the interviewers thought the participants had experienced, one child in the DNE condition reported no information in response to an open-ended free recall question and no information in response to the four cued elaboration reminder card questions, but an unusually large amount of inaccurate information in response to direct questions. In this case, the direct questions were scripted, likely limiting any negative effects due to the interviewer's confirmation bias; however, it still serves as a troubling example of the disastrous consequences that could arise when resorting to specific questions.

In a related line of reasoning, Wood and Garven (2000) distinguished between improper interviewing, which involves employing techniques that have been widely criticized by experts (e.g., suggestiveness, undue social pressure, reinforcement for certain responses, inviting the child to pretend) and clumsy interviewing, which involves not employing all or many of the techniques that experts agree are desirable in child forensic interviews. They note that while clumsy interviewing may not lead to the same negative outcomes (e.g., false allegations) as improper interviewing, clumsy interviewing is still considered "bad interviewing" because it can lead to a less coherent, detailed, and convincing disclosure, "if a disclosure is made at all" (p. 112). To drive this point home, Wood and Garven described a potential cascade of negative outcomes as a result of clumsy interviewing: Because the child's feeble statement is less likely to be detailed and convincing, a caseworker may be less inclined to judge it as credible, judges and attorneys may treat the allegations with more skepticism, and prosecutors may view the child as a poor witness and be more reluctant to accept the case. If they do accept the case, the piecemeal statement elicited from the child during the clumsy interview may become more of a liability than an asset to the case. Thus, they argued, the child is often the biggest loser in the event of a clumsy interview.

Certainly, no interviewer purposefully sets out to conduct either an improper or a clumsy interview, and, fortunately, evidence suggests that most contemporary interviewers avoid the improper and suggestive interview practices of the early days (Johnson et al., 2015; Lamb, 2016). Nevertheless, as previously noted, research spanning a wide range of countries and cultures has found that forensic interviews with children rarely incorporate all of the developmentally sensitive, internationally recognized best practice techniques that researchers currently agree are desirable (Johnson et al., 2015; Korkman et al., 2008; Lamb, 2015; Sumampouw et al., 2020), suggesting that these interviews are, at best, clumsy (Wood & Garven, 2000).

Notwithstanding Poole and Dickinson's (2013) assertion that investigative interviewing is a specialized skill, Hanway and colleagues (2021) argued that "interviewing is a complex cognitive task for the interviewer" (p. 26) who must "actively listen, accurately remember information, think of questions to ask, make judgements, and seek clarification, whilst conducting interviews with witnesses, victims, or suspects" (p. 25; see also Hanway & Akehurst, 2018; Lafontaine & Cyr, 2016). Add to this list of cognitive tasks the imperative that the child forensic interviewer accommodate every aspect of the interview to the child's developmental needs (assuming the child is functioning at their developmental level and doesn't need further accommodations based on developmental or mental health differences), and it is not surprising that the interviewer's increased cognitive load negatively impacts their performance (Hanway et al., 2021).

Based on findings that interviewers often stray from best practice guidelines when conducting interviews in the field, especially when conducting interviews with children the interviewer perceived to be uncooperative (Lamb, 2016; Lamb et al., 2018), research has turned to examining the effectiveness of different interviewer training programs and modalities for ensuring interviewers adhere to best practice techniques (Akca et al., 2021). The original NICHD Protocol (Lamb et al., 2008) was the most widely used protocol in the field by child forensic interviewers during the initial stages of this research (Fernandes et al., 2023); therefore, most studies investigated interviewer performance with this protocol—with frustratingly disappointing results early on. However, after training programs had been revised to include intensive content instruction plus cumulative training involving coding exercises and practice-focused supervision, researchers found more positive long-term results (e.g., Brubacher et al., 2022; see Lamb et al., 2018 for a review).

Unfortunately, because no research currently exists examining the effectiveness of the DNE in the field, it is unknown whether (or not) interviewers' adherence to best practice interview techniques diminishes over time when using the DNE. All studies to date that have examined the efficacy of the DNE have included standardized, scripted follow-up questions in stage 3 of the core template, leaving a significant and very serious gap in the DNE research base. Given that the DNE has not been tested with alleged victims of abuse, DNE interviewers most likely have not encountered the same degree of uncooperativeness and reluctance that have been documented with such children in the field (Lamb, 2016; London et al., 2008). Thus, researchers in the field can only speculate at this time; however, given previous findings, it might be expected that interviewers' adherence to best practice questioning techniques when using the DNE would mirror that of interviewers when using the NICHD and other interview protocols included in these studies. The DNE must be examined in the field with alleged victims of abuse using nonscripted, interviewer-crafted follow-up questions in step 3 of the core template to even begin to answer these and other important questions mentioned in the following section.

Increasing Children's Cooperation and Decreasing Children's Reluctance to Disclose

Parallel in time with the research on interviewers' lack of adherence to best practice interviewing techniques, research also examined factors associated with children's reluctance to disclose abuse (e.g., Hershkowitz et al., 2005; London et al., 2008; Pipe et al., 2007) including motivational factors, such as embarrassment, fear of negative consequences, and fear of the perpetrator (see Lamb, 2016; Lamb et al., 2018, for reviews). Even in the absence of substantial empirical support, clinical and professional organization guidelines had reached consensus that the success of the forensic interview on overcoming these motivational barriers was largely dependent on how well the interviewer had established rapport with the child (Saywitz et al., 2015).

In accordance with these recommendations, the DNE (Saywitz & Camparo, 2014a) includes several nonsuggestive and developmentally sensitive activities and tools for establishing and maintaining rapport with very shy children, children of different ages, and young children coping with separation anxiety, as well as tools for overcoming reluctance in children of different ages. As with other aspects of the DNE, these tools need to be tested in the field to determine the ease with which they can be implemented, as well as their effectiveness in increasing children's cooperation and willingness to disclose.

Beyond revising the training program for the NICHD, Lamb and colleagues (2018) also revised the original NICHD Protocol itself, creating the NICHD Revised Protocol (NICHD-RP). The NICHD-RP was developed to provide structure and "guidance about how to enhance a child-centered approach to interviewing, by improving rapport and [nonsuggestive/noncontingent] support offered to the child throughout" the interview (Lamb et al., 2018, p. 6). This latter point of extending rapport and support throughout the interview is consistent with Saywitz and colleagues (2017), who stated that ". . . rapport is not static. It waxes and wanes as interviewers move from cursory dialog to sensitive/painful topics, and as children's attention, anxiety, and resistance fluctuate" (p. 316). Thus, the NICHD-RP differs from the original NICHD Protocol in at least three important ways: (a) Rapport building and narrative training immediately following introductions but before explaining and practicing ground rules, (b) guidance on evaluating and maintaining rapport beyond the preliminary phase of the interview, and (c) instructions to terminate the interview before the phase 2 substantive interview and schedule an additional interview for continued rapport building if the interviewer perceives that "the child is not cooperative and remains reluctant" (Lamb et al., 2018, Appendix A, p. 244).

Several field studies examining the effectiveness of the NICHD-RP for enhancing support and increasing children's cooperation and allegation rates in cases where allegation rates were corroborated by independent evidence have found that the NICHD-RP leads to increased allegation rates (Hershkowitz et al., 2014, 2017), which are mediated by children's higher levels of cooperativeness during a second interview (Blasbalg et al., 2021), and perceptions of greater credibility of children's allegations (Hershkowitz & Lamb, 2020). Additionally, Hershkowitz and colleagues (2021) explored the interactional dynamics between children and interviewers when using the NICHD-RP over two interview sessions (i.e., when children had not made an allegation during the first interview session and the interviewer had decided to terminate the interview and schedule a second interview). This study found that higher rates of interviewer rapport development and use of supportive techniques during the first interview session predicted the children's higher rates of cooperation during the rapport building phase of the second interview session, which then predicted the children's more spontaneous allegations, which were associated with interviewers' greater use of open-ended questions. The DNE should also be subjected to a similar examination of bidirectional interviewer–child interactional dynamics (e.g., Melinder et al., 2021). Such an analysis would better inform some of the early positive findings with the DNE; for example, Kulkofsky (2010) found that preschool children interviewed with the VL version of the DNE during step 2 of the core template actually led to improved performance on subsequent responses to misleading questions during step 3.

The Future?

Given these new directions that child forensic interviewing has taken in the years since Karen Saywitz's passing (some of which were guided by Saywitz's and her colleagues' meta-analyses on rapport and support; see also, Chapter 12, this volume), I can only speculate about the direction she would have liked to take the DNE in the future. I know that Dr. Saywitz explicitly argued for "flexibility of toolbox use rather than advocate[ing] for a specific protocol," further stating "that a 'one-protocol-fits all' approach may be too limiting (e.g., for 3-year-olds vs. teenagers, children not willing to disclose in one session, or children who lie to protect an abusive parent)" (Saywitz et al., 2017, p. 311). A toolbox approach allows the interviewer to pick and choose among different evidence-based components of different protocols to customize the interview to the specific child's developmental and individual needs as well as the specific goals of the case. For example, given the scripted nature of the four cued elaboration questions in step 2 of the DNE, this entire step could be used as an empirically tested tool with any protocol currently in use in the field, seamlessly inserting it after an allegation has been made between free recall and direct questions.

In considering future directions, perhaps it's best to end this chapter on the DNE interview protocol with some closing thoughts from Saywitz and colleagues (2017):

> Research has been largely focused on question types, which surely affect the accuracy and completeness of children's reports. However, we still know relatively little about the best ways to interview terrified children, children trying to protect a guilty defendant, children worried about being removed from home, children who are very young (3 years and younger), children with varied cultural backgrounds and children with severe psychopathology or disability. Moreover, accuracy is only one desired outcome of forensic interviews. Although obtaining an accurate and complete report is fundamental, professionals should be concerned with additional issues, such as children's physical and emotional safety, and fact finders' reaching the truth. A perspective that takes a holistic approach might serve children, families and society the best in the end. (p. 324)

REFERENCES

Akca, D., Larivière, C. D., & Eastwood, J. (2021). Assessing the efficacy of investigative interviewing training courses: A systematic review. *International Journal of Police Science & Management, 23*(1), 73–84. https://doi.org/10.1177/14613557211008470

American Professional Society on the Abuse of Children. (2012). *Practice guidelines: Forensic interviewing in cases of suspected child abuse.* https://www.apsac.org/guidelines

Bala, N., Lee, J., & McNamara, E. (2001). Children as witnesses: Understanding their capacities, needs, and experiences. *Journal of Social Distress & the Homeless, 10*(1), 41–68. https://doi.org/10.1023/a:1009429602266

Bell, B. E., & Loftus, E. F. (2006). Degree of detail of eyewitness testimony and mock juror judgements. *Journal of Applied Social Psychology, 18*(14), 1171–1192. https://doi.org/10.1111/j.1559-1816.1988.tb01200.x

Blasbalg, U., Hershkowitz, I., Lamb, M. E., & Karni-Visel, Y. (2021). Adherence to the revised NICHD protocol recommendations for conducting repeated supportive interviews is associated with the likelihood that children will allege abuse. *Psychology, Public Policy, and Law, 27*(2), 209–220. https://doi.org/10.1037/law0000295

Bowen, C. J., & Howie, P. M. (2002). Context and cue cards in young children's testimony: A comparison of brief narrative elaboration and context reinstatement. *Journal of Applied Psychology, 87*(6), 1077–1085. https://doi.org/10.1037/0021-9010.87.6.1077

Briere, J. L., & Marche, T. A. (2023). The comprehensive narrative elaboration technique: Expanding the narrative elaboration technique to increase the quantity and quality of children's autobiographical recall. *North American Journal of Psychology, 25*(4), 751–782.

Brown, A., Rams, B., & Collins, J. (2002, July 30). Samantha Runnion's mother blames jury, but legal experts disagree. *The Orange County Register.*

Brown, D., & Pipe, M. E. (2003a). Individual differences in children's event memory reports and the narrative elaboration technique. *Journal of Applied Psychology, 88*(2), 195–206. https://doi.org/10.1037/0021-9010.88.2.195

Brown, D., & Pipe, M. E. (2003b). Variations on a technique: Enhancing children's recall using narrative elaboration training. *Applied Cognitive Psychology, 17*(4), 377–399. https://doi.org/10.1002/acp.876

Brubacher, S. P., Peterson, C., La Rooy, D., Dickinson, J. J., & Poole, D. A. (2019). How children talk about events: Implications for eliciting and analyzing eyewitness reports. *Developmental Review, 51*, 70–89. https://doi.org/10.1016/j.dr.2018.12.003

Brubacher, S. P., Shulman, E. P., Bearman, M. J., & Powell, M. B. (2022). Teaching child investigative interviewing skills: Long-term retention requires cumulative training. *Psychology, Public Policy, and Law, 28*(1), 123–136. https://doi.org/10.1037/law0000332

Camparo, L. B., & Camparo, J. C. (2011, March 31–April 2). *Developmental differences in children's event memories: Enhancing narrative quality with the narrative elaboration and the verbal labels procedures* [Paper presentation]. Biennial Meeting for the Society for Research on Child Development, Montreal, Canada.

Camparo, L. B., Wagner, J. T., & Saywitz, K. J. (2001). Interviewing children about real and fictitious events: Revisiting the narrative elaboration procedure. *Law and Human Behavior, 25*(1), 63–80. https://doi.org/10.1023/a:1005691926064

Canning, H. S., & Peterson, C. (2020). Encouraging more open-ended recall in child interviews. *Psychiatry, Psychology and Law, 27*(1), 81–94. https://doi.org/10.1080/13218719.2019.1687045

Chae, U., Kulkofsky, S., Debaran, F., Wang, Q., & Hart, S. L. (2014). Low-SES children's eyewitness memory: The effects of verbal labels and vocabulary skills. *Behavioral Sciences and the Law, 32*(6), 732–745. https://doi.org/10.1002/bsl.2145

Cronch, L. E., Viljoen, J. L., & Hansen, D. J. (2006). Forensic interviewing in child sexual abuse cases: Current techniques and future direction. *Aggression and Violent Behavior, 11*(3), 195–207. https://doi.org/10.1016/j.avb.2005.07.009

Dorado, J. S., & Saywitz, K. J. (2001). Interviewing preschoolers from low- and middle-SES communities: A test of the narrative elaboration recall improvement technique. *Journal of Clinical Child Psychology, 30*(4), 568–580. https://doi.org/10.1207/S15374424JCCP3004_12

Fernandes, D., Gomes, J. P., Albuquerque, P. B., & Matos, M. (2023). Forensic interview techniques in child sexual abuse cases: A scoping review. *Trauma, Violence, & Abuse, 25*(2), 1382–1396. https://doi.org/10.1177/15248380231177317

Fisher, R. P., & Geiselman, R. E. (1992). *Memory-enhancing techniques for investigative interviewing: The cognitive interview.* Thomas.

Fisher, R. P., Milne, R., & Bull, R. (2011). Interviewing cooperative witnesses. *Current Directions in Psychological Science, 20*(1), 16–19. https://doi.org/10.1177/0963721410396826

Hanway, P., & Akehurst, L. (2018). Voices from the front line: Police officers' perceptions of real-world interviewing with vulnerable witnesses. *Investigative Interviewing: Research and Practice, 9*, 14–33. https://iiirg.org/wp-content/uploads/2021/02/II-RP-Volume-9-Issue-1-Hanway-Akehurst.pdf

Hanway, P., Akehurst, L., Vernham, Z., & Hope, L. (2021). The effects of cognitive load during an investigative interviewing task on mock interviewers' recall of information. *Legal and Criminological Psychology, 26*(1), 25–41. https://doi.org/10.1111/lcrp.12182

Hershkowitz, I., Ahern, E. C., Lamb, M. E., Blasbalg, U., Karni-Visel, Y., & Breitman, M. (2017). Changes in interviewers' use of supportive techniques during the revised protocol training. *Applied Cognitive Psychology, 31*(3), 340–350. https://doi.org/10.1002/acp.3333

Hershkowitz, I., Horowitz, D., & Lamb, M. E. (2005). Trends in children's disclosure of abuse in Israel: A national study. *Child Abuse & Neglect, 29*(11), 1203–1214. https://doi.org/10.1016/j.chiabu.2005.04.008

Hershkowitz, I., & Lamb, M. E. (2020). Allegation rates and credibility assessment in forensic interviews of alleged child abuse victims: Comparing the revised and standard NICHD protocols. *Psychology, Public Policy, and Law, 26*(2), 176–184. https://doi.org/10.1037/law0000230

Hershkowitz, I., Lamb, M. E., Blasbalg, U., & Karni-Visel, Y. (2021). The dynamics of two-session interviews with suspected victims of abuse who are reluctant to make allegations. *Development and Psychopathology, 33*(2), 739–747. https://doi.org/10.1017/S0954579420001820

Hershkowitz, I., Lamb, M. E., & Katz, C. (2014). Allegation rates in forensic child abuse investigations: Comparing the revised and standard NICHD protocols. *Psychology, Public Policy, and Law, 20*(3), 336–344. https://doi.org/10.1037/a0037391

Johnson, M., Magnussen, S., Thoresen, C., Lønnum, K., Burrell, L. V., & Melinder, A. (2015). Best practice recommendations still fail to result in action: A national 10-year follow-up study of investigative interviews in CSA cases. *Applied Cognitive Psychology, 29*(5), 661–668. https://doi.org/10.1002/acp.3147

Jones, L. M., Cross, T. P., Walsh, W. A., & Simone, M. (2005). Criminal investigations of child abuse: The research behind "best practices." *Trauma, Violence, and Abuse, 6*(3), 254–268. https://doi.org/10.1177/1524838005277440

Korkman, J., Santtila, P., Westeråker, M., & Sandnabba, N. K. (2008). Interviewing techniques and follow-up questions in child sexual abuse interviews. *European Journal of Developmental Psychology, 5*(1), 108–128. https://doi.org/10.1080/17405620701210460

Kulkofsky, S. (2010). The effects of verbal labels and vocabulary skill on memory and suggestibility. *Journal of Applied Developmental Psychology, 31*(6), 460–466. https://doi.org/10.1016/j.appdev.2010.09.002

Kulkofsky, S., & Klemfuss, J. Z. (2008). What the stories children tell can tell about their memory: Narrative skill and children's suggestibility. *Developmental Psychology, 44*(5), 1442–1456. https://doi.org/10.1037/a0012849

LaFontaine, J., & Cyr, M. (2016). A study of the relationship between investigators' persona characteristics and adherence to interview best practices in training. *Psychiatry, Psychology and Law, 23*(5), 782–797. https://doi.org/10.1080/13218719.2016.1152925

Lamb, M. E. (2015). Toward developmentally aware practices in the legal system: Progress, challenge, and promise. *American Psychologist, 70*(8), 686–693. https://doi.org/10.1037/a0039634

Lamb, M. E. (2016). Difficulties translating research on forensic interview practices to practitioners: Finding water, leading horses, but can we get them to drink? *American Psychologist, 71*(8), 710–718. https://doi.org/10.1037/amp0000039

Lamb, M. E., Brown, D. A., Hershkowitz, I., Orbach, Y., & Esplin, P. W. (2018). *Tell me what happened: Questioning children about abuse* (2nd ed.). John Wiley & Sons.

Lamb, M. E., Hershkowitz, I., Orbach, Y., & Esplin, P. W. (2008). *Tell me what happened: Structured investigative interviews of child victims and witnesses*. John Wiley & Sons.

Larsson, A. S., & Lamb, M. E. (2009). Making the most of information-gathering interviews with children. *Infant and Child Development, 18*(1), 1–16. https://doi.org/10.1002/ICD.573

Lee, S., & Shin, M. (2025). Effects of the narrative elaboration technique and open-ended rapport on accuracy of children's recall according to age. *Frontiers in Psychology, 15*, 1298759. https://doi.org/10.3389/fpsyg.2024.1298759

Leonard, J., & Hanley, C. (2002, July 21). Tips led to fast arrest in girl's killing. *Los Angeles Times*. https://www.latimes.com/archives/la-xpm-2002-jul-21-me-kidnap21-story.html

London, K., Bruck, M., Wright, D. B., & Ceci, S. J. (2008). Review of the contemporary literature on how children report sexual abuse to others: Findings, methodological issues, and implications for forensic interviewers. *Memory, 16*(1), 29–47. https://doi.org/10.1080/09658210701725732

Mandler, J. M., & Johnson, N. S. (1977). Remembrance of things parsed: Story structure and recall. *Cognitive Psychology, 9*(1), 111–152. https://doi.org/10.1016/0010-0285(77)90006-8

McWilliams, K. (2016, March). Best-practice guidelines for child forensic interviewing: What we know and where we are going. *APA Division 37 Section on Child Maltreatment Newsletter, 21*(1), 2–3.

Melinder, A., Brennen, T., Husby, M. F., & Vassend, O. (2020). Personality, confirmation bias, and forensic interviewing performance. *Applied Cognitive Psychology, 34*(5), 961–971. https://doi.org/10.1002/acp.3674

Melinder, A., Magnusson, M., & Gilstrap, L. L. (2021). What is a child-appropriate interview? Interaction between child witnesses and police officers. *International Journal on Child Maltreatment: Research, Policy and Practice, 3*(4), 369–392. https://doi.org/10.1007/s42448-020-00052-8

Nathanson, R., Crank, J. N., Saywitz, K. J., & Ruegg, E. (2007). Enhancing the oral narratives of children with learning disabilities. *Reading & Writing Quarterly, 23*(4), 315–331. https://doi.org/10.1080/10573560701501610

Newlin, C., Steele, L. C., Chamberlin, A., Anderson, J., Kenniston, J., Russell, A., Stewart, H., & Vaughan-Eden, V. (2015). *Child forensic interviewing: Best practices.* U.S. Department of Justice, Office of Justice Programs, Office of Juvenile Justice and Delinquency Prevention.

Peterson, C., Warren, K. L., & Hayes, A. H. (2013). Revisiting narrative elaboration training with an ecologically relevant event. *Journal of Cognition and Development, 14*(1), 154–174. https://doi.org/10.1080/15248372.2011.638688

Pipe, M. E., Lamb, M. E., Orbach, Y., & Cederborg, A. C. (Eds.). (2007). *Child sexual abuse: Disclosure, delay, and denial.* Erlbaum.

Poole, D. A., & Dickinson, J. J. (2005). The future of the protocol movement: Commentary on Hershkowitz, Horowitz, and Lamb (2005). *Child Abuse & Neglect, 29*(11), 1197–1202. https://doi.org/10.1016/j.chiabu.2004.12.015

Poole, D. A., & Dickinson, J. J. (2013). Investigative interviews of children. In R. E. Holliday & T. A. Marche (Eds.), *Child forensic psychology: Victim and eyewitness memory* (pp. 157–178). Palgrave Macmillan.

Ryan, L. (2021). In focus: *Children's advocacy centers.* Office of Juvenile Justice and Delinquency Prevention. https://ojjdp.ojp.gov/publications/in-focus-childrens-advocacy-centers.pdf

Saywitz, K., & Camparo, L. B. (1998). Interviewing child witnesses. A developmental perspective. *Child Abuse and Neglect, 22*(8), 825–843. https://doi.org/10.1016/s0145-2134(98)00054-4

Saywitz, K. J., & Camparo, L. B. (2009). Contemporary child forensic interviewing: Evolving consensus and innovation over 25 years. In B. L. Bottoms, C. J. Najdowski, & G. S. Goodman (Eds.), *Children as victims, witnesses, and offenders: Psychological science and the law* (pp. 102–127). Guilford Press.

Saywitz, K. J., & Camparo, L. B. (2014a). *Evidence-based child forensic interviewing: The developmental narrative elaboration interview.* Oxford University Press.

Saywitz, K. J., & Camparo, L. B. (2014b). Interviewing children: A primer. In G. B. Melton, B. A. Asher, J. Cashmore, G. S. Goodman, & N. K. Worley (Eds.), *The SAGE handbook of child research* (pp. 333–349). Sage Publications. https://doi.org/10.4135/9781446294758.n21

Saywitz, K., Camparo, L. B., & Romanoff, A. (2010). Interviewing children in custody cases: Implications of research and policy for practice. *Behavioral Sciences and the Law, 28*(4), 542–562. https://doi.org/10.1002/bsl.945

Saywitz, K. J., Larson, R. P., Hobbs, S. D., & Wells, C. R. (2015). Developing rapport with children in forensic interviews: Systematic review of experimental research. *Behavioral Sciences and the Law, 33*(4), 372–389. https://doi.org/10.1002/bsl.2186

Saywitz, K. J., Lyon, T. D., & Goodman, G. S. (2017). When interviewing children: A review and update. In J. B. Klika & J. R. Conte (Eds.), *The APSAC handbook on child maltreatment* (4th ed., pp. 310–329). Sage Publications.

Saywitz, K. J., & Moan-Hardie, S. (1994). Reducing the potential for distortion of childhood memories. *Consciousness & Cognition, 3*(3–4), 408–425. https://doi.org/10.1006/ccog.1994.1023

Saywitz, K. J., & Snyder, L. (1996). Narrative elaboration: Test of a new procedure for interviewing children. *Journal of Consulting and Clinical Psychology, 64*(6), 1347–1357. https://doi.org/10.1037//0022-006x.64.6.1347

Saywitz, K. J., Snyder, L., & Lamphear, V. (1996). Helping children tell what happened: A follow-up study of the narrative elaboration procedure. *Child Maltreatment, 1*(3), 200–212. https://doi.org/10.1177/1077559596001003003

Saywitz, K. J., Snyder, L., & Nathanson, R. (1999). Facilitating the communicative competence of the child witness. *Applied Developmental Science, 3*(1), 58–68. https://doi.org/10.1207/s1532480xads0301_7

Saywitz, K. J., Wells, C. R., Larson, R. P., & Hobbs, S. D. (2019). Effects of interviewer support on children's memory and suggestibility: Systematic review and meta-analyses of experimental research. *Trauma, Violence, & Abuse, 20*(1), 22–39. https://doi.org/10.1177/1524838016683457

Singer, H., & Donlan, D. (1982). Active comprehension: Problem-solving schema with question generation for comprehension of complex short stories. *Reading Research Quarterly, 17*(2), 166–186. https://doi.org/10.2307/747482

Stein, N., & Glenn, C. (1978). The role of temporal organization in story comprehension (Tech. rep. No. 71). University of Illinois, Center for Study of Reading.

Sumampouw, N. E. J., Otgaar, H., La Rooy, D., & de Ruiter, C. (2020). The quality of forensic child interviewing in child sexual abuse cases in Indonesia. *Journal of Police and Criminal Psychology, 35*(2), 179–181. https://doi.org/10.1007/s11896-019-09342-5

United Nations General Assembly. (1989, November 20). *Convention on the rights of the child.* https://www.ohchr.org/en/instruments-mechanisms/instruments/convention-rights-child

Vygotsky, L. S., & Cole, M. (1978). *Mind in society: Development of higher psychological processes.* Harvard University Press.

Wood, J. M., & Garven, S. (2000). How sexual abuse interviews go astray: Implications for prosecutors, police, and child protection services. *Child Maltreatment, 5*(2), 109–118. http://cmx.sagepub.com/cgi/content/abstract/5/2/109

World Health Organization. (2006). *Preventing child maltreatment: A guide to taking action and generating evidence.* https://www.who.int/publications/i/item/preventing-child-maltreatment-a-guide-to-taking-action-and-generating-evidence

Wyman, J. D., Lavoie, J., & Talwar, V. (2019). Best practices for interviewing children with intellectual disabilities in maltreatment cases. *Exceptionality, 27*(3), 167–184. https://doi.org/10.1080/09362835.2018.1425623

Yuille, J. C., Cooper, B. S., & Hervé, H. F. (2009). The Step-Wise guidelines for child interviews: The new generation. In M. Casonato & F. Pfafflin (Eds.), *Pedoparafile: Psychological perspectives forensic psychiatric.* Franco Angeli.

9

Supportively Questioning Children About Suspected Abuse

Michael E. Lamb, Irit Hershkowitz, Yael Karni-Visel, and Uri Blasbalg

A dearth of information about the factors affecting children's capacities to provide useful accounts of their experiences handicapped the professionals involved in assessing children's allegations in numerous celebrated multivictim preschool cases in the 1980s and early 1990s. Fortuitously, however, the same lacunae also stimulated a wave of research designed to alleviate our shared ignorance. One key point of contention concerned the suggestibility of children, and although experts disagreed vehemently about the extent of children's suggestibility and the associated impact on their competence and reliability, investigators and forensic interviewers quickly concluded that they should avoid asking suggestive questions. As a result, descriptive studies of forensic interviews in subsequent years have revealed dramatic declines in the numbers of suggestive questions posed, at least in Norway (e.g., Johnson et al., 2015), and anecdotal evidence suggests the same trend elsewhere. Those declines can be seen as one of the first concrete achievements of post-McMartin research on forensic interviewing, but our focus in this chapter is not on what interviewers should avoid doing but on what they should aim to do instead. We thus show how interviewers using the revised National Institute of Child Health and Human Development (NICHD) Protocol (Lamb et al., 2018) can help children provide complete accounts of their experiences, without compromising the accuracy of what they report, by providing children with cognitive and socio-emotional scaffolding that facilitates effective functioning and by making use of a child-centered, open-ended style of questioning.

https://doi.org/10.1037/0000492-009
Handbook on Child Witnesses: Improving Psychological Science and Legal Practice,
G. S. Goodman, T. D. Lyon, S. D. Hobbs, and R. Enriquez (Editors)

Despite different services, legislative requirements, legal frameworks, and interviewer training, there is a high level of consensus about evidence-based best practice for interviewing children (e.g., American Professional Society on the Abuse of Children, 2023; Brown & Lamb, 2015, 2022; Lamb et al., 2018; Ministry of Justice, 2022; Newlin et al., 2015; Poole, 2016; Saywitz et al., 2017; Saywitz & Camparo, 2013). Indeed, it is widely believed that effective interviewing is crucial to our collective ability to secure justice and needed interventions for victims, families, and alleged perpetrators, and the goal has been to describe and explain the techniques necessary to help interviewers conduct such interviews. Here we discuss each of the factors or techniques in the order in which they are typically addressed in the interview, rather than in the order in which they were the focus of research.

PREPARING CHILDREN TO BE DETAILED AND ACCURATE INFORMANTS

Before seeking to elicit information from children about personal experiences that might have been frightening, embarrassing, confusing, or shameful, interviewers need to ensure that the children

- understand their role and those of the interviewer and the interview itself,
- feel sufficiently comfortable with the interviewer to discuss such personal information,
- become familiar with the style and approach to questioning that the interviewers will adopt, and
- understand the importance of providing as rich and comprehensive an account as possible in response to the gently probing that will follow.

Accordingly, interviewers are routinely advised to introduce themselves, explain the layout and unusual features of the room (e.g., cameras and microphones), and describe what are often called the ground rules for the interview. However, we have found that, especially with uncooperative and reluctant children, it is better to describe the ground rules after establishing rapport and giving the child an opportunity to describe a neutral recent event in detail.

Rapport Building

Children tend to be reticent when they first encounter unfamiliar adults, especially when there is an air of seriousness and the meeting occurs in an unfamiliar room. Their reticence is likely to affect their willingness to discuss their experiences. Establishing rapport before raising the suspicion under investigation is thus widely viewed as best practice (Saywitz et al., 2015) although few researchers have directly compared the impact of different ways of establishing rapport (Brown et al., 2013; E. A. Price et al., 2016). Studies of rapport building (as with a practice narrative, described later) indicate that an open-ended style of questioning during this phase successfully encourages children to provide lengthy responses with minimal interviewer input (Ahern et al., 2014; E. A. Price et al., 2016).

Like most researchers at the time, we initially focused on cognitive factors (especially question type, language appropriateness, and orientation to the ground rules) and paid little attention to emotional and motivational factors that might affect the behavior of children when they were interviewed. Once we had shown (Lamb et al., 2007, 2008) that use of the standard NICHD Protocol indeed allowed interviewers to conduct more informative and uncontaminated investigative interviews, however, researchers began paying increased attention to the motivational factors that make some children reluctant to disclose abuse (Pipe et al., 2007).

As we later explain, suspected victims often remain silent during formal forensic interviews, despite compelling evidence of abuse. In addition, the interviewer's socioemotional behavior plays a significant role in shaping the children's engagement during these sessions. Children may hesitate to report abuse or participate in interviews for various reasons, including emotional bonds with or loyalty to the abuser; fear of retaliation or being abandoned; feelings of guilt, shame, or complicity; concern about repercussions for others; fear of not being believed and facing punishment; and anxiety about disrupting family dynamics (Collin-Vézina et al., 2015). In these cases, more intensive efforts are needed to ensure that the children not only establish rapport but trust the interviewer enough to reveal details about the abuse. Such trusting relationships are the goal in interviews conducted using the revised NICHD Protocol, which we discuss later. Interviewers following this protocol are encouraged to show kindness, use the children's names frequently, and to attend, acknowledge, and respond to expressions of emotion throughout the interview, including in the presubstantive phase.

Hershkowitz and colleagues (2015) demonstrated that higher levels of interviewer support were linked to decreased reluctance during the presubstantive phase of child interviews. Building on this, Ahern and colleagues (2014) analyzed the same dataset, focusing on the nuanced, turn-by-turn interactions within this phase. Their findings revealed that interviewers' supportive behaviors did not consistently align with the children's cues: reluctant remarks by children were no more likely to elicit support in rapport-building phase of the Revised Protocol interviews than in Standard Protocol ones. However, when reluctance was met with support—specifically in Revised Protocol interviews—it was more effective in fostering cooperative responses than in situations where reluctance received no support. Conversely, the absence of support in Revised Protocol interview settings appeared to reduce children's willingness to engage, suggesting potential adverse effects. Lewy and colleagues (2015) reported similar findings about the consequences of withholding support.

Practice Narratives

The way children are guided to respond to neutral topic questions during the presubstantive phase of forensic interviews significantly influences their responses in subsequent parts of the interview (Roberts et al., 2011). This is especially important because children often do not intuitively grasp that forensic interviews differ from everyday conversations in that they are intended to elicit rich, detailed accounts known only to the children (Lamb & Brown, 2006). Compounding this challenge is the fact that children are still developing narrative skills, such as organizing context, describing locations, identifying characters and their motivations, and articulating consequences (Reese et al., 2011).

Encouraging children to recount recent neutral experiences in the presubstantive phase addresses the following challenges: (a) helping them understand the level and specificity of detail expected in their responses, (b) familiarizing them with the types of prompts used later to foster elaboration, (c) supporting extended rapport building, and (d) giving interviewers insight into each child's individual communication style. Researchers, including Saywitz and colleagues, have extensively studied the value of explicitly training children in narrative recall prior to the substantive phase. Their findings consistently show that such preparation enhances the quality of children's reports (e.g., Brown & Pipe, 2003a, 2003b; Camparo et al., 2001; H. L. Price et al., 2013; Roberts et al., 2004; Saywitz & Camparo, 2013; Saywitz & Snyder, 1993, 1996; Sternberg et al., 1997). Encouraging children to describe specific, neutral events promotes the use of episodic memory during accounts of target events. Focusing on individual episodes from repeated experiences also helps young children indicate the number of occurrences and describe each in greater detail (Brubacher et al., 2011).

Finally, the form of questioning matters: As in the substantive interview phase, broadly open-ended prompts elicit more comprehensive responses than narrowly focused ones (Brown et al., 2013; H. L. Price et al., 2013; Roberts et al., 2004; Sternberg et al., 1997). Importantly, using this open style during practice narratives encourages interviewers to maintain the same approach during substantive questioning, which has been associated with fewer interviewer prompts (H. L. Price et al., 2013) and shorter interview durations overall (Brown et al., 2013).

Ground Rules

Once children have established rapport and shown the ability and willingness to provide detailed narrative accounts of recently experienced events, it is important to ensure that they understand the ground rules that distinguish forensic interviews from other conversations with adults (see Chapter 10, this volume). Such ground rules typically involve explaining to children that, in the interview context, they should provide unrestricted accounts of their experiences (e.g., "tell me everything, even the little things"), report only what they are confident about (e.g., "don't guess, just tell me what you really know"), be cognizant of the interviewers' naivety about what occurred (e.g., "I don't know what happened"), tell the truth (e.g., "only tell me what really happened"), signal when they do not know the answer to a question (e.g., "if you don't know the answer to a question, just say 'I don't know'"), signal when they do not understand a question (e.g., "If I say something that you don't understand, just tell me"), and correct interviewers if they say something wrong (e.g., "If I make a mistake, you should correct me"; Brubacher et al., 2015).

Providing ground rules is believed to help reduce some of the difficulties children encounter during forensic interviews. From a young age, children become able to formulate narratives of their experiences, largely shaped by interactions with caregivers (Fivush, 2011; Nelson & Fivush, 2004; Salmon & Reese, 2015). In doing so, they may learn to emphasize storytelling rather than factual accuracy. For example, Kulkofsky and colleagues (2008) found that children who produced more structured and detailed narratives were often less accurate than those who gave briefer accounts. This tendency to favor engaging storytelling runs counter to the forensic interview's goal of obtaining truthful, detailed information. As such, introducing a ground rule that emphasizes truth-telling can help communicate the seriousness of the interview and reduce the likelihood of distortion or exaggeration.

Children also tend to avoid saying "I don't know" in forensic interviews (Earhart et al., 2014), possibly because they don't recognize it as an acceptable response in this context (Scoboria & Fisico, 2013). In other settings, like interactions with parents or tests at school, children may feel pressured to answer even when uncertain. Similarly, children might hesitate to say they don't understand a question, making explicit instructions encouraging such responses potentially reassuring. Interviewer errors, such as misstatements or misinformation (Roberts & Lamb, 1999), further complicate matters. Without guidance, children often fail to correct these errors, possibly due to social norms discouraging them from challenging or contradicting adults (Brubacher et al., 2015; Evans et al., 2010; Hunt & Borgida, 2001; Roberts & Lamb, 1999). Instructing children on the importance of correcting mistakes during interviews may increase the likelihood that they do so.

Although ground rules are typically introduced collectively, each one targets a specific aspect of children's behavior. Some, such as truth-telling (Evans & Lee, 2010; Lyon & Dorado, 2008; Talwar et al., 2004) and appropriately using "I don't know" (Gee et al., 1999; Saywitz & Moan-Hardie, 1994), are well supported by research. Others, like instructing children not to guess (Warren et al., 1991), informing them that the interviewer lacks knowledge about their personal experiences (Mulder & Vrij, 1996), or encouraging them to correct interviewer errors (Warren et al., 1991), have limited yet promising empirical backing.

Practicing ground rules, rather than simply explaining them, seems vital to ensure that children apply them effectively (Brubacher et al., 2015; Danby et al., 2015; Krackow & Lynn, 2010). Without practice, young children may overuse certain rules, like saying "I don't know," even when they do know the answer (Gee et al., 1999; Saywitz & Moan-Hardie, 1994).

Emerging evidence shows that children's comprehension and use of, and benefit from, ground rule instruction vary with age and cognitive abilities

(Brown et al., 2019). Dickinson and colleagues (2015) found that understanding improves with age, with preschoolers (ages 4–5) struggling most with rules like correcting the interviewer. By around age 7, most children showed adequate understanding during practice, yet even among 8- to 9-year-olds, 39% misunderstood at least one of the seven rules commonly communicated. Danby and colleagues (2015) showed that practicing the "don't know" rule increased its use in interviews, although not necessarily accuracy. Regardless of instruction, children rarely admitted they didn't understand or corrected the interviewer.

Although more research is needed on how ground rules interact with factors that affect the quality of testimony, existing findings suggest there are no harmful effects from discussing them. Still, further studies are needed to determine how best to present these rules across developmental stages, when to introduce them, whether reminders improve adherence, and whether applying them enhances the overall reliability of children's accounts (Brown et al., 2019; Brubacher et al., 2015).

SUBSTANTIVE PHASE

Once the preparatory activities built into the presubstantive phase have been completed and the child is psychologically prepared for the interview, the focus should shift nonsuggestively in the substantive period to the possibility of abuse.

Maintaining Rapport and Providing Support

Although building rapport before discussing the alleged events is essential, it does not guarantee that rapport will be maintained throughout the forensic interview (Saywitz et al., 2015). Concerns have been raised about the potential for supportive interviewer behavior, such as adopting an empathic, therapeutic style, to appear suggestive, thereby potentially compromising the credibility and accuracy of the child's testimony (Saywitz et al., 2015). Alarmingly, Lyon and Dorado's research (2008) demonstrated that in studies involving maltreated children coached not to report instances of forbidden play, supportive remarks could increase the incidence of false reporting. For instance, specific reassurance (e.g., "It's okay if you played with the toy house") decreased false denials but also led to false admissions among children who had not engaged in the activity. In contrast, general reassurance was not associated with increased false reporting, although its impact on accuracy was modest, particularly when children had undergone extensive coaching.

Although prior research recommends offering children reassurance about the consequences of disclosure (Bussey & Grimbeek, 1995), evidence suggests this can be done safely only when the reassurance is general in nature and avoids direct reference to the events under investigation. The central challenge for forensic interviewers, then, is to offer meaningful support without referencing any allegation-specific content.

In the first empirical test of a more supportive Revised NICHD Protocol, Hershkowitz and colleagues (2015) promoted enhanced rapport by having interviewers welcome the children, address them by name, express care and interest in the children's experiences, and to echo, acknowledge, or explore the children's emotions and expressions of reluctance. Thanks, appreciation, and positive reinforcement of the children's efforts, but not their specific contents, were recommended. Similarly, expressions of empathy with the children's expressed feelings or difficulties regarding the interview experience were encouraged, as were supportive interventions such as legitimizing expressions, generalizing and normalizing the child's difficulties in the interview and reassuring him or her when possible.

Hershkowitz and colleagues (2015) found that children interviewed using the Revised Protocol displayed lower levels of reluctance during the presubstantive phase. This was particularly evidenced by fewer omission responses such as "don't know," "not sure," "that's all," and unclear or nonresponses. Regardless of which version of the NICHD Protocol (Standard or Revised) was employed, the quantity of detail provided was associated with children's level of reluctance, age, and the type of prompt used.

Notably, interviewers following the Revised Protocol demonstrated more supportive behavior during the presubstantive and transitional phases than those using the Standard Protocol. However, this increased supportiveness did not carry over into the substantive phase, where discussions of abuse allegations took place. Despite interviewers' initial efforts to facilitate disclosure, they did not maintain elevated levels of support once allegations were introduced. Interestingly, children in the Revised Protocol group still exhibited lower reluctance during the substantive phase, even in the absence of additional support, suggesting that early rapport building had a lasting positive effect on their willingness to participate. Nevertheless, these findings underlined the critical need for interviewers to sustain support throughout the interview and to actively rebuild rapport if it begins to diminish (Saywitz et al., 2015).

Despite the lapse in support during the substantive phase, Hershkowitz and colleagues (2014) found that use of the Revised Protocol was linked to a significantly higher rate of abuse allegations among children whose intrafamiliar victimization was independently corroborated. Of the 426 children in the study, over half disclosed abuse, with 60% doing so in Revised Protocol interviews compared with 50% in Standard Protocol interviews. This effect remained robust even after controlling variables such as interviewer, child age, gender, and prior disclosures. These results demonstrate that the supportive, yet nonsuggestive practices embedded in the Revised Protocol can facilitate valid disclosures. Furthermore, the emphasis on carefully structured, free recall–based prompts mitigated the risk of suggestive influence, as had also been emphasized in the Standard Protocol.

Further research conducted with interviewers who had been more extensively trained to continue their supportive behavior throughout the interview showed that using the Revised Protocol (Hershkowitz et al., 2017) was positively associated with a moderation of reluctance in the presubstantive and substantive phases (Ahern et al., 2019; Blasbalg et al., 2018; Blasbalg, Hershkowitz, Lamb, et al., 2019) as well as with further increases in the rates of initial disclosures (Hershkowitz & Lamb, 2020), the production of forensically relevant information (Blasbalg et al., 2018, 2019; Karni-Visel et al., 2019), statement coherence (Blasbalg, Hershkowitz, Karni-Visel, & Lamb, 2019), and perceived credibility (Hershkowitz & Lamb, 2020).

In a very recent study, Blasbalg and colleagues (2025) provided further insight into the ways in which the supportive behaviors of forensic interviewers helped children provide richer descriptions of their experiences. Specifically, the children's increased informativeness was associated with the interviewers' supportive comments and children's nonsubstantive informativeness in the presubstantive phase, child reluctance in the transitional phase, as well as the interviewers' supportiveness and reliance on open-ended questions and the children's emotional expressiveness in the substantive phase. This was the first study to consider all phases of the interview and thus to show that supportiveness has a cumulative multiphase effect, underlining that expressions of reluctance should be addressed as soon as they arise and throughout the course of the interview.

When children remain reluctant to make allegations, despite the interviewers' focus on rapport building and nonsuggestive support in a first interview, the Revised Protocol guidance suggests that interviewers should not try to explore the possibility of abuse and should instead plan a second interview to allow continued rapport building before exploring possible abuse. Adherence to this two-interview model was positively associated with an increase in the number of children who made allegations of abuse (Blasbalg et al., 2021). Of 202 children who did not disclose during an initial interview, the 104 whose interviews were ended before the possibility of abuse was considered were more likely to make allegations when reinterviewed a few days later than those who were asked exhaustively about abuse in the initial interview. This association was mediated statistically by enhanced cooperativeness on the part of the children in the second interview.

A later study further explored the dynamics of such two-session Revised Protocol interviews, focusing on those who did disclose in the second sessions (Hershkowitz et al., 2021). The study showed that interviewer support during the first session predicted a chain of effects on several variables: children's cooperation during the rapport-building phase of the second session, spontaneous allegations, and the enhanced use of open-ended questions during the substantive phase—all of which mediated the effects of interviewer support on the children's free recall of forensically relevant information.

Recognizing and responding to emotions are crucial to the process of building and maintaining rapport. Discussing emotions fosters better narrating (Laible, 2004), better assimilation of information (Pennebaker, 2012), better decision making (Pekrun, 2011), and better emotional processing and emotional regulation (Laible, 2004). The discussions may also help children cope with conflicts of loyalty and with other emotional barriers to disclosure whereas suppression of emotions may consume cognitive resources, leading to impaired functional abilities (Gilbert et al., 1988). However, children rarely express their emotions spontaneously when describing past events, including incidents of abuse, and their expressions tend to be brief and sporadic (e.g., Pasupathi & Wainryb, 2010), although participating in a dialogue that encourages emotional expression promotes it, at least in the laboratory (Ahern & Lyon, 2013; Klemfuss et al., 2013). In forensic contexts, Lyon and colleagues (2012) found that "how did you feel?" questions often elicited reports of abuse-related evaluative content (descriptions of emotional, cognitive, and physical reactions) while interviewer support was associated with enhanced verbal (Karni-Visel et al., 2019) and nonverbal emotional expressiveness (Karni-Visel et al., 2023). The amount of negative emotion expressed was associated with the number of specific details reported as well as with a decrease in generic details (Karni-Visel et al., 2022). In Karni-Visel and colleagues' (2019) study, using the Revised Protocol was positively associated with the expression of more varied emotions, more expression of abuse-related emotions, and more expression of emotions related to the interview context. Importantly, emotional expression mediated the positive association between support and informativeness, enabling better retrieval of substantive information. These findings suggested that, by supportively encouraging the expression of emotions, interviewers may promote children's cooperativeness and informativeness.

By fostering deeper rapport and offering consistent emotional support, forensic interviewers using the Revised Protocol seem to help children overcome their reluctance to disclose information more effectively. These findings underscore the need for best practice guidelines to emphasize the critical role of supportive, yet nonsuggestive, interviewer behaviors when exploring potential abuse. Moreover, structured interviewing protocols are essential not only for guiding conversations but also for cultivating a relationship dynamic that encourages children to share their experiences more openly (Langer et al., 2011).

Questioning Techniques

Of course, the central purpose of the forensic interview is to elicit detailed and accurate accounts of experienced events. Decades of research have explored and compared the relative effectiveness of the different types of questions which has, in turn, informed training to promote the use of techniques that facilitate the retrieval of uncontaminated information from memory by recognizing children's cognitive limitations and strengths (Brown & Lamb, 2015; Lamb et al., 2018; Poole, 2016).

Our current understanding has been shaped by both laboratory studies, offering high levels of experimental control, and field studies that reveal how interactions between interviewers and children unfold in real-world contexts. Through this dual lens, researchers have explored children's capacity to provide accurate information when questioned in developmentally appropriate ways that support child-led retrieval processes (e.g., Brown et al., 2013; Saywitz & Camparo, 2013), as well as the vulnerabilities that arise when suggestive techniques are employed (Klemfuss & Olaguez, 2020).

Numerous studies have shown that the way questions are framed powerfully affects the recall processes triggered and both the richness and accuracy of the responses provided. At one end of the continuum, very broad open-ended prompts (e.g., "tell me everything you remember about that") are child-led in terms of what information is offered, recall-based in terms of the memory process involved, and elicit the most detailed responses. Such prompts, which we call invitations, along with those that use open-ended prompts to encourage children to elaborate on previously reported information (i.e., cued invitations such as "You told me that he touched your privates. Tell me more about him touching your privates") tend to elicit more accurate (Brown et al., 2013) and more forensically important (Phillips et al., 2012) information, as well as fewer inconsistencies (Lamb & Fauchier, 2001) than closed-ended questions. Children also provide more coherent and organized responses when responding to open as opposed to closed prompts (Feltis et al., 2010), as well as more responses including indices of credibility (Hershkowitz et al., 1997).

Further down the continuum are recall-based questions that ask the child to focus on a particular aspect of the event ('Wh-' questions such as "When did this happen?") and are thus more interviewer-led than invitations. Children typically report fewer details, but also more errors (Brown et al., 2013) and more inconsistencies (Lamb & Fauchier, 2001) when responding to such questions (which we call directive questions) and cued invitations rather than broader open-ended prompts. Very young children (3- and 4-year-olds) tend to be most responsive to these prompts, perhaps because they provide more structure and scaffolding to more immature children attempting to retrieve information and construct their reports (Hershkowitz et al., 2012). From around 5 or 6 years of age, developmental differences in the effectiveness of different prompts become less apparent than during the preschool years (Hershkowitz et al., 2012).

Further down the continuum, closed or option-posing questions (e.g., yes/no, multiple-choice type questions) reflect a great deal of interviewer input and require recognition-based memory processes. When children respond, they report fewer details (Korkman et al., 2006), as well as more errors and inconsistent statements (Lamb & Fauchier, 2001) than to any of the other types of prompts or questions.

Lastly, there are recognition-based suggestive questions, which comprise statements or questions that communicate to the children what answers they should give or in which the interviewer assumes certain information that the children have not disclosed. Tagged questions like "he touched you, didn't he?" are easily recognized, but other types of suggestive questions, such as an interviewer assuming something when formulating a question, may be more difficult to spot. Suggestive questions are highly interviewer led and encourage the child to acquiesce to, or adopt, details that the interviewer provided. Of the different question types, they are associated with the highest rates of error.

Open-ended prompts, which convey minimal interviewer input, are widely regarded as the most effective approach to questioning children. They tend to elicit richer, more detailed narratives, but they do not guarantee accuracy or responsiveness. In fact, open questions are often associated with higher rates of nonresponsiveness than other question types (Korkman et al., 2006; Wolfman et al., 2016). Although children can still produce inaccurate information in response to open-ended questions, the risk is significantly lower than with more directive or suggestive formats.

Building on the general success of recall-based methods, recent research has explored more nuanced analyses of specific question types and the types of information they elicit. For instance, Malloy and colleagues (2017) found that how and why questions—although common—rarely yielded informative answers from preschool-aged children. Similarly, Earhart and colleagues (2018) demonstrated that children aged 5 to 9 provided more detailed responses when initially asked what they were there to talk about, as opposed to why they were present. Other studies have shown that question phrasing can significantly influence clarity; for example, Stolzenberg and Lyon (2017) reported that children offered more descriptive accounts of intermediate clothing placement when asked "Where were your clothes?" than when responding to yes/no questions. Evans and colleagues (2017) observed that yes/no questions beginning with "Do you know" or "Do you remember" often resulted in ambiguous answers, as children tended to reply to the literal prompt about their memory rather than its implied meaning.

Collectively, these findings highlight that even subtle shifts in question formulation can shape the quality of children's responses—underscoring the importance of not only using open-ended questions but crafting them with precision and developmental sensitivity.

CONCLUSION

Participating in a forensic interview is a daunting experience for most children because they need to interact with unfamiliar adults, the topic may be difficult to talk about (for both emotional and cognitive reasons), they may fear the consequences of disclosing what happened to them, and they are unused to taking on the role of an expert and recounting their experiences at length and in minute detail. How children are prepared for such demands and precisely how they are then questioned about any experiences they choose to disclose thus affects how well they are likely to engage and contribute. Preparation is best done within the interview because preinterview preparation or coaching (e.g., by parents) could irrevocably change how children come to remember and describe events. We now understand a great deal about how to help children understand their key role as sources of detailed information, how to share detailed accounts from memory, and how to develop rapport and trusting relationships. The strategies interviewers use to elicit children's evidence—the kinds of questions asked and how those questions are distributed throughout the interviews—are also crucial. A substantial body of evidence now documents the benefits and risks associated with different interviewing strategies. Open-ended invitations best support children's recall even though, despite decades of emphasis by researchers and professional experts, interviewers typically do not rely extensively on such prompts during their interviews.

In recent years our understanding of the role of rapport and socioemotional support in further improving children's forensic statements has been remarkably enhanced. Improved research-based guidelines to help interviewers establish more meaningful rapport with children as well as identify and cope supportively with emotional barriers to disclosure have been implemented and tested. Research showed that effectively managing children's emotional needs and difficulties during the interview further enhanced the amount and quality of the forensic statements they provide. Thus, the combination of both emotionally- and cognitively-based strategies, as in the Revised Protocol, represents another step toward the optimization of children's performance as witnesses and the attainment of just outcomes.

REFERENCES

Ahern, E. C., Hershkowitz, I., Lamb, M. E., Blasbalg, U., & Karni-Visel, Y. (2019). Examining reluctance and emotional support in forensic interviews with child victims of substantiated physical abuse. *Applied Developmental Science, 23*(3), 227–238. https://doi.org/10.1080/10888691.2017.1387057

Ahern, E. C., Hershkowitz, I., Lamb, M. E., Blasbalg, U., & Winstanley, A. (2014). Support and reluctance in the pre-substantive phase of alleged child abuse victim investigative interviews: Revised vs. standard NICHD protocols. *Behavioral Sciences & the Law, 32*(6), 762–774. https://doi.org/10.1002/bsl.2149

Ahern, E. C., & Lyon, T. D. (2013). Facilitating maltreatment children's use of emotional language. *Journal of Forensic Social Work, 3*(2), 176–203. https://doi.org/10.1080/1936928X.2013.854124

American Professional Society on the Abuse of Children Task Force. (2023). *APSAC practice guidelines: Forensic interviewing of children*. Association of Professionals Solving the Abuse of Children. https://apsac.org/wp-content/uploads/2025/08/FI-Guidelines-Updated-V2.pdf

Blasbalg, U., Hershkowitz, I., & Karni-Visel, Y. (2018). Support, reluctance and production in child abuse investigative interviews. *Psychology, Public Policy, and Law, 24*(4), 518–527. https://doi.org/10.1037/law0000183

Blasbalg, U., Hershkowitz, I., Karni-Visel, Y., & Lamb, M. E. (2019, June 26–28). *The effects of interviewer's support on the coherence of child abuse forensic statements: Comparing the revised and standard NICHD Protocols* [Paper presentation]. International Investigative Interviewing Research Group Annual Conference, Stavern, Norway.

Blasbalg, U., Hershkowitz, I., Lamb, M. E., & Karni-Visel, Y. (2021). Adherence to the Revised NICHD Protocol recommendations for conducting repeated supportive interviews is associated with the likelihood that children will allege abuse. *Psychology, Public Policy, and Law, 27*(2), 209–220. https://doi.org/10.1037/law0000295

Blasbalg, U., Hershkowitz, I., Lamb, M. E., & Karni-Visel, Y. (2025). *How does the Revised NICHD Protocol work? Underlying mechanisms* [Under review]. University of Cambridge, Cambridge, United Kingdom.

Blasbalg, U., Hershkowitz, I., Lamb, M. E., Karni-Visel, Y., & Ahern, E. C. (2019). Is interviewer support associated with the reduced reluctance and enhanced informativeness of alleged child abuse victims? *Law and Human Behavior, 43*(2), 156–165. https://doi.org/10.1037/lhb0000303

Brown, D. A., & Lamb, M. E. (2015). Can children be useful witnesses? It depends how they are questioned. *Child Development Perspectives, 9*(4), 250–255. https://doi.org/10.1111/cdep.12142

Brown, D. A., & Lamb, M. E. (2022). *Interviewing children about their experiences*. Routledge. https://doi.org/10.4324/9780367198459-REPRW183-1

Brown, D. A., Lamb, M. E., Lewis, C., Pipe, M. E., Orbach, Y., & Wolfman, M. (2013). The NICHD investigative interview protocol: An analogue study. *Journal of Experimental Psychology: Applied, 19*(4), 367–382. https://doi.org/10.1037/a0035143

Brown, D. A., Lewis, C. N., Lamb, M. E., Gwynne, J., Kitto, O., & Stairmand, M. (2019). Developmental differences in children's learning and use of forensic ground rules during an interview about an experienced event. *Developmental Psychology, 55*(8), 1626–1639. https://doi.org/10.1037/dev0000756

Brown, D. A., & Pipe, M. E. (2003a). Individual differences in children's event memory reports and the narrative elaboration technique. *Journal of Applied Psychology, 88*(2), 195–206. https://doi.org/10.1037/0021-9010.88.2.195

Brown, D. A., & Pipe, M. E. (2003b). Variations on a technique: Enhancing children's recall using narrative elaboration training. *Applied Cognitive Psychology, 17*(4), 377–399. https://doi.org/10.1002/acp.876

Brubacher, S. P., Poole, D. A., & Dickinson, J. J. (2015). The use of ground rules in investigative interviews with children: A synthesis and call for research. *Developmental Review, 36*, 15–33. https://doi.org/10.1016/j.dr.2015.01.001

Brubacher, S. P., Roberts, K. P., & Powell, M. B. (2011). Effects of practicing episodic versus scripted recall on children's subsequent narratives of a repeated event. *Psychology, Public Policy, and Law, 17*(2), 286–314. https://doi.org/10.1037/a0022793

Bussey, K., & Grimbeek, E. J. (1995). Disclosure processes: Issues for child sexual abuse victims. In K. J. Rotenberg (Ed.), *Disclosure processes in children and adolescents* (pp. 166–203). Cambridge University Press. https://doi.org/10.1017/cbo9780511527746.009

Camparo, L., Wagner, J. T., & Saywitz, K. J. (2001). Interviewing children about real and fictitious events: Revisiting the narrative elaboration procedure. *Law and Human Behavior, 25*(1), 63–80. https://doi.org/10.1023/A:1005691926064

Collin-Vézina, D., Sablonnière-Griffin, M., Palmer, A. M., & Milne, L. (2015). A preliminary mapping of individual, relational, and social factors that impede disclosure of childhood sexual abuse. *Child Abuse & Neglect, 43*, 123–134. https://doi.org/10.1016/j.chiabu.2015.03.010

Danby, M. C., Brubacher, S. P., Sharman, S. J., Powell, M. B., & Roberts, K. P. (2015). Children's reasoning about which episode of a repeated event is best remembered. *Applied Cognitive Psychology, 29*(4), 625–633. https://doi.org/10.1002/ACP.3306

Dickinson, J. J., Brubacher, S. P., & Poole, D. A. (2015). Children's performance on ground rules questions: Implications for forensic interviewing. *Law and Human Behavior, 39*(1), 87–97. https://doi.org/10.1037/lhb0000119

Earhart, B., Danby, M. C., Brubacher, S. P., Powell, M. B., & Sharman, S. (2018). A comparison of responses to substantive transition prompts in interviews with children. *Child Maltreatment, 23*(3), 221–225. https://doi.org/10.1177/1077559518756827

Earhart, B., La Rooy, D. J., Brubacher, S. P., & Lamb, M. E. (2014). An examination of "don't know" responses in forensic interviews with children. *Behavioral Sciences & the Law, 32*(6), 746–761. https://doi.org/10.1002/bsl.2141

Evans, A. D., & Lee, K. (2010). Promising to tell the truth makes 8-to 16-year-olds more honest. *Behavioral Sciences & the Law, 28*(6), 801–811. https://doi.org/10.1002/bsl.960

Evans, A. D., Roberts, K. P., Price, H. L., & Stefek, C. P. (2010). The use of paraphrasing in investigative interviews. *Child Abuse & Neglect, 34*(8), 585–592. https://doi.org/10.1016/j.chiabu.2010.01.008

Evans, A. D., Stolzenberg, S. N., & Lyon, T. D. (2017). Pragmatic failure and referential ambiguity when attorneys ask child witnesses "do you know/remember" questions. *Psychology, Public Policy, and Law, 23*(2), 191–199. https://doi.org/10.1037/law0000116

Feltis, B. B., Powell, M. B., Snow, P. C., & Hughes-Scholes, C. H. (2010). An examination of the association between interviewer question type and story-grammar detail in child witness interviews about abuse. *Child Abuse & Neglect, 34*(6), 407–413. https://doi.org/10.1016/j.chiabu.2009.09.019

Fivush, R. (2011). The development of autobiographical memory. *Annual Review of Psychology, 62*(1), 559–582. https://doi.org/10.1146/annurev.psych.121208.131702

Gee, S., Gregory, M., & Pipe, M.-E. (1999). 'What colour is your pet dinosaur?' The impact of pre-interview training and question type on children's answers. *Legal and Criminological Psychology, 4*(1), 111–128. https://doi.org/10.1348/135532599167716

Gilbert, D. T., Krull, D. S., & Pelham, B. W. (1988). Of thoughts unspoken: Social inference and the self-regulation of behavior. *Journal of Personality and Social Psychology, 55*(5), 685–694. https://doi.org/10.1037//0022-3514.55.5.685

Hershkowitz, I., Ahern, B., Lamb, M. E., Blasbalg, U., Karni-Visel, Y., & Breitman, M. (2017). Changes in interviewers' use of supportive techniques during the revised protocol training. *Applied Cognitive Psychology, 31*(3), 340–350. https://doi.org/10.1002/acp.3333

Hershkowitz, I., & Lamb, M. E. (2020). Allegation rates and credibility assessment in forensic investigations of alleged child abuse victims: Comparing the revised and standard NICHD protocols. *Psychology, Public Policy and Law, 26*(2), 176–184. https://doi.org/10.1037/law0000230

Hershkowitz, I., Lamb, M. E., Blasbalg, U., & Karni-Visel, Y. (2021). The dynamics of two-session interviews with suspected victims of abuse who are reluctant to make allegations. *Development and Psychopathology, 33*(2), 739–747. https://doi.org/10.1017/S0954579420001820

Hershkowitz, I., Lamb, M. E., & Katz, C. (2014). Allegation rates in forensic child abuse investigations: Comparing the revised and standard NICHD protocols. *Psychology, Public Policy, and Law, 20*(3), 336–344. https://doi.org/10.1037/a0037391

Hershkowitz, I., Lamb, M. E., Katz, C., & Malloy, L. C. (2015). Does enhanced rapport-building alter the dynamics of investigative interviews with suspected victims of intra-familial abuse? *Journal of Police and Criminal Psychology, 30*(1), 6–14. https://doi.org/10.1007/s11896-013-9136-8

Hershkowitz, I., Lamb, M. E., Orbach, Y., Katz, C., & Horowitz, D. (2012). The development of communicative and narrative skills among preschoolers: Lessons from forensic interviews about child abuse. *Child Development, 83*(2), 611–622. https://doi.org/10.1111/j.1467-8624.2011.01704.x

Hershkowitz, I., Lamb, M. E., Sternberg, K. J., & Esplin, P. W. (1997). The relationships among interviewer utterance type, CBCA scores and the richness of children's responses. *Legal and Criminological Psychology, 2*(2), 169–176. https://doi.org/10.1111/j.2044-8333.1997.tb00341.x

Hunt, J. S., & Borgida, E. (2001). Is that what I said? Witnesses' responses to interviewer modifications. *Law and Human Behavior, 25*(4), 583–603. https://doi.org/10.1023/a:1012754207074

Johnson, M., Magnusson, S., Thoresen, C., Lonnum, K., Burrell, L. V., & Melinder, A. (2015). Best practice recommendations still fail to result in action: A national 10-year follow-up study of investigative interviews in CSA cases. *Applied Cognitive Psychology, 29*(5), 661–668. https://doi.org/10.1002/acp.3147

Karni-Visel, Y., Hershkowitz, I., Lamb, M. E., & Blasbalg, U. (2019). Facilitating the expression of emotions by alleged victims of child abuse during investigative interviews using the revised NICHD protocol. *Child Maltreatment, 24*(3), 310–318. https://doi.org/10.1177/1077559519831382

Karni-Visel, Y., Hershkowitz, I., Lamb, M. E., & Blasbalg, U. (2022). Emotional valence and the types of information provided by children in forensic interviews. *Child Abuse & Neglect, 129*. 105639. https://doi.org/10.1016/j.chiabu.2022.105639

Karni-Visel, Y., Hershkowitz, I., Lamb, M. E., & Blasbalg, U. (2023). Nonverbal emotions while disclosing child abuse: The role of interviewer support. *Child Maltreatment, 28*(1), 66–75. https://doi.org/10.1177/10775595211063497

Klemfuss, J. Z., Milojevich, H. M., Yim, I. S., Rush, E. B., & Quas, J. A. (2013). Stress at encoding, context at retrieval, and children's narrative content. *Journal of Experimental Child Psychology, 116*(3), 693–706. https://doi.org/10.1016/j.jecp.2013.07.009

Klemfuss, J. Z., & Olaguez, A. P. (2020). Individual differences in children's suggestibility: An updated review. *Journal of Child Sexual Abuse, 29*(2), 158–182. https://doi.org/10.1080/10538712.2018.1508108

Korkman, J., Santtila, P., & Sandnabba, N. K. (2006). Dynamics of verbal interaction between interviewer and child in interviews with alleged victims of child sexual abuse. *Scandinavian Journal of Psychology, 47*(2), 109–119. https://doi.org/10.1111/j.1467-9450.2006.00498.x

Krackow, E., & Lynn, S. J. (2010). Event report training: An examination of the efficacy of a new intervention to improve children's eyewitness reports. *Applied Cognitive Psychology, 24*(6), 868–884. https://doi.org/10.1002/acp.1594

Kulkofsky, S., Wang, Q., & Ceci, S. J. (2008). Do better stories make better memories? Narrative quality and memory accuracy in preschool children. *Applied Cognitive Psychology, 22*(1), 21–38. https://doi.org/10.1002/acp.1326

Laible, D. J. (2004). Mother-child discourse surrounding a child's past behavior at 30 months: Links to emotional understanding and early conscience development at 36 months. *Merrill-Palmer Quarterly, 50*(2), 159–180. https://doi.org/10.1353/mpq.2004.0013

Lamb, M. E., & Brown, D. A. (2006). Conversational apprentices: Helping children become competent informants about their own experiences. *British Journal of Developmental Psychology, 24*(1), 215–234. https://doi.org/10.1348/026151005X57657

Lamb, M. E., Brown, D. A., Hershkowitz, I., Orbach, Y., & Esplin, P. W. (2018). *Tell me what happened: Questioning children about abuse* (2nd ed.). Wiley.

Lamb, M. E., & Fauchier, A. (2001). The effects of question type on self-contradictions by children in the course of forensic interviews. *Applied Cognitive Psychology, 15*(5), 483–491. https://doi.org/10.1002/acp.726

Lamb, M. E., Hershkowitz, I., Orbach, Y., & Esplin, P. W. (2008). *Tell me what happened: Structured investigative interviews of child victims and witnesses*. Wiley.

Lamb, M. E., Orbach, Y., Hershkowitz, I., Esplin, P. W., & Horowitz, D. (2007). A structured forensic interview protocol improves the quality and informativeness of investigative interviews with children: A review of research using the NICHD Investigative Interview Protocol. *Child Abuse & Neglect, 31*(11–12), 1201–1231. https://doi.org/10.1016/j.chiabu.2007.03.021

Langer, D. A., McLeod, B. D., & Weisz, J. R. (2011). Do treatment manuals undermine youth–therapist alliance in community clinical practice? *Journal of Consulting and Clinical Psychology, 79*(4), 427–432. https://doi.org/10.1037/a0023821

Lewy, J., Cyr, M., & Dion, J. (2015). Impact of interviewers' supportive comments and children's reluctance to cooperate during sexual abuse disclosure. *Child Abuse & Neglect, 43*, 112–122. https://doi.org/10.1016/j.chiabu.2015.03.002

Lyon, T. D., & Dorado, J. S. (2008). Truth induction in young maltreated children: The effects of oath-taking and reassurance on true and false disclosures. *Child Abuse & Neglect, 32*(7), 738–748. https://doi.org/10.1016/j.chiabu.2007.08.008

Lyon, T. D., Malloy, L. C., Quas, J. A., & Talwar, V. A. (2008). Coaching, truth induction, and young maltreated children's false allegations and false denials. *Child Development, 79*(4), 914–929. https://doi.org/10.1111/j.1467-8624.2008.01167.x

Lyon, T. D., Scurich, N., Choi, K., Handmaker, S., & Blank, K. (2012). "How did you feel?": Increasing child sexual abuse witness' production of evaluative information. *Law & Human Behavior, 36*(5), 448–457. https://doi.org/10.1037/h0093986

Malloy, L. C., Orbach, Y., Lamb, M. E., & Walker, A. G. (2017). "How" and "Why" prompts in forensic investigative interviews with preschool children. *Applied Developmental Science, 21*(1), 58–66. https://doi.org/10.1080/10888691.2016.1158652

Ministry of Justice. (2022). *Achieving best evidence in criminal proceedings: Guidance on interviewing victims and witnesses, and guidance on using special measures* [Report]. Home Office. https://www.gov.uk/government/publications/achieving-best-evidence-in-criminal-proceedings

Mulder, L. B., & Vrij, A. (1996). Explaining conversation rules to children: An intervention study to facilitate children's accurate responses. *Law and Human Behavior, 20*(5), 579–595. https://doi.org/10.1016/0145-2134(96)00050-6

Nelson, K., & Fivush, R. (2004). The emergence of autobiographical memory: A social cultural developmental theory. *Psychological Review, 111*(2), 486–511. https://doi.org/10.1037/0033-295X.111.2.486

Newlin, C., Steele, L. C., Chamberlin, A., Anderson, J., Kenniston, J., Russell, A., Stewart, H., & Vaughan-Eden, V. (2015). *Child forensic interviewing: Best practices* (Juvenile Justice Bulletin No. 19). U.S. Department of Justice, Office of Juvenile Justice and Delinquency Prevention.

Pasupathi, M., & Wainryb, C. (2010). On telling the whole story: Facts and interpretations in autobiographical memory narratives from childhood through midadolescence. *Developmental Psychology, 46*(3), 735–746. https://doi.org/10.1037/a0018897

Pekrun, R. (2011). Emotions as drivers of learning and cognitive development. In *New perspectives on affect and learning technologies* (pp. 23–39). Springer. https://doi.org/10.1007/978-1-4419-9625-1_3

Pennebaker, J. W. (2012). *Opening up: The healing power of expressing emotions*. Guilford Press.

Phillips, E., Oxburgh, G., Gavin, A., & Myklebust, T. (2012). Investigative interviews with victims of child sexual abuse: The relationship between question type and investigation relevant information. *Journal of Police and Criminal Psychology, 27*(1), 45–54. https://doi.org/10.1007/s11896-011-9093-z

Pipe, M. E., Lamb, M. E., Orbach, Y., & Cederborg, A. C. (Eds.). (2007). *Child sexual abuse: Disclosure, delay, and denial*. Lawrence Erlbaum Associates.

Poole, D. A. (2016). *Interviewing children: The science of conversation in forensic contexts*. American Psychological Association. https://doi.org/10.1037/14941-000

Price, E. A., Ahern, E. C., & Lamb, M. E. (2016). Rapport-building in investigative interviews of alleged child sexual abuse victims. *Applied Cognitive Psychology, 30*(5), 743–749. https://doi.org/10.1002/acp.3249

Price, H. L., Roberts, K. P., & Collins, A. (2013). The quality of children's allegations of abuse in investigative interviews containing practice narratives. *Journal of Applied Research in Memory and Cognition, 2*(1), 1–6. https://doi.org/10.1016/j.jarmac.2012.03.001

Reese, E., Haden, C. A., Baker-Ward, L., Bauer, P., Fivush, R., & Ornstein, P. A. (2011). Coherence of personal narratives across the lifespan: A multidimensional model and coding method. *Journal of Cognition and Development, 12*(4), 424–462. https://doi.org/10.1080/15248372.2011.587854

Roberts, K. P., Brubacher, S. P., Powell, M. B., & Price, H. L. (2011). Practice narratives. In M. E. Lamb, D. J. La Rooy, L. C. Malloy, & C. Katz (Eds.), *Children's testimony: A handbook of psychological research and forensic practice* (pp. 129–145). Wiley-Blackwell.

Roberts, K. P., & Lamb, M. E. (1999). Children's responses when interviewers distort details during investigative interviews. *Legal and Criminological Psychology, 4*(1), 23–31. https://doi.org/10.1348/135532599167752

Roberts, K. P., Lamb, M. E., & Sternberg, K. J. (2004). The effects of rapport-building style on children's reports of a staged event. *Applied Cognitive Psychology, 18*(2), 189–202. https://doi.org/10.1002/acp.957

Salmon, K., & Reese, E. (2015). Talking (or not talking) about the past: The influence of parent-child conversation about negative experiences on children's memories. *Applied Cognitive Psychology, 29*(4), 475–486. https://doi.org/10.1002/acp.3186

Saywitz, K. J., & Camparo, L. B. (2013). *Evidence-based child forensic interviewing: The developmental narrative elaboration interview: Interviewer guide*. Oxford University Press.

Saywitz, K. J., Larson, R. P., Hobbs, S. D., & Wells, C. R. (2015). Developing rapport with children in forensic interviews: Systematic review of experimental research. *Behavioral Sciences & the Law, 33*(4), 372–389. https://doi.org/10.1002/bsl.2186

Saywitz, K. J., Lyon, T. D., & Goodman, G. S. (2017). Interviewing children. In J. Conte & B. Klika (Eds.), *APSAC handbook on child maltreatment* (4th ed., pp. 310–329). SAGE.

Saywitz, K. J., & Moan-Hardie, S. (1994). Reducing the potential for distortion of childhood memories. *Consciousness and Cognition, 3*(3–4), 408–425. https://doi.org/10.1006/ccog.1994.1023

Saywitz, K. J., & Snyder, L. (1993). Improving children's testimony with preparation. In G. S. Goodman & B. L. Bottoms (Eds.), *Child victims, child witnesses: Understanding and improving testimony* (pp. 117–146). Guilford Press.

Saywitz, K. J., & Snyder, L. (1996). Narrative elaboration: Test of a new procedure for interviewing children. *Journal of Consulting and Clinical Psychology, 64*(6), 1347–1357. https://doi.org/10.1037//0022-006x.64.6.1347

Scoboria, A., & Fisico, S. (2013). Encouraging and clarifying "don't know" responses enhances the accuracy of children's reports. *Journal of Experimental Psychology, 19*(1), 72–82. https://doi.org/10.1037/a0032067

Sternberg, K. J., Lamb, M. E., Hershkowitz, I., Yudilevitch, L., Orbach, Y., Esplin, P. W., & Hovav, M. (1997). Effects of introductory style on children's abilities to describe experiences of sexual abuse. *Child Abuse & Neglect, 21*(11), 1133–1146. https://doi.org/10.1016/s0145-2134(97)00071-9

Stolzenberg, S. N., & Lyon, T. D. (2017). 'Where were your clothes?' Eliciting descriptions of clothing placement from children alleging sexual abuse in criminal trials and forensic interviews. *Legal and Criminological Psychology, 22*(2), 197–212. https://doi.org/10.1111/lcrp.12094

Talwar, V., Lee, K., Bala, N., & Lindsay, R. C. (2004). Children's lie-telling to conceal a parent's transgression: Legal implications. *Law and Human Behavior, 28*(4), 411–435. https://doi.org/10.1023/B:LAHU.0000039333.51399.f6

Warren, A. R., Hulse-Trotter, K., & Tubbs, E. C. (1991). Inducing resistance to suggestibility in children. *Law and Human Behavior, 15*(3), 273–285. https://doi.org/10.1007/BF01061713

Wolfman, M., Brown, D., & Jose, P. (2016). Taking stock: Evaluating the conduct of forensic interviews with children in New Zealand. *Psychology, Crime & Law, 22*(6), 581–598. https://doi.org/10.1080/1068316x.2016.1168426

10

Research on the Use of Ground Rules in Interviews With Children

Sonja P. Brubacher and Deirdre A. Brown

Interviewer: During that conversation, or at any time, did he offer any incentives for maintaining confidentiality?

7-year-old: Um . . . No.

Consider the brief exchange between the interviewer and a 7-year-old child. How likely is it that the child understood the question? Should we rely on their answer as evidence that they were not induced to keep a secret? Or is it more likely that the child did not understand and simply provided a response to satisfy the interviewer?

Answering adults' questions is habitual for children. Teachers, parents, and family friends ask questions (to which these adults often already know the answer) to practice children's language development, test their memories or vocabularies, and engage with them socially (Kelly & Bailey, 2013; Nelson & Fivush, 2000). In these circumstances, inaccuracies and miscommunications do not have serious consequences, but in other situations, clear communication and accuracy are essential (Malloy & Stolzenberg, 2019). One of these situations—the focus of this chapter—is when children are questioned for legal purposes as part of an investigation or trial. These interviews might inform child protection and police investigations, custody evaluations, and judicial or jury decision-making.

https://doi.org/10.1037/0000492-010
Handbook on Child Witnesses: Improving Psychological Science and Legal Practice,
G. S. Goodman, T. D. Lyon, S. D. Hobbs, and R. Enriquez (Editors)

Due to immaturities in children's social and cognitive development, the way in which children are questioned about their experiences and beliefs has a profound impact on the answers adults elicit from them (Brown & Lamb, 2015; Malloy & Stolzenberg, 2019). Karen Saywitz's work, recognizing and responding to the difficulty that children may have with the questions that interviewers pose to them, made a critical contribution to highlighting the importance of preparing children for the demands of an interview. Beginning with interview instructions to assist children in resisting suggestive questions (Saywitz & Moan-Hardie, 1994), this work culminated in an interview protocol that gives children practice and feedback in narrating a past experience (Developmental Narrative Elaboration interview; Saywitz & Camparo, 2014; Saywitz & Snyder, 1996).

Saywitz's work laid an important foundation for the evidence base underpinning the use of ground rules. This foundational work was associated with a concurrent explosion of research over the past 4 decades broadly concerning how best to elicit information from children. There are now internationally recognized best practices for interviewing young people, as reviewed in this volume, including how to effectively prepare them for their task as an informant (Chapter 12, this volume) and signal the expectations of the interviewer. Delivering some form of instructions (i.e., ground rules) is one of those practices, although it is acknowledged that investigative interviewers vary widely in how and when they deliver the rules (Fessinger et al., 2021; Krähenbühl et al., 2015). Further, while the ability to understand and benefit from ground rules instructions improves with age, it is not at ceiling by the end of childhood (e.g., Brown, Lewis, et al., 2025; see also Dickinson et al., 2015), and research is needed to determine the efficacy of instructions and best format of delivery into adolescence.

WHAT ARE GROUND RULES?

Ground rules are a set of instructions that make communication expectations explicit. They are included, to some extent, in all mainstream interviewing guidance documents for interviews with children (e.g., the Standard and Revised versions of the National Institute of Child Health and Human Development [NICHD] Protocol [Lamb et al., 2018]; the Ten Step interview [Lyon, 2021]; the National Children's Advocacy Center Forensic Interview Structure [NCAC; 2019]; the Standard Interview Method [SIM; Powell & Brubacher, 2020]; see also Walsh et al., 2025, for an international overview). The most widely adopted ground rules are listed in Table 10.1 (left column); these will be discussed individually in later sections of this chapter. Other common rules include telling the child the interviewer may take notes, explaining that questions may be repeated (to ensure the child does not take a repeated question to mean their first response was wrong), encouraging the child to ask for a break when needed, and a reminder that children are the experts about what happened to them.

TABLE 10.1. Widely Adopted Ground Rules and Practice Examples

Rule	Practice examples
Don't Know (DK):	
If I ask you a question and you don't know [or don't remember] the answer, don't guess/say, "I don't know."	• If I asked you, "what's my cat's name?" what would you say? • What did I have for breakfast today? • Do I have a sister?
Don't Understand (DU):	
If I say something you don't understand, I want you to tell me you don't understand/know what I mean.	• If I asked you, "Where is your patella?" what would you say? • What's your ocular pigmentation? • Is my shirt gridelin?
Correct Me (CM):	
If I get something wrong, I want you to tell me I'm wrong/correct me.	• If I said you were 90 years old, what would you say? • How did you like your bus ride to the station? *(When known the child did not arrive by bus).* • Did you have fun at the beach yesterday? *(When known the child was not at the beach).*

This last rule is often referred to as *interviewer naïveté* (e.g., "I wasn't there, so I don't know what happened"; Mulder & Vrij, 1996). Eliciting a promise to tell the truth also typically accompanies ground rule delivery and is discussed in Chapters 13 and 15 of this volume.

Historically, ground rules were introduced into interview guidance documents to overcome children's inclination to answer adults' questions even when those questions are unanswerable, incomprehensible, and nonsensical (Hughes & Grieve, 1980; Pratt, 1990; Waterman et al., 2000, 2004). For both social (e.g., compliance) and cognitive (e.g., lack of memory) reasons, children may also try to answer questions that contain misleading or incorrect details (see Bruck & Ceci, 1999, for a review) and change their initial responses when specific or misleading questions are repeated (Cassel et al., 1996; Poole & White, 1991). Ground rules are intended to minimize contextual and social differences between the dynamics of children's interactions with adults in everyday conversations and those of a forensic interview (Zajac & Brown, 2018). Emphasizing the child as the expert, and the possibility that the interviewer may ask difficult questions or make errors in their statements, ostensibly reduces the authority difference between the interviewer and interviewee and empowers child interviewees to feel like they have some control in the conversation. Use of ground rules may also serve to emphasize the gravitas of the interview, highlight the importance of accurate and complete reporting, and ease a child's sense of obligation to respond to everything asked of them, even in the absence of understanding or knowledge.

HOW SHOULD GROUND RULES BE DELIVERED?

In general, it appears that ground rules are more effective when accompanied by a practice example than when delivered just as a statement (Brubacher et al., 2015). Examples of practice questions can be found in Table 10.1 (right column). Despite this broad conclusion, there is little direct evidence to support it. The conclusion results from the knowledge that, in general, studies that have delivered ground rules without practice examples have not found effects of ground rules (Ellis et al., 2003; Peterson & Grant, 2001), while studies that have delivered them with practice examples or extensive instruction have found some effects (Danby et al., 2015 ["don't know" rule]; Gee et al., 1999; Hamilton, Brubacher, & Powell, 2016; Krackow & Lynn, 2010; Nesbitt & Markham, 1999; Peters & Nunez, 1999; Saywitz et al., 1999; Saywitz & Moan-Hardie, 1994), but there are exceptions to that pattern. When practice examples are brief (Danby et al., 2015 ["don't understand" and "correct me" rules]; McWilliams et al., 2021; Rodriguez Steen & Malloy, 2022), or when someone other than the interviewer delivers the instruction and practice (which is unlikely to occur in forensic interviews), children do not appear to benefit (Geddie et al., 2001).

Notably, brief practice is consistent with existing interviewer guidance for ground rule delivery (e.g., Lamb et al., 2018; Lyon, 2021; Powell & Brubacher, 2020). Our team has recently examined the impact of varying the intensity of ground rules instructions and practice on children's use of the rules when asked difficult questions about a staged event. Children aged 5 to 13 years were given increasing amounts of support to learn ground rules across five conditions: (a) no rule instruction; (b) brief practice instructions included in the NICHD Protocol; (c) brief instructions accompanied by visual cue cards; (d) multiple types of practice questions for each rule that included a yes/no, a "wh-", and an invitation question; and (e) multiple questions plus additional practice and feedback during a practice interview. Preliminary analyses suggest that instructions did not make a difference to how children answered "Don't know" or "Correct me" test questions, but when asked questions testing the "Don't understand" rule, children who were given no instruction in the rules performed worst, whereas those receiving more opportunities to practice (with and without feedback) were most accurate (Brown, Brubacher, et al., 2025). Relatedly, 6- to 11-year-old children who were given periodic reminders (i.e., "Remember, if I ask a question that you don't understand, just say, 'I don't understand'") during the specific question portion of an interview about a staged event were more likely to appropriately use the DU rule than children not given reminders (Rodriguez Steen & Malloy, 2024). Thus, it may not be simply whether the rules are practiced that is important, but also how they are taught, how often they are practiced or repeated, and the kind of feedback children receive.

Readers with a keen eye will notice a few things about the practice examples in Table 10.1 (right column). First, none of the practice examples are broad, open-ended prompts (also described as invitations, e.g., "What happened when . . ." or "Tell me about the part where . . ."), even though interviewers are recommended to prioritize this question type during the main interview. Second, the third example for each rule is phrased as a recognition question, while the first two examples are recall questions. There are reasons to expect that practice applying ground rules to recall versus recognition questions would yield different outcomes.

Recall questions require an interviewee to retrieve (or reconstruct) a response, while *recognition questions* provide a range of answers from which the interviewee may choose their response. Recall questions include broad, open-ended prompts (also called invitations) and interrogative questions (also called direct questions, i.e., who, when, where, why, how, and narrow what). Recognition questions (also called closed) include option posing (also called forced choice or multiple choice) and yes/no (a specific subtype of option-posing question). Children and adults are less likely to guess in response to impossible recall than recognition questions (Waterman & Blades, 2011; Waterman et al., 2000, 2004). Thus, children should more easily pass practice questions that are phrased in a recall format (e.g., a narrowly focused 'what' question; Interviewer: "What did I have for breakfast today?" Child: "I don't know") than a recognition format (e.g., Interviewer: "Do I have a dog?" Child: "Yes?").

A forthcoming study examined children's (aged 5–13 years) spontaneous responses to broad open-ended, interrogative, and closed (multiple choice and yes/no) questions that ought to elicit a ground rule response (in the absence of explicit instruction to use the rules). Children were less likely to accurately use a ground rule response (e.g., saying "I don't know" to an unanswerable question, or "I don't understand" to an incomprehensible one) to closed questions posed about an illustrated story compared to other types of questions. The same pattern was largely observed when children were asked questions about their morning routine (Brown, Lewis, et al., 2025).

An additional concern with ground rules practice questions relates to their context or intent, which does not connect well to that of the questions that the child would likely encounter during the subsequent interview—that is, they are not presented in the context of remembering and describing a past experience in detail. Research examining children's learning in domains such as problem solving, language, categories, and numeracy has shown that both the degree of similarity between practice examples and test problems, and the number of opportunities to practice, affect how well children transfer learning to new problems (Day & Goldstone, 2012). Thus, the typical approach to instructing children about ground rules is not consistent with psychological theories about how learning is promoted; however, we do not know how well these theories would generalize to learning new conversational rules. In our recent research examining children's spontaneous use of ground rules (i.e., in the absence of instruction), we found that children were more accurate in responding to questions when interviewed about their experiences the morning of the interview than when asked questions about an illustrated story or when asked about their conceptual understanding of the rules (Brown, Lewis, et al., 2025). Asking children about a recent past event is recommended as an effective component of preparing children to provide testimony (e.g., Brown & Lamb, 2022). Our findings suggest that using this context to assess and practice ground rule use is more likely to support children to effectively use such responses (and hence receive positive reinforcement for their behavior) than using a hypothetical scenario, such as a vignette or story. This context is more akin to the task of talking about the event(s) under investigation, so children more easily transfer their learning from the ground rule instructions.

Our discussion about ground rules practice questions (and their ability to either improve or predict subsequent interview performance) increases in complexity beyond just question format and practice context. The appropriateness of children's responses to practice questions might even differ depending on the content of the question within a single question format (Dickinson et al., 2015; McWilliams et al., 2021). For example, children may guess more when concepts are more easily generated than not. Indeed, maltreated 4- to 7-year-old children were more likely to guess when asked questions about color or number (common concepts for many children; Tare et al., 2008) compared to other content (McWilliams et al., 2021).

Researchers have speculated that some direct questions may be interpreted by children as an invitation to speculate (e.g., "How do you like being [wrong age]?" compared to "What did you do at the waterpark today?"). Direct questions ask children to search their memories for particular types of information, and so create a response demand that is higher than broader prompts because the category of information is obvious (e.g., asking a "where" question signals a location, "who" a person, "what color" a color word, and so forth). Some children may feel obliged to provide an answer even if they do not know, and so draw upon inference, guessing, or other sources of information to provide a response. The first practice example in this paragraph may be interpreted by children as a hypothetical question (Dickinson et al., 2015). Such response tendencies should signal caution to interviewers about requesting types of information that exceed children's capacity to reliably provide, given that children's answers resulting from a guess or other strategy may be indistinguishable from those that draw upon genuine memory.

RESEARCH ON INDIVIDUAL RULES

Developmental differences have been observed in children's abilities to understand various ground rules during instruction and apply them in interviews about their experiences (Brown et al., 2019; Dickinson et al., 2015). Further, associations between performance on the rules have not been consistently demonstrated; Brown et al. (2019) showed no association, whereas Brown, Lewis, et al. (2025) showed positive correlations between rules, albeit using different tasks. In this section, we discuss the three most widely used ground rules independently: Don't Know (DK), Correct Me (CM), and Don't Understand (DU).

Say I Don't Know (DK)

The DK rule is the most widely studied of the ground rules, probably in part because "I don't know" is an adequate response to any communication failure (even if imprecise), and it is the earliest to develop (Dickinson et al., 2015; Harris et al., 2017; Shatz et al., 1983). Children base their judgments about their own knowledge (metacognition) on whether or not they can produce a response (Rohwer et al., 2012). Thus, any problem in a question that makes the question hard to answer can receive a response of DK.

Despite early use, children's performance on the DK rule may be inconsistent. Some evidence suggests that, with practice, the DK rule would be suitable and helpful for children as young as 4 years of age (Danby et al., 2015; Dickinson et al., 2015). In a sample of maltreated Australian Aboriginal children 16 and under (Hamilton, Brubacher, & Powell, 2016), the DK rule received the highest accuracy rates (72%) in response to practice questions (compared to DU [50%] and CM [52%] questions). The DK rule was also the rule used most frequently by the Aboriginal children during the interview (81% of interviews contained DK utterances, compared to 46% and 51% of DU utterances and explicit corrections, respectively). Yet, an early ground rules study found that 3- to 6-year-olds who practiced the DK rule (in conjunction with an interviewer naïveté rule stating, "I can't help you") were no more accurate in answering closed questions about a staged event than the control group who received placebo conversational rules, such as "we take turns" (Cordón et al., 2005). Field studies suggest that when interviewers reject children's "I don't know" responses, children may change their initial answer even when the children have been provided ground rules instructions (Earhart et al., 2014; Grung et al., 2024; see Memon & Vartoukian, 1996, for foundational experimental research demonstrating the negative effects of repeated closed questions on children's response consistency).

The DK rule has also been associated with overextension of use by children and early adolescents (Gee et al., 1999, study 1; McWilliams et al., 2021; Nesbitt & Markham, 1999; Saywitz & Moan-Hardie, 1994, study 1; Shaw, 2022; *cf.* Earhart et al., 2014; Peterson & Grant, 2001), which may have the overall effect of reducing the accuracy of children's responses. Interpreting "don't know" responses is also a challenge for interviewers—they cannot know whether such responses reflect accurate responding, overextension (which would require a different response from the interviewer), or avoidance. As a result, interviewers are typically encouraged to invite a response when the answer is known (i.e., "but if you do know, I want you to tell me"). An important consequence of overextension is that children may use a DK response in lieu of challenging interviewer inaccuracy: In two studies, giving maltreated 4- to 7-year-old children a DK instruction (and in the second study, an additional "correct me" instruction) reduced the children's tendency to correct interviewers' inaccuracies in questions that they knew the answers to, due to increases in DK responses (McWilliams et al., 2021).

Correct Me (CM)

Even though interviewers are admonished to avoid leading or suggestive questions, they may still make unintentional mistakes. To counter this problem, many interview guidelines contain an instruction to correct the interviewer (e.g., "Tell me I got it wrong"). Research on the effectiveness of the CM rule is mixed but points to the importance of effective practice. Studies that included intensive CM rule practice delivered by the interviewer found benefits (Gee et al., 1999; Krackow & Lynn, 2010; Saywitz & Moan-Hardie, 1994). Yet, when practice examples were brief, researchers have not found the CM rule to improve the responses of nonmaltreated 5- to 9-year-olds (Danby et al., 2015) or maltreated 4- to 7-year-olds (McWilliams et al., 2021). Studies that did not include any practice, or used a different interviewer to deliver the practice, also have not found benefits of the CM rule (Ellis et al., 2003; Geddie et al., 2001).

Recent research suggests that performance on the CM practice questions (rather than simply the act of practicing or not) may predict subsequent use of that rule later in the interview (Brown et al., 2019). It also may be that, among younger children (under 10 years old) at least, practice in this rule must be relatively intensive to confer any changes to behavior.

Say I Don't Understand (DU)

Interviewers may use jargon, difficult words, or concepts that children struggle to comprehend (Cooper et al., 2010). Yet, children do not always realize when they have gaps in their comprehension, whether in story passages (Markman, 1979) or forensic interviews (Malloy et al., 2015). In the latter study, researchers recorded how often children signaled miscomprehension in 91 forensic interview transcripts of 4- to 13-year-old alleged child sexual abuse victims. In 32% of interviews, children made no explicit requests for clarification (implicit responses, such as, "I don't know" were not counted). Children's requests for clarification increased with age (see also Henderson & Lyon, 2021; Rodriguez Steen & Malloy, 2022, 2024).

Young children may identify a miscomprehension by saying, "I don't know" or using expressions like "huh?" or "what?", whereas older children are more likely to say "I don't understand" explicitly. In a sample of 2- to 18-year-old children interviewed about alleged abuse, the mean age for the former response was around 7 years, whereas the mean age for explicit use of the DU rule was nearly 9 years (Henderson & Lyon, 2021), during interview exchanges and responses to the instruction practice questions.

Because children do not always recognize or signal their misunderstanding, interviewers are encouraged to instruct children to say, "I don't understand" (DU) or "I don't know what you mean" when there is a comprehension failure. Until recently, only two published experimental studies explicitly gave children a DU rule (Peters & Nunez, 1999; Saywitz et al., 1999). Across both studies, 4- to 9-year-olds were given intensive training in comprehension monitoring (i.e., practice in identifying problematic questions and applying a rule). This training improved the appropriate use of the DU rule compared to children who did not receive such training.

More recently, Rodriguez Steen and Malloy (2022) asked whether the DU rule would benefit children when it was only practiced with a brief instruction, but found that it did not (see also Danby et al., 2015). They presented a 3-minute health and safety activity to 122 4- to 9-year-old children, who were then immediately interviewed. At the beginning of the interview, children were delivered the DU rule as a statement (control condition) or with comprehension monitoring instructions (in a briefer format than the earlier research) or reassurance instructions (telling the child not to worry if something was unclear and offering reassurance that "it's totally okay" to ask the interviewer for clarification). Children also either received stop method instructions (as in Peters & Nunez, 1999; children should hold out their hand like someone stopping traffic and say, "Stop, I don't understand" if a question was unclear) or did not receive stop method instructions. After receiving initial instructions, children were asked 22 questions, 8 requiring application of the DU rule (Rodriguez Steen & Malloy, 2022). Only 9% of the children requested clarification for all tricky questions, while 85% requested clarification for at least one. The majority of responses to the tricky questions were either explicit clarifications using DU phrasing (49%; see also Malloy et al., 2015) or attempts to answer the question (38%). In 9% of the responses, children said DK.

SKILLS UNDERLYING GROUND RULE USAGE

When delivering ground rules and practice examples, interviewers should consider what is developmentally appropriate for the child being interviewed. They should also be aware that there will be individual variation across children in cognitive processing.

Developmental Differences

In general, children's ability to effectively apply ground rules to challenging questions improves through childhood. With age, children develop greater competency in important underlying skills and gain experience with conversational exchanges. The end of childhood, however, does not appear to signal an end to either challenges or improvements with using ground rules. Emerging research demonstrates that even by the end of childhood, performance is not at ceiling (e.g., Brown, Lewis, et al., 2025; see also Dickinson et al., 2015); young adults continue to answer questions that they should not in lieu of using a ground rule response (Johnson-Hunter et al., 2023), and older adults also frequently attempt to answer questions that should be rejected (Ali et al., 2020). Ground rules clearly do not become redundant in later age groups, despite the increases in relevant cognitive and social skills and experience that accompany maturation. Thus, when considering children's performance with ground rules, we must be careful not to hold them to a higher standard than what an adult would achieve. Further, even among children of the same age, numerous individual differences may motivate rule usage, as we discuss next.

Individual Differences

A variety of cognitive skills are assumed to underlie the abilities to respond to ground rules practice questions and to employ ground rules during the interview (Brown et al., 2019; Brubacher et al., 2015). Younger children require more instruction and practice with ground rules to understand their purpose compared to older children; however, even this initial practice at the beginning of an interview may not be sufficient for younger children to effectively apply the rules in subsequent situations. Ground rules can be thought of as strategies that children develop. During strategy development, children generally progress through three phases before becoming proficient: (a) they do not possess the skill or cannot demonstrate it; (b) they learn the skill and demonstrate it intermittently; and (c) they demonstrate the skill regularly, but may not benefit from use of the strategy (Bjorklund et al., 1997) or generalize the skill to a new task (Borkowski et al., 1988). Researchers have identified at least four cognitive skills that develop in childhood and should be associated with ground rule use: Theory of Mind, metacognition (and metamemory), working memory capacity, and inhibitory control. These are discussed in turn.

Children need to possess a theory of mind—an understanding of one's own and others' mental states (Premack & Woodruff, 1978)—to understand why an interviewer's naïveté matters, or how an interviewer could ask questions that contain errors or prompt for details to which the child does not have access. Indeed, the naïveté rule was found to be more effective for 6-year-olds when presented in combination with other rules, rather than alone, but 8-year-olds were unaffected (Waterman & Blades, 2011). The older children likely did not benefit from the rule because they readily recognized that the interviewer would be unaware of what happened. Children's difficulty with ground rule instructions may also reflect emerging competencies within inferential processing and theory of mind development. Younger children may conflate hearing words in a question with understanding the question, for example. Therefore, they would fail to recognize and/or signal comprehension difficulty to the interviewer (Henderson & Lyon, 2021; see also Markman, 1979), or communicate a need for repetition rather than explanation.

Metacognition is essentially cognition about cognition (and *metamemory* is cognition about memory). It involves reflecting on task-related mental processes, such as strategies to improve performance (Flavell, 1979). Thus, metacognition may underlie the execution of a ground rule; that is, the child reflects on the question asked and their own comprehension or knowledge regarding the content of that question, and then strategically selects the correct response. This is a complicated mental task that relies on first recognizing a mismatch between the external and internal states and then determining that a strategy is needed to combat the problem. From there, two further skills are needed.

The child must inhibit prepotent responses (responses that come quickly without thought, like saying 'yes' to a yes/no question that was incomprehensible) and must have the working memory capacity to select the appropriate strategy. Breakdown in any of these skills, which develop throughout childhood, can result in an inappropriate response. Even nonmaltreated children as old as 11 years may not recognize that they have gaps in their understanding (Markman, 1979), and inhibitory control and effective working memory strategies continue to develop into adolescence (Shing et al., 2010).

Our team recently assessed the relationships between individual differences in theory of mind, inhibitory control, working memory, and language skills with performance on tricky ground rules questions in 3- to 12-year-old children (Lewis et al., 2023). The children were interviewed about their morning and had not been given explicit ground rules instructions. Tricky questions were introduced into the interview to test performance on the DK, DU, and CM ground rules. Theory of mind, working memory, and language skills were positively correlated with all three rules. Our measure of inhibitory control was not associated with performance on any of the rules. When we put the measures into a regression, with age as the first step, all three added additional explanations to predicting the DK rule, theory of mind and working memory added significantly to the model for the DU rule, and theory of mind and language added significantly to the CM rule. Of the social skills measures we collected (assertion, communication, cooperation, and self-control), only assertion added additional explanation to CM performance, but not to DK or DU, and the remaining three measures were not significant predictors for any of the three rules.

In addition to cognitive development, a recent study suggested that prosocial skills (as measured by the Strengths and Difficulties Questionnaire; Goodman, 1997) may be associated with the extent to which ground rules affect children's behavior (Lee & Chung, 2023). A sample of 90 Korean children between the ages of 4 and 11 years took part in a play session and were interviewed after a 10-minute break. The interview consisted of one broad, free-recall question with the remainder being nonsuggestive and suggestive yes/no questions. Half the children received ground rules with practice at the start of the interview, and half received no rules. Children with high prosocial skills provided accurate responses and resistance to suggestion with or without ground rules. For children with low prosocial skills, however, those in the ground rules condition provided more accurate information in free recall and demonstrated greater resistance to the suggestive questions compared to the no ground rules condition (Lee & Chung, 2023).

Field research suggests that interviewers have some insight into the role that children's development plays in their ability to utilize ground rules. Overall, interviewers appear to be less likely to deliver ground rules to younger children (aged 7 and under) than older children (e.g., Fessinger et al., 2021; Teoh & Lamb, 2010). The interviewers may assume that the younger children will not benefit from the rules. Yet, when interviewers do provide ground rules to younger children, they are more likely to practice the rules compared to when they provide ground rules to older children (Earhart et al., 2017; Fessinger et al., 2021). Indeed, the youngest age group (5- to 7-year-olds) in a sample of allegedly maltreated 5- to 15-year-olds benefited when they received more prompts (vs. fewer) associated with the rules (Teoh & Lamb, 2010). The older age groups were not affected.

IMPLICATIONS FOR PRACTICE

When delivering ground rules, many professionals tend to assume that if children can respond accurately to practice questions, they will use the rule reliably during the interview. Yet, as we have outlined, this is not always the case. Being able to apply the rule in the interview relies on the child understanding and remembering the rule, the metacognitive process of recognizing that a rule is needed, inhibiting competing responses, and remembering what rules are available to use (Brown et al., 2019). Periodic reminders of the rules, especially before specific questions are asked, may be helpful (Rodriguez Steen & Malloy, 2024).

Further complicating matters is that the specific practice example given may affect the response (Fessinger et al., 2021; McWilliams et al., 2021; see Brown et al., 2019, p. 1636, for discussion). Studies have shown conflicting results regarding the ages when children perform well on practice questions. This may be partly due to having used different questions. As we discussed earlier, this issue goes beyond simply the format of the question (recall vs. recognition); it also includes the complexities of individual experiences and lexical domains. This means that a single practice example is likely to have neither diagnostic value nor effects on children's interview performance.

Since ground rules may be only minimally effective, interviewers are trained to use the highest-quality questions with children. Interviews dominated by nonleading, broad, open-ended questions, where children are doing most of the talking and hold control of the information flow, will naturally contain fewer questions that could necessitate the use of a ground rule. Yet, despite the recognized limitations of ground rules and the expectations for interviewers to adhere to best practice standards of questioning, experts in child development, memory, and interviewing still recommend their use early in the interview (and as needed throughout the interview). There are at least three reasons for experts to recommend that ground rules be included in interviewing guidelines, which we review in this section.

First, the open-ended nature of a question does not guarantee that the question is free of problems. An open-ended question may inadvertently ask about concepts children have forgotten, include terminology with which the child is unfamiliar (this could be exacerbated for children whose first language is not the language of the interview), and can even contain incorrect details (Guadagno & Powell, 2014). Thus, even interviews dominated by open-ended questions can benefit from ground rules instructions. Of course, this assumes that children will understand and employ the instructions appropriately, and it is evident from the research reviewed in this chapter that their ability to do so is tenuous.

Second, children's performance on ground rules questions may provide interviewers with some indications about how a child might signal incomprehension during an interview (Henderson & Lyon, 2021). Yet, we remind interviewers of the caveats already discussed (i.e., that children's performance may be determined by the specific nature of the practice question they received). Several practice examples of varying formats may be needed to elicit the range of responses a child might use (and the way in which they use them), and to provide sufficient opportunities for feedback and reinforcement.

Perhaps most importantly, the third reason to deliver ground rules is that they may serve a rapport-building function and allow for a structured introduction that provides time for the interviewer and child to settle into the situation (Brown & Lamb, 2022; Johnston et al., 2019; Jol & Stommel, 2024; McWilliams et al., 2021). Most interviewing experts agree that some coverage of ground rules should happen in the introductory phase of the interview (and interviewers are also encouraged to reinforce ground rules throughout the interview; e.g., "It's okay if you don't know," or "Remember, I wasn't there when . . . so I need you to tell me everything that happened . . ."). The best placement for early delivery of the ground rules, however, is unclear. The original version of the NICHD Protocol placed ground rules before narrative practice, to minimize interruption of children's flow developed during the narrative practice phase. Interviewers may worry, however, that rules delivered before rapport building could seem confronting, so the revised NICHD Protocol reversed this order to promote children's emotional comfort and trust. The Revised Protocol has advantages over the original (Lamb et al., 2018), but the effects of ground rule placement have not been directly assessed.

FUTURE RESEARCH

The first step in a future program of research is to systematically investigate developmental differences in children's abilities to answer and use a wide variety of ground rules (varying content and question format). Beyond developmental differences, little consideration has been given to how research on ground rules applies to children with intellectual disabilities (CWID) and across various cultural groups. CWID are at greater risk of maltreatment than their typically developing peers, but they are underrepresented in eyewitness memory research (Brown et al., 2015). CWID are also more likely to need the guidance provided by ground rules instructions compared to children without intellectual disabilities, but simultaneously less likely to understand those instructions (Brown et al., 2019). With respect to maltreatment status and cultural differences, a recent study included maltreated children who were predominantly non-White (around 90%), and the patterns of findings generally replicated what has been found elsewhere (McWilliams et al., 2021); however, despite diversity in ethnicity, the children who participated live in the United States and spoke English. To better determine the role of culture in responsiveness to ground rules, research in other countries and languages is needed.

The applicability of ground rules to Australian Aboriginal children was examined in a set of two studies. In the first, qualitative study, a sample of 28 practitioners from across five Australian states evaluated best practice guidelines regarding their applicability for Australian Aboriginal children (Hamilton, Powell, & Brubacher, 2016). The sample included police, child protection, linguists and speech pathologists, and other legal personnel. All participants had direct and frequent experience working with Aboriginal children, and eight identified as Aboriginal (including five senior Aboriginal community workers). Their perceptions were that ground rules would be helpful for this population and would be suitable with some small modifications. The experts suggested that the use of hypothetical language, particularly with the construction "if . . ." is infrequently used in Aboriginal communities. They recommended modifications to the wording of the rules and practice examples (i.e., instead of saying, "*If* I said [e.g., what's my dog's name]," the wording, "I *might* say/ask . . ." was suggested). (Interested readers can consult Jol & Stommel, 2024, for further discussion on the *if* construction of ground rules questions). In a sample of interviews with Aboriginal children under 16 alleging sexual abuse, nearly all ground rules practice questions used the *if* construction, and children's performance on the practice questions was notably lower than that found in other research (Hamilton, Brubacher, & Powell, 2016). The reasons for this discrepancy probably include that most of the sample did not speak English as their first language, but the construction of the practice question may also have contributed. Interviewers should take care to consider that practice examples are developmentally and culturally appropriate.

Interviews with children play a critical role in the investigation and prosecution of child maltreatment. Many countries allow for a child's interview to be recorded and used in the courtroom in lieu of giving direct evidence. Criminal and judicial decisions may be influenced by what is observed in recordings of children's interviews, or read in the transcripts thereof. The extent to which jury members, legal counsel, police investigators, social workers, and other consumers of children's testimony are influenced by ground rule instructions and children's responses to practice questions is worthy of attention. Anecdotally, we have had several interactions with lawyers who have commented that a child's testimony should be considered with great skepticism, given they were unable to answer "simple" questions about an interviewer's pet—the child's attempt to answer the practice question was taken as a broader indicator of their inclination towards confabulation.

Another area for further investigation is the potential unintended effects of ground rules. Most studies have focused on testing the efficacy of ground rules by examining responses to "challenge" or "tricky" test questions designed to elicit a ground rule response. We know little about whether ground rules have broader effects on children's responses to questions that are answerable or appropriately phrased. Given findings that some children overextend use of the DK rule (e.g., Gee et al., 1999, study 1; Nesbitt & Markham, 1999; Saywitz & Moan-Hardie, 1994), and may be less likely to correct erroneous statements from interviewers (McWilliams et al., 2021), children may inhibit their responding because they are trying to comply with the rules. Some hint of this emerged in the training study by our team described earlier (Brown, Brubacher, et al., 2025): When we looked at the number and accuracy of details reported across the entire interview (not just responses to test questions), we saw that children who received the "gold standard" instruction (extended practice examples plus practice and feedback embedded within the practice narrative) were no more or less accurate than those in the other conditions, but they provided fewer details in their descriptions of the event than children who received no instruction, or extended practice examples without feedback. Thus, in addition to learning more about when and how ground rules might be optimally effective in supporting children's testimony, we must also consider potential costs or risks associated with them.

Some children's sense of comfort and autonomy within the interview may be risked by instructions about what language to use when faced with a difficult question, adding to concerns about how to "get it right" for the interviewer. The impact of ground rule instruction and feedback on rapport and children's engagement may vary according to whether the practice questions are designed to elicit successful performance (and subsequent reinforcement), or failure (and subsequent corrective feedback). Further, holding on to a series of instructions while simultaneously recalling and reporting on their experiences may overtax some children's cognitive resources (Brown et al., 2019). Our team has recently evaluated a streamlined ground rule format, designed to minimize cognitive load on children and allow them to signal when questions were problematic in whatever way they chose, rather than using interviewer-provided responses. Children (aged 5 to 12 years) were interviewed about their morning routine: half received a singular ground rule instruction ("Tell me if the question is tricky"), and the other half received instruction about three ground rules ("I don't know," "I don't understand," and "That's not correct"), modeled on the local forensic interview protocol. Both groups practiced applying the three rules. Neither group of children showed perfect application of their instructed rule when asked tricky questions dispersed throughout an interview about a recent staged event. When using a liberal scoring criteria (allowing for alternate responses to rules—e.g., responding "I don't know" to an "I don't understand" test question), there were no differences in performance between the two groups, suggesting that providing explicit instruction in different kinds of rules does not provide any benefit over and above a more generic instruction. Children who received multiple rule instructions often used alternate responses, especially "I don't know," when posed difficult questions.

Our findings need replication and evaluation within more ecologically valid contexts and tasks, but they indicate that using a single instruction (with practice in the multiple ways that a question might be difficult to answer) is as effective as the more conventional approach to ground rule instruction.

CONCLUSION

Interviewers may use (and consumers of children's testimony may perceive) ground rules as a solution to many of the developmental and social challenges that children might encounter during a forensic interview. We have much to learn about what is commonly acknowledged as a critical component of effectively preparing children to talk about their experiences. Given the developmental differences typically observed in children's performance on ground rule questions, within and across rule types, it is surprising that little attention has been given to the form in which rules should be presented, and how they should be trained, at different stages of development. The current approach embedded in current forensic protocols is unlikely to be effective for children of different ages and stages. Indeed, as the research reviewed above indicates, the typical format does not seem to be fit for purpose for many children.

Current approaches often give minimal practice opportunities, and the test trials and context for practice do not map well onto how children are expected to use the ground rules in the subsequent interview (Jol & Stommel, 2024). We have evidence to suggest that something is better than nothing, but the field would benefit from more exploration of optimal ways to present and practice developmentally sensitive rules. We also know little about whether rule reinstatements and reminders are useful and whether they come with any risk; likewise, little is known about the impact of reinforcement for correct use of the rules on children's subsequent use of them and their responses to answerable questions. Thus, there remains a rich agenda for future scholars to contribute to theoretical knowledge and applied practice. In the meantime, as our review shows, (a) practice with ground rules at the beginning of the interview is more likely to enhance their comprehension and application compared to no practice; (b) but that even with instruction, children will leave many difficult questions unchallenged and instead attempt to answer them; and (c) concurrent with the research on questioning strategies with children, there is nothing more helpful than an appropriate question. Perhaps the solution is not to use ground rules as an intervention, but to continue to encourage interviewers to use good questions and appropriate language as a prevention strategy.

REFERENCES

Ali, M. M., Brubacher, S. P., Earhart, B., Powell, M. B., & Westera, N. J. (2020). The utility of ground rule instructions with younger and older adult witnesses. *Applied Cognitive Psychology, 34*(3), 664–677. https://doi.org/10.1002/acp.3648

Bjorklund, D. F., Miller, P. H., Coyle, T. R., & Slawinski, J. L. (1997). Instructing children to use memory strategies: Evidence of utilization deficiencies in memory training studies. *Developmental Review, 17*(4), 411–441. https://doi.org/10.1006/drev.1997.0440

Borkowski, J. G., Milstead, M., & Hale, C. (1988). Components of children's metamemory: Implications for strategy generalization. In F. E. Weinert & M. Perlmutter (Eds.), *Memory development: Universal changes and individual differences* (pp. 73–100). Erlbaum.

Brown, D. A., Brubacher, S. P., Lewis, C. N., & Lamb, M. E. (2025). *Risks and rewards of ground rules in interviews with children: Testing the impact of different instruction approaches* [Manuscript in preparation]. Department of Psychology, University of Otago, Dunedin, New Zealand.

Brown, D. A., & Lamb, M. E. (2015). Can children be useful witnesses? It depends how they are questioned. *Child Development Perspectives, 9*(4), 250–255. https://doi.org/10.1111/cdep.12142

Brown, D. A., & Lamb, M. E. (2022). *Interviewing children about their experiences*. Routledge. https://doi.org/10.4324/9780367198459-REPRW183-1

Brown, D. A., Lewis, C. N., Brubacher, S. P., & Lamb, M. E. (2025). *Developmental changes in children's understanding of conversational ground rules* [Manuscript in preparation]. Department of Psychology, University of Otago, Dunedin, New Zealand.

Brown, D. A., Lewis, C. N., & Lamb, M. E. (2015). Preserving the past: An early interview improves delayed event memory in children with intellectual disabilities. *Child Development, 86*(4), 1031–1047. https://doi.org/10.1111/cdev.12364

Brown, D. A., Lewis, C. N., Lamb, M. E., Gwynne, J., Kitto, O., & Stairmand, M. (2019). Developmental differences in children's learning and use of forensic ground rules during an interview about an experienced event. *Developmental Psychology, 55*(8), 1626–1639. https://doi.org/10.1037/dev0000756

Brubacher, S. P., Poole, D. A., & Dickinson, J. J. (2015). The use of ground rules in investigative interviews with children: A synthesis and call for research. *Developmental Review, 36*, 15–33. https://doi.org/10.1016/j.dr.2015.01.001

Bruck, M., & Ceci, S. J. (1999). The suggestibility of children's memory. *Annual Review of Psychology, 50*(1), 419–439. https://doi.org/10.1146/annurev.psych.50.1.419

Cassel, W. S., Roebers, C. E., & Bjorklund, D. F. (1996). Developmental patterns of eyewitness responses to repeated and increasingly suggestive questions. *Journal of Experimental Child Psychology, 61*(2), 116–133. https://doi.org/10.1006/jecp.1996.0008

Cooper, A., Wallin, A. R., Quas, J. A., & Lyon, T. D. (2010). Maltreated and nonmaltreated children's knowledge of the juvenile dependency court system. *Child Maltreatment, 15*(3), 255–260. https://doi.org/10.1177/1077559510364056

Cordón, I. M., Saetermoe, C. L., & Goodman, G. S. (2005). Facilitating children's accurate responses: Conversational rules and interview style. *Applied Cognitive Psychology, 19*(3), 249–266. https://doi.org/10.1002/acp.1090

Danby, M. C., Brubacher, S. P., Sharman, S. J., & Powell, M. B. (2015). The effects of practice on children's ability to apply ground rules in a narrative interview. *Behavioral Sciences & the Law, 33*(4), 446–458. https://doi.org/10.1002/bsl.2194

Day, S. B., & Goldstone, R. L. (2012). The import of knowledge export: Connecting findings and theories of transfer of learning. *Educational Psychologist, 47*(3), 153–176. https://doi.org/10.1080/00461520.2012.696438

Dickinson, J. J., Brubacher, S. P., & Poole, D. A. (2015). Children's performance on ground rules questions: Implications for forensic interviewing. *Law and Human Behavior, 39*(1), 87–97. https://doi.org/10.1037/lhb0000119

Earhart, B., Brubacher, S. P., Powell, M. B., Westera, N. J., & Goodman-Delahunty, J. (2017). Judges' delivery of ground rules to child witnesses in Australian courts. *Child Abuse & Neglect, 74*, 62–72. https://doi.org/10.1016/j.chiabu.2017.08.005

Earhart, B., La Rooy, D. J., Brubacher, S. P., & Lamb, M. E. (2014). An examination of "don't know" responses in forensic interviews with children. *Behavioral Sciences & the Law, 32*(6), 746–761. https://doi.org/10.1002/bsl.2141

Ellis, L. M., Powell, M. B., Thomson, D. M., & Jones, C. (2003). Do simple "ground rules" reduce preschoolers' suggestibility about experienced and nonexperienced events? *Psychiatry, Psychology, & Law, 10*(2), 334–345. https://doi.org/10.1375/pplt.2003.10.2.334

Fessinger, M. L. S., McWilliams, K., Bakth, F. N., & Lyon, T. D. (2021). Setting the ground rules: Use and practice of ground rules in child forensic interviews. *Child Maltreatment, 26*(1), 126–132. https://doi.org/10.1177/1077559520910783

Flavell, J. H. (1979). Metacognition and cognitive monitoring: A new area of cognitive developmental inquiry. *The American Psychologist, 34*(10), 906–911. https://doi.org/10.1037/0003-066X.34.10.906

Geddie, L. F., Beer, J., Bartosik, S., & Wuensch, K. L. (2001). The relationship between interview characteristics and accuracy of recall in young children: Do individual differences matter? *Child Maltreatment, 6*(1), 59–68. https://doi.org/10.1177/1077559501006001006

Gee, S., Gregory, M., & Pipe, M. E. (1999). "What colour is your pet dinosaur?" The impact of pre-interview training and question type on children's answers. *Legal and Criminological Psychology, 4*(1), 111–128. https://doi.org/10.1348/135532599167716

Goodman, R. (1997). The Strengths and Difficulties Questionnaire: A research note. *The Journal of Child Psychology & Psychiatry, 38*(5), 581–586. https://doi.org/10.1111/j.1469-7610.1997.tb01545.x

Grung, R. M., Baugerud, G. A., Røed, R. K., & Johnson, M. S. (2024). Examining the impact of interviewer rejections following "Don't know" responses in forensic interviews of alleged preschool-aged victims of abuse. *Applied Cognitive Psychology, 38*(4), e4239. https://doi.org/10.1002/acp.4239

Guadagno, B. L., & Powell, M. B. (2014). An examination of the prevalence of temporally leading questions in child witness interviews. *International Journal of Police Science & Management, 16*(1), 16–25. https://doi.org/10.1350/ijps.2014.16.1.324

Hamilton, G., Brubacher, S. P., & Powell, M. B. (2016). Investigative interviewing of Aboriginal children in cases of suspected sexual abuse. *Journal of Child Sexual Abuse, 25*(4), 363–381. https://doi.org/10.1080/10538712.2016.1158762

Hamilton, G., Powell, M. B., & Brubacher, S. P. (2016). Professionals' perceptions regarding the suitability of investigative interview protocols with Aboriginal children. *Australian Psychologist, 52*(3), 174–183. https://doi.org/10.1111/ap.12196

Harris, P. L., Yang, B., & Cui, Y. (2017). "I don't know": Children's early talk about knowledge. *Mind & Language, 32*(3), 283–307. https://doi.org/10.1111/mila.12143

Henderson, H. M., & Lyon, T. D. (2021). Children's signaling of incomprehension: The diagnosticity of practice questions during interview instructions. *Child Maltreatment, 26*(1), 9–104. https://doi.org/10.1177/1077559520971350

Hughes, M., & Grieve, R. (1980). On asking children bizarre questions. *First Language, 1*(2), 149–160. https://doi.org/10.1177/014272378000100205

Johnson-Hunter, S. F., Brown, D. A., Brubacher, S. J., Lewis, C., & Lamb, M. E. (2023). *How do adults respond to unanswerable questions? Examining understanding and use of common interview ground rules* [Manuscript in preparation]. Department of Psychology, University of Otago, Dunedin, New Zealand.

Johnston, V., Brubacher, S. P., Powell, M., & Fuller-Tyszkiewicz, M. (2019). Patterns of nonverbal rapport behaviors across time in investigative interviews with children. *Journal of Nonverbal Behavior, 43*(3), 411–434. https://doi.org/10.1007/s10919-019-00306-1

Jol, G., & Stommel, W. (2024). Practicing ground rules in police interviews with child witnesses. *Language in Society, 53*(3), 445–469. https://doi.org/10.1017/S0047404523000337

Kelly, K. R., & Bailey, A. L. (2013). Dual development of conversational and narrative discourse: Mother and child interactions during narrative co-construction. *Merrill-Palmer Quarterly, 59*(4), 426–460. https://doi.org/10.1353/mpq.2013.0019

Krackow, E., & Lynn, S. J. (2010). Event report training: An examination of the efficacy of a new intervention to improve children's eyewitness reports. *Applied Cognitive Psychology, 24*(6), 868–884. https://doi.org/10.1002/acp.1594

Krähenbühl, S. J., Blades, M., & Cherryman, J. (2015). A qualitative examination of "ground rules" implementation practice in investigative interviews with children. *Psychiatry, Psychology and Law, 22*(6), 830–841. https://doi.org/10.1080/13218719.2015.1015206

Lamb, M. E., Brown, D. A., Hershkowitz, I., Orbach, Y., & Esplin, P. W. (2018). *Tell me what happened: Questioning children about abuse* (2nd ed.). John Wiley & Sons.

Lee, S., & Chung, H. J. (2023). Effects of guiding ground rules and individual differences on the accuracy of children's free recall and suggestibility. *Journal of Child Sexual Abuse, 32*(7), 829–844. https://doi.org/10.1080/10538712.2023.2261925

Lewis, C. N., Brown, D. A., Brubacher, S. P., & Lamb, M. E. (2023). *Cognitive and social skills contributing to children's understanding and use of common interview ground rules* [Manuscript in preparation]. Department of Psychology, University of Otago, Dunedin, New Zealand.

Lyon, T. D. (2021). *Ten step investigative interview* (Version 3). https://works.bepress.com/thomaslyon/184/

Malloy, L. C., Katz, C., Lamb, M. E., & Mugno, A. P. (2015). Children's requests for clarification in investigative interviews about suspected sexual abuse. *Applied Cognitive Psychology, 29*(3), 323–333. https://doi.org/10.1002/acp.3101

Malloy, L. C., & Stolzenberg, S. N. (2019). Questioning kids: Applying the lessons from developmentally-sensitive investigative interviewing to the research context. *Journal of Child Psychology and Psychiatry, 60*(3), 325–327. https://doi.org/10.1111/jcpp.13005

Markman, E. M. (1979). Realizing that you don't understand: Elementary school children's awareness of inconsistencies. *Child Development, 50*(3), 643–655. https://doi.org/10.2307/1128929

McWilliams, K., Williams, S., Stolzenberg, S. N., Evans, A. D., & Lyon, T. D. (2021). Don't know responding in young maltreated children: The effects of wh- questions type and enhanced interview instructions. *Law and Human Behavior, 45*(2), 124–137. https://doi.org/10.1037/lhb0000404

Memon, A., & Vartoukian, R. (1996). The effects of repeated questioning on young children's eyewitness testimony. *British Journal of Psychology, 87*(3), 403–415. https://doi.org/10.1111/j.2044-8295.1996.tb02598.x

Mulder, M. R., & Vrij, A. (1996). Explaining conversation rules to children: An intervention study to facilitate children's accurate responses. *Child Abuse & Neglect, 20*(7), 623–631. https://doi.org/10.1016/0145-2134(96)00050-6

National Children's Advocacy Center. (2019). *National Children's Advocacy Center's Child Forensic Interview structure*. https://files.calio.org/Other%20NCAC%20pubs/NCAC_CFIS_Feb%202019.pdf

Nelson, K., & Fivush, R. (2000). Socialization of memory. In E. Tulving & F. I. M. Craik (Eds.), *The Oxford handbook of memory* (pp. 283–295). Oxford University Press. https://doi.org/10.1093/oso/9780195122657.003.0018

Nesbitt, M., & Markham, R. (1999). Improving young children's accuracy of recall for an eyewitness event. *Journal of Applied Developmental Psychology, 20*(3), 449–459. https://doi.org/10.1016/S0193-3973(99)00027-1

Peters, W. W., & Nunez, N. (1999). Complex language and comprehension monitoring: Teaching child witnesses to recognize linguistic confusion. *Journal of Applied Psychology, 84*(5), 661–669. https://doi.org/10.1037/0021-9010.84.5.661

Peterson, C., & Grant, M. (2001). Forced-choice: Are forensic interviewers asking the right questions? *Canadian Journal of Behavioural Science, 33*(2), 118–127. https://doi.org/10.1037/h0087134

Poole, D. A., & White, L. T. (1991). Effects of question repetition on the eyewitness testimony of children and adults. *Developmental Psychology, 27*(6), 975–986. https://doi.org/10.1037//0012-1649.27.6.975

Powell, M. B., & Brubacher, S. P. (2020). The origin, experimental basis, and application of the standard interview method (SIM): An information-gathering framework. *Australian Psychologist, 55*(6), 645–659. https://doi.org/10.1111/ap.12468

Pratt, C. (1990). On asking children—and adults—bizarre questions. *First Language, 10*(29), 167–175. https://doi.org/10.1177/014272379001002905

Premack, D., & Woodruff, G. (1978). Does the chimpanzee have a theory of mind? *Behavioral and Brain Sciences, 4*(4), 515–526. https://doi.org/10.1017/S0140525X00076512

Rodriguez Steen, L. A., & Malloy, L. C. (2022). Children's clarification requests in interviews: Testing the effects of age, question characteristics, and brief intervention strategies. *Applied Cognitive Psychology, 36*(1), 121–134. https://doi.org/10.1002/acp.3903

Rodriguez Steen, L. A., & Malloy, L. C. (2024). Encouraging children's clarification requests with "I don't understand" rule reminders. *Applied Cognitive Psychology, 38*(1), e4157. https://doi.org/10.1002/acp.4157

Rohwer, M., Kloo, D., & Perner, J. (2012). Escape from metaignorance: How children develop an understanding of their own lack of knowledge. *Child Development, 83*(6), 1869–1883. https://doi.org/10.1111/j.1467-8624.2012.01830.x

Saywitz, K. J., & Camparo, L. B. (2014). *Evidence-based child forensic interviewing: The developmental narrative elaboration interview*. Oxford University Press.

Saywitz, K. J., & Moan-Hardie, S. (1994). Reducing the potential for distortion of childhood memories. *Consciousness and Cognition, 3*(3–4), 408–425. https://doi.org/10.1006/ccog.1994.1023

Saywitz, K. J., & Snyder, L. (1996). Narrative elaboration: Test of a new procedure for interviewing children. *Journal of Consulting and Clinical Psychology, 64*(6), 1347–1357. https://doi.org/10.1037/0022-006X.64.6.1347

Saywitz, K. J., Snyder, L., & Nathanson, R. (1999). Facilitating the communicative competence of the child witness. *Applied Developmental Science, 3*(1), 58–68. https://doi.org/10.1207/s1532480xads0301_7

Shatz, M., Wellman, H. M., & Silber, S. (1983). The acquisition of mental verbs: A systematic investigation of the first reference to mental state. *Cognition, 14*(3), 301–321. https://doi.org/10.1016/0010-0277(83)90008-2

Shaw, T. (2022). *"You can point to this card": Trialling the use of visual aids in teaching children to use ground rules in forensic interviewing* [Doctoral dissertation]. School of Psychology, Te Herenga Waka-Victoria University of Wellington. https://doi.org/10.26686/wgtn.19809586

Shing, Y. L., Lindenberger, U., Diamond, A., Li, S. C., & Davidson, M. C. (2010). Memory maintenance and inhibitory control differentiate from early childhood to adolescence. *Developmental Neuropsychology, 35*(6), 679–697. https://doi.org/10.1080/87565641.2010.508546

Tare, M., Shatz, M., & Gilbertson, L. (2008). Maternal uses of non-object terms in child-directed speech: Color, number, and time. *First Language, 28*(1), 87–100. https://doi.org/10.1177/0142723707085316

Teoh, Y. S., & Lamb, M. E. (2010). Preparing children for investigative interviews: Rapport building, instruction, and evaluation. *Applied Developmental Science, 14*(3), 154–163. https://doi.org/10.1080/10888691.2010.494463

Walsh, D., Bull, R., & Areh, I. (2025). *International handbook of investigative interviewing and interrogation*. Routledge.

Waterman, A. H., & Blades, M. (2011). Helping children correctly say "I don't know" to unanswerable questions. *Journal of Experimental Psychology: Applied, 17*(4), 396–405. https://doi.org/10.1037/a0026150

Waterman, A. H., Blades, M., & Spencer, C. P. (2000). Do children try to answer nonsensical questions? *British Journal of Developmental Psychology, 18*(2), 211–225. https://doi.org/10.1348/026151000165652

Waterman, A. H., Blades, M., & Spencer, C. P. (2004). Indicating when you do not know the answer: The effect of question format and interviewer knowledge on children's 'don't know' responses. *British Journal of Developmental Psychology, 22*(3), 335–348. https://doi.org/10.1348/0261510041552710

Zajac, R., & Brown, D. A. (2018). Conducting successful memory interviews with children. *Child and Adolescent Social Work Journal, 35*(3), 297–308. https://doi.org/10.1007/s10560-017-0527-z

11

What We Know and Don't Know About Eliciting Disclosures From and Interviewing Adolescent Victims and Witnesses

Victoria W. Dykstra, Rachel E. Dianiska, and Jodi A. Quas

Adolescence is an exciting and important period of development. During this time, exploration and identity formation take center stage as adolescents navigate new schools and situations, engage with new peer groups, and gradually move away from their parents' control. Many adolescents experience a change in responsibilities, for instance, by getting their first job or caring for younger siblings, while they also explore alternative or new perspectives and beliefs, spanning religious, political, and even sexual domains. This same period, though exciting, also poses risks, as adolescents' exploration and expanding relationships increase their potential exposure to harm, including as victims of and witnesses to potential violence at the hands of a wide range of perpetrators. This exposure means that adolescents may be questioned about their experiences by concerned parents or other adults, including law enforcement and legal professionals. How adolescents are questioned—and how they answer—has significant implications for their own protection, reducing further harm, and punishing potential perpetrators.

To date, relatively little attention has been devoted to effective methods of questioning suspected adolescent victims and witnesses, especially in legal settings. The paucity of research is a surprising contrast to the large amount of scientific research devoted to interviewing, memory, suggestibility, and disclosure tendencies in suspected child victims (age 12 and under; Azzopardi et al., 2019; Fernandes et al., 2023; Lavoie et al., 2021; Saywitz et al., 2015).

https://doi.org/10.1037/0000492-011
Handbook on Child Witnesses: Improving Psychological Science and Legal Practice,
G. S. Goodman, T. D. Lyon, S. D. Hobbs, and R. Enriquez (Editors)

The overarching purpose of this chapter is to increase attention on the important topic of questioning adolescents about potential harm. Our main contention is that adolescents have unique needs and capabilities in forensic settings. How well interviewers address those needs will directly affect what adolescents disclose and potentially the accuracy of those disclosures. In this chapter, we review empirical evidence relevant to this contention.

Our chapter is organized as follows: First, we review developmental characteristics that, although normative, both increase adolescents' vulnerability to crime-related experiences and alter their disclosure tendencies. Second, we describe emerging research concerning interviewing approaches for use with adolescents that are attuned to adolescents' unique needs, thereby holding promise for law enforcement and legal professionals. We close by highlighting remaining gaps in the literature concerning adolescents' reporting and interviewing needs, along with policy and practice implications of this research.

Before turning to our review, it is useful to have a sense of how often adolescents might be exposed to crimes and what types of crimes adolescents are likely to encounter and therefore be questioned about. The range is considerable and far greater than the types of crimes to which younger children are routinely exposed. Children most often experience and are legally questioned about maltreatment (e.g., neglect, physical abuse, exposure to domestic violence). Even with maltreatment, though, nearly one-quarter of victims in the United States are adolescents (23%; Children's Bureau, 2020). More broadly, according to the U.S. Bureau of Justice Statistics, adolescents are the second most common age group (following young adults, ages 18–24) to experience violent crime in general (Morgan & Truman, 2020), which includes sexual assault, robbery, aggravated assault, and simple assault. Similar trends have been reported in other countries (Cotter, 2021). According to a national survey of youth in the United Kingdom in 2022, for example, 16% of youth ages 13 to 17 years reported having been the victim of violence in the past year. When the definition was expanded to include victims of or witnesses to violence, that number increased to 46% (Youth Endowment Fund, 2022).

Given that adolescence is a time when teens begin to test and navigate romantic relationships, it is perhaps unsurprising that much of their exposure to violence and risk centers around dating and sexual activity, in both in-person and online settings. In the United States, 1 in 12 high school students report having experienced some form of dating violence (e.g., physical, sexual, psychological aggression, stalking; Basile et al., 2020), and in Canada, one in three high-school students who report having been in a romantic relationship indicate having experienced some type of dating violence as well (physical, sexual, psychological; Exner-Cortens et al., 2021). Online risks include exposure to nonconsensual sexting or online grooming by an adult (Finkelhor et al., 2022, 2023), but also adolescents engaging in harmful exploitative practices on their own. They may share sexual photos and videos of themselves and others, acts that can cause significant harm to youth, who are unlikely to fully understand the permanency of the information or its criminal significance

(Cooper et al., 2016; Finkelhor et al., 2022; Livingstone & Görzig, 2012; Naezer & van Oosterhout, 2021). Finally, a vast majority of victims of commercial and online sexual exploitation (manipulated or coerced into sexual acts or pornography in exchange for cash, goods, or services) are youth under age 18, with nearly 75% of these being adolescent-age victims (aged 12–17 years; Children's Bureau, 2020; National Institute of Justice, 2007).

As is evident, adolescents are personally exposed to a range of significant, harmful, and violent experiences. Some overlap with those to which children are exposed (e.g., maltreatment), and others are new to this developmental stage (e.g., online sexual exploitation, intimate partner violence), but across both categories, many do concern sexual matters. Authority figures, including law enforcement and legal professionals, but also other concerned adults such as parents, teachers, counselors, and health care workers, must, at times, question adolescents about what they have seen or endured to ensure adolescents receive necessary support and assistance and that actions are taken against those who perpetrate acts of harm. It is crucial, therefore, that adolescents fully and accurately report on their experiences. As we turn to next, several facets of adolescent development shape adolescents' ability and willingness to do just this.

DISCLOSURE AND INTERVIEWING IN THE CONTEXT OF ADOLESCENT DEVELOPMENT

A useful starting point to understanding adolescents' risk of harm and disclosure tendencies is with an overview of key hallmark characteristics of adolescence that affect these. Among the many characteristics to consider are those that affect adolescents' motivations, such as their tendencies toward exploration, autonomy, peer influence, and dishonesty, but also those that affect their actual memory and suggestibility. Importantly, these characteristics do not operate independently. As they change across development, they interact with one another to create a context in which, compared to children, adolescents are more vulnerable to harm and less likely to disclose that harm to adults.

Adolescent Development: Exploration, Autonomy, and Peers

Adolescence is a developmentally unique period marked by increased exploration, greater expectations of autonomy, and a growing emphasis on and influence by peers. All of these factors are relevant to disclosure versus concealment of negative behaviors, such as victimization or witnessing negative events.

Exploration and identity development are core aspects of adolescent development (e.g., Erikson, 1968; Luyckx et al., 2006; Waterman, 1993), with exploration of different facets of identity being vital to successfully establishing a sense of self (Arnold, 2017; Erikson, 1968; Waterman, 1993). Opportunities for exploration expand as adolescents spend increasing amounts of time away from parents (unsupervised), experience new social settings (e.g., different schools), and try new recreational activities (e.g., school clubs, extracurricular activities; Saragosa-Harris et al., 2022; Wrzus et al., 2013). This exploration is partly facilitated by adolescents' growing autonomy. Beginning in early adolescence, there is a largely universal assumption, at least in Western cultures, that adolescents will gradually move from parents controlling decisions toward mutual decision making, and ultimately to autonomous decisions (Baumrind, 2005; Smetana et al., 2004; Wray-Lake et al., 2010). Over time, adolescents experience greater distance (physical, psychological) from parents and other adults who had been the near-exclusive source of structure, rules, and discipline. Adolescents use this distance to make more of their own decisions and manage the consequences of those decisions (Baumrind, 2005; Simons-Morton et al., 2010). That same autonomy also facilitates adolescents' self-confidence and self-reliance as they learn to make independent decisions in the face of external influence (Chaika, 2020; De-Juanas et al., 2020; Páez-Gallego et al., 2020).

Autonomy and exploration, though normative, often confer some degree of risk (Saragosa-Harris et al., 2022). For instance, adolescents may try alcohol or illicit substances (Braams et al., 2015), or engage in sexual activity, including without protection (Kaplan et al., 2013; Moilanen, 2015). Novel peer groups may encourage risky or even delinquent behavior (Lemaigre et al., 2017). The growing prevalence of social media (Lenhart, 2015) provides adolescents with an ever-expanding range of individuals with whom to interact in online settings, and adolescents may lack an understanding of the potential risks involved in these interactions. Adolescents' decisions about their behaviors are often made without parental input and with the knowledge that parents and society broadly may well disapprove of these behaviors (Darling et al., 2006; Smetana et al., 2009). Either because adolescents feel adults, including parents, do not have the right to know about their autonomous behaviors or to avoid disapproval, adolescents limit parental or adult awareness of their activities via nondisclosure or other concealment strategies (e.g., keeping secrets, lying, avoiding discussing topics; Guo et al., 2022; Jensen et al., 2004; Rote & Smetana, 2016; Smetana et al., 2009). Adolescents may also be reluctant to disclose because they feel increasingly responsible for their risky decisions (Mergler & Patton, 2007). Insofar as adolescents feel they should be autonomous, or that autonomy is a sign of maturity, they may refrain from seeking parents' input when they encounter serious situations (Grandpre et al., 2003; Simons-Morton et al., 2010). As an example, if adolescents choose to engage in online interactions with a stranger that results in sharing of sexual photos, adolescents may not share that information before this occurs, perhaps because the adolescents believe that they have the autonomy to make decisions about how to interact online. If the interaction turns to exploitation or victimization, adolescents may assume that their own autonomous decision making led to the outcome (e.g., claiming to be in a consensual romantic relationship, failing to recognize manipulative tactics), reducing their willingness to tell others about it (Baird et al., 2020; Lavoie et al., 2019; Lindholm et al., 2014).

Another key characteristic of adolescence that affects what adolescents experience and their disclosure tendencies is the importance of peers, which peaks in adolescence (B. B. Brown, 2004; B. B. Brown & Larson, 2009). For example, at the same time adolescents can logically reason about risky behaviors in "cold" cognitive contexts (e.g., in questionnaires), their decision making in peer presence and the potential social rewards adolescents perceive to gain from engaging in risky behaviors varies, leading to a greater likelihood that adolescents will endorse and engage in risk-taking in the presence of peers (Botdorf et al., 2017; Icenogle et al., 2019; Smith et al., 2014; Steinberg, 2010; Tian et al., 2018).

In addition to peers influencing adolescents' decisions and behaviors, peers are also important in relation to adolescents' disclosure. This is most evident in secret-sharing and keeping, which are integral parts of the development and maintenance of adolescent friendships (Towner et al., 2022). Mutual self-disclosure between peers is vital for nurturing more intimate friendships (Valkenburg et al., 2011; Way, 2013), whereas being unable to keep secrets for friends results in perceptions of untrustworthiness, which can lead to negative outcomes such as rejection (Bauminger et al., 2008; Davis, 2012; Sprecher et al., 2013; Towner et al., 2022; Vijayakumar et al., 2020; Vijayakumar & Pfeifer, 2020). The expectation of keeping secrets extends to keeping these from adults as well (B. B. Brown et al., 2007; Chan et al., 2015). This can create a problematic dynamic, as research suggests adolescents are more likely to disclose negative experiences, such as sexual abuse, to peers rather than to parents (Hershkowitz et al., 2007; Kogan, 2004; Malloy et al., 2013; Manay & Collin-Vézina, 2021; Priebe & Svedin, 2008; Schaeffer et al., 2011; Schönbucher et al., 2012). Friends are then presented with the decision whether to transmit that disclosure, which contradicts their common expectation that friends will not disclose knowledge of the experiences of others, even when such disclosures would protect or prevent harm in others.

Dishonesty

When considered together, the aforementioned hallmark characteristics of adolescence—that is, exploration, autonomy, and peer influence—contribute to adolescents' tendency to conceal information from adults. As such, it is useful to consider how this concealment, or dishonesty more broadly, develops, and what aspects of dishonesty are especially relevant to adolescents. Concealment, which includes lying, is evident across the lifespan, emerges in early childhood and increases in frequency and sophistication with development (Evans & Lee, 2011; Gordon et al., 2014; O'Connor et al., 2020; Talwar & Lee, 2002, 2008; Talwar et al., 2007), peaking in adolescence and decreasing thereafter (Debey et al., 2015; Evans et al., 2025; Levine et al., 2013). Lie-telling in adolescence includes managing adults' awareness of their activities via a range of deceptive strategies, including avoiding the subject, denials, secret-keeping, and disclosing some but not all information (Baudat et al., 2022; Guo et al., 2022; Laird et al., 2013; Rote & Smetana, 2015; Smetana et al., 2019). Adolescents feel they have the right to manage certain types of behaviors on their own, such as romantic relationships, who they spend time with, and online activities, and as such feel justified in managing (largely by limiting) their parents' knowledge of these activities (Gingo et al., 2020; Jensen et al., 2004; Rote & Smetana, 2016). In addition, adolescents' ability to perspective take means that they can consider what others know and how they might react when electing if and what to tell.

Limiting parents' or other adults' knowledge presents an obvious problem when adolescents might have experienced or witnessed events that are risky, serious, and/or harmful to themselves or others, with evidence indeed indicating that adolescents' concealment tendencies extend to such events. For instance, adolescents often elect not to disclose substance use or sexual activity to adults (De Looze et al., 2015; Jensen et al., 2004; Warr, 2007). Not all such circumstances pose a major threat, but the general tendency to conceal such behaviors prevents adult intervention when it may be important or necessary. For example, while adolescents typically consider sexual activity to be under their personal control (Daddis & Randolph, 2010; Jensen et al., 2004), there may be circumstances in which they perceive sexual activity to be consensual when it is not, given their perception of and striving for autonomy in their decisions. Adolescents often perceive relationships with adult partners to be consensual (Tener et al., 2014). This perception is even stronger among some victim populations, such as commercially sexually exploited adolescents, who at times view their trafficker as their boyfriend and the exploitation as under their control (Basson et al., 2012; Ijadi-Maghsoodi et al., 2016; Landers et al., 2017). The latter adolescents, when questioned, can be uncooperative, evasive, and even hostile in an attempt to conceal or minimize disclosure of any information that could implicate the trafficker in harm or wrongdoing.

When adolescents do choose to conceal experiences, they are able to do so in fairly sophisticated ways, which includes monitoring information over time to ensure that their lie is consistent across questions and conversations (Evans & Lee, 2011). These abilities are enhanced by their more advanced (relative to children) cognitive and perspective-taking abilities, which makes detection of adolescents' lies potentially more challenging than detection of children's (Dykstra et al., 2020; Evans et al., 2016). To extrapolate to situations involving violence, harm, or risky relationships or behavior, if adolescents wish to keep those situations private, they are better equipped to do so than are children. The approach that adults take when questioning adolescents, therefore, needs to consider adolescent developmental characteristics broadly and adolescents' ability to maintain dishonest responses. Effective questioning is imperative to identify and intervene on behalf of adolescents who have experienced or witnessed harm.

Memory and Suggestibility

When adolescents do decide to disclose negative experiences, it is useful to consider whether, at a broad level, they have the mnemonic capabilities to recount their experiences accurately and completely, and at the same time resist false suggestions. On the one hand, compared to children, the answer to this consideration is a resounding yes. Adolescents are cognitively capable of reporting quite accurately, and at times in significant detail, on their prior experiences, and their accounts are typically longer, more detailed, and contain fewer errors than do those of children (Calado et al., 2018; Jack et al., 2014; Sheahan et al., 2017). Again, and also compared to children, adolescents are less suggestible and are less easily pressured into making false claims about prior experiences, including those that implicate them in wrongdoing (Eisen et al., 2002; Quas et al., 2014; Redlich & Goodman, 2003; Sauerland et al., 2018).

On the other hand, adolescents' memory reports are still not yet fully adult-like. Adolescents are not able recall as many details as adults (Jack et al., 2014; Sheahan et al., 2017), and adolescents make more errors and are more likely to acquiesce to misinformation (Brainerd et al., 2008; Gudjonsson & Singh, 1984; Redlich & Goodman, 2003; Sauerland et al., 2018), at least when interviews contain high pressure to conform, strongly suggestive questions, and forceful interrogation tactics (Brackmann et al., 2019). Of course, even adults are not immune to errors in response to highly suggestive tactics, and on some types of memory tasks, such as line-ups, adolescents perform as well as adults (Sheahan et al., 2017). Given these trends, it is again perhaps most useful to approach adolescent interviews acknowledging both that they generally outperform children on standard eyewitness tasks, but at times have slightly more difficulties than adults. Stated another way, even in terms of cognitive ability, memory, and suggestibility, adolescents comprise a unique population of witnesses whose reporting tendencies may vary from those of other age groups.

Summary: Adolescent Development, Vulnerability, and Disclosure

Research examining disclosure of victimization has mainly focused on children (age 12 and under), with far less attention being paid to adolescents' disclosures, particularly in terms of how they disclose, the recipients of their disclosures regarding experiences as victims or witnesses, and how developmental factors shape those disclosures. Developmentally, as mentioned, adolescents are likely to be quite reluctant to tell adults about a wide range of experiences, even though they can remember those experiences quite well and, to some extent, resist false suggestions about them. Adolescents may assume responsibility for their decisions and experiences, leading to decreases in disclosure, under the assumption that adults do not have the right to know about those decisions or their outcomes. Alternatively, adolescents may be embarrassed or afraid to tell, assuming that they should be responsible and should not make poor decisions. These reasons are important to distinguish, and there may be interview techniques that prove useful for encouraging disclosures and reporting about those they are embarrassed or worried about sharing, and less effective for issues that they feel should be kept private. Furthermore, the varied reasons for nondisclosure are highly relevant to disclosure of sexual matters in particular, topics adolescents are generally reluctant to discuss with adults and about which secret keeping among peers is common. Yet, these secrets, and hence nondisclosures, can include experiences of sexual violence or assault, experiences about which adults need to know in order to intervene. As we turn to next, these developmental characteristics, especially motivational processes that inhibit adolescents' honesty, must be taken into account when developing effective interviewing approaches for this important population.

ADOLESCENT INTERVIEWING

Research highlights unique challenges that exist when attempting to elicit detailed information from adolescents about potential harm, including victimization. At the same time, limited research has evaluated how best to design interviews for adolescents that address these challenges. Research on forensic interviewing has most often included younger age groups, spanning preschoolers through later childhood and early adolescence. Findings have led to a near consensus regarding effective approaches to elicit disclosures and accurate reports from children about violence exposure, particularly sexual and physical abuse (Fernandes et al., 2023; Lavoie et al., 2021); many of the chapters in this volume highlight important aspects of those approaches. For the purposes of the current chapter, we have divided the approaches into three broad categories of interviewer behavior: (a) how rapport is built, (b) broader provisions of support, and (c) how questions are phrased.

Our perspective is that these same broad categories of effective interviewer behaviors apply to adolescents. However, the precise ways that the approaches are implemented within each category need to take into account the developmental stage of the interviewee—in this case, adolescents' specific needs. Doing so, we contend, will increase adolescents' likelihood of reporting when and if they experienced harm, what occurred, and what their needs are, just as recommendations for children do. Before turning to ways that these recommendations could be modified for adolescents, we first review how the recommendations have been implemented in interviews with children. This review will highlight the importance of each component of forensic interviews and examine its effectiveness with adolescent victims.

Forensic Interviewing With Children

The decades of research concerning best-practices interviewing techniques with children (e.g., National Institute of Child Health and Human Development

[NICHD] Investigative Interview Protocol; Lamb et al., 2018; Developmental Narrative Elaboration interview; Saywitz et al., 2015) suggest it is crucial that techniques (a) effectively build rapport with children at the outset, hence increasing their comfort later disclosing; (b) create a supportive interview context to increase the completeness of what children report and reduce their tendency to err; and (c) phrase questions in a way that maximizes children's narrative productivity and minimizes errors.

First, building rapport with children is considered essential for successful forensic interviewing. It includes two sets of separable but often combined activities, giving children instructions regarding the interview and helping children become comfortable engaging with the interviewer and providing narrative responses via getting-to-know-you questions (Saywitz et al., 2015). Instructions include explaining the purpose of the interview, instructing children to say "I don't know," or to correct the interviewer, and engaging in a truth–lie discussion. These, in combination, help children understand the purpose of the interview and their role as the one with knowledge of a prior event (Lamb et al., 2018; Lyon, 2014).

The getting-to-know-you phase, at times called rapport proper, serves multiple purposes. Overall, it allows an interviewer to begin to build trust and help children feel at ease with the interviewer (Abbe & Brandon, 2013). Yet, how getting-to-know-you questions are asked has emerged as being particularly important. Interviewers are instructed to ask open-ended questions, such as about children's likes and dislikes and about a recent, personally salient event (e.g., holiday, birthday). Children are encouraged both in the questions and follow-up prompts to give lengthy narrative answers, thereby increasing their comfort with talking and setting up expectations for the need for continued lengthy answers. This sort of practice has been shown to increase children's later productivity when discussing positive and negative events (e.g., Dorado & Saywitz, 2001; Quas & Dickerson, 2019; Saywitz & Camparo, 2014; Saywitz et al., 1992; for reviews see Lyon, 2014; Saywitz et al., 2015), presumably because children become more relaxed with the interviewer and know what to expect (Lavoie et al., 2021).

Second, interviewer support, or at times described as a supportive interview context, has emerged as being equally important when questioning suspected child victims and witnesses. In some work, rapport building is considered to be a component of supportive interviewing: Creating a supportive interview context begins with interviewers building rapport. However, support is generally considered a broader set of behaviors spanning the entire interview that creates a warm and encouraging context that increases children's comfort and willingness to report details even about negative events and ability to resist an interviewer's suggestions when details did not occur (Bottoms et al., 2007; Quas & Lench, 2007; see also Saywitz et al., 2019). Supportive interviewers maintain an open body posture and eye contact and use facilitators. Other supportive behaviors include using the child's name periodically, providing positive reinforcement regarding a child's efforts (with the explicit instruction that reinforcement is not contingent upon specific answers; see Cleveland et al., 2018), expressing empathy, and acknowledging and possibly exploring the child's emotions. Combined, these behaviors should foster a sense of well-being and confidence that may have positive effects on children's disclosure (Brubacher et al., 2019; Hershkowitz et al., 2014; McWilliams et al., 2021) but more often on their completeness and accuracy (Hershkowitz et al., 2006), and accuracy (Quas & Lench, 2007).

Third, and the domain where the most extensive research has been conducted, concerns how questions are or should be phrased to maximize children's productivity and accuracy and reduce potential errors. The National Institute for Child Health and Human Development Investigative Interview Protocol, for instance, instructs interviewers to begin with general invitations asking children to report everything they remember about a particular event (see Lamb et al., 2018), given that such invitations, especially when paired with cued follow up prompts (e.g., "You said X, tell me more about X.") are consistently associated with increased productivity. Recommendations then discourage the use of closed-ended questions (e.g., yes/no or forced choice, "Were your pants on?"), leading questions (e.g., "He said he'd hurt you, right?"), and ambiguous question types (e.g., indirect speech acts, "Do you know what you were wearing?"), all of which fail to prompt narratives and can lead children to feel pressure to respond even if they do not know an answer or fail to understand the question; they can also lead to response biases or short and minimally useful answers (Evans & Lyon, 2012; Evans et al., 2014, 2017; Lyon, 2014; Stolzenberg et al., 2020, 2021).

These approaches, in combination, have been shown to help elicit detailed and accurate disclosures from children. Interviewers who follow these broad recommendations, even when discussing negative and at times distressing or traumatic events, are likely to obtain more information, including information that is more apt to be trusted as accurate, than interviewers who do not follow the recommendations. Again, however, a noteworthy omission in the impressive body of literature underlying these recommendations is that most studies typically examine children through age 12 or 13 years and have not included individuals in mid to late adolescence. And, for the reasons we have already laid out, adolescents' developmental needs may well necessitate alternative approaches or at least modifications to the recommendations (cf. Dianiska et al., 2024a; Sauerland et al., 2018).

Forensic Interviewing With Adolescents

It is important to note that adolescents have been included in some studies testing the effects of different interviewing approaches on memory, suggestibility, and even abuse disclosures (Dianiska et al., 2024b; Jack et al., 2014; Klemfuss et al., 2013; Quas et al., 2014, 2016; Sauerland et al., 2018), which have allowed for age-related comparisons in reporting tendencies. Yet, most studies, particularly those focused on evaluating approaches designed to enhance disclosure or reduce errors, have ignored how hallmark developmental characteristics of adolescence, such as adolescents' desire for autonomy, the importance of peer relationships, and their tendency to be reluctant to disclose their experiences to adults, affect their responses or reactions to the approaches. Next, we turn to the three categories (rapport, support, question type), describing how they might be modified for adolescents. When available, we describe emerging findings that are promising in terms of the potential value of modifying recommendations based on adolescents' needs for adolescent victims' and witnesses' reporting.

First, the value of building rapport has been touted not only in forensic interviews with children, but with adult victims and witnesses and even suspects as well (for review, see Gabbert et al., 2020). More so than with children, rapport building with adults is designed to establish trust and set clear expectations for the interview process and outcome. Adolescents, as mentioned, are often untrusting of adults, meaning that effective rapport building to establish some level of trust may be crucial, but so might explaining expectations and goals, if presented in a way that fosters a sense of maturity in or respect for adolescents.

How to best establish rapport with adolescents is not entirely clear. That is, very few studies have tested whether techniques designed to build rapport with children are comparably effective with adolescents, or whether other approaches, such as those typically employed with adults, are needed. Studies examining rapport and ground rule instructions have rarely included adolescents, and those that do typically only go up to 13 years of age (Cyr et al., 2012; Dianiska et al., 2024a; Sauerland et al., 2018; Teoh & Lamb, 2010). Recommended approaches to build rapport with adults do not stress a need for open-ended questions or narrative practice about likes or dislikes, as is done with children. Instead, with adults, the emphasis of rapport is on fostering an interpersonal relationship (Tickle-Degnen & Rosenthal, 1990; Vallano & Schreiber Compo, 2015). Approaches are described in general terms, such as conveying mutual attention (e.g., active listening, backchannel responses), establishing a positive affective relationship (e.g., finding common ground in topics discussed, showing an interest in the interviewee as a person), and developing a shared understanding of expectations (e.g., explaining the interview process).

Given adolescents' desires for autonomy and to be seen as equals (Chen, 2010; Fleming, 2005), rapport-building techniques that convey these ideas may be particularly useful, or at least more useful than just having adolescents practice responding to open-ended questions. With adults, interviewers are encouraged to reveal personal information about themselves when eliciting personal information from an interviewee during rapport building. This "mutual self-disclosure" at the outset is believed to facilitate liking and create opportunities for interviewers to highlight similarities and establish common ground (N. L. Collins & Miller, 1994; Vallano et al., 2015). Mutual self-disclosure has been shown to increase adults' disclosures of negative events in analogue studies (R. Collins et al., 2002; Dianiska et al., 2021; Holmberg & Madsen, 2014; Nash et al., 2016; Wachi et al., 2018) and in the amount of information provided by adult suspects (K. Collins & Carthy, 2019; Kelly et al., 2016) and adult victims of sexual assault (Kim et al., 2020) in field studies.

Evidence from a few recent studies with adolescents confirmed the possibility that mutual self-disclosure could be of value in some contexts. In a recent study we conducted with 14- to 19-year-olds, adolescents filled out an online questionnaire, which included questions about negative experiences and behaviors to which they were exposed. Later, the adolescents completed Zoom interviews with interviewers who began by building rapport in one of three ways: standard yes/no closed-ended questions, open-ended questions (comparable to best practice recommended rapport approaches with children), or open-ended questions paired with mutual disclosure (interviewers sharing personal information after the adolescents did). When asked about the negative events and behaviors, adolescents in the mutual disclosure condition were most productive (word count), whereas adolescents in the closed-ended condition were least productive (Dianiska et al., 2024a, 2024b). We are now expanding this study to evaluate whether similar patterns emerge when adolescents' disclosure of negative or embarrassing information is examined, when accuracy can be assessed, and when interviews are conducted in person (Dianiska et al., 2024b; Simpson et al., 2024). Because adolescents recognize the importance of and value self-disclosure in building friendships and maintaining trust (Bauminger et al., 2008; Towner et al., 2022), mutual disclosure could lead to positive feelings toward the interviewer at the outset, increasing adolescents' willingness later to report more details about their own experiences.

Mutual disclosure is just one potentially valuable rapport strategy. Others, as highlighted by interviewers with expertise questioning suspected adolescent victims, include the importance of being honest and open with adolescents early on about the purpose of the interview and meeting adolescents "where they are" at the outset (Deck et al., 2025). The precise ways to do both of these, that is, how to explain the purpose and how to "meet adolescents where they are," will need to be operationalized, but doing so would allow for empirical research to continue to develop and test rapport-building techniques designed specifically for adolescent victims and witnesses.

The second category of recommendations, interviewer support, is likely an equally influential facet of the context of the interview for adolescents. Some studies of the effects of social support on memory and suggestibility have included younger adolescent age groups along with children. Like children, adolescents (e.g., ages 12–14) are less suggestible and less likely to make line-up errors when questioned by a supportive (e.g., maintaining eye contact, providing noncontingent verbal encouragement) than nonsupportive (e.g., not maintaining eye contact, providing no encouragement) interviewer (Quas et al., 2014; Rush et al., 2014; Saywitz et al., 2019). Yet, support was not tailored specifically for adolescents, and very few studies include participants above the age of 12–14 (Blasbalg et al., 2019; Karni-Visel et al., 2023;

Klemfuss et al., 2013; Quas & Dickerson, 2019; Quas et al., 2014). High-support interviewers built rapport by having a friendly conversation at the start of the interview. They sat close to the adolescents, smiled, maintained eye contact, and provided noncontingent positive feedback.

Larger effects of support might emerge if interviewers' supportive behavior address adolescents' needs. How this might be done has yet to be tested empirically, although interviewers in a recent qualitative study highlighted several potential strategies. In the study (Deck et al., 2025), interviewers were asked about common challenges they face when interviewing suspected adolescent victims and approaches they use to overcome those challenges. The experts emphasized the importance of giving adolescents the opportunity and space to express themselves however they choose. They also encouraged adolescents to express their emotions and use their own style of language (e.g., slang, profanity), giving youth a sense of control over the interview and helping them feel free to be themselves. Increasing adolescents' feelings of autonomy and creating an environment of mutual respect likely creates a more supportive interview context, and may influence adolescents' likelihood of reporting sensitive information about experiences such as sexual victimization.

Another facet of interview support that could be easily modified to address adolescents' needs involves interviewers repeating back what the adolescent said. With children, interviewers often repeat what the child said to ensure that the child knows the interviewer is listening and that they understood what the child meant (e.g., cued invitations; D. A. Brown et al., 2013). Simple repetition with adolescents may not convey the same benefit, particularly if adolescents feel that the interviewer is questioning the adolescent's reports or is treating them like a child. Several expert interviewers in Deck et al.'s (2025) study explained that they listen to adolescents' speech and use similar terms and phrasing (e.g., profanity). This matching, interviewers noted, shows that they respect the adolescents' chosen form of expression, and may be a form of meeting adolescents where they are—here in terms of language. Moreover, by using the same types of language, interviewers may be able to repeat parts of adolescents' narratives, indicating that they are paying attention, which again could enhance the supportiveness of the interview context, a possibility that needs to be tested directly.

Finally, turning to question type, regardless of age, open ended questions are recommended. With children, best practices involve using open-ended questions followed by cued invitations to facilitate narrative responses. With adults, like with children, open-ended recall prompts are considered optimal, allowing adults to provide narrative accounts of their experiences in response to general prompts (Lamb et al., 2018). Closed-ended and leading questions, in contrast, lead to errors and false accounts not only in children but also in adults—the latter evidenced in classic misinformation studies by Loftus in the 1970s (for review see Loftus, 2005). Thus, at a broad level, open-ended recall prompts should be employed as much as possible, and closed-ended and leading questions should be avoided with adolescents.

Yet, nuances in the dynamics of the interaction between interviewers and adolescents, combined with high levels of mistrust among some adolescent victim populations (Fix et al., 2021; Somer & Szwarcberg, 2001), could undermine the value of open-ended questions with adolescents, who may elect not to answer them. They may feel too embarrassed or ashamed to share, they may be afraid of the consequences of disclosing, or they may feel the interviewer has no right to the information. Any one of these reasons could lead to adolescents providing only minimal responses, responding evasively, or otherwise avoiding answering when asked open-ended questions; all are patterns seen in analyses of forensic interviews with some types of adolescent victims (e.g., those potentially exposed to commercial exploitation; Dykstra et al., 2024; Lindholm et al., 2015; Nogalska et al., 2021). An overly simple interpretation of these patterns is that the open-ended questions themselves are problematic, or at least problematic with some types of adolescent victims. However, moving to more direct questioning approaches, such as closed-ended questions, also carries significant risks, particularly because the questions are themselves paired with other interview tactics known to increase errors. Several of the tactics are reminiscent of common—and often manipulative—tactics used in interrogations of adult and adolescent suspects, such as maximization (e.g., emphasizing the seriousness of an offense) and minimization (e.g., offering face-saving justifications, excuses). At times, the tactics appear at face value to appeal to developmentally relevant features of adolescence, such as autonomy, by telling adolescents that they have control over what they say, but these tactics undermine that value once adolescents respond. For instance, interviewers may tell victims that they can choose to answer questions or not, but then not accept the victims' denial and instead continue to press for an answer, thereby invalidating the victims' autonomy (Nogalska et al., 2021).

More broadly, the questions, even if open-ended, are embedded in a context of power and pressure rather than mutual trust and autonomy. Given adolescents' high mistrust of adults and sensitivity to adults' efforts to undermine their feelings of autonomy and respect (see Yeager et al., 2018, for a review), strategies that promote power and reduce adolescents' feelings of control are highly likely to be ineffective. Adolescents who have been sexually exploited, either via an online or in-person perpetrator, maintain their evasive stance across open-ended and closed-ended questions, at times becoming overtly hostile to answering when interviewers use interrogative tactics (Henderson et al., 2021; Nogalska et al., 2021). Furthermore, the use of these tactics is linked to reductions in the amount of detail victims provide, even to open-ended questions about substantive sexual topics (Lindholm et al., 2015); a particularly problematic trend given that such topics comprise key information in a case. Thus, with adolescents, while open-ended questions are certainly crucial, they must be embedded in an interview that is framed around adolescents' developmental needs to elicit full disclosures.

It is important to note that there is a distinction between encouraging more productive and accurate reporting from adolescents when they do disclose versus merely encouraging adolescents to disclose—a problem not unique to adolescents, but one that has been identified in child interviewing as well. Some approaches, such as support, appear to be more influential in increasing children's productivity and less effective at increasing children's likelihood of initial disclosure (e.g., McWilliams et al., 2021). This may also be true of adolescents. Identifying how adolescent-tailored interview approaches (rapport, support, question type) affect disclosure versus productivity (while, of course, also considering accuracy) needs to be studied carefully to develop best-practice recommendations tailored to the specific needs of a given interview.

Interviewing adolescents requires an understanding of the characteristics of this important developmental stage. Adolescents' increased reluctance, cognitive capacity to conceal their experiences, and lack of trust in adults and authority figures all pose significant challenges when attempting to encourage disclosures and elicit full and accurate reports of negative experiences and harm, including violence exposure and sexual assault. Extant research has identified effective approaches for questioning children; these approaches can likely be modified in simple but significant ways to be useful for interviewing adolescents as well. It is crucial to identify these modifications and test their effects empirically to provide evidence-based recommendations to practitioners on best practices for interviewing adolescents.

CONCLUSION

Adolescence is a period of immense change, and this change often results in increased risk of or exposure to violence and victimization. While maltreatment occurs during both childhood and adolescence, adolescents are exposed to new forms of victimization, such as commercial sexual exploitation by romantic partners, dating violence, and online exploitation. Given this increased risk, it is vital to identify effective methods for encouraging adolescents to disclose these experiences, as well as ways to interview them to gain detailed accounts. There are numerous ways that developmentally relevant techniques can be incorporated into interview strategies used with children or adults, such as matching adolescent tone and language, engaging in mutual exchange rapport building, and engaging in questioning practices that allow adolescents to feel autonomy over their reporting. Research examining these adjusted strategies is vital to be able to provide evidence-based recommendations for those who interview adolescents about sensitive experiences.

REFERENCES

Abbe, A., & Brandon, S. E. (2013). The role of rapport in investigative interviewing: A review. *Journal of Investigative Psychology and Offender Profiling, 10*(3), 237–249. https://doi.org/10.1002/jip.1386

Arnold, M. E. (2017). Supporting adolescent exploration and commitment: Identity formation, thriving, and positive youth development. *Journal of Youth Development, 12*(4), 1–15. https://doi.org/10.5195/jyd.2017.522

Azzopardi, C., Eirich, R., Rash, C. L., MacDonald, S., & Madigan, S. (2019). A meta-analysis of the prevalence of child sexual abuse disclosure in forensic settings. *Child Abuse & Neglect, 93,* 291–304. https://doi.org/10.1016/j.chiabu.2018.11.020

Baird, K., McDonald, K. P., & Connolly, J. (2020). Sex trafficking of women and girls in a southern Ontario region: Police file review exploring victim characteristics, trafficking experiences, and the intersection with child welfare. *Canadian Journal of Behavioural Science/Revue Canadienne des Sciences du Comportement, 52*(1), 8–17. https://doi.org/10.1037/cbs0000151

Basile, K. C., Clayton, H. B., DeGue, S., Gilford, J. W., Vagi, K. J., Suarez, N. A., Suarez, N. A., Zwald, M. L., & Lowry, R. (2020). Interpersonal violence victimization among high school students—Youth Risk Behavior Survey, United States, 2019. *MMWR Supplements, 69*(1), 28–37. https://doi.org/10.15585/mmwr.su6901a4

Basson, D., Rosenblatt, E., & Haley, H. (2012). *Research to action: Sexually exploited minors (SEM) needs and strengths.* West Coast Children's Clinic.

Baudat, S., Mantzouranis, G., Van Petegem, S., & Zimmermann, G. (2022). How do adolescents manage information in the relationship with their parents? A latent class analysis of disclosure, keeping secrets, and lying. *Journal of Youth and Adolescence, 51*(6), 1134–1152. https://doi.org/10.1007/s10964-022-01599-0

Bauminger, N., Finzi-Dottan, R., Chason, S., & Har-Even, D. (2008). Intimacy in adolescent friendship: The roles of attachment, coherence, and self-disclosure. *Journal of Social and Personal Relationships, 25*(3), 409–428. https://doi.org/10.1177/0265407508090866

Baumrind, D. (2005). Patterns of parental authority and adolescent autonomy. *New Directions for Child and Adolescent Development, 2005*(108), 61–69. https://doi.org/10.1002/cd.128

Blasbalg, U., Hershkowitz, I., Lamb, M. E., Karni-Visel, Y., & Ahern, E. C. (2019). Is interviewer support associated with the reduced reluctance and enhanced informativeness of alleged child abuse victims? *Law and Human Behavior, 43*(2), 156–165. https://doi.org/10.1037/lhb0000303

Botdorf, M., Rosenbaum, G. M., Patrianakos, J., Steinberg, L., & Chein, J. M. (2017). Adolescent risk-taking is predicted by individual differences in cognitive control over emotional, but not non-emotional, response conflict. *Cognition and Emotion, 31*(5), 972–979. https://doi.org/10.1080/02699931.2016.1168285

Bottoms, B. L., Quas, J. A., & Davis, S. L. (2007). The influence of interviewer-provided social support on children's suggestibility, memory, and disclosures. In M.-E. Pipe, M. E. Lamb, Y. Orbach, & A.-C. Cederborg (Eds.), *Child sexual abuse: Disclosure, delay, and denial* (pp. 135–157). Lawrence Erlbaum Associates.

Braams, B. R., van Duijvenvoorde, A. C., Peper, J. S., & Crone, E. A. (2015). Longitudinal changes in adolescent risk-taking: A comprehensive study of neural responses to rewards, pubertal development, and risk-taking behavior. *The Journal of Neuroscience, 35*(18), 7226–7238. https://doi.org/10.1523/jneurosci.4764-14.2015

Brackmann, N., Sauerland, M., & Otgaar, H. (2019). Developmental trends in lineup performance: Adolescents are more prone to innocent bystander misidentifications than children and adults. *Memory & Cognition, 47*(3), 428–440. https://doi.org/10.3758/s13421-018-0877-6

Brainerd, C. J., Reyna, V. F., & Ceci, S. J. (2008). Developmental reversals in false memory: A review of data and theory. *Psychological Bulletin, 134*(3), 343–382. https://doi.org/10.1037/0033-2909.134.3.343

Brown, B. B. (2004). Adolescents' relationships with peers. In R. M. Lerner & L. Steinberg (Eds.), *Handbook of adolescent psychology* (pp. 363–394). Wiley. https://doi.org/10.1002/9780471726746.ch12

Brown, B. B., Bakken, J. P., Nguyen, J., & Von Bank, H. G. (2007). Sharing information about peer relations: Parent and adolescent opinions and behaviors in Hmong and

African American families. *New Directions for Child and Adolescent Development, 116*, 67–82. https://doi.org/10.1002/cd.189

Brown, B. B., & Larson, J. (2009). Peer relationships in adolescence. *Handbook of adolescent psychology, 2*(Pt I), 74–104. Wiley.

Brown, D. A., Lamb, M. E., Lewis, C., Pipe, M. E., Orbach, Y., & Wolfman, M. (2013). The NICHD investigative interview protocol: An analogue study. *Journal of Experimental Psychology: Applied, 19*(4), 367–382. https://doi.org/10.1037/a0035143

Brubacher, S. P., Poole, D. A., Dickinson, J. J., La Rooy, D., Szojka, Z. A., & Powell, M. B. (2019). Effects of interviewer familiarity and supportiveness on children's recall across repeated interviews. *Law and Human Behavior, 43*(6), 507–516. https://doi.org/10.1037/lhb0000346

Calado, B., Otgaar, H., & Muris, P. (2018). Are children better witnesses than adolescents? Developmental trends in different false memory paradigms. *Journal of Child Custody, 15*(4), 330–348. https://doi.org/10.1080/15379418.2019.1568948

Chaika, G. (2020). Psychological characteristics influencing personal autonomy as a factor of psychological well-being. *Psychological Journal, 6*(1), 18–28. https://doi.org/10.31108/1.2020.6.1.2

Chan, H. Y., Brown, B. B., & Von Bank, H. (2015). Adolescent disclosure of information about peers: The mediating role of perceptions of parents' right to know. *Journal of Youth and Adolescence, 44*(5), 1048–1065. https://doi.org/10.1007/s10964-015-0261-9

Chen, X. (2010). Desire for autonomy and adolescent delinquency: A latent growth curve analysis. *Criminal Justice and Behavior, 37*(9), 989–1004. https://doi.org/10.1177/0093854810367481

Children's Bureau. (2020). *Child maltreatment 2018*. U.S. Department of Health & Human Services, Administration for Children and Families, Administration on Children, Youth and Families. https://www.acf.hhs.gov/sites/default/files/documents/cb/cm2018.pdf

Cleveland, K. C., Quas, J. A., & Lyon, T. D. (2018). The effects of implicit encouragement and the putative confession on children's memory reports. *Child Abuse & Neglect, 80*, 113–122. https://doi.org/10.1016/j.chiabu.2018.03.024

Collins, K., & Carthy, N. (2019). No rapport, no comment: The relationship between rapport and communication during investigative interviews with suspects. *Journal of Investigative Psychology and Offender Profiling, 16*(1), 18–31. https://doi.org/10.1002/jip.1517

Collins, N. L., & Miller, L. C. (1994). Self-disclosure and liking: A meta-analytic review. *Psychological Bulletin, 116*(3), 457–475. https://doi.org/10.1037/0033-2909.116.3.457

Collins, R., Lincoln, R., & Frank, M. G. (2002). The effect of rapport in forensic interviewing. *Psychiatry, Psychology and Law, 9*(1), 69–78. https://doi.org/10.1375/pplt.2002.9.1.69

Cooper, K., Quayle, E., Jonsson, L., & Svedin, C. G. (2016). Adolescents and self-taken sexual images: A review of the literature. *Computers in Human Behavior, 55*, 706–716. https://doi.org/10.1016/j.chb.2015.10.003

Cotter, A. (2021). Criminal victimization in 2019. *Juristat, Statistics Canada Catalogue no. 85-002-X*. https://www150.statcan.gc.ca/n1/en/catalogue/85-002-X202100100014

Cyr, M., Dion, J., McDuff, P., & Trotier-Sylvain, K. (2012). Transfer of skills in the context of non-suggestive investigative interviews: Impact of structured interview protocol and feedback. *Applied Cognitive Psychology, 26*(4), 516–524. https://doi.org/10.1002/acp.2822

Daddis, C., & Randolph, D. (2010). Dating and disclosure: Adolescent management of information regarding romantic involvement. *Journal of Adolescence, 33*(2), 309–320. https://doi.org/10.1016/j.adolescence.2009.05.002

Darling, N., Cumsille, P., Caldwell, L. L., & Dowdy, B. (2006). Predictors of adolescents' disclosure to parents and perceived parental knowledge: Between-and within-person differences. *Journal of Youth and Adolescence, 35*(4), 659–670. https://doi.org/10.1007/s10964-006-9058-1

Davis, K. (2012). Friendship 2.0: Adolescents' experiences of belonging and self-disclosure online. *Journal of Adolescence, 35*(6), 1527–1536. https://doi.org/10.1016/j.adolescence.2012.02.013

Debey, E., Schryver, M. D., Logan, G. D., Suchotski, K., & Verschuere, B. (2015). From junior to senior Pinocchio: A cross-sectional lifespan investigation of deception. *Acta Psychologica, 160*, 58–68. https://doi.org/10.1016/j.actpsy.2015.06.007

Deck, S. L., Quas, J. A., & Powell, M. B. (2025). Unique considerations for forensic interviews with adolescents: An exploration of expert interviewers' perspectives. *Child Maltreatment, 30(2)*, 229–241. https://doi.org/10.1177/10775595241270046

De-Juanas, Á., Bernal Romero, T., & Goig, R. (2020). The relationship between psychological well-being and autonomy in young people according to age. *Frontiers in Psychology, 11*, 559976. https://doi.org/10.3389/fpsyg.2020.559976

De Looze, M., Constantine, N. A., Jerman, P., Vermeulen-Smit, E., & Ter Bogt, T. (2015). Parent–adolescent sexual communication and its association with adolescent sexual behaviors: A nationally representative analysis in the Netherlands. *The Journal of Sex Research, 52*(3), 257–268. https://doi.org/10.1080/00224499.2013.858307

Dianiska, R. E., Simpson, E., & Quas, J. A. (2024a). Rapport building with adolescents to enhance reporting and disclosure. *Journal of Experimental Child Psychology, 238*, 105799. https://doi.org/10.1016/j.jecp.2023.105799

Dianiska, R. E., Simpson, E., & Quas, J. (2024b, March 21–23). *Rapport building to facilitate disclosures from adolescents in in-person and online interviews* [Paper presentation]. American Psychology–Law Society Annual Conference, Los Angeles, CA, United States.

Dianiska, R. E., Swanner, J. K., Brimbal, L., & Meissner, C. A. (2021). Using disclosure, common ground, and verification to build rapport and elicit information. *Psychology, Public Policy, and Law, 27*(3), 341–353. https://doi.org/10.1037/law0000313

Dorado, J. S., & Saywitz, K. J. (2001). Interviewing preschoolers from low-and middle-SES communities: A test of the Narrative Elaboration Recall Improvement technique. *Journal of Clinical Child Psychology, 30*(4), 568–580. https://doi.org/10.1207/S15374424JCCP3004_12

Dykstra, V. W., Dianiska, R. E., Lyon, T. D., & Quas, J. A. (2024, June 17–21). *Question type and reluctant responding in trafficked adolescents* [Paper presentation]. International Investigative Interviewing Group Conference, Ottawa, ON, Canada.

Dykstra, V. W., Willoughby, T., & Evans, A. D. (2020). Perceptions of dishonesty: Understanding parents' reports of and influence on children and adolescents' lie-telling. *Journal of Youth and Adolescence, 49*(1), 49–59. https://doi.org/10.1007/s10964-019-01153-5

Eisen, M. L., Qin, J., Goodman, G. S., & Davis, S. L. (2002). Memory and suggestibility in maltreated children: Age, stress arousal, dissociation, and psychopathology. *Journal of Experimental Child Psychology, 83*(3), 167–212. https://doi.org/10.1016/s0022-0965(02)00126-1

Erikson, E. H. (1968). *Identity, youth, and crisis.* Norton and Company.

Evans, A. D., Bender, J., & Lee, K. (2016). Can parents detect 8- to 16-year-olds' lies? Parental biases, confidence, and accuracy. *Journal of Experimental Child Psychology, 147*, 152–158. https://doi.org/10.1016/j.jecp.2016.02.011

Evans, A. D., Dykstra, V. W., & O'Connor, A. M. (2025). Differences in daily lie-telling patterns from adolescence to older adulthood. *Applied Developmental Science*, 1–15. https://doi.org/10.1080/10888691.2025.2486063

Evans, A. D., & Lee, K. (2011). Verbal deception from late childhood to middle adolescence and its relation to executive functioning skills. *Developmental Psychology, 47*(4), 1108–1116. https://doi.org/10.1037/a0023425

Evans, A. D., & Lyon, T. D. (2012). Assessing children's competency to take the oath in court: The influence of question type on children's accuracy. *Law and Human Behavior, 36*(3), 195–205. https://doi.org/10.1037/h0093957

Evans, A. D., Stolzenberg, S. N., Lee, K., & Lyon, T. D. (2014). Young children's difficulty with indirect speech acts: Implications for questioning child witnesses. *Behavioral Sciences & the Law, 32*(6), 775–788. https://doi.org/10.1002/bsl.2142

Evans, A. D., Stolzenberg, S. N., & Lyon, T. D. (2017). Pragmatic failure and referential ambiguity when attorneys ask child witnesses "do you know/remember" questions. *Psychology, Public Policy, and Law, 23*(2), 191–199. https://doi.org/10.1037/law0000116

Exner-Cortens, D., Baker, E., & Craig, W. (2021). The national prevalence of adolescent dating violence in Canada. *Journal of Adolescent Health, 69*(3), 495–502. https://doi.org/10.1016/j.jadohealth.2021.01.032

Fernandes, D., Gomes, J. P., Albuquerque, P. B., & Matos, M. (2023). Forensic interview techniques in child sexual abuse cases: A scoping review. *Trauma, Violence, & Abuse, 25*(2), 1382–1396. https://doi.org/10.1177/15248380231177317

Finkelhor, D., Turner, H., & Colburn, D. (2022). Prevalence of online sexual offenses against children in the US. *JAMA Network Open, 5*(10), e2234471. https://doi.org/10.1001/jamanetworkopen.2022.34471

Finkelhor, D., Turner, H., & Colburn, D. (2023). Which dynamics make online child sexual abuse and cyberstalking more emotionally impactful: Perpetrator identity and images? *Child Abuse & Neglect, 137,* 106020. https://doi.org/10.1016/j.chiabu.2023.106020

Fix, R. L., Aaron, J., & Greenberg, S. (2021). Experience is not enough: Self-identified training needs of police working with adolescents. *Policing: A Journal of Policy and Practice, 15*(4), 2252–2268. https://doi.org/10.1093/police/paab039

Fleming, M. (2005). Adolescent autonomy: Desire, achievement and disobeying parents between early and late adolescence. *Australian Journal of Educational & Developmental Psychology, 5,* 1–16.

Gabbert, F., Hope, L., Luther, K., Wright, G., Ng, M., & Oxburgh, G. (2020). Exploring the use of rapport in professional information-gathering contexts by systematically mapping the evidence base. *Applied Cognitive Psychology, 35*(2), 329–341. https://doi.org/10.1002/acp.3762

Gingo, M., Roded, A. D., & Turiel, E. (2020). What they don't know won't hurt them: Parents' judgments about lying to their adolescents. *Journal of Research on Adolescence, 30*(1), 95–108. https://doi.org/10.1111/jora.12503

Gordon, H. M., Lyon, T. D., & Lee, K. (2014). Social and cognitive factors associated with children's secret-keeping for a parent. *Child Development, 85*(6), 2374–2388. https://doi.org/10.1111/cdev.12301

Grandpre, J., Alvaro, E. M., Burgoon, M., Miller, C. H., & Hall, J. R. (2003). Adolescent reactance and anti-smoking campaigns: A theoretical approach. *Health Communication, 15*(3), 349–366. https://doi.org/10.1207/S15327027HC1503_6

Gudjonsson, G. H., & Singh, K. K. (1984). Interrogative suggestibility and delinquent boys: An empirical validation study. *Personality and Individual Differences, 5*(4), 425–430. https://doi.org/10.1016/0191-8869(84)90137-5

Guo, Y., Killoren, S., & Campione-Barr, N. (2022). Strategies and reasons for nondisclosure in close relationships during adolescence. *Journal of Youth and Adolescence, 51*(9), 1841–1857. https://doi.org/10.1007/s10964-022-01634-0

Henderson, H. M., Cho, S. J., Nogalska, A. M., & Lyon, T. D. (2021). Identifying novel forms of reluctance in commercially sexually exploited adolescents. *Child Abuse & Neglect, 115,* 104994. https://doi.org/10.1016/j.chiabu.2021.104994

Hershkowitz, I., Lamb, M. E., & Katz, C. (2014). Allegation rates in forensic child abuse investigations: Comparing the revised and standard NICHD protocols. *Psychology, Public Policy, and Law, 20*(3), 336–344. https://doi.org/10.1037/a0037391

Hershkowitz, I., Lanes, O., & Lamb, M. E. (2007). Exploring the disclosure of child sexual abuse with alleged victims and their parents. *Child Abuse & Neglect, 31*(2), 111–123. https://doi.org/10.1016/j.chiabu.2006.09.004

Hershkowitz, I., Orbach, Y., Lamb, M. E., Sternberg, K. J., & Horowitz, D. (2006). Dynamics of forensic interviews with suspected abuse victims who do not disclose abuse. *Child Abuse & Neglect, 30*(7), 753–769. https://doi.org/10.1016/j.chiabu.2005.10.016

Holmberg, U., & Madsen, K. (2014). Rapport operationalized as a humanitarian interview in investigative interview settings. *Psychiatry, Psychology and Law, 21*(4), 591–610. https://doi.org/10.1080/13218719.2013.873975

Icenogle, G., Steinberg, L., Duell, N., Chein, J., Chang, L., Chaudhary, N., Di Giunta, L., Dodge, K. A., Fanti, K. A., Lansford, J. E., Oburu, P., Pastorelli, C., Skinner, A. T., Sorbring, E., Tapanya, S., Uribe Tirado, L. M., Alampay, L. P., Al-Hassan, S. M., Takash, H. M. S., & Bacchini, D. (2019). Adolescents' cognitive capacity reaches adult levels prior to their psychosocial maturity: Evidence for a "maturity gap" in a multinational, cross-sectional sample. *Law and Human Behavior, 43*(1), 69–85. https://doi.org/10.1037/lhb0000315

Ijadi-Maghsoodi, R., Cook, M., Barnert, E. S., Gaboian, S., & Bath, E. (2016). Understanding and responding to the needs of commercially sexually exploited youth: Recommendations for the mental health provider. *Child and Adolescent Psychiatric Clinics, 25*(1), 107–122. https://doi.org/10.1016/j.chc.2015.08.007

Jack, F., Leov, J., & Zajac, R. (2014). Age-related differences in the free-recall accounts of child, adolescent, and adult witnesses. *Applied Cognitive Psychology, 28*(1), 30–38. https://doi.org/10.1002/acp.2951

Jensen, L. A., Arnett, J. J., & Feldman, S. S. (2004). The right to do wrong: Lying to parents among adolescents and emerging adults. *Journal of Youth and Adolescence, 33*(2), 101–112. https://doi.org/10.1023/B:JOYO.0000013422.48100.5a

Kaplan, D. L., Jones, E. J., Olson, E. C., & Yunzal-Butler, C. B. (2013). Early age of first sex and health risk in an urban adolescent population. *Journal of School Health, 83*(5), 350–356. https://doi.org/10.1111/josh.12038

Karni-Visel, Y., Hershkowitz, I., Lamb, M. E., & Blasbalg, U. (2023). Nonverbal emotions while disclosing child abuse: The role of interviewer support. *Child Maltreatment, 28*(1), 66–75. https://doi.org/10.1177/10775595211063497

Kelly, C. E., Miller, J. C., & Redlich, A. D. (2016). The dynamic nature of interrogation. *Law and Human Behavior, 40*(3), 295–309. https://doi.org/10.1037/lhb0000172

Kim, S., Alison, L., & Christiansen, P. (2020). Observing rapport-based interpersonal techniques to gather information from victims. *Psychology, Public Policy, and Law, 26*(2), 166–175. https://doi.org/10.1037/law0000222

Klemfuss, J. Z., Milojevich, H. M., Yim, I. S., Rush, E. B., & Quas, J. A. (2013). Stress at encoding, context at retrieval, and children's narrative content. *Journal of Experimental Child Psychology, 116*(3), 693–706. https://doi.org/10.1016/j.jecp.2013.07.009

Kogan, S. M. (2004). Disclosing unwanted sexual experiences: Results from a national sample of adolescent women. *Child Abuse & Neglect, 28*(2), 147–165. https://doi.org/10.1016/j.chiabu.2003.09.014

Laird, R. D., Marrero, M. D., Melching, J. A., & Kuhn, E. S. (2013). Information management strategies in early adolescence: Developmental change in use and transactional associations with psychological adjustment. *Developmental Psychology, 49*(5), 928–937. https://doi.org/10.1037/a0028845

Lamb, M. E., Brown, D. A., Hershkowitz, I., Orbach, Y., & Esplin, P. W. (2018). Interviewing children about abuse. In M. E. Lamb, D. A. Brown, I. Hershkowitz, Y. Orbach, & P. W. Esplin (Eds.), *Tell me what happened* (pp. 1–10). John Wiley & Sons. https://doi.org/10.1002/9781118881248.ch1

Landers, M., McGrath, K., Johnson, M. H., Armstrong, M. I., & Dollard, N. (2017). Baseline characteristics of dependent youth who have been commercially sexually exploited: Findings from a specialized treatment program. *Journal of Child Sexual Abuse, 26*(6), 692–709. https://doi.org/10.1080/10538712.2017.1323814

Lavoie, J., Dickerson, K. L., Redlich, A. D., & Quas, J. A. (2019). Overcoming disclosure reluctance in youth victims of sex trafficking: New directions for research, policy, and practice. *Psychology, Public Policy, and Law, 25*(4), 225–238. https://doi.org/10.1037/law0000205

Lavoie, J., Wyman, J., Crossman, A. M., & Talwar, V. (2021). Meta-analysis of the effects of two interviewing practices on children's disclosures of sensitive information: Rapport practices and question type. *Child Abuse & Neglect, 113*, 104930. https://doi.org/10.1016/j.chiabu.2021.104930

Lemaigre, C., Taylor, E. P., & Gittoes, C. (2017). Barriers and facilitators to disclosing sexual abuse in childhood and adolescence: A systematic review. *Child Abuse & Neglect, 70*, 39–52. https://doi.org/10.1016/j.chiabu.2017.05.009

Lenhart, A. (2015). *Teens, social media & technology overview 2015*. Pew Research Center. https://www.pewresearch.org/internet/2015/04/09/teens-social-media-technology-2015/

Levine, T. R., Serota, K. B., Carey, F., & Messer, D. (2013). Teenagers lie a lot: A further investigation into the prevalence of lying. *Communication Research Reports, 30*(3), 211–220. https://doi.org/10.1080/08824096.2013.806254

Lindholm, J., Börjesson, M., & Cederborg, A. C. (2014). "What happened when you came to Sweden?": Attributing responsibility in police interviews with alleged adolescent human trafficking victims. *Narrative Inquiry, 24*(2), 181–199. https://doi.org/10.1075/ni.24.2.01lin

Lindholm, J., Cederborg, A. C., & Alm, C. (2015). Adolescent girls exploited in the sex trade: Informativeness and evasiveness in investigative interviews. *Police Practice & Research: An International Journal, 16*(3), 197–210. https://doi.org/10.1080/15614263.2014.880839

Livingstone, S., & Görzig, A. (2012). 'Sexting': The exchange of sexual messages online among European youth. In S. Livingstone, L. Haddon, & A. Görzig (Eds.), *Children, risk and safety on the internet* (pp. 151–164). Policy Press. https://doi.org/10.51952/9781847428844.ch012

Loftus, E. F. (2005). Planting misinformation in the human mind: A 30-year investigation of the malleability of memory. *Learning & Memory, 12*(4), 361–366. https://doi.org/10.1101/lm.94705

Luyckx, K., Goossens, L., Soenens, B., & Beyers, W. (2006). Unpacking commitment and exploration: Preliminary validation of an integrative model of late adolescent identity formation. *Journal of Adolescence, 29*(3), 361–378. https://doi.org/10.1016/j.adolescence.2005.03.008

Lyon, T. D. (2014). Interviewing children. *Annual Review of Law and Social Science, 10*(1), 73–89. https://doi.org/10.1146/annurev-lawsocsci-110413-030913

Malloy, L. C., Brubacher, S. P., & Lamb, M. E. (2013). 'Because she's one who listens': Children discuss disclosure recipients in forensic interviews. *Child Maltreatment, 18*(4), 245–251. https://doi.org/10.1177/1077559513497250

Manay, N., & Collin-Vézina, D. (2021). Recipients of children's and adolescents' disclosures of childhood sexual abuse: A systematic review. *Child Abuse & Neglect, 116*(Pt 1), 104192. https://doi.org/10.1016/j.chiabu.2019.104192

McWilliams, K., Stolzenberg, S. N., Williams, S., & Lyon, T. (2021). Increasing maltreated and nonmaltreated children's recall disclosures of a minor transgression: The effects of back-channel utterances, a promise to tell the truth, and a post-recall putative confession. *Child Abuse & Neglect, 116*(Pt 1), 104073. https://doi.org/10.1016/j.chiabu.2019.104073

Mergler, A., & Patton, W. (2007). Adolescents talking about personal responsibility. *The Journal of Student Wellbeing, 1*(1), 57–70. https://doi.org/10.21913/JSW.v1i1.113

Moilanen, K. L. (2015). Predictors of latent growth in sexual risk taking in late adolescence and early adulthood. *The Journal of Sex Research, 52*(1), 83–97. https://doi.org/10.1080/00224499.2013.826167

Morgan, R., & Truman, J. (2020). *Criminal victimization, 2019*. Bureau of Justice Statistics. https://www.bjs.gov/content/pub/pdf/cv19.pdf

Naezer, M., & van Oosterhout, L. (2021). Only sluts love sexting: Youth, sexual norms and non-consensual sharing of digital sexual images. *Journal of Gender Studies, 30*(1), 79–90. https://doi.org/10.1080/09589236.2020.1799767

Nash, R. A., Nash, A., Morris, A., & Smith, S. L. (2016). Does rapport-building boost the eyewitness eyeclosure effect in closed questioning? *Legal and Criminological Psychology, 21*(2), 305–318. https://doi.org/10.1111/lcrp.12073

National Institute of Justice. (2007, December). *Commercial sexual exploitation of children: What do we know and what do we do about it?* (Report No. NCJ 215733). U.S. Department of Justice. https://www.ojp.gov/pdffiles1/nij/215733.pdf

Nogalska, A. M., Henderson, H. M., Cho, S. J., & Lyon, T. D. (2021). Police interviewing behaviors and commercially sexually exploited adolescents' reluctance. *Psychology, Public Policy, and Law, 27*(3), 328–340. https://doi.org/10.1037/law0000315

O'Connor, A. M., Dykstra, V. W., & Evans, A. D. (2020). Executive functions and young children's lie-telling and lie maintenance. *Developmental Psychology, 56*(7), 1278–1289. https://doi.org/10.1037/dev0000955

Páez-Gallego, J., Gallardo-López, J. A., López-Noguero, F., & Rodrigo-Moriche, M. P. (2020). Analysis of the relationship between psychological well-being and decision making in adolescent students. *Frontiers in Psychology, 11*, 1195. https://doi.org/10.3389/fpsyg.2020.01195

Priebe, G., & Svedin, C. G. (2008). Child sexual abuse is largely hidden from the adult society: An epidemiological study of adolescents' disclosures. *Child Abuse & Neglect, 32*(12), 1095–1108. https://doi.org/10.1016/j.chiabu.2008.04.001

Quas, J. A., & Dickerson, K. L. (2019). Implicit encouragement: Enhancing youth productivity when recounting a stressful experience. *International Journal on Child Maltreatment, 2*(4), 239–254. https://doi.org/10.1007/s42448-019-00031-8

Quas, J. A., & Lench, H. C. (2007). Arousal at encoding, arousal at retrieval, interviewer support, and children's memory for a mild stressor. *Applied Cognitive Psychology, 21*(3), 289–305. https://doi.org/10.1002/acp.1279

Quas, J. A., Rush, E. B., Yim, I. S., Edelstein, R. S., Otgaar, H., & Smeets, T. (2016). Stress and emotional valence effects on children's versus adolescents' true and false memory. *Memory, 24*(5), 696–707. https://doi.org/10.1080/09658211.2015.1045909

Quas, J. A., Rush, E. B., Yim, I. S., & Nikolayev, M. (2014). Effects of stress on memory in children and adolescents: Testing causal connections. *Memory, 22*(6), 616–632. https://doi.org/10.1080/09658211.2013.809766

Redlich, A. D., & Goodman, G. S. (2003). Taking responsibility for an act not committed: The influence of age and suggestibility. *Law and Human Behavior, 27*(2), 141–156. https://doi.org/10.1023/a:1022543012851

Rote, W. M., & Smetana, J. G. (2015). Acceptability of information management strategies: Adolescents' and parents' judgments and links with adjustment and relationships. *Journal of Research on Adolescence, 25*(3), 490–505. https://doi.org/10.1111/jora.12143

Rote, W. M., & Smetana, J. G. (2016). Beliefs about parents' right to know: Domain differences and associations with change in concealment. *Journal of Research on Adolescence, 26*(2), 334–344. https://doi.org/10.1111/jora.12194

Rush, E. B., Quas, J. A., Yim, I. S., Nikolayev, M., Clark, S. E., & Larson, R. P. (2014). Stress, interviewer support, and children's eyewitness identification accuracy. *Child Development, 85*(3), 1292–1305. https://doi.org/10.1111/cdev.12177

Saragosa-Harris, N. M., Cohen, A. O., Reneau, T. R., Villano, W. J., Heller, A. S., & Hartley, C. A. (2022). Real-world exploration increases across adolescence and relates to affect, risk taking, and social connectivity. *Psychological Science, 33*(10), 1664–1679. https://doi.org/10.1177/09567976221102070

Sauerland, M., Brackmann, N., & Otgaar, H. (2018). Rapport: Little effect on children's, adolescents', and adults' statement quantity, accuracy, and suggestibility. *Journal of Child Custody, 15*(4), 268–285. https://doi.org/10.1080/15379418.2018.1509759

Saywitz, K. J., & Camparo, L. B. (2014). Interviewing children: A primer. In G. Melton, A. Ben-Arieh, J. Cashmore, G. Goodman, & N. Worley (Eds.), *The SAGE handbook of child research* (pp. 371–390). SAGE. https://doi.org/10.4135/9781446294758.n21

Saywitz, K. J., Geiselman, R. E., & Bornstein, G. K. (1992). Effects of cognitive interviewing and practice on children's recall performance. *Journal of Applied Psychology, 77*(5), 744–756. https://doi.org/10.1037/0021-9010.77.5.744

Saywitz, K. J., Larson, R. P., Hobbs, S. D., & Wells, C. R. (2015). Developing rapport with children in forensic interviews: Systematic review of experimental research. *Behavioral Sciences & the Law, 33*(4), 372–389. https://doi.org/10.1002/bsl.2186

Saywitz, K. J., Wells, C. R., Larson, R. P., & Hobbs, S. D. (2019). Effects of interviewer support on children's memory and suggestibility: Systematic review and meta-analyses of experimental research. *Trauma, Violence, & Abuse, 20*(1), 22–39. https://journals.sagepub.com/doi/full/10.1177/1524838016683457

Schaeffer, P., Leventhal, J. M., & Asnes, A. G. (2011). Children's disclosures of sexual abuse: Learning from direct inquiry. *Child Abuse & Neglect, 35*(5), 343–352. https://doi.org/10.1016/j.chiabu.2011.01.014

Schönbucher, V., Maier, T., Mohler-Kuo, M., Schnyder, U., & Landolt, M. A. (2012). Disclosure of child sexual abuse by adolescents: A qualitative in-depth study. *Journal of Interpersonal Violence, 27*(17), 3486–3513. https://doi.org/10.1177/0886260512445380

Sheahan, C. L., Pica, E., Pozzulo, J. D., & Nastasa, C. (2017). Eyewitness recall and identification abilities of adolescent and young adults. *Journal of Applied Developmental Psychology, 53*, 86–95. https://doi.org/10.1016/j.appdev.2017.09.008

Simons-Morton, B., Pickett, W., Boyce, W., ter Bogt, T. F., & Vollebergh, W. (2010). Cross-national comparison of adolescent drinking and cannabis use in the United States, Canada, and the Netherlands. *International Journal on Drug Policy, 21*(1), 64–69. https://doi.org/10.1016/j.drugpo.2009.02.003

Simpson, E., Dianiska, R. E., & Quas, J. A. (2024, March 21–23). *Adolescents as eyewitnesses: Unique interview approaches for a unique developmental population* [Paper presentation]. American Psychology–Law Society Annual Conference, Los Angeles, CA, United States.

Smetana, J., Robinson, J., Bourne, S. V., & Wainryb, C. (2019). "I didn't want to, but then I told": Adolescents' narratives regarding disclosure, concealment, and lying. *Developmental Psychology, 55*(2), 403–414. https://doi.org/10.1037/dev0000646

Smetana, J. G., Campione-Barr, N., & Daddis, C. (2004). Longitudinal development of family decision making: Defining healthy behavioral autonomy for middle-class African American adolescents. *Child Development, 75*(5), 1418–1434. https://doi.org/10.1111/j.1467-8624.2004.00749.x

Smetana, J. G., Villalobos, M., Tasopoulos-Chan, M., Gettman, D. C., & Campione-Barr, N. (2009). Early and middle adolescents' disclosure to parents about activities in different domains. *Journal of Adolescence, 32*(3), 693–713. https://doi.org/10.1016/j.adolescence.2008.06.010

Smith, A. R., Chein, J., & Steinberg, L. (2014). Peers increase adolescent risk taking even when the probabilities of negative outcomes are known. *Developmental Psychology, 50*(5), 1564–1568. https://doi.org/10.1037/a0035696

Somer, E., & Szwarcberg, S. (2001). Variables in delayed disclosure of childhood sexual abuse. *American Journal of Orthopsychiatry, 71*(3), 332–341. https://doi.org/10.1037/0002-9432.71.3.332

Sprecher, S., Treger, S., Wondra, J. D., Hilaire, N., & Wallpe, K. (2013). Taking turns: Reciprocal self-disclosure promotes liking in initial interactions. *Journal of Experimental Social Psychology, 49*(5), 860–866. https://doi.org/10.1016/j.jesp.2013.03.017

Steinberg, L. (2010). A dual systems model of adolescent risk-taking. *Developmental Psychobiology, 52*(3), 216–224. https://doi.org/10.1002/dev.20445

Stolzenberg, S. N., Morse, S. J., Haverkate, D. L., & Garcia-Johnson, A. M. (2020). The prevalence of declarative and indirect yes/no questions when children testify in criminal cases of child sexual abuse in the United States. *Applied Cognitive Psychology, 34*(1), 194–204. https://doi.org/10.1002/acp.3607

Stolzenberg, S. N., Williams, S., McWilliams, K., Liang, C., & Lyon, T. D. (2021). The utility of direct questions in eliciting subjective content from children disclosing sexual abuse. *Child Abuse & Neglect, 116*(Pt. 1), 103964. https://doi.org/10.1016/j.chiabu.2019.02.014

Talwar, V., Gordon, H. M., & Lee, K. (2007). Lying in the elementary school years: Verbal deception and its relation to second-order belief understanding. *Developmental Psychology, 43*(3), 804–810. https://doi.org/10.1037/0012-1649.43.3.804

Talwar, V., & Lee, K. (2002). Development of lying to conceal a transgression: Children's control of expressive behaviour during verbal deception. *International Journal of Behavioral Development, 26*(5), 436–444. https://doi.org/10.1080/01650250143000373

Talwar, V., & Lee, K. (2008). Social and cognitive correlates of children's lying behavior. *Child Development, 79*(4), 866–881. https://doi.org/10.1111/j.1467-8624.2008.01164.x

Tener, D., Walsh, W. A., Jones, L. M., & Kinnish, K. (2014). "It all depends on the guy and the girl": A qualitative study of youth experiences with statutory victimization relationships. *Journal of Child Sexual Abuse, 23*(8), 935–956. https://doi.org/10.1080/10538712.2014.960635

Teoh, Y. S., & Lamb, M. E. (2010). Preparing children for investigative interviews: Rapport-building, instruction, and evaluation. *Applied Developmental Science, 14*(3), 154–163. https://doi.org/10.1080/10888691.2010.494463

Tian, L., Yuan, J., & Li, Y. (2018). Effects of peer presence and self-esteem on adolescent risk-taking behavior: Evidence from an ERP study. *Acta Psychologica Sinica, 50*(1), 47. https://doi.org/10.3724/sp.j.1041.2018.00047

Tickle-Degnen, L., & Rosenthal, R. (1990). The nature of rapport and its nonverbal correlates. *Psychological Inquiry, 1*(4), 285–293. https://doi.org/10.1207/s15327965pli0104_1

Towner, E., Grint, J., Levy, T., Blakemore, S. J., & Tomova, L. (2022). Revealing the self in a digital world: A systematic review of adolescent online and offline self-disclosure. *Current Opinion in Psychology, 45*, 101309. https://doi.org/10.1016/j.copsyc.2022.101309

Valkenburg, P. M., Sumter, S. R., & Peter, J. (2011). Gender differences in online and offline self-disclosure in pre-adolescence and adolescence. *British Journal of Developmental Psychology, 29*(2), 253–269. https://doi.org/10.1348/2044-835X.002001

Vallano, J. P., Evans, J. R., Schreiber Compo, N., & Kieckhaefer, J. M. (2015). Rapport-building during witness and suspect interviews: A survey of law enforcement. *Applied Cognitive Psychology, 29*(3), 369–380. https://doi.org/10.1002/acp.3115

Vallano, J. P., & Schreiber Compo, N. (2015). Rapport-building with cooperative witnesses and criminal suspects: A theoretical and empirical review. *Psychology, Public Policy, and Law, 21*(1), 85–99. https://doi.org/10.1037/law0000035

Vijayakumar, N., Flournoy, J. C., Mills, K. L., Cheng, T. W., Mobasser, A., Flannery, J. E., Allen, N. B., & Pfeifer, J. H. (2020). Getting to know me better: An fMRI study of intimate and superficial self-disclosure to friends during adolescence. *Journal of Personality and Social Psychology, 118*(5), 885–899. https://doi.org/10.1037/pspa0000182

Vijayakumar, N., & Pfeifer, J. H. (2020). Self-disclosure during adolescence: Exploring the means, targets, and types of personal exchanges. *Current Opinion in Psychology, 31*, 135–140. https://doi.org/10.1016/j.copsyc.2019.08.005

Wachi, T., Kuraishi, H., Watanabe, K., Otsuka, Y., Yokota, K., & Lamb, M. E. (2018). Effects of rapport building on confessions in an experimental paradigm. *Psychology, Public Policy, and Law, 24*(1), 36–47. https://doi.org/10.1037/law0000152

Warr, M. (2007). The tangled web: Delinquency, deception, and parental attachment. *Journal of Youth and Adolescence, 36*(5), 607–622. https://doi.org/10.1007/s10964-006-9148-0

Waterman, A. S. (1993). Developmental perspectives on identity formation: From adolescence to adulthood. In J. E. Marcia, A. S. Waterman, D. R. Matteson, S. L. Archer, & J. L. Orlofsky (Eds.), *Ego identity: A handbook for psychosocial research* (pp. 42–68). Springer-Verlag.

Way, N. (2013). Boys' friendships during adolescence: Intimacy, desire, and loss. *Journal of Research on Adolescence, 23*(2), 201–213. https://doi.org/10.1111/jora.12047

Wray-Lake, L., Crouter, A. C., & McHale, S. M. (2010). Developmental patterns in decision-making autonomy across middle childhood and adolescence: European American parents' perspectives. *Child Development, 81*(2), 636–651. https://doi.org/10.1111/j.1467-8624.2009.01420.x

Wrzus, C., Hänel, M., Wagner, J., & Neyer, F. J. (2013). Social network changes and life events across the life span: A meta-analysis. *Psychological Bulletin, 139*(1), 53–80. https://doi.org/10.1037/a0028601

Yeager, D. S., Dahl, R. E., & Dweck, C. S. (2018). Why interventions to influence adolescent behavior often fail but could succeed. *Perspectives on Psychological Science, 13*(1), 101–122. https://doi.org/10.1177/1745691617722620

Youth Endowment Fund. (2022). *Children, violence and vulnerability 2022.* https://youthendowmentfund.org.uk/wp-content/uploads/2022/10/YEF-Children-violence-and-vulnerability-2022.pdf

12

Rapport and Social Support in Children's Forensic Interviews

Sue D. Hobbs, Rakel P. Larson, and Christine R. Wells

It is not easy to interview children. Even in the best circumstances, children's responses are often lacking in detail. It is not uncommon for a 5-year-old child who is asked, "'What did you do after school today?' to respond with 'We played'" (Saywitz & Camparo, 2014, p. 6). If children provide such limited responses about routine school activities, consider the challenges when trying to interview a child who has witnessed or experienced a traumatic event, such as child maltreatment.

For decades, researchers have worked to identify best practices for interviewing children. When interviewed correctly, children can provide accurate accounts of their experiences (e.g., Saywitz et al., 2018). Conversely, with improper or inadequate interviewing, it can be difficult to obtain reliable reports from children and to be confident in the veracity of these reports. In certain instances, such as child sexual abuse, children are often the only witnesses (Goodman, 2006). Thus, obtaining accurate and reliable reports from children is of utmost importance. Not doing so can be disastrous, resulting in a false conviction and imprisonment of an innocent person or in an acquittal of a guilty party, leaving the perpetrator free to continue abusing children.

Participating in the legal system is often necessary for child victims and witnesses. However, the experience can be traumatic, and children are at risk for experiencing secondary trauma when they do (Cooper, 2012). Thus, in addition to focusing on the reliability of children's reports, it is necessary to consider children's social-emotional well-being during interviews. Indeed,

https://doi.org/10.1037/0000492-012
Handbook on Child Witnesses: Improving Psychological Science and Legal Practice,
G. S. Goodman, T. D. Lyon, S. D. Hobbs, and R. Enriquez (Editors)

most best practice guidelines for interviewing children recommend creating a supportive psychosocial environment during forensic interviews (Lamb et al., 2007; Saywitz et al., 2016, 2018). One way to accomplish this is through rapport-building and being emotionally supportive.

RAPPORT AND SUPPORT: DEFINITIONS AND THEORETICAL MODELS

Rapport is essential for optimal child forensic interviewing. Emotionally supportive interviewing helps maintain rapport. Although they may be discussed separately, in reality, interviewers cannot build rapport without being emotionally supportive (Hershkowitz et al., 2014). Rapport and support are closely intertwined. Thus, when we discuss rapport and support during forensic interviews, we are referring to the psychosocial setting that fosters and maintains rapport throughout the interview process.

Baker et al. (2020) define rapport as "the emotional experience of high-quality interactions" (p. 3), reinforcing the concept that rapport-building is not a one-time event that occurs at the beginning of interviews, but rather a part of a supportive psychosocial environment. In the clinical psychology literature, clinicians define rapport as present when interviewers demonstrate interest and acceptance of clients and when they are supportive and nonjudgmental (Ovsiannikova et al., 2021; Villa & Reitman, 2010). Rapport involves synchronous and harmonious interactions between active participants (Bernieri & Gillis, 2001). Similarly, clinicians Cepeda and Gotanco (2017) describe rapport-building as "engagement," which includes expressing warmth, interest, compassion, acceptance, and empathy to build a symbiotic and trusting relationship between two people (e.g., therapist and client). This requires interpersonal sensitivity, which includes the ability to accurately sense and respond to others' nonverbal cues.

Providing a supportive interview environment is backed by numerous theories (e.g., therapeutic rapport, processing efficiency, attentional control, self-determination, evolutionary-neurodevelopment, and attachment theory). Based on these theories, which we will describe next, it makes sense that children's interview performance is superior under conditions of greater social support. Consistent with the clinical and social psychology literature, the Tickle-Degnen and Rosenthal (1990) theoretical model describes rapport as a "dynamic structure of three interrelating components: mutual attentiveness, positivity, and coordination" (p. 285), all three of which help increase the quality of interactions with others. Mutual attentiveness occurs when participants are focused on and interested in one another. Positivity includes friendliness and warmth, and in some cases, mutual respect (Cuddy et al., 2008; Wojciszke et al., 2009). Coordination occurs when cooperation and synchrony develop between participants as the interview progresses. Attention, positivity, and coordination are interrelated, but they are also distinct, as they develop and change at different rates, and one can develop without the others. All three are important for building and maintaining rapport within a supportive interview environment, and they are reflected in multiple other theories on the effects of psychosocial interviewing contexts (Tickle-Degnen & Rosenthal, 1990).

Therapeutic rapport models focus on medical situations. Medical practitioners' (e.g., medical doctors, therapists) and patients' interactions describe an alliance that emerges through both cognitive empathy and affective empathy. Cognitive empathy entails true curiosity, and affective empathy involves feelings of warmth and caring (Norfolk et al., 2007). Curiosity and warmth are exhibited through engaging behaviors such as smiling, acknowledging, mirroring, caring, and openness. As physicians exhibit more understanding and empathy toward patients, the patients disclose more, which in turn increases physicians' understanding of patient needs and expectations. Thus, the building and maintenance of rapport involves reciprocal interactions between physician and patient.

Other theoretical frameworks propose that psychosocial support during stressful situations increases feelings of competence, self-efficacy, and autonomy and helps individuals regulate their emotions (Lakey & Cohen, 2000). Per processing efficiency and attentional control theories (Derakshan & Eysenck, 2009; Eysenck & Calvo, 1992), anxiety and worry can negatively affect attention and working memory. When anxious, individuals focus more attention on threatening stimuli and use working-memory resources to regulate emotions. This taxing of working memory resources makes it more difficult to process information. Social support during stressful situations helps temper the body's physiological stress response (Quas & Lench, 2007). Thus, a supportive interview environment can help mitigate the negative effects stress has on cognitive processing and memory.

Self-determination theory identifies autonomy, competence, and relatedness as fundamental psychological needs (Deci & Ryan, 2000). As previously stated, a supportive psychosocial interview environment can help increase children's feelings of autonomy. Moreover, individuals feel connection (relatedness) with others when they believe that their autonomy is genuinely supported, and the need for competence can be met when participants feel they are effectively and openly communicating with each other (Baker et al., 2020). In research with mother–adolescent dyads, when mothers engaged in more autonomy-supportive behavior, such as active and reflective listening, showing interest and empathetic understanding, conversations were more reciprocal, adolescents felt more connected with their mothers and disclosed more information (Wuyts et al., 2018).

The evolutionary-neurodevelopmental theory of child development and the differential sensitivity hypothesis propose that some children are more biologically sensitive to social and environmental contexts (Belsky, 2005). Biological sensitivity is multifaceted and can include genetic variations and polymorphisms (e.g., dopamine receptor D4 gene; serotonin transporter gene, 5-HTTLPR), physiological reactivity to the environment, vagal and immune system functioning, and neuropsychological processing (Bakermans-Kranenburg & van IJzendoorn, 2011; Ellis et al., 2011; Somers & Luecken, 2021). These biological variations predict children's vulnerability to adversity as well as their responses to positive experiences (Ellis et al., 2011; Pluess, 2017; Pluess & Belsky, 2013). For example, individual differences in temperament predict coping strategies used by children when they are faced with stressful situations (see Wachs, 2006, for a review). Compared to children who use flexible active self-regulatory coping strategies, children who are more behaviorally inhibited and those low in positive emotionality, approach, and activity, are more likely to use nonproductive, avoidant coping strategies (Carson & Bittner, 1994; Lengua & Sandler, 1996; Penela et al., 2015). These evolutionary-neurodevelopmental frameworks suggest that supportive contexts should most benefit children who are more biologically susceptible to stressful or adverse conditions (Belsky & Pluess, 2009; Ellis et al., 2011).

Supportive interviewing may also be particularly beneficial for children with disrupted, insecure, or disorganized attachments. From the attachment theory perspective (Bowlby, 1969/1982), the mostly dormant attachment system becomes active during times of distress—that is, during situations in which children may need more support or comfort (Alexander et al., 2002). Secure attachment can serve as a model for how to build and maintain rapport with children (Izard, 1990). The development of attachment security is predicted by caregiver sensitivity and responsiveness to children's signals. For example, compared with mothers of insecurely attached infants, mothers of securely attached babies are more attentive to their children's cues, participate in mutual gaze, and show more coordinated behaviors (de Wolff & van IJzendoorn, 1997). Drawing from the attachment literature, positive rapport and supportive interviewing can be characterized by mutual trust, a sense of warmth, reduced anxiety, openness in sharing personal details, a calm demeanor, and children perceiving adults as approachable and dependable (Rotenberg et al., 2003).

Children exposed to harsh, abusive, or neglectful parenting can have difficulties building strong interpersonal connections and having open communication with adults (Bretherton & Munholland, 2008). Attachment theory would predict that children with a history of maltreatment may be wary of new interpersonal interactions, given prior experiences with caregivers where their signals for help, comfort, and support were rejected or punished. For example, compared to their nonmaltreated peers, maltreated adolescents have difficulty forming alliances with mental health professionals, even when controlling for psychopathology levels (Eltz et al., 1995). More intensive rapport-building and supportive efforts may therefore be needed for maltreated children, who are more likely to have insecure or disorganized attachments (Cyr et al., 2010).

RAPPORT AND SUPPORT IN CHILDREN'S FORENSIC INTERVIEW PROTOCOLS

For many years, researchers and forensic interviewers proclaimed the necessity of rapport-building before interviewing children about suspected child abuse. However, rapport-building was not clearly defined in the experimental studies.

Some researchers have highlighted the role of narrative practice in building rapport (e.g., Brown et al., 2013; Hardy & Van Leeuwen, 2004; Roberts et al., 2004). Narrative practice is a preliminary interview phase that gives children the opportunity to practice discussing a previous, neutral event before they begin discussing the critical event—the event that brought them to the interview to begin with (Saywitz et al., 2018). Of interest, in Fischer et al.'s (1993) research about children's storytelling, children who experienced social support (in the form of adults modeling expected behavior) performed better compared to children who did not receive this support. Thus, there is evidence that modeling and practicing desired behavior can improve children's performance, and in some cases, this can be considered a form of social support. However, although research shows that narrative practice increases children's productivity once they have chosen to disclose (Lyon et al., 2014; Yi & Lamb, 2018), it is unclear if narrative practice or modeling builds rapport. In none of these studies on narrative practice did researchers evaluate the waxing and waning of rapport or assess whether children felt rapport with interviewers.

Building and/or maintaining rapport are key elements in most, if not all, techniques for forensic interviews of children. However, the methods used to build rapport vary, as does the emphasis on providing a supportive interview environment (Fernandes et al., 2024). In the original National Institute of Child Health and Human Development (NICHD) interview protocol (Lamb et al., 2007), rapport-building occurred after the introductory phase of the interview and included efforts to set children at ease and opportunities for children to describe events that are unrelated to allegations of abuse. Tom Lyon's Ten Step Protocol (2021) is modeled after the NICHD Protocol. In Lyon's (2021) protocol, rapport-building starts with ground rules instruction and then moves to narrative practice, during which interviewers ask children to describe recent events involving things they like to do, things they don't like to do, and their last birthdays. Children's statements are followed up with "What happened next?" questions. This gives children the opportunity to become more comfortable while also learning how to respond to interview questions. During this phase, interviewers respond with interest to children's answers to help demonstrate to children that they will not be judged or criticized for anything they say during the interview (Lyon, 2016).

The Developmental Narrative Elaboration (DNE) interview, developed by Saywitz and Camparo (2014), contains similar elements such as establishing ground rules and narrative practice. However, in the DNE interview, rapport-building does not just occur at the beginning of the interview. Consistent with the clinical literature, proponents of the DNE interview agree that rapport waxes and wanes throughout an interview, and they seek to build and maintain rapport throughout the process by engaging with children in a supportive and nonsuggestive manner (Saywitz et al., 2018). Similarly, the Revised NICHD Protocol, which builds upon and improves the Standard NICHD Protocol, focuses on using supportive interviewing to build and maintain rapport (Hershkowitz et al., 2014). In the Revised NICHD Protocol, interviewers begin developing rapport before ground rules instructions (see Chapter 9, this volume). In addition to narrative practice, interviewers engage in socially supportive behaviors, such as smiling, using children's names, and expressing care for children and interest in their experiences. The most recent Association of Professionals Solving the Abuse of Children (APSAC; formerly the American Professional Society on the Abuse of Children) Practice Guidelines (APSAC Taskforce, 2023) instruct interviewers to be mindful of rapport throughout the process. Interviewers begin brief rapport-building during the introductory phase by asking children to "Tell me something about you," or "Tell me about things you like to do" (p. 20). However, rapport does not stop there. Interviewers maintain rapport by providing a supportive atmosphere and showing genuine interest in children.

CREATING A SUPPORTIVE INTERVIEW ENVIRONMENT

Therapeutic rapport models describe supportive interviewing and maintaining rapport as communicating in a warm manner to make an interviewee feel at ease and comfortable during the process (Burleson et al., 1994; Norfolk et al., 2007). In experimental research on the effects of support on children's interviews, researchers define support in various ways, including being warm and friendly, using children's names, having open body posture, making eye contact, showing interest, smiling, demonstrating empathy, providing positive feedback or praise for children's efforts, using facilitators, such as "uh huh" and "okay" (Cleveland et al., 2018; McWilliams et al., 2021; see also, Saywitz et al., 2016 for a meta-analysis on supportive interviewing). Similarly, researchers on investigative interviews of adults in various capacities (e.g., suspects, witnesses, therapy clients) assert that rapport is built and maintained through supportive interview behaviors like those listed and by considering others' perspectives, engaging in reciprocity, being calm, and treating interviewees with respect (Collins & Carthy, 2018; Gabbert et al., 2020; Walsh & Bull, 2012; see also Abbe & Brandon, 2013, 2014, for reviews). The role of rapport-building and supportive interviewing is to develop and maintain coordination and synchrony between parties, thus maintaining the interviewee's ease and comfort. Overall, interviewer supportiveness includes a range of warm and empathic nonverbal and verbal behaviors that are provided across the entire interaction.

There are, however, some caveats to the use of supportive behaviors during interviews. Timing is important. If encouragement is or appears to be contingent on children's responses, the interview becomes suggestive instead of supportive (Saywitz et al., 2015; Schreiber et al., 2006). Moreover, supportiveness can backfire when it is forced or disingenuous. For example, pseudo or false rapport can occur when an interviewer adopts an open posture and responds with "interest" to interviewee comments but is not truly sincere or paying attention. This pseudo or false rapport can damage the relationship between parties if the interviewee realizes or perceives that the behaviors meant to demonstrate sincerity, interest, and positivity are faked (Gabbert et al., 2020; Johnston et al., 2019).

Clinicians recommend that interviewers do not assume to know what children need but to take cues from children and to consider their developmental needs. For example, in their review on building rapport with children who have experienced crises, Ovsiannikova et al. (2021) recommend using stuffed animals, puppets, and toys, or showing magic tricks, depending on children's age, development, and needs. Clinicians also recommend maintaining a supportive environment by using open-ended questions about pleasant activities and minimal follow-up prompts to clarify children's answers. They suggest avoiding questions that could prompt social desirability responses from children (Villa & Reitman, 2010). Regardless of the method used, researchers and clinicians agree that rapport and support are meant to help children feel a sense of comfort and safety with interviewers and a sense that it is safe to tell interviewers the truth.

Generally, when someone receives psychological and social support, they perceive or know that they are cared for and valued and have assistance from others to meet their needs during stressful events (Cohen, 2004; Uchino, 2009). As previously stated, the definitions, behaviors, and purposes of both rapport and supportive interviewing are similar. The purpose of both is to create a sense of safety during interviews. In the literature with children and adults, researchers assert that rapport must be built initially and maintained throughout interviews (Gabbert et al., 2020; Johnston et al., 2019; Lavoie et al., 2021). When rapport is maintained, interviewers obtain fuller and more complete accounts, as we will discuss in more detail later. Conversely, interviews are less effective when attentiveness and engagement break down, and rapport is not maintained (Hershkowitz et al., 2006; Walsh & Bull, 2012).

FINDINGS FROM THE RESEARCH: SUPPORTIVE INTERVIEW ENVIRONMENTS AND CHILDREN'S REPORTS

A supportive environment can affect the reliability and quality of children's reports in several ways (Lavoie et al., 2021; Saywitz et al., 2016). According to processing efficiency and attentional control theories, anxiety reduces cognitive resources that would otherwise be used to process information, and supportive interviewing affects children's anxiety levels and stress responses. Children interviewed in a supportive manner exhibit decreased biological stress responses and report less anxiety compared to children questioned in a nonsupportive manner (Davis & Bottoms, 2002; Quas & Lench, 2007; Saywitz et al., 2016). Research demonstrates that decreased anxiety predicts improved memory performance, especially in younger and highly emotionally reactive children (Quas & Lench, 2007; Quas et al., 2014). Conversely, lack of supportive behaviors (e.g., frustration, disapproval, contradiction, inattentiveness) has a negative effect and inhibits children from telling what they know (e.g., Almerigogna et al., 2007; Lewy et al., 2015; Zajac et al., 2012).

More recent research has emerged in which intentional rapport-building methods were assessed in children's interviews. Foster et al. (2023) compared narrative practice with interactional rapport-building, which is based on Tickle-Degnen and Rosenthal's (1990) model of rapport. To build mutual attentiveness, positivity, and coordination, interviewers and children (10- to 13-year-olds) worked together to learn and perform a magic trick. Children's feelings of rapport were assessed, and those in the interactional rapport-building condition felt significantly more rapport with interviewers compared to children in the narrative practice condition. Children in the interactional rapport-building condition were significantly more likely to provide reliable reports compared to younger children (7- to 9-year-olds) and children in the narrative practice condition.

Attachment theory suggests that a supportive psychosocial environment would be especially helpful for maltreated children. Child witnesses in cases of maltreatment express real and imagined fears of negative consequences of disclosure (e.g., harm to self or loved ones; adult anger, disappointment) that can heighten interview anxiety (Lamaigre et al., 2017). Moreover, maltreatment is a risk factor for anxiety symptoms and difficulties with attention (e.g., Krug et al., 2002). Children who have experienced child abuse or neglect may have low expectations about adults being supportive and offering help when it is needed (Bowlby, 1969/1982, 1980; Bretherton & Munholland, 2008; Lyon et al., 2010; Toth et al., 1997). Psychological support can ease tension and help build feelings of trust and safety during forensic interviews (Ovsiannikova et al., 2021). The body of literature would benefit from added research with children who have trauma histories to help interviewers understand how supportive interviewing can help or hinder the reports of these vulnerable children (Hershkowitz et al., 2014). More ethically conducted laboratory research is needed so we can learn how to help maltreated children feel safe during interviews without increasing a social desirability response in an effort to please supportive, friendly interviewers.

Memory Accuracy and Suggestibility

Multiple theories suggest that supportive interviewing should enhance memory accuracy and decrease suggestibility by reducing anxiety-related cognitive interference. Children often (but not always) provide more correct responses and fewer incorrect responses when interviewed in a supportive compared to a nonsupportive manner (e.g., Almerigogna et al., 2007; Peter-Hagene et al., 2014; Quas et al., 2005, 2014, see Saywitz et al., 2016 for a systematic review and meta-analysis). These results vary depending on children's ages, question type (e.g., specific nonleading, yes/no, suggestive, free recall), and the delay between the target event and interview. In many studies, researchers interview children a short time after the to-be-remembered event (i.e., a few minutes to 2 weeks), although in some, children are interviewed much later. Researchers' findings are mixed regarding whether interviewer supportiveness facilitates children's recall after shorter delays, such as one week (see e.g., Brubacher et al., 2019; Quas et al., 2005). Research suggests that supportiveness can improve children's responses to open-ended questions after approximately one month (Goodman et al., 1991) and one year (Peter-Hagene et al., 2014). Given that children who experience traumatic events are not typically interviewed immediately afterward, and maltreated children often delay disclosures of abuse, the findings on supportiveness after longer delays are especially relevant (Berliner & Conte, 1995; Goodman-Brown et al., 2003).

Supportive interviewing may not always elicit more accurate responses from children. In a systematic literature review and meta-analysis (Saywitz et al., 2016), researchers identified three studies in which supportiveness did not have the anticipated effect on children's responses (Goodman et al., 1995; Imhoff & Baker-Ward, 1999; Quas et al., 2004). In the Goodman et al. study, supportiveness was negatively correlated with children's accuracy. The researchers suggested that, rather than children becoming less informative in response to support, interviewers may have become more supportive in attempts to engage uncooperative children. In the latter two studies, researchers found no differences in children's memory accuracy or suggestibility when comparing supportive and nonsupportive interviews, which may have occurred because the nonsupportive interviews were more neutral than truly nonsupportive. These findings illustrate the importance of additional research to help unpack how the dynamic nature of interviews may affect children's reports.

Eisen et al. (2019) conducted research with 3- to 12-year-old children who were involved in maltreatment investigations—the children to whom laboratory research is meant to generalize. All children were inpatients at a forensic hospital for 5 days while authorities investigated allegations of maltreatment. The study events—a beanbag game and interview 30 minutes later—both occurred in the hospital. The study findings were complex and somewhat unexpected. Compared to younger children, older children (6- to 12-year-olds) more frequently answered "no" to questions that should have been answered "yes." In other words, older children exhibited a "'no' bias" in response to specific questions, resulting in more omission errors compared to preschool-aged children in the same condition. Consistent with previous research, preschool children made more commission errors compared to older children, no matter the interview condition. However, preschool children made more commission errors in the support condition compared to the nonsupport condition. When interviewed in a supportive context, preschool children said "yes" to questions that should have been answered "no" (a "yes" bias). These findings demonstrate the need for additional research on children's reports in supportive and nonsupportive interview contexts, especially among children who have experienced child maltreatment.

Completeness and Productivity of Reports

Self-determination theory emphasizes autonomy and competence as fundamental psychological needs, providing a framework for understanding how supportive interviewing enhances children's reports. Consistent with this theoretical framework, children who experience supportive interviews are less reluctant to provide information compared to children who experience nonsupportive or neutral interviews (Blasbalg et al., 2019; Hershkowitz et al., 2006; Lavoie et al., 2021; but see Quas et al., 2014).[1] Moreover, supportive interviewing elicits more detailed, informative, and forensically relevant responses (Blasbalg et al., 2019; Hershkowitz et al., 2015; Lavoie et al., 2021). A psychosocially supportive environment may help increase autonomy and feelings of competence by decreasing the perceived power differential between children and the adults interviewing them, enabling children to overcome feelings of mistrust (e.g., Goodman et al., 1991; Ponizovsky-Bergelson et al., 2019; van Os et al., 2020).

Tickle-Degnen and Rosenthal's (1990) theoretical model, along with therapeutic rapport frameworks, can help explain how interviewer behaviors like implicit encouragement (e.g., facilitators) affect children's responses. In two studies, researchers assessed 3- to 9-year-old children's disclosures about a staged event in which they accidentally broke something (Cleveland et al., 2018; McWilliams et al., 2021). With implicit encouragement, children who disclosed breaking a toy provided more details (McWilliams et al., 2021). In the Cleveland et al. (2018) study, developmental differences emerged; children's productivity during free recall increased with age, but only in a high implicit encouragement condition. Of interest, developmental differences may influence interviewer behavior, which can affect children's responses. Forensic interviewers tend to be more talkative and less supportive with younger rather than older children, and more talkativeness is negatively correlated with the amount of information children provide (Teoh & Lamb, 2013). Thus, interviewers must be mindful of how they verbally respond to children's reports when attempting to provide a supportive atmosphere.

Individual Differences

Multiple theoretical frameworks posit that individual difference factors should influence children's responsiveness to supportive interviewing. For instance, evolutionary-neurodevelopmental theory and the differential sensitivity hypothesis predict that children who are highly reactive to the environment would benefit from supportive interviewing. Research supports this prediction, showing that highly reactive children provide more correct responses when interviewed in a high-support condition than when interviewed in a low-support condition (Quas et al., 2004). This is of interest, given that forensic interviews can be emotionally arousing and maltreated children may be

[1]Children provided more details about an emotionally arousing laboratory event when they were interviewed in a nonsupportive condition. However, the effect size was small ($\eta^2 = .04$), and the authors reasoned that children may have provided more information in an effort to elicit more support from nonsupportive interviewers.

especially sensitive to the interview environment (Bakermans-Kranenburg & van IJzendoorn, 2011; see also Hobbs et al., 2023, for review).

Parental attachment orientation can interact with interviewer support to affect memory accuracy (Chae et al., 2021; Peter-Hagene et al., 2014). Consistent with attachment theory (Bowlby, 1969/1982), parents with more attachment avoidance and/or anxiety may be less likely to support their children during distressing events compared with more securely attached parents. Parents with insecure attachment histories may provide their children with fewer coping strategies during the event itself and be less likely to rehearse the event with their children afterward, which can impair later memory retrieval and accuracy (Chae et al., 2011, 2014). Chae et al. (2021) found that children of avoidant parents were less accurate on free-recall questions when interviewed by a nonsupportive interviewer; however, they did not find any significant differences in memory accuracy for the supportive condition. When interviewed by a nonsupportive interviewer, children of avoidant parents may feel more intimidated, anxious, or emotionally dysregulated, but these memory errors are minimized when they are interviewed in a supportive fashion.

SUMMARY AND IMPLICATIONS FOR FORENSIC AND CLINICAL PRACTICE

Children can provide accurate reports about what has happened to them. Interviewers can facilitate this by ensuring that the interview environment is supportive and that children feel comfortable enough to disclose their experiences. Research with children and adults across various domains (e.g., therapy, eyewitness and victim testimonies, qualitative studies, interrogations, laboratory experiments) clearly demonstrates that building rapport and providing a supportive context during interviews are crucial factors for obtaining comprehensive and accurate information. A supportive interview environment helps maintain rapport, decreases suggestibility, and increases completeness and accuracy of children's responses. Based on the aforementioned research, we make the following recommendations for developing and maintaining rapport with children in a supportive interview context:

Adopt an Interpersonally Warm, Positive, and Attentive Stance

Supportive interviewing involves being warm, friendly, and interested in what children have to say. Interviewers can help put children at ease by smiling, addressing children by name, making eye contact, and using an open and relaxed body posture (Saywitz et al., 2015). We recommend that interviewers provide children with their undivided attention (Johnston et al., 2019). Be aware that children's needs fluctuate as rapport waxes and wanes, and they move from answering introductory questions to answering questions about sensitive and/or painful events (Saywitz et al., 2018).

Keep Supportive Behaviors Noncontingent and Nonsuggestive

Be careful that interviews do not involve selective reinforcement for certain types of answers. This can increase suggestibility and decrease accuracy (Quas et al., 2007; Schreiber et al., 2006).

Maintain a Supportive Interview Environment When Children Are Reluctant

Some interviewers may become frustrated and nonsupportive when children do not respond to them (Hershkowitz et al., 2006). When faced with uncooperative children, interviewers may ask fewer open-ended questions, increase the use of closed-ended and leading questions, and become more forceful and insistent when children are reluctant to talk to them (Gilstrap & Ceci, 2005; Hershkowitz et al., 2006). This approach can backfire and result in inaccurate reports and increased resistance (Rohrabaugh et al., 2016). However, maintaining social support in response to reluctance can increase children's cooperation (Ahern et al., 2014).

Additionally, interviewers can help avoid reluctance by not asking sensitive or abuse-related questions until children are comfortable and cooperative (Hershkowitz et al., 2006). It is imperative that interviewers remain supportive when children are uncooperative. This can be challenging, especially when interviewers feel pressured by impatient observers. Training and supervision can help interviewers to continue supportive interviewing even when children are reluctant and external pressures are present (Hershkowitz et al., 2017).

Be an Empathic Listener

As described in the clinical psychology literature, empathic listening involves noticing and understanding, not action or therapeutic intervention (e.g., Tustonja et al., 2024). Empathic listening does not require interviewers to eliminate children's negative affect states—sometimes anger or sadness are important parts of a memory. Efforts to tell children not to feel nervous or worried may only serve to devalue their feelings. Interviewers may have to tolerate negative feelings, listen patiently, and accept that these feelings exist, without showing disappointment, discomfort, frustration, anger, or rejection. Children's forensic interviewers would do well to heed therapist Carl Rogers' instructions. Listen without judgment (Rogers, 1975).

Create a Safe, Private, Child-Friendly Setting With Minimal Distraction

Interviews should be conducted in child-friendly settings, such as playrooms or offices with comfortable, age-appropriate furniture and decorations (e.g., Ovsiannikova et al., 2021; Saywitz & Camparo, 2014; Saywitz et al., 2018).

CONCLUSION

The evidence base on interviewer supportiveness is clear. A socially supportive interview environment can reduce mistrust, decrease anxiety, enhance honesty, and facilitate self-disclosure. Interviewers can provide a supportive atmosphere without compromising children's accuracy. Interviewer supportiveness may be a key variable in promoting the feeling that children are being listened to by adults whom they can trust and who perceive them as competent sources of information. Society has two compelling interests when children are involved in the legal system: an interest in discovering the truth and an interest in safeguarding children's physical and mental well-being. Although interviewers are only temporary figures in children's lives, they are present at pivotal moments and can make a difference in obtaining reliable reports from children while maintaining children's well-being.

REFERENCES

Abbe, A., & Brandon, S. E. (2013). The role of rapport in investigative interviewing: A review. *Journal of Investigative Psychology and Offender Profiling, 10*(3), 237–249. https://doi.org/10.1002/jip.1386

Abbe, A., & Brandon, S. E. (2014). Building and maintaining rapport in investigative interviews. *Police Practice and Research, 15*(3), 207–220. https://doi.org/10.1080/15614263.2013.827835

Ahern, E. C., Hershkowitz, I., Lamb, M. E., Blasbalg, U., & Winstanley, A. (2014). Support and reluctance in the pre-substantive phase of alleged child abuse victim investigative interviews: Revised versus Standard NICHD Protocols. *Behavioral Sciences & the Law, 32*(6), 762–774. https://doi.org/10.1002/bsl.2149

Alexander, K. W., Quas, J. A., & Goodman, G. S. (2002). Theoretical advances in understanding children's memory for distressing events: The role of attachment. *Developmental Review, 22*(3), 490–519. https://doi.org/10.1016/S0273-2297(02)00004-7

Almerigogna, J., Ost, J., Bull, R., & Akehurst, L. (2007). State of high anxiety: How non-supportive interviewers can increase the suggestibility of child witnesses. *Applied Cognitive Psychology, 21*(7), 963–974. https://doi.org/10.1002/acp.1311

APSAC Taskforce. (2023). *APSAC practice guidelines: Forensic interviewing of children*. Association of Professionals Solving the Abuse of Children (APSAC). https://apsac.org/wp-content/uploads/2025/08/FI-Guidelines-Updated-V2.pdf

Baker, Z. G., Watlington, E. M., & Knee, C. R. (2020). The role of rapport in satisfying one's basic psychological needs. *Motivation and Emotion, 44*(2), 329–343. https://doi.org/10.1007/s11031-020-09819-5

Bakermans-Kranenburg, M. J., & van IJzendoorn, M. H. (2011). Differential susceptibility to rearing environment depending on dopamine-related genes: New evidence and a meta-analysis. *Developmental Psychopathology, 23*(1), 39–52. https://doi.org/10.1017/S0954579410000635

Belsky, J. (2005). Differential susceptibility to rearing influences: An evolutionary hypothesis and some evidence. In B. Ellis & D. Bjorklund (Eds.), *Origins of the social mind: Evolutionary psychology and child development* (pp. 139–163). Guilford Press.

Belsky, J., & Pluess, M. (2009). Beyond diathesis stress: Differential susceptibility to environmental influences. *Psychological Bulletin, 135*(6), 885–908. https://doi.org/10.1037/a0017376

Berliner, L., & Conte, J. R. (1995). The effects of disclosure and intervention on sexually abused children. *Child Abuse & Neglect, 19*(3), 371–384. https://doi.org/10.1016/S0145-2134(94)00138-3

Bernieri, F. J., & Gillis, J. S. (2001). Judging rapport: Employing Brunswik's lens model to study interpersonal sensitivity. In J. A. Hall & F. J. Bernieri (Eds.), *Interpersonal sensitivity: Theory and measurement* (pp. 67–88). Erlbaum. https://doi.org/10.4324/9781410600424

Blasbalg, U., Hershkowitz, I., Lamb, M. E., Karni-Visel, Y., & Ahern, E. C. (2019). Is interviewer support associated with the reduced reluctance and enhanced informativeness of alleged child abuse victims? *Law and Human Behavior, 43*(2), 156–165. https://doi.org/10.1037/lhb0000303

Bowlby, J. (1980). *Sadness and depression* (Attachment and Loss, Vol. 3). Basic Books.

Bowlby, J. (1982). *Attachment: Vol. 1. Attachment and Loss.* Basic Books. (Original work published 1969)

Bretherton, I., & Munholland, K. A. (2008). Internal working models in attachment relationships: Elaborating a central construct in attachment theory. In J. Cassidy & P. Shaver (Eds.), *Handbook of attachment: Theory, research, and clinical applications* (pp. 102–130). Guilford Press.

Brown, D. A., Lamb, M. E., Lewis, C. N., Pipe, M. E., Orbach, Y., & Wolfman, M. (2013). The NICHD investigative interview protocol: An analogue study. *Journal of Experimental Psychology: Applied, 19*(4), 367–382. https://doi.org/10.1037/a0035143

Brubacher, S. P., Poole, D. A., Dickinson, J. J., La Rooy, D., Szojka, Z. A., & Powell, M. B. (2019). Effects of interviewer familiarity and supportiveness on children's recall across repeated interviews. *Law and Human Behavior, 43*(6), 507–516. https://doi.org/10.1037/lhb0000346

Burleson, B. R., Albrecht, T. L., Goldsmith, D. J., & Sarason, I. G. (1994). Introduction: The communication of social support. In B. R. Burleson, T. L. Albrecht, & I. G. Sarason (Eds.), *Communication of social support* (pp. 11–30). SAGE.

Carson, D. K., & Bittner, M. T. (1994). Temperament and school-aged children's coping abilities and responses to stress. *Journal of Genetic Psychology: Research and Theory on Human Development, 155*(3), 289–302. https://doi.org/10.1080/00221325.1994.9914779

Cepeda, C., & Gotanco, L. (2017). *Psychiatric interview of children and adolescents.* American Psychiatric Association Publishing.

Chae, Y., Goodman, G. S., & Edelstein, R. S. (2011). Autobiographical memory development from an attachment perspective: The special role of negative events. In J. B. Benson (Ed.), *Advances in Child Development and Behavior* (Vol. 40, pp. 1–49). Academic Press. https://doi.org/10.1016/b978-0-12-386491-8.00001-3

Chae, Y., Goodman, G. S., Larson, R. P., Augusti, E. M., Alley, D., VanMeenen, K. M., Culver, M., & Coulter, K. P. (2014). Children's memory and suggestibility about a distressing event: The role of children's and parents' attachment. *Journal of Experimental Child Psychology, 123,* 90–111. https://doi.org/10.1016/j.jecp.2014.01.005

Chae, Y., Goodman, G. S., Wang, Y., Goodman, M., McWilliams, K., Shaver, P. R., Thompson, R. A., & Widaman, K. F. (2021). Parents' attachment orientation, interviewers' support, and children's memory for a mildly distressing event. *Memory, 29*(10), 1384–1395. https://doi.org/10.1080/09658211.2021.1988644

Cleveland, K. C., Quas, J. A., & Lyon, T. D. (2018). The effects of implicit encouragement and the putative confession on children's memory reports. *Child Abuse & Neglect, 80,* 113–122. https://doi.org/10.1016/j.chiabu.2018.03.024

Cohen, S. (2004). Social relationships and health. *American Psychologist, 59*(8), 676–684. https://doi.org/10.1037/0003-066X.59.8.676

Collins, K., & Carthy, N. (2018). No rapport, no comment: The relationship between rapport and communication during investigative interviews with suspects. *Journal of Investigative Psychology and Offender Profiling, 16*(1), 18–31. https://doi.org/10.1002/jip.1517

Cooper, T. A. (2012). Sacrificing the child to convict the defendant: Secondary traumatization of child witnesses by prosecutors, their inherent conflict of interest, and the need for child witness counsel. *Cardozo Public Law, Policy, and Ethics Journal, 9*, 239–286. http://ssrn.com/abstract=2174482

Cuddy, A. J. C., Fiske, S. T., & Glick, P. (2008). Warmth and competence as universal dimensions of social perception: The stereotype content model and the BIAS map. *Advances in Experimental Social Psychology, 40*, 61–149. https://doi.org/10.1016/S0065-2601(07)00002-0

Cyr, C., Euser, E. M., Bakermans-Kranenburg, M. J., & Van IJzendoorn, M. H. (2010). Attachment security and disorganization in maltreating and high-risk families: A series of meta-analyses. *Development and Psychopathology, 22*(1), 87–108. https://doi.org/10.1017/S0954579409990289

Davis, S. L., & Bottoms, B. L. (2002). Effects of social support on children's eyewitness reports: A test of the underlying mechanism. *Law and Human Behavior, 26*(2), 185–215. https://doi.org/10.1023/A:1014692009941

Deci, E. L., & Ryan, R. M. (2000). The "what" and "why" of goal pursuits: Human needs and the self-determination of behavior. *Psychological Inquiry, 11*(4), 227–268. https://doi.org/10.1207/S15327965PLI1104_01

Derakshan, N., & Eysenck, M. W. (2009). Anxiety, processing efficiency, and cognitive performance: New developments from attentional control theory. *European Psychologist, 14*(2), 168–176. https://doi.org/10.1027/1016-9040.14.2.168

de Wolff, M., & van IJzendoorn, M. H. (1997). Sensitivity and attachment: A meta-analysis on parental antecedents of infant attachment. *Child Development, 68*(4), 571–591. https://doi.org/10.1111/j.1467-8624.1997.tb04218.x

Eisen, M. L., Goodman, G. S., Diep, J., Lacsamana, M. T., Olomi, J., Goldfarb, D., & Quas, J. A. (2019). Effects of interviewer support on maltreated and at-risk children's memory and suggestibility. *International Journal on Child Maltreatment: Research, Policy, and Practice, 2*(1–2), 255–278. https://doi.org/10.1007/s42448-019-00016-7

Ellis, B. J., Boyce, W. T., Belsky, J., Bakermans-Kranenburg, M. J., & van IJzendoorn, M. H. (2011). Differential susceptibility to the environment: An evolutionary-neurodevelopmental theory. *Development and Psychopathology, 23*(1), 7–28. https://doi.org/10.1017/S0954579410000611

Eltz, M. J., Shirk, S. R., & Sarlin, N. (1995). Alliance formation and treatment outcome among maltreated adolescents. *Child Abuse & Neglect, 19*(4), 419–431. https://doi.org/10.1016/0145-2134(95)00008-V

Eysenck, M. W., & Calvo, M. G. (1992). Anxiety and performance: The processing efficiency theory. *Cognition & Emotion, 6*(6), 409–434. https://doi.org/10.1080/02699939208409696

Fernandes, D., Gomes, J. P., Albuquerque, P. B., & Matos, M. (2024). Forensic interview techniques in child sexual abuse cases: A scoping review. *Trauma, Violence, Abuse, 25*(2), 1382–7396. https://doi.org/10.1177/15248380231177317

Fischer, K. W., Bullock, D. H., Rotenberg, E. J., & Raya, P. (1993). The dynamics of competence: How context contributes directly to skill. In R. Wozniak & K. W. Fischer (Eds.), *Development in context: Acting and thinking in specific environments* (pp. 93–117). Erlbaum.

Foster, I., Talwar, V., & Crossman, A. (2023). The role of rapport in eliciting children's truthful reports. *Applied Developmental Science, 27*(3), 221–237. https://doi.org/10.1080/10888691.2022.2058507

Gabbert, F., Hope, L., Luther, K., Wright, G., Ng, M., & Oxburgh, G. (2020). Exploring the use of rapport in professional information gathering contexts by systematically mapping the evidence base. *Applied Cognitive Psychology, 35*(2), 329–341. https://doi.org/10.1002/acp.3762

Gilstrap, L. L., & Ceci, S. J. (2005). Reconceptualizing children's suggestibility: Bidirectional and temporal properties. *Child Development, 76*(1), 40–53. https://doi.org/10.1111/j.1467-8624.2005.00828.x

Goodman, G. S. (2006). Children's eyewitness memory: A modern history and contemporary commentary. *Journal of Social Issues, 62*(4), 811–832. https://doi.org/10.1111/j.1540-4560.2006.00488.x

Goodman, G. S., Bottoms, B. L., Schwartz-Kenney, B. M., & Rudy, L. (1991). Children's testimony about a stressful event: Improving children's reports. *Journal of Narrative & Life History, 1*(1), 69–99. https://doi.org/10.1075/jnlh.1.1.05chi

Goodman, G. S., Sharma, A., Thomas, S. F., & Considine, M. G. (1995). Mother knows best: Effects of relationship status and interviewer bias on children's memory. *Journal of Experimental Child Psychology, 60*(1), 195–228. https://doi.org/10.1006/jecp.1995.1038

Goodman-Brown, T. B., Edelstein, R. S., Goodman, G. S., Jones, D. P. H., & Gordon, D. S. (2003). Why children tell: A model of children's disclosure of sexual abuse. *Child Abuse & Neglect, 27*(5), 525–540. https://doi.org/10.1016/S0145-2134(03)00037-1

Hardy, C. L., & Van Leeuwen, S. A. (2004). Interviewing young children: Effects of probe structures and focus of rapport-building talk on the qualities of young children's eyewitness statements. *Canadian Journal of Behavioural Science/Revue Canadienne des Sciences du Comportement, 36*(2), 155–165. https://doi.org/10.1037/h0087226

Hershkowitz, I., Ahern, E. C., Lamb, M. E., Blasbalg, U., Karni-Visel, Y., & Breitman, M. (2017). Changes in interviewers' use of supportive techniques during the revised protocol training. *Applied Cognitive Psychology, 31*(3), 340–350. https://doi.org/10.1002/acp.3333

Hershkowitz, I., Lamb, M., & Katz, C. (2014). Allegation rates in forensic child abuse investigations: Comparing the revised and standard NICHD protocols. *Psychology, Public Policy, and Law, 20*(3), 336–344. https://doi.org/10.1037/a0037391

Hershkowitz, I., Lamb, M. E., Katz, C., & Malloy, L. C. (2015). Does enhanced rapport-building alter the dynamics of investigative interviews with suspected victims of intra-familial abuse? *Journal of Police and Criminal Psychology, 30*(1), 6–14. https://doi.org/10.1007/s11896-013-9136-8

Hershkowitz, I., Orbach, Y., Lamb, M. E., Sternberg, K. J., & Horowitz, D. (2006). Dynamics of forensic interviews with suspected abuse victims who do not disclose abuse. *Child Abuse & Neglect, 30*(7), 753–769. https://doi.org/10.1016/j.chiabu.2005.10.016

Hobbs, S. D., Chae, Y., & Noriega, I. (2023). Autobiographical memory and health in childhood and adolescence. In B. Halpern-Felsher (Ed.), *Encyclopedia of child and adolescent health* (Vol. 2, pp. 50–63). Elsevier. https://doi.org/10.1016/B978-0-12-818872-9.00107-2

Imhoff, M. C., & Baker-Ward, L. (1999). Preschooler's suggestibility: Effects of developmentally appropriate language and interviewer supportiveness. *Journal of Applied Developmental Psychology, 20*(3), 407–429. https://doi.org/10.1016/S0193-3973(99)00022-2

Izard, C. E. (1990). Personality, emotion, expressions, and rapport. *Psychological Inquiry, 1*(4), 315–317. https://doi.org/10.1207/s15327965pli0104_10

Johnston, V., Brubacher, S. P., Powell, M., & Fuller-Tyszkiewicz, M. (2019). Patterns of nonverbal rapport behaviors across time in investigative interviews with children. *Journal of Nonverbal Behavior, 43*(3), 411–434. https://doi.org/10.1007/s10919-019-00306-1

Krug, E. G., Dahlberg, L. L., Mercy, J. A., Zwi, A. B., & Lozano, R. (Eds.). (2002). *World report on violence and health*. World Health Organization.

Lakey, B., & Cohen, S. (2000). Social support: Theory, measurement, and intervention. In B. H. Gottlieb, L. G. Underwood, & S. Cohen (Eds.), *Social support measurement and intervention: A guide for health and social scientists* (pp. 29–52). Oxford University Press.

Lamaigre, C., Taylor, E. P., & Gittoes, C. (2017). Barriers and facilitators to disclosing sexual abuse in childhood and adolescence: A systematic review. *Child Abuse & Neglect, 70*, 39–52. https://doi.org/10.1016/j.chiabu.2017.05.009

Lamb, M. E., Orbach, Y., Hershkowitz, I., Esplin, P. W., & Horowitz, D. (2007). A structured forensic interview protocol improves the quality and informativeness of investigative interviews with children: A review of research using the NICHD investigative interview protocol. *Child Abuse & Neglect, 31*(11–12), 1201–1231. https://doi.org/10.1016/j.chiabu.2007.03.021

Lavoie, J., Wyman, J., Crossman, A. M., & Talwar, V. (2021). Meta-analysis of the effects of two interviewing practices on children's disclosures of sensitive information: Rapport practices and question type. *Child Abuse & Neglect, 113*, 104930. https://doi.org/10.1016/j.chiabu.2021.104930

Lengua, L. J., & Sandler, I. N. (1996). Self-regulation as a moderator of the relation between coping and symptomatology in children of divorce. *Journal of Abnormal Child Psychology, 24*(6), 681–701. https://doi.org/10.1007/BF01664734

Lewy, J., Cyr, J., & Dion, J. (2015). Impact of interviewers' supportive comments and children's reluctance to cooperate during sexual abuse disclosure. *Child Abuse & Neglect, 43*, 112–122. https://doi.org/10.1016/j.chiabu.2015.03.002

Lyon, T. D. (2016). Investigative interviewing of the child. In D. N. Duquette, A. M. Haralambie, & V. S. Sankaran (Eds.), *Child welfare law and practice: Representing children, parents, and state agencies in abuse, neglect, and dependency cases* (3rd ed., pp. 87–113). National Association of Counsel for Children.

Lyon, T. D. (2021). *Ten Step Investigative Interview* (Version 3). https://drive.google.com/file/d/1JTrEH6eK4pHwCqr7HU5-Bg1CYFUyWrER/view?usp=sharing

Lyon, T. D., Ahern, E. C., Malloy, L. C., & Quas, J. A. (2010). Children's reasoning about disclosing adult transgressions: Effects of maltreatment, child age, and adult identity. *Child Development, 81*(6), 1714–1728. https://doi.org/10.1111/j.1467-8624.2010.01505.x

Lyon, T. D., Wandrey, L., Ahern, E., Licht, R., Sim, M. P., & Quas, J. A. (2014). Eliciting maltreated and nonmaltreated children's transgression disclosures: Narrative practice rapport building and a putative confession. *Child Development, 85*(4), 1756–1769. https://doi.org/10.1111/cdev.12223

McWilliams, K., Stolzenberg, S. N., Williams, S., & Lyon, T. D. (2021). Increasing maltreated and nonmaltreated children's recall disclosures of a minor transgression: The effects of back-channel utterances, a promise to tell the truth and a post-recall putative confession. *Child Abuse & Neglect, 116*(1), 104073. https://doi.org/10.1016/j.chiabu.2019.104073

Norfolk, T., Birdi, K., & Walsh, D. (2007). The role of empathy in establishing rapport in the consultation: A new model. *Medical Education, 41*(7), 690–697. https://doi.org/10.1111/j.1365-2923.2007.02789.x

Ovsiannikova, Y., Liebiedieva, S., Pokhilko, D., Onishchenko, N., Gontarenko, L., & Shyrobokov, Y. (2021). The modern approach to rapport building with children affected by crisis events. *BRAIN. Broad Research in Artificial Intelligence and Neuroscience, 12*(4), 532–542. https://doi.org/10.18662/brain/12.4/263

Penela, E. C., Walker, O. L., Degnan, K. A., Fox, N. A., & Henderson, H. A. (2015). Early behavioral inhibition and emotion regulation. *Child Development, 86*(4), 1227–1240. https://doi.org/10.1111/cdev.12384

Peter-Hagene, L., Bottoms, B. L., Davis, S. L., & Nysse-Carris, K. L. (2014, March 6–8). *Social support effects on children's suggestibility after one year* [Poster presentation]. American Psychology–Law Society Conference, New Orleans, LA, United States.

Pluess, M. (2017). Vantage sensitivity: Environmental sensitivity to positive experiences as a function of genetic differences. *Journal of Personality, 85*(1), 38–50. https://doi.org/10.1111/jopy.12218

Pluess, M., & Belsky, J. (2013). Vantage sensitivity: Individual differences in response to positive experiences. *Psychological Bulletin, 139*(4), 901–916. https://doi.org/10.1037/a0030196

Ponizovsky-Bergelson, Y., Dayan, Y., Wahle, N., & Roer-Strier, D. (2019). A qualitative interview with young children: What encourages or inhibits young children's participation? *International Journal of Qualitative Methods, 18,* 1–9. https://doi.org/10.1177/1609406919840516

Quas, J. A., Bauer, A., & Boyce, W. T. (2004). Physiological reactivity, social support, and memory in early childhood. *Child Development, 75*(3), 797–814. https://doi.org/10.1111/j.1467-8624.2004.00707.x

Quas, J. A., & Lench, H. C. (2007). Arousal at encoding, arousal at retrieval, interviewer support, and children's memory for a mild stressor. *Applied Cognitive Psychology, 305*(3), 289–305. https://doi.org/10.1002/acp.1279

Quas, J. A., Malloy, L. C., Melinder, A., Goodman, G. S., D'Mello, M., & Schaaf, J. M. (2007). Developmental differences in the effects of repeated interviews and interviewer bias on young children's event memory and false reports. *Developmental Psychology, 43*(4), 823–837. https://doi.org/10.1037/0012-1649.43.4.823

Quas, J. A., Rush, E. B., Yim, I. S., & Nikolayev, M. (2014). Effects of stress on memory in children and adolescents: Testing causal connections. *Memory, 22*(6), 616–632. https://doi.org/10.1080/09658211.2013.809766

Quas, J. A., Wallin, A. R., Papini, S., Lench, H. C., & Scullin, M. H. (2005). Suggestibility, social support, and memory for a novel experience in young children. *Journal of Experimental Child Psychology, 91*(4), 315–341. https://doi.org/10.1016/j.jecp.2005.03.008

Roberts, K. P., Lamb, M. E., & Sternberg, K. J. (2004). The effects of rapport-building style on children's reports of a staged event. *Applied Cognitive Psychology, 18*(2), 189–202. https://doi.org/10.1002/acp.957

Rogers, C. R. (1975). Empathetic: An unappreciated way of being. *The Counseling Psychologist, 5*(2), 2–10. https://doi.org/10.1177/001100007500500202

Rohrabaugh, M., London, K., & Hall, A. K. (2016). Planning the forensic interview. In W. T. O'Donohue & M. Fanetti (Eds.), *Forensic interviews regarding child sexual abuse. A guide to evidence-based practice* (pp. 197–218). Springer.

Rotenberg, K., Eisenberg, N., Cumming, C., Smith, A., Singh, M., & Terlicher, E. (2003). The contribution of adults' nonverbal cues and children's shyness to the development of rapport between adults and preschool children. *International Journal of Behavioral Development, 27*(1), 21–30. https://doi.org/10.1080/01650250143000571

Saywitz, K. J., & Camparo, L. B. (2014). *Evidence-based child forensic interviewing: The developmental narrative elaboration interview.* Oxford University Press.

Saywitz, K. J., Larson, R. P., Hobbs, S. D., & Wells, C. R. (2015). Developing rapport with children in forensic interviews: A systematic review of experimental research. *Behavioral Sciences and the Law, 33*(4), 372–389. https://doi.org/10.1002/bsl.2186

Saywitz, K. J., Lyon, T. D., & Goodman, G. S. (2018). When interviewing children: A review and update. In J. B. Klika & J. R. Conte (Eds.), *APSAC Handbook on Child Maltreatment* (4th ed., pp. 310–329). Sage.

Saywitz, K. J., Wells, C. R., Larson, R. P., & Hobbs, S. D. (2016). Effects of interviewer support on children's memory and suggestibility: Systematic review and meta-analysis of experimental research. *Trauma, Violence, & Abuse, 20*(1), 22–39. https://doi.org/10.1177/1524838016683457

Schreiber, N., Bella, L. D., Martinez, Y., McLaurin, K. A., Strok, R., Garven, S., & Wood, J. M. (2006). Suggestive interviewing in the McMartin Preschool and Kelly Michaels daycare abuse cases: A case study. *Social Influence, 1*(1), 16–47. https://doi.org/10.1080/15534510500361739

Somers, J. A., & Luecken, L. J. (2021). Socioemotional mechanisms of children's differential response to the effects of maternal sensitivity on child adjustment. *Parenting, Science, and Practice, 21*(3), 241–275. https://doi.org/10.1080/15295192.2020.1809955

Teoh, Y. S., & Lamb, M. (2013). Interviewer demeanor in forensic interviews with children. *Psychology, Crime & Law, 19*(2), 145–159. https://doi.org/10.1080/1068316X.2011.614610

Tickle-Degnen, L., & Rosenthal, R. (1990). The nature of rapport and its nonverbal correlates. *Psychological Inquiry, 1*(4), 285–293. https://doi.org/10.1207/s15327965pli0104_1

Toth, S. L., Cicchetti, D., Macfie, J., & Emde, R. N. (1997). Representations of self and other in the narratives of neglected, physically abused, and sexually abused preschoolers. *Development and Psychopathology, 9*(4), 781–796. https://doi.org/10.1017/S0954579497001430

Tustonja, M., Topić Stipić, D., Skoko, I., Čuljak, A., & Vegar, A. (2024). Active listening–A model of empathetic communication in the helping professions. *Medicina Academica Integrativa, 1*(1), 42–47. https://doi.org/10.47960/3029-3316.2024.1.1.42

Uchino, B. N. (2009). Understanding the links between social support and physical health: A life-span perspective with emphasis on the separability of perceived and received support. *Perspectives on Psychological Science, 4*(3), 236–255. https://doi.org/10.1111/j.1745-6924.2009.01122.x

van Os, E. C. C., Zijlstra, A. E., Knorth, E. J., Post, W. J., & Kalverboer, M. E. (2020). Finding keys: A systematic review of barriers and facilitators for refugee children's disclosure of their life stories. *Trauma, Violence & Abuse, 21*(2), 242–260. https://doi.org/10.1177/1524838018757748

Villa, M., & Reitman, D. (2010). *Sage reference handbook of clinical interviewing with children.* Sage. https://doi.org/10.4135/9781412982740

Wachs, T. (2006). Contributions of temperament to buffering and sensitization processes in children's development. *Annals of the New York Academy of Sciences, 1094*(1), 28–39. https://doi.org/10.1196/annals.1376.004

Walsh, D., & Bull, R. (2012). Examining rapport in investigative interviews with suspects: Does its building and maintenance work? *Journal of Police and Criminal Psychology, 27*(1), 73–84. https://doi.org/10.1007/s11896-011-9087-x

Wojciszke, B., Abele, A. E., & Baryla, W. (2009). Two dimensions of interpersonal attitudes: Liking depends on communion, respect depends on agency. *European Journal of Social Psychology, 39*(6), 973–990. https://doi.org/10.1002/ejsp.595

Wuyts, D., Soenens, B., Vansteenkistke, M., & Van Petegem, S. (2018). The role of observed autonomy support, reciprocity, and need satisfaction in adolescent disclosure about friends. *Journal of Adolescence, 65*(1), 141–154. https://doi.org/10.1016/j.adolescence.2018.03.012

Yi, M., & Lamb, M. E. (2018). The effects of narrative practice on children's testimony and disclosure of secrets. *Applied Cognitive Psychology, 32*(3), 326–336. https://doi.org/10.1002/acp.3385

Zajac, R., O'Neill, S., & Hayne, H. (2012). Disorder in the courtroom? Child witnesses under cross-examination. *Developmental Review, 32*(3), 181–204. https://doi.org/10.1016/j.dr.2012.06.006

13

Mechanisms of Denial

Children's Deception and Secrecy

Angela M. Crossman and Victoria Talwar

One of the most consistent challenges facing practitioners who work with child witnesses is how to elicit their accurate and honest reports about true events in the context of countervailing motivations. These can be influences that lead children to intentionally provide inaccurate reports through deception or that undermine their willingness to disclose accurate reports through secrecy. Research has explored each behavior over the past century, growing and deepening our understanding of deception and secrecy among children.

This chapter examines the implications of this understanding for child witnesses and the practitioners who work with them. We first define the related constructs of lying and secrecy and differentiate between them, describing the development of and motivations for each. The research on these constructs has considerable overlap, and they are discussed together in many places throughout the chapter. We examine evidence-based approaches for encouraging honesty, concluding with legal and practical implications to help guide work with child witnesses.

DIFFERENTIATING LYING FROM SECRECY: DISTINCTION WITHOUT A DIFFERENCE?

Lying and secrecy often go hand-in-hand, as both involve withholding true information. Generally speaking, *lying* occurs when one makes an intentionally false statement, meaning that what is communicated differs from what

https://doi.org/10.1037/0000492-013
Handbook on Child Witnesses: Improving Psychological Science and Legal Practice,
G. S. Goodman, T. D. Lyon, S. D. Hobbs, and R. Enriquez (Editors)

the speaker believes is true (to explore the nature of deception in depth, e.g., Bok, 1978; Lee, 2013). Sometimes termed *lies of commission*, the individual knowingly provides false and/or fabricated information to actively mislead while withholding the truth (Ekman, 1985, terms this *falsification*). One can also intentionally omit information to mislead (e.g., when asked to describe what they saw, a witness withholds identifying information about the perpetrator), sometimes called a *lie of omission*. Ekman (1985) calls this concealment or lying by withholding information "without actually saying anything untrue" (p. 28), though others may consider this to be secret-keeping rather than lying (for discussion, see Williams et al., 2020).

Secrecy is the intentional withholding of information from another person (Bok, 1984). To keep a secret, one must avoid revealing the contents of the secret, which can be a challenge. Under questioning, one could continue to keep the secret, reveal the truth (e.g., Gordon et al., 2014), or lie by commission, adding or substituting false information. Secrecy, through secret-telling, can also involve selectively sharing information with a restricted and trusted audience, such as a close friend, perhaps to relieve the burden of keeping the secret or to build intimacy (Watson & Valtin, 1997b). Although these constructs are related, one can keep a secret without necessarily lying, but lying implicitly involves keeping secret some aspect of the truth. Here, we will refer to providing false information (i.e., lie of commission) as lying, and withholding information (without providing false information) as secret-keeping or concealment.

Deception and secret-keeping often co-occur and share a number of characteristics as they evolve. Both can have positive and negative intentions, committed for self-serving purposes and/or the intention of helping others. Both telling the truth and disclosing a secret can impact one's relationships with others, particularly those who might be implicated. Also, both constructs are imbued with nuance in how they are socialized, perceived, and enacted culturally, with children likely receiving mixed messages about each. For instance, although "lying" tends to be universally proscribed as bad in theory (e.g., denying a transgression), some lies may be condoned and even encouraged in practice (e.g., parents asking children to tell polite lies; Lavoie et al., 2016). Similarly, although some secrets may be "good" and are encouraged by parents and other adults (i.e., keeping a surprise party secret), other secrets are "bad" and unsafe for children to keep, putting themselves or others in jeopardy. It is therefore important to clarify how children learn to understand the difference between lies and secrets that are culturally acceptable versus hazardous, and how practitioners can best support children's honest disclosures across motivational contexts (e.g., Dunkerley & Dalenberg, 2000; Fisher et al., 2016).

DEVELOPMENT OF CHILDREN'S LYING AND SECRET-KEEPING BEHAVIOR

Although most daily communications with others are truthful, individuals occasionally tell lies and keep secrets for a variety of reasons (DePaulo et al., 1996; Serota et al., 2010). Some lies and secrets are self-serving, used primarily to protect oneself from harm or for personal gain. Research suggests these are the earliest types of lies children tell, typically to escape imminent punishment and/or to hide misdeeds, emerging before 3 years of age for some children (Evans & Lee, 2013; Leduc et al., 2017; Stouthamer-Loeber, 1986; Williams et al., 2016). Parents in one study, for instance, kept diaries of their preschoolers' lies and reported that the most frequent lies children told were to avoid discomfort and negative consequences to themselves (Newton et al., 2000). In legal contexts, children may lie or keep secrets out of fear of getting in trouble for having done something wrong or being blamed for the repercussions when the truth or secret is disclosed. Self-protective lies continue to be told with age to help mitigate negative consequences to individuals' self-interest in different contexts. Adolescents, for example, are more likely to conceal their activities to avoid parental censure when they expect their parents to disapprove (Bureau & Mageau, 2014; Smetana et al., 2009).

Another motivation to lie is for personal gain. Such "instrumental lies" may initially be told in an effort to obtain material benefits (e.g., to obtain a prohibited treat), while later lies may be told in pursuit of social rewards (e.g., enhancing self-presentation, reputation). For example, children as young as 5 years of age will tell self-presentation lies to appear "positive" or enhance their image with others (Klafka & Liszkowski, 2021). For the same reason, children may keep secret personal information that they feel detracts from their reputation or of which they feel ashamed (Lavoie, Nagar, & Talwar, 2017). In forensic settings, children may tell self-serving lies for material gain or rewards, to evade punishment, to appease others, or to enhance their perceived importance or credibility in the eyes of adults (Evans & Lyon, 2011).

Children learn to lie to benefit or protect another from harm as well. These "prosocial lies" are evaluated less negatively compared to self-serving lies and are sometimes encouraged by adults (Lavoie et al., 2016). For example, polite lies may be told to avoid hurting someone's feelings or to smooth social interactions or relationships. In contrast, lying about or keeping secret another's transgression for their protection or benefit may be more problematic, such as an adolescent lying to assist a peer doing something illegal or concealing the identity of a known perpetrator to protect a peer from punishment. Such lies and secrets about negative behaviors, though intended for the benefit of another, would nevertheless not be evaluated as socially acceptable (Watson & Valtin, 1997a) and are of particular concern in legal settings. Children might lie about or conceal a perpetrator's wrongdoing to protect them, as well as to avoid negative consequences for themselves, perhaps out of fear of being blamed. Given their particular relevance to child witness testimony, the current chapter thus focuses on children's lies and secrets concerning their own or another person's wrongdoing.

CHILDREN'S UNDERSTANDING AND EVALUATION OF LIES AND SECRETS

How children understand and evaluate lies and secrets can have implications for their forthcomingness and credibility as witnesses. Whereas children lie and keep secrets for various reasons, their conceptual and moral understanding of lying develops with age, shifting from a concrete, literal perspective to one that is more abstract and nuanced (e.g., Bussey, 1992; Peterson et al., 1983; Piaget, 1932/1965; Strichartz & Burton, 1990). Children learn initially that lies are false statements, before learning that they are intentionally false. That is, children as young as 2 years of age have been found to reliably accept true statements and reject false statements, and children can reliably understand factuality to correctly label true and false statements between 3.5 and 4 years of age, with 5-year-olds having close to 90% accuracy (Lyon et al., 2013). Hence, children's conceptual understanding of lies begins to emerge during the preschool years, initially based on statement factuality.

More nuanced understanding of lies develops in the school years (Peterson et al., 1983; Piaget, 1932/1965; Strichartz & Burton, 1990; Wimmer et al., 1984). With age, children begin to differentiate among false statements using intentions and motivations, understanding that beliefs can be false (as with mistakes), and false statements can be uttered without the intent to deceive (as with jokes, sarcasm), narrowing the definition of lies. In terms of motivations, Bussey (1999) reported that most children aged between 4 and 11 years classify all types of untruthful statements as lies regardless of whether they were told for self-oriented or other-oriented reasons. In contrast, Lee and Ross (1997) showed that 12- to 14-year-olds and college students were less likely to identify false statements as "lies" when they were motivated by a desire to help than when they were motivated by a desire to harm. Thus, as they grow older, children become increasingly capable of distinguishing lies from honest errors, guesses, exaggerations, jokes, and, eventually, more complex forms of communication, such as sarcasm and irony, using the speaker's beliefs, intentions, and motivations as cues (Creusere, 2000; Rothermich et al., 2020).

Children's moral judgments of lying also develop with age. Preschoolers tend to view lying—especially when self-serving in nature—as a negative behavior (e.g., Talwar et al., 2002; Wagland & Bussey, 2005). Nevertheless, nuanced evaluations have emerged even among 4-year-olds, some of whom evaluate lies differentially depending on a speaker's intentions (e.g., to harm vs. protect someone; Bussey, 1992, 1999; Siegal & Peterson, 1996). Moreover, children tend to evaluate lies told for the benefit of others more positively with increasing age (e.g., Popliger et al., 2011). Hence, as children grow, their conceptual and moral understanding of lying becomes more refined, reflecting an increasing sensitivity to speakers' beliefs, intentions, and the social contexts of their lies. By early adolescence, most children possess a level of understanding about lying and truth-telling that resembles that of adults.

Not unlike lying, children's secret-keeping precedes their conceptual understanding of secrecy, which deepens across middle childhood (Watson & Valtin, 1997b). Children as young as 5 years old differentiate between secrets and nonsecrets (Anagnostaki et al., 2010, 2013) and understand that surprises involve secrecy from an early age (Watson & Valtin, 1997a). Nevertheless, preschoolers may struggle to identify a "bad" secret (e.g., a child asked not to report accidental breakage), and their early reluctance to keep some secrets may rely on their deference to authority figures to whom revelation is due (Watson & Valtin, 1997b).

As they move into middle childhood, children's understanding of the informational and relational aspects of secrecy grows, along with their ability to distinguish among different types of secrets (Anagnostaki et al., 2010, 2013). For instance, Watson and Valtin (1997a, 1997b) found that younger children (i.e., 5- to 6-year-olds) failed to recognize that the desire to reveal a secret may conflict with keeping that secret. Older children (i.e., 11- to 12-year-olds) could reconcile such conflicts depending on the circumstances, understanding that some secrets are safe to keep to maintain friendships, while others are not and must be disclosed for safety. With age, children come to understand the social norms and expectations regarding the roles of secret-keeping and secret-sharing in harming or maintaining relationships (Liberman, 2020). Perhaps as a result, older children and adolescents are more likely to initially disclose abuse to peers than are younger children, who more often disclose to mothers (Manay & Collin-Vézina, 2021). Overall, then, children's evolving understanding and evaluation of secrets and lies can have implications for their ability and willingness to provide testimony as child witnesses.

CHILDREN'S MAINTENANCE SKILLS—LIES ABOUT THEIR OWN WRONGDOING

Children's lie-telling behavior appears and increases rapidly at an early age. Researchers find that while fewer than half of 3-year-olds typically lie to conceal their own transgressions (Evans & Lee, 2013; Leduc et al., 2017; Talwar & Lee, 2002), the majority of 4- to 7-year-olds do so (Talwar & Lee, 2002, 2008). Older children also tell such lies, with a peak in adolescence that decreases into adulthood (Debey et al., 2015; Evans & Lee, 2010). Lies for personal gain also begin to emerge in the preschool years (Lavoie, Leduc, et al., 2017; Peskin, 1992), but relative proportions of lie types used seems to shift with age. Older children seem to tell more other-oriented lies than do younger children (Lavoie, Leduc, et al., 2017).

Despite early use, however, young children are not skilled liars. To lie convincingly, a liar must manage verbal and nonverbal behaviors to avoid provoking suspicion—not just during the initial lie statement, but throughout all follow-up discussions. This is not easy, particularly for young children. Nonetheless, while some children may display a few different nonverbal signs of deception, there are no reliable nonverbal indicators to consistently distinguish lie-tellers from truth-tellers or enable adults to reliably detect children's lies (e.g., Talwar & Lee, 2002; Talwar et al., 2007). Verbal leakage, however, is more common among younger children, as preschoolers struggle to verbally sustain an elaborate lie beyond mere denial (Talwar & Lee, 2008; Talwar et al., 2007). This difficulty extends to concealment as well.

A mega-analysis of seven hundred fifty-two 4- to 9-year-olds found that verbal leakage during interview rapport-building was highest among younger children (Williams et al., 2020). Another study found that, after falsely denying wrongdoing, younger children were highly likely to disclose incriminating details in later statements, while roughly half of 6- and 7-year-olds successfully concealed the truth in response to follow-up questions (Talwar & Lee, 2002). When later asked to evaluate transcripts of their reports, adult raters readily detected the younger children who verbally revealed their transgressions, but they could not distinguish between the older children who lied versus those who told the truth. Subsequent research has confirmed similar patterns, showing that the ability to sustain lies in later statements improves across childhood and into adolescence (Evans & Lee, 2011; Prodan et al., 2024; Talwar & Lee, 2008; Talwar et al., 2007).

Given the limitations in their lie maintenance skills, young children are not effective liars, partly due to their limited understanding of how lying works. For instance, some children between 2 and 3 years of age make false statements that seem to reflect a desire for wish fulfillment rather than an intention to create a false belief (Talwar & Lee, 2008). Not until 3.5 years or older do children seem able to effectively maintain false statements (Ahern et al., 2011). Consistent with findings that children become more skilled at concealing their lies verbally with age (e.g., Talwar et al., 2007), evidence suggests that this ability is related to children's maturing mental state understanding (Leduc et al., 2017; Ma et al., 2015).

Lying is a complex cognitive task. To lie successfully, individuals must consider what others know, generate a statement that alters what they believe is true, and carefully manage both verbal and nonverbal behaviors to appear credible and consistent. Children's lie-telling skills evolve through their first decade of life, and these improvements coincide with significant advancements in cognition (Sai et al., 2021; Talwar & Crossman, 2011; Talwar & Lee, 2008). Theory of mind and various executive functioning skills, in particular, support the development and evolution of lie-telling ability (Sai et al., 2021). Younger children's rudimentary lies involve simple false denials, and they lack the skills to maintain those lies. Yet, as theory of mind and executive functioning skills mature (i.e., inhibitory control, working memory, planning, cognitive flexibility), children can tell more elaborate lies and maintain them under questioning. Thus, early lying reflects early cognitive maturation (e.g., Ding et al., 2015; Lavoie & Talwar, 2020; Ma et al., 2015; Talwar, Lavoie, Leduc, et al., 2017), whereas children with related cognitive deficits (e.g., autism spectrum disorder) show delays in lying (e.g., Li et al., 2010; Talwar et al., 2012). Moreover, lying proficiency seems to peak in young adulthood and decline through adulthood, as does inhibitory control (Debey et al., 2015). Thus, the ability to lie is a marker of cognitive maturity as children come to understand others' mental states and develop and apply their executive functioning abilities to control their own behaviors to mislead.

CHILDREN'S LIE MAINTENANCE SKILLS—LIES ABOUT ANOTHER'S WRONGDOING

Of particular legal concern are cases in which children testify about transgressions committed by another person, such as abuse or in custody disputes (Bala & Schuman, 1999; Crossman et al., 2002). In abuse cases, children are usually providing testimony about an adult's wrongdoing during incidents that involved direct interaction between the child and the adult. They may ask the child to lie to protect them and keep parts of the events secret (Arenzon et al., 2024; Lyon et al., 2008; Talwar et al., 2004). For example, in a study by Bottoms et al. (2002), mothers "accidentally" broke a toy and instructed their child to keep it a secret, explaining that she might get in trouble. Older children tended to comply by withholding information to keep the secret, while younger children did not. In another study (Talwar et al., 2004), parents committed a minor transgression (i.e., broke a puppet) and then coached their children not to tell because the parent might get in trouble. When interviewed later, with or without parents present, most children told the truth and disclosed the transgression. However, children were more likely to lie on behalf of their parent once it was clear that they would not be held responsible for breaking the puppet (Talwar et al., 2004). These findings suggest that some children may lie to protect a parent, but they may be willing to do so only when telling such a lie does not conflict with their own self-interest. This may be true for unrelated adults as well. A study with children awaiting a court appearance in the Los Angeles County Dependency Court found that some children would lie to conceal an adult experimenter's transgression and fabricate event details at that adult's request, following coaching to do so (Lyon et al., 2008). These findings highlight how critical it is to understand how coaching can induce children to report false events or false details of an event to protect another person.

Beyond convincing children to lie about or conceal misdeeds, coaching can also impact how effective children are at maintaining lies for others. Talwar, Hubbard et al. (2018) examined the influence of heavy versus light coaching by their parent on children's reports about others' behavior. Most children who received minimal parental coaching confessed during the interview. However, the majority of children who received extensive coaching (at least 45 minutes) maintained their fabrication during the interview. In another study (Talwar, Yachison, et al., 2018), children received no coaching, light coaching, or extensive coaching from a confederate who had broken a forbidden toy. As expected, younger children (5 and under) maintained the false story poorly. Yet, with extensive coaching, including help creating a cover story, children were significantly better at maintaining the false story throughout the interview. With light or no coaching, young children were not able to maintain the lie. For older children, who are better at maintaining a false story, even light coaching improved their ability to maintain false reports significantly. Overall, findings suggest that robust coaching can both spur children to produce inaccurate reports and help them maintain those reports, making it more difficult to distinguish false reports from the truth. However, this impact may be attenuated by a child's age and general ability to provide detailed reports. Furthermore, the types of questions asked (e.g., free-recall vs. closed-ended) may also differentially impact children's disclosures (Wyman et al., 2019, 2020).

Children who are reluctant to disclose a transgression that involves themselves and others in response to open-ended questions may be more likely to disclose if asked closed-ended questions (e.g., Bottoms et al., 2002; Lyon et al., 2014; Pipe & Wilson, 1994). However, closed-ended questions must be used with caution and interviewers are warned to avoid these questions because they can be suggestive (Lamb et al., 2011; Stolzenberg et al., 2017). Instead, starting an interview with open-ended recall questions and cued prompts (e.g., "What happened next?"; "You said X, tell me everything about that.") is encouraged. Older children may be more likely to disclose in response to such recall questions (Williams et al., 2020). Notably, younger children may actually disclose information that they have been asked to keep secret early in an interview, during the rapport-building phase (e.g., Williams et al., 2020). However, since many children will not disclose in response to recall questions, later in the interview, nonsuggestive yes–no questions can be added incrementally to obtain further information. For instance, while 21% of children in one study disclosed witnessing a theft in answer to a free-recall question, 9% disclosed with repeated recall prompts, and 15% more disclosed the theft later, in response to closed-ended, yes–no questions (Foster et al., 2022, 2023).

CHILDREN'S SECRET-KEEPING SKILLS

Children learn that they can conceal information in the preschool years and are capable of keeping a secret by 5 years of age (Bottoms et al., 2002; Peskin, 1992). They begin to keep secrets in the preschool years, with 5- and 6-year-olds more likely to keep a secret than 3-year-olds, and more likely to keep an adult stranger's secret than 9-year-olds, particularly in the presence of the transgressor (Watson & Valtin, 1997b). However, children's ability to do so effectively improves with age as their understanding of the concept improves.

As with lying, secret-keeping seems to be related to children's developing cognitive abilities (Watson & Valtin, 1997a). For instance, Gordon et al. (2014) examined secret-keeping in children 4 to 12 years of age. Children saw their parents commit a transgression (i.e., break a toy) and were asked to promise to keep the transgression a secret. Children were then interviewed with open-ended and closed-ended questions. Overall, secret-keeping increased with age; although promising to keep the secret led to fewer initial disclosures, disclosure rates increased over the course of the interviews. Children who did keep the secret had more generalized trust beliefs in others and more mature executive functioning abilities.

Some secrets are likely easier for children to keep than others and may not be defined by them in the same way as adults (e.g., "bad" secrets; Watson & Valtin, 1997a, 1997b). Younger children might be more influenced by the presence of a transgressor in keeping versus revealing a secret than are older children, suggesting a less stable understanding of secrecy (Watson & Valtin, 1997a, 1997b). Surprises may be easier for children to grasp than other types of secrets. Lavoie and Talwar (2020) examined children between 4 and 11 years of age who made crafts with a researcher as a surprise gift for their parents. The majority of children kept the gift a secret by deflection (e.g., "I don't want to tell you, it's a secret!") or by not talking about it ("we did stuff"). A third of children lied to throw their parent off the scent (e.g., "the surprise was the Smarties the researcher gave me"). Younger children (ages 4–7 years) were more likely to excitedly disclose the "surprise" to their parents. However, children with better theory of mind and working memory abilities were more likely to avoid fully disclosing the secret.

Beyond cognition, the relationship with the "instigator" or person with whom children share a secret is likely important, particularly for older children. In middle childhood, as children's understanding of the relational aspects of secrecy grows, children become more likely to keep a secret for a parent or a peer (Gordon et al., 2014; Watson & Valtin, 1997b). This is particularly true as their understanding of the role of secrecy in intimacy and friendship matures (Watson & Valtin, 1997a, 1997b). For example, Lyon et al. (2010) found that maltreated children were less likely to endorse disclosure of a parent's transgressions to the police compared to nonmaltreated children. Yet, nonmaltreated children tended to endorse less disclosure against parent transgressors with age, but not maltreated children, findings that may reflect maltreated children's lack of trust in parental figures (Lyon et al., 2010).

What secrets do children keep? Lavoie and colleagues (2017) interviewed children about keeping secrets and telling lies, and children kept a diary of secrets over 3 days. On average, participants recorded telling 2 lies and keeping 2 secrets per day. Younger participants, between 8 and 11 years of age, said they would keep secrets with good friends or keep mean gossip a secret. Younger children also talked about kids keeping secrets to conceal misdeeds and avoid getting in trouble. Older youth between the ages of 12 and 15 tended to keep secret personal information that they did not want to share with anyone because it was embarrassing or could hurt someone. Overall, participants felt that if they were asked to keep a secret by a friend, it was not acceptable to tell it to others, but they realized that it was acceptable to tell someone they could trust about secrets that were dangerous or that could cause someone to get hurt (Lavoie, Nagar, & Talwar, 2017).

In a longitudinal study with adolescents, Dykstra et al. (2020) found that lying to and keeping secrets from parents increased with age. This may reflect an increasing desire to have autonomy in their activities and personal choices. In Lavoie, Nagar, & Talwar (2017), youth indicated that they felt their "secrets" belonged to them and they had the right to be in control of what information was shared. To that end, Darling and colleagues (2006) found that adolescents who perceived their parents would disagree with their choice of leisure activities were more likely to omit or conceal information about those activities. Thus, teens may keep secrets to prevent what they perceive as privacy invasion and/or to protect their autonomy.

Together, these findings suggest the importance of recognizing how a relationship can be used to facilitate children keeping "bad" secrets (e.g., grooming), particularly among younger children who might not yet understand their implications. For these children, understanding there is a transgression may facilitate their disclosure of another person's wrongdoing. Older children may be more willing to keep secrets for those with whom they share an important relationship, but highlighting the salience of danger may be an important antidote to such secret-keeping.

Detecting Children's Lies and Secrets

Research consistently shows that adults tend to detect deception by other adults at near chance levels (e.g., Bond & DePaulo, 2006; Hartwig & Bond, 2011), and the same seems to be true for children. A meta-analysis found that adults' detection rate was 54% overall (Gongola et al., 2017). Adults were better at classifying children's true reports (63.8% accuracy) than false reports (47.5% accuracy) and, consistent with children's developmental improvements, detection rates were higher for younger children (aged 3–5 years; 60%) than middle (aged 6–9 years; 56.7%) and older children (aged 10–15 years; 52.5%). Yet, detection rates were not high, even for the youngest children. Moreover, police officers tend to be no better than laypeople at detecting children's deception (Leach et al., 2004). Techniques that enhance the likelihood of children revealing cues to secrets and lies are likely more productive, such as increasing cognitive load or engaging in more elaborate questioning, which might enhance discriminability of truths and lies or elicit secrets (Talwar & Crossman, 2012; Wyman et al., 2019).

The difference in detection rates as a function of veracity is notable. Adults may be more accurate with true reports because people are honest much of the time. This may lead to a presumption of honesty and a bias towards classifying statements as true (Levine, 2019). There may also be a difference in detection as a function of the type of report. For instance, Wyman et al. (2018) examined the accuracy of adults' veracity judgments for children's initial denials or accusations about an alleged theft, which were either true or false, and subsequent recantations/reversals, which were the opposite in veracity. True allegations were more accurately detected than false allegations, whereas false denials were more accurately detected than false allegations or true denials. Children's denials (whether true or false) tended to be rated as more credible in the recanted reports than were accusations that followed denials. Finally, adults' perceptions of a child may affect their classification of that child's statements as true or false. Talwar et al. (2006) found that adult raters' assessments of child mock-witness veracity were predicted by perceptions of the child's maturity, suggestibility, and integrity. Additional research is needed to clarify conditions that impact the detection of children's lies and secrets.

Promoting Truth-Telling

Given that we are poor at detecting children's secrets and lies, research focus has shifted toward different techniques to promote truth-telling among child witnesses. Promising to tell the truth has emerged as one of the most effective honesty promotion techniques to date (e.g., Bender et al., 2018; Evans & Lee, 2010; Evans & Talwar, 2023; Heyman et al., 2015; Lyon & Dorado, 2008; Quas et al., 2018; Talwar et al., 2002). The word *promise* creates a sense of obligation, as it demonstrates a commitment or intention to act (Bussey, 2010). For instance, Talwar et al. (2004), found that children were less likely to lie for their parents after promising to tell the truth. Similarly, Lyon et al. (2008) found that maltreated children were more likely to truthfully disclose an adult's wrongdoing after promising to tell the truth. However, although the technique is effective with children 5 years and older, it may be less effective with preschoolers and maltreated children under some circumstances (Bender et al., 2018; Evans & Talwar, 2023; Heyman et al., 2015; Lyon & Evans, 2014; Quas et al., 2018; Talwar et al., 2002; see also Chapter 15, this volume). Given the importance of eliciting their reports, more research is needed on how best to promote children's truthful and accurate disclosures (e.g., Evans et al., 2018; McWilliams et al., 2019; Quas et al., 2018; Talwar et al., 2025).

Understanding mechanisms that underlie effective truth-promotion techniques can inform future efforts to support child witness veracity. Bandura's (2014) social cognitive theory of moral action suggests that an individual's behavior is largely shaped by their expectations about the outcomes of different actions. Through socialization, children's behavior is influenced by external and internal factors. Early on, young children depend on external guidance, such as physical consequences (i.e., punishment) or social incentives (i.e., praise for pleasing others). As they internalize cultural moral standards, internal motivations—like feeling good about doing the "right" thing—also begin to influence their behavior. Consistent with the theory, one study found that children were less likely to lie about wrongdoing when questioners appealed to either external or internal reasons to tell the truth, but not when external consequences were emphasized (Talwar et al., 2015). In other studies, moral stories that emphasize the positive consequences of truthfully telling an adult about wrongdoing promote children's truthfulness (Ding et al., 2024; Lee et al., 2014; Talwar et al., 2016, 2018). When stories include both a character modeling honesty and positive consequences as a result, they seem to be even more effective at eliciting children's honesty about their own wrongdoing (Evans & Talwar, 2023). In fact, some research indicates that these techniques can promote honesty even among children who have been coached to lie (Lyon et al., 2008; Talwar et al., 2018). Further investigation is necessary to determine the limits and conditions under which truth-promotion techniques are most effective with child witnesses. Nonetheless, the evidence suggests that strengthening children's internal motivations to be truthful may enhance social incentives for honesty while reducing competing social obstacles to honesty.

Belief and Action

To evaluate their competency to testify, child witnesses are often questioned about their understanding of the concepts of lies and truth (or their commitment to telling the truth; e.g., take an oath), whether in court or in investigative interviews (Bala et al., 2010; Lyon, 2011; Ministry of Justice & National Police Chiefs' Council, 2022; O'Connell et al., 2020). This type of questioning is founded on the assumption that, if children know that lying is bad and commit to telling the truth, they remain honest and forthcoming. It should be noted that despite knowing that lying is generally viewed as morally wrong (Batson & Thompson, 2001) and that perjury laws exist to enforce honesty among witnesses in court, adults still lie. Similarly, a child's understanding of the concept of lying does not guarantee truthful statements, just as a limited understanding does not necessarily mean they are unwilling to be honest. Indeed, children tell the truth well before they can define it (Lyon, 2014). For a thorough discussion of the relationship between children's understanding of lying and court procedures for assessing competence, see Chapter 15, this volume.

Legal Implications and Conclusions

Research on children's deception and secrecy has legal and practical implications for child witnesses and the practitioners who work with them. Forensic professionals are especially concerned with the truthfulness of children's testimony. When undetected in an investigative interview or court context, children's secrets and lies can carry grave sociolegal ramifications. Believing a child who falsely denies experiencing abuse to protect themselves or the abuser may have harmful consequences for that child and others, such as continued victimization. Believing a child who falsely reports all or part of an event that did not occur can harm innocent suspects. It is important to note that this does not suggest that children are any more dishonest than adults. Adults often lie (DePaulo et al., 1996), and children tend to lie for similar reasons. However, children's lies are generally less sophisticated, and they often struggle to maintain them under questioning, particularly younger children. As a result, the potential for harm from children's lying in court is, at most, comparable to that posed by adult witnesses.

The need for advanced cognitive skills to produce elaborate lies has important implications for assessing the reliability of child witness testimony. It indicates that children with cognitive challenges, such as developmental delays or specific disorders like autism spectrum disorder, are less likely to generate or maintain credible false reports. Additionally, younger child witnesses tend to be less effective at lying when detailed verbal reports are required. While children can be coached on behalf of others, these lies generally emerge later and less readily than self-protective lies.

Children must also decide when to lie, and their decisions are influenced by their assessment of the potential consequences if detected and a desire to minimize negative outcomes for themselves and others. Certainly, escaping negative consequences is a powerful motivator from an early age. Child witnesses may be motivated to lie or keep a secret to hide an event they view as a transgression because they expect punishment if they tell the truth. Younger children, in particular, may be affected by their fear of potential punishment (Wagland & Bussey, 2005), underscoring the importance of providing reassurance during interviews with children. One study found that children who were in a school that relied on corporal punishment were more likely to lie, and were better at maintaining lies, than children attending a school without corporal punishment (Talwar & Lee, 2011). In a harshly punitive environment, children may learn that they have nothing to lose by lying; lying becomes a more adaptive choice than being honest (Gingo & Carter, 2024; Talwar & Crossman, 2022). Indeed, other research has found that when inequalities and injustices exist in a hierarchical system, some people cope using deception to resist and protect themselves (Turiel, 2002). Research has yet to sufficiently examine racial and cultural dynamics that could impact children's forthcomingness in investigative interviews (e.g., Dunkerley & Dalenberg, 2000; Fisher et al., 2016).

Likewise, children appear more likely to lie on behalf of another when the personal costs or consequences are minimized. That is, with age, children likely weigh different factors in relation to themselves and others as part of a cost–benefit analysis. Younger children may focus on immediate benefits or costs to themselves (Popliger et al., 2011), while older children and adolescents weigh both short-term and longer-term consequences, such as the interpersonal costs of getting caught lying (e.g., disappointing parents, being rejected by peers) or the relational implications of disclosing a secret (Liberman, 2020). Consequently, when seeking to obtain honest, complete reports from children (and overcome potential inducements or motivations to lie or keep a secret), interviewers should keep in mind how children perceive the consequences of lying and keeping secrets, versus disclosing the truth. It may help to highlight the importance and benefits of honesty, along with asking children to make a promise to tell the truth.

Note that much of the literature discussed here examined children's lying and secret-keeping using experimental paradigms that lack external validity. Studies that involve breaking a toy as a transgression differ from cases where children conceal or lie about abuse. Due to ethical constraints, researchers cannot replicate legal cases involving abuse, so they rely on creating analogous, naturalistic situations with higher stakes, such as staging a mock crime where the perpetrator asks the child to keep a secret. Hence, more research is needed that better approximates the types of secrets and lies children may tell in legal contexts, requiring creativity to design situations that are both ecologically valid and ethically acceptable.

Gaps in existing research highlight the need for continued innovation in procedures that can help to encourage and enhance children's motivations for revealing the truth and thus facilitate the work of forensic practitioners. Findings to date suggest that investigators should assess children's developmental maturity and address motivations that might underlie their honesty and forthcomingness, as a function of developmental stage. Providing reassurance to children that telling the truth serves their self-interests, emphasizing the importance of disclosing "bad" secrets, and minimizing negative consequences for honesty would be beneficial. Additionally, obtaining children's promises to tell the truth (or using other truth-induction techniques) may increase the salience of honesty and help shift their motivation toward truth-telling. Future research should continue to describe and differentiate the development of children's lie-telling and secret-keeping abilities and further develop methods that help ensure the accuracy and honesty of child witness testimony.

Although secrets and lies are inevitable in human communication, we hope to eventually eliminate any impact they might have on children and adults in the legal system through ongoing, practice-informed research innovation.

REFERENCES

Ahern, E. C., Lyon, T. D., & Quas, J. A. (2011). Young children's emerging ability to make false statements. *Developmental Psychology, 47*(1), 61–66. https://doi.org/10.1037/a0021272

Anagnostaki, L., Wright, M. J., & Bourchier-Sutton, A. J. (2010). The semantics of secrecy: Young children's classification of secret content. *The Journal of Genetic Psychology, 171*(4), 279–299. https://doi.org/10.1080/00221325.2010.493186

Anagnostaki, L., Wright, M. J., & Papathanasiou, A. (2013). Secrets and disclosures: How young children handle secrets. *The Journal of Genetic Psychology, 174*(3), 316–334. https://doi.org/10.1080/00221325.2012.672350

Arenzon, V., Crossman, A. M., Foster, I., Flory, I. M., & Talwar, V. (2024). Examining the influence of children's temperament, externalising and internalising problems on crime disclosure. *Canadian Journal of Behavioural Science/Revue Canadienne des Sciences du Comportement, 57*(1), 44–52. https://doi.org/10.1037/cbs0000412

Bala, N., Lee, K., Lindsay, R. C. L., & Talwar, V. (2010). The competency of children to testify: Psychological research informing Canadian law reform. *International Journal of Children's Rights, 18*(1), 53–77. https://doi.org/10.1163/157181809x458544

Bala, N., & Schuman, J. (1999). Allegations of sexual abuse when parents have separated. *Canadian Family Law Quarterly, 17*(2), 191–243.

Bandura, A. (2014). Social cognitive theory of moral thought and action. In W. M. Kurtines, J. L. Gewirtz, & J. L. Lamb (Eds.), *Handbook of moral behavior and development* (Vol. 1, pp. 69–128). Psychology Press.

Batson, C. D., & Thompson, E. R. (2001). Why don't moral people act morally? Motivational considerations. *Current Directions in Psychological Science, 10*(2), 54–57. https://doi.org/10.1111/1467-8721.00114

Bender, J., O'Connor, A. M., & Evans, A. D. (2018). Mirror, mirror on the wall: Increasing young children's honesty through inducing self-awareness. *Journal of Experimental Child Psychology, 167*, 414–422. https://doi.org/10.1016/j.jecp.2017.12.001

Bok, S. (1978). *Lying: Moral choice in public and private life*. Quartet Books.

Bok, S. (1984). *Secrets: On the ethics of concealment and revelation*. Oxford University Press.

Bond, C. F., Jr., & DePaulo, B. M. (2006). Accuracy of deception judgments. *Personality and Social Psychology Review, 10*(3), 214–234. https://doi.org/10.1207/s15327957pspr1003_2

Bottoms, B. L., Goodman, G. S., Schwartz-Kenney, B. M., & Thomas, S. N. (2002). Understanding children's use of secrecy in the context of eyewitness reports. *Law & Human Behavior, 26*(3), 285–313. https://doi.org/10.1023/A:1015324304975

Bureau, J. S., & Mageau, G. A. (2014). Parental autonomy support and honesty: The mediating role of identification with the honesty value and perceived costs and benefits of honesty. *Journal of Adolescence, 37*(3), 225–236. https://doi.org/10.1016/j.adolescence.2013.12.007

Bussey, K. (1992). Lying and truthfulness: Children's definitions, standards, and evaluative reactions. *Child Development, 63*(5), 129–137. https://doi.org/10.1111/j.1467-8624.1992.tb03601.x

Bussey, K. (1999). Children's categorization and evaluation of different types of lies and truths. *Child Development, 70*(6), 1338–1347. https://doi.org/10.1111/1467-8624.00098

Bussey, K. (2010). The role of promises for children's trustworthiness and honesty. In K. J. Rotenberg (Ed.), *Interpersonal trust during childhood and adolescence* (pp. 155–176). Cambridge University Press. https://doi.org/10.1017/CBO9780511750946.008

Creusere, M. A. (2000). A developmental test of theoretical perspectives on the understanding of verbal irony: Children's recognition of allusion and pragmatic insincerity. *Metaphor and Symbol, 15*(1–2), 29–45. https://doi.org/10.1207/s15327868ms151&2_3

Crossman, A. M., Powell, M. B., Principe, G. F., & Ceci, S. J. (2002). Child testimony in custody cases. *Journal of Forensic Psychology Practice, 2*(1), 1–31. https://doi.org/10.1300/J158v02n01_01

Darling, N., Cumsille, P., Caldwell, L. L., & Dowdy, B. (2006). Predictors of adolescents' disclosure to parents and perceived parental knowledge: Between-and within-person differences. *Journal of Youth and Adolescence, 35*(4), 659–670. https://doi.org/10.1007/s10964-006-9058-1

Debey, E., De Schryver, M., Logan, G. D., Suchotzki, K., & Verschuere, B. (2015). From junior to senior Pinocchio: A cross-sectional lifespan investigation of deception. *Acta Psychologica, 160*, 58–68. https://doi.org/10.1016/j.actpsy.2015.06.007

DePaulo, B. M., Kashy, D. A., Kirkendol, S. E., Wyer, M. M., & Epstein, J. A. (1996). Lying in everyday life. *Journal of Personality and Social Psychology, 70*(5), 979–995. https://doi.org/10.1037/0022-3514.70.5.979

Ding, X. P., Cheng, J. K. T., Cheng, Q., & Heyman, G. D. (2024). An assessment of when moral stories promote children's honesty. *Applied Developmental Science, 28*(3), 292–301. https://doi.org/10.1080/10888691.2023.2195182

Ding, X. P., Wellman, H. M., Wang, Y., Fu, G., & Lee, K. (2015). Theory-of-mind training causes honest young children to lie. *Psychological Science, 26*(11), 1812–1821. https://doi.org/10.1177/0956797615604628

Dunkerley, G. K., & Dalenberg, C. J. (2000). Secret-keeping behaviors in Black and White children as a function of interviewer race, racial identity, and risk for abuse. *Journal of Aggression, Maltreatment & Trauma, 2*(2), 13–35. https://doi.org/10.1300/J146v02n02_02

Dykstra, V. W., Willoughby, T., & Evans, A. D. (2020). A longitudinal examination of the relation between lie-telling, secrecy, parent–child relationship quality, and depressive symptoms in late-childhood and adolescence. *Journal of Youth and Adolescence, 49*(2), 49–59. https://doi.org/10.1007/s10964-019-01183-z

Ekman, P. (1985). *Telling lies: Clues to deceit in the marketplace, politics, and marriage*. Norton.

Evans, A. D., & Lee, K. (2010). Promising to tell the truth makes 8- to 16-year-olds more honest. *Behavioral Sciences & the Law, 28*(6), 801–811. https://doi.org/10.1002/bsl.960

Evans, A. D., & Lee, K. (2011). Verbal deception from late childhood to middle adolescence and its relation to executive functioning skills. *Developmental Psychology, 47*(4), 1108–1116. https://doi.org/10.1037/a0023425

Evans, A. D., & Lee, K. (2013). Emergence of lying in very young children. *Developmental Psychology, 49*(10), 1958–1963. https://doi.org/10.1037/a0031409

Evans, A. D., & Lyon, T. D. (2011). Assessing children's competency to take the oath in court: The influence of question type on children's accuracy. *Law & Human Behavior, 36*(3), 195–205. https://doi.org/10.1037/h0093957

Evans, A. D., O'Connor, A. M., & Lee, K. (2018). Verbalizing a commitment reduces cheating in young children. *Social Development, 27*(1), 87–94. https://doi.org/10.1111/sode.12248

Evans, A. D., & Talwar, V. (2023). Encouraging honesty: Developmental differences in the influence of honesty promotion techniques. *Developmental Psychology, 60*(3), 481–490. https://doi.org/10.1037/dev0001640

Fisher, A. K., Mackey, T. D., Langendoen, C., & Barnard, M. (2016). Child and interviewer race in forensic interviewing. *Journal of Child Sexual Abuse, 25*(7), 777–792. https://doi.org/10.1080/10538712.2016.1208705

Foster, I., Talwar, V., & Crossman, A. (2022). The role of rapport in eliciting children's truthful reports. *Applied Developmental Science, 27*(3), 221–237. https://doi.org/10.1080/10888691.2022.2058507

Foster, I., Talwar, V., & Crossman, A. (2023). 'I like you so . . .': How transgressor and interviewer likeability and familiarity influence children's disclosures. *Psychiatry, Psychology and Law, 31*(5), 797–815. https://doi.org/10.1080/13218719.2023.2214931

Gingo, M., & Carter, S. (2024). Subverting parental overreach: Children endorse defiance and deception as legitimate modes of moral resistance and social opposition. *Journal of Experimental Child Psychology, 238*, 105800. https://doi.org/10.1016/j.jecp.2023.105800

Gongola, J., Scurich, N., & Quas, J. A. (2017). Detecting deception in children: A meta-analysis. *Law & Human Behavior, 41*(1), 44–54. https://doi.org/10.1037/lhb0000211

Gordon, H. M., Lyon, T. D., & Lee, K. (2014). Social and cognitive factors associated with children's secret-keeping for a parent. *Child Development, 85*(6), 2374–2388. https://doi.org/10.1111/cdev.12301

Hartwig, M., & Bond, C. (2011). Why do lie-catchers fail? A lens model meta-analysis of human lie judgments. *Psychological Bulletin, 137*(4), 643–659. https://doi.org/10.1037/a0023589

Heyman, G. D., Fu, G., Lin, J., Qian, M. K., & Lee, K. (2015). Eliciting promises from children reduces cheating. *Journal of Experimental Child Psychology, 139*, 242–248. https://doi.org/10.1016/j.jecp.2015.04.013

Klafka, M., & Liszkowski, U. (2021). The emergence of lying for reputational concerns in 5-year-olds. *Frontiers in Psychology, 12*, 700695. https://doi.org/10.3389/fpsyg.2021.700695

Lamb, M. E., Hershkowitz, I., Orbach, Y., & Esplin, P. W. (2011). *Tell me what happened: Structured investigative interviews of child victims and witnesses*. John Wiley & Sons.

Lavoie, J., Leduc, K., Arruda, C., Crossman, A. M., & Talwar, V. (2017). Developmental profiles of children's spontaneous lie-telling behavior. *Cognitive Development, 41*, 33–45. https://doi.org/10.1016/j.cogdev.2016.12.002

Lavoie, J., Leduc, K., Crossman, A. M., & Talwar, V. (2016). Do as I say and not as I think: Parent socialization of lie-telling behaviour. *Children & Society, 30*(4), 253–264. https://doi.org/10.1111/chso.12139

Lavoie, J., Nagar, P. M., & Talwar, V. (2017). From Kantian to Machiavellian deceivers: Development of children's reasoning and self-reported use of secrets and lies. *Childhood, 24*(2), 197–211. https://doi.org/10.1177/0907568216671179

Lavoie, J., & Talwar, V. (2020). Care to share? Children's cognitive skills and concealing responses to a parent. *Topics in Cognitive Science, 12*(2), 485–503. https://doi.org/10.1111/tops.12390

Leach, A., Talwar, V., Lee, K., Bala, N., & Lindsay, R. C. L. (2004). Intuitive lie detection of children's deception by law enforcement officials and university students. *Law & Human Behavior, 28*(6), 61–685. https://doi.org/10.1007/s10979-004-0793-0

Leduc, K., Williams, S., Gomez-Garibello, C., & Talwar, V. (2017). The contributions of mental state understanding and executive functioning to preschool-aged children's lie-telling. *British Journal of Developmental Psychology, 35*(2), 288–302. https://doi.org/10.1111/bjdp.12163

Lee, K. (2013). Little liars: Development of verbal deception in children. *Child Development Perspectives, 7*(2), 91–96. https://doi.org/10.1111/cdep.12023

Lee, K., & Ross, H. J. (1997). The concept of lying in adolescents and young adults: Testing Sweetser's folkloristic model. *Merrill-Palmer Quarterly, 43*(2), 255–270.

Lee, K., Talwar, V., McCarthy, A., Ross, I., Evans, A., & Arruda, C. (2014). Can classic moral stories promote honesty in children? *Psychological Science, 25*(8), 1630–1636. https://doi.org/10.1177/0956797614536401

Levine, T. R. (2019). An overview of detecting deceptive communication. In T. Docan-Morgan (Ed.), *The Palgrave handbook of deceptive communication* (pp. 289–301). Palgrave Macmillan. https://doi.org/10.1007/978-3-319-96334-1_15

Li, A. S., Kelley, E. A., Evans, A. D., & Lee, K. (2010). Exploring the ability to deceive in children with autism spectrum disorders. *Journal of Autism and Developmental Disorders, 41*(2), 185–195. https://doi.org/10.1007/s10803-010-1045-4

Liberman, Z. (2020). Keep the cat in the bag: Children understand that telling a friend's secret can harm the friendship. *Developmental Psychology, 56*(7), 1290–1304. https://doi.org/10.1037/dev0000960

Lyon, T. D. (2011). Assessing the competency of child witnesses: Best practice informed by psychology and law. In M. E. Lamb, D. La Rooy, L. C. Malloy, & C. Katz (Eds.), *Children's testimony: A handbook of psychological research and forensic practice* (pp. 69–85). Wiley-Blackwell.

Lyon, T. D. (2014). Interviewing children. *Annual Review of Law and Social Science, 10*(1), 73–89. https://doi.org/10.1146/annurev-lawsocsci-110413-030913

Lyon, T. D., Ahern, E. C., Malloy, L. C., & Quas, J. A. (2010). Children's reasoning about disclosing adult transgressions: Effects of maltreatment, child age, and adult identity. *Child Development, 81*(6), 1714–1728. https://doi.org/10.1111/j.1467-8624.2010.01505.x

Lyon, T. D., & Dorado, J. S. (2008). Truth induction in young maltreated children: The effects of oath-taking and reassurance on true and false disclosures. *Child Abuse & Neglect, 32*(7), 738–748. https://doi.org/10.1016/j.chiabu.2007.08.008

Lyon, T. D., & Evans, A. D. (2014). Young children's understanding that promising guarantees performance: The effects of age and maltreatment. *Law & Human Behavior, 38*(2), 162–170. https://doi.org/10.1037/lhb0000061

Lyon, T. D., Malloy, L. C., Quas, J. A., & Talwar, V. A. (2008). Coaching, truth induction, and young maltreated children's false allegations and false denials. *Child Development, 79*(4), 914–929. https://doi.org/10.1111/j.1467-8624.2008.01167.x

Lyon, T. D., Quas, J. A., & Carrick, N. (2013). Right and righteous: Children's incipient understanding and evaluation of true and false statements. *Journal of Cognition and Development, 14*(3), 437–454. https://doi.org/10.1080/15248372.2012.673187

Lyon, T. D., Wandrey, L., Ahern, E., Licht, R., Sim, M. P., & Quas, J. A. (2014). Eliciting maltreated and nonmaltreated children's transgression disclosures: Narrative practice rapport building and a putative confession. *Child Development, 85*(4), 1756–1769. https://doi.org/10.1111/cdev.12223

Ma, F., Evans, A. D., Liu, Y., Luo, X., & Xu, F. (2015). To lie or not to lie? The influence of parenting and theory-of-mind understanding on three-year-old children's honesty. *Journal of Moral Education, 44*(2), 198–212. https://doi.org/10.1080/03057240.2015.1023182

Manay, N., & Collin-Vézina, D. (2021). Recipients of children's and adolescents' disclosures of childhood sexual abuse: A systematic review. *Child Abuse & Neglect, 116*(Pt. 1), 104192. https://doi.org/10.1016/j.chiabu.2019.104192

McWilliams, K., Stolzenberg, S. N., Williams, S., & Lyon, T. D. (2019). Increasing maltreated and nonmaltreated children's recall disclosures of a minor transgression: The effects of back-channel utterances, a promise to tell the truth and a post-recall putative confession. *Child Abuse & Neglect, 116*(1), 104073. https://doi.org/10.1016/j.chiabu.2019.104073

Ministry of Justice and National Police Chiefs' Council. (2022). *Achieving best evidence in criminal proceedings: Guidance on interviewing victims and witnesses, and guidance on using special measures.* https://assets.publishing.service.gov.uk/media/6492e26c103ca6001303a331/achieving-best-evidence-criminal-proceedings-2023.pdf

Newton, P., Reddy, V., & Bull, R. (2000). Children's everyday deception and performance on false-belief tasks. *British Journal of Developmental Psychology, 18*(2), 297–317. https://doi.org/10.1348/026151000165706

O'Connell, F., Cherryman, J., & Warmelink, L. (2020). Mock juror's perceptions of a child witness passing or failing a truth and lies discussion or promising to tell the truth. *Applied Cognitive Psychology, 34*(1), 285–292. https://doi.org/10.1002/acp.3612

Peskin, J. (1992). Ruse and representations: On children's ability to conceal information. *Developmental Psychology, 28*(1), 84–89. https://doi.org/10.1037//0012-1649.28.1.84

Peterson, C. C., Peterson, J. L., & Seeto, D. (1983). Developmental changes in ideas about lying. *Child Development, 54*(6), 1529–1535. https://doi.org/10.2307/1129816

Piaget, J. (1932/1965). *The moral judgment of the child* (M. Gabain, Trans.). The Free Press.

Pipe, M. E., & Wilson, J. C. (1994). Cues and secrets: Influences on children's event reports. *Developmental Psychology, 30*(4), 515–525. https://doi.org/10.1037//0012-1649.30.4.515

Popliger, M., Talwar, V., & Crossman, A. M. (2011). Predictors of children's prosocial lie-telling: Motivation, socialization variables, and moral understanding. *Journal of Experimental Child Psychology, 110*(3), 373–392. https://doi.org/10.1016/j.jecp.2011.05.003

Prodan, N., Ding, X. P., & Visu-Petra, L. (2024). Truthful yet misleading: Elementary second-order deception in school-age children and its sociocognitive correlates. *Journal of Experimental Child Psychology, 237,* 105759. https://doi.org/10.1016/j.jecp.2023.105759

Quas, J. A., Stolzenberg, S. N., & Lyon, T. D. (2018). The effects of promising to tell the truth, the putative confession, and recall and recognition questions on maltreated and nonmaltreated children's disclosure of a minor transgression. *Journal of Experimental Child Psychology, 166,* 266–279. https://doi.org/10.1016/j.jecp.2017.08.014

Rothermich, K., Caivano, O., Knoll, L. J., & Talwar, V. (2020). Do they really mean it? Children's inference of speaker intentions and the role of age and gender. *Language and Speech, 63*(4), 689–712. https://doi.org/10.1177/0023830919878742

Sai, L., Shang, S., Tay, C., Liu, X., Sheng, T., Fu, G., Ding, X. P., & Lee, K. (2021). Theory of mind, executive function, and lying in children: A meta-analysis. *Developmental Science, 24*(5), e13096. https://doi.org/10.1111/desc.13096

Serota, K. B., Levine, T. R., & Boster, F. J. (2010). The prevalence of lying in America: Three studies of self-reported lies. *Human Communication Research, 36*(1), 2–25. https://doi.org/10.1111/j.1468-2958.2009.01366.x

Siegal, M., & Peterson, C. C. (1996). Breaking the mold: A fresh look at children's understanding of questions about lies and mistakes. *Developmental Psychology, 32*(2), 322–334. https://doi.org/10.1037/0012-1649.32.2.322

Smetana, J. G., Villalobos, M., Tasopoulos-Chan, M., Gettman, D. C., & Campione-Barr, N. (2009). Early and middle adolescents' disclosure to parents about activities in different domains. *Journal of Adolescence, 32*(3), 693–713. https://doi.org/10.1016/j.adolescence.2008.06.010

Stolzenberg, S. N., McWilliams, K., & Lyon, T. D. (2017). The effects of the hypothetical putative confession and negatively valenced yes/no questions on maltreated and non-maltreated children's disclosure of a minor transgression. *Child Maltreatment, 22*(2), 167–173. https://doi.org/10.1177/1077559516673734

Stouthamer-Loeber, M. (1986). Lying as a problem behavior in children: A review. *Clinical Psychology Review, 6*(4), 267–289. https://doi.org/10.1016/0272-7358(86)90002-4

Strichartz, A. F., & Burton, R. V. (1990). Lies and the truth: A study of the development of the concept. *Child Development, 61*(1), 211–220. https://doi.org/10.2307/1131060

Talwar, V., Arruda, C., & Yachison, S. (2015). The effects of punishment and appeals for honesty on children's truth-telling behavior. *Journal of Experimental Child Psychology, 130*, 209–217. https://doi.org/10.1016/j.jecp.2014.09.011

Talwar, V., & Crossman, A. (2011). From little white lies to filthy liars: The evolution of honesty and deception in young children. In J. Benson (Ed.), *Advances in child development and behavior* (Vol. 40, pp. 139–179). Academic Press. https://doi.org/10.1016/b978-0-12-386491-8.00004-9

Talwar, V., & Crossman, A. (2022). Liar, liar . . . sometimes: Understanding social-environmental influences on the development of lying. *Current Opinion in Psychology, 47*, 101374. https://doi.org/10.1016/j.copsyc.2022.101374

Talwar, V., & Crossman, A. M. (2012). Children's lies and their detection: Implications for child witness testimony. *Developmental Review, 32*(4), 337–359. https://doi.org/10.1016/j.dr.2012.06.004

Talwar, V., Crossman, A. M., Block, S., Brubacher, S., Dianiska, R., Espinosa Becerra, A. K., Goodman, G., Huffman, M. L., Lamb, M. E., London, K., La Rooy, D., Lyon, T. D., Malloy, L. C., Maltby, L., Greco, V. P. N., Powell, M., Quas, J., Rood, C. J., Spyksma, S. D., . . . Wylie, B. (2025). Urgent issues and prospects on investigative interviews with children and adolescents. *Legal and Criminological Psychology, 30*(1), 61–82. https://doi.org/10.1111/lcrp.12269

Talwar, V., Gordon, H., & Lee, K. (2007). Lying in the elementary school years: Verbal deception and its relation to second-order belief understanding. *Developmental Psychology, 43*(3), 804–810. https://doi.org/10.1037/0012-1649.43.3.804

Talwar, V., Hubbard, K., Saykaly, C., Lee, K., Lindsay, R. C. L., & Bala, N. (2018). Does parental coaching affect children's false reports? Comparing verbal markers of deception. *Behavioral Sciences & the Law, 36*(1), 84–97. https://doi.org/10.1002/bsl.2331

Talwar, V., Lavoie, J., Gomez-Garibello, C., & Crossman, A. M. (2017). Influence of social factors on the relation between lie-telling and children's cognitive abilities. *Journal of Experimental Child Psychology, 159*, 185–198. https://doi.org/10.1016/j.jecp.2017.02.009

Talwar, V., & Lee, K. (2002). Development of lying to conceal a transgression: Children's control of expressive behaviour during verbal deception. *International Journal of Behavioral Development, 26*(5), 436–444. https://doi.org/10.1080/01650250143000373

Talwar, V., & Lee, K. (2008). Social and cognitive correlates of children's lying behavior: Conceptual understanding of lying, executive functioning, and false beliefs. *Child Development, 79*(4), 866–881. https://doi.org/10.1111/j.1467-8624.2008.01164.x

Talwar, V., & Lee, K. (2011). A punitive environment fosters children's dishonesty: A natural experiment. *Child Development, 82*(6), 1751–1758. https://doi.org/10.1111/j.1467-8624.2011.01663.x

Talwar, V., Lee, K., Bala, N., & Lindsay, R. C. L. (2002). Children's conceptual knowledge of lying and its relation to their actual behaviors: Implications for court competence examinations. *Law & Human Behavior, 26*(4), 395–415. https://doi.org/10.1023/A:1016379104959

Talwar, V., Lee, K., Bala, N., & Lindsay, R. C. L. (2004). Children's lie-telling to conceal parents' transgressions: Legal implications. *Law & Human Behavior, 28*(4), 411–435. https://doi.org/10.1023/B:LAHU.0000039333.51399.f6

Talwar, V., Lee, K., Bala, N., & Lindsay, R. C. L. (2006). Adults' judgments of children's coached reports. *Law & Human Behavior, 30*(5), 61–570. https://doi.org/10.1007/s10979-006-9038-8

Talwar, V., Yachison, S., & Leduc, K. (2016). Promoting honesty: The influence of stories on children's lie-telling behaviours and moral understanding. *Infant and Child Development, 25*(6), 484–501. https://doi.org/10.1002/icd.1949

Talwar, V., Yachison, S., Leduc, K., & Nagar, P. M. (2018). Practice makes perfect? The impact of coaching and moral stories on children's lie-telling. *International Journal of Behavioral Development, 42*(4), 416–424. https://doi.org/10.1177/0165025417728583

Talwar, V., Zwaigenbaum, L., Goulden, K. J., Manji, S., Loomes, C., & Rasmussen, C. (2012). Lie-telling behavior in children with autism and its relation to false-belief understanding. *Focus on Autism and Other Developmental Disabilities, 27*(2), 122–129. https://doi.org/10.1177/1088357612441828

Turiel, E. (2002). *The culture of morality: Social development, context and conflict.* Cambridge University Press.

Wagland, P., & Bussey, K. (2005). Factors that facilitate and undermine children's beliefs about truth telling. *Law & Human Behavior, 29*(6), 639–655. https://doi.org/10.1007/s10979-005-7371-y

Watson, A. J., & Valtin, R. (1997a). Secrecy in middle childhood. *International Journal of Behavioral Development, 21*(3), 431–452. https://doi.org/10.1080/016502597384730

Watson, A. J., & Valtin, R. (1997b). A structural analysis of children's concepts of secrecy. *Australian Journal of Psychology, 49*(1), 49–54. https://doi.org/10.1080/00049539708259850

Williams, S., Leduc, K., Crossman, A., & Talwar, V. (2016). Young deceivers: Executive functioning and antisocial lie-telling in preschool aged children. *Infant and Child Development, 26*(1), e1956. https://doi.org/10.1002/icd.1956

Williams, S., McWilliams, K., & Lyon, T. (2020). Children's concealment of a minor transgression: The role of age, maltreatment, and executive functioning. *Journal of Experimental Child Psychology, 191*, 104664. https://doi.org/10.1016/j.jecp.2019.104664

Wimmer, H., Gruber, S., & Perner, J. (1984). Young children's conception of lying: Lexical realism—Moral subjectivism. *Journal of Experimental Child Psychology, 37*(1), 1–30. https://doi.org/10.1016/0022-0965(84)90055-9

Wyman, J., Foster, I., Crossman, A., Colwell, K., & Talwar, V. (2019). The efficacy of free-recall, cognitive load, and closed-ended questions when children are asked to falsely testify about a crime. *Applied Cognitive Psychology, 33*(4), 544–560. https://doi.org/10.1002/acp.3494

Wyman, J., Foster, I., Lavoie, J., Tong, D., & Talwar, V. (2018). Detecting children's false allegations and recantations of a crime. *Psychology, Crime & Law, 24*(6), 652–671. https://doi.org/10.1080/1068316x.2017.1402018

Wyman, J., Saykaly, C., & Talwar, V. (2020). The effectiveness of free-recall, cognitive instruction and closed-ended questions when students with and without disabilities provide eyewitness reports of another's transgression. *Psychology, Crime & Law, 27*(9), 1–20. https://doi.org/10.1080/1068316X.2020.1852564

14

Child Victims and Witnesses With Autism

Interactions With the Legal System

Rayna Enriquez, Katie Maras, and Lucy A. Henry

Children with disabilities are at a high risk of victimization (Christoffersen, 2019; Fang et al., 2022; Jones et al., 2012). The distinctive characteristics of their disabilities can make them particularly vulnerable, and they might also be the only witness to observe criminal acts (e.g., interpersonal violence; Cooke et al., 2024). The types of support and adaptations required for the unique needs of individuals with disabilities have become a major topic in research and the legal system. Although there are varying sociocognitive propensities for individuals with disabilities such as autism, research indicates that tailored, supportive interviewing techniques and facilitative interactions can aid most autistic individuals to provide evidence of similar volume and accuracy to typically developing (TD) populations (e.g., Almeida et al., 2019; Denne et al., 2024; Henry, Crane, et al., 2017; Wilcock et al., 2019).

Prior chapters in this book focus on TD children's interactions with the legal system as victims and witnesses. We begin this chapter by outlining the key sociocognitive characteristics of individuals with autism. Then, we review the existing research literature on interviewing autistic individuals and consider others' perceptions of these individuals' credibility. Next, we provide an overview of the long-term effects of autistic individuals' involvement in the legal system. Finally, we discuss how this research informs policy and influences practice in the legal system to accommodate autistic individuals.

https://doi.org/10.1037/0000492-014
Handbook on Child Witnesses: Improving Psychological Science and Legal Practice,
G. S. Goodman, T. D. Lyon, S. D. Hobbs, and R. Enriquez (Editors)

AUTISM

The *Diagnostic and Statistical Manual of Mental Disorders, Fifth Edition* (*DSM-5*; American Psychiatric Association, 2013), combined what was known in previous versions of the *DSM* as high-functioning autism, Asperger's disorder, and pervasive developmental disorder into one diagnosable disorder labeled autism spectrum disorder. Approximately 1 in 54 children in the United States are diagnosed with autism (Maenner et al., 2020). Autism is characterized by differences in social communication and emotional understanding along with restrictive or repetitive behaviors. Research comparing sociocognitive functioning between TD and autistic individuals has shown challenges and differences in social communication, theory of mind, sense of self, and episodic memory (Bowler et al., 2011; Desaunay et al., 2020; Frith & Happé, 1999; Lind & Bowler, 2009; Lyons & Fitzgerald, 2013). These characteristics can present unique challenges when an individual diagnosed with autism interacts with the legal system.

Importantly, an autism diagnosis is on a scale or spectrum; therefore, the level at which an individual's functioning is affected can vary from less impacted (requiring lower or minimal support needs) to more impacted (those with higher and more complex support needs). Social communication challenges are a specific characterization associated with an autism diagnosis; therefore, individuals diagnosed with autism may have trouble processing social cues or social elements in interpersonal interactions (Frith & Happé, 1999; Kristen et al., 2014; Norris & Maras, 2021), but they may have enhanced processing of nonsocial components (Mottron et al., 2006). Approximately 44% of children with autism have an intelligence quotient (IQ) score in the average to above-average range (Maenner et al., 2020); however, due to differences in theory of mind (Baron-Cohen, 1995), social activities such as understanding and partaking in social roles and relationships, engaging in social interactions or affective experiences, orienting to a social stimulus, and effectively communicating their own experiences and understanding the experiences of others can be challenging (Ford & McLean, 2023; Macintosh & Dissanayake, 2006). Early signs of these differences in social skills can be seen in preschool, elementary school, and early adolescent settings, where maintaining peer relationships can be more challenging compared to TD individuals (Bradshaw et al., 2021).

Central to the social challenges observed in autism is the construct of *theory of mind*, the capacity to attribute mental states, such as beliefs, intentions, and desires, to oneself and others (Baron-Cohen, 1995; Happé, 1994). Autistic individuals are argued to encounter "mindblindness," which manifests as challenges in understanding others' minds, interpreting social cues, predicting others' behavior, and engaging in reciprocal social interactions (Baron-Cohen, 1995). Reliance on concrete, observable cues rather than abstract, mentalistic representations when deciphering social situations can make it challenging to take other perspectives and comprehend nuanced social interactions (Happé, 1994). Critical to legal involvement is that during social interactions, differences in theory of mind can lead to misunderstandings around an autistic individual's ability to understand their role as an informant and the expectations of the interviewer (Frith & Happé, 1999).

More recently, researchers have evolved from interpretations of theory of mind "difficulties" to expressing interactions with autistic individuals as a "two-way street," in which the issue of communication lies in both the autistic and nonautistic person. The *double-empathy problem* (Milton, 2012) is used to describe a concept that expresses a mutual and interpersonal misunderstanding between an autistic and nonautistic individual, where both individuals experience challenges in empathizing and comprehending the other person's state of mind, causing a barrier in communication (Milton et al., 2022). Within this misunderstanding, the interviewer is just as responsible for not understanding the autistic individual's state of mind as the autistic person is for not understanding the interviewer's state of mind. This new outlook on social interactions with autistic individuals can reframe the understanding of social communication and focus on best practices for social and emotional support.

Metamemory is linked to differences in theory of mind in autistic individuals, suggesting they may experience challenges with understanding and communicating their own memories (Grainger et al., 2014; Kristen et al., 2014). Autobiographical memory in autistic individuals can be affected by challenges in processing self-oriented thoughts, theory of mind, and cognitive functioning (Crane & Maras, 2018). Compared to TD individuals, autistic individuals may retrieve autobiographical memories more slowly, with fewer, less specific details (e.g., Crane et al., 2009, 2012; Goddard et al., 2014). They can also face difficulties in recalling episodic memories, or memories of specific events (Geng et al., 2024). Cognitive-self theory posits that TD individuals use self-related frameworks to organize and encode event details, aiding in memory retrieval and goal setting, a process beginning around ages 3 to 4 years old. In contrast, autistic individuals may have a fragmented sense of self compared to TD individuals (e.g., Lind & Bowler, 2009; Lombardo et al., 2007; but see Lind et al., 2020), potentially linked to theory-of-mind differences (Baron-Cohen, 1995; Hobson, 2010). This may affect their recall of autobiographical memories in relation to their self-system.

OVERVIEW OF RESEARCH ON INTERVIEWING CHILDREN WITH AUTISM

A growing body of eyewitness research has examined how the cognitive differences experienced by autistic individuals influence their ability to recall events. Evidence to date indicates that the recall of both autistic children (e.g., Almeida et al., 2019; Bruck et al., 2007; Henry, Crane, et al., 2017; Henry, Messer, et al., 2017; Henry et al., 2020; Mattison et al., 2015; McCrory et al., 2007) and adults (e.g., Maras & Bowler, 2011; Maras et al., 2012) is less complete following open-ended prompts; that is, autistic individuals tend to freely recall less information than their nonautistic peers. Findings regarding accuracy and error reporting are less consistent: Some studies find autistic individuals to be less accurate (e.g., Maras & Bowler, 2010, 2011; Maras et al., 2012, 2013; Mattison et al., 2015), whereas others find no differences in accuracy between autistic and nonautistic individuals (e.g., Almeida et al., 2019; Bruck et al., 2007; Henry, Crane, et al., 2017; Henry, Messer, et al., 2017; Henry et al., 2020; Maras et al., 2020; McCrory et al., 2007). When details are coded for type, autistic individuals' recall of people and/or actions can be diminished (Henry, Crane, et al., 2017; Maras & Bowler, 2010, 2012; Mattison et al., 2015), whereas reporting of surroundings and object information is often good (Maras & Bowler, 2010, 2012; but see Henry, Crane, et al., 2017; Mattison et al., 2015). Only one study has looked at the narrative coherence of autistic witnesses' accounts. Henry et al. (2020) applied a story grammar framework to code autistic and nonautistic children's eyewitness recall and found that, although the autistic children recalled fewer event details, they did not differ from nonautistic children on narrative coherence, narrative length, or semantic diversity. This finding underscores the reliability of autistic children's testimony, even if it is sometimes less complete.

Importantly, the completeness and/or accuracy of autistic individuals' recall is often improved when more questioning support is provided; for example, more specific questioning, sketching, physical reinstatement of context, concrete visual prompts, or segmenting recall into more manageable chunks (e.g., Bruck et al., 2007; Denne et al., 2024; Henry, Crane, et al., 2017; Henry, Messer, et al., 2017; Maras & Bowler, 2012; Maras et al., 2012, 2020; Mattison et al., 2015, 2018; McCrory et al., 2007). These findings are in line with Bowler and colleagues' task support hypothesis (Bowler et al., 2004), which posits that autistic individuals' memory performance is enhanced on tasks that provide more supportive questioning for the to-be-remembered material.

In the first investigation of retrieval support for autistic witnesses, Maras and Bowler (2010) tested autistic adults with the aid of the cognitive interview (Fisher & Geiselman, 1992)—a widely used, evidence-based police interviewing technique, shown to increase the amount of correct information that adult witnesses recall with only a slight increase in errors (for a meta-analysis, see Memon et al., 2010). In addition to social communication techniques, such as rapport-building and transferring control of the interview to the witness, the cognitive interview contains various cognitive mnemonics, including instructions from the interviewer to mentally reinstate the context that was experienced during the target event, as well as varied retrieval attempts such as recalling the details in a different order or changing the perspective of recall (Dando et al., 2015). Contrary to the task support hypothesis, however, Maras and Bowler (2010) found that the cognitive interview failed to elicit more correct details from autistic adults compared to a structured comparison interview (with the same number of retrieval attempts and follow-up questions, but without the cognitive mnemonics), and in fact reduced the accuracy of the information that the autistic adults did recall (Maras & Bowler, 2012;

Maras et al., 2013). It has been posited that the open-ended and socially demanding nature of the cognitive interview may be sociocognitively burdensome for autistic individuals, limiting their ability to retrieve, monitor, and recall an event in its entirety (Maras, 2021).

No published research has examined the developmental effect of the cognitive interview with autistic children, but Mattison et al. (2015, 2018) assessed the effectiveness of the 'mental reinstatement of context' component—using an adapted "sketch reinstatement of context" (Sketch-RC) with autistic children and adolescents. The Sketch-RC was developed to help witnesses construct a narrative by asking them to sketch what reminded them of the event, while verbally describing what they were drawing (Dando, 2013). This enables witnesses to generate retrieval cues that are (crucially) salient to them, while also shifting focus to drawing and away from the social pressure of the interviewer–interviewee interaction. Legal practitioners report regularly using drawing for vulnerable witnesses and perceive it to be an effective interviewing tool (Mattison & Dando, 2020). In line with previous findings with autistic adults (Maras & Bowler, 2010, 2012), the mental reinstatement of context procedure was problematic for autistic children. Whereas sketching improved their recall accuracy of an episodic event to the level of their nonautistic peers, it had no tangible influence on the completeness of their recall in either the free narrative or questioning phase that followed (Mattison et al., 2015, 2018).

In an ambitious study with 71 autistic and 199 nonautistic children (aged 6–11 years), Henry, Crane, et al. (2017) tested the effectiveness of different types of interviewing support compared to a standard best practice (control) interview. There was no significant effect of sketching on autistic children's completeness, and they furthermore failed to replicate Mattison et al.'s (2015, 2018) finding that sketching improved accuracy. In another condition, Henry et al. tested children using a technique referred to as verbal labels, which involved providing "Tell me more" prompts after free recall, in relation to people, settings, objects, actions, and conversations (Brown & Pipe, 2003). Although verbal labels significantly improved the completeness of nonautistic children's recall, no statistically significant benefit was found for autistic children. However, although the autistic group recalled around one-third fewer correct details than the nonautistic children when interviewed with the best practice interview, additional prompting in the form of verbal labels and sketching techniques resulted in a notable but nonsignificant increase in the completeness of their recall (Henry, Crane, et al., 2017).

Little evidence is available regarding effective interventions to accommodate social and memory differences for autistic children, especially in forensic settings. Hsu and Teoh (2017) tested the effect of implementing a moderated social interview interaction with children who experienced a live event before being interviewed either in person or via an avatar. Challenges were not observed in the autistic group when the modality of the interview was administered via virtual reality; however, differences were noted with the in-person interview between autistic and TD children.

However, the notion that autistic individuals need more direction during interviews has received empirical support. For example, a variation of verbal labels, with the addition of a visual pie chart cueing witnesses to recall details about who, what, where, etc. (visual-verbal prompting), was effective in improving the specificity of autistic adults' responses (Norris et al., 2020). Similarly, interviewers need to give autistic children more prompting during their interviews (Henry, Messer, et al., 2017). Open-ended invitations, refocusing attention to a particular point (e.g., "You mentioned that a fight broke out. . . . Tell me everything about that") are the most effective type of question in eliciting more details from both autistic and nonautistic children (Almeida et al., 2019; see also Chapter 9, this volume). Even with such questions, however, autistic children often recall fewer details than their nonautistic counterparts (Almeida et al., 2019).

Thus, free-recall questions are an area of difficulty for autistic people because questions should be based on what a witness has already said. If free recall is reduced, there is less for protocol-informed interviewers to follow up on, and testimony is less complete as a result. Asking more questions in an attempt to bolster the otherwise relatively scant free recall risks decreasing the accuracy of responses; specific or closed questions can heighten suggestibility and elicit more errors as child witnesses are tempted to guess (Cotterill, 2022, Chapter 7; see also Chapter 7, this volume). Despite widely held beliefs within the legal system that autistic witnesses are more suggestible (e.g., George et al., 2018), studies that have examined this concern report no differences between autistic children or autistic adults and their nonautistic IQ-matched peers in susceptibility to suggestive questioning (Bruck et al., 2007; Maras & Bowler, 2011, 2012; McCrory et al., 2007). Both autistic and nonautistic children become less accurate when questions become more closed, specific, or suggestive (Almeida et al., 2019). Differences may appear in practice, however: If autistic children freely recall less detail in the first instance, they may be more likely to be asked closed, suggestive, and leading questions (Mattison & Dando, 2020). There is worrying evidence that autistic adults may be more compliant (Chandler et al., 2019), although to date, no work has examined compliance in legal contexts with autistic children.

To overcome these issues that autistic witnesses experience with free recall, while mindful of the need for a nonleading, witness-led approach, an alternative witness-aimed first account (WAFA) interview technique has been developed for autistic adults (Maras et al., 2020). Here, the witness is asked to self-segment their memory of the event into their own discrete parameter-bound "topic boxes" at the outset, before engaging in an exhaustive free-recall retrieval attempt (followed by interviewer probing) within the parameters of each topic box in turn. Displaying the topic boxes on sticky notes serves as a reminder of the structure of the event and reduces the amount of event information that they must hold "online," freeing up cognitive resources and allowing the witness to focus their search and retrieval strategies within individual segments. Findings indicate that the WAFA interview elicits more detailed and accurate recall from both autistic and nonautistic adult witnesses than a standard structured (free recall followed by questioning) interview (Maras et al., 2020), although research to adapt and test this technique with children is needed.

In sum, theoretically informed and evidence-based alternative interviewing techniques have been developed that accommodate differences in how autistic people remember and communicate past events, enabling more detailed and reliable accounts during police interviews (e.g., Bagnall & Maras, 2025; Maras et al., 2020; Mattison et al., 2015, 2018). However, these advancements focus on the police investigative stages, with scant evidence on how autistic individuals fare in court and if adaptations (e.g., "special measures" for vulnerable witnesses in England and Wales; Ministry of Justice and National Police Chiefs' Council, 2022) are effective in assisting them during trial. This is critical as, in contrast to police interviewing (where the focus is on assisting interviewees to provide detailed and reliable evidence and where leading questions may result in an interview being inadmissible), there is little prohibition on questioning style in court. The effect of cross-examination on autistic children's testimony remains to be tested, but is likely to be detrimental (Henry et al., 2021).

PERCEPTIONS OF CHILD WITNESSES AND VICTIMS

It is important that child witnesses testify, especially since their testimony might be the main evidence available in cases of child sexual abuse, where physical evidence is often limited, particularly in less severe instances (Lamb et al., 2007). In such cases, prosecutors may have little choice but to put the child on the stand in a court of law if prosecution is deemed important to pursue. Furthermore, research on TD children's attitudes following testimony in criminal court reveals that some children report more negative feelings about the legal system if the case is dropped, the alleged offender obtains a light sentence, or the offender is not convicted (Goodman et al., 1992; Quas & Goodman, 2012). This may result in feelings of being unheard by the justice system and foster long-term negative attitudes toward the legal system. Hence, it may be crucial for child victims to testify, ideally with necessary accommodations provided, particularly for child victims with disabilities.

Although autistic children's legal participation is important, they still encounter challenges related to how others perceive their behavior and testimony. Mock jurors often perceive autistic child witnesses as less credible than TD child witnesses (Crane et al., 2020; Logos et al., 2021), which has been attributed to differences in the amount of recall, the detail provided, and behavioral demeanor (Crane et al., 2020). Although adapted questioning, such as more explicit, parameter-bound questions, may provide the assistance autistic witnesses need to successfully recall information, it may also present challenges around how jurors interpret this additional support and whether they believe it is altering the child's testimony (McAuliff et al., 2015).

Another significant individual difference that affects jurors' perceptions of credibility is the behaviors exhibited by autistic children. According to expectancy violation theory (Burgoon, 1993, 2015), people hold expectations for others' behaviors based on social norms and personal beliefs about how they should express themselves in certain contexts. When expectations are violated, the observer becomes distracted by the violation and directs more attention to the behavior rather than what is said. Autistic individuals' behaviors, such as differences in paralanguage, eye contact, emotional expression, and repetitive movements, may influence perceptions of deception (Benes & Lund, 2024; Logos et al., 2021). Additionally, Crane et al. (2020) gathered ratings of behavioral characteristics comparing TD and autistic children, in which the autistic child was rated as less composed, less coherent, and less focused than the TD child. These perceptions may be attributed to autistic individuals' differences in social interactions and communication (e.g., atypical eye contact, limited/asynchronous gestures and body movements, atypical speech characteristics, unusual expressions of emotion). Observing these behaviors during recall of emotionally distressing events can lead to lower judgments of credibility (McCrory et al., 2007).

Age is also a factor in judgments of credibility. TD child witnesses are often susceptible to misinformation or coaching from adults (Antrobus et al., 2016; Brown & Lewis, 2013; Melinder et al., 2016), and as teenagers, TD teens are less believable than younger children due to the former's knowledge of sexuality (Bottoms & Goodman, 1994). The risk of child witnesses' susceptibility to misinformation has led to questions about the credibility of their testimony. Thus, it is important to consider how age might influence the perceived credibility of child witnesses, including those with autism. A research study examined the effect of age on adults' judgments of credibility in autistic children. Although sexual knowledge was not at issue in this study, older children with or without autism were rated as more credible, honest, and coherent than younger children with or without autism (Enriquez et al., 2024). Therefore, it is important to recognize that age may play a role in shaping perceptions of credibility.

It is also critical to understand if and how adaptations, such as the provision of special measures in England and Wales (which include the provision of a registered intermediary, communication aids, and giving evidence via live link and prerecorded videos if allowed by the judge), influence others' perceptions of autistic victims' credibility. Social communication and behavioral differences in autistic people are often exacerbated under stress (Duvekot et al., 2017), which may diminish jurors' perceptions of them during the socially, emotionally, and cognitively demanding nature of unmodified court proceedings (Tallon et al., 2015). Thus, if courtroom special measures are effective in reducing autistic individuals' anxiety, this may have a concomitant benefit on perceived credibility. Provision of special measures, especially for autistic youth, may also serve as a reminder of a witness's vulnerable status and provide an explanation for behaviors that may otherwise be perceived as manifesting a lack of credibility or sincerity.

Conversely, prosecutors may be reluctant to have witnesses give evidence via "link" (closed-circuit TV) due to concerns that juries would find evidence given remotely, such as via video conferencing, as less credible (Fairclough, 2020; Goodman et al., 1998). Despite earlier evidence with TD children that their presence in a courtroom has a positive effect on mock jurors' perceptions (Landström & Granhag, 2010), a recent review found no reliable evidence that the use of video evidence influences verdict outcomes (Munro, 2018). This may differ for autistic individuals, however, depending on whether differences in their demeanor are magnified under the close camera focus (Zwi & Irving, 2020) or whether online, remote questioning reduces behavioral differences while also improving the quality of their evidence. This is an urgent issue for future research.

One way to improve perceptions of credibility during an autistic individual's testimony is by making jurors and legal officials aware of an autism diagnosis and providing information on the characteristics and effects of the diagnosis (Crane et al., 2020; Maras et al., 2018, 2019). Mock jurors tend to rate autistic children as credible as TD children, and in some cases, as more credible than TD children (Berryessa, 2016; Crane et al., 2020; Logos et al., 2021; see also Maras et al., 2019 for findings with autistic adults). Disclosure of an autism diagnosis may also counteract any negative perceptions an autistic child witness may receive if they require a support person or aid while testifying, allowing autistic individuals to feel more comfortable during their testimony.

LONG-TERM SOCIAL AND EMOTIONAL OUTCOMES OF LEGAL INVOLVEMENT

Autistic individuals, particularly children, are highly vulnerable to traumatic experiences and adverse outcomes when involved in the criminal justice system (D. S. Cooper et al., 2022; Holloway et al., 2020; Salerno & Schuller, 2019). This vulnerability is compounded when their diagnosis is not disclosed, leading to a higher risk of being discredited or not receiving necessary emotional and social support. Without proper understanding and accommodation, autistic children may not be recognized for their specific needs and capabilities as witnesses, which could severely impact their ability to participate effectively in legal proceedings (Salerno & Schuller, 2019). The limited available research on the long-term effect of interacting with the legal system for autistic individuals highlights that prior negative experiences with police can lead to distrust and fear (e.g., Gibbs & Haas, 2020; Salerno & Schuller, 2019). These experiences often result in trauma and a reluctance to seek help in true emergencies (Salerno & Schuller, 2019), underscoring the importance of educating law enforcement and court personnel about autism to foster better interactions and support mechanisms.

Although no directly relevant research exists, autistic children's ability to cope with and understand legal proceedings likely varies with age. Capacity for coping and understanding legal proceedings, believed to be independent of language and attention (Saywitz et al., 2017), is also a key predictor of recall ability. Younger TD children often struggle more with comprehension and communication, necessitating age-appropriate adjustments in how information is presented to them (Quas et al., 2009). Developmental factors, in combination with the challenges of an autism diagnosis, mean that visual aids and simplified language are crucial tools in helping these children navigate the legal process (Henry, Crane, et al., 2017). However, positive outcomes have been reported by some parents and caregivers regarding interactions between their autistic children and law enforcement, with studies noting that the police response often had a calming effect (Tint et al., 2017, 2019). This suggests that with proper training and approach, law enforcement can effectively engage with autistic individuals.

POLICY AND PRACTICE

Most of the relevant research on autism and interviewing adaptations comes from the United Kingdom. In England and Wales, all victims and witnesses under the age of 18 are classed as vulnerable under the Youth Justice and Criminal Evidence Act (1999). The guidance produced by the U. K.'s Ministry of Justice (Ministry of Justice & National Police Chief's Council, 2022), *Achieving Best Evidence: Guidance on Interviewing Victims and Witnesses, and Guidance on Using Special Measures* (ABE; see also Fairclough, 2020; Farrugia & Maras, 2022) sets out how vulnerable witnesses should be interviewed in a developmentally appropriate manner. ABE advocates for the use of a phased approach, following (a) rapport, (b) free recall, (c) questions, and (d) closure.

Despite detailed ABE guidance emphasizing the importance of using more open-ended questions, in practice, interviewers have difficulty maintaining this, often reverting to the use of closed questions (Lamb, 2016). This is unsurprising given that TD children's recall is often sparse under open-ended questions (Brown & Lamb, 2015), and autistic children's recall can be even more so (e.g., Almeida et al., 2019; Bruck et al., 2007; Henry, Crane, et al., 2017; Henry, Messer, et al., 2017; Henry et al., 2020; Mattison et al., 2015; McCrory et al., 2007). However, ABE also outlines strategies to aid vulnerable witnesses with the process of providing evidence, including the use of communication aids, props, and the appointment of a registered intermediary—an impartial, trained professional who facilitates communication between vulnerable witnesses and members of the justice system.

The Witness Intermediary Scheme was introduced in England and Wales in 2004 (P. Cooper & Mattison, 2017) to provide the option of a registered intermediary for vulnerable witnesses. Assistance may be provided at various stages, from before trial at the investigative interview through to court, where the intermediary can recommend court adaptations and directly facilitate communication during cross-examination (whether prerecorded or live during the trial). Although initial feedback from those involved in the Witness Intermediary Scheme has been positive, notwithstanding logistical issues (Plotnikoff & Woolfson, 2015; Victims' Commissioner, 2019), there is scant data from empirical research (Fairclough, 2020; Majeed-Ariss et al., 2021). Only one experimental study to date has tested the efficacy of registered intermediaries for obtaining evidence with autistic children, and this focused on the police investigative interview stages. Henry, Crane, et al. (2017) reported that although the assistance of a registered intermediary improved the volume of correct information recalled by TD children's accounts, it had no discernible effect on the volume of correct information in autistic children's accounts. However, the authors note that the beneficial effect of registered intermediary assistance for autistic witnesses may not be in relation to the parameters measured in their study, leaving open the possibility that they are key to autistic witnesses being able to give any evidence at all (Dando et al., 2018).

A key development for vulnerable witnesses in England and Wales (yet to be empirically tested for autistic witnesses at court) is the introduction of special measures permitting adaptations to how evidence is gathered and presented in criminal courts. Measures include allowing (a) evidence-in-chief to be presented in the form of a prerecorded investigative (police) interview, (b) witnesses to give evidence in court from behind a screen, (c) evidence being provided in private (closing the public gallery), (d) removal of court dress (wigs and gowns), (e) communication through a registered intermediary, (f) the use of live-link for cross-examination (from within the court building where the trial is taking place, or from an authorized remote location), and (g) prerecorded cross-examination (via live-link). This last measure, recently rolled out in England and Wales, allows for cross-examination to be conducted in advance of a trial, negating the need for vulnerable witnesses to attend court and provide evidence during a live trial. However, as outlined earlier, prosecutors are often reluctant to utilize video evidence due to concerns about its effect on juror perceptions (Fairclough, 2020). One solution may be to use supportive techniques with all child witnesses, rather than only with autistic children, given that such adaptations tend to be universally beneficial.

Research on supportive practices for autistic individuals in legal settings in the United States is scarce and mainly focuses on autistic adult defendants, but highlights several strategies and initiatives aimed at improving their experiences and ensuring fair treatment. The Americans With Disabilities Act (ADA; 1990) in the United States provides individuals with disabilities, such as autistic individuals, protection against discrimination due to their disability. This also requires courts to provide reasonable accommodations under the ADA to ensure that autistic individuals can participate fully in legal proceedings. In parallel with this legal obligation, recent years have seen a growing body of research aimed at enhancing interactions between the legal system and individuals with disabilities.

One crucial initiative to improve autistic individuals' interactions with the legal system is a person-centered approach tailored to the unique needs of autistic individuals, considering intersecting individual, interpersonal, and environmental factors (Bagnall & Maras, 2025). This might include adjusting the court environment to reduce sensory overload and anxiety (e.g., modifying lighting and noise levels), and using clear, simple language and visual aids to explain procedures. Support persons or advocates trained in autism may be key to facilitating such adjustments during legal proceedings. These advocates help autistic children understand the proceedings and communicate effectively with legal professionals. Such strategies have been studied in TD populations, in which victim witness advocates function as a resource to provide children with emotional and informational support during legal proceedings (McAuliff et al., 2015). Children benefited from having a supportive adult in the courtroom with them, highlighting the importance of providing a support person to children diagnosed with autism.

Training for legal professionals is also essential. Several states in the United States, such as New Jersey (Kelly & Hassett-Walker, 2016) and Pennsylvania (Pennsylvania General Assembly, 2015), have mandatory autism awareness training for law enforcement officers; however, most states do not cover autism in law enforcement training. In research regarding court settings, Berryessa (2016) surveyed judges on the effect of knowing an individual has autism on defendant sentencing. The judges indicated that the autism diagnosis was a potential mitigating factor, leading to the consideration that the autistic offender's actions could have been a result of the characteristics of their diagnosis. Lawyers surveyed indicated that autistic clients are predominantly given reasonable adjustments in courtrooms (Slavny-Cross et al., 2022). Programs designed to educate judges, lawyers, law enforcement, and court staff about autism can enhance the ability to interact appropriately and sensitively with autistic child victims and witnesses. Such training should cover understanding autism-related behaviors, effective communication strategies, and the importance of accommodating sensory sensitivities. Overall, more research is needed in the United States to further examine the best practices for interviewing autistic child witnesses in legal settings.

CONCLUSION

The interaction of autistic individuals, especially children, with the legal system presents numerous challenges that require targeted interventions and accommodations to ensure fair treatment and effective participation. As reviewed, research consistently highlights that autistic children are productive, accurate, and credible witnesses when provided with appropriate accommodations, such as visual aids and clear, simple language. However, without these accommodations, their ability to testify effectively can be compromised. Key strategies for improving the experiences of autistic children in legal settings include the use of registered intermediaries, who can facilitate communication between the child and legal professionals, and the implementation of special measures, which adjust the court environment to reduce stress and sensory overload.

Despite the challenges, positive outcomes are achievable. Properly trained law enforcement and legal personnel can create supportive interactions, helping autistic individuals feel more secure and understood. More accommodating legal environments for autistic children not only enhance their abilities to participate in legal proceedings but also help in mitigating the long-term social and emotional effects of their involvement in the legal system. Continued research and the implementation of evidence-based practices are essential for ensuring that the legal system meets the needs of all individuals, regardless of their neurodevelopmental profile.

REFERENCES

Almeida, T. S., Lamb, M. E., & Weisblatt, E. J. (2019). Effects of delay, question type, and socioemotional support on episodic memory retrieval by children with autism spectrum disorder. *Journal of Autism and Developmental Disorders, 49*(3), 1111–1130. https://doi.org/10.1007/s10803-018-3815-3

American Psychiatric Association. (2013). *Diagnostic and statistical manual of mental disorders* (5th ed.). https://doi.org/10.1176/appi.books.9780890425596

Americans With Disabilities Act of 1990, 42 U.S.C. § 12101 *et seq.* (1990). https://www.ada.gov/pubs/adastatute08.htm

Antrobus, E., McKimmie, B. M., & Newcombe, P. (2016). Mode of children's testimony and the effect of assumptions about credibility. *Psychiatry, Psychology and Law, 23*(6), 922–940. https://doi.org/10.1080/13218719.2016.1152927

Bagnall, R., & Maras, K. (2025). Autism and police interviewing: An individual, interpersonal, and environmental model of vulnerability. In S. Macdonald & D. Peacock (Eds.), *The Routledge handbook of disability, crime, and justice* (pp. 197–218). Routledge.

Baron-Cohen, S. (1995). *Mindblindness: An essay on autism and theory of mind.* MIT Press.

Benes, C., & Lund, E. (2024). Knowledge and perspectives of developmental language disorders: The pilot development of a survey of professionals working in law enforcement. *American Journal of Speech-Language Pathology, 33*(2), 969–989. https://doi.org/10.1044/2023_AJSLP-22-00374

Berryessa, C. M. (2016). Brief report: Judicial attitudes regarding the sentencing of offenders with high functioning autism. *Journal of Autism and Developmental Disorders, 46*(8), 2770–2773. https://doi.org/10.1007/s10803-016-2798-1

Bottoms, B. L., & Goodman, G. S. (1994). Perceptions of children's credibility in sexual assault cases. *Journal of Applied Social Psychology, 24*(8), 702–735. https://doi.org/10.1111/j.1559-1816.1994.tb00608.x

Bowler, D., Gaigg, S., & Lind, S. (2011). Memory in autism: Binding, self and brain. In I. Roth & P. Rezaie (Eds.), *Researching the autism spectrum: Contemporary perspectives* (pp. 316–346). Cambridge University Press. https://doi.org/10.1017/CBO9780511973918.013

Bowler, D. M., Gardiner, J. M., & Berthollier, N. (2004). Source memory in adolescents and adults with Asperger's syndrome. *Journal of Autism and Developmental Disorders, 34*(5), 533–542. https://doi.org/10.1007/s10803-004-2548-7

Bradshaw, J., McCracken, C., Pileggi, M., Brane, N., Delehanty, A., Day, T., Federico, A., Klaiman, C., Saulnier, C., Klin, A., & Wetherby, A. (2021). Early social communication development in infants with autism spectrum disorder. *Child Development, 92*(6), 2224–2234. https://doi.org/10.1111/cdev.13683

Brown, D. A., & Lamb, M. E. (2015). Can children be useful witnesses? It depends how they are questioned. *Child Development Perspectives, 9*(4), 250–255. https://doi.org/10.1111/cdep.12142

Brown, D. A., & Lewis, C. N. (2013). Competence is in the eye of the beholder: Perceptions of intellectually disabled child witnesses. *International Journal of Disability,*

Development and Education, 60(1), 3–17. https://doi.org/10.1080/1034912X.2013.757132

Brown, D. A., & Pipe, M. E. (2003). Individual differences in children's event memory reports and the narrative elaboration technique. *Journal of Applied Psychology, 88*(2), 195–206. https://doi.org/10.1037/0021-9010.88.2.195

Bruck, M., London, K., Landa, R., & Goodman, J. (2007). Autobiographical memory and suggestibility in children with autism spectrum disorder. *Development and Psychopathology, 19*(1), 73–95. https://doi.org/10.1017/S0954579407070058

Burgoon, J. K. (1993). Interpersonal expectations, expectancy violations, and emotional communication. *Journal of Language and Social Psychology, 12*(1–2), 30–48. https://doi.org/10.1177/0261927x93121003

Burgoon, J. K. (2015). Expectancy violations theory. In C. R. Berger, M. E. Roloff, S. R. Wilson, J. P. Dillard, J. Caughlin, & D. Solomon (Eds.), *The international encyclopedia of interpersonal communication* (pp. 1–9). Wiley. https://doi.org/10.1002/9781118540190.wbeic102

Chandler, R. J., Russell, A., & Maras, K. L. (2019). Compliance in autism: Self-report in action. *Autism: The International Journal of Research and Practice, 23*(4), 1005–1017. https://doi.org/10.1177/1362361318795479

Christoffersen, M. N. (2019). Violent crime against children with disabilities: A nationwide prospective birth cohort study. *Child Abuse & Neglect, 98,* 104150. https://doi.org/10.1016/j.chiabu.2019.104150

Cooke, K., Ridgway, K., Pecora, L., Westrupp, E., Hedley, D., Hooley, M., & Stokes, M. A. (2024). Individual, social, and life course risk factors for experiencing interpersonal violence among autistic people of varying gender identities: A mixed methods systematic review. *Research in Autism Spectrum Disorders, 111,* 102313. https://doi.org/10.1016/j.rasd.2023.102313

Cooper, D. S., Uppal, D., Railey, K. S., Blank Wilson, A., Maras, K., Zimmerman, E., Bornman, J., & Shea, L. L. (2022). Policy gaps and opportunities: A systematic review of autism spectrum disorder and criminal justice intersections. *Autism, 26*(5), 1014–1031. https://doi.org/10.1177/13623613211070341

Cooper, P., & Mattison, M. (2017). Intermediaries, vulnerable people and the quality of evidence: An international comparison of three versions of the English intermediary model. *The International Journal of Evidence & Proof, 21*(4), 351–370. https://doi.org/10.1177/1365712717725534

Cotterill, B. F. (2022). *Are children reliable witnesses*? Palgrave Macmillan. https://doi.org/10.1007/978-3-031-10382-7

Crane, L., Goddard, L., & Pring, L. (2009). Specific and general autobiographical knowledge in adults with autism spectrum disorders: The role of personal goals. *Memory, 17*(5), 557–576. https://doi.org/10.1080/09658210902960211

Crane, L., Goddard, L., & Pring, L. (2012). Autobiographical memory in adults with autism spectrum disorder: The role of depressed mood, rumination, working memory and theory of mind. *Autism, 17*(2), 205–219. https://doi.org/10.1177/1362361311418690

Crane, L., & Maras, K. (2018). General memory abilities for autobiographical events in adults with autism spectrum disorder. In J. L. Johnson, G. S. Goodman, & P. C. Mundy (Eds.), *The Wiley handbook of memory, autism spectrum disorder, and the law* (pp. 146–178). Wiley. https://doi.org/10.1002/9781119158431

Crane, L., Wilcock, R., Maras, K. L., Chui, W., Marti-Sanchez, C., & Henry, L. A. (2020). Mock juror perceptions of child witnesses on the autism spectrum: The impact of providing diagnostic labels and information about autism. *Journal of Autism and Developmental Disorders, 50*(5), 1509–1519. https://doi.org/10.1007/s10803-018-3700-0

Dando, C. J. (2013). Drawing to remember: External support of older adults' eyewitness performance. *PLOS One, 8*(7), e69937. https://doi.org/10.1371/journal.pone.0069937

Dando, C. J., Geiselman, R. E., MacLeod, N., & Griffiths, A. (2015). Interviewing adult witnesses and victims. In G. Oxburgh, T. Myklebust, T. Grant, & R. Milne (Eds.), *Communication in investigative and legal contexts: Integrated approaches from forensic psychology, linguistics, and law enforcement* (pp. 79–106). Wiley-Blackwell. https://doi.org/10.1002/9781118769133.ch5

Dando, C. J., Ormerod, T. C., Cooper, P., Marchant, R., Mattison, M., Milne, R., & Bull, R. (2018). No evidence against sketch reinstatement of context, verbal labels or the use of registered intermediaries for children with autism spectrum disorder: Response to Henry et al. (2017). *Journal of Autism and Developmental Disorders, 48*(7), 2593–2596. https://doi.org/10.1007/s10803-018-3479-z

Denne, E., Brubacher, S., Simpson, K., Adams, D., Dargue, N., & Powell, M. (2024). Examining autistic and non-autistic children's productivity in response to subtypes of open-ended prompts. *International Journal on Child Maltreatment: Research, Policy and Practice,* 7(2), 257–266. https://doi.org/10.1007/s42448-023-00186-5

Desaunay, P., Briant, A. R., Bowler, D. M., Ring, M., Gérardin, P., Baleyte, J. M., Guénolé, F., Eustache, F., Parienti, J. J., & Guillery-Girard, B. (2020). Memory in autism spectrum disorder: A meta-analysis of experimental studies. *Psychological Bulletin, 146*(5), 377–410. https://doi.org/10.1037/bul0000225

Duvekot, J., van der Ende, J., Verhulst, F. C., Slappendel, G., van Daalen, E., Maras, A., & Greaves-Lord, K. (2017). Factors influencing the probability of a diagnosis of autism spectrum disorder in girls versus boys. *Autism: The International Journal of Research and Practice, 21*(6), 646–658. https://doi.org/10.1177/1362361316672178

Enriquez, R., Johnson, J. L., Wang, Y., Mundy, P., & Goodman, G. S. (2024). Adults' ratings of youths with autism spectrum disorder when recalling a stressful event. *Applied Cognitive Psychology, 38*(6), e70009. https://doi.org/10.1002/acp.70009

Fairclough, S. (2020). *Special measures literature review.* Office of the Victims Commissioner for England and Wales. https://s3-eu-west-2.amazonaws.com/jotwpublic-prod-storage-1cxo1dnrmkg14/uploads/sites/6/2021/12/OVCSpecial-Measures-Literature-Review-July-2020.pdf

Fang, Z., Cerna-Turoff, I., Zhang, C., Lu, M., Lachman, J. M., & Barlow, J. (2022). Global estimates of violence against children with disabilities: An updated systematic review and meta-analysis. *The Lancet Child & Adolescent Health, 6*(5), 313–323. https://doi.org/10.1016/S2352-4642(22)00033-5

Farrugia, L., & Maras, K. (2022). Achieving best evidence from victims and witnesses. In G. E. Oxburgh, T. Myklebust, M. Fallon, & M. Hartwig (Eds.), *Interviewing and interrogation: A review of research and practice since World War II* (pp. 389–412). Torkel Opsahl Academic EPublisher.

Fisher, R. P., & Geiselman, R. E. (1992). *Memory enhancing techniques for investigative interviewing: The cognitive interview.* Charles C Thomas.

Ford, R. M., & McLean, T. (2023). Self-processing and social functioning in autistic preschoolers. *The British Journal of Developmental Psychology, 42*(1), 36–48. https://doi.org/10.1111/bjdp.12468

Frith, U., & Happé, F. (1999). Theory of mind and self-consciousness: What is it like to be autistic? *Mind & Language, 14*(1), 82–89. https://doi.org/10.1111/1468-0017.00100

Geng, K., Wang, Y., Fu, W., Chen, S., & Yang, Y. (2024). Episodic memory impairment and its influencing factors in individuals with autism spectrum disorder: Systematic review and meta-analysis. *European Archives of Psychiatry and Clinical Neuroscience.* https://doi.org/10.1007/s00406-024-01889-7

George, R., Crane, L., Bingham, A., Pophale, C., & Remington, A. (2018). Legal professionals' knowledge and experience of autistic adults in the family justice system. *Journal of Social Welfare and Family Law, 40*(1), 78–97. https://doi.org/10.1080/09649069.2018.1414381

Gibbs, V., & Haas, K. (2020). Interactions between the police and the autistic community in Australia: Experiences and perspectives of autistic adults and parents/carers.

Journal of Autism and Developmental Disorders, 50(12), 4513–4526. https://doi.org/10.1007/s10803-020-04510-7

Goddard, L., Dritschel, B., Robinson, S., & Howlin, P. (2014). Development of autobiographical memory in children with autism spectrum disorders: Deficits, gains, and predictors of performance. *Development and Psychopathology, 26*(2), 215–228. https://doi.org/10.1017/S0954579413000904

Goodman, G. S., Taub, E. P., Jones, D. P. H., England, P., Port, L. K., Rudy, L., & Prado, L. (1992). Testifying in criminal court: Emotional effects on child sexual assault victims. *Monographs of the Society for Research in Child Development, 57*(5), i–159. https://doi.org/10.2307/1166127

Goodman, G. S., Tobey, A. E., Batterman-Faunce, J. M., Orcutt, H., Thomas, S., Shapiro, C., & Sachsenmaier, T. (1998). Face-to-face confrontation: Effects of closed-circuit technology on children's eyewitness testimony and jurors' decisions. *Law and Human Behavior, 22*(2), 165–203. https://doi.org/10.1023/a:1025742119977

Grainger, C., Williams, D. M., & Lind, S. E. (2014). Metacognition, metamemory, and mindreading in high-functioning adults with autism spectrum disorder. *Journal of Abnormal Psychology, 123*(3), 650–659. https://doi.org/10.1037/a0036531

Henry, L. A., Crane, L., Fesser, E., Harvey, A., Palmer, L., & Wilcock, R. (2020). The narrative coherence of witness transcripts in children on the autism spectrum. *Research in Developmental Disabilities, 96*, 103518. https://doi.org/10.1016/j.ridd.2019.103518

Henry, L. A., Crane, L., Millmore, A., Nash, G., & Wilcock, R. (2021). Intermediaries and cross-examination resilience in children: The development of a novel experimental methodology. *Applied Cognitive Psychology, 35*(6), 1387–1404. https://doi.org/10.1002/acp.3869

Henry, L. A., Crane, L., Nash, G., Hobson, Z., Kirke-Smith, M., & Wilcock, R. (2017). Verbal, visual, and intermediary support for child witnesses with autism during investigative interviews. *Journal of Autism and Developmental Disorders, 47*(8), 2348–2362. https://doi.org/10.1007/s10803-017-3142-0

Henry, L. A., Messer, D. J., Wilcock, R., Nash, G., Kirke-Smith, M., Hobson, Z., & Crane, L. (2017). Do measures of memory, language, and attention predict eyewitness memory in children with and without autism? *Autism & Developmental Language Impairments, 2*, 2396941517722139. https://doi.org/10.1177/2396941517722139

Hobson, R. P. (2010). Explaining autism: Ten reasons to focus on the developing self. *Autism, 14*(5), 391–407. https://doi.org/10.1177/1362361310364142

Holloway, C. A., Munro, N., Jackson, J., Phillips, S., & Ropar, D. (2020). Exploring the autistic and police perspectives of the custody process through a participative walk-through. *Research in Developmental Disabilities, 97*, 103545. https://doi.org/10.1016/j.ridd.2019.103545

Hsu, C. W., & Teoh, Y. S. (2017). Investigating event memory in children with autism spectrum disorder: Effects of a computer-mediated interview. *Journal of Autism and Developmental Disorders, 47*(2), 359–372. https://doi.org/10.1007/s10803-016-2959-2

Jones, L., Bellis, M. A., Wood, S., Hughes, K., McCoy, E., Eckley, L., Bates, G., Mikton, C., Shakespeare, T., & Officer, A. (2012). Prevalence and risk of violence against children with disabilities: A systematic review and meta-analysis of observational studies. *The Lancet, 380*(9845), 899–907. https://doi.org/10.1016/S0140-6736(12)60692-8

Kelly, E., & Hassett-Walker, C. (2016). The training of New Jersey emergency service first responders in autism awareness. *Police Practice and Research, 17*(6), 543–554. https://doi.org/10.1080/15614263.2015.1121390

Kristen, S., Rossmann, F., & Sodian, B. (2014). Theory of own mind and autobiographical memory in adults with ASD. *Research in Autism Spectrum Disorders, 8*(7), 827–837. https://doi.org/10.1016/j.rasd.2014.03.009

Lamb, M. E. (2016). Difficulties translating research on forensic interview practices to practitioners: Finding water, leading horses, but can we get them to drink? *American Psychologist, 71*(8), 710–718. https://doi.org/10.1037/amp0000039

Lamb, M. E., Orbach, Y., Hershkowitz, I., Esplin, P. W., & Horowitz, D. (2007). Structured forensic interview protocols improve the quality and informativeness of investigative interviews with children: A review of research using the NICHD Investigative Interview Protocol. *Child Abuse & Neglect, 31*(11–12), 1201–1231. https://doi.org/10.1016/j.chiabu.2007.03.021

Landström, S., & Granhag, P. A. (2010). In-court versus out-of-court testimonies: Children's experiences and adults' assessments. *Applied Cognitive Psychology, 24*(7), 941–955. https://doi.org/10.1002/acp.1606

Lind, S. E., & Bowler, D. M. (2009). Recognition memory, self-other source memory, and theory-of-mind in children with autism spectrum disorder. *Journal of Autism and Developmental Disorders, 39*(9), 1231–1239. https://doi.org/10.1007/s10803-009-0735-2

Lind, S. E., Williams, D. M., Nicholson, T., Grainger, C., & Carruthers, P. (2020). The self-reference effect on memory is not diminished in autism: Three studies of incidental and explicit self-referential recognition memory in autistic and neurotypical adults and adolescents. *Journal of Abnormal Psychology, 129*(2), 224–236. https://doi.org/10.1037/abn0000467

Logos, K., Brewer, N., & Young, R. L. (2021). Countering biased judgments of individuals who display Autism-characteristic behavior in forensic settings. *Human Communication Research, 47*(3), 215–247. https://doi.org/10.1093/hcr/hqab002

Lombardo, M. V., Barnes, J. L., Wheelwright, S. J., & Baron-Cohen, S. (2007). Self-referential cognition and empathy in autism. *PLOS One, 2*(9), e883. https://doi.org/10.1371/journal.pone.0000883

Lyons, V., & Fitzgerald, M. (2013). Atypical sense of self in autism spectrum disorders: A neuro-cognitive perspective. In M. Fitzgerald (Ed.), *Recent advances in autism spectrum disorders* (Vol. 1). IntechOpen. https://doi.org/10.5772/53680

Macintosh, K., & Dissanayake, C. (2006). Social skills and problem behaviours in school-aged children with high-functioning autism and Asperger's disorder. *Journal of Autism and Developmental Disorders, 36*(8), 1065–1076. https://doi.org/10.1007/s10803-006-0139-5

Maenner, M. J., Warren, Z., Robinson Williams, A., Amoakohene, E., Bakian, A. V., Bilder, D. A., Durkin, M. S., Fitzgerald, R. T., Furnier, S. M., Hughes, M. M., Ladd-Acosta, C. M., McArthur, D., Pas, E. T., Salinas, A., Vehorn, A., Williams, S., Esler, A., Grzybowski, A., Hall-Lande, J., . . . Shaw, K. A. (2020). Prevalence of autism spectrum disorders among children aged 8 years—Autism and developmental disabilities monitoring network. *Surveillance Summaries, 69*(4), 1–12. https://doi.org/10.15585/mmwr.ss7202a1

Majeed-Ariss, R., Brockway, A., Cook, K., & White, C. (2021). 'Could do better': Report on the use of special measures in sexual offences cases. *Criminology & Criminal Justice, 21*(1), 89–106. https://doi.org/10.1177/1748895819840396

Maras, K. (2021). Obtaining testimony from autistic people. In F. R. Volkmar, R. Loftin, A. Westphal, & M. Woodbury-Smith (Eds.), *Handbook of autism spectrum disorder and the law* (pp. 145–183). Springer. https://doi.org/10.1007/978-3-030-70913-6_7

Maras, K., & Bowler, D. M. (2011). Brief report: Schema consistent misinformation effects in eyewitnesses with autism spectrum disorder. *Journal of Autism and Developmental Disorders, 41*(6), 815–820. https://doi.org/10.1007/s10803-010-1089-5

Maras, K., Dando, C., Stephenson, H., Lambrechts, A., Anns, S., & Gaigg, S. (2020). The witness-aimed first account (WAFA): A new technique for interviewing autistic witnesses and victims. *Autism: The International Journal of Research and Practice, 24*(6), 1449–1467. https://doi.org/10.1177/1362361320908986

Maras, K., Marshall, I., & Sands, C. (2019). Mock juror perceptions of credibility and culpability in an autistic defendant. *Journal of Autism and Developmental Disorders, 49*(3), 996–1010. https://doi.org/10.1007/s10803-018-3803-7

Maras, K. L., & Bowler, D. M. (2010). The cognitive interview for eyewitnesses with autism spectrum disorder. *Journal of Autism and Developmental Disorders, 40*(11), 1350–1360. https://doi.org/10.1007/s10803-010-0997-8

Maras, K. L., & Bowler, D. M. (2012). Context reinstatement effects on eyewitness memory in autism spectrum disorder. *British Journal of Psychology, 103*(3), 330–342. https://doi.org/10.1111/j.2044-8295.2011.02077.x

Maras, K. L., Gaigg, S. B., & Bowler, D. M. (2012). Memory for emotionally arousing events over time in autism spectrum disorder. *Emotion, 12*(5), 1118–1128. https://doi.org/10.1037/a0026679

Maras, K. L., Memon, A., Lambrechts, A., & Bowler, D. M. (2013). Recall of a live and personally experienced eyewitness event by adults with autism spectrum disorder. *Journal of Autism and Developmental Disorders, 43*(8), 1798–1810. https://doi.org/10.1007/s10803-012-1729-z

Mattison, M., Dando, C. J., & Ormerod, T. C. (2018). Drawing the answers: Sketching to support free and probed recall by child witnesses and victims with autism spectrum disorder. *Autism, 22*(2), 181–194. https://doi.org/10.1177/1362361316669088

Mattison, M. L., & Dando, C. J. (2020). Police officers' and Registered Intermediaries' use of drawing during investigative interviews with vulnerable witnesses. *Psychology, Crime & Law, 26*(2), 167–185. https://doi.org/10.1080/1068316X.2019.1652744

Mattison, M. L., Dando, C. J., & Ormerod, T. C. (2015). Sketching to remember: Episodic free recall task support for child witnesses and victims with autism spectrum disorder. *Journal of Autism and Developmental Disorders, 45*(6), 1751–1765. https://doi.org/10.1007/s10803-014-2335-z

McAuliff, B. D., Lapin, J., & Michel, S. (2015). Support person presence and child victim testimony: Believe it or not. *Behavioral Sciences & the Law, 33*(4), 508–527. https://doi.org/10.1002/bsl.2190

McCrory, E., Henry, L. A., & Happé, F. (2007). Eye-witness memory and suggestibility in children with Asperger syndrome. *Journal of Child Psychology and Psychiatry, 48*(5), 482–489. https://doi.org/10.1111/j.1469-7610.2006.01715.x

Melinder, A. M. D., Burrell, L., Eriksen, M. O., Magnussen, S., & Wessel, E. (2016). The emotional child witness effect survives presentation mode. *Behavioral Sciences & the Law, 34*(1), 113–125. https://doi.org/10.1002/bsl.2232

Memon, A., Meissner, C., & Fraser, J. (2010). The cognitive interview: A meta-analytic review and study space analysis of the past 25 years. *Psychology, Public Policy, and Law, 16*(4), 340–372. https://doi.org/10.1037/a0020518

Milton, D., Gurbuz, E., & Lopez, B. (2022). The 'double empathy problem': Ten years on. *Autism: The International Journal of Research and Practice, 26*(8), 1901–1903. https://doi.org/10.1177/13623613221129123

Milton, D. E. M. (2012). On the ontological status of autism: The 'double empathy problem'. *Disability & Society, 27*(6), 883–887. https://doi.org/10.1080/09687599.2012.710008

Ministry of Justice and National Police Chiefs' Council. (2022). *Achieving best evidence in criminal proceedings: Guidance on interviewing victims and witnesses, and guidance on using special measures*. Ministry of Justice. https://www.gov.uk/government/publications/achieving-best-evidence-in-criminal-proceedings

Mottron, L., Dawson, M., Soulières, I., Hubert, B., & Burack, J. (2006). Enhanced perceptual functioning in autism: An update, and eight principles of autistic perception. *Journal of Autism and Developmental Disorders, 36*(1), 27–43. https://doi.org/10.1007/s10803-005-0040-7

Munro, V. (2018). *The impact of the use of pre-recorded evidence on juror decision making: An evidence review*. Crime and Justice Social Research, Scottish Government. https://wrap.warwick.ac.uk/id/eprint/103606/

Norris, J. E., Crane, L., & Maras, K. (2020). Interviewing autistic adults: Adaptations to support recall in police, employment, and healthcare interviews. *Autism: The International Journal of Research and Practice, 24*(6), 1506–1520. https://doi.org/10.1177/1362361320909174

Norris, J. E., & Maras, K. (2021). Supporting autistic adults' episodic memory recall in interviews: The role of executive functions, theory of mind, and language abilities. *Autism, 26*(2), 513–524. https://doi.org/10.1177/13623613211030772

Pennsylvania General Assembly. (2015). *Judicial code (42 PA.C.S.) and municipalities code (53 PA.C.S.): Continuing education requirements, powers and duties of municipal police officers' education and training commission.*

Plotnikoff, J., & Woolfson, R. (2015). *Intermediaries in the criminal justice system: Improving communication for vulnerable witnesses and defendants.* Bristol University Press. https://doi.org/10.2307/j.ctt1t89326

Quas, J. A., & Goodman, G. S. (2012). Consequences of criminal court involvement for child victims. *Psychology, Public Policy, and Law, 18*(3), 392–414. https://doi.org/10.1037/a0026146

Quas, J. A., Wallin, A. R., Horwitz, B., Davis, E., & Lyon, T. D. (2009). Maltreated children's understanding of and emotional reactions to dependency court involvement. *Behavioral Sciences & the Law, 27*(1), 97–117. https://doi.org/10.1002/bsl.836

Salerno, J. M., & Schuller, R. A. (2019). The impact of prior police contact on victims and witnesses with autism spectrum disorder. *Psychiatry, Psychology and Law, 26*(5), 816–829.

Saywitz, K. J., Lyon, T. D., & Goodman, G. S. (2017). When interviewing children: A review and update. In J. B. Klika & J. R. Conte (Eds.), *The APSAC handbook on child maltreatment* (4th ed., pp. 310–329). Sage.

Slavny-Cross, R., Allison, C., Griffiths, S., & Baron-Cohen, S. (2022). Autism and the criminal justice system: An analysis of 93 cases. *Autism Research, 15*(5), 904–914. https://doi.org/10.1002/aur.2690

Tallon, J. A., Daftary-Kapur, T., & Penrod, S. (2015). Defendant remorse and publicity in capital trials: Is seeing truly believing? *Criminal Justice and Behavior, 42*(12), 1282–1302. https://doi.org/10.1177/0093854815602500

Tint, A., Weiss, J. A., & Lunsky, Y. (2017). Identifying the key factors associated with emergency department visits for youth with autism spectrum disorder. *Autism Research, 10*(6), 1191–1200.

Tint, A., Weiss, J. A., & Lunsky, Y. (2019). Emergency service experiences of youth with autism spectrum disorder and their families: A narrative review. *Journal of Clinical Medicine, 8*(3), 792–795. https://doi.org/10.1177/1362361318760294

Victims' Commissioner for England and Wales. (2019, July 1). *2018/19 Annual report* (HC 2280). https://victimscommissioner.org.uk/document/annual-report-of-the-victims-commissioner-2018-to-2019/

Wilcock, R., Crane, L., Hobson, Z., Nash, G., Kirke-Smith, M., & Henry, L. A. (2019). Eyewitness identification in child witnesses on the autism spectrum. *Research in Autism Spectrum Disorders, 66,* 101407. https://doi.org/10.1016/j.rasd.2019.05.007

Youth Justice and Criminal Evidence Act. (1999). *Youth Justice and Criminal Evidence Act 1999.* England and Wales.

Zwi, A., & Irving, A. (2020). Practice and procedure: Cross-examination by video in the COVID-19 context. *Law Society Journal, 70,* 76–77. https://search.informit.org/doi/10.3316/informit.368355227429808

III

PERCEPTIONS OF CHILDREN IN COURT

15

Children's Competency and the Effects of Direct- and Cross-Examination on Children's Accuracy and Productivity

Stacia N. Stolzenberg, Colleen E. Sullivan, and Lea Sobrilsky

Children are called to testify regularly in court proceedings in the United States, with some estimating that over 100,000 children appear annually in court (Ceci & de Bruyn, 1993; Pantell et al., 2017). Many more children experience victimization (Finkelhor, 2011). However, they tend to testify only when they are central to the case and in instances where critical evidence cannot be obtained through other individuals or forms of evidence. For example, in one national survey of prosecutors, researchers found that children testify most commonly in cases of alleged sexual abuse, followed by physical abuse and witnessing family violence (Goodman et al., 1999). Those who investigate children's claims have clear evidence-based guidelines during the forensic interview due to decades of work on how to elicit accurate and complete reports (Lamb et al., 2018). Yet, these guidelines do not directly correspond to how children are questioned in court.

Courtroom questioning is distinct. Although forensic interviewers utilize open prompts to facilitate children's uninterrupted narratives in the hopes of achieving the purest report, this is not the goal in court. Attorneys are advised to keep control of witnesses, both to maintain their arguments and to facilitate expediency (Myers, 1987). The U.S. legal system is adversarial, with prosecutors corroborating children's reports and defense attorneys advocating zealously for their clients (Myers, 2017). This process is stressful for children

https://doi.org/10.1037/0000492-015
Handbook on Child Witnesses: Improving Psychological Science and Legal Practice,
G. S. Goodman, T. D. Lyon, S. D. Hobbs, and R. Enriquez (Editors)

(Goodman et al., 1992; Zajac et al., 2012), and many other countries have modified their procedures, adjusting how, whether, and when children testify (Bussey, 2009; Henderson & Lamb, 2017; Henderson et al., 2019). Many of these reforms are unlikely to happen in the United States, given the Confrontation Clause of the Amendment VI and the Supreme Court's interpretation, making it important for defense attorneys to cross-examine children on the stand (Lyon & Dente, 2012; Lyon & Stolzenberg, 2014).

Still, in recent decades, researchers have examined how children testify in court, as well as best practices for doing so. The purpose of this chapter is to examine the current research on how children are questioned in court. We will review how children are assessed for competency to testify, as well as how attorneys elicit information from children during testimony. Throughout, we will pay particular attention to how legal practices may affect children's ability to provide accurate and productive accounts of their experiences.

COMPETENCY

Whether a child is deemed competent determines if they will be allowed to testify. This is an important determination; in many cases where children testify, their testimonial evidence is foundational to the charges themselves (Stolzenberg & Lyon, 2014a). In the United States, children's competency relies on three basic criteria: (a) whether they can observe, recall, and communicate about events; (b) whether they can understand the seriousness of an oath; and (c) whether they understand the necessity of telling the truth while testifying (Pantell et al., 2017). These criteria can be conceptualized as two types of competency: basic competency and truth–lie competency (Lyon, 2011).

Basic Competency

Basic competency is defined as children's ability to perceive, remember, and communicate (Hoyano & Keenan, 2007). A common concern is that children may be too young to meet these requirements. As such, some countries and most U.S. states allow for inquiries into whether the child exhibits basic competency (Hoyano & Keenan, 2007; Lyon, 2011). Yet, assessing the basic competency of children is unstandardized.

Some argue that a practical assessment is determining children's basic language skills, which can be accomplished by seeing whether children are able to respond to simple questions from the judge (Klemfuss & Ceci, 2012; Myers, 1997). Yet, this does not fully assess whether children can sufficiently remember past events and communicate effectively about those experiences. Others argue that it might be appropriate to let children testify without conducting competency assessments; one can evaluate the credibility of the child after assessing their testimony performance (Hoyano & Keenan, 2007). However, there is concern that allowing the testimony of children who are unable to remember or communicate clearly may benefit the party who presents the child as a witness regardless of the child's lack of competence (Lyon, 2011).

When competency assessments are required, a more appropriate assessment might involve narrative practice (Lyon, 2011), which is a component of several interviewing protocols (Lamb et al., 2018; Saywitz & Camparo, 2014). Although commonly used in forensic interviews, courtrooms rarely do much rapport-building (Ahern et al., 2015). Courts could adapt narrative practice rapport-building for their own needs, whereby they might ask children to narrate a recent event prior to asking about abuse allegations (e.g., "Tell me about things you like to do?" "I like to go to the park." "Tell me everything that happened the last time you went to the park."). This might be multifunctional in court, as it is in forensic interviews. It can allow a child to respond to simple questioning and demonstrate that they can remember and narrate prior events, but it can also go beyond, allowing children to practice narrating in a way that they might need to do as they describe victimization (e.g., distinguishing an event from many that have been recurrent); practicing what an interview will look like can be an effective method for increasing children's recall performance (Saywitz et al., 1992). Specifically, narrative practice rapport-building can help children to feel comfortable talking while also increasing the productivity of their responses. It helps to establish rapport between the questioner and child, while also training children to provide narrative responses to open-ended questions (Hershkowitz, 2009; Lyon, 2011; Lyon et al., 2014).

Truth–Lie Competency and the Oath

Truth–lie competency is defined as children's ability to distinguish truth from lies, while also understanding the importance of telling the truth. In courtrooms, this corresponds with a requirement to take an oath to tell the truth. The concern regarding truth–lie competency is that young children might struggle to distinguish truth from lies, or they may be unable to understand the moral ramifications of telling falsehoods. Here, we rely on developmental science to assess how and when children can distinguish truth from lies, and how to encourage truth-telling.

Developmental Research on Truth–Lie Understanding

Scientists find that young children can recognize when statements are true and begin to connect that to morality. Lyon and colleagues (2013) presented 2- to 5-year-olds with true and false statements about vignettes and found the youngest children could reliably accept true statements and dismiss falsehoods. By 3.5 to 4 years old, children could reliably label statements as true or false, and label true and false statements as good and bad; children's ability to evaluate the morality paralleled their recognition of the truthfulness or falsity of the statement (Lyon et al., 2013). These findings echo those of others, where researchers find that young children can identify statements as truthful or not and connect that to positive or negative assessments (Bussey, 1992; Talwar et al., 2002).

Much of the research on truth–lie understanding focuses on typically developing children. In courtrooms, it is important to know whether maltreated children hold the same understanding, as maltreated children are known to present with cognitive delays. Here, most maltreated children understand what is the truth versus what is a lie by around 5 years of age (Lyon & Saywitz, 1999). However, young children struggle to explain the difference between truth and lies, meaning they may find it challenging to explain why lying is bad or to define the terms (e.g., truth, lie). This is important in the context of how courts should assess children's truth–lie understanding and children's ability to promise to tell the truth during testimony.

How to Encourage Truth Telling in Court

The U.S. legal system has some of the most rigorous truth–lie competency requirements, in that some form of an oath is near universal (Lyon, 2011). In an investigation of how 4- to 15-year-olds respond to truth–lie competency questions in courtroom testimony, Evans and Lyon (2012) found that nearly all young children (around 90% for 4- to 9-year-olds) were asked truth–lie competency questions; of the children who testified in court and were asked truth–lie competency questions, the researchers did not identify a single instance where a child was found incompetent to testify (which could mean that children who failed the competency questions before trial were not presented as witnesses). They also found that the children showed significant variability in how they responded to questions depending on how they were asked, meaning that contemporary courtroom truth–lie questioning may underestimate children's understanding. As such, it is important to utilize research to assess how to elicit the truth from children who testify. First, we will focus on how children are questioned about truth–lie in court, before examining the effectiveness of asking children to promise to tell the truth.

Truth–lie questioning in court. As previously noted, courtroom questioning is likely to underestimate children's understanding of truth-telling, as well as their understanding of the associated morality. But what does this look like? Examining children's testimonies, Evans and Lyon (2012) found that about half of truth–lie competency questions were focused on the meaning of these terms and half on the moral implications of lying (e.g., whether it is good to tell the truth). For questions about meaning, children provided more inaccurate responses when asked to define the terms, as opposed to when asked to identify if statements were truthful or if they knew the difference between true and untrue statements. For questions about morality, children provided the most inaccurate statements when asked about the consequences of lying (e.g., "Does anything happen to someone who tells a lie?") versus when they were asked to evaluate the morality of truth (e.g., "Is it good to tell the truth?").

Furthermore, the form of the question mattered. Children erred most when asked a "Do you know" question (DYK; e.g., "Do you know what it means to tell the truth?"). These questions may be challenging for children because they have both an explicit question ("Do you know") and an implicit question ("What does it mean to tell the truth?"; Evans et al., 2014, 2017; Stolzenberg et al., 2020). In this context, DYK questions about truth–lie may have artificially increased children's "no" responses, out of desire to avoid acknowledging knowing negative information (Evans & Lyon, 2012). It is likely that hypothetical questions about the meaning of lying and the consequences of lying underestimate children's ability because their awareness of the negativity of lying make them reluctant to discuss lies (Evans & Lyon, 2012; Lyon & Saywitz, 1999).

Taken together, courtroom questioning about truth–lie competency likely underestimates children's understanding of the concepts, particularly given that many courtroom questions are unnecessarily difficult and sometimes altogether unnecessary (Evans & Lyon, 2012). As such, courtroom questioning about truth–lie competency is not a clear way of determining whether children understand the concepts themselves or if children's responses to them are predictive of whether they will be honest (Lyon, 2011) or accurate (Goodman et al., 1991). Therefore, many have asserted that they provide little value, and more focus should be placed on whether children will promise to tell the truth.

The effectiveness of promising to tell the truth. It might be more effective to focus on whether children will explicitly promise to tell the truth and how this might influence children's truthfulness. Promising requires an interpersonal commitment and may also appeal to children's sense of morality by both telling the truth and maintaining trust (Lyon & Evans, 2014). Numerous early laboratory studies found that asking children to promise to tell the truth appeared to increase children's willingness to disclose adult wrongdoing without increasing false reporting (Lyon & Dorado, 2008; Lyon et al., 2008; Talwar et al., 2002). Yet, researchers have questioned whether this effect is consistent across different groups of children.

In a few laboratory studies, researchers found that young children may be less influenced by a promise to tell the truth (Lyon et al., 2008; Quas et al., 2018; Talwar et al., 2002). Lyon and colleagues (2008) found that when asked about an adult's transgression, 4- to 5-year-olds' responses were similar in both the control group and those asked to promise. It's possible that because young children find promises less meaningful than older children, they do not yet fully comprehend the binding nature of a promise, where, when broken, can undermine the trust between those individuals (Quas et al., 2018). McWilliams and colleagues (2021) tested the effectiveness of the promise between maltreated and nonmaltreated 4- to 9-year-olds in a laboratory setting with an adult who committed a minor transgression. They found that promising to tell the truth did increase children's accurate reporting of a minor adult transgression, but only for nonmaltreated children. Maltreated children could have an increased motivation to conceal adult transgressions (McWilliams et al., 2021). It is also likely that as the challenges of keeping a promise increase, the effectiveness of the promise will likely decrease (McWilliams et al., 2021).

However, these data directly conflict with prior studies where researchers found that making a promise to tell the truth may work for maltreated children (Lyon & Dorado, 2008; Lyon et al., 2008). An unchallenged finding is that for maltreated children, utilizing a promise reduces their false allegations (Lyon et al., 2014); what appears more difficult is to reduce their false negatives, particularly when they feel implicated in a joint transgression and are questioned about it.

So where does this leave legal practitioners with truth–lie competency assessments? Questioning children about their understanding of truth, lies, and the importance of telling the truth is challenging, error-inducing, and does not predict whether children will tell the truth (Lyon, 2011). When legal requirements in the United States necessitate that children demonstrate truth–lie competency, a promise to tell the truth may be more effective; however, this may not work as well for young and maltreated children. Practically though, very young children are unlikely to testify. According to recent data, nearly all child victims who testify are at least 6 years old (Stolzenberg et al., 2020). As such, the concerns about effectiveness for younger children (e.g., 4- and 5-year-olds) are less relevant to courtroom competency evaluations than the concern about effectiveness for maltreated children. Researchers need to continue to conduct more examinations of how a promise to tell the truth may differentially influence maltreated children, as they are likely to testify. In practice, the issue does not seem to be whether children will be willing to promise to tell the truth—almost all are willing to do so—but whether the promise will be associated with their increased accuracy. As such, the current research does not suggest that courtrooms should avoid asking children to promise to tell the truth but instead do so with an understanding that it might have limited efficacy in some cases.

DIRECT- AND CROSS-EXAMINATION

After children are deemed competent, they testify. Here, attorneys have different goals. It is necessary for prosecutors to establish children's credibility in direct examination. In doing so, prosecutors need to preempt or rebuff concerns that may come up by the defense. Their main goal is to corroborate the child's allegations in a manner that makes the child look credible (Myers, 2017). Whereas in the interest of advocating for the defendant, it is the job of the defense attorney to question the child's credibility during cross-examination; they must evaluate whether allegations are honest or suggestively influenced, are consistent across time, and are plausible (Denne et al., 2020). Fundamentally, the goal of the defense attorney is to undermine the child's credibility in the hope that jurors will deem the child inaccurate or untruthful (Myers, 2017).

The stakes are high. If a false allegation is deemed credible, an outcome may include imprisonment for an innocent suspect. If a true allegation is found to lack credibility, children may be unprotected from a perpetrator. Given these dynamics, researchers have devoted effort to understanding how children are questioned in court, with a focus on how methods might undermine or facilitate children's accuracy and productivity. Generally, researchers focus on two related elements: the style of questioning and the content of the questions.

Questioning Style and the Influence on Children's Testimony

Although our focus is on children in court, the style of pretrial questioning (during forensic interviews) has implications for how children should be questioned when on the stand. Forensic interviewers have clear guidelines for how to question children. Some child advocacy centers rely on some form of the most well-researched approach to interviewing—the National Institute of Child Health and Human Development (NICHD) Protocol—and many others look to the research on interviewing for guidance on structuring their interviews. The NICHD Protocol was developed from foundational laboratory and field research documenting how to question children about their prior experiences (Lamb et al., 2018). One central tenet of the NICHD Protocol (and others like it), which is foundational to eliciting accurate and complete reports from children, concerns the precise phrasing of the questions themselves (e.g., the words the questioner uses). In essence, researchers find that the way in which a question is asked greatly influences how children will respond, including what kinds of details children will report, whether those details will be accurate, how many details will be reported, and whether those details will accurately reflect the experience in question. This is important because when children provide cohesive, thoughtful, and clear accounts of their allegations, this resonates with jurors as credible (Pichler et al., 2020).

One can think about the linguistic form of questions as spanning a continuum from open to leading (Lamb et al., 2018; Stolzenberg et al., 2020). Although more granular distinctions are available, some simplify the categorization by denoting that questions can be categorized as open-ended (e.g., requesting an elaborative response) or closed-ended (requiring a single word or detail; Malloy & Stolzenberg, 2019). In the most succinct summary, guidelines recommend that questioners need to ask nonsuggestive, open-ended questions, which result in longer, more detailed, and more accurate responses (Lamb et al., 2018). It is commonly accepted that asking closed-ended questions, which are typically defined as yes/no or forced-choice questions, as well as more suggestive questions that communicate an expected response from children by presupposing information that the questioner had not previously mentioned (e.g., "He hurt you, didn't he?"), are more likely to elicit inaccurate and incomplete responses from children (Lamb et al., 2018).

Closed-Ended Questioning in Children's Courtroom Testimony

In criminal court, closed-ended questions predominate; multiple teams of researchers, across multiple countries, find that most questions during testimony can be answered with unelaborated responses (Andrews & Lamb, 2016;

Hanna et al., 2012; Henderson et al., 2019; Stolzenberg et al., 2020; Zajac & Cannan, 2009; Zajac et al., 2012). In the most recent sample of U.S. criminal trials, Stolzenberg and colleagues (2020) found that 75% of questions asked of children during direct- and cross-examination were closed-ended. The problem is that these questions are likely to elicit underinformative responses—younger children, such as those from 3 to 6 years old, will give simple yeses, nos, or proffered responses (e.g., selecting one of the options from a question stem; Stolzenberg et al., 2017b). Some have referred to this as formal reticence (Stolzenberg & Lyon, 2017; Stolzenberg et al., 2020). The concern is that children are predisposed to produce easily retrievable and minimally sufficient responses to questions based on the question form and that such responses can mislead those who are evaluating children's reports (Lyon et al., 2019; Stolzenberg et al., 2017a, 2020).

Children's unelaborated responses can lead to problematic miscommunications, because they simplify or misconstrue the truth. In an investigation about how children describe clothing placement, children provided minimally sufficient responses by only offering unelaborated responses about whether clothes were "on" or "off" when the question allowed them to do so (e.g., yes/no questions "Were the clothes on?"; forced-choice "Were the clothes on or off?"), but provided intermediate descriptions of clothing placement (e.g., describing the clothes as partially removed, "The pants were pulled down") when asked open-ended questions (e.g., "Where were the clothes?"; Stolzenberg et al., 2017b). In cases of alleged child sexual abuse, these discussions about clothing placement are common when children testify, and children received open-ended questions about clothing placement only 9% of the time during direct- and cross-examination, with the remainder of the questions about clothing placement taking various forms of closed-ended questioning (Stolzenberg & Lyon, 2017). Although prosecutors were more likely to ask Wh- questions (12% of their questions about clothing placement) than defense attorneys (4%), the percentages were small. This likely led to miscommunications, particularly given the parallel laboratory findings where 3- to 6-year-olds misreported clothing placement if asked a closed-ended question when clothing was intermediately placed (Stolzenberg et al., 2017b; Wylie et al., 2021). Beyond formal reticence, children are likely to contradict themselves in response to closed-ended questions (Andrews & Lamb, 2016).

Across samples, researchers find that both prosecuting and defense attorneys exhibit little sensitivity to the age of the child, meaning there are few differences in how they phrase questions for younger and older children (Andrews et al., 2015a, 2015b, 2016; Evans et al., 2009; Klemfuss et al., 2014; Stolzenberg & Lyon, 2014b). As such, the frequency of closed-ended questions in court likely undermines children's ability to provide productive, accurate, and coherent reports. However, it is important to note that the use of focused questions, including some closed-ended questions (such as yes/no questions) may be necessary in court depending on the child's age or state of fear; courtrooms can be very stressful environments for children that is challenging to duplicate in the lab or in child advocacy centers (Goodman et al., 1992).

Suggestive questioning. Some closed-ended questions, especially those that are linguistically suggestive or grammatically complex, hold additional concerns (Brennan & Brennan, 1988). Suggestive questions communicate the questioner's intended response (Cassel et al., 1996). Some forms include *negative term questions* (e.g., yes/no question beginning with a negative term, "Didn't it hurt?"), *declarative questions* (e.g., turning a statement into a question, "And he didn't hurt you?"), and *tag questions* (e.g., tags at the end of declarative statements, "It hurt, didn't it?"). These questions are common during children's testimony (Klemfuss et al., 2014; Stolzenberg & Lyon, 2014b; Stolzenberg et al., 2020). In one assessment of 5- to 17-year-olds testifying about alleged child sexual abuse, tag and negative term questions represented 8% of questioning and declarative questions represented another 21% (see Stolzenberg et al., 2020). Here, researchers found that defense attorneys asked over twice as many tag questions as prosecutors, whereas both attorneys asked many declarative questions. Linguistically suggestive questions, particularly tag and negative term questions, are likely to cause increased problems for children's accuracy and productivity (Cassel et al., 1996; Lamb et al., 2018). Children provide more unelaborated and nonsubstantive responses to suggestive questions compared to other kinds of closed-ended questions (Stolzenberg et al., 2020). Declarative questions (e.g., "You were scared?") need further study independent of other question types, as researchers have rarely examined how their suggestiveness affects children's responses.

Attorney Goals and the Linguistic Form of Questioning

There is a misfit between the kinds of questions attorneys ask and methods that produce accurate reports. By asking many closed-ended and suggestive questions, attorneys risk children's inaccurate and inconsistent reporting, which undermines the ability to ascertain the truth (Cheit, 2014; Lyon et al., 2017). Indeed, children may be particularly susceptible to defense attorneys' questioning (Cheit, 2014; Lyon & Stolzenberg, 2014; Stolzenberg & Lyon, 2014b): Researchers find that defense attorneys' questions are more linguistically complex (Zajac & Hayne, 2003; Zajac et al., 2003). Yet, using forensic interviewing protocols in court is unlikely given the adversarial nature of the U.S. system (and other countries with similar systems). Prosecutors and defense attorneys have varying goals and competing truths. Defense attorneys are allowed to be leading during cross-examination (Mueller & Kirkpatrick, 2007); their ultimate role is to advocate for their client and do so persuasively. They will want to highlight inconsistencies and incoherence by asking complex, leading, and difficult questions. Defense attorneys likely see a benefit in decreasing children's productivity and maximizing miscommunications as well as contextualizing children's narratives as confusing or lacking credibility (Stolzenberg et al., 2020). Here, it is the job of prosecutors and judges to intervene when children are asked inappropriate questions and questions they cannot comprehend or cannot answer well (Myers, 2017).

Although prosecutors are generally more aligned with best practices, they still ask mostly closed-ended questions (Bruer et al., 2022). Here, the logic is less clear. Prosecutors have the goal of trying to present children's reports in the best light, so it would be safe to presume that they want to elicit accurate and coherent reports. Yet it is possible that prosecutors may know what is considered best practice for questioning children, but they may choose to use more direct means to maintain control (Myers, 1987; Stolzenberg et al., 2020), not recognizing how much this might undermine children's productivity, accuracy, and coherence. Prosecutors maintain the ability to ask children to clarify their reports during redirect, which gives an opportunity to correct misinterpretations that arise previously. However, it would be better to prevent inconsistencies and miscommunications from the start. As such, prosecutors should aim to elicit accurate and coherent details throughout. They can do so by asking more focused wh- questions during direct- and redirect examination in place of more yes/no questions; in doing so they can still maintain some control and facilitate better responses. Indeed, researchers find that wh- questions can be more productive than yes/no questions in trial testimony (Andrews et al., 2016; Szojka et al., 2023). In addition, prosecutors need to object when children are asked inappropriate questions during cross-examination. Although there may be practical reasons why prosecutors may not want to object (e.g., fear of angering the judge, odds of it getting overruled), research has found that prosecutors rarely object during cross-examination, even when it seems most appropriate to do so (Andrews & Lamb, 2017; Andrews et al., 2015b). For example, when looking specifically at the asked-and-answered objection, Andrews and colleagues (2015b) found that on 61 occasions in criminal trial testimonies of 6- to 12-year-olds, questions to children were repeated at least nine or more times without objection. In addition, fewer than 25% of cases included an objection to this type of questioning during the child's testimony, even though repeated questions occurred with regularity in nearly every case (Andrews et al., 2015b).

Another approach for prosecutors is to pair closed-ended questions with open-ended ones. As Stolzenberg and colleagues (2020) described, attorneys concerned with both control and expediency might narrow the child's scope of testimony by using a closed-ended question (e.g., "Did you tell your mom about what happened with X?") and then asking the child to elaborate through focused wh- questions (e.g., "What did you tell your mom?"). Such an approach might present a reasonable avenue for prosecutors to better facilitate accurate reports for children while still allowing them to maintain control over the flow of information.

Questioning Content and the Influence on Children's Testimony

The complex language in questioning often interacts with difficult content. Beyond the form of the question itself being difficult, children are asked about topics they may struggle to discuss, and the difficulty of the two (linguistics and content) can increase misunderstandings. Denne and colleagues (2020) examined trial transcripts and found that most questions asked in testimony focused on whether children had been suggestively influenced, the plausibility of what children described, and whether children were consistently reporting details across time. Here, potential for miscommunication and confusion abound. Furthermore, Andrews and Lamb (2018) found that 40% of questioning during testimony focused on peripheral details, which may be particularly challenging for children to report.

Suggestive Influence

Attorneys are motivated to establish or undermine the truthfulness of children's reports. One intensified element with children is whether they have been suggestively influenced. In fact, during testimony nearly all children are asked many questions about their prior conversations, with the average child asked about five different prior disclosure recipients (Stolzenberg & Lyon, 2014b). Attorneys do this as a means of assessing what was said to whom and under what circumstances, to evaluate the likelihood of influence, coaching, and the plausibility of disclosures (Lyon & Stolzenberg, 2014). In addition, they do so as a means of bringing in prior disclosures as admissible corroborative evidence that abuse occurred. When they do so, the words that attorneys use matter. Research has found that 6- to 11-year-olds assent that they were told something when they were asked, depending on the question form, and the ability to distinguish between "ask" and "tell" increases with age (Stolzenberg et al., 2017a; Wylie, McWilliams, et al., 2022).

Attorneys, and particularly defense attorneys, may ask children about whether they have been coached or otherwise suggestively influenced through indirect means (e.g., "Did your mom help you remember?" "Did you practice what to say with the detective?"; St. George, Sullivan, et al., 2022). These questions imply something positive to the child (e.g., an adult being helpful) and something negative to other adults (e.g., the helpful adult is shaping the child's report). Research has found that when compared to more explicit questions, implicatures result in increased assents from children, which wrongly imply coaching occurred when it did not (Wylie et al., 2023; Wylie, St. George, et al., 2022). In an assessment of trials, St. George, Sullivan, and colleagues (2022) found that 66% of attorneys' questions about suggestive influence or truthfulness were indirect accusations ("Did your mom practice with you before coming to court?"). Defense attorneys made more indirect accusations about suggestive influence than prosecutors, but prosecutors still accounted for 46% of all indirect accusations; the researchers found that defense attorneys' questions tended to be more implicit, whereas prosecutors still asked many implicit questions about these topics that could be quite tricky for children testifying. Although defense attorneys may purposefully ask children indirectly, prosecutors may be unintentionally asking children difficult questions about suggestive influence, leading to clear miscommunications.

Plausibility

Attorneys are often focused on the details of children's reports. Yet, in some cases, asking about these details may be developmentally inappropriate. For example, attorneys spend an enormous amount of time questioning children about specific details like the location of events, timing of events, and other witnesses who could know information or have been present during allegations (Andrews & Lamb, 2018). Attorneys often question children about the sequencing of events and spatial relations within the alleged abuse incident(s) (St. George et al., 2022b). Research has found that young children have a difficult time explaining the temporal elements of abuse, such as the order of episodes, duration, frequency, and the location of specific acts in time, relative to specific dates (McWilliams et al., 2019, 2023; Wandrey et al., 2012). Because children's ability to describe timing and spatial relations develops with age, these questions may be particularly difficult for young children (particularly those 6 to 10 years old).

Yet children's difficulty is not specific to these topics. For example, in a recent examination of criminal testimonies of 5- to 12-year-olds in alleged sexual abuse cases, Sullivan, St. George, and colleagues (2022) found that questions about the mechanics of abuse (e.g., precise descriptions of physical interactions), which are difficult to describe, often interacted with poor questioning, and this corresponded to underinformative responses from children as well as clear miscommunications. Relatedly, young children (4- to 9-year-olds) may struggle to report touching, particularly when asked yes/no questions, compared to open-ended questions, and the ability to report varying forms of touch (e.g., being touched with the mouth instead of a hand) improves with age; researchers find that young children do not think that nonmanual touching or touching with an object constitutes touching (Sullivan, Stolzenberg, et al., 2022). This is not uncommon across various topics that arise in direct- and cross-examination. What attorneys are really trying to get at with these questions is a sense of whether the child's report is plausible; whether there is a reasonable likelihood that the events could have unfolded as the child described them (St. George et al., 2022b). To understand whether children's reports are believable, attorneys seek to elicit specific details of victimization, such as the mechanics of how abuse occurred and the context of the abuse.

However, plausibility relies on more than just asking about specific details. As described by St. George and colleagues (2022b), when assessing plausibility, attorneys can highlight misconceptions about victimization, discuss unbelievable statements or descriptions, and simultaneously offer alternative explanations for the child's statements or reports. In these ways, defense attorneys are likely to capitalize on commonly held misconceptions about victimization to undermine believability (Denne et al., 2023). Descriptions of abuse, particularly sexual abuse, can be counterintuitive, and jurors' perceptions are influenced by myths and misperceptions about victimization, such as abuse always involves force (St. George et al., 2022a). Defense attorneys may highlight the counterintuitive features of abuse to exploit jurors' misperceptions, thereby calling allegation plausibility into question. In an assessment of trials, St. George and colleagues (2022b) found that 57% of defense attorneys' plausibility questions highlighted misperceptions about abuse. Furthermore, by assessing jurors' questions after children testified in criminal cases, researchers found that jurors often question these common misconceptions and myths about abuse, even after redirect examination (St. George et al., 2020).

Consistency

Attorneys will assess children's credibility by asking about the consistency of the child's report across time. Indeed, attorney guides recommend that defense attorneys attempt to impeach children through inquiring about prior inconsistent statements (Myers, 1987), and prosecutors are instructed to address inconsistencies as well (Bailey & Rothblatt, 1985). Here, defense attorneys will do so to highlight children as unbelievable or lacking credibility. However, it is likely that children may have a difficult time explaining inconsistencies. In addition, inconsistency does not necessarily mean the child is lying.

There are multiple reasons why children might be inconsistent when reporting victimization. First, children may be inconsistent because a long period of time has passed between when they originally reported abuse and when they are testifying; just the time between when a prosecutor files charges and when the child testifies is often at least 8 months (Stolzenberg & Lyon, 2014b). This does not account for the delay that is typical between when abuse begins and when children disclose (McElvaney, 2015). In addition, when children are exposed to repeated questioning, which is common in trials, this can increase their inconsistent responses (Andrews & Lamb, 2014, 2021). Indeed, prior to trial, children are usually interviewed numerous times when reporting abuse, so experiencing repeated questioning across interviews is very likely (Malloy et al., 2007). All these factors may be exacerbated with suggestive questioning, as well as when children experienced repeated abuse and must rely on source memory to distinguish between specific episodes of abuse (Brubacher & La Rooy, 2014; Denne et al., 2020). And yet, nearly all children who testify are victims of repeated abusive episodes (Stolzenberg & Lyon, 2014a), meaning that children may struggle to give consistent and coherent accounts of what occurred in specific instances (Quas et al., 2007). As such, expecting children to report consistent details, particularly when asked such a large proportion of questions about specific details, is a very high bar indeed. Prosecutors should do their best to avoid repeated questions and be prepared to both address and rehabilitate child witnesses by educating jurors about realistic expectations regarding consistency.

SUGGESTIONS AND FUTURE DIRECTIONS

Children are likely to testify in court in the United States, given the rate of child victimization, as well as the structure of our legal system. Even though this process is likely quite stressful for children (Goodman et al., 1992), it is unlikely to change. Still, there are pathways for reform to ensure that children can provide their best testimony and experience the least amount of stress possible.

Practically, children who testify in court are likely to pass competency assessments (Evans & Lyon, 2012). Children's responses to contemporary competency assessments can provide information for legal practitioners that may help assess children's overall ability to provide testimony. When legal practitioners must assess basic competency, they should utilize some form of narrative practice rapport-building. Doing so will allow them to ascertain how well children can narrate about a prior event, which will likely have additional positive consequences for children's subsequent testimony (e.g., providing more details throughout). In assessing truth–lie competency, questions about children's definitional understanding can be challenging to phrase well and are not always predictive of children's later honesty. When truth–lie competency is assessed, relying on children's promises to tell the truth may be effective. There is mixed research on the efficacy of this practice for maltreated children, but there are also some data to support the practice (Evans & Lyon, 2012). Researchers should continue to assess how taking an oath might differentially affect younger and maltreated children compared to other groups of children.

Currently, the practices in direct- and cross-examination are likely to increase children's miscommunications and contradictions, while producing inaccurate information from children. There is much we can do to improve the quality of information we receive from children testifying. Limiting the scope of cross-examination is unlikely; defense attorneys are allowed to lead on cross-examination and have an inherent benefit in eliciting miscommunications and contradictions from children. But others in the courtroom can work to reduce inappropriate questions. One avenue is for prosecutors to increase their objections to developmentally inappropriate questions; currently, researchers find that prosecutors do so only infrequently (Andrews & Lamb, 2017; Andrews et al., 2015b). Another avenue is to train judges to exercise greater control over what they allow to occur during cross-examination. If they are trained to understand the linguistic and content challenges posed by various questions, they can prohibit these questions and ensure queries are rephrased so that children can understand (Myers, 2017). A final avenue might be better preparing children for what they might experience during cross-examination; researchers find that children who receive pretrial practice on cross-examination style questioning about unrelated topics do better later (Irvine et al., 2016). This might be a way of reducing the detrimental effects of cross-examination for children.

Furthermore, researchers can continue to work with prosecutors to examine and train attorneys on best practices for direct examination (Powell, 2005). Prosecutors can reduce the linguistic complexity of their questions, focus on the necessary parts of a child's narrative while asking fewer questions about unnecessary details, pair closed-ended questions with open-ended questions, and ensure that they ask about developmentally difficult content in ways that researchers have found to produce the most accurate reports from children. If prosecutors can reduce contradictions and miscommunications in direct examination, this will have cascading effects for children's later testimony.

Furthermore, prosecutors can add questions that may repair or benefit children's perceived credibility. For example, asking children about their subjective reactions to abuse (e.g., "How did your body feel?") can elicit responses from children that make their narratives more well-rounded and believable (Ahern & Lyon, 2013; Stolzenberg et al., 2021).

CONCLUSION

Although there is questionable efficacy of courtroom questioning in eliciting accurate and productive reports from children, the reality is that children will testify in direct- and cross-examination in the United States. Researchers and legal practitioners need to be aware of best practices for encouraging children to provide their most truthful, complete, and coherent reports, and then be able to apply these practices within the framework of our legal system to best serve children, their families, and those accused of crimes.

REFERENCES

Ahern, E. C., & Lyon, T. D. (2013). Facilitating maltreated children's use of emotional language. *Journal of Forensic Social Work, 3*(2), 176–203. https://doi.org/10.1080/1936928X.2013.854124

Ahern, E. C., Stolzenberg, S. N., & Lyon, T. D. (2015). Do prosecutors use interview instructions or build rapport with child witnesses? *Behavioral Sciences & the Law, 33*(4), 476–492. https://doi.org/10.1002/bsl.2183

Andrews, S. J., Ahern, E. C., Stolzenberg, S. N., & Lyon, T. D. (2016). The productivity of wh- prompts when children testify. *Applied Cognitive Psychology, 30*(3), 341–349. https://doi.org/10.1002/acp.3204

Andrews, S. J., & Lamb, M. E. (2014). The effects of age and delay on responses to repeated questions in forensic interviews with children alleging sexual abuse. *Law and Human Behavior, 38*(2), 171–180. https://doi.org/10.1037/lhb0000064

Andrews, S. J., & Lamb, M. E. (2016). How do lawyers examine and cross-examine children in Scotland? *Applied Cognitive Psychology, 30*(6), 953–971. https://doi.org/10.1002/acp.3286

Andrews, S. J., & Lamb, M. E. (2017). The structural linguistic complexity of lawyers' questions and children's responses in Scottish criminal courts. *Child Abuse & Neglect, 65*, 182–193. https://doi.org/10.1016/j.chiabu.2017.01.022

Andrews, S. J., & Lamb, M. E. (2018). Cross-examining young alleged complainers in Scottish criminal courts. *Criminal Law Review, 2018*(1), 34–57. https://keele-repository.worktribe.com/output/409337/cross-examining-young-alleged-complainers-in-scottish-criminal-courts

Andrews, S. J., & Lamb, M. E. (2021). Lawyers' question repetition and children's responses in Scottish criminal courts. *Journal of Interpersonal Violence, 36*(1–2), 276–296. https://doi.org/10.1177/0886260517725739

Andrews, S. J., Lamb, M. E., & Lyon, T. D. (2015a). The effects of question repetition on responses when prosecutors and defense attorneys question children alleging sexual abuse in court. *Law and Human Behavior, 39*(6), 559–570. https://doi.org/10.1037/lhb0000152

Andrews, S. J., Lamb, M. E., & Lyon, T. D. (2015b). Question types, responsiveness and self-contradictions when prosecutors and defense attorneys question alleged victims of child sexual abuse. *Applied Cognitive Psychology, 29*(2), 253–261. https://doi.org/10.1002/acp.3103

Bailey, F. L., & Rothblatt, H. B. (1985). *Successful techniques for criminal trials* (2nd ed.). Lawyers Cooperative Publishing.

Brennan, M., & Brennan, R. E. (1988). *Strange language: Child victims under cross examination*. Riverina Murray Institute of Higher Education.

Brubacher, S. P., & La Rooy, D. (2014). Witness recall across repeated interviews in a case of repeated abuse. *Child Abuse & Neglect, 38*(2), 202–211. https://doi.org/10.1016/j.chiabu.2013.06.010

Bruer, K. C., Williams, S., & Evans, A. D. (2022). Lawyers' experience questioning children in Canadian court. *Child Abuse & Neglect, 134*, 105930. https://doi.org/10.1016/j.chiabu.2022.105930

Bussey, K. (1992). Lying and truthfulness: Children's definitions, standards, and evaluative reactions. *Child Development, 63*(1), 129–137. https://doi.org/10.2307/1130907

Bussey, K. (2009). An international perspective on child witnesses. In B. L. Bottoms, C. J. Najdowski, & G. S. Goodman (Eds.), *Children as victims, witnesses, and offenders: Psychological science and the law* (pp. 209–232). Guilford Press.

Cassel, W. S., Roebers, C. E. M., & Bjorklund, D. F. (1996). Developmental patterns of eyewitness responses to repeated and increasingly suggestive questions. *Journal of Experimental Child Psychology, 61*(2), 116–133. https://doi.org/10.1006/jecp.1996.0008

Ceci, S. J., & de Bruyn, E. (1993). Child witnesses in court: A growing dilemma. *Children Today, 22*(1), 5–9.

Cheit, R. E. (2014). *The witch-hunt narrative: Politics, psychology, and the sexual abuse of children*. Oxford University Press.

Denne, E., St. George, S., & Stolzenberg, S. N. (2023). Myths and misunderstandings about child sexual abuse in criminal investigations. *Journal of Interpersonal Violence, 38*(1–2), NP1893–NP1919. https://doi.org/10.1177/08862605221093679

Denne, E., Sullivan, C., Ernest, K., & Stolzenberg, S. N. (2020). Assessing children's credibility in courtroom investigations of alleged child sexual abuse: Suggestibility, plausibility, and consistency. *Child Maltreatment, 25*(2), 224–232. https://doi.org/10.1177/1077559519872825

Evans, A. D., Lee, K., & Lyon, T. D. (2009). Complex questions asked by defense lawyers but not prosecutors predicts convictions in child abuse trials. *Law and Human Behavior, 33*(3), 258–264. https://doi.org/10.1007/s10979-008-9148-6

Evans, A. D., & Lyon, T. D. (2012). Assessing children's competency to take the oath in court: The influence of question type on children's accuracy. *Law and Human Behavior, 36*(3), 195–205. https://doi.org/10.1037/h0093957

Evans, A. D., Stolzenberg, S. N., Lee, K., & Lyon, T. D. (2014). Young children's difficulty with indirect speech acts: Implications for questioning child witnesses. *Behavioral Sciences & the Law, 32*(6), 775–788. https://doi.org/10.1002/bsl.2142

Evans, A. D., Stolzenberg, S. N., & Lyon, T. D. (2017). Pragmatic failure and referential ambiguity when attorneys ask child witnesses "do you know/remember" questions. *Psychology, Public Policy, and Law, 23*(2), 191–199. https://doi.org/10.1037/law0000116

Finkelhor, D. (2011). Prevalence of child victimization, abuse, crime, and violence exposure. In J. W. White, M. P. Koss, & A. E. Kazdin (Eds.), *Violence against women and children: Vol. 1. Mapping the terrain* (pp. 9–29). American Psychological Association. https://doi.org/10.1037/12307-001

Goodman, G. S., Hirschman, J. E., Hepps, D., & Rudy, L. (1991). Children's memory for stressful events. *Merrill-Palmer Quarterly, 37*(1), 109–157. http://www.jstor.org/stable/23087341

Goodman, G. S., Quas, J. A., Bulkley, J., & Shapiro, C. (1999). Innovations for child witnesses: A national survey. *Psychology, Public Policy, and Law, 5*(2), 255–281. https://doi.org/10.1037/1076-8971.5.2.255

Goodman, G. S., Taub, E. P., Jones, D. P., England, P., Port, L. K., Rudy, L., & Prado, L. (1992). Testifying in criminal court: Emotional effects on child sexual assault victims.

Monographs of the Society for Research in Child Development, 57(5), i–159. https://doi.org/10.2307/1166127

Hanna, K., Davies, E., Crothers, C., & Henderson, E. (2012). Questioning child witnesses in New Zealand's criminal justice system: Is cross-examination fair? *Psychiatry, Psychology and Law, 19*(4), 530–546. https://doi.org/10.1080/13218719.2011.615813

Henderson, H. M., Andrews, S. J., & Lamb, M. E. (2019). Examining children in English high courts with and without implementation of reforms authorized in Section 28 of the Youth Justice and Criminal Evidence Act. *Applied Cognitive Psychology, 33*(2), 252–264. https://doi.org/10.1002/acp.3472

Henderson, H. M., & Lamb, M. (2017). Pre-recording children's trial testimony: Effects on the criminal justice system. *Criminal Law Review, 5*, 345–356.

Hershkowitz, I. (2009). Socioemotional factors in child sexual abuse investigations. *Child Maltreatment, 14*(2), 172–181. https://doi-org.ezproxy1.lib.asu.edu/10.1177/1077559508326224

Hoyano, L., & Keenan, C. (2007). *Child abuse: Law and policy across boundaries*. Oxford University Press.

Irvine, B., Jack, F., & Zajac, R. (2016). Preparing children for cross-examination: Do the practice questions matter? *Psychology, Crime & Law, 22*(9), 858–878. https://doi.org/10.1080/1068316X.2016.1197224

Klemfuss, J. Z., & Ceci, S. J. (2012). Legal and psychological perspectives on children's competence to testify in court. *Developmental Review, 32*(3), 268–286. https://doi.org/10.1016/j.dr.2012.06.005

Klemfuss, J. Z., Quas, J. A., & Lyon, T. D. (2014). Attorneys' questions and children's productivity in child sexual abuse criminal trials. *Applied Cognitive Psychology, 28*(5), 780–788. https://doi.org/10.1002/acp.3048

Lamb, M. E., Brown, D. A., Hershkowitz, I., Orbach, Y., & Esplin, P. W. (2018). *Tell me what happened: Questioning children about abuse*. John Wiley & Sons.

Lyon, T. D. (2011). Assessing the competency of child witnesses: Best practice informed by psychology and law. In M. E. Lamb, D. J. La Rooy, L. C. Malloy, & C. Katz (Eds.), *Children's testimony: A handbook of psychological research and forensic practice* (pp. 69–85). Wiley-Blackwell.

Lyon, T. D., & Dente, J. A. (2012). Child witnesses and the confrontation clause. *The Journal of Criminal Law & Criminology, 102*(4), 1181–1232. https://scholarlycommons.law.northwestern.edu/jclc/vol102/iss4/3

Lyon, T. D., & Dorado, J. S. (2008). Truth induction in young maltreated children: The effects of oath-taking and reassurance on true and false disclosures. *Child Abuse & Neglect, 32*(7), 738–748. https://doi.org/10.1016/j.chiabu.2007.08.008

Lyon, T. D., & Evans, A. D. (2014). Young children's understanding that promising guarantees performance: The effects of age and maltreatment. *Law and Human Behavior, 38*(2), 162–170. https://doi.org/10.1037/lhb0000061

Lyon, T. D., Malloy, L. C., Quas, J. A., & Talwar, V. A. (2008). Coaching, truth induction, and young maltreated children's false allegations and false denials. *Child Development, 79*(4), 914–929. https://doi.org/10.1111/j.1467-8624.2008.01167.x

Lyon, T. D., McWilliams, K., & Williams, S. (2019). Child witnesses. In N. Brewer & A. B. Douglass (Eds.), *Psychological science and the law* (pp. 157–181). Guilford Press.

Lyon, T. D., Quas, J. A., & Carrick, N. (2013). Right and righteous: Children's incipient understanding and evaluation of true and false statements. *Journal of Cognition and Development, 14*(3), 437–454. https://doi.org/10.1080/15248372.2012.673187

Lyon, T. D., & Saywitz, K. J. (1999). Young maltreated children's competence to take the oath. *Applied Developmental Science, 3*(1), 16–27. https://doi.org/10.1207/s1532480xads0301_3

Lyon, T. D., & Stolzenberg, S. N. (2014). Children's memory for conversations about sexual abuse: Legal and psychological implications. *Roger Williams University Law Review, 19*(2), 411–450. https://docs.rwu.edu/rwu_LR/vol19/iss2/5

Lyon, T. D., Stolzenberg, S. N., & McWilliams, K. (2017). Wrongful acquittals of sexual abuse. *Journal of Interpersonal Violence, 32*(6), 805–825. https://doi.org/10.1177/0886260516657355

Lyon, T. D., Wandrey, L., Ahern, E., Licht, R., Sim, M. P., & Quas, J. A. (2014). Eliciting maltreated and nonmaltreated children's transgression disclosures: Narrative practice rapport building and a putative confession. *Child Development, 85*(4), 1756–1769. https://doi.org/10.1111/cdev.12223

Malloy, L. C., Lyon, T. D., & Quas, J. A. (2007). Filial dependency and recantation of child sexual abuse allegations. *Journal of the American Academy of Child & Adolescent Psychiatry, 46*(2), 162–170. https://doi.org/10.1097/01.chi.0000246067.77953.f7

Malloy, L. C., & Stolzenberg, S. N. (2019). Questioning kids: Applying the lessons from developmentally-sensitive investigative interviewing to the research context. *Journal of Child Psychology and Psychiatry, and Allied Disciplines, 60*(3), 325–327. https://doi.org/10.1111/jcpp.13005

McElvaney, R. (2015). Disclosure of child sexual abuse: Delays, non-disclosure and partial disclosure. What the research tells us and implications for practice. *Child Abuse Review, 24*(3), 159–169. https://doi.org/10.1002/car.2280

McWilliams, K., Lyon, T. D., & Quas, J. A. (2019). Maltreated children's ability to make temporal judgments using a recurring landmark event. *Journal of Interpersonal Violence, 34*(4), 873–883. https://doi.org/10.1177/0886260516645812

McWilliams, K., Stolzenberg, S. N., Williams, S., & Lyon, T. (2021). Increasing maltreated and nonmaltreated children's recall disclosures of a minor transgression: The effects of back-channel utterances, a promise to tell the truth, and a post-recall putative confession. *Child Abuse & Neglect, 116*(1), 104073. https://doi.org/10.1016/j.chiabu.2019.104073

McWilliams, K., Williams, S., Henderson, H. M., Evans, A. D., & Lyon, T. D. (2023). Pseudotemporal invitations: 6-to 9-year-old maltreated children's tendency to misinterpret invitations referencing "time" as solely requesting conventional temporal information. *Child Maltreatment, 28*(2), 265–274. https://doi.org/10.1177/10775595221104829

Mueller, C. B., & Kirkpatrick, L. C. (2007). *Federal evidence* (3rd ed.). Aspen Publishers.

Myers, J. E. (1987). The child witness: Techniques for direct examination, cross-examination, and impeachment. *Pacific Law Journal, 18*(3), 801–942.

Myers, J. E. (1997). *Evidence in child abuse and neglect cases*. Aspen Publishers.

Myers, J. E. (2017). Cross-examination: A defense. *Psychology, Public Policy, and Law, 23*(4), 472–477. https://doi.org/10.1037/law0000131

Pantell, R. H., Yogman, M., Gambon, T., Lavin, A., Mattson, G., Rafferty, J. R., & Wissow, L. S. (2017). The child witness in the courtroom. *Pediatrics, 139*(3), e20164008. https://doi.org/10.1542/peds.2016-4008

Pichler, A. S., Sharman, S. J., Powell, M., Westera, N., & Goodman-Delahunty, J. (2020). Association between interview quality and child sexual abuse trial outcome. *Journal of Family Violence, 35*(4), 395–403. https://doi.org/10.1007/s10896-019-00051-5

Powell, M. B. (2005). Improving the reliability of child witness testimony in court: The importance of focusing on questioning techniques. *Current Issues in Criminal Justice, 17*(1), 137–143. https://doi.org/10.1080/10345329.2005.12036342

Quas, J. A., Davis, E. L., Goodman, G. S., & Myers, J. E. B. (2007). Repeated questions, deception, and children's true and false reports of body touch. *Child Maltreatment, 12*(1), 60–67. https://doi.org/10.1177/1077559506296141

Quas, J. A., Stolzenberg, S. N., & Lyon, T. D. (2018). The effects of promising to tell the truth, the putative confession, and recall and recognition questions on maltreated and non-maltreated children's disclosure of a minor transgression. *Journal of Experimental Child Psychology, 166*, 266–279. https://doi.org/10.1016/j.jecp.2017.08.014

Saywitz, K. J., & Camparo, L. B. (2014). *Evidence-based child forensic interviewing: The developmental narrative elaboration interview*. Oxford University Press.

Saywitz, K. J., Geiselman, R. E., & Bornstein, G. K. (1992). Effects of cognitive interviewing and practice on children's recall performance. *Journal of Applied Psychology, 77*(5), 744–756. https://doi.org/10.1037/0021-9010.77.5.744

St. George, S., Denne, E., & Stolzenberg, S. N. (2022a). Blaming children: How rape myths manifest in defense attorneys' questions to children testifying about child sexual abuse. *Journal of Interpersonal Violence, 37*(17–18), NP16623–NP16646. https://doi.org/10.1177/08862605211023485

St. George, S., Denne, E., & Stolzenberg, S. N. (2022b). 'This incident happened when there were 10 people in the house?' Exploring a framework to categorize defense attorneys' plausibility questioning in CSA trials. *Psychology, Crime & Law, 30*(6), 556–582. https://doi.org/10.1080/1068316X.2022.2104277

St. George, S., Garcia-Johnson, A., Denne, E., & Stolzenberg, S. N. (2020). "Did you ever fight back?" Jurors' questions to children testifying in criminal trials about alleged sexual abuse. *Criminal Justice and Behavior, 47*(8), 1032–1054. https://doi.org/10.1177/0093854820935960

St. George, S., Sullivan, C., Wylie, B. E., McWilliams, K., Evans, A. D., & Stolzenberg, S. N. (2022). Did your mom help you remember? An examination of attorneys' subtle questioning about suggestive influence to children testifying about child sexual abuse. *Journal of Interpersonal Violence, 37*(15-16), NP13902–NP13927. https://doi.org/10.1177/08862605211006369

Stolzenberg, S. N., & Lyon, T. D. (2014a). Evidence summarized in attorney's closing arguments predicts acquittals in criminal trials of child sexual abuse. *Child Maltreatment, 19*(2), 119–129. https://doi.org/10.1177/1077559514539388

Stolzenberg, S. N., & Lyon, T. D. (2014b). How attorneys question children about the dynamics of sexual abuse and disclosure in criminal trials. *Psychology, Public Policy, and Law, 20*(1), 19–30. https://doi.org/10.1037/a0035000

Stolzenberg, S. N., & Lyon, T. D. (2017). 'Where were your clothes?' Eliciting descriptions of clothing placement from children alleging sexual abuse in criminal trials and forensic interviews. *Legal and Criminological Psychology, 22*(2), 197–212. https://doi.org/10.1111/lcrp.12094

Stolzenberg, S. N., McWilliams, K., & Lyon, T. D. (2017a). Ask versus tell: Potential confusion when child witnesses are questioned about conversations. *Journal of Experimental Psychology: Applied, 23*(4), 447–459. https://doi.org/10.1037/xap0000136

Stolzenberg, S. N., McWilliams, K., & Lyon, T. D. (2017b). The effects of the hypothetical putative confession and negatively valenced yes/no questions on maltreated and nonmaltreated children's disclosure of a minor transgression. *Child Maltreatment, 22*(2), 167–173. https://doi.org/10.1177/1077559516673734

Stolzenberg, S. N., Morse, S. J., Haverkate, D. L., & Garcia-Johnson, A. M. (2020). The prevalence of declarative and indirect yes/no questions when children testify in criminal cases of child sexual abuse in the United States. *Applied Cognitive Psychology, 34*(1), 194–204. https://doi.org/10.1002/acp.3607

Stolzenberg, S. N., Williams, S., McWilliams, K., Liang, C., & Lyon, T. D. (2021). The utility of direct questions in eliciting subjective content from children disclosing sexual abuse. *Child Abuse & Neglect, 116*(Pt. 1), 103964. https://doi.org/10.1016/j.chiabu.2019.02.014

Sullivan, C., St. George, S., Stolzenberg, S. N., Williams, S., & Lyon, T. D. (2022). Imprecision about body mechanics when child witnesses are questioned about sexual abuse. *Journal of Interpersonal Violence, 37*(13–14), NP12375–NP12397. https://doi.org/10.1177/0886260521997941

Sullivan, C. E., Stolzenberg, S. N., Williams, S., & Lyon, T. D. (2022). Children's under-extended understanding of touch. *Psychology, Public Policy, and Law, 28*(4), 505–514. https://doi.org/10.1037/law0000374

Szojka, Z. A., Moussavi, N., Burditt, C., & Lyon, T. D. (2023). Attorneys' questions and children's responses referring to the nature of sexual touch in child sexual abuse trials. *Child Maltreatment, 28*(3), 438–449. https://doi.org/10.1177/10775595231161033

Talwar, V., Lee, K., Bala, N., & Lindsay, R. C. (2002). Children's conceptual knowledge of lying and its relation to their actual behaviors: Implications for court competence examinations. *Law and Human Behavior, 26*(4), 395–415. https://doi.org/10.1023/a:1016379104959

Wandrey, L., Lyon, T. D., Quas, J. A., & Friedman, W. F. (2012). Maltreated children's ability to estimate temporal location and numerosity of placement changes and court visits. *Psychology, Public Policy, and Law, 18*(1), 79–104. https://doi.org/10.1037/a0024812

Wylie, B., Stolzenberg, S. N., McWilliams, K., Evans, A. D., & Lyon, T. D. (2021). Young children's ability to describe intermediate clothing placement. *Child Maltreatment, 26*(1), 87–94. https://doi.org/10.1177/1077559520930825

Wylie, B. E., Evans, A. D., McWilliams, K., & Stolzenberg, S. N. (2023). Children's understanding of implied coaching questions: Does acquiescence influence perceptions of believability? *Journal of Applied Developmental Psychology, 85,* 101510. https://doi.org/10.1016/j.appdev.2022.101510

Wylie, B. E., McWilliams, K., Stolzenberg, S. N., Evans, A. D., & Lyon, T. D. (2022). Young children's understanding of the epistemic and deontic meanings of ask and tell. *Journal of Experimental Child Psychology, 224,* 105516. https://doi.org/10.1016/j.jecp.2022.105516

Wylie, B. E., St. George, S., McWilliams, K., Evans, A. D., & Stolzenberg, S. N. (2022). Children's acquiescence to polysemous implicature questions about coaching: The role of parental support. *Journal of Applied Developmental Psychology, 78,* e101370. https://doi.org/10.1016/j.appdev.2021.101370

Zajac, R., & Cannan, P. (2009). Cross-examination of sexual assault complainants: A developmental comparison. *Psychiatry, Psychology and Law, 16*(Suppl. 1), 36–54. https://doi.org/10.1080/13218710802620448

Zajac, R., Gross, J., & Hayne, H. (2003). Asked and answered: Questioning children in the courtroom. *Psychiatry, Psychology and Law, 10*(1), 199–209. https://doi.org/10.1375/pplt.2003.10.1.199

Zajac, R., & Hayne, H. (2003). I don't think that's what really happened: The effect of cross-examination on the accuracy of children's reports. *Journal of Experimental Psychology: Applied, 9*(3), 187–195. https://doi.org/10.1037/1076-898X.9.3.187

Zajac, R., O'Neill, S., & Hayne, H. (2012). Disorder in the courtroom? Child witnesses under cross-examination. *Developmental Review, 32*(3), 181–204. https://doi.org/10.1016/j.dr.2012.06.006

16

Mock Jurors' Perceptions of Child Sexual Abuse Victims

A Review

Jonathan M. Golding, Margaret C. Stevenson, Kelly C. Burke, and Mary M. Levi

In the courtroom, children often appear as crime victim witnesses, typically in child sexual abuse (CSA) cases. Their testimony is critical to the outcome of CSA cases (Myers et al., 1999), because CSA cases often lack physical evidence. However, jurors have difficulty discriminating accurate from inaccurate child testimony (Golding, Malik, et al., 2020). Given jurors' inability to reliably determine the validity of a child's testimony, what influences juror decision making in child abuse cases? Understanding factors influencing CSA case outcomes remains important, as CSA is a pervasive issue within the U.S. legal system. In 2023, 546,159 cases of child maltreatment were substantiated in the United States (Children's Bureau, 2025), a conservative estimate of actual rates. Of these cases, 7.5% were sexually abused. Yet only a fraction of CSA cases (20%) analyzed between 2009–2013 led to prosecution, many of which were later dropped (53%), and only a small proportion of CSA cases proceeded to trial (12%; Block et al., 2022).

Empirical research examining legal and extralegal factors affecting perceptions of child abuse victims in court has grown rapidly within the last few decades (for prior reviews, see Bottoms et al., 2007; Golding et al., 2009; Golding, Malik, et al., 2020). This chapter provides an updated state of the field by reviewing the impact of various factors (e.g., gender, race, intellectual disability status, etc.) on these perceptions, focusing on CSA and extending a recent review (Golding, Malik, et al., 2020). Given the broad scope of the field, our report is necessarily noncomprehensive. Therefore, we focus predominantly

https://doi.org/10.1037/0000492-016
Handbook on Child Witnesses: Improving Psychological Science and Legal Practice,
G. S. Goodman, T. D. Lyon, S. D. Hobbs, and R. Enriquez (Editors)

on courtroom research (i.e., mock trial studies) and emphasize more recently published studies. We encourage interested readers to refer to previous chapters (Bottoms et al., 2007; Golding et al., 2009) for more detail regarding studies that were published over 10 years ago.

MOCK TRIAL METHODOLOGY, CHALLENGES, AND STRENGTHS

Research investigating perceptions of CSA (and all forms of child abuse) in a legal context typically employs a mock trial methodology. Participants (undergraduates and/or community members) serving as mock jurors receive a fictious or actual case summary, a transcript in written text, or a videotaped trial. After the trial summary, participants render a verdict and offer other case judgments (e.g., victim credibility). Often, researchers measure mock jurors' individual verdict preferences, but in some studies, jurors deliberate before rendering verdicts (Fine et al., 2023).

Mock trial researchers attempt to use ecologically valid materials that follow the general framework of actual trials; however, one concern is that lab studies do not exactly replicate a real trial experience (Diamond, 1997). Nonetheless, this research is generalizable to some extent. In fact, studies employing less representative undergraduate samples typically generalize to those involving more representative community members (Bornstein et al., 2017). Moreover, by offering experimental control, lab studies ensure scientific integrity, allowing causal conclusions to be drawn about the effects of a particular factor on mock jurors' decisions. This would not be possible if researchers were to study actual cases, which are unique in many ways and do not allow for rigorous experimental control.

MOCK JUROR CHARACTERISTICS

Although various mock juror individual differences and attitudes predict CSA judgments, mock juror gender has emerged as a pervasive and widely replicated predictor of CSA case decisions (for reviews, see Bottoms et al., 2007; Golding et al., 2009; Golding, Malik, et al., 2020; Voogt & Klettke, 2017). Generally, women, more than men, render pro-child victim case judgments in CSA cases (i.e., perceive a child victim as credible and not responsible, blame defendants, render guilty verdicts; Font, 2013; Rawn et al., 2023). Gender differences in such case judgments might stem from internalized gender roles that disproportionately place women in child-caretaking roles (Hochschild, 1989/2003). Also, women's greater likelihood of being sexually victimized might foster a greater tendency to empathize with CSA victims (Bottoms, 1993; Haegerich & Bottoms, 2000). Women score higher than men on empathy toward CSA victims, opposition to adult–child sex, positive attitudes toward women, and CSA victim credibility (Bottoms et al., 2014), whereas men score higher on fear of being falsely accused of CSA (Jones et al., 2020). These attitudes, emotions, and beliefs statistically mediate (i.e., explain the relation between) the effect of mock juror gender on case judgments (e.g., verdicts) in hypothetical CSA cases (Bottoms et al., 2014; Jones et al., 2020).

Much like the general body of mock jury research, most studies documenting gender differences in CSA cases have been conducted with individual mock jurors and have not included deliberations. Studies that included deliberation reveal that women are somewhat more likely than men to shift from a guilty to a not guilty verdict after deliberation, in turn, attenuating gender differences in verdicts (e.g., Bottoms et al., 1998). A woman's greater tendency to shift to acquittal postdeliberation likely stems from women's disproportionate predeliberation conviction proneness and jurors' general tendency to shift toward acquittal postdeliberation in criminal cases (i.e., a leniency bias) due to the reasonable doubt standard's high threshold for guilt (MacCoun & Kerr, 1988). In support, Bottoms and colleagues (1998) found no gender differences in persuasive behaviors among undergraduate mock jurors during deliberations about a CSA case (speaking frequency, speaking turns, interruptions, etc.). Of importance, deliberation might not fully attenuate gender differences in CSA cases. For example, Golding and colleagues (2007) experimentally manipulated mock jury gender distribution such that juries were either mostly women versus not mostly women (i.e., mostly men or equal numbers of men and women). Mock jurors in this experiment read a fictional trial summary of a first-degree sexual assault case in which a stepfather allegedly abused his 6-year-old stepdaughter. Although women were more likely than men to shift to acquittal postdeliberation, women-majority juries (vs. nonwomen-majority juries) were more likely to switch from not guilty to guilty verdicts (and vice versa). Of interest, women-majority juries rendered the highest conviction rates. Although less extensively studied, women also tend to be more pro-prosecution oriented than men in cases of nonsexual child abuse including child physical abuse (Pettalia et al., 2017), neglect, and psychological abuse (Pettalia et al., 2017; Rawn et al., 2022).

Despite the considerable empirical evidence of mock juror gender effects in child abuse cases, very few studies have examined mock juror race effects in cases of child abuse, and results are mixed. Holcomb and Jacquin (2007) presented a student sample with a fictional trial summary of a CSA case involving an adult male perpetrator and female child victim but found no effects of mock juror race on verdicts or sentence recommendations. In contrast, Bottoms and colleagues (2004, experiment 1) found evidence of ingroup favoritism. That is, when the CSA victim's race matched that of mock jurors, jurors rendered higher degree-of-guilt ratings. Foley and Chamblin (1982) found similar results among White mock jurors; however, Black jurors were more punitive in intraracial cases (involving Black and White victims and defendants). Yet, the effects were no longer significant after controlling for the perceived socioeconomic status of victim and defendant (Golding et al., 2007; Golding, Malik, et al., 2020).

Although juror gender and juror race might influence decisions in child abuse cases, the *Batson v. Kentucky* (1986) and *J.E.B. v. Alabama* (1994) U.S. Supreme Court decisions prevent the exclusion of jurors based on race and gender. Even so, attorneys are free to attempt to use various other attitudes and life experiences as the basis for excluding a prospective juror for cause. There may be some merit to this strategy: Various mock juror attitudes, including low trait empathy, negative attitudes toward women, and less opposition to adult-child sex (Bottoms et al., 2014) predict diminished perceived child victim credibility.

Not surprisingly, in CSA cases attorneys and judges routinely assess prospective jurors' own CSA experiences during *voir dire* (Cramer et al., 2009), suggesting they believe a jurors' history of CSA will influence their decisions in such cases. But do they? Meta-analytic data revealed that, compared to nonvictims, mock jurors who experienced CSA (or knew someone who did) were more likely to empathize with a CSA victim, which in turn mediated effects on increased perceived victim credibility and guilty verdicts (Jones et al., 2020). Jones and colleagues (2020), however, cautioned against using prospective jurors' abuse history to unilaterally dismiss them from serving in such cases. At a practical level, predicting individual juror behavior from group trends will only produce a better-than-chance result over many cases, and only if combined with other, more targeted *voir dire* strategies. That is, disproportionately eliminating women or those with a history of experiencing CSA is likely to produce only minimal increases in the number of not guilty verdicts—gains that would only be detectable over the course of hundreds of trials. From a legal perspective, it is also worth considering the reverse perspective—whether jurors without abuse experiences are biased against CSA victims. Jones and colleagues (2020) argued that a fair jury comprises various people who bring disparate experiences and knowledge to bear to the case at hand, just as law instructs them to do (Diamond, 2007). Finally, it is important to consider that whereas it is legally permissible to exclude prospective jurors on the grounds of their history of CSA victimization or other CSA-related attitudes (e.g., CSA victim empathy), such practices will disproportionately eliminate women, jeopardizing jury representativeness.

VICTIM CHARACTERISTICS

Of course, not only do juror characteristics have the potential to shape child abuse case outcomes; child victim characteristics also have an impact. Some scholars theorize that jurors associate child sexual victimization more with girls than with boys (Sepler, 1990). Myths that boys are rarely sexually assaulted, and that those who are abused are effeminate, weak, and enjoy it (Donnelly & Kenyon, 1996), might help explain why a sample of French men blamed a boy CSA victim more than a girl, especially when the perpetrator was female (Esnard & Dumas, 2013; see also Fromuth et al., 2010, 2013). In contrast, reviews of mock trial studies revealed little evidence of victim gender effects on CSA case judgments and conflicting results when such effects manifested (Golding et al., 2007; Golding, Malik, et al., 2020; Voogt & Klettke, 2017).

Only one study to date involved an experimental manipulation of a CSA victim's gender, gender identity, and sexual orientation (Miller & London, 2023). In this study, mock jurors read a case summary of an alleged sexual abuse incident between a 15-year-old victim and 34-year-old male teacher. Findings revealed bias against gender-minority victims, such that mock jurors rendered more pro-prosecution judgments (e.g., guilt) when the victim was portrayed as cisgender versus transgender—effects that were most evident when the victim was portrayed as a transgender boy (vs. a transgender girl).

Just as some child victims may be discriminated against based on gender identity, child victims of color experience considerable risk of racial discrimination in the legal system (Stevenson et al., 2020). Such findings might, in part, stem from harmful stereotypes linking race with child abuse (Najdowski & Bernstein, 2018). CSA cases involving children of color (especially Black children) are also less likely to be substantiated (Stevenson & Rivers, 2023), or to result in an alleged perpetrator's arrest, prosecution, or conviction (Sedlak et al., 2005). Moreover, stereotypes associating Black (vs. White) children with dishonesty (O'Connor et al., 2023), hypersexuality, and promiscuity (e.g., Donovan, 2007), and perceptions that they are older and less innocent (Goff et al., 2014), may lead jurors to respond more negatively to CSA victims of color.

Yet few mock trial studies examine CSA victim race effects. Although Bottoms and colleagues (2004) found no effects of child victim race (Black, White, Hispanic) or of White mock jurors' preexisting racial prejudice on verdicts, jurors considered Black and Latina CSA victims (aged 12, 16) as more responsible for their own abuse than a White counterpart. In a recent CSA mock trial, undergraduate mock jurors' endorsement of the Jezebel stereotype (i.e., associating Black girls with promiscuity/hypersexuality) predicted more negative evaluations of a Black (but not White) CSA victim (e.g., lower credibility; Alley et al., 2019).

One explanation for why racial attitudes are sometimes unrelated to mock juror verdicts may be their use of explicit measures: Participants might attempt to avoid appearing prejudiced by dishonestly self-reporting their racial attitudes. Indeed, O'Connor and colleagues (2023) found that community member mock jurors' explicit racial bias was unrelated to their verdicts in a child physical abuse case. Yet, mock jurors' implicit racial bias (i.e., associating photographs of Black children with dishonest words and White children with honest words) predicted a lower likelihood of finding a coach guilty when the child victim was Black, but not White. Of note, victim race does not operate in isolation but often interacts with defendant race to influence jurors' case judgments. For example, Bottoms and colleagues (2004, experiment 2) found that although there were no significant main effects of victim or defendant race (Black vs. White) on verdicts in a mock CSA case, mock jurors rendered significantly higher guilt ratings when victim and defendant race matched versus differed from each other—effects driven by a belief that same-race CSA is more plausible than interracial CSA (see also Foley & Chamblin, 1982).

Unlike victim gender and race, victim age manifests as a factor that reliably predicts mock jurors' decisions in CSA cases (see Golding et al., 2007; Golding, Malik, et al., 2020; but see Johnson & Shelley, 2014). Bottoms and Goodman (1994) theorized that younger children were perceived as having more limited cognitive abilities/competence than older children and adults, and this undermines jurors' perceptions of child testimony in bystander eyewitness cases (e.g., a car accident)—effects confirmed by mock trial studies involving experimental manipulations of victim age (see Golding et al., 2007; Golding, Malik, et al., 2020; Pozzulo, 2017). In contrast, they theorized that younger children are considered more credible than older children specifically in the context of CSA cases—Younger children are too naïve and sexually ignorant to be able to fabricate a claim of sexual victimization. These assumptions lead mock jurors to be less conviction prone in cases involving older children (12 and older), who they consider as more capable of lying about sexual victimization (Bottoms et al., 2007)—effects similarly confirmed by considerable mock trial experiments (Golding et al., 2007; Golding, Malik, et al., 2020).

Victim age effects might also depend on abuse type. Sheahan and colleagues (2021) manipulated abuse type (physical vs. sexual) and victim age (12 vs. 20) in the context of abuse perpetrated by an assistant soccer coach. Although there were no significant effects on verdicts, participants perceived the 12-year-old as more credible than the 20-year-old when the alleged abuse was physical. In contrast, jurors perceived the 12-year-old as less credible than the 20-year-old when the alleged abuse was sexual—perhaps because the victims in both age conditions were 12 and older, the age at which sexual abuse victims lose perceived credibility (Bottoms & Goodman, 1994).

Like child age, child intellectual disability status has the potential to shape child abuse case judgments. Of importance, children with intellectual disabilities are at heightened risk of experiencing abuse (Byrne, 2018). Although prosecutors might be reluctant to criminally charge defendants in CSA cases involving victims with intellectual disabilities due to concern that such witnesses will appear noncredible, evidence suggests that cases with such victims are no less likely to result in conviction (Golding et al., 2007). With respect to CSA, just as mock jurors perceive younger children as particularly credible (due to their sexual naivety), mock jurors similarly perceived an intellectually disabled 16-year-old sexual abuse victim as less likely to have lied about her own abuse; they were more likely to convict compared to participants in a control condition in which the victim was described as of average intelligence (Bottoms et al., 2003). Yet, when children are called on as eyewitnesses to events not related to sexual abuse, mock jurors perceive the testimony of children labeled as intellectually disabled as less credible than children without an intellectual disability (Henry et al., 2011), but as no less honest (Brown & Lewis, 2013). Even so, mock jurors were no more likely to convict a father accused of murdering his infant when the infant was described as intellectually disabled (vs. not), and, in fact, rendered shorter sentences and felt less empathy for the victim when they believed the infant was intellectually disabled (Bottoms et al., 2011).

Finally, a few mock trials have explored the potential for child demeanor or mental illness to shape case outcomes. Although time since abuse and pretrial preparation might ease the potential for trauma when a child testifies in court, it might also dampen the child's emotion expression. Yet, mock jurors expect children to be emotional when testifying about their own sexual victimization (Bederian-Gardner & Goldfarb, 2014; Myers et al., 1999), and when these expectations are violated, they are less conviction prone (Golding, Malik, et al., 2020). Similarly, child witness mental illness diagnoses might influence case outcomes (Crane et al., 2020). Mock jurors randomly assigned to believe that a CSA victim was diagnosed with posttraumatic stress disorder (compared to no such diagnosis) were more likely to convict the defendant—an effect mediated by belief that the abuse occurred (Wang & Stevenson, 2023).

VICTIM CASE ISSUES

In addition to victim characteristics, various victim case issues might also affect perceptions of a child abuse victim in the courtroom. For instance, child victims may be afforded various types of courtroom assistance to protect them from a stressful experience (Malloy et al., 2007), such as allowing in-court testimony to be replaced by testimony via closed-circuit television (CCTV) or a videotaped interview (McAuliff & Kovera, 2012). Mock trial studies on this issue are equivocal (Golding, Malik, et al., 2020), with some finding no effect of presentation type on verdicts (Antrobus et al., 2016); but others finding that video testimony leads to more guilty verdicts than in-court testimony (Landström & Granhag, 2010). In addition, a child can be assisted through the presence of a support person. McAuliff and colleagues (2015) presented community members with a CSA video mock trial with or without a female support person seated next to the victim, finding that the presence (vs. absence) of the support person led to fewer guilty verdicts.

Expectations about how courtroom accommodations affect children's behavior can also shape how jurors perceive victims. Compared to a CSA victim providing traditional live testimony, mock jurors expected a child providing accommodated testimony (e.g., with a support person, via CCTV/videotape) to be less fidgety, more confident, more cooperative, clearer, and more fluent in their responses (McAuliff & Kovera, 2012). Yet, children providing accommodated testimony are not more likely to behave this way (e.g., Murray, 1995). This may be problematic because violated expectations for a CSA victim's behavior might reduce perceived victim credibility (e.g., Landström & Granhag, 2010).

Another accommodation is to interview children at child advocacy centers, which offer developmentally appropriate and socially supportive approaches.

But do such accommodations bias jurors' perceptions of a child's testimony? To test this, Johnson and Shelley (2014) asked undergraduates to read a case vignette involving stepfather-perpetrated CSA and manipulated descriptions of forensic interview setting and the Standard Protocol used in each (police department vs. child advocacy center). In the police condition, the forensic interviewer explained that the interview was conducted in an isolated room containing adult furniture, and that legal professionals did not observe the interview but were allowed to pose questions for the interviewer to ask later. In the child advocacy condition, the interviewer explained that the interview was conducted in a bright room containing toys for children, and that legal professionals were allowed to observe the interview via a one-way mirror and pose questions. No significant differences emerged on any measures (e.g., child credibility, degree-of-guilt), suggesting that conducting interviews in socially supportive settings does not harm how jurors perceive children's testimony. Caution is warranted, however, because the questions posed during police versus child advocacy center interviews were likely to influence jurors to a greater extent than mere differences in the setting where the interview was conducted. Of note, interviews at child advocacy centers are conducted by forensic interviewers trained to employ best practices for yielding accurate child testimony, which can also shape jurors' perceptions. Indeed, undergraduate and community member mock jurors perceived a child eyewitness to domestic violence as more credible and truthful after she passed the Canadian promise to tell the truth (a best practice) or passed a truth-and-lie ceremony as compared to failing the truth-and-lie ceremony, although there were no effects on defendant guilt (O'Connell et al., 2020). Thus, promising to tell the truth was better than seeing the child fail the truth-and-lie ceremony, and as good as seeing the child pass the truth-and-lie ceremony, which supports best practices.

Child abuse victims can also have other, corroborating eyewitnesses to their abuse (e.g., the Sandusky case at Penn State University, where adult witnesses to the alleged sexual abuse testified). The earliest example of published research on this issue involved community members as mock jurors who considered a video depiction of a CSA trial (Duggan et al., 1989; see also Bottoms & Goodman, 1994; Golding et al., 2015; Holcomb & Jacquin, 2007). When the video included corroborating testimony (from another child or adult), as compared to no corroboration, the corroborating witness, regardless of the witness' age, did not increase guilty verdicts among female participants, but significantly increased pro-victim judgments (e.g., guilt) among men.

Other evidentiary issues include medical evidence (e.g., DNA) and expert testimony. The former is important because during a trial, the strength of legal evidence is the most important factor impacting legal decision making (Devine et al., 2001). Golding and colleagues (2000) presented undergraduates with a case summary in which a 6-year-old girl accused her neighbor of forcing her to have sexual intercourse—supported or not by DNA evidence. The presence (vs. absence) of DNA evidence increased jurors' positive perceptions of the child's credibility and convictions.

To assist the court, the judge may allow prosecution or defense expert testimony (Lyon et al., 2020), each of which can influence jurors' decisions. Compared to no expert testimony, prosecution expert testimony can increase guilty verdicts (Golding et al., 2015; Golding, Malik, et al., 2020; Horner et al., 2012), and defense expert testimony can lead to decisions in favor of the defendant (Khurshid & Jacquin, 2013; but see Buck et al., 2011). When both sides present expert testimony, however, the experts cancel each other out (e.g., Khurshid & Jacquin, 2013). Quality of expert testimony is also important: McAuliff and Duckworth (2010) presented community members with a CSA case in which a defense expert presented his own study on eyewitness memory—the study did or did not have threats to internal validity (e.g., missing control group) and was published or unpublished. Only when the control group was missing, were participants more likely to vote guilty if the study was published (vs. unpublished).

A final case issue to note is delayed reporting/repression. Although it would be best for a victim to report a crime immediately and completely, in child abuse cases this is rare (Pipe et al., 2007). Yozwiak and colleagues (2004; see also Miller et al., 2022; but see Bottoms et al., 1997) presented community members with a CSA case involving a 6-year-old victim. There were fewer guilty verdicts when the victim fully disclosed the crime on two occasions as compared to when there was a delay in disclosure. Research on delayed reporting also includes studies of repression (i.e., a traumatic memory exists in one's unconscious but can be recovered many years later; American Psychological Association, 1998; Freud, 1894/1962). Loftus and colleagues (1993) first examined repression in court, having undergraduates read a sexual abuse trial involving a 20-year-old adult who claimed to have forgotten (i.e., repressed) abuse that occurred 10 years earlier or been abused but kept it a secret for 10 years. Participants were more skeptical of repressed memories than memories that had always been remembered but kept secret. Later, Golding and colleagues (1995; see also Bornstein & Muller, 2001) included a control condition (i.e., victim reported the CSA immediately) and found fewer verdicts favoring the victim for the combined repressed/no-repressed condition than the control condition. Note, however, that if a defendant claimed to have repressed being sexually assaulted for 30 years, they were convicted of murder less often than when the abuse was not repressed (Lynch et al., 2014).

DEFENDANT CHARACTERISTICS

Perceptions of child abuse victims in court are impacted by characteristics of the child but may also be affected by defendants' characteristics. Although researchers have examined the latter, there are relatively few mock trial studies to do so. The lack of research on defendant gender may be due to the assumption that women rarely commit abuse (Golding, Malik, et al., 2020). Whereas this assumption is true of CSA (88.7% perpetrators are male compared to 8.4% female), the gender of perpetrators of all forms of child maltreatment (i.e., neglect, physical abuse, sexual abuse) are more evenly split between men (47.3%) and women (51.9%; Children's Bureau, 2023). The few existing mock trial studies (Golding, Malik, et al., 2020) examined defendant gender in different ways. Some only manipulated defendant gender, finding that community members rendered more guilty verdicts in CSA cases with a female child when the defendant was male versus female (e.g., McCoy & Gray, 2007; but see Stanziani & Cox, 2021). Others examined defendant and victim gender in the context of teacher–student CSA. Although not a mock trial study, the earliest of these revealed that male teacher/female student CSA led to harsher sentence recommendations than female teacher/male student CSA (e.g., Fromuth et al., 2010). Quas and colleagues (2002; see also Anderson et al., 2018) examined this type of abuse case in criminal court, finding fewer guilty verdicts in the female teacher/male student CSA condition than the male teacher/male student CSA case (but see Pica et al., 2023; Pozzulo et al., 2010). Likewise, in a plea-bargain context (i.e., defendant waives their right to trial and pleads guilty in exchange for reduced charges/sentence), Pals and colleagues (2022) found lower plea-bargain support for male versus female teachers.

A few studies have focused on issues of sexual orientation. Herek (2002) found that nearly 20% of male respondents endorsed a belief that gay men molested children. Moreover, some participants rate same-gender CSA as more abusive than opposite-gender interactions (Golding, Malik, et al., 2020). One example is Wiley and Bottoms' study (2009; see also Stawiski et al., 2012), which specifically (unlike other studies) noted that the defendant was gay or straight. Those who perceived the defendant to be gay (vs. straight) convicted more often; and, for male-victim cases, moral outrage mediated the effect of defendant sexual orientation on verdict and degree of guilt.

Laypeople tend to perceive White (vs. non-White) individuals as the most likely perpetrators of CSA (Livingston et al., 2022) and perceive White and Black individuals (vs. other racial/ethnic groups) to be the most likely perpetrators of child abuse generally (Skorinko & Spellman, 2013). Yet, few laboratory studies have examined the role of defendant race in child abuse cases, and those that have typically find that the effect of defendant race interacts with victim race to affect jurors' judgments. Moreover, cumulative racial bias at every stage within the legal system (police stops/searches, detainment, arrest, bail, prosecution, conviction, probation terms, sentencing; Najdowski & Stevenson, 2022), places defendants of color at heightened risk of experiencing similarly negative outcomes in child abuse legal contexts.

One other characteristic that has been examined is defendant age. Specifically, Pozzulo and colleagues (2010) manipulated defendant age (15 vs. 40 years old) in a case involving a 12-year-old CSA victim, but found that it did not impact outcome judgments for their undergraduate participants (also Redlich et al., 2008). Similarly, Pica and colleagues (2023) examined defendant age (25 or 55 years old) and social status (high or low) among a sample of undergraduates who read a mock trial transcript of a child trafficking case yet found no effects of either independent variable.

DEFENDANT CASE ISSUES

Research on defendant case issues is also scant, but several studies raise important concerns related to perceptions of child abuse. First, Stevenson and colleagues (2010) tested a theoretical model explaining how jurors discussed a case in which a criminal defendant convicted of murder in a capital case had a history of child abuse. Testimony from the defense included that the defendant had been physically abused by his father for many years and that the defendant's sister had been sexually abused by their father. The complex deliberation data (11- or 12-person mock juries) indicated that jurors were more likely to argue that other jurors should ignore child abuse as a mitigating factor or use this evidence as an aggravating factor than to use it as a mitigator.

Second, Goodman-Delahunty and Martschuk (2020) investigated the issue of presenting uncharged acts by the defendant in court. They presented community members (serving as mock jurors in a 9- to 13-member jury) with a video trial and manipulated the nature of the offense: indecency or sexual intercourse with a child under 14 years old. They also manipulated the type of trial such that participants received a trial in which there was no evidence of uncharged sexual acts by the defendant; the alleged victim described four uncharged acts of inappropriate touching/grooming by the defendant that occurred before the charged crime; and two other victims described three uncharged acts of indecency and one act of penetration by the defendant. The results showed that juries were reluctant to convict solely based on the complainant's word, and there was little evidence of unfair prejudice to the accused due to the presence of uncharged acts.

Third, Malik and colleagues (2018) examined a defendant accused of CSA testifying in court. Community members read a fictional trial summary in which the defendant either testified or did not testify, and the evidence included the testimony of a sexual assault nurse examiner (strong evidence) or not (weak evidence). Guilty verdicts were more likely when there was strong evidence, and the defendant did not testify; anger toward the defendant mediated the relation between the defendant's lack of testimony and guilty verdicts.

Fourth, Golding, Neuschatz, and colleagues (2020) explored the role of a jailhouse informant (JI) on CSA cases. JI testimony (also called secondary confessions) involves an inmate testifying that a defendant confessed to a crime and is often compelling evidence to jurors (Neuschatz & Golding, 2022). In two experiments, community members read about a sexual assault of a 6-year-old child or a 25-year-old adult (female victim in experiment 1, male victim in experiment 2) in a case that included a JI or did not. The presence of a JI led to more guilty verdicts, regardless of victim age, and this effect was mediated by perceived victim credibility.

Finally, archival research suggests that a defendant's mode of attack and choice of location can influence case outcomes. Lundrigan and colleagues (2020) examined a United Kingdom police database of child stranger rape cases that went to jury trial ($N = 70$) from 2001–2015 to determine which of

19 victim- and offense-related factors predicted verdicts. They found that a weapon and an outdoor location significantly increased the likelihood of conviction.

VICTIM AND DEFENDANT RELATIONSHIP

Another important consideration regarding child abuse cases that cuts across both parties is the relationship between the victim and defendant. Few studies have examined this issue, as most mock trial research focuses on a single relationship context by examining a perpetrator known to the victim (e.g., stepfather; Golding, Malik, et al., 2020). A few studies, however, have found a significant effect of defendant–victim relationship type. One study found that community members had higher confidence in guilty verdicts when the defendant was a stranger versus a parent in a child abuse case (McCoy & Gray, 2007). Pica and colleagues (2019) also investigated the victim–defendant relationship. They presented undergraduates with a case summary that varied witness/victim age (5, 10, 15 years old), victim/witness familiarity with the defendant (familiar-personal: teacher; familiar-casual: pizza delivery guy; stranger), and nature of the crime (personal: victim abducted vs. nonpersonal: victim of theft). Higher guilt ratings emerged in the familiar conditions when the child was abducted, as compared to the other conditions.

IMPLICATIONS FOR PSYCHOLOGY, POLICY, AND LAW

CSA continues to be a societal problem, and the number of reported cases remains high (Children's Bureau, 2023). We hope that the present review of the impact of various factors (e.g., gender, race, intellectual disability status) on perceptions of child abuse victims offers greater understanding of how abused children are perceived in court, while serving as a catalyst for future researchers. Whereas some topics (e.g., juror gender) have garnered a great deal of investigation, other important factors have been overlooked. As was the case many years earlier (Chaffin, 2006), researchers remain more likely to examine perceptions of CSA as compared to other types of abuse (physical, neglect, emotional), which are far more common. Thus, much remains to be learned about how jurors perceive non-CSA cases. Also, only a handful of mock trial studies involving child victimization include jury deliberation, which evidence shows is an important moderator that can change predeliberation study effects (Fine et al., 2023). Finally, although scholars have begun exploring gender identity and race-based discrimination within child abuse decision making, more research is sorely needed. Indeed, racial injustice is particularly pronounced within all legal systems within the United States and several other countries, which ushers in harmful life trajectories for children of color (Stevenson et al., 2020).

CONCLUSION

We urge scholars to embrace important and new directions in their research and call on legal practitioners to harness the existing science in ways that best serve child victims. Attorneys ought to develop cases in ways that anticipate and address the potential for juror bias in cases involving children minoritized by gender identity (Miller & London, 2023), sexual orientation (Stawiski et al., 2012), and race (Alley et al., 2019). Expert witnesses can also harness the science reviewed in this chapter as they plan for how to best educate jurors about a particular case. In this way, we can ensure that the legal system is equipped to use research to successfully prosecute all types of child abuse, and that child victims are treated fairly in the courtroom.

REFERENCES

Alley, D., Silberkleit, G., Bederian-Gardner, D., & Goodman, G. S. (2019). Race-based sexual stereotypes influence ratings of child victims in sexual abuse cases. *International Journal on Child Maltreatment: Research, Policy & Practice, 2*(4), 287–308. https://doi.org/10.1007/s42448-019-00034-5

American Psychological Association. (1998). Final conclusions of the American Psychological Association working group on investigation of memories of childhood abuse. *Psychology, Public Policy & Law, 4*(4), 933–940. https://doi.org/10.1037/1076-8971.4.4.933

Anderson, A., Wingrove, T., Fox, P., McLean, K., & Styer, E. (2018). Who is the rotten apple? Mock jurors' views of teacher–student sexual contact. *Journal of Interpersonal Violence, 33*(9), 1449–1471. https://doi.org/10.1177/0886260515618214

Antrobus, E., McKimmie, B. M., & Newcombe, P. (2016). Mode of children's testimony and the effect of assumptions about credibility. *Psychiatry, Psychology & Law, 23*(6), 922–940. https://doi.org/10.1080/13218719.2016.1152927

Batson v. Kentucky, 476 U.S. 79 (1986). https://www.uscourts.gov/educational-resources/educational-activities/facts-and-case-summary-batson-v-kentucky

Bederian-Gardner, D., & Goldfarb, D. (2014). Expectations of emotions during testimony: The role of communicator and perceiver characteristics. *Behavioral Sciences & the Law, 32*(6), 829–845. https://doi.org/10.1002/bsl.2146

Block, S. D., Johnson, H. M., Williams, L. M., Shockley, K. L., Wang, E., & Widaman, K. F. (2022). Predictors of prosecutorial decisions in reports of child sexual abuse. *Child Maltreatment, 28*(3), 488–499. https://doi.org/10.1177/10775595221074375

Bornstein, B. H., Golding, J. M., Neuschatz, J., Kimbrough, C., Reed, K., Magyarics, C., & Luecht, K. (2017). Mock juror sampling issues in jury simulation research: A meta-analysis. *Law & Human Behavior, 41*(1), 13–28. https://doi.org/10.1037/lhb0000223

Bornstein, B. H., & Muller, S. L. (2001). The credibility of recovered memory testimony: Exploring the effects of alleged victim and perpetrator gender. *Child Abuse & Neglect, 25*(11), 1415–1426. https://doi.org/10.1016/s0145-2134(01)00282-4

Bottoms, B. L. (1993). Individual differences in perceptions of child sexual assault victims. In G. S. Goodman & B. L. Bottoms (Eds.), *Child victims, child witnesses: Understanding and improving testimony* (pp. 229–261). Guilford Press.

Bottoms, B. L., Davis, S. L., & Epstein, M. A. (2004). Effects of victim and defendant race on jurors' decisions in child sexual abuse cases. *Journal of Applied Social Psychology, 34*(1), 1–33. https://doi.org/10.1111/j.1559-1816.2004.tb02535.x

Bottoms, B. L., Diviak, K. R., & Davis, S. L. (1997). Jurors' reactions to satanic ritual abuse allegations. *Child Abuse & Neglect, 21*(9), 845–859. https://doi.org/10.1016/S0145-2134(97)00046-X

Bottoms, B. L., Golding, J. M., Stevenson, M. C., Wiley, T. R. A., & Yozwiak, J. A. (2007). A review of factors affecting jurors' decisions in child sexual abuse cases. In M. P. Toglia, J. D. Read, D. F. Ross, & R. C. L. Lindsay (Eds.), *Handbook of eyewitness psychology* (pp. 509–543). Erlbaum.

Bottoms, B. L., & Goodman, G. S. (1994). Perceptions of children's credibility in sexual assault cases. *Journal of Applied Social Psychology, 24*(8), 702–732. https://doi.org/10.1111/j.1559-1816.1994.tb00608.x

Bottoms, B. L., Kalder, A. K., Stevenson, M. C., Oudekerk, B. A., Wiley, T. R., & Perona, A. (2011). Gender differences in jurors' perceptions of infanticide involving disabled and non-disabled infant victims. *Child Abuse & Neglect, 35*(2), 127–141. https://doi.org/10.1016/j.chiabu.2010.10.004

Bottoms, B. L., Nysse-Carris, K., Harris, L., & Tyda, K. (2003). Juror's perceptions of adolescent sexual abuse victims who have intellectual disabilities. *Law & Human Behavior, 27*(2), 205–227. https://doi.org/10.1023/a:1022551314668

Bottoms, B. L., Peter-Hagene, L. C., Stevenson, M. C., Wiley, T. R. A., Mitchell, T. S., & Goodman, G. S. (2014). Explaining gender differences in jurors' reactions to child sexual assault cases. *Behavioral Sciences & the Law, 32*(6), 789–812. https://doi.org/10.1002/bsl.2147

Bottoms, B. L., Schmidt, E., & Epstein, M. (1998, March 5–7). *Effects of juror gender and verdict preference on persuasion during deliberations in child abuse trials* [Paper presentation]. Biennial meeting of the American Psychology–Law Society, Redondo Beach, CA, United States.

Brown, D. A., & Lewis, C. N. (2013). Competence is in the eye of the beholder: Perceptions of intellectually disabled child witnesses. *International Journal of Disability, Development and Education, 60*(1), 3–17. https://doi.org/10.1080/1034912x.2013.757132

Buck, J. A., London, K., & Wright, D. B. (2011). Expert testimony regarding child witnesses: Does it sensitize jurors to forensic interview quality? *Law & Human Behavior, 35*(2), 152–164. https://doi.org/10.1007/s10979-010-9228-2

Byrne, G. (2018). Prevalence and psychological sequelae of sexual abuse among individuals with an intellectual disability: A review of the recent literature. *Journal of Intellectual Disabilities, 22*(3), 294–310. https://doi.org/10.1177/1744629517698844

Chaffin, M. (2006). The changing focus of child maltreatment research and practice within psychology. *Journal of Social Issues, 62*(4), 663–684. https://doi.org/10.1111/j.1540-4560.2006.00482.x

Children's Bureau. (2023). *Child maltreatment 2022.* U.S. Department of Health & Human Services, Administration for Children and Families, Administration on Children, Youth and Families. https://www.acf.hhs.gov/cb/data-research/child-maltreatment

Children's Bureau. (2025). *Child maltreatment 2023.* U.S. Department of Health & Human Services, Administration for Children and Families, Administration on Children, Youth and Families. https://acf.gov/sites/default/files/documents/cb/cm2023.pdf

Cramer, R. J., Adams, D. D., & Brodsky, S. L. (2009). Jury selection in child sex abuse trials: A case analysis. *Journal of Child Sexual Abuse, 18*(2), 190–205. https://doi.org/10.1080/10538710902743974

Crane, L., Wilcock, R., Maras, K. L., Chui, W., Marti-Sanchez, C., & Henry, L. A. (2020). Mock juror perceptions of child witnesses on the autism spectrum: The impact of providing diagnostic labels and information about autism. *Journal of Autism and Developmental Disorders, 50*(5), 1509–1519. https://doi.org/10.1007/s10803-018-3700-0

Devine, D. J., Clayton, L. D., Dunford, B. B., Seying, R., & Pryce, J. (2001). Jury decision making: 45 years of empirical research on deliberating groups. *Psychology, Public Policy, & Law, 7*(3), 622–727. https://doi.org/10.1037//1076-8971.7.3.622

Diamond, S. S. (1997). Illuminations and shadows from jury simulations. *Law & Human Behavior, 21*(5), 561–571. https://doi.org/10.1023/a:1024831908377

Diamond, S. S. (2007). How jurors deal with expert testimony and how judges can help. *Journal of Law and Policy, 16*(1), 2162–4089. https://brooklynworks.brooklaw.edu/jlp/vol16/iss1/4

Donnelly, D. A., & Kenyon, S. (1996). "Honey, we don't do men": Gender stereotypes and the provision of services to sexually assaulted males. *Journal of Interpersonal Violence, 11*(3), 441–448. https://doi.org/10.1177/088626096011003009

Donovan, R. A. (2007). To blame or not to blame: Influences of target race and observer sex on rape blame attribution. *Journal of Interpersonal Violence, 22*(6), 722–736. https://doi.org/10.1177/0886260507300754

Duggan, L. M., Aubrey, M., Doherty, E., Isquith, P. K., Levine, M., & Scheiner, J. (1989). The credibility of children as witnesses in a simulated child sex abuse trial. In S. J. Ceci, D. F. Ross, & M. P. Toglia (Eds.), *Perspectives on the child witness* (pp. 71–99). SpringerVerlag.

Esnard, C., & Dumas, R. (2013). Perceptions of male victim blame in a child sexual abuse case: Effects of gender, age and need for closure. *Psychology, Crime & Law, 19*(9), 817–844. https://doi.org/10.1080/1068316x.2012.700310

Fine, A., Salerno, J., Phalen, H., Growns, B., Walters, A., Olson, B., & Bussey, L. (2023, March 16–18). *A systematic review of the moderating effects of deliberation* [Paper presentation]. Annual Conference of the American Psychology–Law Society, Philadelphia, PA, United States.

Foley, L. A., & Chamblin, M. H. (1982). The effect of race and personality on mock jurors' decisions. *The Journal of Psychology, 112*(1), 47–51. https://doi.org/10.1080/00223980.1982.9923533

Font, S. A. (2013). Perceptions of juvenile sexual abuse victims: A meta-analysis on vignette-based studies on the effects of victims' age and respondents' gender. *Journal of Child Sexual Abuse, 22*(5), 593–611. https://doi.org/10.1080/10538712.2013.800934

Freud, S. (1962). The neuro-psychoses of defence. In J. Strachey (Ed. & Trans.), *The standard edition of the complete psychological works of Sigmund Freud* (Vol. 3, pp. 41–61). Hogarth Press. (Original work published 1894)

Fromuth, M. E., Kelly, D. B., Wilson, A. K., Finch, L. V., & Scruggs, L. (2013). An exploratory study of the effects of teacher attractiveness on undergraduates' perceptions of teacher–student sexual involvement. *Journal of Child Sexual Abuse, 22*(3), 341–357. https://doi.org/10.1080/10538712.2013.772272

Fromuth, M. E., Mackey, A. L., & Wilson, A. (2010). Effect of student vulnerability on perceptions of teacher–student sexual involvement. *Journal of Child Sexual Abuse, 19*(4), 419–433. https://doi.org/10.1080/10538712.2010.495700

Goff, P. A., Jackson, M. C., Di Leone, B. A. L., Culotta, C. M., & DiTomasso, N. A. (2014). The essence of innocence: Consequences of dehumanizing Black children. *Journal of Personality and Social Psychology, 106*(4), 526–545. https://doi.org/10.1037/a0035663

Golding, J. M., Bradshaw, G. S., Dunlap, E. E., & Hodell, E. C. (2007). The impact of mock jury gender composition on deliberations and conviction rates in a child sexual assault trial. *Child Maltreatment, 12*(2), 182–190. https://doi.org/10.1177/1077559506298995

Golding, J. M., Dunlap, E. E., & Hodell, E. C. (2009). Jurors' perceptions of children's eyewitness testimony. In B. L. Bottoms, C. J. Najdowski, & G. S. Goodman (Eds.), *Children as victims, witnesses, and offenders: Psychological science and the law* (pp. 188–208). Guilford Press.

Golding, J. M., Lynch, K. R., Wasarhaley, N. E., & Keller, P. (2015). Courtroom perceptions of child sexual assault: The impact of an eyewitness. *Criminal Justice & Behavior, 42*(7), 763–781. https://doi.org/10.1177/0093854814568552

Golding, J. M., Malik, S., Jones, T. M., Burke, K. C., & Bottoms, B. L. (2020). Perceptions of child sexual abuse victims: A review of psychological research with implications for law. In J. Pozzulo, E. Pica, & C. Sheahan (Eds.), *Memory and sexual misconduct: Psychological research for criminal justice* (pp. 132–174). Routledge/Taylor & Francis Group.

Golding, J. M., Neuschatz, J. S., Bornstein, B. H., Riederer, A. M., & Wetmore, S. A. (2020). The perception of a jailhouse informant in a sexual assault case. *Journal of Police and Criminal Psychology, 38*(2), 281–292. https://doi.org/10.1007/s11896-020-09400-3

Golding, J. M., Sego, S. A., Sanchez, R. P., & Hasemann, D. (1995). The believability of repressed memories. *Law & Human Behavior, 19*(6), 569–592. https://doi.org/10.1007/bf01499375

Golding, J. M., Stewart, T. L., Yozwiak, J. A., Djdali, Y., & Sanchez, R. P. (2000). The impact of DNA evidence in a child sexual assault trial. *Child Maltreatment, 5*(4), 373–383. https://doi.org/10.1177/1077559500005004009

Goodman-Delahunty, J., & Martschuk, N. (2020). Mock jury and juror responses to uncharged acts of sexual misconduct. *Zeitschrift für Psychologie, 228*(3), 199–209. https://doi.org/10.1027/2151-2604/a000410

Haegerich, T. M., & Bottoms, B. L. (2000). Empathy and jurors' decisions in patricide trials involving child sexual assault allegations. *Law & Human Behavior, 24*(4), 421–448. https://doi.org/10.1023/a:1005592213294

Henry, L., Ridley, A., Perry, J., & Crane, L. (2011). Perceived credibility and eyewitness testimony of children with intellectual disabilities. *Journal of Intellectual Disability Research, 55*(4), 385–391. https://doi.org/10.1111/j.1365-2788.2011.01383.x

Herek, G. M. (2002). Gender gaps in public opinion about lesbians and gay men. *Public Opinion Quarterly, 66*(1), 40–66. https://doi.org/10.1086/338409

Hochschild, A. R. (with Machung, A.). (2003). *The second shift.* Penguin Books. (Original work published 1989)

Holcomb, M. J., & Jacquin, K. M. (2007). Juror perception of child eyewitness testimony in a sexual abuse trial. *Journal of Child Sexual Abuse, 16*(2), 79–95. https://doi.org/10.1300/J070v16n02_05

Horner, G., Thackeray, J., Scribano, P., Curran, S., & Benzinger, E. (2012). Pediatric sexual assault nurse examiner care: Trace forensic evidence, ano-genital injury, and judicial outcomes. *Journal of Forensic Nursing, 8*(3), 105–111. https://doi.org/10.1111/j.1939-3938.2011.01131.x

J.E.B. v. Alabama, 511 U.S. 127 (1994). https://www.uscourts.gov/educational-resources/educational-activities/facts-and-case-summary-jeb-v-alabama

Johnson, J. L., & Shelley, A. E. (2014). Effects of child interview tactics on prospective jurors' decisions. *Behavioral Sciences & the Law, 32*(6), 846–866. https://doi.org/10.1002/bsl.2152

Jones, T. M., Bottoms, B. L., & Stevenson, M. C. (2020). Child victim empathy mediates the influence of jurors' sexual abuse experiences on child sexual abuse case judgments: Meta-analyses. *Psychology, Public Policy, & Law, 26*(3), 312–332. https://doi.org/10.1037/law0000231

Khurshid, A., & Jacquin, K. M. (2013). Expert testimony influences juror decisions in criminal trials involving recovered memories of childhood sexual abuse. *Journal of Child Sexual Abuse, 22*(8), 949–967. https://doi.org/10.1080/10538712.2013.839592

Landström, S., & Granhag, P. A. (2010). In-court versus out-of-court testimonies: Children's experiences and adults' assessments. *Applied Cognitive Psychology, 24*(7), 941–955. https://doi.org/10.1002/acp.1606

Livingston, T. N., Rerick, P. O., & Davis, D. (2022). Race/ethnicity and relationship stereotypes in child sex abuse cases. *Psychological Reports, 127*(1), 112–123. https://doi.org/10.1177/00332941221119414

Loftus, E. F., Weingardt, K., & Hoffman, H. (1993). Sleeping memories on trial: Reactions to memories that were previously repressed. *Expert Evidence, 2*(2), 51–59.

Lundrigan, S., Dhami, M. K., & Agudelo, K. (2020). Factors predicting conviction in child stranger rape. *Child Abuse & Neglect, 101,* 104242. https://doi.org/10.1016/j.chiabu.2019.104242

Lynch, K. R., Golding, J. M., & Wasarhaley, N. E. (2014). Juror perceptions of repressed sexual abuse in an adult parricide case. *American Journal of Forensic Psychology, 32*(1), 19–28.

Lyon, T. D., Williams, S., & Stolzenberg, S. N. (2020). Understanding expert testimony on child sexual abuse after *New Jersey v. J. L. G.*: Ground truth, disclosure suspicion bias, and disclosure substantiation bias. *Behavioral Sciences & the Law, 38*(6), 630–647. https://doi.org/10.1002/bsl.2490

MacCoun, R. J., & Kerr, N. L. (1988). Asymmetric influence in mock jury deliberation: Jurors' bias for leniency. *Journal of Personality and Social Psychology, 54*(1), 21–33. https://doi.org/10.1037//0022-3514.54.1.21

Malik, S. E., Golding, J. M., & Lippert, A. (2018). The impact of a defendant not testifying in a child sexual assault case. *American Journal of Forensic Psychology, 36*(1), 5–29.

Malloy, L. C., Mitchell, E., Block, S., Quas, J. A., & Goodman, G. S. (2007). Children's eyewitness memory: Balancing children's needs and defendants' rights when seeking the truth. In M. P. Toglia, J. D. Read, D. F. Ross, & R. C. L. Lindsay (Eds.), *The handbook of eyewitness psychology: Vol. 1. Memory for events* (pp. 545–574). Erlbaum.

McAuliff, B. D., & Duckworth, T. D. (2010). I spy with my little eye: Jurors' detection of internal validity threats in expert evidence. *Law & Human Behavior, 34*(6), 489–500. https://doi.org/10.1007/s10979-010-9219-3

McAuliff, B. D., & Kovera, M. B. (2012). Do jurors get what they expect? Traditional versus alternative forms of children's testimony. *Psychology, Crime & Law, 18*(1), 27–47. https://doi.org/10.1080/1068316X.2011.613391

McAuliff, B. D., Lapin, J., & Michel, S. (2015). Support person presence and child victim testimony: Believe it or not. *Behavioral Sciences & the Law, 33*(4), 508–527. https://doi.org/10.1002/bsl.2190

McCoy, M. L., & Gray, J. M. (2007). The impact of defendant gender and relationship to victim on juror decisions in a child sexual abuse case. *Journal of Applied Social Psychology, 37*(7), 1578–1593. https://doi.org/10.1111/j.1559-1816.2007.00228.x

Miller, Q. C., Call, A. A., & London, K. (2022). Mock jurors' perceptions of child sexual abuse cases: Investigating the role of delayed disclosure and relationship to the perpetrator. *Journal of Interpersonal Violence, 37*(23–24), NP23374–NP23396. https://doi.org/10.1177/08862605221078812

Miller, Q. C., & London, K. (2023). Mock jurors' perceptions of child sexual abuse cases involving sexual and gender minority victims. *Psychology of Sexual Orientation and Gender Diversity, 10*(2), 311–323. https://doi.org/10.1037/sgd0000541

Murray, K. (1995). *Live television link: An evaluation of its use by child witnesses in Scottish criminal trials*. Scottish Office Central Research Unit.

Myers, J. E., Redlich, A., Goldman, G., Prizmich, L., & Imwinkelried, E. (1999). Jurors' perceptions of hearsay in child sexual abuse cases. *Psychology, Public Policy, & Law, 5*(2), 388–419. https://doi.org/10.1037//1076-8971.5.2.388

Najdowski, C. J., & Bernstein, K. M. (2018). Race, social class, and child abuse: Content and strength of medical professionals' stereotypes. *Child Abuse & Neglect, 86*, 217–222. https://doi.org/10.1016/j.chiabu.2018.10.006

Najdowski, C. J., & Stevenson, M. C. (2022). A call to dismantle systemic racism in criminal legal systems. *Law & Human Behavior, 46*(6), 398–414. https://doi.org/10.1037/lhb0000510

Neuschatz, J. S., & Golding, J. M. (2022). *Jailhouse informants*. NYU Press.

O'Connell, F., Cherryman, J., & Warmelink, L. (2020). Mock juror's perceptions of a child witness passing or failing a truth and lies discussion or promising to tell the truth. *Applied Cognitive Psychology, 34*(1), 285–292. https://doi.org/10.1002/acp.3612

O'Connor, A. M., Hall, W., & Campbell, K. L. (2023). Rating the honesty of White and Black children via implicit and explicit measures: Implications for child victims in the criminal justice system. *Child Maltreatment, 28*(3), 450–461. https://doi.org/10.1177/10775595231173363

Pals, A. M., Golding, J. M., & Levi, M. M. (2022). Perceptions of a plea agreement in cases of teacher and adolescent student sexual assault. *Journal of Child Sexual Abuse, 31*(8), 930–947. https://doi.org/10.1080/10538712.2022.2119911

Pettalia, J., Pozzulo, J. D., & Reed, J. (2017). The influence of sex on mock jurors' verdicts across type of child abuse cases. *Child Abuse & Neglect, 69*, 1–9. https://doi.org/10.1016/j.chiabu.2017.03.025

Pica, E., Hildenbrand, A., Fraser, L., & Pozzulo, J. (2023). Juror decision-making in a child trafficking case: The impact of defendant and victim gender, defendant age, and defendant status. *Journal of Interpersonal Violence, 38*(17-18), 10031–10054. https://doi.org/10.1177/08862605231169760

Pica, E., Pozzulo, J., Sheahan, C. L., & Pratt, K. (2019). 'I know him!': Does witness–defendant familiarity impact mock jurors across different aged witnesses and types of crime? *Applied Psychology in Criminal Justice, 15*(2), 171–184.

Pipe, M. E., Lamb, M., Orbach, Y., & Cedarborg, A. C. (Eds.). (2007). *Child sexual abuse: Disclosure, delay, and denial*. Erlbaum.

Pozzulo, J. (2017). Jurors' perceptions of the young eyewitness. In J. Pozzulo (Ed.), *The young eyewitness: How well do children and adolescents describe and identify perpetrators*? (pp. 136–153). American Psychological Association. https://doi.org/10.1037/14956-009

Pozzulo, J. D., Dempsey, J., Maeder, E., & Allen, L. (2010). The effects of victim gender, defendant gender, and defendant age on juror decision making. *Criminal Justice and Behavior, 37*(1), 47–63. https://doi.org/10.1177/0093854809344173

Quas, J. A., Bottoms, B. L., Haegerich, T. M., & Nysse-Carris, K. L. (2002). Effects of victim defendant, and juror gender on decisions in child sexual assault cases. *Journal of Applied Social Psychology, 32*(10), 1993–2021. https://doi.org/10.1111/j.1559-1816.2002.tb02061.x

Rawn, K. P., Levi, M. M., Pals, A. M., Huber, H., & Golding, J. M. (2023). Impacts of victim resistance and type of assault on legal decision-making in child sexual assault. *Journal of Child Sexual Abuse, 32*(4), 418–437. https://doi.org/10.1080/10538712.2023.2180468

Rawn, K. P., Pals, A., & Golding, J. M. (2022). "He yells because he cares": Jury perceptions of emotional abuse from a sports coach toward child athletes. *Journal of Family Trauma, Child Custody & Child Development, 20*(3), 1–21. https://doi.org/10.1080/26904586.2022.2036287

Redlich, A. D., Quas, J. A., & Ghetti, S. (2008). Perceptions of children during a police interrogation: Guilt, confessions, and interview fairness. *Psychology, Crime, & Law, 14*(3), 201–223. https://doi.org/10.1080/10683160701652542

Sedlak, A. J., Doueck, H. J., Lyons, P., Wells, S. J., Schultz, D., & Gragg, F. (2005). Child maltreatment and the justice system: Predictors of court involvement. *Research on Social Work Practice, 15*(5), 389–403. https://doi.org/10.1177/1049731505277947

Sepler, F. (1990). Victim advocacy and young male victims of sexual abuse: An evolutionary model. In M. Hunter (Ed.), *The sexually abused male: Prevalence, impact, and treatment* (Vol. 1, pp. 73–85). Lexington Books.

Sheahan, C. L., Pica, E., & Pozzulo, J. D. (2021). Abuse is abuse: The influence of type of abuse, victim age, and defendant age on juror decision making. *Journal of Interpersonal Violence, 36*(1-2), 938–956. https://doi.org/10.1177/0886260517731316

Skorinko, J. L., & Spellman, B. A. (2013). Stereotypic crimes: How group-crime associations affect memory and (sometimes) verdicts and sentencing. *Victims & Offenders, 8*(3), 278–307. https://doi.org/10.1080/15564886.2012.755140

Stanziani, M., & Cox, J. (2021). The failure of all mothers or the mother of all failures? Juror perceptions of failure to protect laws. *Journal of Interpersonal Violence, 36*(1–2), NP690–NP711. https://doi.org/10.1177/0886260517736273

Stawiski, S., Dykema-Engblade, A., & Tindle, R. S. (2012). The roles of shared stereotypes and shared processing goals on mock jury decision making. *Basic & Applied Social Psychology, 34*(1), 88–97. https://doi.org/10.1080/01973533.2011.637467

Stevenson, M. C., Bottoms, B. L., & Burke, K. (2020). *The legacy of race for children: Psychology, public policy, and law*. Oxford University Press.

Stevenson, M. C., & Bottoms, B. L., & Diamond, S. S. S. (2010). Jurors' discussions of a defendant's history of child abuse and alcohol abuse in capital sentencing deliberations. *Psychology, Public Policy, & Law, 16*(1), 1–38. https://doi.org/10.1037/a0018404

Stevenson, M. C., & Rivers, M. A. (2023). When disclosure fails to substantiate abuse: Child and perpetrator race predict child sexual abuse substantiation. *Child Maltreatment, 28*(4), 1–13. https://doi.org/10.1177/10775595231157729

Voogt, A., & Klettke, B. (2017). The effect of gender on perceptions of credibility in child sexual assault cases: A systematic review. *Journal of Child Sexual Abuse: Research, Treatment, & Program Innovations for Victims, Survivors, & Offenders, 26*(2), 195–212. https://doi.org/10.1080/10538712.2017.1280576

Wang, Y., & Stevenson, M. C. (2023, April 20–22). *Effects of child sexual abuse victim mental health status on mock jurors' case judgments.* [Paper presentation]. Annual meeting of the Midwestern Psychological Association, Chicago, IL, United States.

Wiley, T. R. A., & Bottoms, B. L. (2009). Effects of defendant sexual orientation on jurors' perceptions of child sexual assault. *Law & Human Behavior, 33*(1), 46–60. https://doi.org/10.1007/s10979-008-9131-2

Yozwiak, J. A., Golding, J. M., & Marsil, D. F. (2004). The impact of type of out-of-court disclosure in a child sexual assault trial. *Child Maltreatment, 9*(3), 325–334. https://doi.org/10.1177/1077559504266518

IV

EMOTIONAL REACTIONS AND COURT PREPARATION PROGRAMS

17

Children's Interactions With the Legal System

Hannah M. Johnson, Michaela G. Ramsey, Alexandria P. Winstead, and Stephanie D. Block

Each year, millions of children interact with the legal system worldwide (United Nations Children's Fund, 2022). Involvement in the legal system often results from reports of child maltreatment, meaning that children are either victims and/or witnesses of abuse. Child abuse is associated with poorer health outcomes in later adult years (Herrenkohl et al., 2012). Some of the known emotional outcomes related to child maltreatment are internalizing symptoms (e.g., depression, anxiety) and externalizing behaviors (e.g., aggression, substance use disorders). For example, child sexual abuse (CSA) is associated with significant detrimental effects on children's mental health, which can result in depression, anxiety, personality disorders, eating disorders, posttraumatic stress disorder, and self-harm (Cummings et al., 2012; Yates et al., 2008).

Understanding the true effect of legal participation on children can be hard to untangle as children involved in the legal system might also have trauma and adverse mental health outcomes (e.g., limited coping skills, poor emotion regulation) related to their maltreatment experience (Quas & Goodman, 2012). Legal proceedings are not designed to accommodate potentially traumatized children, and there is concern about the extent to which they cause children harm (e.g., secondary victimization; Sumalla & Hernández-Hidalgo, 2018). Yet, other research has emphasized some positive outcomes that children experience after participating in court (Goodman et al., 1992); for example,

We would like to thank our anonymous prosecutors who provided the case examples for this chapter.

https://doi.org/10.1037/0000492-017
Handbook on Child Witnesses: Improving Psychological Science and Legal Practice,
G. S. Goodman, T. D. Lyon, S. D. Hobbs, and R. Enriquez (Editors)

children being present and heard during legal hearings predicted better outcomes in child abuse cases (Block et al., 2010; Runyan et al., 1988). This chapter reviews what is known about the emotional impact of children's experiences in child abuse and criminal court and highlights a few case examples throughout that exemplify some of the empirical findings.

When children are the main witnesses, cases typically cannot move forward without some degree of their participation. Their involvement can range from being victims of crime, being eyewitnesses to crime, and/or participation in custody cases. Children might have forensic interviews or provide courtroom testimony (see Chapters 8 to 14, this volume, for more information about forensic interviewing practices). In child abuse court (sometimes referred to as dependency court, juvenile court, or family court), there are all types of maltreatment cases, including neglect, child physical abuse, and/or CSA. This court makes decisions about potential out-of-home/foster care placement and decisions about the potential termination of parental rights (Block et al., 2010). When children testify in criminal court, they most commonly do so in cases of CSA (Goodman et al., 1999; Sedlak et al., 2006). Criminal courts make decisions on guilt or innocence and punish those found guilty. It should be noted that much of the research related to children's involvement in forensic and legal settings addresses factors related to CSA. Each of these interactions can have short- and long-term impacts on the children and their development, some of which are described in this chapter. Extensive research about children as offenders or perpetrators in cases involved in the juvenile justice system is not included. Here our main goal is to review the emotional experiences and outcomes for children involved in the legal system as victims or eyewitnesses.

When children must testify, as is often true in criminal court, several facets of interacting with the legal system are potentially stressful for children (Goodman et al., 1992; Quas et al., 2005, 2009; Troxel et al., 2009). It can be difficult for victims to take the stand (Elmi et al., 2018; Goodman et al., 1992), talk about their abuse in front of strangers (Saywitz & Nathanson, 1993), see their abuser in court (Hobbs et al., 2014), understand the legal process (Quas et al., 2005), or be cross-examined by the defendant's attorney (Szojka et al., 2023). Beyond testifying, Sas and colleagues (1993) found that negative court outcomes (e.g., a perpetrator being found not guilty) and a close relationship to the perpetrator (e.g., if the perpetrator was a family member) increased children's emotional distress. Additionally, delays in court proceedings can prolong emotional recovery; for example, children may stay anxious for longer (Goodman et al., 1992; Runyan et al., 1988) or take more time to resolve their depression symptoms (Whitcomb et al., 1994).

Individual differences and case factors also may affect how children fare. Legal involvement can differ across age, gender, and case factors, such as caregiver support and severity of abuse (Goodman et al., 1992; Quas et al., 2005, 2009). Emotional outcomes may differ across racial groups. Qualitative analyses have revealed that underrepresented children involved in child abuse court felt they were not believed or listened to (Block et al., 2010). Regardless of these individual differences and case factors, the pathway to legal justice typically relies on children's participation. It is crucial to understand the emotional outcomes associated with legal involvement and the ways in which innovative practices are used to reduce negative consequences and bolster positive experiences.

CHILD ABUSE COURT INVOLVEMENT

The goal of child abuse court is to protect children from future harm and ensure they have a safe home/place to live (Sedlak et al., 2006). Child abuse court can be a lengthy process (e.g., years), which involves numerous hearings, meetings, and court appearances (Malloy et al., 2007). Children involved in child abuse court are often victims of substantiated abuse, most often involving physical abuse and especially neglect (Sedlak et al., 2006). Child abuse court can be traumatic for all involved. Shdaimah and Summers (2014) surveyed adult stakeholders regarding their perceptions of the child abuse court process in Baltimore, Maryland, finding that the court environment itself was stressful. The environment was described as hectic and frantic, with no space for the children, families, or other professionals to meet (Shdaimah & Summers, 2014). Additionally, Stephens and colleagues (2021) interviewed social workers, attorneys, parent advocates, and parents involved in child abuse court who described the court process as harsh and antitherapeutic, where race and class bias can compound the traumatic experience of legal involvement, which puts already at-risk children in an environment that adults describe as chaotic.

In addition to the actual court environment, research indicates that other factors, such as understanding the court proceedings, may influence the mental health of children involved in child abuse court hearings. Quas and colleagues (2009) found that children who did better answering questions about the legal system also reported lower levels of distress concerning their court involvement. This does not necessarily mean a better understanding of court proceedings led to lower distress; it is possible that increased distress affected children's ability to respond to questions about the legal system (Quas et al., 2009). Children in child abuse court want the opportunity to meaningfully participate in decisions that affect them. This requires more involvement of children and families in the decision-making process through feedback mechanisms that support this involvement (Cashmore, 2025).

Children involved in child abuse court can be removed from their homes and can experience multiple housing placements, with some data indicating that children in foster care can experience up to 15 to 20 (or more) placements during their time in care (Hartman et al., 2023; Newton et al., 2000). Many of these children are separated from their siblings, families, schools, and communities. Such disruptions put children at risk for internalizing and externalizing symptoms (Hindt & Leon, 2022), therefore children in the court system are already potentially vulnerable. Many children involved in child abuse court report just wanting to go home (Block et al., 2010), even if they are experiencing maltreatment there.

Block and colleagues (2010) found that child abuse court knowledge was quite low for 7- to 10-year-olds and was not significantly predicted by child factors (e.g., mental state, ethnicity). Positive attitudes toward child abuse courts were more likely for younger children and children who had lower levels of anxiety (Block et al., 2010). Comparing children's attitudes toward criminal and/or child abuse courts, children appearing in child abuse court expressed more positive attitudes about seeing the perpetrator in court than children appearing in criminal court. These child victims and witnesses had more positive attitudes about answering questions in court (both child abuse and criminal court) when they were younger (perhaps more naïve) and when the abuse was less severe (Hobbs et al., 2014).

Lastly, waiting to testify is a potentially important factor to consider in how children might fare. For instance, children who testified in child abuse court showed improvement after testimony and were able to more quickly resolve symptoms of anxiety related to testifying than the children who were still awaiting trial at the time of the final interview (Runyan et al., 1988). In summary, positive attitudes of children appearing in child abuse court relate to child characteristics (e.g., lower age), case details (e.g., lower severity of abuse), and timing associated with resolution of the case. Because participating in child abuse court can be distressing, there is a need to provide intervention, support, and resources to children to lessen these negative experiences.

Supporting Children in Child Abuse Court

Some of the procedures implemented to support children who are involved in child abuse court include court preparation programs, *guardian ad litems* (GALs), court-appointed special advocates (CASAs), and legislation aimed at reducing the length of court proceedings. Interventions aimed at providing legal education to children could help reduce the negative outcomes associated with child abuse court involvement (Block et al., 2010; Quas et al., 2009). Court preparation programs are a way some of these interventions can be implemented (see Chapter 18, this volume, for more information on court preparation programs). GALs and CASAs are professionals assigned to work with children involved in child abuse court cases. Their main role is to advocate for the children; specifically, GALs often act as legal advocates, reporting to judges on what is in the best interest of the children. There is limited empirical work examining the effectiveness of GALs on reducing the negative outcomes for children involved in child abuse court.

The CASA program is one protective program that has undergone numerous evaluations for effectiveness. There are over 900 CASA programs in the United States (National CASA/GAL Association for Children, 2022). Although there are differences between jurisdictions, the CASA programs have the same goals—to advocate for the needs of children and to help them achieve permanency by presenting formal reports to the courts (Gershun & Terrebonne, 2018). Having a support person in court has a positive impact on children's well-being.

Children with CASAs have more frequent contact with a supportive adult and as well as improved access to services. Having a CASA is associated with children having less negative behavior and better educational outcomes compared to those who do not have a CASA (Gershun & Terrebonne, 2018). The effectiveness of the CASA program highlights the important support these volunteers provide to children during their time in court. Unfortunately, there are not enough volunteers for the CASA programs (Felix et al., 2017; Gershun & Terrebonne, 2018). Cases with children who are older and with more than one type of maltreatment reported were more likely to be assigned CASA workers compared to younger children and those with one type of abuse reported (Osborne et al., 2019). More work needs to be accomplished to ensure that all children in child abuse court can access this type of support to buffer the negative effects this court may have on children.

Targeted legislation to reduce delays in court proceedings in child abuse courts has been implemented in countries such as England and Wales. The goal of this legislation is to give children speedier access to permanency plans and closure. Specifically, the Children and Family Act 2014 introduced a 26-week rule to reduce the timeline for proceeding through child abuse court. There is a paucity of research about positive changes this act is having on children involved in child abuse court; however, there has been no documented increase in negative outcomes for children (Beckett et al., 2016). With further evaluation, this may be a promising innovation to help reduce the hardships children experience when participating in potentially lengthy and repeated child abuse court proceedings. It is important to note that sometimes cases require delays because of the case context; for example, if parental rights are being terminated, there should be a thorough investigation or if parents need time to complete treatment programs (Masson et al., 2017).

In conclusion, child abuse courts seek to protect children from future harm (Sedlak et al., 2006), yet lengthy and repeated court proceedings, conflicting opinions of professionals about what should happen with the case (Malloy et al., 2007), and multiple out-of-home placements (Newton et al., 2000) likely cause additional trauma. Many parents and their representatives report that the court environment itself can be stressful and chaotic for children, families, and other professionals (Shdaimah & Summers, 2014; Stephens et al., 2021). Cashmore (2024) highlights the need for the decision makers to include the child in the process, facilitate a respectful dialogue, and ground their decisions in evidence-based practices. There have been some promising innovations initiated to address some of these concerns; however, more resources, evaluation, and support are needed to further help children involved in child abuse court and reduce the harm related to child abuse court involvement.

CRIMINAL COURT INVOLVEMENT

This section turns to the impact on children of criminal court involvement. As previously mentioned, it can be hard to disentangle the effect of testifying from the detrimental effects of abuse (Ghetti et al., 2002). There are many ways to measure success in CSA cases. A verdict is one measure, such that when a child comes forward and an offender is found guilty, many might feel that justice has been served. In any case, it is important to consider the perspective and bearing on the child in the following examples.

> ***Case Study 1:***[1] A child was the victim of rape by a friend's father. This child, like many, was threatened that if he told anyone, his parents would be killed. At first, he did not tell anyone because of that threat. Eventually, he made a partial disclosure, and when his parents did not die, the child eventually told more. The victim's parents were supportive and wanted him to go through with the trial and testify. There was concern from the therapists about how the child would fare emotionally if there was a not guilty verdict. He testified, and the verdict was guilty. After the sentencing, the child realized that his friend's father was now going to jail. He felt so guilty—incorrectly feeling that it was his fault that his friend's dad was now in prison. This child victim ended up hospitalized with severe mental health concerns.

> ***Case Study 2:*** A very young child fell into the rare percentage of children who are assaulted by a stranger. This child was molested in a public setting and testified in a trial where the verdict was not guilty. Interestingly, the parents never told the child the case outcome or complained that the system failed them, and they only told the child that the child did a great job. Over a decade later, the same stranger was charged with assaulting someone else, and the initial victim, now a successful and happy college student, was contacted by investigators. It was only then that the initial child learned that the stranger had been found not guilty in the first trial. In the second trial, the perpetrator was found guilty.

These case studies demonstrate the importance of focusing not just on the verdict, but on the perspective and framing of the criminal trial/outcome to the children through a developmental lens. In most states, it is necessary for children to testify in criminal court because they are typically the primary evidence in the case, particularly in sexual abuse cases (Lamb et al., 2008). In fact, the American Academy of Pediatrics estimates that substantially more than 100,000 children appear as witnesses in court every year (Pantell, 2017). Children's testimony has been identified as a critical piece of evidence in prosecuting child maltreatment (Cross & Whitcomb, 2017). When they testify, children face the accused perpetrator in the courtroom. Prosecutors understand that legal involvement can be distressing for children and attempt to prepare them for court proceedings. However, despite this awareness and attempts to promote a better understanding of the court process, child maltreatment cases rely heavily on children's testimony (Cross & Whitcomb, 2017) making it difficult to minimize the children's involvement in their cases.

Goodman and colleagues (1992) conducted one of the first studies that examined the effect of legal involvement on children's well-being. They interviewed children who testified in criminal court and children who did not testify. As judged by parents, children who testified had more behavioral problems 7 months after their testimony compared to children who did not testify.

[1]The clinical material used in this chapter has been disguised to protect patient confidentiality.

Of interest, once the prosecution concluded, and in the cases where the children had supportive caregivers, the negative effects of testifying lessened (Goodman et al., 1992). After 10 years, Quas and colleagues (2005) conducted a follow-up study on the outcomes of legal involvement with the same children that Goodman and colleagues (1992) had studied. Children who experienced both severe sexual abuse and testified multiple times had an increased risk for trauma-related symptoms (e.g., sexualized behaviors), externalized behaviors (e.g., aggression, delinquency), and internalized behaviors (e.g., anxiety, depression). Furthermore, several children reported negative outcomes after not testifying, especially when defendants received lighter sentences (Quas et al., 2005). Younger children had more difficulty enduring their legal involvement, and younger age was associated with increased externalized behaviors over time. There is some evidence that younger children (under 8 years old) are less stressed when testifying compared to older children (Whitcomb et al., 1994). One potential explanation for this finding is that the courts were in some ways more protective of younger victims.

More recently, Elmi and colleagues (2018) examined emotional and mental health outcomes in a sample of children referred to a children's advocacy center following a report of abuse, in which 38% of the children testified in court. Results indicated that all the children ($N = 344$) showed significant improvement after two years, but that children who testified in court more than once showed higher levels of emotional distress (e.g., hypervigilance, avoidance, depression, anxiety). Numerous studies reveal that testifying multiple times might be especially challenging for children (Goodman et al., 1992; Quas et al., 2005).

Research has consistently found that children report anxiety about facing their alleged perpetrators, recounting their abuse to strangers, and other fears related to being embarrassed, accused of lying, or crying during their testimony (Back et al., 2011; Murtha, 2021; Troxel et al., 2009). Children who appear in criminal court express more negative attitudes about seeing the defendant in court than do children appearing in child abuse court (Hobbs et al., 2014). In the presence of their abuser, children's trauma symptoms can increase and affect their ability to communicate (Goodman et al., 1992). Experiencing high levels of stress can negatively impact detailed memory recall (Wolf, 2017). Thus, minimizing stress in the courtroom can be important to facilitate children's abilities to communicate accurately which is beneficial for promoting just outcomes (refer to Chapters 3, and 7, this volume, for more information on childhood memory and suggestibility within the legal system).

In court, witnesses are subjected to cross-examination, potentially years after abuse and/or initial disclosures occurred. Cross-examination can be distressing for children. During cross-examination, some attorneys use developmentally inappropriate terminology and sentence phrasing, designed to confuse children, while harshly questioning them in court (R. Zajac et al., 2012). Although there is much research on the appropriate way to elicit accurate information from children (including this book), attorneys are not required to use these empirically based techniques when questioning children. Both prosecutors and defense attorneys rely on yes–no and forced-choice questions when interviewing child witnesses (Szojka et al., 2023). When cross-examining victims or witnesses, defense attorneys often rely on suggestive questions, which can be confusing and problematic for children (R. Zajac et al., 2012). In fact, Lyon and colleagues (2012) found that defense attorneys asked 79% of the suggestive questions posed to children testifying in felony CSA trials. When these and other poor practices are used, children can experience new trauma, which can influence their ability to recover from engaging in the legal process (Westcott & Page, 2002).

Supports in Criminal Court

Given the high level of stress surrounding children's testimony, several measures exist to reduce courtroom stress for children who testify, including court preparation programs (see Chapter 18, this volume), closed-circuit television (CCTV; Goodman et al., 1998), service animals, victim advocates, and caregiver support. CCTV, sometimes referred to as live link, is a protective measure where children can testify from another location (e.g., private room in the courthouse), to reduce stress by addressing fears of testifying (e.g., facing abusers, being on the witness stand, and crying in court; Eastwood, 2003; Sas et al., 1991). The use of CCTV and prerecorded interviews has been widely implemented in many countries (e.g., United Kingdom, Australia, New Zealand, Sweden). In the United States, however, the Confrontation Clause (Amendment VI of the U.S. Constitution) guarantees the right for the defendant to have a face-to-face confrontation with their accuser(s) when charged with a criminal offense, and CCTV can be seen as a violation of this right. Yet, a defendant's right to confrontation can be restricted if children are under emotional distress or unable to communicate in court due to the presence of their abusers. To date, 24 U.S. states have addressed this challenge and have created statutes allowing for CCTV testimonies (Murtha, 2021). The use of CCTV for types of crimes varies greatly. For example, statutes in seven states, including Florida, Colorado, Illinois, Mississippi, Rhode Island, Vermont, and New York, allow CCTV for sexual offense crimes only. Arizona, Arkansas, Kansas, and Wisconsin will allow CCTV for any crime (Bennett, 2004). The accessibility of CCTV also varies for child victims. According to Bennett (2004), 16 states will allow the use of CCTV only for victims; 21 states will allow child victims and witnesses to testify via CCTV. Children who used CCTV during their testimony expressed gratitude and relief due to not having to face their abusers (Eastwood, 2003). Although CCTV is allowed in numerous states, Goodman and colleagues (1999) conducted a nationwide survey of prosecutors and found that they are less likely to use CCTV due to the negative perceptions associated with children's testimony.

Facility dogs (i.e., accredited service dogs) are professionally trained to assist individuals, typically children, who may experience psychological, emotional, or physical difficulties and are used as a therapeutic measure for children. These dogs help decrease anxiety and stress (Crenshaw & Stella, 2011) and help the interviewer build rapport with abused children (Howell et al., 2021; Spruin et al., 2020). Research has assessed the effect of having a dog present during police interviews for CSA victims and found that children had decreased stress when a dog was present (Krause-Parello et al., 2018). To expand further on a facility dog's role in legal interviews, Spruin and colleagues (2020) administered a survey to sexual assault survivors to assess the use of a facility dog in building rapport and providing support during legal interviews. The use of facility dogs reduced anxiety in survivors and helped them feel more comfortable in legal environments. These positive outcomes contributed to improvements in the interviewer's ability to establish rapport and build trust with the witness (Spruin et al., 2020). Even with these positive outcomes, there is concern that the use of dogs will increase bias (for children/against defendants) among jurors. Burd and McQuiston (2019) examined potential mock juror bias by having children testify alone, with a facility dog, or while holding a teddy bear for comfort. Mock jurors' experience of emotion toward the defendant and likelihood of conviction were measured. Findings indicated that the use of teddy bears for support increased participants' feelings of disgust toward the defendant and the likelihood of conviction; however, the use of facility dogs decreased participants' feelings of disgust and anger toward the defendant. Further, authors reported that jurors did not attribute ownership of the dog to the victim (Burd & McQuiston, 2019). See Chapter 18, this volume, for more details on the use of facility dogs.

Sometimes, children simply want someone present in the courtroom when they testify. In fact, there are federal funds that can be used to help children have access to support persons during their cases (Child Abuse Prevention and Treatment Act, 1974/2018). Children often are assigned victim advocates, who work in concert with the prosecutors' offices and are present in the courtroom. These victim advocates can explain the court process to the children and their families throughout their cases. Victim advocates and other professionals are essential support for children involved in criminal court and can be even more important if caregivers do not provide optimal support to their children. In the following case study, a child is highly supported by the prosecutorial team and a foster parent.

> ***Case Study 3:*** A prosecutor told us about a 5-year-old girl who was raped by her mother's boyfriend. The mother supported the boyfriend in the trial, even shouting at her child on the way to court, "you f***ing little lying b**ch wh*re." The child was placed in foster care. The child testified in court and afterward told the prosecutor, "I told the truth, and I didn't die!" That night was the first night the child slept through the night and didn't wake up with a nightmare. Those who knew the child reported an immediate change in the child's demeanor when she came off the stand. The child was eventually adopted by the foster parent and went on to graduate from college.

One clearly documented protective factor related to the child's well-being, especially for CSA victims, is support from caregivers and family. Supportive caregivers display an overall concern for the child's well-being and safety

(Bick et al., 2014). For example, one dimension of support is protection; caregivers can protect their child by ensuring the perpetrator no longer has access to the child and/or removing the perpetrator from the home (Johnson et al., 2024). Victims of CSA experience reduced anxiety, better long-term adjustment (Elliott & Carnes, 2001; van Toledo & Seymour, 2013; K. Zajac et al., 2015), and an increased ability to cope postdisclosure when they have supportive caregivers (Cyr et al., 2013; see also Everson et al., 1989).

Caregivers also play a vital role in the investigation and prosecution of children's CSA cases. Block and colleagues (2023) and Duron (2018) found that CSA cases reported to prosecutors' offices were more likely to move forward with prosecution when there was documentation of caregiver support. As previously discussed, when children testify, regardless of case outcome, support from their caregivers, specifically their mothers, helps ease the stress of testifying in court (Goodman et al., 1992). However, not all CSA cases go to trial. Some of these cases are settled outside the courtroom via plea bargains and settlement agreements (Block et al., 2023). It is important that victims continue to be provided with high levels of support throughout and beyond the legal proceedings.

Caregivers can affect their children's exposure to various resources. They may need to coordinate and provide transportation to appointments (e.g., court-related appointments, medical exams, therapy sessions). Often the caregivers are the ones responsible for getting the children access to recommended services and support during the legal process. To do so, caregivers need access to resources of their own to increase their ability to support their children. Caregivers consistently report needing access to their own mental health resources, social support, and financial support (Johnson, 2022; van Toledo & Seymour, 2013). McPherson and colleagues (2012) discuss the value of caregivers receiving their own mental health support, specifically if they were victims of CSA. In a qualitative study interviewing nonoffending caregivers, individual support (e.g., therapy, social support from friends and family) was rated as the most helpful resource to help them cope with their children's cases; seven out of 11 participants had access to their own therapy. One caregiver noted, "I needed my own therapy for parenting problems and court issues and all this . . . I'm not using my kid's therapy time to talk about parenting issues" (Johnson, 2022, n.p.). Other caregivers reported needing access to more community support to help with the whole process of their children's cases. However, there are few evidence-based community resources available to caregivers to help them support their children through the legal process (Hernandez et al., 2009). Future research should further study ways to bolster support for caregivers to increase their capacity to support their children and potentially reduce the negative effect of criminal court involvement.

The criminal legal system is not designed for children, and how children are treated throughout the criminal court process influences their experiences and potentially the case outcomes (Quas & Goodman, 2012). Future research related to children's involvement in criminal court should examine the different nuances of cases and how those nuances emotionally affect the child victims. For example, Quas and colleagues (2023) examined the differences between cases of child sex trafficking and CSA and found victims of sex trafficking were noted to be uncooperative and have a lack of caregiver support—important nuances. Future research should explore how cooperation affects case outcomes for both trafficking victims and CSA victims (see Chapter 11, this volume, for more about trafficking victims' cooperation during forensic interviews).

CONTEXTUAL FACTORS AND CONSIDERATIONS

When child abuse victims are involved in the legal system, our observations lead us to make a few recommendations. Communities need more education on how they can participate in abuse prevention efforts, protect victims and families, and identify evidence of child maltreatment when they serve on juries (Williams et al., 2022). There is a need for further research on the feasibility of recommendations provided to families when their children's cases are closed in the legal system, regardless of the case outcome (Williams et al., 2022).

Children involved in the legal system indicate a need to be protected, to be seen and heard, to be believed, and to be supported (Field & Katz, 2022). Not receiving appropriate support to manage negative emotional outcomes can have far-reaching consequences for children, their families, and the community; for example, some children engage in juvenile offending behavior such as truancy, substance use, and other risk-taking behavior. Reports indicate 9% to 30% of child victims engage in juvenile offending behavior (Ryan & Testa, 2005). This percentage can increase to 38% if there are no interventions in place to support the child victim (Widom, 1989). The following case example highlights this concern.

> ***Case Study 4:*** The stepdad had raped the child from around ages 5 to 15. The mom and whole family supported the stepdad. The child victim was 15 at the time of indictment and 17 at the time of testimony. She testified about the long-standing rape and horrific abuse, and the stepdad was convicted. The victim had no other support system in place and was disowned by her mother. After the trial, the child ended up delinquent and in the system herself as an offender.

To mitigate the negative effects of abuse, children need access to protective factors, which include supportive adults and appropriate services to address their emotional needs. Communities and policies also need to acknowledge and address the abundance of evidence within the U.S. criminal legal system of racial bias (Kovera, 2019) and how this could potentially influence reporting and handling of these cases. Race of the victim affects legal decision-making processes ranging from protective order determinations, to police arrests, to judicial sentencing (Burke et al., 2020; Hunt, 2015; Winstead & Stevenson, 2021). Even within the child welfare system, Black children are overrepresented, experience slower exit rates, and are more likely to be removed from their homes

(Lu et al., 2004; Putnam-Hornstein et al., 2013). A longitudinal study followed children aged 5 to 10 years and found that direct racism (e.g., hate crimes) was associated with increased risk of mental health symptoms (e.g., suicide risk), and continued indirect racism (e.g., structural racism) increased the odds of sleep difficulties and poor mental health (Shepherd et al., 2017). It is not surprising that these experiences of racism have long-term developmental effects, indicating a need for increased support services and debiasing strategies to address this unfair treatment of children. Children and their families who are disproportionately represented, whose families feel in any way targeted, or who have a general distrust of the criminal legal system due to concerns of racism or racial trauma, might be more susceptible to negative emotional (and health-related) outcomes (Sanders-Phillips et al., 2014). Frequently reviewing policies and procedures to make sure all children and families are receiving equitable access to support is essential (Rosenberg et al., 2024). Research needs to investigate what policies and procedures would lead to more equitable outcomes for families and children and then implement these evidence-based procedures into practice. Future research should further explore these topics to enhance the well-being of children and families interacting with the legal system.

CONCLUSION

Child abuse and criminal courts present different challenges to children enduring stress and other negative emotional outcomes related to involvement with the legal system (e.g., testifying in court). Whether a case moves forward with prosecution or not, child victims and witnesses need access to many resources to appropriately cope with the actual and potential trauma of violence as well as the impact of participating in the legal system. First, we acknowledge that the research on the emotional effects of court is studying children who are, for the most part, already at risk and/or traumatized. Limited longitudinal research has examined the influence of testimony and participating in various phases of the legal system. Additionally, some of the research described in this chapter is observational and not experimental; therefore, we need to be cautious about assuming legal involvement is causing the observed distress.

There are a multitude of factors that can predict how any child will fare. As described earlier, having a supportive caregiver is associated with positive outcomes (Block et al., 2023; Goodman et al., 1992). Limiting the number of times that a child testifies may also be important (Elmi et al., 2018; Quas et al., 2005). Future research should examine the many reasons that children can testify multiple times (e.g., there could be multiple defendants in a different trial, in the case of a hung jury with a subsequent retrial) and the impact this could have on various children and case outcomes. Additionally, the length of court cases can be problematic for children, who want to move on from their cases. In Massachusetts (like many other states), CSA cases take an average of about 2 years to go to trial (Block & Williams, 2019). After COVID-19, some trials did not begin for up to 4 years. Waiting to testify can increase anxiety in children (Runyan et al., 1988). However, in some cases, having more time before a trial is viewed as a positive if children are supported and become more capable of coping with the challenges of a trial (Williams et al., 2022).

This chapter detailed children's fears about testifying in court, many of which are, unfortunately, valid. Despite some limited changes in the law, most children who testify will do so facing their perpetrator and will have to recall specific details of their abuse to strangers. Many will be accused of lying, and some will cry during their testimonies. Most attorneys do not ask children questions in developmentally appropriate ways and tend to use forced-choice or yes–no questions rather than open-ended questions when asking children about sexual touch (Szojka et al., 2023). Defense attorneys ask questions designed to discredit child witnesses and sometimes ask questions that are intentionally confusing (R. Zajac et al., 2012). And still, many children (and their families) make the decision to participate in these trials. Trials can provide a sense of closure and justice, and trials can give children a sense of control (Brannon, 1994). Some victims report enduring trials in the hopes of protecting future victims from their perpetrators. From a social safety perspective, when guilty defendants remain free, there is a concern about future victims (Collings, 2011). Research indicates that involvement in the legal system can be beneficial for child victims, despite potential stress and anxiety (Goodman et al., 1992). In Berliner and Conte's (1995) interviews with child maltreatment victims and families about their experience with the legal system, many victims reported that although the prospect of participating in the legal system can elicit negative emotions (e.g., anxiety), with support they would prefer to participate.

Most criminal maltreatment cases cannot go forward without the participation of child victims and their families. Some do not want to participate because of their concerns about court-related stress. There are evidence-based innovations we can use to buffer this experience for children. There is a benefit to having support animals and/or support people (including victim advocates, CASAs) available to children (Spruin et al., 2020). Although our court systems could be designed to better protect children, we can use CCTV or other methods to make this experience less traumatic for children. These measures reduce some of the negative emotional outcomes of involvement in the legal process (see Chapter 18, this volume, about court preparation programs); however, more work should take place to implement these supports for child victims and witnesses throughout the country. Of interest, these techniques not only reduce stress for children, they also have been shown to increase children's memory accuracy (Wolf, 2017), promoting justice. Despite research on the effectiveness of innovations and techniques to reduce stress for children, we have seen limited use of such programs in the United States.

The U.S. court system has not applied some of the science designed to reduce stress for children in courtroom settings; courts are not designed to support child victims and child witnesses. While courts must balance the rights of defendants and children, more collaboration and cross-disciplinary training is needed for professionals working with children in these settings (Kletzka & Siegfried, 2008). Although there are individual differences in how child victims and witnesses might respond to their participation in the legal process, legal professionals would benefit from education on child development to reduce unnecessary stress. Better training and communication between legal professionals can buffer the potential emotional effects of testifying in court for children. Future research exploring the implementation of cross-disciplinary training and education with legal professionals can help increase the use of evidence-based effective practices for legal professionals (Herbert et al., 2021).

Finally, much is already known about ways we can both reduce stress and promote children's well-being in legal settings and especially after legal involvement. It is our responsibility as scientists to advocate for the implementation of empirically-based policy and change in the courtroom, and throughout the legal process to reduce stress on children.

REFERENCES

Back, C., Gustafsson, P. A., Larsson, I., & Bertero, C. (2011). Managing the legal proceedings: An interpretative phenomenological analysis of sexually abused children's experience with the legal process. *Child Abuse & Neglect, 35*(1), 50–57. https://doi.org/10.1016/j.chiabu.2010.08.004

Beckett, C., Dickens, J., & Bailey, S. (2016). *Outcomes for children of shorter court decision-making processes: A follow-up study of the Tri-borough care proceedings pilot.* Centre for Research on Children and Families, School of Social Work, University of East Anglia. https://ueaeprints.uea.ac.uk/id/eprint/62005/1/Tri_borough_outcomes_report_October_2016_UEA.docx.pdf

Bennett, K. J. (2004). Legal and social issues surrounding closed-circuit television testimony of child victims and witnesses. *Journal of Aggression, Maltreatment & Trauma, 8*(3), 233–271. https://doi.org/10.1300/J146v08n03_02

Berliner, L., & Conte, J. R. (1995). The effects of disclosure and intervention on sexually abused children. *Child Abuse & Neglect, 19*(3), 371–384. https://doi.org/10.1016/s0145-2134(94)00138-3

Bick, J., Zajac, K., Ralston, M. E., & Smith, D. (2014). Convergence and divergence in reports of maternal support following childhood sexual abuse: Prevalence and associations with youth psychosocial adjustment. *Child Abuse & Neglect, 38*(3), 479–487. https://doi.org/10.1016/j.chiabu.2013.11.010

Block, S. D., Johnson, H. M., Williams, L. M., Shockley, K. L., Wang, E., & Widaman, K. F. (2023). Predictors of prosecutorial decisions in reports of child sexual abuse. *Child Maltreatment, 28*(3), 488–499. https://doi.org/10.1177/10775595221074375

Block, S. D., Oran, H., Oran, D., Baumrind, N., & Goodman, G. S. (2010). Abused and neglected children in court: Knowledge and attitudes. *Child Abuse & Neglect, 34*(9), 659–670. https://doi.org/10.1016/j.chiabu.2010.02.003

Block, S. D., & Williams, L. M. (2019). *The prosecution of child sexual abuse: A partnership to improve outcomes.* U.S. Department of Justice Office of Justice Programs. https://www.nij.ojp.gov/library/publications/prosecution-child-sexual-abuse-partnership-improve-outcomes

Brannon, L. C. (1994). The trauma of testifying in court for child victims of sexual assault vs. the accused's right to confrontation. *Law & Psychology Review, 18,* 439.

Burd, K. A., & McQuiston, D. E. (2019). Facility dogs in the courtroom: Comfort without prejudice? *Criminal Justice Review, 44*(4), 515–536. https://doi.org/10.1177/0734016819844298

Burke, K. C., Petty, T., Jones, T. M., Stevenson, M. C., Silberkleit, G., & Bottoms, B. L. (2020). Adults' perceptions of law-involved minority children and youth: Implications for researchers and professionals. In M. C. Stevenson, B. L. Bottoms, & K. C. Burke (Eds.), *The legacy of racism for children: Psychology, law and public policy* (pp. 189–210). Oxford University Press. https://doi.org/10.1093/med-psych/9780190056742.003.0011

Cashmore, J. (2024). Procedural justice and the impact of court and other decision-making processes on children and families in the child protection system. *Children Australia, 46*(2), 3035. https://doi.org/10.61605/cha_3035

Cashmore, J. (2025). The role of children's voices and feedback mechanisms in family justice. *Child & Family Social Work*. Advance online publication. https://doi.org/10.1111/cfs.13303

Child Abuse Prevention and Treatment Act, 42 U.S.C. 5106 (1974 & rev. 2018). https://www.govinfo.gov/content/pkg/USCODE-2017-title42/html/USCODE-2017-title42-chap67.htm

Collings, S. J. (2011). Professional services for child rape survivors: A child-centered perspective on helpful and harmful experiences. *Journal of Child & Adolescent Mental Health, 23*(1), 5–15. https://doi.org/10.2989/17280583.2011.594244

Crenshaw, D. A., & Stella, L. (2011). The play therapist as advocate for children in the court system. *International Journal of Play Therapy, 6*(4), 6–9.

Cross, T. P., & Whitcomb, D. (2017). The practice of prosecuting child maltreatment: Results of an online survey of prosecutors. *Child Abuse & Neglect, 69*, 20–28. https://doi.org/10.1016/j.chiabu.2017.04.007

Cummings, M., Berkowitz, S. J., & Scribano, P. V. (2012). Treatment of childhood sexual abuse: An updated review. *Current Psychiatry Report, 14*(6), 599–607. https://doi.org/10.1007/s11920-012-0316-5

Cyr, M., McDuff, P., & Hébert, M. (2013). Support and profiles of nonoffending mothers of sexually abused children. *Journal of Child Sexual Abuse, 22*(2), 209–230. https://doi.org/10.1080/10538712.2013.737444

Duron, J. F. (2018). Legal decision-making in child sexual abuse investigations: A mixed-methods study of factors that influence prosecution. *Child Abuse & Neglect, 79*, 302–314. https://doi.org/10.1016/j.chiabu.2018.02.022

Eastwood, C. (2003). The experiences of child complainants of sexual abuse in the criminal justice system. *Trends & Issues in Crime and Criminal Justice, 250*, 1–6. Australian Institute of Criminology. https://www.aic.gov.au/publications/tandi/tandi250

Elliott, A. N., & Carnes, C. N. (2001). Reactions of nonoffending parents to the sexual abuse of their child: A review of the literature. *Child Maltreatment, 6*(4), 314–331. https://doi.org/10.1177/1077559501006004005

Elmi, M. H., Daignault, I. V., & Hébert, M. (2018). Child sexual abuse victims as witnesses: The influence of testifying on their recovery. *Child Abuse & Neglect, 86*, 22–32. https://doi.org/10.1016/j.chiabu.2018.09.001

Everson, M. D., Hunter, W. M., Runyon, D. K., Edelsohn, G. A., & Coulter, M. L. (1989). Maternal support following disclosure of incest. *American Journal of Orthopsychiatry, 59*(2), 197–207. https://doi.org/10.1111/j.1939-0025.1989.tb01651.x

Felix, S. N., Agnich, L. E., & Schueths, A. (2017). An evaluation of a court appointed special advocates (CASA) program in the rural south. *Children and Youth Services Review, 83*, 48–56. https://doi.org/10.1016/j.childyouth.2017.10.025

Field, N., & Katz, C. (2022). The experiences and perceptions of sexually abused children as participants in the legal process: Key conclusions from a scoping literature review. *Trauma, Violence, & Abuse, 24*(4), 2758–2771. https://doi.org/10.1177/15248380221111463

Gershun, M., & Terrebonne, C. (2018). Child welfare system interventions on behalf of children and families: Highlighting the role of court appointed special advocates. *Current Problems in Pediatric and Adolescent Health Care, 48*(9), 215–231. https://doi.org/10.1016/j.cppeds.2018.08.003

Ghetti, S., Alexander, K. W., & Goodman, G. S. (2002). Legal involvement in child sexual abuse cases: Consequences and interventions. *International Journal of Law and Psychiatry, 25*(3), 235–251. https://doi.org/10.1016/s0160-2527(02)00104-8

Goodman, G. S., Quas, J. A., Bulkley, J., & Shapiro, C. (1999). Innovations for child witnesses: A national survey. *Psychology, Public Policy, and Law, 5*(2), 255–281. https://doi.org/10.1037/1076-8971.5.2.255

Goodman, G. S., Taub, E. P., Jones, D. P. H., England, P., Port, L. K., Rudy, L., & Prado, L. (1992). Testifying in criminal court: Emotional effects on child sexual assault victims. *Monographs of the Society for Research in Child Development, 57*(5), i–159. https://doi.org/10.2307/1166127

Goodman, G. S., Tobey, A. E., Batterman-Faunce, J. M., Orcutt, H., Thomas, S., Shapiro, C., & Sachsenmaier, T. (1998). Face-to-face confrontation: Effects of closed-circuit technology on children's eyewitness testimony and jurors' decisions. *Law and Human Behavior, 22*(2), 165–203. https://doi.org/10.1023/A:1025742119977

Hartman, D. T., Wang, Y., Wu, Y., Goldfarb, D., Vidales, D., Qin, J., Eisen, M. L., & Goodman, G. S. (2023). Childhood sexual abuse: A longitudinal study of disclosures and denials. *Child Maltreatment, 28*(3), 462–475. https://doi.org/10.1177/10775595231165335

Herbert, J., Ghan, N., Salveron, M., & Walsh, W. (2021). Possible factors supporting cross-agency collaboration in child abuse cases: A scoping review. *Journal of Child Sexual Abuse, 30*(2), 167–191. https://doi.org/10.1080/10538712.2020.1856994

Hernandez, A., Ruble, C., Rockmore, L., McKay, M., Messam, T., Harris, M., & Hope, S. (2009). An integrated approach to treating non-offending parents affected by sexual abuse. *Social Work in Mental Health, 7*(6), 533–555. https://doi.org/10.1080/15332980802301440

Herrenkohl, T. I., Hong, S., Klika, J. B., Herrenkohl, R. C., & Russo, M. J. (2012). Developmental impacts of child abuse and neglect related to adult mental health, substance use, and physical health. *Journal of Family Violence, 28*(2), 191–199. https://doi.org/10.1007/s10896-012-9474-9

Hindt, L. A., & Leon, S. C. (2022). Ecological disruptions and well-being among children in foster care. *American Journal of Orthopsychiatry, 92*(1), 39–50. https://doi.org/10.1037/ort0000584

Hobbs, S. D., Goodman, G. S., Block, S. D., Oran, D., Quas, J. A., Park, A., Widaman, K. F., & Baumrind, N. (2014). Child maltreatment victims' attitudes about appearing in dependency and criminal courts. *Children and Youth Services Review, 44*, 407–416. https://doi.org/10.1016/j.childyouth.2014.07.001

Howell, T. J., Hodgkin, S., Modderman, C., & Bennett, P. C. (2021). Integrating facility dogs into legal contexts for survivors of sexual and family violence: Opportunities and challenges. *Anthrozoös, 34*(6), 863–876. https://doi.org/10.1080/08927936.2021.1938406

Hunt, J. S. (2015). Race in the justice system. In B. L. Cutler & P. A. Zapf (Eds.), *APA handbook of forensic psychology: Vol. 2. Criminal investigation, adjudication, and sentencing outcomes* (pp. 125–161). American Psychological Association. https://doi.org/10.1037/14462-005

Johnson, H. M. (2022). *Exploring the support of non-offending caregivers of child victims of sexual abuse* [Doctoral dissertation]. Department of Psychology, University of Massachusetts Lowell.

Johnson, H. M., Block, S. D., Gonzales, J. E., Ramsey, M. G., Shockley, K. L., & Williams, L. M. (2024). Predictors of non-offending caregiver support in cases of child sexual abuse. *Child Abuse & Neglect, 149*, 106650. https://doi.org/10.1016/j.chiabu.2024.106650

Kletzka, N. T., & Siegfried, C. (2008). Helping children in the child welfare systems heal from trauma: A systems integration approach. *Juvenile and Family Court Journal, 59*(4), 7–20. https://doi.org/10.1111/j.1755-6988.2008.00018.x

Kovera, M. B. (2019). Racial disparities in the criminal justice system: Prevalence, causes, and a search for solutions. *Journal of Social Issues, 75*(4), 1139–1164. https://doi.org/10.1111/josi.12355

Krause-Parello, C. A., Thames, M., Ray, C. M., & Kolassa, J. (2018). Examining the effects of a facility dog on stress in children undergoing forensic interview for allegations of child sexual abuse. *Journal of Child Sexual Abuse, 27*(3), 305–320. https://doi.org/10.1080/10538712.2018.1443303

Lamb, M. E., Hershkowitz, I., Orbach, Y., & Esplin, P. W. (2008). *Tell me what happened: Structured investigative interviews of child victims and witnesses*. John Wiley & Sons. https://doi.org/10.1002/9780470773291

Lu, Y. E., Landsverk, J., Ellis-Macleod, E., Newton, R., Ganger, W., & Johnson, I. (2004). Race, ethnicity, and case outcomes in child protective services. *Children and Youth Services Review, 26*(5), 447–461. https://doi.org/10.1016/j.childyouth.2004.02.002

Lyon, T. D., Scurich, N., Choi, K., Handmaker, S., & Blank, R. (2012). "How did you feel?": Increasing child sexual abuse witnesses' production of evaluative information. *Law & Human Behavior, 36*(5), 448–457. https://doi.org/10.1037/h0093986

Malloy, L. C., Lyon, T. D., & Quas, J. A. (2007). Filial dependency and recantation of child sexual abuse allegations. *Journal of the American Academy of Child & Adolescent Psychiatry, 46*(2), 162–170. https://doi.org/10.1097/01.chi.0000246067.77953.f7

Masson, J., Dickens, J., Bader, K., Garside, L., & Young, J. (2017). Achieving positive change for children? Reducing the length of child protection proceedings: Lessons from England and Wales. *Adoption & Fostering, 41*(4), 401–413. https://doi.org/10.1177/0308575917730007

McPherson, P., Scribano, P., & Stevens, J. (2012). Barriers to successful treatment completion in child sexual abuse survivors. *Journal of Interpersonal Violence, 27*(1), 23–39. https://doi.org/10.1177/0886260511416466

Murtha, C. (2021). Standing by to protect child abuse victims: Utilizing standby counsel in lieu of personal cross-examination. *Penn State Law Review, 126*(1), 249–272.

National CASA/GAL Association for Children. (2022). *History*. Retrieved April 5, 2022, from https://nationalcasagal.org/about-us/history/

Newton, R. R., Litrownik, A. J., & Landsverk, J. A. (2000). Children and youth in foster care: Disentangling the relationship between problem behaviors and number of placements. *Child Abuse & Neglect, 24*(10), 1363–1374. https://doi.org/10.1016/s0145-2134(00)00189-7

Osborne, C., Warner-Doe, H., & Lawson, J. (2019). Who gets a CASA? Selective characteristics of children appointed a CASA advocate. *Children & Youth Services Review, 98*, 65–71. https://doi.org/10.1016/j.childyouth.2018.12.020

Pantell, R. H. (2017). The child witness in the courtroom. *Pediatrics, 139*(3), 1–9. https://doi.org/10.1542/peds.2016-4008

Putnam-Hornstein, E., Needell, B., King, B., & Johnson-Motoyama, M. (2013). Racial and ethnic disparities: A population-based examination of risk factors for involvement with child protective services. *Child Abuse & Neglect, 37*(1), 33–46. https://doi.org/10.1016/j.chiabu.2012.08.005

Quas, J. A., & Goodman, G. S. (2012). Consequences of criminal court involvement for child victims. *Psychology, Public Policy, and Law, 18*(3), 392–414. https://doi.org/10.1037/a0026146

Quas, J. A., Goodman, G. S., Ghetti, S., Alexander, K. W., Edelstein, R., Redlich, A. D., & Jones, D. P. H. (2005). Childhood sexual assault victims: Long-term outcomes after testifying in criminal court. *Monographs of the Society for Research in Child Development, 70*(2), v, 118–128. https://doi.org/10.1111/j.1540-5834.2005.00337.x

Quas, J. A., Mukhopadhyay, S., Winks, K. M., Dianiska, R. E., & Lyon, T. D. (2023). Successful criminal prosecutions of sex trafficking and sexual abuse of minors: A comparative analysis. *Child Maltreatment, 28*(3), 500–516. https://doi.org/10.1177/10775595231176432

Quas, J. A., Wallin, A. R., Horwitz, B., Davis, E., & Lyon, T. D. (2009). Maltreated children's understanding of and emotional reactions to dependency court involvement. *Behavioral Sciences & the Law, 27*(1), 97–117. https://doi.org/10.1002/bsl.836

Rosenberg, R., Williams, S. C., Martinez, V., & Ball, J. C. (2024). Mandated reporting policies and the detection of child abuse and neglect. *Children and Youth Services Review, 159*, 107499. https://doi.org/10.1016/j.childyouth.2024.107499

Runyan, D. K., Everson, M. D., Edelsohn, G. A., Hunter, W. M., & Coulter, M. L. (1988). Impact of legal intervention on sexually abused children. *Pediatrics, 113*(4), 647–653. https://doi.org/10.1016/S0022-3476(88)80373-1

Ryan, J. P., & Testa, M. F. (2005). Child maltreatment and juvenile delinquency: Investigating the role of placement and placement instability. *Children and Youth Services Review, 27*(3), 227–249. https://doi.org/10.1016/j.childyouth.2004.05.007

Sanders-Phillips, K., Kliewer, W., Tirmazi, T., Nebbitt, V., Carter, T., & Key, H. (2014). Perceived racial discrimination, drug use, and psychological distress in African American youth: A pathway to child health disparities. *Journal of Social Issues, 70*(2), 279–297. https://doi.org/10.1111/josi.12060

Sas, L., Austin, G., Wolfe, D., & Hurley, P. (1991). *Reducing the system-induced trauma for child sexual abuse victims through court preparation, assessment, and follow-up* [Report]. National Welfare Grants Division, Health and Welfare Canada.

Sas, L. D., Hatch, A., Malla, S., Dick, T., & Hurley, P. (1993). *Three years after the verdict: A longitudinal study of the social and psychological adjustment of child witnesses referred to the child witness project.* Child Witness Project, London Family Court Clinic.

Saywitz, K. J., & Nathanson, R. (1993). Children's testimony and their perceptions of stress in and out of the courtroom. *Child Abuse & Neglect, 17*(5), 613–622. https://doi.org/10.1016/0145-2134(93)90083-H

Sedlak, A. J., Schultz, D., Wells, S. J., Lyons, P., Doueck, H. J., & Gragg, F. (2006). Child protection and justice systems processing of serious child abuse and neglect cases. *Child Abuse & Neglect, 30*(6), 657–677. https://doi.org/10.1016/j.chiabu.2005.11.010

Shdaimah, C., & Summers, A. (2014). Families in waiting: Adult stakeholder perceptions of family court. *Children and Youth Services Review, 44*, 114–119. https://doi.org/10.1016/j.childyouth.2014.06.004

Shepherd, C. C. J., Li, J., Cooper, M. N., Hopkins, K. D., & Farrant, B. M. (2017). The impact of racial discrimination on the health of Australian Indigenous children aged 5–10 years: Analysis of national longitudinal data. *International Journal for Equity in Health, 16*(1), Article 116. https://doi.org/10.1186/s12939-017-0612-0

Spruin, E., Mozova, K., Dempster, T., & Freeman, R. (2020). The use of facility dogs to bridge the justice gap for survivors of sexual offending. *Social Sciences, 9*(6), 96. https://doi.org/10.3390/socsci9060096

Stephens, T. N., Katz, C. C., Pisciotta, C., & Lens, V. (2021). The view from the other side: How parents and their representatives view family court. *Family Court Review, 59*(3), 491–507. https://psycnet.apa.org/doi/10.1111/fcre.12590

Sumalla, J. M. T., & Hernández-Hidalgo, P. (2018). Victims of child sexual abuse: Understanding their need for justice. *International Journal of Law, Crime and Justice, 54*, 11–20. https://doi.org/10.1016/j.ijlcj.2018.06.003

Szojka, Z. A., Moussavi, N., Burditt, C., & Lyon, T. D. (2023). Attorneys' questions and children's responses referring to the nature of sexual touch in child sexual abuse trials. *Child Maltreatment, 28*(3), 438–449. https://doi.org/10.1177/10775595231161033

Troxel, N. R., Ogle, C. M., Cordon, I., Lawler, M., & Goodman, G. S. (2009). Child witnesses in criminal court. In B. L. Bottoms, C. Najdowski, & G. S. Goodman (Eds.), *Children as victims, witnesses, and offenders: Psychological science and the law* (pp. 150–166). Guilford Press.

United Nations Children's Fund. (2022, January 31). *Justice for children: Justice systems worldwide are failing to protect children and to uphold their most basic rights.* https://www.unicef.org/protection/justice-for-children

van Toledo, A., & Seymour, F. (2013). Interventions for caregivers of children who disclose sexual abuse: A review. *Clinical Psychology Review, 33*(6), 772–781. https://doi.org/10.1016/j.cpr.2013.05.006

Westcott, H. L., & Page, M. (2002). Cross-examination, sexual abuse and child witness identity. *Child Abuse Review, 11*(3), 137–152. https://doi.org/10.1002/car.730

Whitcomb, D., Goodman, G., Ruynan, D. K., & Hoak, S. (1994). *The emotional effects of testifying on sexually abused children.* U.S. Department of Justice, Office of Justice Programs, National Institute of Justice.

Widom, C. S. (1989). The cycle of violence. *Science, 244*(4901), 160–166. https://doi.org/10.1126/science.2704995

Williams, L. M., Block, S. D., Johnson, H. M., Ramsey, M. G., & Winstead, A. P. (2022). *Prosecution of child sexual abuse: Challenges in achieving justice.* Wellesley Centers for Women. https://www.wcwonline.org/Fact-Sheets-Briefs/prosecution-of-child-sexual-abuse-challenges-in-achieving-justice

Winstead, A. P., & Stevenson, M. C. (2021). Effects of intimate partner violence perpetrator and victim race on protective order determinations. *Journal of Interpersonal Violence, 37*(19–20), NP17454–NP17472. https://doi.org/10.1177/08862605211028164

Wolf, O. T. (2017). Stress and memory retrieval: Mechanisms and consequences. *Current Opinion in Behavioral Sciences, 14*, 40–46. https://doi.org/10.1016/j.cobeha.2016.12.001

Yates, T. M., Carlson, E. A., & Egeland, B. (2008). A prospective study of child maltreatment and self-injurious behavior in a community sample. *Development and Psychopathology, 20*(2), 651–671. https://doi.org/10.1017/S0954579408000321

Zajac, K., Ralston, M. E., & Smith, D. W. (2015). Maternal support following childhood sexual abuse: Associations with children's adjustment post-disclosure and at 9-month follow-up. *Child Abuse & Neglect, 44*, 66–75. https://doi.org/10.1016/j.chiabu.2015.02.011

Zajac, R., O'Neill, S., & Hayne, H. (2012). Disorder in the courtroom? Child witnesses under cross-examination. *Developmental Review, 32*(3), 181–204. https://doi.org/10.1016/j.dr.2012.06.006

18

Children's Advocacy Centers and Kids in Court Preparation Programs

Rebecca Nathanson

Children are important participants in the judicial process, testifying in criminal, family, juvenile, and civil court, especially in cases of alleged sexual abuse (Ceci & de Bruyn, 1993; Pantell, 2017). Their testimony is often essential to the fact-finding process and discovery of the truth in child sexual abuse cases. States can vary regarding the ages of children who are typically put on the stand as no minimum age exists for children's testimony (Myers, 1986). In some jurisdictions (e.g., Nevada), children as young as 5 years of age routinely testify in cases of abuse and neglect. How do we protect children from further trauma during the investigative and judicial processes and adequately prepare children for the daunting task of testifying, while maintaining the integrity of the legal process and without infringing on the rights of the accused? This chapter will review the literature on the establishment, expansion, and evaluation of children's advocacy centers (CACs) and will review the literature on court preparation programs for children.

CHILDREN'S ADVOCACY CENTERS

To obtain more successful prosecutions of child sexual abuse cases and provide a more child-friendly, less traumatic environment for interviewing child witnesses, District Attorney Robert E. "Bud" Cramer coordinated efforts to create a better system to support abused children (National Children's

https://doi.org/10.1037/0000492-018
Handbook on Child Witnesses: Improving Psychological Science and Legal Practice,
G. S. Goodman, T. D. Lyon, S. D. Hobbs, and R. Enriquez (Editors)

Alliance, n.d.). As a result, the first CAC was established in Huntsville, Alabama, in 1985 (Cramer, 1985). Instead of being subjected to interviews by multiple professionals, such as law enforcement, criminal justice, child protective services (CPS), and medical professionals, or interviews in a police station, at CPS, and at school, children had a single forensic interviewer, in a child-friendly environment, with a team of multidisciplinary professionals observing through a one-way mirror.

CACs began to emerge throughout the nation. In 1988, representatives from these CACs formed the National Network for Children's Advocacy Centers to provide direction and training. In 1998, this network was renamed the National Children's Alliance (National Children's Alliance, n.d.).

In 1992, then Congressman Bud Cramer introduced the *National Children's Advocacy Program Act of 1992* (H.R.4729–102nd Congress [1991–1992]) "to provide information, services, and assistance so that communities can establish multidisciplinary programs that respond to child abuse" (para. 1, line 2). While Cramer's Act was never formally adopted, language from his proposal was used to amend the *Victims of Child Abuse Act of 1990* and other child protection legislation (Office of Juvenile Justice and Delinquency Prevention, 2025).

CACs are responsible for coordinating the investigation, treatment, and prosecution of child abuse cases; to be accredited, CACs must include the following (National Children's Alliance, 2017):

- child-appropriate facilities
- multidisciplinary teams (e.g., child protection, victim advocacy, law enforcement, prosecution, physical and mental health)
- designated legal entity responsible for program and fiscal operations
- culturally competent policies and practices
- forensic interviews
- medical evaluation and treatment
- therapeutic intervention
- victim support/advocacy
- case review and tracking

Since the inception of the first CAC in 1985, the model has been widely accepted and is highly regarded both in the United States and abroad, prompting continual growth in the number of CACs (St-Amand et al., 2023). Most recently, according to the National Children's Alliance (2024), 959 CACs served more than 372,000 children in the United States. The international community has also increasingly implemented the multidisciplinary team approach of the CAC model, and there are now CACs in more than 41 countries (National Children's Advocacy Center, 2025). Unlike the United States, there is not a central repository for international programs, so information regarding the specifics of these centers is limited (Cullen et al., 2024). In 1989, Israel first established a network of child advocacy councils aimed at providing a model for implementing advocacy centers for children similar to CACs in the United States (Rauche-Elnekave, 1989). There are now 40 CACs in Canada, or child and youth advocacy centers as they are often called there, with additional centers in various stages of development (Child & Youth Advocacy Centres, 2021). Parkerville Children and Youth Care opened Australia's first CAC—now known as a Child, Youth and Family Centre—in Western Australia in 2011, and a second in 2019 (Parkerville Children and Youth Care, 2025). The Barnahus model, which was developed in Iceland in 1998 and is similar to the CAC model, includes all Nordic countries and is presently the recommended best-practice model in Europe (Johansson & Stefansen, 2020). To turn the tide of child abuse, Rowland suggested the establishment of CACs in the United Kingdom (Rowland, 2014). More recently, Cook and colleagues (2022) conducted a study aimed at eliciting children's input regarding the design of an advocacy center, suggesting that "the creation of an Advocacy House (Advocacy Centre) model based on the U.S. model should be considered as a national initiative in the U.K." (p. 3).

Evaluation of Children's Advocacy Centers

Although the number of CACs has continued to grow, both in the United States and abroad, research on the effectiveness of the centers has been limited (Jones et al., 2007). In the first quasi-experimental national evaluation of CACs, researchers at the University of New Hampshire Crimes Against Children Research Center conducted three studies and examined medical evaluations (Walsh et al., 2007), child forensic interviewing (Cross et al., 2007), and child and parent satisfaction (Jones et al., 2007) across four well-established CACs. Data were compared to non-CAC facilities.

Walsh and colleagues (2007) examined the medical evaluations of child sexual abuse victims and found that children suspected of being sexually abused were twice as likely to have a medical evaluation when they were interviewed at a CAC than children who were interviewed elsewhere. Further analysis of the data also revealed that females, children who were younger, White children, children injured while being abused, and children suspected of being penetrated, were more likely to receive a medical exam than others. Moreover, children who were not suspected of being penetrated but were interviewed at a CAC were four times more likely to receive a medical examination than children interviewed at a non-CAC. Although Walsh and colleagues (2007) concluded that the results of their study suggested that CACs are effective at providing more medical exams for children suspected of being sexually abused, they did not find a relation between medical exams and offenders being charged. The finding of increased medical exams in children interviewed at CACs is encouraging in that it supports the notion that more comprehensive services are provided at CACs compared to the services of children interviewed elsewhere (Walsh et al., 2007). However, that a relation was not found between medical exams and offenders being charged is disappointing given that one of the primary initial goals in the establishment of CACs was to obtain more successful prosecutions of child sexual abuse cases

(Walsh et al., 2007). Although disappointing, these results were not surprising. The lack of effect of increased medical examinations on offenders being charged may be due to the rarity with which medical examinations produce corroborating evidence of abuse. Heger and colleagues (2002), for example, found that of 2,384 children referred for medical evaluation of sexual abuse, only 4% had abnormal examinations at the time of evaluation. Additional research examining the primary factors that lead to increased prosecution in sexual abuse cases may be beneficial. The benefits of medical evaluations, which in and of themselves may be traumatic to young children, also should be further evaluated.

Cross and colleagues (2007) examined child forensic interview practices across children interviewed at CACs compared to children interviewed at other locations (e.g., CPS offices, police stations, home, school) and found that children interviewed in both CACs and non-CAC environments typically engaged in two or less interviews. Interviews of children conducted at CACs were significantly more likely, however, to involve police, multidisciplinary team interviews, case reviews, joint police/CPS interviews, and videotaping of interviews (Cross et al., 2007). Cross and colleagues (2007) concluded that although CACs did not reduce the number of interviews children are subjected to, CACs appeared to have greater coordination on investigations and child forensic interviewing. This is an important finding and is in alignment with the goals of the National Children's Alliance. Although not evaluated in Cross and colleagues' study, greater coordination of investigations and child interviews may lead to decreased secondary trauma for children as well as an increase in prosecutions of child abuse and neglect cases. This is an area where further evaluation is needed.

In examining parent and child satisfaction with child interviews held at CACs compared to the satisfaction of families whose children were interviewed elsewhere, Jones and colleagues (2007) found that caregivers of children interviewed at CACs were more satisfied with the investigative process than caregivers of children interviewed in alternate settings. These differences were not found in child satisfaction, where children interviewed at CACs and at alternative settings both rated the investigation process relatively favorably, although children who were interviewed at CACs reported that they were less frightened (Jones et al., 2007). Jones et al. (2007) concluded that "the CAC model shows promise for improving families' experiences" (p. 1070). Although the lack of differences found between the satisfaction of children interviewed at CACs and elsewhere is somewhat disappointing, the fact that children interviewed at CACs reported being less frightened or anxious is very encouraging given that a primary goal in the establishment of CACs was to provide a less traumatic environment for interviewing child witnesses (National Children's Alliance, n.d.). Moreover, the finding that caregivers were more satisfied with the investigative process when children were interviewed at a CAC is also important as caregiver satisfaction may lead to greater support for the child, which in turn may improve child outcomes (Malloy & Lyon, 2006; National Children's Alliance, 2017).

In a 2015 review of the literature on CACs, Elmquist and colleagues (2015) concluded that although there are preliminary data to support the notion that CACs reduce the stress and trauma placed on children during the investigation of alleged abuse, additional research, including larger sample sizes, longitudinal studies, and expanded outcome measures, is needed to further evaluate the policies and practices of CACs. They suggest that CACs might benefit from incorporating ongoing research into the CAC model and accreditation standards. More recently, Cross and colleagues (2022) also noted that, given small sample sizes, data are limited on CAC practices across the country, specifically in the types of services that are offered to children and their families.

Given the limited data on CAC practices in the United States, Cross and colleagues (2022) surveyed CAC directors to examine the composition of the multidisciplinary teams utilized and the forms of assistance CACs provided. Findings indicated that most multidisciplinary teams were comprised of professionals recommended by the National Children's Alliance (e.g., child protection, victim advocacy, law enforcement, prosecution, physical and mental health). Cross and colleagues (2022) suggested adding other professionals such as rape crisis counselors, juvenile court professionals, and domestic violence service providers to the teams. Their findings also indicated that

> although most CACs are meeting assistance standards set forth by the National Children's Alliance (e.g., child-appropriate facilities, multidisciplinary teams, fiscal responsibility, culturally competent practices, forensic interviews, medical evaluations, therapeutic intervention, victim support, case tracking), CACs tended to vary in the specific forms of assistance they provide. (p. 10)

Summary of Children's Advocacy Centers

CACs have evolved significantly since they were first established in 1985. The first quasi-experimental national evaluation of CACs was conducted in 2007. Findings from research conducted on CACs in the United States, while limited, are promising. For example, the use of multidisciplinary teams and greater coordination in child abuse investigations were reported in most CACs (Cross et al., 2007, 2022). Additionally, most CACs were found to be meeting assistance standards set by the National Children's Alliance (Cross et al., 2022). Information regarding the specifics of international centers is limited, however, since there is not a central repository for these programs.

The findings of the research conducted on CACs in the United States, while limited, is promising. For example, the use of multidisciplinary teams and greater coordination in child abuse investigations were reported in most CACs (Cross et al., 2007, 2022). Most CACs were found to be meeting assistance standards set by the National Children's Alliance (Cross et al., 2022). Overall, the research on CACs thus far focuses primarily on investigations of abuse and delivery of services and not, for the most part, on prosecution outcomes resulting from CAC investigations—a primary objective in the establishment of the CAC model. Additional research is needed to further examine the relation between CAC characteristics and prosecution outcomes. Perhaps legal outcomes other than successful prosecutions should also be examined, as cases of abuse are often not criminally prosecuted (Faller & Palusci, 2007). Instead, child abuse cases are frequently adjudicated in removal proceedings in family or juvenile court, they have the responsibility of ensuring safe, timely permanency for maltreated children (Children's Bureau, 2022). It may also be important to reconsider what the primary goal of CACs should be. Although prosecution outcomes are important for obvious reasons, reduced secondary trauma child witnesses encounter in the investigation and prosecution of child abuse cases is just, if not more, important. Additional evaluations of not only child satisfaction, but the effects of the CAC model on children's anxiety and trauma are important to consider.

CHILDREN AS WITNESSES

Investigations held at CACs are an important first step in reducing system-related stress in child witnesses (Walker, 2011). Successful prosecution of sexual abuse cases often relies on children's testimony in court (Hartley et al., 2013; Myers, 2002). Concern remains, however, regarding the credibility of children as witnesses and the emotional trauma they may endure from testifying. Children's legal knowledge, memory, communication, and emotional abilities have all been shown to affect child witness credibility. For example, a substantial amount of research has examined children's legal knowledge, indicating that children's knowledge of the legal system is limited and is typically characterized by significant misunderstandings of the legal process (Block et al., 2010; Cooper et al., 2010; Eltringham & Aldridge, 2000; Flin et al., 1989; Freshwater & Aldridge, 1994; Peterson-Badali et al., 1997; Saywitz, 1989; Saywitz et al., 1990; Warren-Leubecker et al., 1989). Children's memory and suggestibility have also been examined, with some researchers questioning the reliability of children's recollections (Bruck & Ceci, 1999) and others finding that children can be quite credible witnesses (Bottoms & Goodman, 1996).

A significant area of concern is the potential trauma children endure while participating in the legal process. In a United States Supreme Court opinion, Justice Harold "Harry" Blackmun, in a dissent joined by Justice William Rehnquist, commented that "the fear and trauma associated with a child's testimony can cause psychological injury to the child and can prevent the possibility of effective testimony, undermining the truth-finding function of the trial itself" (*Coy v. Iowa*, 487 U.S. 1012, 1988). Children's anxiety related to testifying has been well-documented in the literature (Goodman et al., 1992; Nathanson & Saywitz, 2003, 2015; Sas, 1993; Sas et al., 1991). The courtroom itself can also be quite anxiety-provoking for children. In examining the effects of the courtroom environment on children's memory and anxiety, Nathanson and Saywitz (2003) found significantly greater heart rate variability, indicative of a stress response, in children who were interviewed in a moot courtroom when compared to children interviewed in a small, private room. In fact, heart rates of children interviewed in the small room ranged from 60 to 120 beats per minute, whereas heart rates of children interviewed in the courtroom ranged from 60 to over 240 beats per minute. Study participants were questioned about an innocuous event and were not actual victims of abuse, illustrating that merely being in the courtroom environment can cause significant anxiety for children. In addition, memory of children interviewed in the courtroom was impaired, with children interviewed in the small room recalling twice as much correct information as children interviewed in the courtroom. Although the courtroom experience can be traumatic for children, research has shown that children who are adequately prepared for court can provide more complete and accurate testimony (Quas & Goodman, 2012; Sas et al., 1991).

COURT EDUCATION AND PREPARATION PROGRAMS

In response to concerns about the potentially traumatic effects of testifying on children, court preparation and education programs for child victims/witnesses have continued to emerge over the past 20 years throughout the United States and in numerous other countries, predominantly in Canada and the United Kingdom (e.g., Cunningham & Stevens, 2011; Davies et al., 2004; Nathanson, 2004; Peterson et al., 2020; Plotnikoff & Woolfson, 2000, 2009). The programs vary widely in terms of content, methodology, and service delivery model. Whereas most programs focus primarily on the child, other programs aim at aiding professionals and/or caregivers working with children going to court. For example, Kristi House Children's Advocacy Center in Florida developed a step-by-step guidebook for professionals and advocates to prepare children and caregivers for court (Ramirez & Costa, 2022). Cunningham and Stevens (2011) developed a guide, *Helping a Child Be a Witness in Court: 101 Things to Know, Say, and Do,* with essential information for supporting child witnesses; and the Canadian Child Abuse Association (2025) developed an online court preparation facilitator program designed to train adults to provide assistance to child witnesses.

Child-centered witness preparation programs include in-person individual and group sessions, as well as videos to teach children about the court process (Ramirez & Costa, 2022) and online child witness court preparation programs on YouTube (Canadian Child Abuse Association, 2020). Use of a support dog (courthouse facility dog) is one of the most recent attempts to decrease the court-related trauma child witnesses may endure and are a source of comfort for witnesses before, during, and after testimony (McDonald & Rooney, 2016). Although the use of support dogs in the courtroom has garnered increased attention in recent years, there is limited research on the effects of support dogs on witnesses or the court process. In one study, Capparelli and colleagues (2020) examined whether the use of dogs increased the quantity of verbal reports for emotional events in undergraduate student participants. Results revealed that the use of dogs during interviews resulted in greater information reported when discussing negative events. No effect was found on reports of positive events. The authors suggest that canine-assisted interviews may provide comfort to people, resulting in more extensive reports about negative stressful events. In two additional studies, Burd and McQuiston (2019) examined the impact of courtroom facility dogs on mock jurors' perceptions of child witnesses. In both studies, they found that the use of courtroom dogs was not prejudicial to defendants and suggested that, contrary to due process arguments, facility dogs may not influence verdict, verdict confidence, or sentencing. Although the popularity of courtroom facility dogs has increased significantly in recent years, the use of these dogs has not been universally practiced or accepted (McDermott et al., 2021). In 2021, however, the American Bar Association approved Resolution 101A, which urges all jurisdictions to permit specially-trained dogs to accompany anxious or traumatized individuals who are testifying in court (American Bar Association, 2021). Currently, over 40 states have enacted statutes that allow for support dogs (Alicea-Lozada, 2022).

Although the methods and delivery models for court preparation programs for children vary widely, the primary goals of the programs are consistent—educating children about court procedures and reducing their anxiety while participating in the process. In 2002, Hurley, Scarth, and Stevens identified five components necessary for effective court education and support programs: education, role play and practice, relaxation and anxiety management, court accompaniment and support, and debriefing and follow-up (as cited in Walker, 2011). Building on the recommendations of Hurley and colleagues (2002) and guiding literature from the field, Walker (2011) developed a preparation program aimed at (a) demystifying the court process through education, (b) reducing fear and anxiety about testifying through stress reduction techniques, and (c) empowering children through emotional support. Walker (2011) also suggested that comprehensive child witness preparation programs should include a separate group for nonoffending parents/caregivers to provide support for the child throughout court involvement.

Additional established programs have emerged over the past two decades, including Kids' Court School at the University of Nevada, Las Vegas (Nathanson, 2004); Kids and Teens in Court at the Chadwick Center for Children and Families in San Diego, California (Chadwick Center, n.d.); Kids' Court in King County, Washington (Chadwick Center, n.d.); Kristi House's Court Prep for Kids in Miami, Florida (Ramirez & Costa, 2022); and the Court Preparation and Accompaniment Facilitator Training Program (Canadian Child Abuse Association, 2023). All programs include court education; most have some form of stress reduction with many including role play in an actual or moot courtroom, and some including preparation for caregivers or support persons. Session offerings vary in terms of the numbers of children taught at any given time, with some programs providing individual sessions to children and other programs offering small or large groups. The number of sessions also varies, ranging from one to several. Background and training of court preparation providers vary as well with some taught by licensed personnel with advanced degrees and others taught by graduate students.

EVALUATION OF COURT PREPARATION EFFECTIVENESS

Although the number of court preparation programs for children and youth has continued to grow both in the United States and abroad, research on the evaluation of preparation programs is limited. In one of the first evaluations of a court preparation program for children, Sas and colleagues (1991) conducted an evaluation of the London Family Court Clinic Child Witness Project. They randomly assigned 144 children referred to the child witness clinic to either a tour of the courtroom or to one of two more intensive preparation protocols that involved three to eight individual sessions with a therapist focused on court education and stress reduction, plus a tour of the courtroom, follow-up interviews, and booster sessions as needed. As compared with a courtroom tour, more intense individualized preparation resulted in greater legal knowledge and helped children deal with their stress and anxieties related to the abuse and to testifying. In addition, children who received the individual preparation were rated by attorneys as "doing better on the stand and having a better orientation to court."

Doueck and colleagues (1997) examined issues that arose for children and families who participated in the child victim witness program. Developed in 1988, this program, "in response to legislative changes that sought to make the Canadian judicial system more responsive to children's needs" (p. 115), is designed to prepare child witnesses, as well as to coordinate the efforts of child protection, law enforcement, and prosecution personnel in the investigation and prosecution of child abuse cases. Social workers who also serve as advocates teach the program's child preparation component, and the number and type of sessions vary depending on individual needs. Doueck and colleagues (1997) found that there are significant benefits to providing court education to children and their families, with written materials and the establishment of a support person viewed as important by both children and their families.

In a study with similar goals, preparing child witnesses and coordinating interagency efforts, Davies and colleagues (2004) conducted a two-year evaluation of a pilot program in New Zealand that provides education for child witnesses and their primary caregivers on the court process and procedures, with the aid of age-appropriate booklets and videos; the program also aims to facilitate interagency collaboration. In addition to court education, the program addresses both children's fears about testifying and choosing a support person for court. Davies and colleagues (2004) found that all stakeholders agreed that the program was an important initiative and recommended its implementation nationwide. Moreover, the child participants reported that the program made them feel less stressed and nervous about going to court.

Numerous studies have evaluated the effectiveness of the Child Witness Pack, a program developed in the United Kingdom in 1992 to provide support for child witnesses and their families. The Child Witness Pack program materials consist of three booklets focused on the experience of going to court: two activity booklets with word games and coloring that teach children about the court process and roles of courtroom participants that provide guidance for answering questions in court; and one booklet for caregivers that describes how they can support their children in court (Gersch et al., 1999). With the aid of the booklets, program personnel answer children's questions about court and communicate the child's needs to the prosecution and to the court (Plotnikoff & Woolfson, 1995). It was also strongly suggested that an independent adult accompany the child to court whenever possible (Gersch et al., 1999).

In an evaluation of the Child Witness Pack, Gersch and colleagues (1999) examined whether children's knowledge and understanding of the court process, as well as their emotional response to court, was altered after attending the program. The authors also examined children's, teachers', and educational psychologists' perception of the program. Results indicated that children's knowledge and understanding of the court system significantly increased after program participation. However, the program did not decrease children's negative emotional response to court. For example, words such as "court," "judge," and "trial" continued to produce anxiety and fear in children. Overall, children, teachers, and educational psychologists positively evaluated the Child Witness Pack and viewed it as a valuable way of preparing children for court.

In another evaluation of the Child Witness Pack, Plotnikoff and Woolfson (1995) examined "a wide range of views about the Pack, the extent to which the Pack is used to prepare child witnesses, and explored more about the characteristics, functions, and training of the independent adult who is responsible for preparing the child for court" (p. 45). Consistent with the findings of Gersch and colleagues (1999), Plotnikoff and Woolfson found that children, caregivers, law enforcement, and court personnel viewed the Pack positively and found the materials useful.

Subsequent to their evaluation of the Child Witness Pack, Plotnikoff and Woolfson (2005) conducted the first national survey in the United Kingdom of child witnesses across England, Wales, and Northern Ireland to assess the experiences of 50 child witnesses ranging from 7 to 17 years old. Their findings indicated that despite policies and procedures that were intended to facilitate children's testimony, a significant gap existed between the intended policies and actual delivery of services across the country.

In a 2009 follow-up study, Plotnikoff and Woolfson examined whether the implementation gap between child witness policies and procedures had narrowed since 2005. Although policies indicate that children are entitled to support that enables them to provide optimal testimony with limited stress and anxiety (Crown Prosecution Service, 2006), Plotnikoff and Woolfson found that there was still a significant gap "between the vision of policy and the reality of many children's experiences" (p. 3). These findings were derived from interviews with 182 child witnesses between 5 and 19 years old, and their caregivers. With regard to child witness preparation and support, although policy indicates that child witnesses are entitled to support, Plotnikoff and Woolfson (2009) found that only 50% of children toured the courtroom prior to trial, 54% met with a court preparation support person prior to trial, and

44% never met with a support person or visited the courtroom before the day of the trial. In addition, two-thirds of the child witnesses were accompanied to court by a support person they had never met. It was also reported that although the Child Witness Pack booklets were given to 70% of child witnesses, only 31% of these children had a support person who went through the booklet with them. However, consistent with previous research (i.e., Gersch et al., 1999; Plotnikoff & Woolfson, 1995), the children did describe the materials as helpful. In the 2009 evaluation, Plotnikoff and Woolfson found that pretrial support was beneficial to child witnesses who received it. For example,

> 95% of children who met with a support person prior to trial said that it made them feel better about going to court, 84% of child witnesses who toured the courtroom prior to trial said it helped them feel more confident or to know what to expect at trial; and over one-third of children and their caregivers said that contact with a support person prior to trial was what made it possible for the child to go to court. (p. 5)

In one of the first evaluations of an established, manualized program, Nathanson and Saywitz (2015) conducted a quasi-experimental evaluation of the effects of the Kids' Court School (KCS) on the anticipatory anxiety of child witnesses. KCS is a well-established court preparation program that has served over 1,700 children at the University of Nevada, Las Vegas (UNLV; Nathanson, 2004). Child witnesses ages 4 through 17 years old with impending legal proceedings attend two individual or small group sessions, comprised of legal knowledge education and stress inoculation training, 1 to 2 weeks prior to appearing in court. The first session focused on legal knowledge education, addressing the pretrial and trial processes and the roles and functions of courtroom participants. The role of the witness was emphasized, as this is the child's role in court. The importance of being a witness, truth-telling, taking an oath, and speaking so that the child can be heard and understood were discussed. Children were also taught that if they do not remember or know the answer to a question that they are asked, it is appropriate to simply express that they do not remember, do not know, or do not understand. The second session of KCS focused on stress inoculation training. Children's court-related fears were elicited, current coping strategies assessed, and deep-breathing and positive self-talk taught and encouraged as coping skills to reduce anxiety while testifying. The second session concluded with a mock trial in a moot courtroom. Law students functioned in the roles of the prosecuting and defense attorneys, bailiff, and defendant. Children took turns playing both the roles of judge and witness. On the witness stand, children were questioned through direct and cross-examination, and were exposed to objections, as in a real trial.

To evaluate the effects of KCS on children's court-related anticipatory anxiety, Nathanson and Saywitz administered the Court-Related Stress Scale–Revised (CRSS-R; Saywitz & Nathanson, 2006) to 193 KCS participants between the ages of 4 and 17 years with impending legal proceedings, just prior to participating in the first session of KCS. The CRSS-R is a 10-item instrument that assesses children's perceptions of the degree of stress associated with various court-related experiences such as having an attorney ask them questions or answering embarrassing questions in court. Participants rate each experience on a 5-point scale (e.g., 1 = *not stressful, not upsetting*; 3 = *upsetting*; 5 = *very, very stressful*). One week after the first session, children were taught the second session, followed by the mock trial. After the mock trial, the CRSS-R posttest was administered. Results revealed that children's overall court-related anticipatory anxiety significantly decreased after attending KCS (Nathanson & Saywitz, 2015). Moreover, anxiety associated with seven of the 10 individual court-related experiences also significantly decreased after participation in the KCS program.

In a related study, Nathanson and Messina (2022) evaluated the effects of remote delivery of the KCS program on children's court-related anticipatory anxiety. During the COVID-19 pandemic, UNLV, like most universities across the country, cancelled in-person instruction and implemented remote delivery of its courses. The university was closed to the community. The approximately 100 child victims/witnesses who attend KCS at UNLV each year were no longer permitted to be on campus, despite these children continuing to be subpoenaed to testify in court about allegations of abuse and neglect. In response to the need to continue the KCS program, the program was adapted for remote delivery through Zoom. Analyses of children's pre and post ratings of their court-related stress, as indicated on the CRSS-R, revealed data consistent with Nathanson and Saywitz's (2015) findings. Children rated their anticipatory anxiety as significantly lower after attending KCS (Nathanson & Messina, 2022).

In another evaluation of an established court preparation program for children and youth, Peterson and colleagues (2020) evaluated the Kids and Teens in Court (KTIC) program at the Chadwick Center in San Diego, California. The program, which serves approximately 250 children and nonoffending caregivers each year, was established in partnership with San Diego district attorney's office in 1997. The goals of the program are to decrease children's court-related anxiety, ensure relevant legal knowledge of both children and their caretakers, and improve children's ability to effectively testify in court (Peterson et al., 2020). The manualized KTIC curriculum is an "empirically grounded, trauma-informed, comprehensive model for court preparation and education" (p. 37). The curriculum, which is taught by trauma-informed clinical social workers, includes court education, relaxation training, and mock trials; caregiver/support person preparation; as well as the use of court support dogs (Peterson et al., 2020). Children and youth, in a group format, attend three 2-hour sessions over a one-month period. The first session is held at the CAC, with subsequent sessions held at the courthouse.

Although thousands of children in San Diego County have participated in the KTIC program for more than two decades, the program has only recently been formally evaluated. Utilizing the CRSS-R, Peterson and colleagues (2020) evaluated the effects of the KTIC program on the court-related stress of 175 children and youth who attended one, two, or three sessions at KTIC. Results revealed that children's court-related stress decreased significantly after each individual session and after the three sessions from start to finish. Peterson and colleagues (2020) concluded that KTIC "benefits children who have experienced trauma and will be testifying in court and reduces the concern of further trauma from the court process itself" (p. 41).

The finding of reduced court-related stress in child witnesses after participation in the KTIC program is consistent with evaluations of the KCS (i.e., Nathanson & Messina, 2022; Nathanson & Saywitz, 2015). In all these studies a reduction in children's anticipatory court-related stress was found. Thus, children are not as anxious about going to court after participating in these programs, which is promising. However, while reducing children's anticipatory anxiety is important and the trauma of going to court is lessened, it is also imperative to note that testifying itself may still evoke anxiety and secondary trauma in child witnesses. It is vital for future research to examine anxiety during testimony (e.g., physiological measures, observations) and/or afterward (e.g., self-report, observations) to evaluate the effects of court preparation programs on anxiety during testimony itself and after. The unique aspects of the anxiety reduction components of preparation programs such as stress inoculation through deep breathing and self-talk (Nathanson & Saywitz, 2015) and trauma-informed treatment through relaxation and cognitive coping skills (Peterson et al., 2020) should also be examined.

Research on the effectiveness of court preparation programs for children is limited; however, research in this area is expanding, with evaluation of manualized programs emerging in recent years. Although programs varied in content, methodology, and delivery models, the aim of programs was typically the same: to reduce the trauma that child witnesses often experience while participating in the judicial process. Most programs contained court education and stress reduction components. Some programs were taught individually while others were taught in groups. The number of sessions tended to vary between programs. The educational background and training of the program providers also varied; some were taught by graduate students, some by therapists, and some by social workers with expertise in child trauma and trauma-focused mental health treatment.

Evaluations of programs have also produced varied positive outcomes. Some children gained greater legal knowledge by participating in a court preparation program (Gersch et al., 1999; Sas et al., 1991). Other children reported less anxiety about going to court after program participation (Davies et al., 2004; Nathanson & Saywitz, 2015; Peterson et al., 2020; Sas et al., 1991). One program did not reduce children's negative emotional response to court, although children did rate the overall program as positive (Gersch et al., 1999). Additional programs were also evaluated positively by children and families (Doueck et al., 1997; Gersch et al., 1999; Plotnikoff & Woolfson, 2009, 1995); others garnered professional support (Davies et al., 2004; Gersch et al., 1999; Plotnikoff & Woolfson, 1995). Sas and colleagues (1991) found that children who participated in the London Family Court Clinic Child Witness Project did better on the stand after participating in the program. Despite these positive outcomes,

Plotnikoff and Woolfson (2009) found that gaps still existed between the policies and procedures that had been put in place in the United Kingdom to support children and the services children actually received.

DIRECTIONS FOR FUTURE RESEARCH

Although researchers have reported encouraging outcomes of various preparation programs, further research is needed to establish guidelines for best practices in child witness preparation. The individual components of existing preparation programs should be evaluated to determine which are most beneficial for children. If the aim of court preparation is to decrease children's system-induced stress, then the components of the programs need to be evaluated to determine which are most likely to succeed. Does increasing children's knowledge of the court process reduce court-related anxiety? Are specific stress reduction strategies needed, and if so, which strategies are most beneficial? Participation in the KCS in Las Vegas, Nevada, for example, reduced children's anticipatory court-related stress (Nathanson & Saywitz, 2015). The program is comprised of legal education, stress inoculation, and a mock trial. Are all three of these components necessary to reduce children's anxiety? Or can anxiety be reduced with just one or two of these components? Participation in the KTIC program in San Diego, California, reduced children's court-related stress as well (Peterson et al., 2020). The KTIC program consists of psychoeducational components as well as relaxation training and affect regulation, modeled after components of trauma-focused cognitive behavior therapy (TF-CBT). In fact, the authors suggest that due in part to this unique aspect of the program, as well as the use of licensed clinical social workers with specialized training in child trauma and trauma-focused mental health treatment, the KTIC program "bridges the gap between the mental health/trauma treatment process and the court process" (Peterson et al., 2020, p. 7). Was the TF-CBT component primarily responsible for the reduction in children's court-related anxiety? Did the fact that highly trained professionals with expertise in trauma-focused mental health teach the program influence the outcome? Further research examining these questions can aid the development of cost-effective and efficient preparation programs that are important given the limited time constraints child witnesses have due to impending court dates and conflicting multiple appointments children involved in the judicial process often encounter.

The inclusion of support for caregivers in child witness preparation programs and the presence of a support person for children has also been shown to be important (Davies et al., 2004; Doueck et al., 1997; Gersch et al., 1999). One study, however, found that a significant number of children had never met their support person prior to their first court appearance (Plotnikoff & Woolfson, 2009). Is an unfamiliar support person as beneficial for a child as a support person who has an established relationship with a child? Although the research appears clear that child witnesses can benefit from a support person, there is a lack of clarity as to who that person should be (e.g., professional, family member) and how they are chosen.

Additional research on the effects of the use of courtroom facility dogs on child witnesses, as well as on the court process itself, is also needed. As noted, the use of courtroom dogs has increased significantly in recent years, although studies in this area are limited. It would be interesting to see if courtroom dogs decrease the anxiety children endure during participation in the court process, either when used to augment other child witness preparation methods or when used independently. In addition, legal arguments concerning due process when facility dogs are used can also be addressed through empirical evaluation of the effects of dogs in the courtroom on issues such as adjudications and witness credibility.

Methodology and models of delivery of preparation programs must also be further evaluated. For example, is there a benefit to individual court preparation compared to preparation of groups of children? It may be more cost effective to prepare children in groups, but children may learn at different rates or may feel uncomfortable learning about court and talking about court-related fears in the presence of other children. Alternatively, it may be comforting for children to know that they are not alone as victims of abuse. For example, although actual cases are never discussed at the KCS, during one session with a small group of girls, one of the girls looked at the other and said, "Did something happen to you, too?" Both girls appeared relieved when the second child answered "Yes." The number and timing of sessions should also be evaluated. Is it best to prepare a child just prior to going to court so that the information learned is fresh in their minds, or is it better to allow ample time for children to practice anxiety reduction strategies before going to court?

Models of delivery of court preparation programs are another area that needs further exploration. Child-centered preparation programs include videos, on-line web-based programs, as well as in-person programs for children. Several remote programs have also been developed, and some have shown promise for decreasing children's court-related stress (Nathanson & Messina, 2022). Online delivery can be beneficial for children who live in remote areas where in-person services are not available, as well as for children who have limited transportation resources and/or scheduling conflicts with other mandated services typical of children involved in the judicial process. Davies and colleagues (2004), however, suggests that "written and audiovisual materials are not a substitute for the necessary contact between an educator and the child and family" (p. 228). Moreover, contemporary research in online learning suggests that synchronous live sessions are more effective and help close the communication gap that is often described as feeling disconnected to the content (Quezada et al., 2020; Roca et al., 2020; Tso & Park, 2020). Thus, it may be important to teach online preparation programs synchronously so that we actively engage child victims, who already may feel disconnected to the world around them, as they navigate the judicial system.

Lastly, although an early study found that court preparation programs could lead to doing better on the stand (Sas et al., 1991), additional research is important not only to examine the effects of child witness preparation on anxiety and trauma, but its effects on testimony and legal outcomes as well.

CONCLUSION

CACs and child witness preparation programs are central to reducing the trauma often associated with children's participation in the legal process. Reduced trauma may also lead to more successful prosecution in abuse and neglect cases—primary goal in the establishment of CACs (Cramer, 1985). More important, reduced trauma in child witnesses may enhance the truth-finding function of the trial itself, which Justices Blackmun and Rehnquist suggest can be undermined by the trauma of testifying (*Coy v. Iowa*, 487 U.S. 1012, 1988), thus, simultaneously protecting children and protecting the rights of the accused. Article 12 of the *Convention on the Rights of the Child* (1989) establishes the right of every child to have their voice heard in decisions that affect them. Society has a responsibility to help facilitate children's voices by providing an appropriate interview environment and court preparation for children. Perhaps a 6-year-old participant in the KCS program said it best: "I want to go to court and talk to the judge. This is about my life, and my life is important" (R. Nathanson, personal communication, October 31, 2002).

REFERENCES

Alicea-Lozada, D. (2022). *Support for child witnesses: From dogs to "court school."* National Center for State Courts. https://www.ncsc.org/information-and-resources/trending-topics/archived-articles/child-in-court

American Bar Association. (2021). *Resolution 101A* [Report]. https://www.americanbar.org/content/dam/aba/administrative/tips/animal-law/res-101a.pdf

Block, S. D., Oran, H. S., Oran, D., Baumrind, N., & Goodman, G. S. (2010). Abused and neglected children in court: Knowledge and attitudes. *Child Abuse & Neglect, 34*(9), 659–670. https://doi.org/10.1016/j.chiabu.2010.02.003

Bottoms, B. L., & Goodman, G. S. (1996). *International perspectives on child abuse and children's testimony: Psychological research and law.* Sage Publications.

Bruck, M., & Ceci, S. J. (1999). The suggestibility of children's memory. *Annual Review of Psychology, 50*(1), 461–489. https://doi.org/10.1146/annurev.psych.50.1.419

Burd, K. A., & McQuiston, D. E. (2019). Facility dogs in the courtroom: Comfort without prejudice? *Criminal Justice Review, 44*(4), 1–22. https://doi.org/10.1177/0734016819844298

Canadian Child Abuse Association. (2020, July 16). *CCAA court preparation* [Video]. YouTube. https://youtu.be/DwNiQoVex0U?si=eqyTGJTO2u8qfozk

Canadian Child Abuse Association. (2025). *Court preparation and accompaniment facilitator training program.* Retrieved September 24, 2025, from https://ccaa.org/ccaa-online-training-cwcpp/

Capparelli, A. L., Miller, Q. C., Wright, D. B., & London, K. (2020). Canine-assisted interviews bolster informativeness for negative autobiographical memories. *Psychological Reports, 123*(1), 159–178. https://doi.org/10.1177/0033294119851803

Ceci, S. J., & de Bruyn, E. (1993). Child witnesses in court: A growing dilemma. *Children Today, 22*(1), 5–9.

Chadwick Center. (n.d.). *Kids and teens in court program.* Retrieved September 29, 2025, from https://www.chadwickcenter.org/kids-and-teens-in-court/

Child & Youth Advocacy Centres. (2021). *Child & Youth Advocacy Centres: Building better services for children and youth who are victims or witnesses of crime in Canada* [Homepage]. https://cac-cae.ca

Children's Bureau. (2022). *Understanding child welfare and the courts.* Child Welfare Information Gateway, U.S. Department of Health and Human Services. https://www.childwelfare.gov/resources/understanding-child-welfare-and-courts/

Cook, D. L., Livesley, J., Long, T., Sam, M., & Rowland, A. G. (2022). The need for children's advocacy centers: Hearing the voices of children. *Comprehensive Child and Adolescent Nursing, 45*(4), 368–382. https://doi.org/10.1080/24694193.2021.1989085

Cooper, A., Wallin, A. R., Quas, J. A., & Lyon, T. D. (2010). Maltreated and non-maltreated children's knowledge of the juvenile dependency system. *Child Maltreatment, 15*(3), 255–260. https://doi.org/10.1177/1077559510364056

Coy v. Iowa, 487 U.S. 1012 (1988).

Cramer, R. E., Jr. (1985). The district attorney as a mobilizer in a community approach to child sexual abuse. *University of Miami Law Review, 40,* 209–216. https://repository.law.miami.edu/umlr/vol40/iss1/11

Cross, T., Jones, L., Walsh, W., Simone, M., & Kolko, D. (2007). Child forensic interviewing in Children's Advocacy Centers: Empirical data on a practice model. *Child Abuse & Neglect, 31*(10), 1031–1052. https://doi.org/10.1016/j.chiabu.2007.04.007

Cross, T. P., Whitcomb, D., & Maran, E. (2022). *Practice in U.S. children's advocacy centers: Results of a survey of CAC directors.* Children and Family Research Center, University of Illinois at Urbana-Champaign.

Crown Prosecution Service. (2006). *Children and young people: CPS policy on prosecuting criminal cases involving children and young people as victims and witnesses.*

Cullen, P., Williams, A., Troullinou, P., Nathans, C., & Gabriele, T. (2024). *International child safeguards: Gaps, challenges, and opportunities for collaboration* [White paper]. Trilateral Research. https://trilateralresearch.com/wp-content/uploads/2024/08/ICS-Whitepaper-report-final.pdf

Cunningham, A. J., & Stevens, L. (2011). *Helping a child to be a witness in court: 101 things to know, say and do.* London, Ontario Centre for Children and Families in the Justice System (London Family Court Clinic).

Davies, E., Devere, H., & Verbitsky, J. (2004). Court education for young witnesses: Evaluation of the pilot service in Aotearoa, New Zealand. *Psychiatry, Psychology and Law, 11*(2), 226–235. https://doi.org/10.1375/1321871042707179

Doueck, H. J., Weston, E. A., Filbert, L., Beekhuis, R., & Redlich, H. F. (1997). A child witness advocacy program: Caretakers' and professionals' views. *Journal of Child Sexual Abuse, 6*(1), 113–122. https://doi.org/10.1300/J070v06n01_08

Elmquist, J., Shorey, R. C., Febres, J., Zapor, H., Klostermann, K., Schratter, A., & Stuart, G. L. (2015). A review of children's advocacy centers' (CACs) response to cases of child maltreatment in the United States. *Aggression and Violent Behavior, 25,* 26–34. https://doi.org/10.1016/j.avb.2015.07.002

Eltringham, S., & Aldridge, J. (2000). The extent of children's knowledge of court as estimated by guardians. *Child Abuse Review, 9*(4), 275–286. https://doi.org/10.1002/1099-0852(200007/08)9:4<275::aid-car618>3.3.co;2-n

Faller, K. C., & Palusci, V. J. (2007). Children's advocacy centers: Do they lead to positive outcomes? *Child Abuse & Neglect, 31*(10), 1021–1029. https://doi.org/10.1016/j.chiabu.2007.09.001

Flin, R. H., Stevenson, Y., & Davies, G. M. (1989). Children's knowledge of court proceedings. *British Journal of Psychology, 80*(3), 285–297. https://doi.org/10.1111/j.2044-8295.1989.tb02321.x

Freshwater, K., & Aldridge, J. (1994). The knowledge and fears about court of child witnesses, schoolchildren, and adults. *Child Abuse Review, 3*(3), 183–195. https://doi.org/10.1002/car.2380030307

Gersch, I. S., Gersch, A. N., Lockhart, R., & Moyse, S. A. (1999). The child witness pack: An evaluation. *Educational Psychology in Practice, 15*(1), 45–50. https://doi.org/10.1080/0266736990150108

Goodman, G. S., Taub, E. P., Jones, D. P. H., England, P., Port, L. K., Rudy, L., & Prado, L. (1992). Testifying in criminal court: Emotional effects on child sexual assault victims. *Monographs of the Society for Research in Child Development, 57*(5), i–159. https://doi.org/10.2307/1166127

Hartley, D. J., Mullings, J. L., & Marquart, J. W. (2013). Factors impacting prosecution of child sexual abuse, physical abuse, and neglect cases processed through a children's advocacy center. *Journal of Child & Adolescent Trauma, 6*(4), 260–273. https://doi.org/10.1080/19361521.2013.836586

Heger, A., Ticson, L., Velasquez, O., & Bernier, R. (2002). Children referred for possible sexual abuse: Medical findings in 2,384 children. *Child Abuse & Neglect, 26*(6–7), 645–659. https://doi.org/10.1016/s0145-2134(02)00339-3

H.R.4729–102nd Congress. (1991–1992). *Summary.* https://www.congress.gov/bill/102nd-congress/house-bill/4729

Hurley, P., Scarth, K., & Stevens, L. (2002). *Children as witnesses: Helping young people give their evidence in court, helping courts hear the evidence of children.* Centre for Children and Families in the Justice System. https://web.archive.org/web/20180924033708/http://scarthmckillop.ca/research/childwitness.pdf

Johansson, S., & Stefansen, K. (2020). Policy-making for the diffusion of social innovations: The case of the Barnahus model in the Nordic region and the broader European context. *Innovation: The European Journal of Social Science Research, 33*(1), 4–20. https://doi.org/10.1080/13511610.2019.1598255

Jones, L., Cross, T., Walsh, W., & Simone, M. (2007). Do children's advocacy centers improve families' experiences of child sexual abuse investigations? *Child Abuse & Neglect, 31*(10), 1069–1085. https://doi.org/10.1016/j.chiabu.2007.07.003

Malloy, L. C., & Lyon, T. D. (2006). Caregiver support and child sexual abuse: Why does it matter? *Journal of Child Sexual Abuse, 15*(4), 97–103. https://doi.org/10.1300/J070v15n04_06

McDermott, C. M., Marsh, S., Miller, M. K., & Forte, T. (2021). From the doghouse to the courthouse: Facility dogs as trial aids for vulnerable witnesses. *Trends in State Courts (2021), 47–51.* http://cdm16501.contentdm.oclc.org/cdm/ref/collection/facilities/id/263

McDonald, S., & Rooney, L. (2016). Let's "paws" to consider the possibility: Using support dogs with victims of crime. *Victims of Crime Research Digest, 7,* 1–12. http://www.justice.gc.ca/eng/rp-pr/cj-jp/victim/rd7-rr7/p4.html

Myers, J. E. B. (1986). Testimonial competence of children. *Journal of Family Law, 25*(2), 287–356.

Myers, J. E. B. (2002). The legal system and child protection. In J. E. B. Myers, L. Berliner, J. Briere, C. T. Hendrix, C. Jenny, & T. A. Reid (Eds.), *The APSAC handbook on child maltreatment* (2nd ed., pp. 55–78). Sage.

Nathanson, R. (2004). *Kids' court school.* University of Nevada Las Vegas. https://law.unlv.edu/kids-court-school

Nathanson, R., & Messina, E. L. (2022, March 17–19). *Preparing children for court during COVID: Evaluation of remote delivery of a model program* [Paper presentation]. American Psychology–Law Society Annual Conference, Denver, CO, United States.

Nathanson, R., & Saywitz, K. J. (2003). The effects of the courtroom context on children's memory and anxiety. *Journal of Psychiatry & Law, 31*(1), 67–98. https://doi.org/10.1177/009318530303100105

Nathanson, R., & Saywitz, K. J. (2015). Preparing children for court: Effects of a model court education program on children's anticipatory anxiety. *Behavioral Sciences and the Law, 33*(4), 459–475. https://doi.org/10.1002/bsl.2191

National Children's Advocacy Center. (2025). *Training and resources: Child abuse professionals.* Retrieved September 24, 2025, https://www.nationalcac.org/child-abuse-professionals/

National Children's Alliance. (n.d.). *History of NCA.* https://www.nationalchildrensalliance.org/history-of-nca/

National Children's Alliance. (2017). *Standards for accredited members.* https://www.nationalchildrensalliance.org/wp-content/uploads/2015/06/NCA-Standards-for-Accredited-Members-2017.pdf

National Children's Alliance. (2024). *2024: National CAC statistics.* https://www.nationalchildrensalliance.org/wp-content/uploads/2025/03/2024_Annual_CAC_Service_Stats.pdf

Office of Juvenile Justice and Delinquency Prevention. (2025). *Children's advocacy centers: Literature review: A product of the Model Programs Guide.* https://ojjdp.ojp.gov/model-programs-guide/literature-reviews/childrens-advocacy-centers#0-0

Pantell, R. (2017). The child witness in the courtroom. *Pediatrics, 139*(3), e20164008. https://doi.org/10.1542/peds.2016-4008

Parkerville Children and Youth Care. (2025). *Child, youth and family centres.* Retrieved September 24, 2025, from https://parkerville.org.au/what-we-do/child-youth-and-family-centres

Peterson, L., Rolls Reutz, J. A., Hazen, A. L., Habib, A., & Williams, R. (2020). Kids and teens in court (KTIC): A model for preparing child witnesses for court. *American Journal of Community Psychology, 65*(1–2), 35–43. https://doi.org/10.1002/ajcp.12390

Peterson-Badali, M., Abramovitch, R., & Duda, J. (1997). Young children's legal knowledge and reasoning ability. *Canadian Journal of Criminology, 39,* 145–170.

Plotnikoff, J., & Woolfson, R. (1995). *Child witness pack: An evaluation* (NCJ Number 161796). Program/Project Evaluation (UK). https://www.ojp.gov/ncjrs/virtual-library/abstracts/child-witness-pack-evaluation

Plotnikoff, J., & Woolfson, R. (2000). *An evaluation of child witness support.* Scottish Executive Central Research Unit.

Plotnikoff, J., & Woolfson, R. (2005). *In their own words: The experiences of 50 young witnesses in criminal proceedings* [Report]. Policy Practice Research Series, National Society for the Prevention of Cruelty to Children and Victim Support. https://www.researchgate.net/publication/344177101_In_their_own_words_The_experences_of_50_young_witnesses_in_criminal_proceedings_The_NSPCC_in_partnership_with_Victim_Support

Plotnikoff, J., & Woolfson, R. (2009). *Measuring up? Evaluating implementation of government commitments to young witnesses in criminal proceedings.* National Society for the Prevention of Cruelty to Children. https://doi.org/10.13140/RG.2.2.23728.51206

Quas, J. A., & Goodman, G. S. (2012). Consequences of criminal court involvement for child victims. *Psychology, Public Policy, and Law, 18*(3), 392–414. https://doi.org/10.1037/a0026146

Quezada, R. L., Talbot, C., & Quezada-Parker, K. B. (2020). From bricks and mortar to remote teaching: A teacher education program's response to COVID-19. *Journal of Education for Teaching, 46*(4), 472–483. https://doi.org/10.1080/02607476.2020.1801330

Ramirez, V., & Costa, J. (2022, March 15). *Court prep for kids.* Kristi House Children's Advocacy Center. https://kristihouse.org/services/court-prep-for-kids/

Rauche-Elnekave, H. (1989). Advocacy and ombuds work for children: Implications of the Israeli experience. *Child Welfare, 68*(2), 101–112.

Roca, E., Melgar, P., Gairal-Casadó, R., & Pulido-Rodríguez, M. A. (2020). Schools that 'open doors' to prevent child abuse in confinement by COVID-19. *Sustainability, 12*(11), 4685. https://doi.org/10.3390/su12114685

Rowland, A. G. (2014). *Living on a railway line.* The Winston Churchill Memorial Trust, The Pennine Acute Hospitals NHS Trust and The University of Salford. http://www.wcmt.org.uk/users/andrewrowland2014

Sas, L., Austin, G., Wolfe, D. A., & Hurley, P. (1991). *Reducing the system-induced trauma for child sexual abuse victims through court preparation, assessment and follow-up* [Final report, Project No. 4555-1-125]. National Welfare Grants Division, Health and Welfare Canada, London Family Court Clinic.

Sas, L. D. (1993). *Three years after the verdict: A longitudinal study of the social and psychological adjustment of child witnesses referred to the child witness project* [Final Report, Project No. 4887-06-91-026]. Family Violence Prevention Division of Health Canada, London Family Court Clinic.

Saywitz, K. J. (1989). Children's conceptions of the legal system: Court is a place to play basketball. In S. J. Ceci, D. F. Ross, & M. P. Toglia (Eds.), *Perspectives on children's testimony* (pp. 131–157). Springer. https://doi.org/10.1007/978-1-4613-8832-6_7

Saywitz, K. J., Jaenicke, C., & Camparo, L. (1990). Children's knowledge of legal terminology. *Law and Human Behavior, 14*(6), 523–535. https://doi.org/10.1007/BF01044879

Saywitz, K. J., & Nathanson, R. (1993). Children's testimony and their perceptions of stress in and out of the courtroom. *Child Abuse & Neglect, 17*(5), 613–622. https://doi.org/10.1016/0145-2134(93)90083-H

Saywitz, K. J., & Nathanson, R. (2006). *Court-Related Stress Scale–Revised (CRSS-R)* [Unpublished instrument].

St-Amand, A., Rimer, P., Nadeau, D., Herbert, J., & Walsh, W. (2023). *Innovative practices in child and youth advocacy centre models.* Presses de l'Université du Quebec.

Tso, I. F., & Park, S. (2020). Alarming levels of psychiatric symptoms and the role of loneliness during the COVID-19 epidemic: A case study of Hong Kong. *Psychiatry Research, 293*, 113423. https://doi.org/10.1016/j.psychres.2020.113423

United Nations General Assembly. (1989). *Convention on the rights of the child.* https://www.unicef.org/media/52626/file

Walker, J. (2011). If I'm the party, where's the cake? The need for comprehensive child-witness court preparation programs. *Center Piece, 3*(1), 1–6.

Walsh, W., Cross, T., Jones, L. M., Simone, M., & Kolko, D. J. (2007). Which sexual abuse victims receive a forensic medical examination? *Child Abuse & Neglect, 31*(10), 1053–1068. https://doi.org/10.1016/j.chiabu.2007.04.006

Warren-Leubecker, A., Tate, C. S., Hinton, I. D., & Ozbek, I. N. (1989). What do children know about the legal system and when do they know it? First steps down a less traveled path in child witness research. In S. J. Ceci, D. F. Ross, & M. P. Toglia (Eds.), *Perspectives on children's testimony* (pp. 158–183). Springer. https://doi.org/10.1007/978-1-4613-8832-6_8

INDEX

B

D

M

N

O

Q

R

S

ABOUT THE EDITORS

Gail S. Goodman, PhD, is Distinguished Professor of Psychology, Emerita, at the University of California, Davis. Dr. Goodman received many national and international awards and grants for her writings and research on child witnesses. Her research is widely cited, including, pivotally, in U.S. Supreme Court decisions concerning child witnesses and courtroom testimony. She obtained her doctoral degree in psychology from the University of California, Los Angeles. For many years she published with Dr. Karen J. Saywitz, and they were close friends. Dr. Goodman and Dr. Saywitz are often credited with starting the modern scientific study of children's eyewitness memory and children in the legal context.

Thomas D. Lyon, JD, PhD, is the Judge Edward J. and Ruey L. Guirado Chair in Law and Psychology at the University of Southern California Gould School of Law. After graduating from Harvard Law School, he worked as an attorney for the Children's Services Division of the Los Angeles County Counsel. He obtained a PhD in developmental psychology from Stanford University and was a postdoctoral researcher with Karen J. Saywitz, PhD, at the University of California, Los Angeles. His work has been funded by the National Institute of Child Health and Development, the National Science Foundation, and the Department of Justice.

Sue D. Hobbs, PhD, is Professor of Child and Adolescent Development and Chair of Undergraduate Studies in Education in the College of Education at California State University, Sacramento. Dr. Hobbs obtained her doctoral degree in developmental psychology from the University of California, Davis. She received the Karen Saywitz Early Career Award for Outstanding Contributions to Research/Practice in the Field of Child Maltreatment from Division 37 (Society for Child and Family Policy and Practice) of the American Psychological Association. As a graduate student, she collaborated with Dr. Saywitz on research for the Swedish government that resulted in multiple publications and was later extended into their coauthored book on the experiences of youth in foster care. Her research and peer-reviewed publications focus on children's eyewitness memory, forensic interviewing techniques, and the experiences of foster youth in the legal system. She has authored numerous peer-reviewed publications on child witnesses, foster care outcomes, and children's testimony in maltreatment cases.

Rayna Enriquez, PhD, works at the National Institute of Justice and holds a doctoral degree in developmental psychology from the University of California, Davis. Dr. Enriquez obtained her bachelor's degree in psychology with a specialization in law, forensics, and criminality from the University of Southern California. As part of her training, she served as a researcher of forensic interviewing techniques for children in court actions. She specializes in eyewitness memory and perceptions of children with developmental disorders, as well as in true and false memory in adults.